CRIMINOLOGY

SECOND EDITION

Chris Hale
Professor of Criminology
University of Kent

Keith Hayward
Senior Lecturer in Criminology and Sociology
University of Kent

Azrini Wahidin
Reader in Criminology and Criminal Justice
Queen's University, Belfast

Emma Wincup
Senior Lecturer in Criminology and Criminal Justice
University of Leeds

OXFORD
UNIVERSITY PRESS

OXFORD

UNIVERSITY PRESS

Great Clarendon Street, Oxford OX2 6DP

Oxford University Press is a department of the University of Oxford.
It furthers the University's objective of excellence in research, scholarship,
and education by publishing worldwide in

Oxford New York

Auckland Cape Town Dar es Salaam Hong Kong Karachi
Kuala Lumpur Madrid Melbourne Mexico City Nairobi
New Delhi Shanghai Taipei Toronto

With offices in

Argentina Austria Brazil Chile Czech Republic France Greece
Guatemala Hungary Italy Japan Poland Portugal Singapore
South Korea Switzerland Thailand Turkey Ukraine Vietnam

Oxford is a registered trade mark of Oxford University Press
in the UK and in certain other countries

Published in the United States
by Oxford University Press Inc., New York

British Library Cataloguing in Publication Data

Data available

Library of Congress Control Number: 2009925563

Typeset by Newgen Imaging Systems (P) Ltd, Chennai, India
Printed in Great Britain
on acid-free paper by
L.E.G.O. S.p.A.

ISBN 978–0–19–922729–7

10 9 8 7 6 5 4 3 2 1

Eight miles from Manhattan is the largest penal colony in the world, a place most New Yorkers could not point to on the map and many do not know exists. Home to 15,000 inmates, Riker's Island is just over the waterway 100 yards from La Guardia International airport. It is a place of invisibility from where, paradoxically, the inmates have an extraordinary view of one of the most famous skylines in the world: a tantalizing sight which no doubt only serves to increase their misery. Such a world of secret punishment sets us a whole series of puzzles for the criminologist—for the sociologist as sleuth! Why, first of all, is punishment hidden when in the past, as the French philosopher Michael Foucault pointed out in *Discipline and Punish*, it was out front and ostentatious: witness the public gallows, the whipping post, the village stocks. And why do so many people need to be punished in a rich, developed country that, supposedly, is the homeland of liberal democracy? In the United States there are 2.1 million people behind bars at any one time, and prison building, management, and maintenance has become a giant industry, vigorously competed for by state and local authorities because of its promise of employment and a pollution-free environment.

But let us look a little closer at Riker's Island: it is the size of a small town of 20,000 inhabitants (including staff) with its own schools, bakers, tailor shop, recreation, medical centre, nursery, and religious facilities. Yet it is scarcely economically sufficient: Riker's costs the US taxpayer over $800 million a year to run. Indeed the average cost of keeping an inmate is $60,000 a year—compare that to the average US wage of $37,000. And as for efficiency, about 75% of inmates will return to Riker's within a year of release. Let us say at this stage that such a paradox is repeated across the developed world—it is not an idiosyncrasy of the United States, however much the scale of imprisonment is exceptional. So a further and seemingly perennial problem occurs for the criminologist: how is such an irrational process possible and why does it persist? But the puzzles do not end here. Let us look at the inmates themselves: what strikes one immediately is that the demographic profile of Riker's is scarcely representative of the wider society. First of all they are over 90% Black and Latino, secondly they are nearly all men, thirdly one quarter have been treated for mental illness and 80% have a history of substance abuse. Lastly and perhaps most definitively, they are poor: 30% are homeless and 90% lack a high school diploma. And such a profile of race, gender, mental instability, and desperate poverty could be repeated in prisons around the globe. Why, then, is the criminal justice system skewed in such a way? Is this the shape of criminality? Each of these dimensions of the inmate population throws up its own series of questions. Is the racial disproportionality of the prison due to racism inherent in the criminal justice system or does it truly reflect the differences in levels of crime between ethnic groups? Is there some genetic characteristic of men compared to women that makes them more aggressive and liable to crime? To what extent can the mentally disturbed be held responsible for their crimes? And are the poor incarcerated the world over because it is the deviance of the poor that we call crimes? Or is all this just another example of the golden rule: it is the people with gold who make the rules?

The study of criminology begs all these questions. It encompasses questions of sociology and psychology, of legal theory and social philosophy, of biology and the social sciences. It is at the crossroads of all these disciplines and more—it is never a marginal concern but one that takes us immediately into the relations of normality and deviance, of order and disorder, of crime and punishment, and indeed of good and evil. Because of this, crime has always been a major staple of the mass media: it is on the news every night. It is the core theme of detective fiction and of 'cops and robbers' drama on television. It alarms us and makes us fearful, but it also entertains and thrills us. We are attracted and beguiled by these images yet so many of them are patently false. The serial killer is an extreme rarity, yet it becomes a major genre of thriller fiction, its depiction a caricature of reality, a 'pornocopia' of sex and violence. Crime in the real world is frequently not detected—the criminal usually gets away. In fiction the intuitive skills and resourcefulness of the detective inevitably lead to the apprehension of the crook yet reality has no such denouement. The depiction of the violent attack from Hollywood blockbusters to video games revolves around 'stranger danger'—the threat of the unknown, of the malicious 'Other'. In most parts of the world this is the very inverse of truth. If you want to know your most likely murderer, look in the mirror. You are most likely to kill yourself, to commit suicide, than be killed by others; of those around you, your best friends and your nearest and dearest, then casual acquaintances are more likely to be your killer than those unknown to you. The stranger will only rarely look back at you, and when it does, the face looking out will be the same age, the same class, the same colour of skin as you. The only exception to this is if you are a woman: a man's face will look back at you (you are most likely to be killed by your husband or boyfriend) and, tragically, if you are a child, it is your mum or dad who will look back at you—only rarely will it be a stranger.

Criminology is intrigued by crime and the images of crime: each 'fact' which seems obvious becomes problematic on examination; each stereotype that we take for granted appears dubious or even prejudiced when we inspect it at close quarters. Our task, then, must be to untangle stereotype from reality, fact from fiction. And the search for the answers to all these questions that we have posed—and many more besides—is an endeavour of great practical importance, for it is only by their solution that we can help ameliorate both the impact of crime and the pains of imprisonment.

It is with such thoughts in mind that I recommend this book to students, practitioners and interested members of the public alike. The editors are to be congratulated for having brought together a group of contributors that pose these and many other related questions surrounding criminology and its uses in an accessible and thought-provoking way. I am certain that this book will be a cornerstone of criminology and criminal justice programs for many years to come.

Jock Young, New York City, NY

OUTLINE CONTENTS

DETAILED CONTENTS

LIST OF FIGURES

LIST OF TABLES

LIST OF CONTRIBUTORS

Jeff Ferrell *Professor of Sociology, Texas Christian University, USA, and Visiting Professor of Criminology, University of Kent*

Marian FitzGerald *Visiting Professor of Criminology, University of Kent*

Frank Furedi *Professor of Sociology, University of Kent*

Hannah Goodman *Chong Research Fellow, De Montfort University*

Chris Greer *Senior Lecturer in Criminology, City University*

Chris Hale *Professor of Criminology, University of Kent*

Keith Hayward *Senior Lecturer in Criminology, University of Kent*

Tim Hope *Professor of Criminology, University of Keele*

Richard Jones *Lecturer in Criminology, Edinburgh University*

Trevor Jones *Reader in Criminology, Cardiff University*

Derek Kirton *Reader in Social Policy and Social Work, University of Kent*

Roger Matthews *Director of Crime Reduction and Community Safety Research Unit, London South Bank University*

Wayne Morrison *Professor of Law, Director of the External Laws Programme of the University of London*

Mike Presdee *Senior Lecturer in Criminology, University of Kent*

Paddy Rawlinson *Lecturer in Criminology, London School of Economics*

Larry Ray *Professor of Sociology, University of Kent*

Heather Shore *Senior Lecturer in Social and Cultural History, Leeds Metropolitan University*

Catrin Smith *Reader in Criminology, University of Chester*

Terry Thomas *Professor in Criminal Justice Studies, Leeds Metropolitan University*

Steve Tombs *Professor of Sociology, Liverpool John Moores University*

Peter Traynor *Research officer, University of Leeds*

Steve Uglow *Professor of Criminal Justice, University of Kent*

Azrini Wahidin *Reader in Criminology and Criminal Justice, Queen's University, Belfast*

The late Brian Williams *formerly Professor of Community Justice and Victimology, De Montfort University*

Emma Wincup *Senior Lecturer in Criminology and Criminal Justice, University of Leeds*

Anne Worrall *Professor of Criminology, Keele University*

Guide to the book

Chris Hale, Keith Hayward, Azrini Wahidin, and Emma Wincup

Criminology's phenomenal expansion has shown no sign of abating since we remarked upon it in the Guide to the First Edition of this book. Once taught exclusively as a post-graduate subject, criminology is now offered in an ever-expanding range of undergraduate courses at all levels across the university system. To put this into perspective, in the UK alone there are now 934 courses related to criminology offered by 98 institutions. One could also point to a large increase in the number of 'applied criminology' courses, such as community justice and police studies aimed at professionals already working within the criminal justice system or those who hope to pursue a career in criminal justice.

Inevitably such rapid expansion has precipitated the arrival of a whole host of text-books, dictionaries, and handbooks that have sought to introduce developments in criminology and criminal justice to this new generation of students. For all their various merits, few of these works have been able to provide undergraduate criminologists with a single comprehensive and authoritative source that serves as an accessible overview of the most pertinent issues currently facing the discipline. *Criminology* is specifically intended to meet this requirement. It has been produced as a complete package both for students new to criminology and their lecturers. We also hope that *Criminology* will serve as a useful resource for criminal justice practitioners and interested members of the general public.

For students, *Criminology* offers 27 chapters on core criminological issues that can be used to help them prepare for a seminar discussion, or as the foundation stone for a presentation or undergraduate essay. Each chapter is self-contained, although links are made to relevant discussions in other chapters. Students are also encouraged to use the index to research the topic further. In addition to the substantive discussion, a number of pedagogical features are included. Chapters are accompanied by review questions, suggestions for further reading, and relevant websites. Where appropriate, students are guided to additional resources such as sources of data. Key concepts are collated in a glossary at the end of the text. All of this, we hope, adds up to a book that is pitched at an appropriate level for students with no prior knowledge of criminology, yet at the same time is challenging enough to equip them with the skills and knowledge needed for future study.

For lecturers, *Criminology* proffers sufficient material for a module spanning the whole academic year, and allows lecturers responsible for one term/semester modules to dip into the book and select an appropriate mix of topics. Each chapter is complemented by questions that can be used to structure discussions within seminars.

Accompanying this textbook is an extensive website carefully designed both to assist students with little background understanding of criminology, and to provide module leaders with a range of pedagogic tools aimed at enhancing the student learning experience. The most important resources are links to relevant websites, which allow students to access additional information at the click of a button in order to update and augment the chapter discussions. This is particularly vital given the ever-changing nature of criminal justice policy and shifting patterns of offending and victimization. For lecturers, the website offers brief lecture notes and Powerpoint® slides for each topic included in the book. The website also contains a 'Testbank' of approximately 300 multiple-choice questions. These can be used by students to test their understanding of the material covered in each chapter and employed by lecturers to assess students on a formal and informal basis. Each question is accompanied by feedback to enable students to further their understanding of criminological issues.

This book is arranged around four themes. As its name suggests Part One, 'Introducing Crime and Criminology', introduces students to the core concepts and issues needed for the study of criminology today. To begin with, Wayne Morrison tackles what is perhaps the discipline's most fundamental question: what is crime? Whilst for the uninitiated this may appear a straightforward topic, he moves quickly beyond simple definitions to consider questions of power and legitimacy, each reviewed within a historically and culturally informed discussion of how criminologists define their object of study. In her chapter, 'The History of Crime', Heather Shore provides an overview of the history of crime in Britain by exploring the changing construction of criminality and the historical development of the criminal justice system. Bringing the story up to date and using material from recent government and independent reviews of crime statistics, Tim Hope provides a comprehensive discussion of the changing and sometimes conflicting uses to which they are put. In particular he problematizes such important questions as: How do we know the level of crime? What information is available and how reliable is it? Going far beyond the standard discussions, he presents a provocative and informed account of the problems of measuring crime either from police figures or by using surveys. Shifting gear, the next chapter provides the student with a comprehensive introduction to how criminological theory has developed and is used. While all the chapters in this book are theoretically informed, Keith Hayward and Wayne Morrison offer the reader a series of theoretical vignettes, each one of which provides both an accessible introduction to a particular theory and informed signposts to more detailed readings. The following chapter by Emma Wincup focuses on the production of criminological knowledge and encourages students to adopt a critical stance when interpreting it. She charts the development of the empirical research tradition in criminology, outlines the range of research designs and methods available to criminological researchers, draws attention to the particular challenges criminologists face when conducting research, and identifies new methodological developments currently influencing criminology.

Whilst the main thrust of this text is sociological we freely acknowledge the substantial influence psychology has exerted on criminology. In Chapter 6 Keith Hayward casts a sympathetic but critical eye on the interface between these two disciplines, presenting and assessing some of the major psychological theories of crime and their impact on the study of crime and criminal justice. This interdisciplinary approach is further evidenced in Jeff Ferrell's chapter on the cultural significance of crime. His central aim is to examine the way in which crime and culture intertwine within the lived experiences of everyday life. He asserts that a whole host of urban crimes are perpetuated by actors for whom transgression serves a number of purposes. Ferrell charts a world of underground graffiti artists, gang members, street hustlers, pimps, and other 'outsider' criminals, whose distinctive subcultures are increasingly the subject of media, corporate, and political interest. Continuing this cultural theme, Chris Greer focuses specifically on the interconnections between crime and the media. In a world in which crime is often packaged as entertainment and refracted in so-called 'reality television', Greer asks us to reflect on and unpick these increasingly pervasive relationships. After critically discussing the dominant theoretical, conceptual, and methodological approaches, he considers the evidence for the 'effects' of media representations, both on criminal behaviour and importantly on fear of crime, exploring the implications of living in a media-saturated era for crime and its control.

Part Two, 'Forms of Crime' moves beyond introduction to look at some of the various types of crimes prevalent in late-modern society. Starting with our daily round, Mike Presdee examines the way crime is woven into the fabric of everyday life. He looks at the day-to-day offences that constitute the major part of the recorded crime figures, arguing that while, historically, volume crime has meant property crime (burglary, theft, and criminal damage), now low-level activities labelled 'anti-social' are increasingly coming to dominate the volume crime discourse. Picking up on these themes, Emma Wincup and Peter Traynor's chapter also focuses on crimes which are a feature of many people's daily lives. Problematic use of drugs and alcohol are often linked with volume *and* violent crime, although the relationship between drug and alcohol use and crime is more complex than is typically portrayed in media and political discussions.

While violence inevitably features in the previous two chapters, Larry Ray takes discussion to another level providing a systematic overview of some of the main sociological and criminological debates in the area. But more than this he explores changing sociocultural responses to crimes involving high levels of aggression and violence. Using data from the British Crime Survey, he provides figures on the prevalence of different types of violence within England and Wales and discusses the impact of hate, homophobic, and racist crimes. In Chapter 12, Terry Thomas tackles the subject and nature of sexual offending. He examines the forms it takes as well as social and criminal justice responses made to sex offending over the last ten years.

A very different type of crime, but one that again is often ignored in student texts, is the vitally important area of corporate crime. Steve Tombs examines the emergence of this concept, discussing its meaning and reviewing the extent to which it represents a crime problem. He then considers various dimensions of corporate crime, its visibility, causation, and control, questioning society's will to censure and punish company directors and other 'rogue' capitalists. While criminology has tended to concentrate on more 'traditional' forms of criminality, the burgeoning of organized crime on a global scale has provoked increasing academic interest. Paddy Rawlinson looks at a number of its current and previous manifestations, from US street gangs of the 1920s, to the Italian-based family 'mafia' groups, and on to the newer organized crime groups that have emerged from places as geographically and culturally distinct as the former Soviet Union and Colombia. Similarly marginalized from the criminological gaze is terrorism. While other disciplines have begun to engage with this subject in the wake of 9/11, criminology has been slow to regard the dynamics of international terrorism as one of its primary concerns. Addressing this lacuna Frank Furedi provides a general introduction to the subject and poses a series of important questions about how one actually defines terrorism against a backdrop of contemporary fears in a risk-averse society.

In Part Three, 'Social Dimensions of Crime' the authors examine how offending, victimization, and experiences of the criminal justice system (CJS) may be affected by people's class, gender, and ethnicity. Beginning with the complex relationships between crime, economic marginalization, and social exclusion, Chris Hale provides a clear introduction to the key issues and debates. Again, moving beyond the standard textbook approach of focusing on crime and unemployment, he provides a more rounded critical analysis of the impact of economic factors on offending and victimization. Next, Catrin Smith and Emma Wincup explore the connections between gender and crime. They examine the different kinds of crimes in which men and women are involved, and consider the complex and changing relationship between masculinity(ies), femininity(ies), and crime. They deconstruct how these relations have been typically understood in criminological theory and look at the different ways in which men and women are dealt with by the CJS.

The treatment ethnic minority groups receive, both as victims and suspects, has rightly had an increasingly high profile in the last three decades. In her chapter on race and ethnicity Marian FitzGerald begins by exploring the meaning of both terms in the context of discussions of crime. She critically examines the debates surrounding this vexed (and always controversial) issue and argues the need for renewed rigour and clarity to avoid repeating past mistakes and confusions.

Anti-social behaviour, binge drinking, and street gangs are some of the latest manifestations of society's perennial concerns about young people and their problem behaviour. Dealing with such matters is the focus of Derek Kirton's chapter. He outlines the key principles around which youth justice has evolved and how the balance between welfare and punishment has shifted over time in line with broader social and political changes. He provides, too, a profile of youth crime, making links between age and other social divisions. Young people are not the only age group to experience special problems within the CJS. In the final chapter in this section, Azrini Wahidin examines the relationship between later life, crime, imprisonment, and the criminal justice system. She examines the key issues and current debates surrounding often neglected older offenders in the criminal justice system.

In Part Four, 'Responses to Crime', the focus shifts to consider how society responds to crime through its treatment of both offenders and victims. Here we see crime's inherently political nature. The process and delivery of criminal justice, the practices of the agencies involved in 'crime control', and the treatment of victimized communities and individuals are all framed by public and political debate. In their chapter Chris Hale and Marian FitzGerald examine the rise in punitive and retributive discourses against broader economic and social changes. Echoing earlier chapters on youth crime, street crime, and public disorder, Hale and FitzGerald document how these have led to an unseemly competition between the political parties to be the 'toughest team in town'.

Picking up this theme, Steve Uglow outlines and critiques the role of the CJS in England and Wales. He provides a comprehensive and accessible account of the different parts of the criminal justice system (including recent significant changes such as the creation of the Ministry of Justice), and highlights the linkages and tensions between them.

Exploring further the themes of intensified social control discussed by Hale and FitzGerald, Richard Jones looks at how social control now operates in a different register. Over the last two decades, a range of new electronic and digital technologies have come to be employed as tools of formal control, security, exclusion, and punishment, bringing with them 'new' social practices which many commentators, rightly or wrongly, have argued are likely to have profound consequences for established civil liberties. Jones's chapter offers the reader a general introduction to theoretical debates surrounding surveillance. It then proceeds with an overview of these new technologies of social control, including the forms they currently take, how they function, and their usage. These uses include both the private sector as a form of surveillance and physical exclusion, and in the public domain as an instrument of criminal justice—for example, the electronic tagging and monitoring of offenders.

Brian Williams' chapter on victimology examines how from its early stereotyping of victims as blameworthy (contributing in some way to their own problems), victimology—the study of victims—has developed a more critical edge. The chapter introduces the reader to the study of victims of crime and to the political and social changes which have brought victims to the centre of debates about crime.

Trevor Jones's discussion of policing draws out the important distinction between 'policing' and the public organizational structure 'the police'. He achieves this task by exploring the workings of a number of agencies, in both the public and private sector, engaged in governance and regulation. After outlining the historical development of the police in Britain and exploring the multitude of roles performed by the police, he considers the different models of policing in operation today and their perceived effectiveness. The key role of discretion, and how this can lead to the exercise of police powers in a discriminatory manner, is also critically assessed. This opens up an analysis of 'cop culture' and attempts by the police to overcome allegations of racial discrimination and poor relations with minority ethnic and other 'hard to reach' communities.

The final two chapters look at the treatment of convicted offenders. Anne Worrall begins by exploring the development of punishment in the community from the nineteenth century onwards and the emergence of the new discourse of offender management in the twenty-first century. Focusing mainly, but not exclusively, on England and Wales, it deals largely with the punishment of adult offenders. She highlights the range of community penalties available to sentencers, and their evolution over the past 100 years, and summarizes the debates about their effectiveness as a means of reducing re-offending and diverting offenders from custody. In a thought-provoking chapter, Roger Matthews provides a critical discussion on the history of prisons, the use of imprisonment, and why imprisonment has become the dominant form of punishment in western societies for the last 200 years.

The production of this book has been a mammoth undertaking involving 26 contributors from 16 different institutions. Whilst this has inevitably thrown up a number of editorial headaches, once again, we think the end result has been worth the struggle. Building upon the tremendous success of the First Edition, we believe we have once again produced an invaluable and comprehensive undergraduate text for criminology students and anyone else interested in the study of crime, deviance, and criminal justice. Thus, we would like to take a moment here to thank all the contributors for their patience and good grace in the face of our editorial diktats!

Likewise we must also thank our editorial team at Oxford University Press for their enthusiasm for the project. Tom Young originally commissioned the second edition of the book before moving on to other projects at OUP, and helped us to decide what revisions needed to be made. His replacement, Jo Godfrey, was instrumental in keeping the project on track, and we were sad to lose her as our editor before the project was complete. We welcomed Helen Swann as our final editor shortly before submitting the manuscript and appreciated her efforts to ensure the handover to the production team was a smooth one.

Above all we would like to dedicate this book to the interested criminological reader. We hope you find it a useful resource and aid to study. Welcome to the wonderful and exciting world of criminological research.

Chris Hale, Keith Hayward, Azrini Wahidin, and Emma Wincup
Canterbury, Belfast, and Leeds
October 2008

Guide to the online resource centre

Criminology is accompanied by an interactive Online Resource Centre, which you can access at www.oxfordtextbooks.co.uk/orc/hale2e/. The Online Resource Centre is closely integrated with the book, and provides students and lecturers with ready-to-use teaching and learning resources. The resources are available free-of-charge, designed to complement the textbook, and offer additional materials which are suited to electronic delivery. All these resources can be downloaded and are fully customizable, allowing them to be incorporated into an institution's existing virtual learning environment ('VLE').

Lecturer resources

These resources are password-protected to ensure that only lecturers can gain access. Lecturers may use these free resources to complement their own teaching materials or as a platform to update and restructure their courses. Registering is easy: go to 'Lecturer

Resources' on the Online Resource Centre, complete a simple registration form, and access will granted within three working days (subject to verification). Each registration is personally checked to ensure the security of the site.

Test bank

The test bank is a fully customizable resource containing ready-made assessments with which to test students. It offers versatile testing tailored to the contents of each particular chapter and there are questions in several different formats: multiple choice; multiple response; matching; fill in the blanks; true/false; and short answer. The test bank is downloadable into Questionmark Perception, Blackboard, WebCT, and most other virtual learning environments (VLEs). The test bank questions are also downloadable in formats suitable for printing directly by the lecturer.

PowerPoint slides and lecturer notes

These complement each chapter of the book and are a useful resource for preparing lectures and handouts. They allow lecturers to guide their students through the key concepts, ideas and theories and can be fully customized to meet the needs of the course, enabling lecturers to focus on the areas most relevant to their students.

Student resources

These are accessible to all students, with no registration or password access required, enabling students to get the most out of the textbook.

Chapter synopses

Succinct overviews of each chapter help you to locate relevant material easily and quickly.

Web links

A selection of annotated web links, chosen by the chapter authors, allows you to research easily those topics that are of particular interest. These links are checked and updated regularly to ensure they remain relevant and up to date.

Glossary

A useful one-stop reference point for all the keywords used within the textbook. In addition to a standard, alphabetical glossary, you will also find key term 'flashcards' and interactive 'crosswords', both of which allow you to test your knowledge of important criminology vocabulary.

Further reading

Sources recommended by the chapter authors for additional reading, to assist you in understanding important issues and developing a broader knowledge of the subject.

Part One

INTRODUCING CRIME AND CRIMINOLOGY

1

What is crime?
Contrasting definitions
and perspectives

Wayne Morrison

INTRODUCTION

Crime, we are told, is today a salient fact, an integral part of the risks we face in everyday life. In both scholarly and public opinion crime is associated with harm and violence; harm to individuals, destruction of property, and the denial of respect to people and institutions. It is clear that we face pressing problems of a practical and scholarly nature in understanding crime. But we lack agreement on the most basic question, namely *what is crime*? This battle over definitions, of categorizing events as crimes or other things, is no tame affair. In a bid to make sense of the diversity of opinions, definitions, and perspectives surrounding this question, this chapter will introduce some of the complex interrelationships surrounding the various ways that crime is constructed and objectified, before setting out some of the different perspectives that people actually take towards defining crime in practice. Many of the issues outlined in this chapter will be picked up in the substantive chapters that follow in this text.

BACKGROUND

Crime operates as a core concept in mod... ...ems like a common sense category but this is only a superficial appearance ... ...r, makes it necessary to ask what boundaries can be placed ar... ...its use mean for us, individually, as speakers of th... ...oncept? Who has the power to make their ...laims stick? These questions raise issues ...elativism; is there a settled or 'objective' ...s and different territorial institutions or m... ...d within a particular locality or group, bu... ...account? What is the role, function, and ... ...ncepts, such as 'punishment') as an orga... ...analysis onto the acts of power of the a... ...ithin the nation state, the legislature, a... ...erms of that speech, notably the police a... ...ts of coercive social control (see Chapters... ...t part of the question while the framewor... ...sed in the following sections.

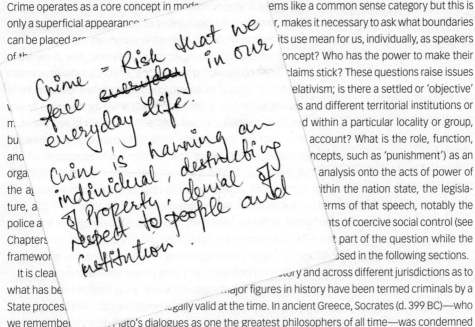

It is clea... ...tory and across different jurisdictions as to what has be... ...ajor figures in history have been termed criminals by a State proces... ...egally valid at the time. In ancient Greece, Socrates (d. 399 BC)—who we remember ... ...ato's dialogues as one the greatest philosophers of all time—was condemned by a court for the crime of corrupting the youth of Athens with his teachings. He died by taking hemlock after refusing the aid of his supporters to free him. In Roman-occupied Palestine, Jesus Christ was condemned and crucified along with 'two common thieves'; Martin Luther King was imprisoned for his role in the 1960's US civil rights movement. While in prison he wrote his *Letter From Birmingham Jail*, an essay that stands as one of the classic writings on civil disobedience (in which he argues that one has a duty to disobey unjust laws, but also to abide by the lawful processes of the State including any punishment so ordered). Likewise, Nelson Mandela was convicted for activities against the apartheid State of South Africa and served 26 years in prison before his release. He subsequently became the first democratically elected President of South Africa. Are we to call individuals like these 'criminals'? Or do we say that it was a mistake to have ever called them that?

Writing in the late nineteenth century, the French sociologist Emile Durkheim—often referred to as the 'father figure of sociology'—pointed out that a great deal of social change has occurred as the result of people going against the settled rules and opposing the interests of those in power (see Chapter 4 below). According to Durkheim, a society that had no crime would be 'pathologically over-controlled':

> According to Athenian law, Socrates was a criminal, and his condemnation was no more than just. However, his crime, namely, the independence of his thought, rendered a service not only to humanity but to his country. It served to prepare a new morality and faith which the Athenians needed, since the traditions by which they had lived until then were no longer in harmony with the current conditions of life. (Durkheim, 1966: 71)

Following Durkheim we do not look at 'crime' as something that exists in abstraction, or define it as reflecting some form of simple, 'plain-fact' situation. Instead 'crime' is a complex interaction of many processes: from the creation of a concept of 'crime', to people identifying some event as a crime; from the responses to the event so called, to the behaviour and formal activities of state agencies (or in the emerging global arena supra-national bodies such as the International Criminal Court or the International Criminal Tribunal for Yugoslavia) that may or may not process the persons responsible as 'criminals' and punish them. These interactions all take place against the backdrop of the cultural world inhabited at that time. In understanding these interactions it is also important to notice what was not done, what was avoided, as much as cataloguing what was done. This is the subject of the next section.

Defining crime: confronting events and understanding processes

Reflecting upon the processes involved in claiming certain actions or events as crimes serves as a route into analysing differences and similarities in actual events and their role within the sets of beliefs, understandings, and reactions to others that enables our societies to cohere. Consider the following examples of social events. Are they crimes?

- In 1781 The *Zong* was a slave ship owned by a large Liverpool slaving company employed on the well-tried route from Liverpool to West Africa and thence with a cargo of slaves to the Caribbean. On 6 September it sailed from West Africa with a cargo of 470 slaves bound for Jamaica. Twelve weeks later, closing on its destination, the *Zong* had already lost more than 60 Africans and seven of the 17-man crew because of dysentery brought on by severe overcrowding. The *Zong's* captain ordered that sick slaves should be thrown overboard both to preserve dwindling supplies of water and to allow the shipping company to claim their loss against insurance. One hundred and thirty-one slaves were thrown overboard and drowned, even though it had rained and there was plenty of water. None of the sick sailors were thrown overboard.

- On 5 July 1884, the yacht the *Mignonette*, crewed by three men and a cabin boy, sank in a storm 1,600 miles off the Cape of Good Hope. The crew escaped in a small open boat with no supply of food or water except a can of turnips. By 24 July, all four were in a terrible condition and one of the men, Dudley, killed the cabin boy, who was delirious, with a knife and all three drank his blood and fed on his body. Four days later a passing boat picked them up. It is accepted that the boy would not have lived and the men probably would have died if they had not eaten him.

- On 6 August 1945, US forces dropped an atomic bomb called 'Little Boy' on the Japanese city of Hiroshima. Three days later they dropped another called 'Fat Man' on Nagasaki. By the end of 1945, less than six months later, the Hiroshima bomb had caused 140,000 deaths, and the Nagaski bomb 70,000. Five years later the totals were 200,000 and 140,000. At the time the reason put forward was that the use of atomic devices was necessary to shorten the war and save allied lives. Was this a crime? Does it matter to your opinion that at the Tokyo International Military Tribunal set up to judge Japanese war criminals, the only judge with any previous experience of 'international law', the Indian judge Pal, issued a full dissenting judgment? He refused to accept the prosecution of the Japanese defendants as he considered that the Allies too should be tried and punished for crimes committed during the war, in particular for the dropping of the atomic bomb.

- In 1994, after the plane carrying the President of Rwanda was shot down, government military forces along with perhaps as many as 50,000 civilians armed with knives and machetes systematically killed more than 800,000 out of the 1,000,000 minority Tutsi population and at least 20,000 moderate Hutu in a three-month killing spree. This received very little international attention and the United Nations withdrew its small peacekeeping force due to an absence of Security Council pressure to protect anyone. Most commentators believe that if international action had been taken the majority of the 800,000-plus people killed would have been saved.

- In 1999, the government of a major European country facing legitimacy problems have their secret service agents stage a 'terrorist attack' on their own citizens, killing 200. They then blame the attack upon separatist 'terrorist' movements in one of the other provinces of the country. As a result they engage in a military crackdown in which a reputed 100,000 civilians lose their lives. Four years later militant separatists, several of whom have lost their families in the military action, seize a school and take hostages. Government forces try to free the children, but in the following action 400 hostage children lose their lives.

- On 11 September 2001, the Twin Towers in New York, once the tallest buildings in the world, were struck by planes hijacked by members of the 'terrorist' group Al-Qaeda (literally 'a base'; the origins of Al-Qaeda can be traced to the Muslim Brotherhood in Egypt, as they developed they were aided and financed by the US CIA and factions within Saudi Arabia as part of the Afghanistan Mojahaden waging Jihad against the Soviet occupation of Afghanistan). The crashed planes started intense fires which collapsed the towers with the loss of nearly 3,000 lives. Some commentators, including the US Sectary of State, called this a massive crime but quickly they were redefined as 'acts of war'. The US President in a State of the Nation speech divided the world up into a civilized group that were with the US and others that stood against them. The US Congress and Senate authorized the President to 'use all necessary and appropriate force against those nations, organizations, or persons *he determines* planned, authorized, committed, or aided the terrorist attacks...or harbored such organizations or persons' (115 Stat 224, 18 September 2001: Authorizations for Use of United Stated Armed Forces).

- Inmates in a government prison learn that another inmate sentenced for a relatively minor crime has admitted to a cellmate that he has sexually abused children in the past. The inmates convene their own court, try the inmate, and find him guilty. As a sentence they beat him up, breaking both his legs and kneecaps, and leave him permanently crippled. Are their actions a crime, or are they justly punishing him?

- The owner of a factory operates in breach of health and safety regulations and keeps the fire escape exits locked. As a result of a fire on the premises many of the factory staff burn to death. Is this a crime, or an industrial accident?

- In 2003 many thousands of abortions were carried out in the US in accordance with the valid law. Members of the pro-life movement claim that the doctors carrying out the operations are guilt of murder—are they? One pro-life member shoots and kills a well-known abortion-performing doctor, because he says the doctor was breaking God's will and he needed to be punished.

The examples could be multiplied. Certainly all 'crimes' are unique events; however, are there common characteristics to some of these events that mark them off for special recognition and thus mean they are crimes? Is there a coherent way of distinguishing key factors and ensuring that 'we', that is the representatives of a community, come to an agreement as to what makes up a crime, or, indeed, what should then follow from agreeing that a crime has taken place? Or does the issue of agreeing on what is crime actually show how divided 'we' are? If we answer each event with a yes, that those events should be accepted as a crime, are we merely being emotive? (Emotivism is defined as a use of language that asserts something which cannot logically be backed up in such a way that it convinces the majority of others to agree.) Can we separate what *is* legally a crime (that is, it is contrary to the valid law) from what we feel ought to be a crime? Or is this way of distinguishing things a mistake? Is it a lazy way out of the dilemma of our responsibility towards the world? What then can we learn from following through the above examples?

- The *Zong* actually went to trial as an insurance case. The boat owners had claimed insurance on the dead slaves as they said they were simply 'property' that had been thrown overboard out of necessity. The original jury agreed and ordered the underwriters to pay insurance on them, but the underwriters appealed and we do not know if any insurance money was ever paid out. Meanwhile, a group of people around a prominent individual called Glanvill Sharp tried to get the authorities to prosecute the crew for murder, but they were unsuccessful. The system did not want this to be called a crime (see Gearey, Morrison, and Jago, 2009, chapter 2). As Walvin (1992) argues, if this event had been called 'murder', it would have unpicked the legality of the whole slave system and the international trade in it. As a result people around Glanvill Sharp got together and formed an anti-slavery and abolitionist movement that ultimately changed the system.

- In the case of the cabin boy who was killed and eaten, the men were prosecuted and the case of Dudley and Stephens (1884) became a leading case for the proposition that necessity cannot be a defence against the charge of murder in English law. The judge who heard the case made a wonderful statement that it was always the duty of the captain of a ship to look after his passengers and crew before himself. Of course the *Zong* was not mentioned in argument! The men were sentenced to death, but this was reduced to six months' imprisonment. In fact it was a custom of the sea for men in similar conditions to cast lots and the person with the shortest lot to be killed and eaten (Simpson, 1984). In this example the men had agreed to do this, but the cabin boy was so weak that they decided to kill him without casting lots. The Admiralty opposed the trial as they did not want the customs of the sea upset, but another government department insisted on charges.

- No one has ever faced charges in respect of the atomic bomb, although Sellars (2002: 66), relying upon a biography of the US President Harry Truman (written by his daughter, Margaret) relates a stag dinner hosted by Truman in early 1953. At this dinner, the famous wartime British leader, Winston Churchill, had the bad manners to ask Truman if he had his response ready for when they both were to stand before St Peter and told to justify using the atomic bombs. This caused considerable shock, which was alleviated when the party organized a mock trial of Churchill with Truman as judge and a jury consisting of the US Secretary of State and other close US colleagues and Generals. Acquittal resulted, though Sellars could not find in Margaret Truman's account the reason; perhaps, Sellars surmised, 'they sensed that their own hands were dipped in blood. Or perhaps, they reasoned that it did not matter anyway. After all, even in real life tribunals, no one ever punishes a victor.'

Let us pause for reflection. What are the consequences if we accept the definition of crime that is presented in most criminal law textbooks, namely a crime is some conduct (an act or omission) which, when it leads to a certain state of affairs, is treated in that jurisdiction as being capable of leading to prosecution and punishment? Glanville Williams (1955: 107), for example, defined crime as 'an act that is capable of being followed by criminal proceedings, having one of the types of outcome (punishment etc) known to follow these proceedings'. This in practice is the definition of crime most commonly accepted, as was brought out by Tappan's famous injunction that criminology accepts as its object of study crime, defined as 'an intentional act or omission in violation of criminal law (statutory and case law), committed without defence or justification, and sanctioned by the State as a felony or misdemeanor' (1947: 100). But this means that there is no common element to a crime other than the fact of the prior legal procedure defining such and such act or omission as a crime. It also means that so far in the events considered only the act of killing the cabin boy was a crime, and that was a near thing. In the great age of sail it is probable that many cases occurred where crews ended up in open boats or stranded on desolate shores and one of their company was killed and eaten. But they drew lots, thus when they were picked up everyone could be satisfied that the custom of the sea had been followed and no crime occurred and the authorities were never involved.

- In the case of Rwanda we face a situation, which most commentators now say, was the most easily preventable mass crime of the twentieth century. The attention of the world's media was on events in South Africa where Nelson Mandela was elected President and apartheid ended peacefully. When the first killings began ten Belgian UN soldiers were killed with the result that the UN withdrew the mission and all attempts to get intervention failed, in particular because of US reluctance caused in part by the previous killing of 18 US servicemen in Somalia. The subsequent official US line was that they did not have proper information; they did not appreciate the full picture. We now know that they knew fully what was going on and that President Clinton had ordered that the term 'genocide' not be used as that might trigger calls for the US to intervene, not to mention the quasi-legal obligation to take action as a country that had ratified the Genocide Convention (see, for example, 'US chose to ignore Rwandan genocide', *The Guardian*, 31 March 2004). Thus, deliberate US inactivity was one of the crucial factors that condemned to death the equivalent of the US domestic homicide total for 1950–2000. It would be literally unthinkable for President Clinton to face penal sanctions in connection with these deaths; for his deliberate inactivity to be called a 'crime'. He was, however, pursued by extremely expensive legal proceedings (costing more than a UN force that would have deterred or at least stopped the main killings of the genocide) for most of his second term in office. The question to be ascertained in those particular proceedings, which included impeachment hearings, was did he commit a crime or misdemeanour when he stated that an activity with a certain female intern at the White House, later found to be an oral sexual act, did not constitute 'sexual relations'. He was acquitted (his defence was that he used the term in a precise legal sense, i.e. that it defined penetrative sexual intercourse which he had not engaged in).

- The situation with the 'major European country' and terrorism equates to what many have claimed the situation was between Russia and Chechnya. In the context of the current 'war on terror', most governments say that Chechnya is an internal matter for Russia, in effect closing their eyes to massive human rights violations, death, and destruction.

- The action of the prison inmates constitutes 'self-help'. It is deemed a crime and not justified 'punishment' in part because one of the principles that modern society is founded on is that the State claims a monopoly upon legitimate violence. There are many examples of groups that organize themselves in such a way that they almost constitute a State within a State—such as the Mafia or transnational drug dealing organizations—taking on State-like roles and procedures. In doing so they pose a threat to the State's existence and since the sixteenth century the dominant mode of large-scale social organization has been the 'nation state'. It is the nation state that has the authority to define what sort of activities can be deemed crimes within its boundaries and only officials of the nation state are authorized to carry out punishments. (When the first edition of this chapter was written, October 2004, American and Iraqi forces were waiting until after the US election to attack the Iraqi city of Falluja to establish government control. A key point has been that 'in Falluja, the insurgents are free to carry out their own brand of justice, like the public lashings of people suspected of theft and rape, and the videotaped beheading of...one of the city's National Guard commanders' (Filkins, 2004).) The English for capital punishment comes in part from the Latin word capitalis which means 'of the head', and was originally by decapitation, literally 'a capital offence'. The symbolism of the beheading is the denial of the legitimacy and the ability of the State to function and its replacement by a counter-state group.

- The consequences of the response to the events of 11 September 2001 are many; at the time of revising this chapter (September 2008) they include the invasion of Iraq and Afghanistan with great division in world opinion as to the legality of those actions and the bloody insurgency that opposes the foreign presence. If the choice had been made to call 11 September 2001 a 'crime' then the response might have been an international policing action determined to bring the perpetrators to the justice of an international court; the choice of war seems to many to have weakened the movement for international or global justice.

- The final three examples are simplified examples based on real cases. They allow us in the words of the Norwegian criminologist, Nils Christie, to hold up the processes in which crime is identified and reacted to as a mirror revealing a picture of social relations not otherwise seen. Take the example of the factory owners. In the early 1990s similar fires caused the deaths of hundreds of workers in the US, Thailand, and China.

In the North Carolina Chicken Processing Plant fire of 1991, 25 workers died and 49 were injured when a fire broke out and all but one of the nine fire escapes was locked. The owners had locked the doors and boarded up the windows to prevent the staff stealing food; however, no security fence had been constructed or any security guard hired. Nineteen of the 25 dead were single mothers, predominantly black—blacks had only been allowed to work in the factories of the south since the 1970s and even then they were nonunionized and unable to bargain for reasonable conditions. Blame for the fire was attributed to various local, federal, and State agencies. It had not been visited by health and safety officers for over 11 years and had already experienced several minor fires that year. There was no trial, the owner pleaded guilty to 25 counts of manslaughter, while his son and another manager went free as part of the plea bargain arrangement. To the extent that it was reported and picked up in the media, the fire revealed the conditions of work for many in the semi-rural areas of the US and demonstrated the divided nature of social life in the US. But if one thought that defining something as a crime invokes sympathy for the victims and that political measures would be likely to be taken to reduce victimhood or harm, this case is sobering; for less than two years later insurance companies and the business lobby in North Carolina got together and introduced legislation to reduce compensation for injured workers. Moreover, crime in Anglo-American jurisprudence is an individualist responsibility; in other words crime usually can only be proven when specific individuals are implicated and responsibility can be fixed upon them. Thus, it is individuals who are blamed and not the system. This can be seen even more clearly from another case where on 10 May 1993, fire broke out at the Kader toy factory outside Bangkok, Thailand. Managers had locked exit doors to make sure the workers could not steal the toys. Hundreds of workers, mostly young women, were trapped inside. Officially 188 were killed, with 469 injured, many seriously, after they were forced to leap from second, third, and fourth floors of the buildings to avoid being burnt to death. Blame was fixed on the managers. But did the fault lie only with the managers? The fire occurred at the height of the Simpsons craze and the factory was producing Simpson toys: a melted Bart became the symbol of the tragedy and the consequences of the new global capitalist/consumer economy. The following quote is from a Malaysian labour activist, Tian Chua, who writes from prison where he had been detained from April 2001, without being charged, for attempting to organize Malaysian workers without government permission (you may note the politics here, for if she was actually charged with a 'crime' most jurisdictions require a court appearance where at least a minimal level of proof is brought forward in order that the person remains in custody!).

> The bodies of Bart Simpson scattered all over the ground—some half burned, some without heads or limbs, some half completed...Kader was one of the largest toy manufactures in Asia. It was also a typical multinational company which moved around for cheap labour. Kader was jointly owned by Thai and Hong Kong capitalists. It mainly produced toys for European & American markets...The toy industry is a sector which produces fun and joy. Toys bring laughter to children and parents. However, the tragedy of Kader fire revealed the sorrows and suffering behind toy manufacturing. Kader made us aware that workers use their sweat, tears and blood to exchange happiness for children around the world. (quoted, 2Bangkok.com, accessed 19/10/04)

In 1993, another fire broke out in the Zhili Toy factory in Shenzhen, China, with 87 deaths. Here we come to the difference between a sociological/critical criminological reading of these events as crimes and a more legalist or narrowly focused criminological interpretation of the event. From the sociological or critical criminological perspective, the international connections between market driven consumption, demands for cheap but well-produced products, and the avoidance of operating according to full health and safety measures are apparent and have considerable bearing on the fire. From a more narrowly focused understanding of crime, those factors are all 'externalities'; what is of concern in ascertaining whether the events were a crime is then only the immediate actions and mental states of those who locked the doors and those who should have ordered them to be open. Moreover, what of the issue of responding to the victims and preventing future similar incidents? Whereas earlier, well published industrial fires, such as the Triangle Shirtwaist Factory fire of 1911 in New York (where nearly 150 people died because of locked fire exits), led to labour agitation and improved regulations of working conditions, the conditions for workers in the so-called developing world are at the mercy of multinational corporations that can quickly relocate to cheaper, less regulated locations. The international press gave Kader some attention, but today writers say very little has improved:

> Thailand's limited building and safety codes, minimal wage levels and factory regulations are not enforced. Indeed, the government in Thailand attracts foreign capital to its shores by

openly advertising the lack of restrictions on the exploitation of workers. The Kader factory was no aberration. All the horrors of nineteenth century European capitalism—child labor, dirty and unsafe working conditions, shanty housing—are on display everywhere in Bangkok. (Symonds, 1997: 58–9)

So, even if we were to agree to call this a crime, the consequence may be that a small group of individuals are blamed and punished, but the wider social conditions that caused social harm are pushed to one side and overlooked. This leads several criminologists to say we should not concentrate upon 'crime' as an organizing concept, but replace it instead with 'social harm' or protection of 'human rights' (see, for example, Hillyard *et al.*, 2004).

To summarize this section: we are therefore talking about complicated and changing interactions of governmental and discursive power, public concerns, and the different roles of officials who control key decision-making processes (see Chapter 21) as well as the media that highlights certain issues and downplays others (see Chapters 7 and 8). There are complex factors at work that influence how the edifice of public administration—including what the literature refers to as 'the criminal justice system'—relates to and processes events that may or may not be termed crimes.

REVIEW QUESTIONS

1 Under the law of society X, it is lawful to keep slaves and any slave that escapes or attempts to escape commits a serious offence; it is also a crime for any person to consciously assist in the escape of a slave or not to report a slave to the authorities if they come across an escaped slave [assume that there are no international conventions concerning slavery]. While on holiday in X you meet a person you realize is an escaped slave but do not report them; in fact you allow them to stay in your hotel room. Are you a criminal? Is the slave? Your partner decides that they must obey the law and they report you to the authorities with the result that you and the slave are sent to prison. Has your partner done anything wrong?

2 Using Internet sources and the library, research the Bhopal disaster in India 1984. Who was at fault and has justice been achieved in response to that event? What role if any does racism or corruption play?

Frameworks of choice and logic: the politics of criminology and the definition of crime

So far we have explored matters with respect to practical examples. We have seen how in practice and in the literature there is much disagreement over defining exactly what a crime is. McCabe (1983: 49) says 'there is no word in the whole lexicon of legal and criminological terms which is so elusive of definition as the word "crime"'! How then can a discipline that has as its common focus the study of crime ever have a settled focus? The history of criminology can be read as revolving around this question. It has been said that most definitions of crime involve a drastic circularity and that criminological explanations relying upon them become tautologies. Perhaps it is the effect of this, but criminology as a scholarly discipline has moved in circles over many of its central issues. One problem is that the definition of crime adopted by an individual reflects the whole world perspective of that individual and the social groups they reside within. We are faced with various distinctions, controversies, and frameworks of logic that are related to our view of the world and mankind's place in it. These include choices between the following assertions or claims:

- Crime is some action or omission that causes harm in a situation that the person or group responsible 'ought' to be held accountable and punished, irrespective of what the law books of a state say.

- Crime is an action against the law of God, whether as revealed in the holy books, such as The Bible, Koran, or Torah, or that we instinctively recognize as against God's will, irrespective of what the law books of a State say. If the State law books allow something that we know to be against God's will this does not change its status—it is still a crime.

- Crime is an act or omission that is defined by the validly passed laws of the nation state in which it occurred so that punishment should follow from the behaviour. Only such acts or omissions are crimes.

- If there is no public authority capable or ready to police social activity and punish offenders, then there is no crime. Crimes and criminals only exist when a public body has judged them such according to accepted procedures. Without the State and the criminal law there is no crime. Without criminal justice systems there are no criminals.

- Crime is an irrelevant concept as it is tied to the formal social control mechanism of the State; deviance is a concept that is owned by sociology, thus our study should be the sociology of deviance, rather than criminology.

We can identify at least four frameworks in which to make sense of how crime is defined:

(a) crime as a social construction;

(b) crime as a product of religious authority/doctrine;

(c) crime as a reflection of nation-state legality;

(d) more recent concepts beyond the nation-state derived from social and political theory.

Criminology and, indeed, our present position more generally contain the legacy of the earlier positions. Let us look briefly at each in turn.

Social construction

Social construction is a highly influential and controversial current perspective. In summary it argues that our concepts and the practical consequences that flow from using them are the products (constructions) of social interaction and only make sense within the communities in which that interaction takes place. In other words, 'crime' is a label created in social interaction, but once created it has both a symbolic and practical reality.

We endow the world with symbols and respond to the meanings contained in them. Language and other symbolic systems codify these meanings and by using language we impose a grid on reality; the law is a particularly strong grid system. In this case we create terms of crime and punishment that enable us to identify and distinguish different events. But these terms also impose certain consequences, as in the following statement from a very influential book on criminal justice: 'When a crime is committed, justice must be done...a failure to punish crime is wrong and a community that does not punish its criminals is derelict in its moral duty' (Gross, 1979: xv and 18). In many accounts crime and punishment are linked as if they were unproblematic concepts reflecting a reality in which crimes are committed as a matter of identifiable facts and once the person responsible is identified certain processes must logically follow. However, those who accept social construction argue that since language and other symbolic systems are social products, this is a socially constructed grid. It is a social choice to recognize such and such an event as a crime, or such and such a person as a 'criminal'. Some other term and therefore some other course of action could be used. Two consequences follow. In one we have a research project of following through the creation of the use of the concept crime and its actual allocation to particular events or situations (the process of criminalization). A second consequence is that we can argue that there is no particular natural level of use of the concept crime, that it can imprison us in particular techniques of social ordering, and it may be better to abolish its use. This was stated clearly by the Dutch abolitionist lawyer, Louk Hulsman:

> categories of 'crime' are given by the criminal justice system rather than by victims of society in general. This makes it necessary to abandon the notion of 'crime' as a tool in the conceptual framework of criminology. Crime has no ontological reality. Crime is not the object but the product of criminal policy. Criminalization is one of the many ways of constructing social reality. (Hulsman, 1986: 34–5)

Drawing upon anthropological evidence of how different social groups identified troublesome situations and individuals, the American criminologist Howard Becker (1963) and others developed an influential school of thought in sociology known as labelling theory (see Chapter 4). This holds that the terms crime, deviance, or punishment are labels, variously applied by acts of power and not some natural reflection of events. The full potential of labelling theory was not realized. When Becker wrote, for example, he only mentioned in passing the gender divide in which men made the rules in society for other men and women. Today, in the hands not only of feminists but deconstructionists, labelling theory leads in a more radical social constructionist theory in which a multi-sided account of criminalization is given (see Chapter 4). In its abolitionist forms, such as with the Norwegian criminologist Nils Christie (2004), the major challenge for criminology is to understand the social processes of the application of these basic labels and, by implication, if we follow through the process we might come to an understanding that may lead to a lowering of the rate of 'crime' by abandoning the entire processes of criminalization. His central assertion undercuts the common-sense views of crime and disorder:

> Crime does not exist. Only acts exist, acts often given different meanings within various social frameworks. Acts and the meanings given to them are our data. Our challenge is to follow

the destiny of acts through the universe of meanings. Particularly, what are the social conditions that encourage or prevent giving the acts the meaning of being crime? (Christie, 2004: 3)

Crime does not exist. Only acts exist, acts often given different meanings within various
social frameworks. Acts, and the meanings attached to them . . . but is this actually so and
even if this was the case, could humans really accept such a radical view?

Crime in 'the city of God'

The phrase 'city of God' comes from the Christian writer St Augustine (354–410), but
could with only slight modification be used to describe Islamic or Judaic systems; it refers
to the world view where we humans live in a universe created by God and his commands.
Social construction theory is denied by many people who see in it the consequences
of human ambition to position ourselves as the masters of the world and our destiny.
Instead, very significant numbers of people believe that God created the universe and
allocated a place for humans within his creation. To enable us to know something of
his intentions God also sent messages to humanity through prophets and other forms
of revelation; these messages were collected in books of authority of which the Koran,
the Bible, and the Torah are best known. Each lays out various rules in terms of imperatives and warnings of the consequences if these are not followed. Let us fear God, says
the Koran, 'verily, God is witness over all'. God will prepare shameful woe for those
who disobey his rules. To the followers, the laws of God lay out the path to heaven and
redemption. There is no problem of the legitimacy of these rules and the definition of
what should be crime since God's will is the ultimate driving force of creation—even if
humans have been endowed with free will and the capacity not to see the truth. There
are numerous problems for social order in a complex grouping: a crucial one is who can
agree on the exact message from God, what happens to constrain conflicting interpretations? As Blaise Pascal put it, 'men never do evil so openly and contentedly as when
they do it from religious conviction'. Take as examples two crime-related words that have
found their way into our English dictionary: thuggery and assassination. The derivation
of thuggery is from the Sanskrit sthag, to conceal. For centuries a religious sect existed in
India to rob and murder. A conservative estimate is that they killed well over a million
people between 1740 and 1840 until suppressed by British colonial authorities. Thugs
were devotees of the goddess Bhowani or Kali, the 'Black Mother', the Hindu goddess
of death and destruction. Gangs of men operated to murder and rob, strangling their
victims as sacrifices to Kali. When caught Thugs looked forward to their execution as a
quick route to paradise. The English word assassination comes from the Muslim world,
where after the death of the prophet Muhammad, three of his early successors were killed
with daggers. A group, 'assassins', was founded by Hasan Ibn al-Sabbsh, whose followers
killed rival Sunni Muslims, and many Muslim caliphs (ultimate leaders) have been killed
over the subsequent centuries. The Assassins killed as acts of piety and sought to replace
an allegedly corrupt Sunni regime with a supposedly ideal Shiite one; when caught they
accepted their death.

Throughout the western world the horrors of the massive religious conflicts of the
late middle ages resulted in the separation of Church and State. The city of God became

replaced by the city of man, and religious belief was deemed in practice to be a personal matter. For much of its history criminology has been a secular discipline, an applied science of the nation state; but there are now serious arguments that it has been badly compromised by neglecting to engage with the religious belief systems that many people live by (Knepper, 2001).

Nation-state legality

From the seventeenth century, slowly and with many oppositions, a secular view of crime arose where crime is understood as an act or omission as defined by the sovereign authority in factual charge of a specific territory—the nation state. It is important to note the full implications of this view. First, the substance of what is made criminal is a matter of the 'will' of the sovereign body, the Parliament, the courts, and the Senate. Second, as liberal jurisprudential writers, such as H.L.A. Hart (1961) emphasize, the fact that something is made a crime does not necessarily mean it is immoral. While in practice many crimes will be based on the shared perceptions of the people, arising from customs, religious beliefs, and common-sense conceptions of what is acceptable and unacceptable; crimes are simply posited by the rule-making power centres of the State. Third, it follows that to be called a criminal is a status conferred by the legal and political process of the State, there is no such thing as a natural criminal or a born criminal (cf Chapter 4). As Korn and McCorkle express it, this was forgotten by much individualist focused criminology, which took a naturalist view of the terms 'crime' and 'criminality'.

> The use of the term criminal to identify persons occupying a potential and removable status is in sharp contrast to the view that criminality is a sickness, a biological condition, or a type. The failure to distinguish between the ideas of status and type has led to costly errors and lost directions in criminology. It has led many to mistake the fact of a fairly clear legal category for the existence of an equally identifiable category of persons with similar characteristics. It has led brilliant investigators into life-long searches for common biological, social, or psychological traits. Despite the failure of these investigations to isolate within the offender a single characteristic not found in the law-abiding, the search for common factors continues to preoccupy those who are still unaware that the object of their quest is the product of a semantic confusion. (Korn and McCorkle, 1959: 48)

Those authors were also 'realists', saying that 'irrespective of laws, an act is not a crime until the offender is caught, tried and punished'. The consequences for criminology were clear since the knowledge base requires first the achievement of political control by a State over territory, secondly institutional processes of recognition and interpretation of activity as criminal, and lastly the scholarly reflection upon that ascription and processes of dealing with those defined. By implication where the State has not instituted a situation of 'continuous political control' there can be no criminological reflection; criminology (at least in its conventional or mainstream forms) was the applied science of the nation state and where the nation state did not define crime, there was no criminological knowledge (see Hogg, 2002, and Morrison, 2005, for arguments for a contemporary criminology beyond the nation state).

Beyond nation-state definitions of crime

Modern western societies have largely defined crime in the terms laid down by the nation state. A crime is an act or omission that leads to penal sanction in accordance with the constitutionally valid procedures of that nation state. Thus nation state A will prohibit the smoking of cannabis, while nation state B may say that within specified areas (for example, the coffee shops of Amsterdam) it is allowed. The examples can be multiplied; thus relativism—and, say some, the holocaust. It does not take a great leap of the imagination to see the policy of the extermination of European Jews (and all others if the State could have power over them) written into the manifesto of Hitler and adopted when the legitimate sovereign of the German people. Hitler's aggressive expansionist policies brought about World War II and after it several of the surviving Nazis were tried for the crime of waging aggressive war and associated crimes against humanity. While we now see the Holocaust as the icon of crime in the twentieth century, at the time and today many commentators say that logically it would not have been a crime if the extermination of the Jews had remained an internal state policy. Perhaps no writer has expressed this better than George Steiner:

> I wonder what would have happened if Hitler had played the game after Munich, if he had simply said, 'I will make no move outside the Reich so long as I am allowed a free hand inside my borders'. [The death camps of] Dachau, Buchenwald, and Therasienstadt would have operated in the middle of twentieth-century civilisation until the last Jew had been made soap. There would have been brave words on Trafalgar Square and in Carnegie Hall, to audiences diminishing and bored. Society might, on occasion, have boycotted German wines. But no foreign power would have taken action. Tourists would have crowded the Autobahn and spars of the Reich, passing near but not too near to the death-camps. (Steiner, 1967: 150)

Even if we were to agree with Steiner as a tragic matter of fact, this would clearly be an affront to notions of our common humanity. Hence it is essential that we engage in a movement to construct a framework for defining crime that is neither tied to any one particular view of religion, nor to the confines of the nation state.

Within criminology a well-known attempt was made by the Schwendigers who asked if criminologists were 'defenders of order or guardians of human rights'? They suggested that our individualist focused conceptions of crime needed to be broadened so that we could define whole 'social systems as criminal'. They argued that an expanded definition of 'crime as a label for social systems' become a 'warrant not for controlling atomistic individuals, or preventing an atomistic act, but rather for the regulation or elimination of social relationships, properties of social systems, or social systems as a whole' (Schwendiger and Schwendiger 1975: 136). Post World War II, a number of international conventions have tried to create a system for the recognition and processing of international crime under such titles as 'crimes against humanity' or 'genocide'. This is an expanding framework, though at present it is characterized more by words than actual deeds, and instances of international intervention are controversial (see Morrison 2004, 2005).

One other attempt may be noted, perhaps the most common within the sociological imagination, namely to replace crime by the concept of 'deviance'. Many of the works published within the criminological enterprise from the 1960s focused on the 'sociology of deviance' in order that criminality might escape from legality and create its own frame of reference. The problem was that deviance was, and remained, a sociological construct. In the public consciousness crime was the dominant and seemingly the most useful category.

This failure of sociological criminology to create a discourse that could engage successfully with the public and the political power centres is reflected in *The Culture of Control* by David Garland (2001), one of the most respected writers in criminology and the sociology of punishment. Garland highlighted the current dilemma surrounding the question of 'what is crime?' by pointing out the practical ways in which crime is approached and perceived in contemporary society. Garland did not refer to crime merely as an increasing factual reality (which is in itself a contestable proposition), nor indeed did he refer to the more complex category of the social fear of crime and ask how we can distinguish the reality of crime from the public and media image of crime; his theme was that *crime was now a core category of governing.* In his narrative, the perception that crime had increased had given rise to a new culture particularly in the US and UK, which he termed the 'culture of control'. His text was published shortly before the terrorist attacks of 11 September 2001, but those events—and the huge changes to notions of security throughout the western and Muslim worlds—have demonstrated the interdependence of the actions of defining events as crimes and modes of social governance. Some called the events of 11 September a great crime. Others called it an act of war, while still others, alternatively, said that the terms used were unimportant, for the real task was to inquire as to why certain people were motivated to carry them out? How one reacted to those events, however, was in considerable part a result of controlling how one defined their nature. Or put it another way: the consequences that the acts invoked were not predetermined, there was a range of possible reactions; once those events were defined in such or such a way, then the range of social reactions was constrained. Thus we end where we began, by re-emphasizing the diversity of opinions, definitions, perspectives, and complex interrelationships that surround what at first sight may seem a simple question: what is crime?

Given that the traditional frame of reference for doing criminology, including locating the processes whereby 'crime' was defined, has been the nation state, current scholarship that attempts to come to grips with globalization should revolutionize criminology (its impact so far has been minor). We are told that state sovereignty, the legitimate definer of crime in a territory, is being undercut. At its strongest the argument is that the State can no longer produce sovereignty—if so, this impacts on all aspects of the State's performance. In the field of crime control this results in ambivalent tactics. State sovereignty asserts itself even when it lacks control over the economy by a wave of popularism in the arena of security seeking public support of its power displays in war on crime, or war on drugs, or war on terror. Consider the effect of defining the events of 11 September 2001 as war and not a crime. The choice of 'crime' would have allowed for an international policing action, working through (and building) international moves towards international criminal courts, and a board coalition. The struggle to bring the 'terrorists' to justice would have been a global justice and not the 'justice of this nation' as George W. Bush had stated. Declaring a war on terror has led to the invasion of Afghanistan and Iraq, the destabilization of a number of countries, dramatically divided world opinion, and to the clear double standards concerning the treatment of civilian deaths in the US and those of the invaded countries. The events at the 'Abu Ghraib' prison in Iraq became shorthand for the abuse of power and the 'crimes' committed in several dozen detention centres in Iraq, Afghanistan, and at Guantanamo Bay. At last Pentagon count, no less than 27 detainee deaths were criminal homicides. The CIA has admitted to using 'water boarding' (near drowning), unmistakably a form of torture. And documents released in 2005 under the Freedom of Information Act have confirmed some of the more outrageous accounts of detainee abuse. In commenting on images of US soliders killing a wounded insurgent, the war correspondent Max Hastings sums up the moral distaste the hypocrisy of this 'war for civilization' engenders:

This is a scene straight out of Platoon or Full Metal Jacket. A soldier gazing down on a prostrate enemy sees him move and shouts: 'He's f***ing faking he's dead.' Another soldier fires a single contemptuous shot into the wounded man's head, and says laconically: 'Well, he's dead now.'

On Saturday in Fallujah, that shocking melodrama was played out for real. US marines shot a wounded and helpless Iraqi—in a mosque, of all places—while an NBC television news camera recorded every detail. The images have flashed across the world, into the homes of thousands of millions of people, many of whom already hate what America is doing in Iraq.

...Here are the crusaders for democracy, as George Bush and Tony Blair portray themselves and their soldiers, acting like animals. Even before this atrocity, the world recoiled from the spectacle of Fallujah shattered in the name of freedom...

...Two months ago in Basra, a British officer said to me: 'We were appalled by those pictures from Abu Ghraib. They seemed to cut the legs off the whole moral basis for our presence here.' So they did. So, likewise, does the film footage from Fallujah.

Americans pursue a doctrine of firepower which causes Nato allies to think them unfit for any role in which 'hearts and minds' must be won. The fact is that the American way leaves few hearts and minds alive to parley with. American soldiers possess a contempt for people of alien races, which cost them defeat in Vietnam and could well cost them failure in Iraq.

...It is not enough for George Bush to declare from the distant citadels of Washington that the Coalition's forces are pursuing an honourable cause. On the battlefield, they must also be seen to be fighting in an honourable way.

...Not only have they abused Iraqis, they have been shown before the world to abuse Iraqis. The damning visual evidence is there.

...whatever happens afterwards to the Iraqi people, the way Bush has waged his war in Iraq has inflicted lasting injury on the cause of democracy. Who can again take seriously this President's claim to be fighting for freedom and virtue, when metaphorically he delivers such proclamations from the wreckage of Fallujah?

...I would suggest that what happened in Fallujah this weekend is arguably more the handiwork of Bush, Rumsfeld and Cheney than of the wretched marine who fired the shot.

...only a fool in the White House would suppose that he can win the War Against Terror through so much blood recklessly shed, such mountains of rubble so carelessly created.

Every frame of film of Saturday's murder in Fallujah is worth another legion of recruits to al-Qaeda.

...Why shouldn't people hate George Bush? (Max Hastings, 'Marine atrocities mock US cause', *The Daily Mail*, 17 November 2004)

Different States play the sovereignty games differently and what is crime in one area may not be crime in another, additionally the efforts of one State to fight crime or drugs may actively cause crime in another. In this negative argument the decline of the State as the body that laid out the conditions of territorial security means that the State is increasingly part of the 'crime problem' and not the solution; the need then is to go beyond the State in the process of locating the foundations for defining what is crime and what are proper and legitimate responses to it.

REVIEW QUESTIONS

1 'The criminal law is the source of crime; without the law we would not have crime'. Discuss.

2 What value is there in advocating an 'abolitionist' approach, such as that espoused by Nils Christie or Louk Hulsman?

CONCLUSION

Defining crime is not a matter of common sense or simply following an accepted procedure. In the examples given in this chapter we can see some of the complex political and economic forces that shape how what is a crime is defined in practice—such as US domestic political pressure to downplay knowledge of the events in Rwanda, and to ensure that the specific term that would have described them as a great crime, genocide, was not used, while other domestic political pressures were behind the desperate attempts to define Clinton's explanation of his 'personal' life as a crime. What can we learn? The case of the *Zong*, for example, may seem a long time ago, but:

> On Boxing Day 1996, the crew of an old rusting freighter the *Yiohan* forced over 300 passengers off the ship and on to a small craft designed for a third of that number. Over 280 were drowned when the boat went down. Four years later, fishermen in Sicily were still hauling in corpses and body parts with their catches (*Observer*, 10 June 2001). The tragedy received very little press coverage: only the *Observer* ran the story, as an exposé of the ship's captain. (Webber, 2004: 133)

Webber's point is that of course this was not seen as a modern crime created out of the economic imbalances of the global system; rather the problem was that of the illegal immigrants and those individuals that preyed upon them (who were not apprehended or punished). In the case of the *Zong*, the demand for cheap labour fed the eighteenth-century slave system of enforced migration. Today we enforce barriers and impose the label criminal on those who seek to voluntarily migrate outside the strict 'legal' conditions governing official migration. In August 2008 the Italian Prime Minister Silvio Berlusconi, who also owns much of the Italian media outlets and has constantly used his political position to frustrate judicial investigations into his operations and tangled ownership relations, launched a crackdown on crime, which many Italians and his media associate with illegal immigration. A number of new 'crimes' were legislated, including making it an offence punishable by up to four years jail to enter the country illegally. Expulsions have increased but the Italian authorities often find the countries of origin of illegal arrivals reluctant to accept them back if they are deported. In a highly symbolic measure troops have been deployed in joint anti-crime patrols with police in some of Italy's major cities. Some 20,000 people out of the 55,000 prisoners currently serving sentences or awaiting trial in Italian jails are foreigners, a number set to increase due to the expense and difficulty of executing expulsions ordered by the judiciary. This sense of national emergency is part of his political agenda, creating targets whereby he can show to the citizens that he can tackle the sources of their feelings of insecurity and unease. Yet in so doing the task of facing up to the global interconnections is downplayed.

We have a lot to learn from history in this area. Even if we can only conclude that in defining crime there is no easy answer, only controversy and struggle.

QUESTIONS FOR DISCUSSION

1 Why is it so difficult to agree upon a definition of crime?

2 'The crimes that the public are most concerned about are not the real risks that we face.' Discuss.

3 'The solution to the problems of defining crime will be found only by escaping from the confines of the nation state. We need some universal standards to use as our reference to define crime.' Discuss.

4 Take an area, such as drug prohibition, and follow through how and when this was prohibited. Ask whose interests are served by this criminalization policy? Is criminalization a cause of social harm?

GUIDE TO FURTHER READING

Most textbooks have either a chapter or a section on defining crime. These vary drastically in quality and can be repetitive.

The classic discussion is Keith Bottomley, 'What is Crime?', Chapter 1 of *Criminology in Focus* (1979, Oxford: Martin Robertson).

One of the better recent discussions is John Tierney, *Criminology: Theory and Context* (1996, London: Prentice Hall), Chapter 1 'Criminology, Crime and Deviance: some Preliminaries', and Chapter 2 'Measuring Crime and Criminality'.

Perhaps the best recent single chapter is Stuart Henry and Dragan Milovanovic, *Constitutive Criminology: Beyond Postmodernism* (1996, London: Sage), Chapter 5, 'Definitions of Crime and Constructions of the Victim'.

See also Chapter 2 'A Crime by Any Other Name . . .' in Jeffrey Reiman's *And the Poor Get Prison: Economic Bias in American Criminal Justice* (1996, Needham Heights: Allyn & Bacon) for examples of industrial accidents and other events that cause great harm not being called crimes.

On the rise and fall of the sociology of deviance Colin Sumner's 'The Sociology of Deviance: an Obituary' (1994, Buckingham: Open University Press) is wonderful reading.

For an instructive and relevant essay on the contrast between mainstream criminology and more realist conceptions of harm see Phil Scraton's 'Defining "power" and challenging "knowledge": critical analysis as resistance in the UK' in *Critical Criminology: Issues, Debates, Challenges*, Kerry Carrington and Russell Hogg (eds) (2002, Devon: Willan).

Nils Christie's *A Suitable Amount of Crime* (2004, London: Routledge) is an excellent consistent analysis of the proposition that 'crimes are in endless supply. Acts with the potentiality of being seen as crimes are like an unlimited natural resource. We can take out a little in the form of crime—or a lot' (p. 10).

The best argument that crime needs to be replaced by concepts of social harm is *Beyond Criminology: Taking Harm Seriously*, Paddy Hillyard, Christina Pantazis, Steve Tombs and Dave Gordon (eds) (2004, London: Pluto).

For a counter argument which analyses why western societies appear to be treating every imaginable source of harm as a crime see *Crime in an Insecure World*, Richard Ericson (2006: Oxford: Polity).

For the need for criminology to move beyond the nation state see Wayne Morrison's, *Criminology, Civilisation and the New World Order* (2006, London: Routledge/Cavendish).

For an alternative criminology textbook that stresses the importance of meaning and power in the construction of crime and law, see Jeff Ferrell, Keith Hayward, and Jock Young's *Cultural Criminology: An Invitation* (2008, London: Sage).

WEB LINKS

Lexis ONE
http://www.lexisone.com

A free legal research site providing searchable case law and a whole host of other useful research aids.

The Emile Durkheim Archive
http://durkheim.itgo.com/anomie.html

A detailed website dedicated to the French sociologist.

Amnesty International
http://www.amnesty.org

Find out more about the campaign for international human rights legislation and human rights abuses.

REFERENCES

Becker, H. (1964) *Outsiders*. New York: Free Press.

Brown, D. and Hogg, R. (1992) 'Law and order politics—left realism and radical criminology: a view from "down under"', in R. Mathews and J. Young (eds), *Issues in Realist Criminology*. London: Sage.

Christie, N. (2004) *A Suitable Amount of Crime*. London: Routledge.

Durkheim, E. (1966) *The Rules of Sociological Method* (trans S.A. Solovay and J.H. Mueller, (ed) G.E.G. Catlin). New York: Free Press.

Filkins, D. (2004) 'List of Iraqi cities where US troops won't go is growing longer'. International Herald Tribune, 6 September.

Garland, D. (2001) *The Culture of Control*. Oxford: Oxford University Press.

Gearey, A., Morrison, W., and Jago, R. (2009) *The Politics of the Common Law: Perspectives, Rights, Processes, Institutions,* London: Routledge-Cavendish.

Gross, H. (1979) *A Theory of Criminal Justice*. New York: Oxford University Press.

Hart, H.L.A. (1961) *A Concept of Law*. Oxford: Clarendon Press.

Hogg, R. (2002) 'Criminology beyond the nation state: global conflicts, human rights and the "new world disorder"', in K. Carrington and R. Hogg, *Critical Criminology*. Cullompton: Willan.

Knepper, P. (2001) *Explaining Criminal Conduct*. Durham, North Carolina: Carolina Academic Press.

Korn, R. and McCorkle, L. (1959) *Criminology and Penology*. New York: Henry Holt & Co.

McCabe, S. (1983) 'Crime', in D. Walsh and A. Poole (eds) *A Dictionary of Criminology*. London: Routledge and Kegan Paul, pp. 49–52.

Morrison, W. (2004) 'Criminology, genocide, and modernity: remarks on the companion that criminology ignored', in Sumner C. (ed) *The Blackwell Companion to Criminology*. Oxford: Blackwell.

Morrison, W. (2005) 'Rethinking narratives of penal change in global context' in J. Pratt, *et. al.* (eds.) *The New Punitiveness*. Devon, Willan.

Morrison, W. (2006) *Criminology, Civilisation and the New World Order*. London: Routledge. Cavendish.

Schwendiger, H. and Schwendiger, J. (1975) 'Defenders of Order or Guardians of Human Rights?' in Ian Taylor *et al.* (eds) *Critical Criminology*. London: Routledge & Kegan Paul.

Sellars, K. (2002) *The Rise and Rise of Human Rights*. Phoenix Mill: Sutton.

Simpson, A.W.B. (1984) *Cannibalism and the Comman Law*. Chicago and London: University of Chicago Press.

Symonds, P. (1997) *Industrial Inferno: The Story of the Thai Toy Factory Fire*. London: Labour Press Books.

Tappan, P. (1947) 'Who is the Criminal?', *American Sociological Review* 12: 96–102.

Walvin, J. (1992) *Black Ivory: A History of British Slavery*. London: HarperCollins.

Webber, F. (2004) 'The war on migration', in Paddy Hillyard *et al.* (eds) *Beyond Criminology: Taking Harm Seriously*. London: Pluto Press.

Williams, G. (1955) 'The Definition of Crime', 8, *Current Legal Problems*.

Website accessed: <http://www.2bangkok.com/2bangkok>, posted articles 'melted Bart', May 4, 2003; 'Bart Simpson and the Kader fine commemoration' May 21, 2005.

2

History of crime

Heather Shore

INTRODUCTION

The aim of this chapter is to provide readers with an overview of the history of crime in Britain. But why does a student of criminology need to know about history? Or more specifically, why do criminologists need a history of crime? Modern day penological theory and penal practices, criminal law, policing, juvenile justice, and public order, all have a historical context. It is important for students to understand the evolution of the practices, institutions, theories, and systems with which they are concerned. The purpose of this chapter, then, is to explore these developments and their broader historical contexts, and in doing so to clarify the various issues and paradigms which have come to characterize the history of crime. This chapter is divided into four sections. The first will consider the nature and definition of criminality over time, looking particularly at youth crime and the idea of the 'criminal class'. The following three sections will explore the different stages of criminal justice, focusing on the process of prosecution, the role of policing, and the theory and practice of punishment over time.

BACKGROUND

Arguably, the earliest influential theoretician of law was Sir William Blackstone who published his, *Commentaries on the Laws of England* between 1765 and 1769. The *Commentaries* were the first document to fully elucidate the form and function of the English criminal law, which had undergone considerable change since the constitutional changes and crisis of the seventeenth century.[1] Indeed, the eighteenth century, was something of a watershed in terms of theories of criminality and penality. From the mid-eighteenth century a number of commentators published on the problems of policing and prostitution, the care of disorderly youth, the state of the prisons, and the nature of punishment. Thus, Henry and John Fielding (1707–54 and 1721–80), Jonas Hanway (1712–86), John Howard (1726–90), Patrick Colquhoun (1745–1820), and Jeremy Bentham (1748–1832) were the most important voices in the shaping of eighteenth and early nineteenth century criminal justice.[2] Whilst their reputation and contribution has been recognized historically, we should also remember that most of these figures had what we might call a practitioner role in the criminal justice system. For example, the Fieldings were magistrates, Hanway founded the Marine Society, an institution for delinquent boys, Howard was a county sheriff, and Colquhoun was a magistrate (Emsley, 2005). The connection between practice and theory continued in the nineteenth century, but broader social and political contexts shifted the focus. Increasingly, theories of criminality were to be shaped by scientific and medical discourses, and in the later nineteenth century the work of the anthropologist Cesare Lombroso (1876) has been seen as highly significant (Pick, 1989). However, the earlier history of such pseudo-sciences as *physiognomy* and *phrenology* which had been discredited by the 1850s, were also influential in the shaping of European criminal justice responses.

It has become one of the paradigms of the history of crime that both traditional and *revisionist* approaches have tended to focus on the eighteenth and nineteenth centuries. Whilst, as this chapter will show, earlier histories of crime had their place, it was the periods of more dramatic shifts in society and the social order which have caught historians' attention. Moreover, as we can see from the development of theory, it was in these periods that contemporaries started making the clearest connections between social action, domestic policy, and the control of crime. In the early eighteenth century, criminal justice was overwhelmingly local, the community and the parish controlled law enforcement, punishment was a matter of discretion and negotiation, and where it did take place, served to some extent as a public mechanism for order and stability. By the late nineteenth century, the State had taken over much of the running of the justice system, and it was state agencies and institutions that played out criminal justice at both a local and national level. Moreover, whilst public and private conceptions of justice were not mutually exclusive, the establishment of a professional police force, the formalization of summary jurisdiction and rationalization of criminal trial, the development of the *total institution*, and the professionalization of the criminal justice sector were significant watersheds.

However, the history of crime that is available to us as researchers, teachers, and students is also shaped by access to, and survival of, sources. Historians' methodologies have often been shaped by parallel developments in other disciplines and by broader political developments. Until the 1960s much of the history of crime that existed was uncritically based on a narrative reading of mainly elite sources. Thus, the parliamentary blue books, covering Select Committees, Inquiries, and Royal Commissions were the key sources that defined the '*Whiggish*' histories of the earlier twentieth century. Most of these traditional approaches focused on the idea of progress, on the achievements of the 'great' men and women, the Fieldings, Howards, Peels, and Frys, and on the triumph of a humanitarianism which was implicitly shaped by Victorian liberal ideas of modernity.[3] This was gradually to change in the post-World War II period when a combination of factors saw a new generation of historians entering into the profession. The product of an expanded higher education system in the 1960s and 1970s was a body of vigorous young researchers who had been politicized by an era characterized by the anti-war movement, by sexual politics, by civil rights, and to some extent by theoretical Marxism. Moreover, the emergence of the social sciences encouraged a more interdisciplinary approach to history and those historians who were constructing, '*history from below*'.

Critical *positivist* approaches were particularly influential to historians of crime, who started to appreciate the value of *quantitative* methods in understanding crime over time. This focus on the counting of crime, complemented by the focus on non-elite readings of criminality, put the archive and particularly the county-archive at the centre of historical research into crime. However, by the later 1980s the limitations of *quantitative* methods were the subject of considerable debate. Survival of records was inconsistent across time and place; moreover, the statistics constructed by historians, as well as those left by our forebears, were not always reliable (Emsley, 2005: 21–55; Sharpe, 1999: 59–63). Methodologies were questioned, and the realization that interpretation was based on the limitations of 'known' crimes resulted in the emergence of new wave of approaches and perspectives. Nowadays, empiricism and *quantitative* methods tend to be incorporated within a more holistic approach. The impact of postmodernist theory and more cultural readings of sources have made historians of crime think twice about their own interpretation of primary material. Currently, a stronger engagement has been sought between historians of crime and criminologists, and to some extent with practitioners in the criminal justice system. Arguably, a more nuanced approach to understanding our criminal past will emerge out of these relationships and collaborations. I hope that the student reading this chapter will gain an understanding of the importance of such an interdisciplinary approach.

Defining crime

The problem of the 'hardened' offender, and, as an extension, of the 'criminal classes', was one that was continually to exercise the minds of the Victorians. Yet, as historians of crime have recognized, these typologies can be found in descriptions of London's social life at least from the Elizabethan period (McMullan, 1984). By the eighteenth century the impact of population growth, immigration, and manufacture helped increase public as well as State anxiety about crime. The metropolis was perceived as the nerve centre for crime, and increasingly contemporaries were thinking in terms of some sort of economic organization (Howson, 1970). The criminal gang, the highwayman, the street-robber, and the thief-whore were key figures in the criminal typologies that can be found in the biographies and literatures of crime that proliferated in this period. Despite the State's anxieties about crime, and the prevalence of the picturesque, reading the eighteenth-century texts the abiding concern seems to have been about the juxtaposition of wealth and poverty, the closeness of the city streets crowding all classes, not only the criminal, into the urban melting-pot. Criminality was seen as part of a lifestyle risk, to which we could all succumb. This view of crime was to stay substantially the same until the early decades of the nineteenth century. In this period the changes in criminal justice paralleled by a sense of deepening social crisis, resulted in a reformulation of ideas about criminality. At the start of the century, these reformulations focused upon the most vulnerable members of society: the young.

Juvenile offenders

From the early nineteenth century, juvenile delinquency was increasingly being singled out as a social problem. In 1815 the Committee for Investigating the Causes of the Alarming Increase of Juvenile Delinquency in the Metropolis was formed, and the report that they published the following year opened the floodgates to a rush of parliamentary Select Committees, investigations, and pamphlets concerned with juvenile crime. Recent work has suggested that the main motivations behind this groundswell was a mixture of generational fears, coincident with the end of the French wars, a re-focusing of attention on the outdated prison system, and the growing influence of reform (King, 1998; Shore, 1999). Increasingly, the need to separate children from adults throughout the whole of the criminal justice system became paramount. In the 1820s a number of acts were passed which were partially designed with the juvenile in mind. The Malicious Trespass Act of 1820, the Vagrancy Act of 1824, and the Larceny Act of 1827 allowed for varying forms of summary processing to be resorted to in the case of petty crimes and minor theft. Overwhelmingly, these acts singled out the trivial and mundane crimes which juvenile offenders were most likely to commit. Moreover, as Susan Magarey argued in her important article, the passage of the 1829 Metropolitan Police Act reinforced this process by focusing the early energies of the new police on petty offences and more vulnerable offenders (1978). As discussed above, the development of summary jurisdiction and juvenile justice in Britain went hand-in-hand, a relationship that was formalized with the passage of the Juvenile Offenders Act of 1847, which allowed children under the age of 14 to be tried in petty sessions summarily, and a further Act of 1850 which allowed the age limit to be raised to 16. From this point on criminal children were increasingly diverted to summary jurisdiction, although the Juvenile Court was not established until the early twentieth century, under the 1908 Children's Act. The legislative journey of the later nineteenth century was to focus almost wholly on the institutional care of the juvenile.

Strategies to deal with juveniles in institutions developed in two ways. On the one hand, the State felt that the new prisons and penitentiary, the apparatus of reform, were adequate to house and to reform juvenile offenders. Peel's Gaol Act of 1824 allowed for greater classification and separation of juveniles. Institutions would be rebuilt or refurbished with separate juvenile-specific accommodation. On the other hand, the philanthropic sector established a number of refuges and schools where juvenile offenders could be given useful training. Ultimately the passage of the Industrial and Reformatory Schools Acts between 1854 and 1857 incorporated elements of both the State and voluntary systems. The principle of separate confinement of juvenile offenders was to be finalized in 1876 under the Education Act, which established day industrial schools and truant schools. As a result of the reformatory movement of the later century, there was a significant decline of children in prison, and most children placed in prison were there on remand, or in lieu of paying a fine. This was addressed by the Industrial Schools Act of 1866, which detained such children in the workhouse, and more successfully in the Youthful Offenders Act of 1901, which empowered the courts to remand a child 'into the custody of any "fit person"... who is willing to receive him' (Radzinowicz and Hood, 1986: 627–8).

The drive to separate the child from the adult prisoner was underpinned by the desire to nip crime in the bud. Increasingly, commentators saw the control of and intervention in juvenile offenders' lives as the key to preventing future generations of 'hardened' recidivist criminals. Partly this seems to have been a reflection of real concern about marginalized children, and the need to provide viable solutions. However, it was also a reflection of the shifting attitudes to criminality in this period. Contemporaries were increasingly seeking to categorize juvenile offenders by the nature and level of their offending (Carpenter, 1851; Shore, 1999: 95). The classification and categorization of criminals, both juvenile and adults, was largely engendered by the new forms of disciplinary institutions which were being built and developed in this period. Thus, in theory at least, the new penality allowed for the matching of sanction to prisoner. However, arguably, the classification of the criminal was also a reflection of broader attempts to discipline the poor, and the new industrial classes (Ignatieff, 1978). From the mid-nineteenth century the idea of the working class was to be paralleled by the emergence of a much more threatening criminal class.

The criminal class

Allusions to the criminal class became common from the mid-century. Whilst fears about criminal subcultures have most frequently, and understandably, been based on the metropolis, Glasgow, Cardiff, Liverpool, Birmingham, and most of the ports and other growing urban and industrial conurbations, had areas identified as belonging to the criminal class (Jones, 1982: 85–116). In reality, the identification of certain areas as 'criminal districts' owed much to concerns about public health and sanitation issues, and to increased police surveillance. Whilst such areas had always been present, the portrayal of criminality became more intense in the later nineteenth century. The combination of more effective policing, the rise of social evangelicalism, the impact of imperial racist discourses, and the emergence of a threatening casual labour class, all helped bring attention to the 'criminal classes'. Gareth Stedman-Jones' groundbreaking study of the economic and political disenfranchisement of the London poor in Victorian society has shown how changes to the labour market resulted in the emergence of a threatening casual labouring class, located overwhelmingly in the east of the city (1971). The problematization of the casual poor was further underlined by political reform. The reform acts of 1832 and 1867 which resulted in the enfranchisement of a significant proportion of the working class arguably contributed to the further disenfranchisement of the remaining poor. Whilst charitable schemes provided morally cleansed housing and recreation for the respectable working man and his family, the residuum were physically ghettoized, and perceived in opposition to the respectable working class. For many Victorian commentators the poor were synonymous with the criminal class.

The 'mission' to rescue the urban poor was legitimized by the 'othering' of the poor. In the context of Victorian imperialism, where missionaries and politicians were evangelicalizing to the native 'other' in Africa and India, the comparisons with outcast London were, for too many contemporaries, startling (Marriott, 1999: xi–l). From the mid-nineteenth century, the influence of the natural sciences, of physiological approaches to criminality like *phrenology*, and the impact of organic and hereditary explanations for crime, typified by the work of Cesare Lombroso (1835–1909) and Havelock Ellis (1859–1939) in the later nineteenth century, saw the criminal and the 'criminal class' biologically identified as 'other'. Moreover, the fact of massive Irish and Jewish immigration from the 1840s, and 1890s respectively, and particularly the presence of the politically dangerous refugee, emphasized the notion of the underworld as the 'otherworld'. The casual residuum then was increasingly constructed through a new set of agendas based on the impact of mass immigration, the revelations of slum clearance (particularly anxieties about public health and disease), and the re-formulation of imperial and racial discourses.

Finally, changes in law enforcement, increasingly centred on the identification, surveillance, and supervision of criminal districts in London. After 1829, the increase in police activity clearly aided in the redefinition of criminal and poor space in towns and cities, and surveillance and supervision was now seen as a key role of the new police. With the establishment of a Detective Branch in 1842, and its reformation as the CID in 1877 (Petrow, 1994), criminals and criminal networks were much more effectively mapped and identified. The police identification and, consequently, stigmatization of certain areas as 'dangerous', added to the creation of the underworld and the criminal class who were its inhabitants. The perception of a threatening 'criminal class' enabled a system which labelled and categorized convicts, culminating in the passage of the Habitual Criminals Act of 1869.

Gender and crime

New conceptions and reconceptualizations of gender were a feature of the attempts to categorize the 'criminal class' and the more pedestrian criminality and deviance of the urban poor. Judicial discretion often punished male and female offenders in different ways (Palk, 2006). Contemporary rhetoric about crime and criminality was also subject to gendered differences. The female offender was seen as increasingly deviant during the nineteenth century, an issue reflected in the parallel medicalization of prostitution through the Contagious Diseases Acts of 1864, 1866, and 1869 (Zedner, 1991; Walkowitz, 1980). Other concerns about the relationship between crime and gender focused on the problem of inter-personal violence. It has been argued that the overall decline of customary displays of brutality (the privatization of public executions, the attack on blood sports) reflected a decreasing tolerance for violence in Victorian society (Carter Wood, 2004). The State stepped in to control the displays of public disorder which had been a feature of the eighteenth-century metropolis; the preservation of order in public spaces became a concern both for parishes and the State in urbanizing society (Shoemaker, 2004). During the nineteenth century the criminal law increasingly punished violence in a more systematic way, and at least ostensibly Victorian society became characterized by restraint and self-mastery (Wiener, 2004). This decreasing tolerance for violence, however, also highlighted particular problems of interpersonal conflicts. Arguably, these concerns about violence were shaped by a particular set of gendered understandings. Relationships between husbands and wives were to be increasingly subjected to gaze of the State. Conflict in such relationships has been characterized as 'everyday' where violence is located at the core of people's daily lives (D'Cruze, 2000). Recent historiography has explored the 'everyday' in the context of female participation in street-gangs (Davies, 2000), new-born child murder (Arnot, 2000), and sexual violence (D'Cruze, 1998). Whilst public displays of violence may have been privatized to some degree, within the complex web of relationships of family and community, 'traditional' ways of solving conflict were still resorted to. What differentiates the Victorian period and early twentieth century from the pre-modern is the increasing willingness of the State and its agencies to intervene in 'everyday' violence. For example, the introduction of women police from the early twentieth century marked an important development in the policing of families (Jackson, 2006).

REVIEW QUESTIONS

1 Historians have argued that the Victorian period was one in which there was an 'invention' of the juvenile delinquent. Do you agree with this assessment? In which ways was the juvenile 'invented'?

2 How far did the fundamental changes to late eighteenth and nineteenth century society and culture affect understandings of and attitudes to crime and criminality? What was the impact of industrialization, urbanization, immigration, and the increasing secularization of society on public and private responses to crime?

3 Why did the Victorians believe in the existence of the 'criminal class'? Is it fair to argue that the 'criminal 'class' was predominately an urban problem?

The criminal justice system

The way in which criminal justice systems evolve over time is undoubtedly central to the student of crime. However, for the historian of crime the mechanics of that change is less significant than the political and social shifts which structured and propelled it. Moreover, for most historians it is the impact of developments in criminal justice upon its subjects that most concern them. Thus, the processes and institutions of criminal justice take precedence over the technicalities of legislation. These latter are left more properly to historians of legal process (Radzinowicz, 1948–86; Baker, 2002).

Prosecution

The major difference between the system of prosecution in the eighteenth century and the one which was to evolve by the end of the nineteenth century was that the former was essentially victim-led. Thus, historically the English legal system provided for any private citizen to initiate a prosecution. Justice was essentially a face-to-face matter between victim and offender. However, if you were a victim of crime it was not always necessary or desirable to prosecute the offender. The costs of prosecution were prohibitive, particularly for those who could neither afford legal advice, nor to lose valuable wages. Moreover, alternative sanctions were available. Communities were not averse to dispensing forms of rough justice as a way of disciplining petty offenders, and maintaining social stability (Sharpe, 1999: 123–5). If the offender was known to you, a servant say, or relative, you might agree to enter into private negotiations and settlement rather than take the person to court. Other victims would use newspapers or handbills as a way of advertising for the return of their stolen goods, offering a reward in return for no questions asked (Emsley, 2005: 225). As a result of these informal responses to crime, entrepreneurial systems of law enforcement flourished, with rewards and gratuities for informers often providing the incentive to deal with crimes through extra-legal means. This system was countered by legislation passed during the later eighteenth and early nineteenth centuries that allowed expenses towards the cost of prosecution. By the time of Peel's Criminal Justice Act of 1826, expenses were paid to all prosecutors where there was a conviction, to witnesses, and in the case of some misdemeanours as well as felonies.

However, financial considerations were not the only factor to encourage prosecution. The increasing abolition of the capital sentence during the early nineteenth century, for example for picking pockets in 1808, and in 1820 for shoplifting, meant that people were more willing to consider prosecution.

Police prosecution

The most significant shift in the prosecution process was to come with the formalization and professionalization of law enforcement from the mid-nineteenth century. With the establishment of the metropolitan police in 1829, the police were to take a much more significant role in the prosecution process. Petty street crime and public order offences were increasingly seen as the remit of the police. With the extension of professional policing to the counties and boroughs during the 1830s, the police role in prosecution was strengthened, and by the late nineteenth century the police had come to dominate the prosecution process (Emsley and Storch, 1993).

Institutions

The nature of the court setting was also to change over the course of the eighteenth and nineteenth centuries. The extension of summary jurisdiction (the transfer of offences from quarter session to petty session) during the early nineteenth century was to have its greatest impact on the trial of young offenders (Shore, 1999: 29–34). Traditionally, the prosecution of crime had to go through a series of stages before it reached court, depending on the nature of the crime. Petty crimes such as gambling, assault, trespass, regulatory offences, certain poaching offences, and other misdemeanours were tried summarily in front of a magistrate or two, sitting informally in his front parlour or in a room in a local tavern (Shoemaker, 1991: 6). However, if a case brought before the magistrate was judged a felony, the offender would then be committed to trial at a higher court. An indictment would be prepared, which would then be submitted to the Grand Jury, who would then decide whether the case should proceed. If your case was sent to a higher court, it would be heard either at the Quarter Sessions or at the Assize court. The former met four times a year in counties and towns, the latter met twice a year in most major county towns. Assizes were generally reserved for the more heinous of crimes, and special assizes could be called if a local example needed to be made. For metropolitan London, the equivalent of the Assizes was the Old Bailey, which was to be re-housed and renamed the Central Criminal Court in 1834. In practice, at all these stages there was a level of discretion and negotiation (King, 2000). As a consequence, the course of eighteenth-century prosecution has been controversially debated by a number of historians in the 1970s and 1980s, most importantly through the work of Douglas Hay who contended that the English criminal law was one of the instruments of ideological control and terror available to the ruling class at this time (Hay, 1975).

The greatest shift in this process during the nineteenth century was, as has already been suggested, the extension of summary jurisdiction, and the wider role of the police as prosecutors. After the mid-nineteenth century these functions increasingly combined with the advent of the police court, which dispensed justice in the case of misdemeanours and some petty crime. The concept of the petty session, the magistrate hearing, was also expanded. In political terms this restructuring of summary jurisdiction was most vociferously shaped by the proponents of juvenile justice. A series of acts were passed during the nineteenth century which led to the increase in the numbers of offenders tried in front of magistrates in a petty session (without a jury present), and a decrease in those tried at the higher courts. This was a rationalization of criminal justice that by the late nineteenth century would bear much more relation to modern court systems.

Policing

Traditionally, historians have focused on the 1829 Metropolitan Police Act as the great watershed of British law enforcement history. Before this time, it is argued, progress in policing could mainly be pinpointed to a few far-sighted individuals. However, it took the emergence of a new humanitarianism, along with the social anxieties engendered by urbanization, population rise, and industrialization, to really fuel change. This is a largely benign view of police history, focused narrowly on the interplay between administrative and legislative shift on the one hand, and the biography of police reformers on the other. Not surprisingly, with the advent of social history in the 1970s, and the influence of Marxism, a much more conflictual version of police history has now been established alongside these more traditional accounts. However, both approaches tend to see the early nineteenth century as the key period for the making of the English police. More recently though, historians of the early modern period have done much to enlarge and extend our understanding of law enforcement over time.

Policing before the police

The common stereotype of pre-modern forms of policing is one of ineptitude, followed closely by corruption. Yet, many early modern communities had systems of law enforcement that worked, and once we take a closer look at the early nineteenth century we see that there are more continuities with the earlier period than was previously acknowledged. Whilst there was no formal police force prior to the nineteenth century, there were lots of different forms of policing. The major difference with the earlier period was that policing was effected on a local, parochial basis, and as a result of this, the local community, usually in the form of the parish vestry, had a greater involvement in the policing of their village, or parish. The other difference was that policing was effectively unpaid. Stipendiary magistrates did not appear until the eighteenth century, and until this time magistrates, constables, and the watch were largely dependent on a variety of rewards and handouts to make their position worthwhile (parishes did hire full-time watchmen, but the extent to which this was an organized system varied from parish to parish).[4] James Sharpe makes the point that police in the early modern period need to be understood in a much broader sense, to encompass forms of urban and parochial government, not just uniformed and professional law-enforcement officers (1999: 261–2).

Eighteenth century law enforcement has suffered something of a bad press from historians. The passage of various royal proclamations in London and its suburbs from the late seventeenth century, as a response to worries about what we might effectively call street crime, created a situation which encouraged entrepreneurial forms of policing to flourish. Hence, the system of rewards that came into prominence in the early eighteenth century seemed, at least in the metropolis, to engender high levels of corruption amongst its law enforcement officials. However, by concentrating on corrupt thief-takers like the notorious, and often ubiquitous Jonathan Wild (Howson, 1970), historians have sometimes undermined more serious analysis of eighteenth century policing.[5] The intricacies of the reward system have been expertly handled by Leon Radzinowicz (1948–86, vol. 3); however, more recently historians like Elaine Reynolds (1998) and John Beattie (1986, 2001) have readdressed this situation with much fuller examinations of policing on the ground. Their work has shown how local policing was often very effective and suited the needs of early eighteenth century communities. Community involvement in street policing, particularly in a period where the victim was more centrally involved in the prosecution process, was considerable. Self-interested parish vestries were keen to control the behaviour of the 'idle and disorderly' in their neighbourhoods. From the late seventeenth century, in urban centres, a combination of local parishioners, reforming magistrates, and constables came together to form the Societies for the Reformation of Manners, whose implicit concern was to clean the streets of prostitutes, vagrants, and others whose behaviour was defined as disorderly (Shoemaker, 1992). These societies colluded with criminal justice in the early eighteenth century, in the face of heightened concern about street crime, often relying on the activities of informers and the more surreptitious elements of law enforcement. As a result, by the 1730s a popular backlash against the reforming societies saw them driven underground, though they were briefly resurrected towards the end of the century. The eighteenth century was punctuated by calls for reform: of the police, of the prisons, of the criminal justice system. However, it was a combination of factors such as urbanization, population growth, and migration, but also changing attitudes to street life, and public space, which prompted both reformers and parishioners to push for change.

Evolution and watersheds

The role of the police evolved rapidly over the course of the nineteenth century. By the latter part of the century the police were still subject to a considerable amount of public criticism. Much has been written, in recent years, to undermine the traditional Whig narrative of police reform in the nineteenth century. The watersheds of police reform were, in essence, the 1790s, and the 1820s–30s. In 1795 Patrick Colquhoun published *A Treatise on the Police of the Metropolis* (1795). In 1792 the Middlesex Justices Act was passed, establishing seven police offices for London, manned by stipendiary magistrates. In 1798, generally attributed to the influence of Colquhoun, a private police force was set up to guard the commerce of the river Thames; in 1800 this organization was taken over by the Government and remodelled as the Thames River Police (Emsley, 1996). The later period was marked by the passage of the Metropolitan Police Act of 1829, the

Rural Constabulary Act of 1839, and the County and Borough Police Act of 1856. Recent research has concentrated on two areas. First, as discussed above, it has focused on the continuities between the old police and the new. Second, it has considered the evolution of law enforcement outside London.

Because it was the seat of government and because of its size and concerns about metropolitan crime, London tended to host most new initiatives in policing. However, the concentration on London belies the extent of policing experiments in other parts of the country. The Cheshire Police Act had also been passed in 1829, and many provincial towns had efficient police by the 1830s. More generally, the combination of the Lighting and Watching Act (1833) and the Municipal Corporations Act (1835) gave local authorities in Britain a considerable amount of power and leeway to reorganize their systems of police. The shift to considering provincial police reform has necessarily broadened research on issues connected with rural policing. Recent work has shown how crucial the permissive 1839 Constabulary Act was in rural areas. The country gentry put their resolve firmly behind Peel's message of prevention, and whilst the installation of a police force was piecemeal and more gradual in the countryside, by the mid-nineteenth century it was clear that both urban and rural England had seen the transition to a 'policed' society (Phillips and Storch, 1999). However, the police were not greeted universally with open arms, and resistance has been well documented. Robert Storch's classic articles on police resistance in class-conscious working-class communities, particularly those of the northern textile towns, show how they opposed the presence of the police through extra-parliamentary means, such as anti-police disturbances (1975; 1976). However, working-class victims of crime could also see the advantages of the 'new police'. As we have already seen, one of the major effects of the establishment of the police was the transfer of the prosecution process from the victim to the police. As a result working-class people were more willing to report petty crime, and even to involve the police in domestic altercations (Jones, 1992: 214). By the end of the nineteenth century, the police were a central institution in British society. Moreover, it was not only in preventative policing that developments had occurred. The emergence of more specialized branches of police work was to be a major feature of the later nineteenth and early twentieth centuries (Emsley, 1996).

REVIEW QUESTIONS

1 How effective was law enforcement in the eighteenth and early nineteenth centuries?

2 How fair is it to describe law enforcement prior to 1829 as fundamentally corrupt and unworkable?

3 In 'Whiggish' accounts of police history, the work of police reformers such as Henry and John Fielding, Patrick Colquhoun, and Robert Peel has been seen as key to the development of the British police. How significant were these reformers? How would you assess their contribution?

4 What was the impact of the 1829 Metropolitan Police Act?

5 To what extent was it a success or failure?

Punishment

For governments, practitioners, and academics, punishment—its level, economic viability, application, and appropriateness—has dominated much of the discussion about crime and its control (Morgan, 1994: 891). Moreover, the nature of imprisonment is at the centre of that debate. The soaring prison population, combined with much higher numbers of long-term sentences, problems of disorder, and unpalatable conditions have meant that penality is a constant challenge for home secretaries. Historically, at least superficially, these concerns seem very familiar. Certainly, if we consider the middle decades of the nineteenth century, when debates about the specific nature of penal servitude were played out alongside a widespread programme of penitentiary building, it is often tempting to draw parallels. However, if we take a broader view of punishment over time, we can trace both continuities and some very marked changes in such responses to crime.

Gallows to penitentiary

Perhaps the most distinct shift in the punishment of offenders historically has been the move from public, physical sanctions, such as whipping, but more notoriously, forms of torture, and execution, to the more 'private' punishment of penal servitude. This dichotomy is one that has been argued persuasively and famously by the late French philosopher, Michel Foucault, in his groundbreaking study of English and French criminal justice, *Discipline and Punish: The Origins of the Prison* (1977). Foucault's analysis of the prison is shaped by a broader understanding of the shifts and strains of eighteenth and nineteenth century society. Thus, the growth of the State, and of a surveillance society, paralleled by the professionalization of medicine, and the development of psychiatry are key determinants in Foucault's version of penality. Other historians have seen the rise of the penitentiary as more closely related to the impact of the industrial revolution, and the predominance of new forms of work and workplace, which called for a more disciplined and controllable workforce (Ignatieff, 1978). Nevertheless, there are a number of difficulties with the way in which historians have considered this undoubted watershed. One of these is the assumption that early modern forms of penality and punishment were necessarily problematic. Until the nineteenth century, punishment took the form of a variety of physical and fiscal sanctions. Besides execution, whipping and branding had also been used, alongside the extensive use of fines. The house of corrections and bridewells already combined the idea of discipline, work and punishment, in a way which has become more readily identified with nineteenth century reforms. The existing gaols and prisons were designed as remand institutions for prisoners awaiting trial. However, the dominant image of early modern punishment is the public execution. Perhaps unsurprisingly, much of historians' debate about continuity and change in punishment has focused on the capital sentence (Innes and Styles, 1993).

In the swath of penal debates which were to appear in Britain from the later eighteenth century, the dominant model was improvement and reformation (through physical conditions and education and religious strategies). The enlightenment penal reformers such as Cesare Beccaria (1738–94) on the continent and John Howard (1726–90) in England posited a more rational prison system which, they argued, would move away from the barbaric system of the past. Writing at a time when their contemporaries were very receptive to new ideas about penality, these authors had a significant impact on the development of political debates. Yet, the linear progressive model of prison reform has been undermined by historians. Clearly, this was a system in need of some overhaul. Conditions in many of the old penal institutions were undoubtedly poor, and it was not uncommon for early modern gaols to be managed as a commercial venture (Forsythe, 1983). Moreover, as Joanna Innes (1987) has pointed out, reformatory institutions such as the houses of correction and bridewells were considered a largely appropriate way of dealing with petty offenders, including vagrants and prostitutes. Reform in the eighteenth century then was not a sudden break with the past, but more a combination of enlightenment ideas, a new sensibility about institutions and institutional life that could also be seen reflected in attitudes to the lunatic asylum or the workhouse, broader social, ideological and economic factors, such as the emergence of an increasingly industrialized workforce and workplace, and only in part a response to what were seen as the excesses of the 'bloody code'.

This was a legislative trend that extended the death penalty by statute after 1688. During the course of the eighteenth century, the number of crimes for which you could be executed dramatically increased (from around 50 in 1660 to 160 by 1750 and 288 by 1815). Historians such as Douglas Hay (1975) and Edward Thompson (1975) argued that the ruling classes of the eighteenth century used the criminal law as an ideological tool, exploring the role of justice, mercy, terror, and discretion in the criminal justice system. However, closer examination of the Bloody Code has revealed that it frequently remade the definition of crime, rather than created 'new' offences. Often the legislation was incredibly specific, thus 'Destroying Westminster Bridge' was a single offence; 'Destroying Fulham Bridge' was another (Emsley, 2005: 256). Indeed the majority of people who were executed in the eighteenth century were done so under legislation which had much older roots (Innes and Styles, 1993: 243–5). Finally, it should be noted that there was a considerable gap between the number of capital sentences and actual executions during the eighteenth century (Emsley 2005: 256–8). Douglas Hay has seen the threat of the capital statute, and the use of exemplary executions, as a way in which the ruling class maintained its power (1975: 17–63).

Punishment or reformation?

By the late eighteenth century, the various strands of debate about criminal justice had crystallized into a penal strategy that focused centrally on the reformation of the offender. However, the nature of this reformation was not so straightforward, and for much of the nineteenth century the tension between the more punitive and reformatory elements of punishment were to dominate both discourse and actual practice. Much of this debate was focused upon the prison, in particular newly built penitentiaries which were to be the site of many of the penal experiments of the nineteenth century. However, other, older forms of punishment persisted. Transportation to Australia replaced transportation to the American colonies as a major penalty for those found guilty of serious crime from the late eighteenth century.

During the early nineteenth century Britain embraced what has been described as the age of the 'great confinement'. The old system was replaced with one that was to become dominated by penal servitude. For much of the nineteenth century, penality was under review, with contemporaries seeking a balance between punishment and reformation. Perhaps the most startling element of the new penality was the emergence of the penitentiaries, realized in the building of Millbank penitentiary in 1816. The idea of the penitentiary was to combine the disciplinary regimes of silence and separation with educational and religious instruction. The 1778 penitentiary act created two national penitentiaries (male and female) which were to be centrally administered. For a variety of reasons, but not least due to the disruption of the French wars, the scheme took several decades to materialize. The war itself was to contribute to the shifting opinions of the Government regarding penality. The administration of substantial numbers of prisoners of war for a relatively long period undoubtedly influenced plans for the national penitentiaries (Emsley, 2005: 271). Moreover, the ideals of Jeremy Bentham's Panopticon were also incorporated in the recommendations of the Holford Committee (1810), which met to look into the question of the prisons (McConville, 1981: 111–12). Bentham's architectural realization of the prison was closely bound with adherence to three principles. First, there was the rule of lenity, which signalled the move from bodily suffering associated with the old penal system. Second, there was the rule of severity, which posited the principle of less eligibility. Third, there was the rule of economy, that the system should essentially be cost effective. The Holford Committee generally shared these views, and to a greater or lesser degree, they underpinned the regimes established in Britain's institutions over the next few decades.

The system that was to evolve by the end of the nineteenth century had learnt from the lessons of the past. Whilst elements of the silent and separate system (also known as the Auburn and Philadelphia system which had been established in North America) could still be found, the worst excesses of the penal experiments of the early nineteenth century were removed. That system had not lived up to its reformatory promise, solitary confinement had a counter-productive effect on the morale of prisoners, and a number of highly publicized cases of suicide and insanity brought it into discredit. The separation of prisoners had more success. This was to be engendered by the classification of different categories of prisoner, particularly through the Gaol Acts of the 1820s, though this theory was not always put into practice. Despite this, the principles of Benthamite penality were to be echoed in the Penal Servitude Acts of 1853, 1857, and 1864. Penal servitude differed from a sentence of imprisonment in a number of ways, and was envisaged as a direct replacement for transportation, seven years transportation equalling seven years' penal servitude. Essentially penal servitude consisted of a mixture of separate confinement and hard labour, followed by probation in the form of a ticket-of-leave. It was kept for those convicted of more serious crimes (those who would previously have been transported) and thus went hand-in-hand with the Habitual Criminals Act, and the Prevention of Crimes Act which was passed in 1871, and tightened supervision of convicted criminals (Petrow, 1994: 75–82).

REVIEW QUESTIONS

1 To what extent was the 'Bloody Code' a real reflection of punishment in the eighteenth century?

2 How 'reformatory' was the penal system of the nineteenth century? What methods were used to effect reform?

3 Why was the death penalty increasingly replaced by penal servitude in the nineteenth century? To what extent can it be argued that this was the product of a more humanitarian society?

CONCLUSION

This chapter has sought to explain some of the continuities and changes which have characterized the attitudes to crime and management of criminal justice in the past. Historians interested in society and in the lives of the poor have frequently turned to the criminal justice system. Such studies have illuminated many areas which are central to the work of historians, sociologists, and criminologists alike. Historians, of course, have to work within the limitations of their sources, and for the most part this means that we are largely looking at elite perceptions of crime. Nevertheless, an understanding of historical sources such as quarter sessions and assize records, police reports, legal documents, newspapers, parliamentary papers, as well as the vast literature that reformers and social commentators produced, is crucial if we are going to understand the complexities of modern day criminal justice.

In this chapter I have shown that the later eighteenth and the nineteenth centuries have been a key reference point for historians of crime. Whilst recognizing strong continuities with the early modern period, the broader developments in State and society that occur from the later eighteenth century have left us a legacy that modern practitioners still at times grapple with. In penality, in particular, we see the legacy of the past in the Victorian prisons that are still in use. The prison system is faced with problems of overcrowding, rather than as in the past when inmates were denied a nutritional diet and basic education.

In this volume Roger Matthews has discussed the role of modern prisons. Anne Worrall has considered the current vogue to return to community punishment, echoing the traditions of pre-modern society, where community justice was a key form of control in both village and urban parishes. The juvenile justice system also owes much to its earlier manifestations. The public and the penal definition of what a juvenile delinquent is and the appropriate treatment for them, as Derek Kirton shows in this volume, is still in conflict. Modern policing is still characterized by tensions. Corruption charges, public inquiries, and internal reorganization continue much as they did in the nineteenth century. Nevertheless, historical systems of criminal justice do need to be considered in the contexts of the societies in which they developed. Elsewhere in this volume, Chris Greer, Jeff Ferrell, and Mike Presdee have considered the relationship between crime and broader social and cultural forms.

Indeed, it is important for the student of criminology to have some basic understanding of the economic upheaval, social conflict, cultures, and political development of the eighteenth and nineteenth centuries, to understand the changes I have discussed. The impact of industrialization, of the market economy, the demographic changes that led to a shift to an urban-based population, the reorganization of local government, new forms of State management, all combine in this period to produce new reformulations of crime and responses to it. What we also have to remember, is that these were changes in society that did not only affect the criminal justice system, but reached in many ways into the lives of the working class people who formed the vast majority of those who moved through the criminal justice system. In 1834 the reorganization of the poor relief system led to a re-evaluation and revamping of the workhouse system. Indoor relief in the workhouse paralleled the prison, as did a series of institutions for the poor. The workplace also changed dramatically in this period, urban manufactories and later factories fundamentally changed traditional patterns of work and workplace practices. Developments in public health, education, and housing should also be taken into account. The student of criminology, I would argue, needs some sense of the historical framework. This now provides the benchmark to understanding the developments and background to the institutions that both serve to protect and punish us both in terms of policy and practice.

QUESTIONS FOR DISCUSSION

1   What are the potential problems with using historical criminal statistics?

2   To what extent do you agree with Douglas Hay's assessment that eighteenth-century society 'was a society with a bloody penal code, an astute ruling class who manipulated it to their advantage, and a people schooled in the lessons of Justice, Terror and Mercy' (1975)?

3   Why did the criminal justice system undergo so much change during the nineteenth century? How far was this a break with the past?

4   How far is it possible to argue that the nineteenth century was subject to periodic 'moral panics' about violent crime?

5   The Old Bailey Sessions Papers were journalists' accounts of the crimes tried at the Old Bailey from the late seventeenth century. They are available at the Old Bailey Online (website address provided below). What sort of crimes did people commit in the eighteenth century? How were offenders sentenced? What age/gender patterns can be traced?

GUIDE TO FURTHER READING

Beattie, J.M. (1986) *Crime and the Courts in England, 1660–1800*, Oxford: Clarendon Press.

A classic and exhaustive account of the mechanisms of criminal justice in late seventeenth-century and eighteenth-century Surrey. Despite its local focus, this book has become a handbook for students seeking to understand how courts actually worked in the past.

Emsley, C. (2005) *Crime and Society in England, 1750–1900* (3rd edn), London: Longman.

This is the most useful and authoritative overview of the history of crime from the later eighteenth century and in the nineteenth century. An invaluable introductory text book.

Hay, D., Linebaugh, P., and Thompson, E.P. *et al.* (1975) *Albion's Fatal Tree: Crime and Society in Eighteenth Century England*, London: Allen Lane.

Since its publication in 1975 this collection of essays by many of the luminaries of the crime history field has provoked much debate and some controversy. In particular Douglas Hay's groundbreaking chapter has become a classic contribution to our understanding of the eighteenth century criminal justice system.

King, P. (1998) 'The Rise of Juvenile Delinquency in England, 1780–1840', *Past and Present*, 160: 116–66.

A useful overview of the perceived rise of juvenile crime from the late eighteenth century, this provides an empirical and *quantitative* analysis of the subject, with a survey of the reform texts of the time.

Zedner, L. (1991) *Women, Crime, and Custody*. Oxford: Clarendon Press.

A gendered reading of the nineteenth century criminal justice system. This book adds much to our understanding of penality in the Victorian period, and the relationship between broader cultural and social attitudes and criminal justice.

WEB LINKS

http://www.met.police.uk/history/index.htm

The History of the Metropolitan Police Service, including a timeline of police history.

http://www.oldbaileyonline.org/

The Proceedings of the Old Bailey Online, records of the trials that have taken place at the Old Bailey from 1674 to 1913.

http://www.rossbret.org.uk/

Rossbret UK Institutions includes information and links on British institutions including prisons, reformatories, workhouses, asylums, and industrial schools.

http://www.evergreen.loyola.edu/%7Ecmitchell/

The Tyburn Tree: Public Execution in Early Modern England, history of execution in England, includes contemporary images and last dying speeches.

REFERENCES

Arnot, M. (2000) 'Understanding Women Committing New Born Child Murder in Victorian England', in Shani D'Cruze (ed.) *Everyday Violence in Britain, 1850–1950: Gender and Class*. Harlow: Longman, 55–69.

Baker, J.H. (2002) *An Introduction to Legal History* (4th edn). London: Butterworths.

Beattie, J.M. (1986) *Crime and the Courts in England, 1660–1800*. Oxford: Clarendon Press.

Beattie, J.M. (2001) *Policing and Punishment in London, 1660–1750: Urban Crime and the Limits of Terror*. Oxford: Oxford University Press.

Beccaria, C. (1767) *Dei Delitti e Delle Pene*. London.

Carpenter, M. (1851) *Reformatory Schools for the Children of the Perishing and Dangerous Classes and for Juvenile Offenders*. London: C. Gilpin.

Carter Wood, J. (2004) *Violence and Crime in Nineteenth-Century England: The Shadow of Our Refinement*. London: Routledge.

Davies, A. (2000) 'Youth gangs, gender and violence, 1870–1900', in Shani D'Cruze (ed) *Everyday Violence in Britain, 1850–1950. Gender and Class*. Harlow: Longman, 70–85.

D'Cruze, S. (1998) *Crimes of Outrage: Sex, Violence and Victorian Working Women*. London: UCL Press.

D'Cruze, S. (ed) (2000) *Everyday Violence in Britain, 1850–1950: Gender and Class*. Harlow: Longman.

Emsley, C. (1996) (2nd edn). *The English Police*. London: Longman.

Emsley, C. (2005) (3rd edn) *Crime and Society in England, 1750–1900* (2nd edn). London: Longman.

Emsley, C. and Storch, R. (1993) 'Prosecution and the Police in England Since 1700', *Bulletin of the International Association for the History of Crime and Criminal Justice*. 18: 45–57.

Forsythe, W.J. (1983) *A System of Discipline. Exeter Borough Prison, 1819–1863*. Exeter: University of Exeter.

Foucault, M. (1977) *Discipline and Punish: The Origins of the Prison.* London: Allen Lane.

Hay, D. (1975) 'Property, authority and the criminal law', in D. Hay, P. Linebaugh, E.P. Thompson (*et al.*), in *Albion's Fatal Tree: Crime and Society in Eighteenth Century England.* London: Allen Lane, 17–63.

Howard, J. (1777) *The State of the Prisons in England and Wales.* Warrington.

Howson, G. (1970) *Thief-Taker General: The Rise and Fall of Jonathan Wild.* London: Hutchinson.

Ignatieff, M. (1978) *A Just Measure of Pain: The Penitiary in the Industrial Revolution, 1750–1850.* London: Macmillan.

Innes, J. (1987) 'Prisons for the poor: English Bridewells, 1550–1800', in F. Snyder, D. Hay (eds), *Labour, Law and Crime: An Historical Perspective.* London: Tavistock Press.

Innes, J. and Styles, J. (1993) 'The crime wave: recent writing on crime and criminal justice in eighteenth-century England', in A. Wilson (ed), *Rethinking Social History.*

Jackson, L. (2006) *Women Police: Gender, Welfare and Surveillance in the Twentieth Century.* Manchester: Manchester University Press.

Jones, D. (1982) *Crime, Protest, Community and Police in Nineteenth-Century Britain.* London: Routledge & Kegan Paul.

Jones, D. (1992) *Crime in Nineteenth Century Wales.* Cardiff: University of Wales Press.

King, P. (1998) 'The Rise of Juvenile Delinquency in England, 1780–1840', *Past and Present*, 160: 116–66.

King, P. (2000) *Crime, Justice and Discretion in England, 1740–1820.* Oxford: Oxford University Press.

Magarey, S. (1978) 'The Invention of Juvenile Delinquency in Early Nineteenth-Century England', *Labour History* [Canberra], 34: 11–27. (Reprinted in Muncie, J., McLaughlin, E. and Hughes, G. (2002), *Youth Justice: Critical Readings in History, Theory and Policy.* London: Sage, pp. 159–72).

Marriott, J. (1999) 'Introduction', in J. Marriott and M. Matsumura (eds), *The Metropolitan Poor: Semi-Factual Accounts, 1795–1910*, 5 vols. London: Pickering and Chatto, vol. 1, xi–l.

McConville, S. (1981) *A History of English Prison Administration, volume 1: 1750–1877.* London: Routledge & Kegan Paul.

McMullan, J. (1984) *The Canting Crew: London's Criminal Underworld, 1550–1700.* New Brunswick, New Jersey: Rutgers University Press.

Morgan, R. (1994) 'Imprisonment', in M. Maguire, R. Morgan and R. Reiner (eds), *The Oxford Handbook of Criminology.* Oxford: Clarendon Press, 889–948.

Palk, D. (2006), *Gender, Crime and Judicial Discretion, 1780–1830.* Woodbridge: Royal Historical Society.

Petrow, S. (1994) *Policing Morals: The Metropolitan Police and the Home Office, 1870–1914.* Oxford: Clarendon Press.

Phillips, D. and Storch, R. (1999) *Policing Provincial England, 1829–1856: The Politics of Reform.* Leicester: Leicester University Press.

Pick, D. (1989) *Faces of Degeneration: A European Disorder, c. 1848–1918.* Cambridge: Cambridge University Press.

Radzinowicz, L. (1948–86, 5 volumes) *A History of the English Criminal Law.* London: Stevens & Son.

Radzinowicz, L. and Hood, R. (1986) *A History of the English Criminal Law: Volume 5, The emergence of penal policy in Victorian and Edwardian England.* Oxford: Clarendon Press.

Reynolds, E. (1998) *Before the Bobbies: the Night Watch and Police Reform in Metropolitan London, 1720–1830.* Basingstoke: Macmillan.

Sharpe, J.A. (1999) *Crime in Early Modern England, 1550–1750* (2nd edn). London: Longman.

Shoemaker, R. (1991) *Prosecution and Punishment: Petty Crime and the Law in London and Rural Middlesex, c. 1660–1725.* Cambridge: Cambridge University Press.

Shoemaker, R. (1992) 'Reforming the city: the reformation of manners campaign in London, 1690–1738', in L. Davison, *et al.* (eds), *Stilling the Grumbling Hive: the Response to Social and Economic Problems in England, 1689–1750.* Stroud: Alan Sutton, 99–120.

Shoemaker, R. (2004), *The London Mob: Violence and Disorder in Eighteenth Century London.* London: Hambledon Continuum.

Shore, H. (1999) *Artful Dodgers: Youth and Crime in Early Nineteenth Century London.* London: Royal Historical Society.

Stedman-Jones, G. (1971) *Outcast London: A Study in the Relationship Between Classes in Victorian Society.* Oxford: Clarendon Press.

Storch, R.D. (1975) 'The Plague of Blue Locusts: Police Reform and Popular Resistance in Northern England, 1840–57', *International Review of Social History*, 20: 61–90.

Storch, R.D. (1976) 'The policeman as domestic missionary: urban discipline and popular culture in northern England, 1850–80', *Journal of Social History*, Summer: 481–509.

Thompson, E.P. (1975) *Whigs and Hunters: The Origins of the Black Act*. London: Allen Lane.

Walkowitz, J. (1980) *Prostitution and Society: Women, Class and the State*. Cambridge: Cambridge University Press.

Wiener, M. (2004) *Men of Blood: Violence, Manliness and Criminal Justice in Victorian England*. Cambridge: Cambridge University Press.

Zedner, L. (1991) *Women, Crime and Custody in Victorian England*. Oxford: Clarendon Press.

NOTES

1. The crisis of the English Civil War (1642–8), and the subsequent *restoration* of the monarchy in 1660, wrought significant developments in the law, the operation of the State, and the role of parliament and other government institutions.

2. Henry and John Fielding were police magistrates and social reformers (Henry was also the author of the influential pamphlet, *An Inquiry into the Causes of the late Increase of Robbers, etc*, (1751) and novels including *Tom Jones* (1749)). Jonas Hanway was also a social reformer, and the founder of the Marine Society (1756) in London, which trained delinquent boys for service in the navy. John Howard was a penal reformer, and the author of *The State of Prisons in England and Wales* (1777). Patrick Colquhoun was a magistrate and police reformer. Jeremy Bentham was a philosopher and jurist. In the 1780s he devised a plan for the 'Panopticon'—a model prison where all prisoners would be observable by (unseen) guards at all times.

3. Robert Peel was home secretary from 1822, and is credited as the main architect of the 1829 Metropolitan Police Act (he was later Prime Minister between 1834–5 and 1841–6). Elizabeth Fry (1780–1845) was a Quaker and prison reformer, noted for her work with female prisoners.

4. The watch were paid civilians who guarded and patrolled the streets at night. They were eventually superseded by the passage of the various metropolitan and county police acts of the nineteenth century.

5. Jonathan Wild (c. 1682–1725) was a receiver of stolen goods, informer, and prototype organized crime chief who operated in London in the early eighteenth century. He was executed at Tyburn in 1725.

3

What do crime statistics tell us?

Tim Hope

INTRODUCTION

Other chapters in this book explore the meaning of the concept 'crime' (Morrison, Chapter 1). In this chapter, the definition of 'crime' refers to a category of human acts that are proscribed by law and for which those responsible, if found guilty, are liable to some form of judicial punishment. The custodian of these kinds of acts is, of course, the State. In this sense, then, crime is a 'property' of the State (Christie, 2004). So, too, are 'statistics'. Dictionary definitions point to the origins of the term, even before the adoption of numerical systems of accounting, as arising out of the act of administration and government itself—of state affairs, or statecraft. This is true still: even though other, non-government bodies can collect statistics (Statistics Commission, 2006), and alternative analyses and interpretations of statistics are possible, there is a real sense that 'statistics' are the 'arithmetic of politics' (Dorling and Simpson, 1999). In contemporary society, statistics have become an important medium of governance—simultaneously informing and obscuring the various risks, including crime, around which we increasingly orient our daily lives and from which we expect our governments to protect us (Rose, 1999). Thus, both 'crime' and 'statistics', as they will be discussed in this chapter, are bound-up fundamentally with the operation and function of the State itself. Crime statistics, then, are *the accounts* that the State compiles of the actions of its agencies concerning those acts which the law proscribes.

BACKGROUND

There are broadly two polar views held about crime statistics within criminology: on the one hand, there is what we might call the *realist* view. This sees the official record as an indicator of the state of crime in society. Thus, even though there may be a 'dark figure' of crime out there—which ultimately may be unfathomable—in this view, it remains possible to refine and develop our statistics so that they aspire to, if not actually ever perfectly achieve, an accurate reflection of the underlying extent, pattern and trend of crime in society. Clearly, experience may suggest that some indicators—for example, statistics of crime recorded by the police—can be inaccurate and subject to biases of various kinds, some of which will be discussed below. Other measurement and estimation techniques have emerged, for example, *crime victimization surveys*, which promise improvements in accuracy and corrections of bias. Nevertheless, the intention is to use these statistics as indices of the amount of crime in society. There are two broad traditions of use here: first, *administration*, where crime statistics provide government (and the electorate) with intelligence about society that assists in the deployment and management of the State's criminal justice resources. As a Government *Review of Crime Statistics for England and Wales* puts it: 'there is general agreement that the overarching purpose for collecting information on crime should be to reduce the impact of crime on society' (Home Office, 2000: 9). A second use is *research*, which sees social statistics as 'social facts'—that is, indicators of the condition of society as a whole—the analysis of which reveals something about how society operates. The progenitor of this tradition is Emile Durkheim's classic nineteenth-century study of suicide (Durkheim, 1979).

Against the realist position, there is the *constructivist* perspective. In contemporary criminology this view stems largely from Aaron Cicourel's study of *The Social Organisation of Juvenile Justice* (1968). Based on research into the organization of juvenile justice in an American city, and how the various officials and others saw the process, Cicourel concluded that official statistics could be understood only with reference to the way in which the agencies responsible for them carried out their work. In this view, official statistics tell us as much, if not more, about the organization that produces them than about the phenomenon—that is crime—that they are supposed to measure. Because they are *social constructs*, statistics do not give a clear or objective view of the phenomena they purport to measure because they confuse details about crime with the way it is reacted to and dealt with by the relevant authorities.

Should the student of criminology bother with crime statistics at all? At one extreme, there may be those—at one time disparagingly referred to as 'positivists'—who still believe that crime statistics can be used (more or less) as an objective measure of the state of crime in society. Sections of the public, media, and politicians may still think this. They will want to use crime statistics as true measures of the level of crime, or worse, the moral health of society. Nowadays, no criminologist would take such a naive and uncritical view of official statistics. Nevertheless, official crime statistics continue to be used in many studies. Largely, this is for *pragmatic* reasons: the questions asked of them are interesting and important. For example, how much crime is there, has it increased or declined? But there are no more reliable alternative ways available to measure them. For all their faults, official statistics of crime are public records, whose cost of collection is borne by the State. They have a comprehensive, standard coverage of all of the jurisdictions for which the State is custodian, and can be related to other state statistics, particularly those taken from the national Census of Population to provide profiles of levels of crime in different types of community. Criminologists will continue to use official statistics in their work, not least because governments themselves also use them as tools for measuring the performance of criminal justice agencies, particularly the police, and for accounting to the public.

At the other extreme are those who might be thought of as 'impossibilists', who see official crime statistics as fatally flawed not just because they cannot measure crime separately from the actions of the agencies that produce them, but because the important social and cultural processes that go to make up the process of defining and reacting to crime and deviance are themselves not amenable to statistical measurement and analysis. In this view, quantitative measurement of cultural definitions—meanings and linguistic tropes about crime—is impossible. On the contrary, the analysis of such phenomena has its own logic and canon of procedures that are inimical to the mathematically-based logic of statistics and risk analysis.

Students of criminology will need to make up their own minds as to where they stand on these issues—of course, after a careful reading of this and the other chapters in this book! The stance taken here is pragmatic. It will be realistic enough to say that there are phenomena 'out there' that are capable of being measured in principle and that the careful use of statistics can illuminate many issues that may not be grasped properly by more subjectively oriented approaches to understanding. However, it also recognizes the constructivist argument that the various phenomena of crime in society cannot be divorced from the practices of the agencies that define, report, and record them. This is an important area of social enquiry itself. If, philosophically, crime cannot be divorced from its control, statistics nevertheless can be used to illuminate the interplay between the two or, at the very least, the operation of control itself. Nor is this merely an academic exercise. The more politicians, government, and the media use and cite statistics in justification of their actions, or lack thereof, the more that citizens—including students of criminology—will need to know about how those statistics are produced and how reliable they are as a basis for political decisions, especially if democracy is to work properly. Thus, this chapter will offer a brief 'consumers' guide' to some of the key issues concerning the construction of crime statistics.

What is a crime statistic?

In this chapter, we will focus on arguably one of the most popular of the crime statistics—the *crime rate*—that is, the measure that gives an index of crime occurring in a particular jurisdiction for a specific time period. Police records have been the main source for constructing crime rates. In recent years, however, governments have begun to look for other ways to collect crime statistics—usually commissioning large-scale population (that is, crime victimization) surveys for the purpose. There are broadly two reasons for this. First, a realization that the various potential biases in official records (discussed below) result in an inaccurate measure of the extent, scale, and pattern of crime in society, which causes particular problems in trying to compare jurisdictions, to estimate trends over time, or to explain patterns and trends. Second, reliable statistics have become even more important as governments concern themselves with assessing the performance of criminal justices agencies, particularly the police, whose purpose is seen increasingly as a 'service' to the community, especially to reduce crime and provide security and protection for citizens (see, for example, Home Office, 2003).

As with all 'statistics' there are three different components or uses. These are:

- *Counts*—that is, the actual number of offences occurring within a given referent of time and space—for example, the number of burglary offences in England and Wales per year.
- *Frequencies*—that is, how the counts of criminal offences are distributed amongst a population—for example, how many people are victims, and how frequently are they victimized?
- *Rates*—that is, expressing the count of criminal incidents as an indicator or characteristic of the population or jurisdiction that produced it, typically as a ratio of another characteristic of the population; for example, the rate of burglary per 10,000 residents of the County of Staffordshire.

The following sections of this chapter will look, first, at the social and political context of statistics concerning 'the crime rate', and subsequently on each of these three 'statistics' in turn. Particular attention is paid to how they are defined and how their measurement is constructed.

REVIEW QUESTIONS

1 What is the difference between a 'realist' and a 'constructivist' view of crime statistics? What is the approach adopted here?

2 What are the three different components of a crime statistic?

The social and political context of crime statistics in England and Wales

This section focuses on the social and political context of crime statistics, taking England and Wales (a jurisdiction within the United Kingdom) as an example, and drawing upon the findings of a review by the UK Statistics Commission (Statistics Commission, 2006; Fox *et al.*, 2006).

Contemporary uses of crime statistics continue to evolve, shaped by changes in society and politics. Some of these are listed in Table 3.1:

Table 3.1 Societal change and the impact on the use and availability of crime statistics

Societal change	Impact on the use and availability of crime statistics
The data explosion	The IT revolution in society has made it possible to collate and analyse information to an unprecedented scale and complexity, and such facilities are set to continue.
The Information/ Risk Society	Information and data has become increasingly central to most people's lives throughout society; people are now expected, and demand, more by way of information to assist them in their everyday decision-making.
The culture of crime	Crime and punishment have become far more salient in contemporary society and politics, and have become attached to other values and evaluations of policies and programmes. People are concerned about how crime will affect them in managing their everyday lives, and as an issue with which to evaluate government and public services, to unprecedented degrees.
Decline of moral orthodoxy	Behaviours that are crimes are also practised widely in the population (e.g. drug misuse). Deviance and 'criminality' are widespread; while most of the population support the statutory definitions, crime is also frequently practised in the breach.
Decline of trust in authority	The pronouncements of authority (including government statistics) are no longer taken on trust in the way they once were. The media has played a role here in the fostering of a more open but also a more sceptical society.
Governance	Contemporary forms of government are placing data and information in a far more central role in facilitating governance: particularly influential has been the adoption of market processes into the public sector and the 'new public management', including 'governing-at-a-distance', the separation of 'steering' and 'rowing' functions, consumer choice, local accountability, partnership working, etc.
Modernization of public services	For at least the past 25 years, Government has pursued an agenda to modernize and reform public services, especially those delivered locally.
Criminal justice reform	Reflecting the above, there has been a greater emphasis on the reform of the criminal justice system (CJS). Whereas the reform process in the health and education sectors has been lengthier and more developed, reform initiatives in the CJS have been more recent and, as yet, more limited. Nevertheless, the pace of change, particularly in policing (following the Police Reform Act 2002) is gaining considerable momentum

Source: Statistics Commission (2006: 43).

All of the above changes have had a major impact on the role and significance of crime statistics in society.

A number of reviews of crime statistics have been undertaken over recent years. While the basic elements of the modern system of recording crime statistics stem from the review carried out by the Perks Committee in the 1960s (Home Office, 1967), major recent changes to the official crime statistics derive from a series of reviews carried out more recently. A thematic inspection by HM Inspectorate of Constabulary (HMIC, 2000) and Home Office Research Study 204 (Burrows *et al.*, 2000) both identified significant deficiencies in the quality of police-recorded crime data. These issues were also taken up in 2000 in the *Simmons Review* (Home Office, 2000) which looked widely across the range of issues concerning both the production and presentation of crime statistics. Latterly, the UK Statistics Commission published a report on users' perspectives on crime statistics (Statistics Commission, 2006) while the Home Secretary (whose jurisdiction covers England and Wales only) commissioned an 'independent review' of crime statistics, chaired by Professor Adrian Smith (Home Office, 2006). This range of activity demonstrates that crime statistics and the challenges they pose in terms of reporting, presentation and interpretation, are both high profile and politically sensitive.

What are the main types of crime statistics?

There are a number of different sources of crime data. The main official statistics are police-recorded crime and surveys.

Police-recorded crime

In England and Wales police-recorded crime is composed of categories of crime that are outlined in the Home Office Counting Rules[1] and known as 'notifiable offences'. These include: violence against the person, sexual offences, robbery, burglary, theft, handling stolen goods, fraud and forgery, criminal damage, drug offences, and 'other offences'. Over time, there have been changes in the way that police have been asked to record crime such as amendments to the Counting Rules introduced in 1998 and the introduction of the National Crime Recording Standard (NCRS) in April 2002. The NCRS requires that the police record a crime if 'the circumstances as reported amount to a crime as defined by law and there is no credible evidence to the contrary'.[2] The record will remain unless evidence emerges to disprove that a crime has occurred. The NCRS was introduced to ensure standardization of police recording practices' between types of complainant, types of incident, and within and between police services.[3] The coverage of available crime statistics is limited by the omission of 'summary offences' from the published recorded data (in England and Wales) and the omission of data from certain specific police forces such as the British Transport Police (although the Smith Review recommends that these should now be included as crime statistics). In Scotland, police-recorded crime statistics are more highly aggregated than those in England and Wales. Instead of the NCRS, Scotland has the Scottish Crime Recording Standard (SCRS), designed to reflect its distinct legal system. Northern Ireland adheres to the NCRS and follows similar principles to those in England and Wales.

Crime victimization surveys

There are a number of crime victimization surveys within the UK. The largest is the British Crime Survey (BCS), which actually covers only England and Wales. This survey asks approximately 45,000 adults in private households per year about levels of crime and public attitudes to crime. The survey asks about crime the individuals have experienced within the last year, including crimes *that were not reported* to the police. This enables estimates of victimization at police-force-area level and allows robust estimates of lower incidence crimes. The BCS also includes questions relating to attitudes to crime, such as the level of worry about crime, and also questions about measures taken to avoid crime. The BCS has a range of uses. It provides:

- a measure of crime victimization, independent of police-recorded crime statistics;
- a means of 'auditing' police-recorded crime statistics. Without the BCS it would not be possible to distinguish between trends in police figures generated by changes in crime and the public's propensity to report crime to the police, as opposed merely to changes in police recording practices;
- data on people's perceptions of crime such as worry and fear; and
- data to help policy makers identify those groups most likely to be at risk of crime.

Scotland was incorporated in the first BCS, but since then, the Scottish Crime Survey (SCS) has been independent of the BCS. Recent surveys—re-designated as the Scottish Crime and Justice Survey (SCJS)—now involve continuous data collection, with a much larger, rolling monthly sample of adults across Scotland that, as with BCS, involves adults over 16.

Other surveys include:

- a Commercial Victimization Survey (CVS) run by the Home Office in 1994 and 2002. This survey involves crime against small- and medium-sized retail and manufacturing premises in England and Wales;
- the Offending Crime and Justice Survey (OCJS), which examines the extent of offending, anti-social behaviour and drug use among the household population, and in particular, among young people aged from 10 to 25.

Who are the users of crime statistics?

According to research carried out for the Statistics Commission review (Fox *et al.*, 2006), the primary 'users' of crime statistics are:

- the public—increasingly, people want to find out about crime and policing issues in their own neighbourhoods, and about what their local government and police force are doing about it; in particular, statistics are of concern to those from or interested in demographic groups that are most commonly perceived to be the subject of discrimination;
- central government—as a basis for policy making and the presentation of their policies to the electorate; and

- organizations responsible at a local level for the delivery of the criminal justice system and crime reduction—in particular the police and other partners within local Crime and Disorder Reduction Partnerships (CDRPs).

However, other groups also have an interest as 'secondary users'. These include the research community (both academic and commercial), private sector organizations who make use of crime statistics to sell services, or for business information purposes. These groups provide services based upon crime statistics to the primary users. Similarly, many individuals and organizations, including the media, parliamentarians, academics, and the voluntary sector also have an interest in crime statistics, ultimately *pro bono* on behalf of the public and its interests.

What are the purposes of crime statistics?

The role played by crime statistics in government has changed considerably. Whereas in the past, the official crime statistics were part of a system of national accounts of the condition of British society, now crime statistics play a central role within *the modern regime of statutory governance* intended to regulate the criminal justice system and its agencies. Crime statistics now not only measure the needs of society but are also used to manage the performance of criminal justice agencies and partnerships. This specifically instrumental definition of the use of crime statistics is a relatively new one, largely emerging as part of a political modernization agenda, and reflecting the policy priorities of the Government, including police reform.

Understanding the purposes for which the public use crime statistics is difficult. The 2006 Statistics Commission review suggested the following five uses that private citizens might make of crime statistics:

- assessing the performance of the authorities in tackling crime;
- understanding policy development by government;
- understanding the causes of crime, victimization, and offending;
- determining personal risk and susceptibility to crime; and
- informing the public of criminal activity in their area.

The Review also suggested that although the public have some understanding of crime statistics, on the whole they do not specifically make an effort to keep abreast of trends. In particular, crime statistics are only one of a number of sources of information that the public use when making decisions in their everyday lives, and that they do not use them to make precise calculations about the risks they could face from crime. Indeed, although the public may use crime-related statistics to assess performance of local agencies, or who to vote for, and to assess levels of risk of victimization, they are probably more strongly influenced by local factors. So, for instance, anecdotal 'evidence' from friends and family are more likely to influence perceptions than crime figures, which are not always robust, and which do not facilitate easy comparison of one area with another. Furthermore, there is by no means a perfect correlation between individuals' actual risk of crime and their fear of it. For instance, analysis of the British Social

Attitudes Survey suggested that worry about crime was linked to a range of other social attitudes.

Are crime statistics 'fit for purpose'?

National government and local delivery organizations have three main purposes that they use crime statistics to help fulfil:

- policy and implementation;
- performance management;
- communicating with the public.

Making policy

The Statistics Commission Review concluded that, allowing for the fact that policy makers can commission bespoke research and *ex ante* evaluation to support policy-making decisions, the available crime statistics are broadly fit for policy-making purposes. However, a number of issues relating to specific types of crime statistics were highlighted. It has long been recognized that police-recorded crime statistics are an imperfect measure of crime and hence not an adequate basis for policy. They are highly dependent on:

- recording practices and counting rules,
- the relevant authorities' (limited) ability to detect the occurrence of crime, and
- the public's (including victim's) varying propensities to report crime occurrences to the authorities.

Variations in these factors between places and over time (discussed later in this chapter) greatly reduce the reliability of crime statistics as measures of the need for crime control policy or measures of performance in delivering it.

The data that have been available hitherto have been provided by local police forces in summary form, according to agreed counting rules. The data set contains limited case and contextual information that would be of interest to policy makers, for example, details of offences and the demographics of victims. Future plans for the direct supply of crime records to the Home Office (through a proposed National Management Information System (NMIS)) may go some way to change this position, providing a more flexible, standardized and detailed crime record information system. Yet, currently, the Home Office has been vague about when the long-planned NMIS might be brought online, or about its ideas for standardizing the recording of 'incidents' reported to the police via local force command and control systems. It was partly because of the recognized limitations of recorded crime statistics in supporting policy making—especially in failing to capture the extent of unreported crime victimization—that the BCS was originally introduced in 1981.

Performance

The capacity of the crime statistics to meet performance needs of central government and local delivery organizations varies, with the statistics more appropriate to central government purposes than the needs of local organizations. However, the Statistics Commission Review concluded that generally, crime statistics are not 'fit for purpose' as a means of managing performance. It was concluded that the substantial investment that has gone into the various improvements in the official crime statistics in recent years would seem primarily determined by the needs of central government. Issues concerning the investment in crime statistics and statistical systems that might be needed to meet the increased expectations that have been placed on local agencies, including police forces, have not been addressed to the degree to which national government's needs have been addressed.

Home Office policy makers and HM Inspectorate of Constabulary (HMIC) use crime statistics to assess the performance of local criminal justice agencies, including police forces and Crime and Disorder Reduction Partnerships (CDRPs). Performance assessment has become much more systematized in recent years, for example, with the introduction of the Police Performance Assessment Framework (PPAF). Historically, recorded crime statistics have been used in national-level performance measurement, and are now available publicly for Police Forces Areas (PFA), Basic Command Units (BCUs), and CDRPs. The National Crime Recording Standard (NCRS) was introduced in 2001 primarily to bring about a standardization in crime recording practice across the country, itself necessary to facilitate a consistent standard of comparison between PFAs over time. There seems to be widespread agreement that the NCRS has now put in place the best standard of crime recording obtained to date. This has been due to its recording procedures, its administrative system, and the programme of auditing of compliance carried out by the Audit Commission on behalf of the Home Office. Although compliance was at first incomplete, the programme of auditing substantially improved levels of compliance nationally.

Despite improvements brought about by the NCRS, the extent to which recorded crime statistics are dependent on counting rules and the collection process will remain a serious limitation to their use. The strongest examples of this abiding problem are violent crime and anti-social behaviour. Despite the priority afforded to these offences in government policy, they are the ones that pose the greatest problems of definition, recording, and the greatest volatility in public reporting.

Local criminal justice agencies, especially police BCUs and CDRPs have been required both to assess their performance, and to base their operational and strategic decision-making, upon the use of crime statistics. Unlike national government, local government requirements have had to be met by recorded crime statistics alone, since the Government maintains that the cost to the Exchequer of mounting local surveys equivalent to the BCS would be prohibitive.

British Crime Survey

Both BCS and recorded crime data are used by the Home Office to report on its performance under the relevant Public Service Agreements (PSAs) required by HM Treasury. However, the importance of the PSA framework, along with the deficiencies of recorded crime data, now means that the BCS has become the primary source of crime statistics for Home Office performance management at national and Government Office (England and Wales) level. It is also now accepted that performance targets for anti-social behaviour will be measured chiefly through perceptual information; again, only to be gleaned from Survey data. Despite the importance now attached to the BCS as the primary national source of important data on crime, and a significant increase in its sample size to provide more frequent measurement at police force area (PFA) level, its basic methodology has remained substantially unchanged since its inception 25 years ago. Not only has its cost increased substantially but like all social surveys, the BCS encounters a range of methodological issues that can affect its reliability and validity substantially. These are discussed below. Neither the range of problems, nor the methodological solutions arrived at (including the re-design applied in 2001) have been sufficiently transparent to either afford independent or public scrutiny. Although work was commissioned by the Home Office around sampling methodology, it is not clear whether the Home Office have taken full advantage of the methodological expertise available in the wider expert community, or whether necessary steps have been taken to ensure that public interests in the reliability of the BCS and value-for-money issues are properly balanced. Despite an increased sample size, the BCS lacks the *granularity* to provide reliable statistics on areas of a scale lower than PFA; again, this is inconsistent with the direction of policy and practice, and the now regular output of recorded crime statistics at BCU and CDRP level.

Communication

National government and local crime reduction and criminal justice delivery organizations wish to communicate with the public. However, because it is not always clear what it is that governments want to communicate to the public (since it is difficult to answer the question as to whether politicians are always inclined to speak the whole truth) it is difficult to assess whether the crime data available is fit for the purpose of political communication. In particular, there seems a fundamental ambiguity in the publication of criminal statistics between the Government's duties to report to the public on social conditions and its wish to communicate messages about its own performance to its electorate. Currently, the Home Office publishes regular statistical bulletins that include both findings from the BCS and recorded crime statistics that focus on national crime trends. Potentially this leads to confusion for the public regarding key messages, especially if the statistical series diverge.

It is even harder to define the purposes for which the public would wish to use crime statistics. Nevertheless, it seems unlikely that the general public has any clearly articulated view as to how crime statistics could assist their purposes. The Statistics Commission Review concluded, not surprisingly, that the absence of clarity about the public's interests in crime statistics is shared by professionals in both government and local crime reduction and criminal justice delivery organizations. Rather, the public rely upon others—including not only central and local government but also commentators in the media and academia—to assist them with defining their needs and in interpreting how the crime statistics might help them. In turn, this requires:

- government/producers to release crime statistics appropriately;
- media to report/communicate the statistics accurately; and
- government/academics/commentators/interest groups to provide valid interpretations of the statistics and to demonstrate the applicability of statistics to meeting the public's needs.

In sum, the Statistics Commission Review, along with the Government's own independent review (Home Office, 2006), concluded that crime statistics are generally not fit for purpose as a means of political communication with the public. Key reasons underpinning this conclusion are:

- *limitations with the crime statistics themselves*—for instance, the lack of neighbourhood-level statistics and the extent to which statistics reflect public perceptions of crimes such as violence;

- *the role of the media as a mediator between crime statistics as published and their consumption by the public*—it was recognized that the media pursue a range of agendas and interests and tend to focus on stories about individual, atypical crimes rather than statistics. Although journalists who specialize in Home Affairs do sometimes have a good understanding of the crime statistics, the wider media sometimes distorts statistical information it reports due to a lack of understanding;

- *the lack of public trust in government statistics*—this lack of trust is not specific to crime statistics and may reflect a lack of trust in government more generally;

- *the public's ability to interpret crime statistics*—neither survey data nor police-recorded crime is well understood by the public. In particular the relationship between the BCS and recorded crime statistics causes confusion, particularly since the Home Office now uses both sources in regularly reporting to the public, which does not dispel the impression that ministers pick the particular statistics that suit their purposes at particular times.

REVIEW QUESTIONS

1 What are the social and political forces that have influenced the current use of crime statistics?

2 How do police-recorded crime statistics differ from those obtained from crime victimization surveys?

3 What are the three main types of users of crime statistics?

4 How has the Government's use of crime statistics changed?

5 How do the public perceive and use crime statistics?

6 Are crime statistics fit for the following purposes: (a) policy and implementation; (b) performance management; and (c) communicating with the public?

Counting crime

What is counted?

Many things that people experience, witness, or perpetrate could be classified as crime. Sometimes, for instance, people do not know that these incidents are crimes. The retort 'I'll get you!' during a heated exchange between, say, two irate neighbours could end up as an offence of 'threatening behaviour'. Or people do not want incidents to be considered as crimes, or more particularly do not want the police to intervene in what they see as their 'private' disputes, even if there is good reason that they should. For instance, the abused woman in domestic violence may be too afraid to report her abusive partner to the police, while the abuser will not want his abusive behaviour to be known about or punished. Sometimes, people are not even aware they have been victims of crime—after all, the most successful confidence tricks or Internet scams are those where the victim remains completely oblivious, even while their pockets or bank accounts are being pillaged.

The police have little knowledge about most crime at the time it occurs and without victims or witnesses telling them about it they will remain ignorant. Thus, the British Crime Survey (BCS), a sample survey of people's crime victimization experiences (see below), found that the police were present at the scene in only about 3 per cent of incidents experienced by respondents. Generally, there are more incidents and events in people's everyday lives that might warrant a police response than are ever brought to their attention.

Not only is there a 'dark figure' of unreported crime, but there is also a 'grey figure' (Bottomley and Pease, 1986)—the disparity between estimates of what members of the public say they report to the police and the number of crimes actually recorded. The difference is considerable. For instance, from estimates from the 1999 BCS, of the two-fifths of incidents experienced by victims that they said they had reported to the police, only slightly over half appear to have been recorded in the returns made by police to Government (Kershaw, *et al.*, 2000). Thus, there are two sources of 'bias' in police-recorded counts of crime—*the propensity of the public to report crime* and *the practice of the police in recording it.*

Where is the count of crime recorded?

There are three generic sources of statistical information on crime counts:

- *Official statistics.* In many jurisdictions, local police forces are obliged by statute to report the occurrence of certain crimes to the State. In England and Wales these are called 'notifiable offences'. How these are to be reported is set out in the *Home Office Counting Rules*[4] which describe how, and in what ways, occurrences of crime which have come to police attention are to be counted as criminal offences in police forces' returns. There is an extensive range of different offence codes for recorded crime, though for publication purposes these are aggregated into broader categories of offences, which include: violence against the person, sexual offences, robbery, burglary, theft, handling stolen goods, fraud and forgery, criminal damage, drug offences, and 'other offences'. Motor vehicle offences under the Road Traffic Acts are recorded separately. In England and Wales, historically, the Home Office published an official, annual series of *Criminal Statistics*, though this was discontinued following a review (Home Office, 2000). Nowadays a more limited range of police-recorded statistics are presented as an annual 'snapshot of crime' in the *Home Office Statistical Bulletin* series, along with other statistical information, mostly from the BCS. Published summaries of official crime statistics are already available on the Internet[5] <http://

www.crimestatistics.org.uk> and, in future, the statistical information reported to the Home Office may also become available directly via the Internet.

- *Crime victimization surveys.* These are large-scale, representative sample surveys of private citizens (though businesses are sometime surveyed too), in which respondents are asked about the crime they have experienced, usually over the previous year, including crimes *which were not reported* to the police. While a range of crimes are included, an effort is made to collect information on a 'basket' of crimes comparable to official crime statistics in order to compare patterns and trends between them. There are a number of regular crime victimization surveys in the UK, including the BCS (which actually only covers England and Wales) and the Scottish Crime Victimization Survey (SCVS), run by the Scottish Government for its separate jurisdiction. Such surveys tend to be quite large—the BCS now surveys year round a sample of approximately 45,000 adults in private households. While their original purpose was to provide an alternate means of estimating the amount of crime occurring (by finding out about unrecorded crime), surveys such as the BCS are also used increasingly as a means for Government to assess the performance of criminal justice agencies, particularly the police (Allen, 2007).

- *Administrative records.* Police forces also collate and store statistical information on crime as a by-product of their administrative and operational activities. The police record information as it is reported to them by the public, via the emergency telephone system (the '999' number in the UK) and from other sources, including their own officers. Incoming calls for police service and assistance are usually logged as *incident data*, while attending and investigating officers may compile *crime reports* from them. As noted, some of this information is extracted, and recorded as notifiable offences. Police incident and crime report data are not usually published, though they may be accessible for research purposes on request (or not).

Access, control, and governance of crime statistics in England and Wales

Issues concerning access and control of crime data, including recent Freedom of Information legislation in the UK has made, in principle, some unpublished statistical information on crime more accessible to the public on request. Data Protection legislation generally tends to exempt from public access police records held in connection with criminal investigations. The activities of local police forces in England and Wales, including their crime-recording practices, come under the independent scrutiny both of the Audit Commission for England and Wales and Her Majesty's Inspectorate of Constabulary (equivalent bodies pertain in Scotland). As a government department, the crime-recording practices of the Home Office are scrutinized by the National Audit Office, which reports directly to Parliament. Recent legislation in England and Wales is bringing about a series of changes to the constitution of the National Statistics. Although all government statistics come under the auspices of the National Statistics Board for quality control purposes, crime statistics remain *official* rather than *national* statistics since administrative responsibility remains (in England and Wales) with the Home Office, a ministry of state.

REVIEW QUESTIONS

1 What are the 'dark', 'grey', and 'light' figures of crime?

2 What are the three sources of statistical information about crime?

3 Who oversees crime statistics; who controls access to them?

Recording incidents as criminal offences

The decision by the police to record an incident reported to them as an offence is a *negotiated outcome*, with the police balancing a number of considerations, usually with some permitted (and some acquired) discretion. There is only one reason for the police to record a complaint or reported incident as a crime—*prima facie* evidence that an offence might have been committed—but there are a variety of reasons why the police do *not* record incidents.

Variation in discretionary police recording practice has most often been seen as the main influence on disparities in the recording (as distinct from the reporting) of crime.

The most recent overhaul of the Counting Rules occurred in 1998, largely as an effort to improve the correspondence between numbers and types of incidents and recorded offences. Some of the disparity in recording is also due to different approaches taken when incidents are reported. The *Review of Crime Statistics for England and Wales* (Home Office, 2000) discovered the existence of two recognizable models of police recording practice: a *prima facie* model which faithfully records as crime the details of allegations made by the public; and an *evidential* model which subjects complaints to some investigative selection prior to recording (Burrows *et al.*, 2000); the former tending to produce a greater number of recorded crimes than the latter. As an illustration of how these approaches might affect the counting of crime, some years ago, a study estimated that the much greater crime rate of Nottinghamshire, compared to its surrounding counties, was due largely to zealous, *prima facie* recording of incidents, including the counting of a series of milk-bottle thefts from doorsteps as separate incidents! (Farrington and Dowds, 1985). Efforts to standardize recording practices amongst police forces have resulted in the implementation of the National Crime Recording Standard (NCRS), including further amendment of the Counting Rules, with effect from April 2002.

There are a number of reasons why a reported incident may not be recorded:

- The police decide there is insufficient evidence that a crime has occurred. For example, a mobile phone reported stolen may have been found and returned.

- There is little chance of an offender being detected and prosecuted successfully.

- The victim (complainant) withdraws the complaint and thus will not be willing to give evidence in court.

- The police exercise discretion in the recording of incidents, for example, as a result of police cultural prejudices and biases against certain types of complainant or complaint (Reiner, 1992). For example, until relatively recently, the police tended not to record officially incidents of 'domestic violence' reported to them.

- The police feel an obligation to record crime because other parties may require an official recognition of an incident. For instance, insurance companies usually require victims to report incidents to the police as a condition of meeting their claims regarding loss of property. In part, this helps protect insurers against the possibility of victims fraudulently claiming compensation for losses from burglaries that have not taken place, since this would entail lying to the police as well. Thus, 78 per cent of BCS burglaries with loss are reported to the police, with 98 per cent of these recorded by the police. In contrast, 49 per cent of attempts and no-loss burglaries are reported to the police, with only 44 per cent of these recorded.

- The police are under pressure to record, or not, as part of accounting for their individual or organizational performance (Bottomley and Pease, 1986). The Government nowadays sets the police targets for reductions in crime, leading to the use of crime statistics as a measure of police 'performance'. In the past, the so-called 'clear-up rate'—the proportion of recorded crimes detected or otherwise dealt with—was also used as a measure of police performance, but was much criticized because it could be manipulated through various recording practices (McCabe and Sutcliffe, 1978).

- The police may employ a range of 'covert' practices to massage the figures (for many reasons, including those noted above), generally known as cuffing (Bottomley and Coleman, 1981), where complaints are deliberately not recorded.

- Offenders frequently want their admissions to be 'taken into consideration'—that is, as 'TICs'—in the hope of more lenient treatment in sentencing. Sometimes these admissions just affect the rate of detection. Sometimes, though, when offenders admit to committing offences that have not been recorded hitherto (known as *secondary detections*) they result in increasing the number of recorded offences as well.

Comparing counts of incidents and offences

For many years in Britain, the police have kept a record—or log—of incidents attended by officers. With the advent of computer systems, and the widespread use of telephones to report incidents, manual recording of incidents has given way to computerized systems. Typically, calls for police service, either through the emergency '999' system or to a local police station, are received at a call centre; details are then taken by a despatcher who assigns available police officers to investigate. Having conducted their enquiries and taken necessary action, the officers will confirm the nature of the incident and an outcome code will then be assigned to the incident log. If officers have evidence that a crime has been committed, they will complete a *crime report* that will be entered onto the police crime recording information system. For future reference, there is usually a link between the incident log and the crime recording system. Numbers or details of incidents attended by the police are not usually published. Counts of *notifiable offences* (defined according to the Home Office Counting Rules) are extracted from the police forces' crime recording systems and returned to the Home Office for processing, eventually finding their way in aggregate form into the Criminal Statistics.

In recent years, the computerization of police records and information systems has helped to provide a picture of how the profile of 'incidents' reported to and/or attended by the police matches the profile of 'crime' recorded by them. As might be expected, there is nothing like a perfect match. Yet what a comparison of the profiles of incidents and crimes reveals is not so much whether the police are providing a good or bad service as the contrast between police work as a service to the public, and police work in the control of crime.

Most research-based answers to the enquiry 'what do the police do?' point to the plethora of different kinds of calls-for-service from the public and the range of responses by the police—from emergency assistance, informal handling, referral, counselling, note-taking, as well as crime-recording. The same raw material provides information on two separate but related activities—police work, and crime. However, both rest fundamentally upon the same basis—the relationship between the public and the police. For each incident, the public take decisions to invoke (call-up) police authority with regard to their 'troubles' and concerns—these include, but are not necessarily restricted to, matters that are criminal as defined by statute. The police make decisions about treating those troubles as a public concern. Different kinds of incident reported to them evoke different kinds of responses. The part played by the police can vary, as can their role as law officers or as a public 'emergency' service. In some incidents where the evidence and attitude of the complainant point clearly towards a crime having been committed, the police responsibility is to record it as a notifiable offence. Other incidents, such as traffic accidents (or the proverbial 'cats-up-trees') are usually not considered to be crimes at all; and in between, there is a grey area where police officers can, and are usually entitled to, exercise substantial discretion as to whether or not to record an incident as an offence.

Basic differences between incident-based and crime-based profiles of police work are illustrated in a study undertaken with my colleagues Professor Susanne Karstedt and Dr Stephen Farrall of Keele University.[6] The research was carried out in an English county, comprising some 1.4 million residents, covering (for England) a large geographic area, with a representative spread of communities—from affluent to poor, including ethnic minorities—and land uses—from the densely urban to the sparsely rural. As part of a research project, access was given to data from both the incident and crime information systems for the entire calendar year of 2000. The incident data contained records of incidents attended by police officers, mostly in response to calls from members of the public. The crime information system contained records of 'crime reports', initiated by attending or investigating police officers. In the research, we sought to count the number of reported incidents and the number of recorded crimes. In order to make some comparison, we needed to group incidents and crimes into broadly similar categories. The classification was not always easy, nor exactly equivalent, other than within broad classes of incidents and crimes. Nevertheless, the results are illustrated in Table 3.2.

Table 3.2 shows that there were over six times more incidents than there were recorded crimes (the third column of Table 3.2). Second, just over a half of all reported incidents did not have criminal equivalents, comprising a wide and diverse range of incidents, accidents, other emergencies, and duties where a police presence was needed, including road traffic matters. Yet, even when comparing recorded crimes with incidents that could be construed as criminal, the respective profiles of incidents and recorded crimes differed quite considerably. It is possible that some of this disparity could have been due to multiple calls from the public about the same offence. Nevertheless, different types of criminal incident had different levels of 'excess' reporting, relative to the number of crimes recorded. Thus, anti-social and violent criminal incidents involving people, including incidents of nuisance, conflict, and violence, comprised the majority of calls

Table 3.2 Incidents reported ('calls') and notifiable offences ('crimes') recorded by an English County Constabulary for the year 2000 (percentages)

	Incidents	Crimes	Ratio of incidents to crimes
Nuisances and conflicts	24	30	4.9
Violence	9	9	6.0
Burglaries and thefts	14	58	1.5
Other incidents	41	–	
Other crimes	–	3	109.0
Roads and related incidents	11	–	
Total number	733,695	118,503	6.2

Note: These records were compiled for a period before the changes brought in by the National Crime Recording Standard, implemented in April 2002.

from the public to the police about incidents where an offence might have been committed (that is, 69 per cent of all possibly criminal incidents), while acquisitive property crime (largely burglaries and thefts of various kinds) comprised the majority of recorded crimes (58 per cent). Anti-social and violent incidents exceeded recorded crimes by a ratio of five reported incidents to one recorded crime, while acquisitive incidents exceeded crimes by only one-and-a-half to one. Thus, the profiles of public reporting and police recording differed both in volume and type of incident.[7]

As already noted, the police may be responding to the nature of the incident in question but they may also be responding to the different needs of the community. For example, concern about 'anti-social behaviour'—including noisy neighbours or young people scuffling in public—may be made by residents whose primary concern is for the police to control the situation or to move on the troublemakers. In these situations, an arrest (and resulting crime report) may be the last resort when other means have failed. In sum, comparing the different profiles of incident and recorded crime statistics can tell us something about the extent of crime, the public's demands on the police service, and the way in which the police respond to such demands.

REVIEW QUESTIONS

1 What are the different reasons for the police under-recording crime?

2 What is meant by the 'prima facie' and 'evidential' approaches to recording crime?

3 What is the purpose of the Home Office Counting Rules, and of the National Crime Recording Standard?

4 To what kinds of incident are the police called most frequently? How does the profile of incidents differ from the profile of recorded crime?

Reporting crime to the police

We have already seen how the official statistics of crime might be affected by the recording of crime by the police. Yet, because of the fact that people do not necessarily report all the crime victimization they experience (for reasons described below), it is possible that differences in official crime rates between communities, or trends in crime rates over time, also may reflect the public's propensity to report crime to the police. As noted, crime victimization surveys—such as the BCS or the US National Crime Victimization Survey (NCVS)—have evolved as an alternative measure of crime in the community. Typically, these are (large-scale) sample surveys of general populations. Their method is usually described as *self-report* since it asks respondents to tell the survey's interviewers about incidents in which they have been a victim, usually over the past six to twelve months. Yet, if crime victimization surveys aim to give a more accurate estimate than official statistics, how accurate are they in turn? Broadly, their accuracy depends upon two things: the *coverage* of the survey; and its accuracy of *measurement*.

Coverage of household crime victimization surveys

Crime victimization surveys may not measure all crime for the following reasons:

- They are surveys of *private individuals*, who are asked to report on both their personal crime victimization experiences (for example, violence, robbery, and theft) and on property crime victimization suffered by their household (for example, burglary, car crime, vandalism). Crimes against *corporate organizations*—including, firms, retailers, local authorities, hospitals, and educational establishments—are not included, amounting to a sizeable number of offences.

- They are samples of the population and may have particular *sample-selection biases*. The BCS does not capture the experiences of young people (below 16 years) because it does not sample this age group. It also only samples people in their homes, thus failing to reach both the homeless, and those living in institutions. Generally, certain population groups are harder for interviewers to find at home than others, especially young people and inner-city dwellers, whose lifestyles lead them to be out and about a lot. Telephone surveys, though cheaper than face-to-face interviews, obviously rely on widespread telephone ownership.[8] Nowadays, the BCS uses a postal address system for sampling. Previously, surveys used the Register of Electors; however, non-registration for the 'Poll Tax' during the 1980s led to large numbers of people disappearing from the Electoral Register; likewise, increasing non-voting generally (and non-registration to vote) has led to the Electoral Register ceasing to be a reliable sampling frame. And some people, for a variety of reasons, simply refuse to take part. Unfortunately, research suggests that all these population groups tend to have substantial experience of crime victimization and/or abuse, thus leading to an underestimation of the count in victimization surveys, and a biased profile of victimization risk for the population as a whole.

- *Measurement of offences*—because surveys rely upon the self-report method, they may not include offences where victims are *unaware* they have been victimized (as in the case of successful frauds, or crimes committed against them by corporate bodies, because they are not usually asked such questions), and so-called *victimless crimes*, such as prostitution or drug misuse.

- *Rarity of crime*—statistically speaking, crime victimization is a relatively rare event, experienced by few people in the population at any one time (see the section on frequency below). Thus, in order to gain sufficient counts of victims and offences for reliable statistical analysis, it is necessary to have large samples, and long(ish) recall periods. In practice, only central governments (and occasionally local or regional governments) can afford to sponsor crime victimization surveys on a regular basis. In 2000, the Home Office increased the sample size of the BCS to around 40,000 partly in order to obtain reliable estimates of crime for the 43 police force areas of England and Wales.

- *Geographic clustering*—crime is not distributed equally amongst communities; the majority of victims, and of offences, occur in relatively few areas (see section on rates below). Alongside their large scale, surveys also have to selectively sample particular areas—usually 'inner city' residential areas—in order to obtain reliable samples of victims. Unfortunately, this means that the sample can become less representative of the population as a whole, who are mostly non-victims, living in lower crime areas. Surveys such as the BCS that employ face-to-face interviewing also select their samples in geographically-clustered areas, so as to reduce survey costs, such as the travelling time for interviewers. Generally, although the clustering of respondents can produce biased estimates—because 'birds of a feather flock together' (people living near each other are often similar socially)—these biases can be handled mostly by statistical correction. However, there remains the potential for bias if the survey's cluster selection method 'misses' to some extent the geographical clustering of groups at risk of crime victimization.

Accuracy of measurement in crime surveys

This set of issues and biases arise from the process of interviewing.[9]

- *Knowledge of incidents*—the BCS interviews one respondent per household to answer questions both about personal experiences of victimization and those of the household collectively (usually property crimes). However, respondents may not know about, and will not report, the crime experiences of other household members.

- *Not telling*—there are various reasons for respondents not telling survey interviewers about crime victimization, including: *load and fatigue*—too many crime experiences or too many questions may make the respondent unwilling to divulge all their experiences; *concealing*, for instance, if there is a personal relationship between the victim and the offender (as in domestic violence) because of feelings of shame, or fear of reprisal, or if the victim feels culpable or responsible for the incident in some way (for example, an assailant receiving an unlucky blow in a fight may end up the 'victim'). Means of ensuring greater anonymity, sympathy, and/or confidentiality during the interview process may help to reduce concealment (for instance, a change to the use of Computer Assisted Personal Interviewing (CAPI) by laptop, with an element of anonymous self-completion, may have increased the count of domestic violence in the British Crime Survey).

- *Memory-decay*—or less politely, forgetting. The more distant the event, the less likely respondents are to remember it.

- *Telescoping*—conversely, especially serious or worrying events which occurred some time ago (that is, outside the survey's recall period) may be brought forward in time—as in, 'it only seemed like yesterday'—because they remain a worrying memory from which victims may not have recovered fully.

- *Education*—surveys ask questions, and rely on people's understanding and memory. Education trains people in understanding and remembering (all those exams!); so, the more educated you are, the more likely you are to recall incidents, and also to cooperate fully with the interviewer (for which, read examiner!).

- *Multiple and series incidents*—in order to make their counts comparable to official crime counts, surveys try to measure crime as discrete, unrelated, incidents, but for some people—again, 'domestic violence' is an illustrative example—their experience of crime is so frequent, and the 'crime' itself is so much a condition of their everyday lives that it is nearly impossible to count or separate instances of these crimes into separate incidents.

- *Interview conditions*—who the interviewer is, where the interview takes place, whether others are present, what procedures of recording (for example, the CAPI example above), ensuring confidentiality and so on, are all likely to produce different responses, greater or less recall, different admission rates, etc. Matching interviewers with interviewees may also affect response rates if it creates greater understanding or trust between interviewer and respondent—for example, appropriate matching according to ethnicity, gender, age, culture, and linguistic background can all increase trust and response.

What do crime surveys tell us about the reporting of crime?

The main reason given in official reports of the results of crime victimization surveys for the differential reporting of incidents to the police is the intrinsic characteristics of *incidents*. Comparison between reporting rates for different types of offence (for example, Kershaw *et al.*, 2001), alongside questions directly asked of victims about their decisions to report incidents (Mayhew *et al.*, 1993), point to assessments of the seriousness or triviality of the offence, as well as to the more ambiguous responses of perceived police ineffectiveness and being able to deal with matters privately (Coleman and Moynihan, 1996).[10] Where applicable, considerations of loss and the validation of insurance claims are also likely to affect victims' assessments. These are especially likely to result in high reporting and recording rates where insurance is widespread, as in household contents insurance, or compulsory, as in theft of cars, where insurance claims are likely to be made. Thus, according to the 1996 BCS, victims of motor vehicle theft reported 97 per cent of incidents to the police, while only 36 per cent of attempted vehicle thefts were reported.

Against this view is another which points to the 'discriminatory' nature of reporting decisions applied by, and recording practices applied to, particular *types of complainant* which biases official statistics. Observational research on police–public encounters has generally found person-based selectivity on the part of the police in their decisions to record complaints and allegations from and against particular types of people, including selective treatment of particular social groups such as young people, members of ethnic minorities, the unemployed, and the economically disadvantaged (Reiner, 1992; Black, 1980; Reiss, 1971). Yet it is difficult to distinguish between what Reiner terms 'discrimination'—'a pattern of exercise of police powers which results in some social categories being overrepresented as targets for police action' (1992: 157)—and 'differentiation'—a disproportionate exercise of police powers against some social categories relative to their presence in the population. A general difficulty is that 'social' selectivity in the types of incident, and person, coming to police attention—for instance, young members of Black and Ethnic Minority (BEM) groups being out and about on the streets—is confounded with the potential for 'institutional bias' in police culture and practice in the way they respond to persons coming to their attention—for instance, while on patrol, or being called by 'worried residents'.

A difficulty for research is separating out the *general propensity* of different population groups to report crime to the police, even if they are witnesses rather than victims (which may be due to differences in their confidence in the police, or their sense of public duty, or community spirit), from the specific *need* to report crime because they have been a victim (where victims are seeking some kind of service, or are obliged to report by their insurers). The BCS only asks victims about their actual reporting of their current incidents reported in the survey and not the general population about its general propensities in reporting incidents to the police. Likewise, 'incident-tracking' studies pre-select from amongst incidents reported to the police 'those which either definitely, *or might have*, incorporated allegations of crime' (Burrows *et al.*, 2000, original emphasis; see also Farrington and Dowds, 1985).

The greater disparity between calls and crimes for incidents of nuisance and disorder, than for incidents of acquisitive crime (Table 3.2) may reflect differences between the reporting of incidents witnessed by members of the public and the reporting of crime experienced by victims. A study of victims of property crime, identified in the BCS, used statistical techniques to estimate general propensities to report crime by taking into account differences in risk of victimization as well as incident-specific characteristics (MacDonald, 2001). Having done this, the research still found that younger, male, or unemployed victims were less likely, while people of Indian Subcontinental ethnic origin were more likely, to report their victimization to the police. Further, victims who had a low opinion of police efficacy were less likely, while those who were worried about burglary were more likely, to report incidents. It would seem, at least with regard to their own personally experienced victimization, that members of the public exercise a degree of choice—albeit constrained—over their decision to call the police, and that this may reflect their perceptions of the likely response of the police to them as well as their own need to call.

Summary: counting crime

Much of the attention paid to the reporting and recording of incidents to the police has been concerned with matters of bias of the resulting indicators extracted from them.

Much of this preoccupation reflects a particular, instrumental way of viewing these figures; that is, as an index of a *real* phenomenon (crime) calling for a specific control response—criminal justice—by the State. Yet, since most of the incidents that find their way into the official accounts would not come to the attention of the State without being initiated by private citizens, these figures also represent a *social construction*, the 'policing of communications about risk in late modern society' (Ericson and Haggerty, 1997; 70). Here, the public are communicating their needs to the police as much as the police are collating evidence on behalf of the State of the need for crime control. Thus a *crime rate*, rather than being simply a record of police activity, or an indicator of the demand for crime control, may actually represent the aggregated outcome of the interaction of two processes—the *invocation of police authority* by the public in respect of difficult and troubling incidents—and the *criminalization of incidents* through the application of the criminal law by the police in respect of those incidents. In their own ways, both recorded criminal statistics and the crime victimization surveys that seek to supplement them are each the outcome of *dialogues* between the citizen and the State; as with all dialogues, they reflect both what is being said, and how it is being received.

REVIEW QUESTIONS

1 What are the factors that lead to unrepresentative (biased) results from sample surveys of crime victimization?

2 What are the factors that affect the accuracy of measurement in crime victimization surveys?

3 What are the kinds of reasons victims have for reporting crime to the police?

The frequency of crime victimization[11]

Sample surveys of general populations such as the BCS generate *counts* of crime-victimization events experienced by their respondents. Typically they ask their respondents to report the numbers of incidents of a set of offences that they or their households have experienced over a particular recall period (usually no more than the previous 12 months). Naturally, tabulations of responses to such questions yield frequency distributions for the number of crime victimizations experienced by the sampled respondents over the recall period. Typically also, those experiencing one or more incidents are usually considered to be 'victims', and thus distinguished from non-victims (i.e. people not reporting any incidents), while persons reporting more than one incident have come to be termed 'multiple victims' or, following Farrell and Pease (1993), 'repeat victims'. Because the surveys are representative samples, so also have these categories come to be thought of as representative of the crime victimization experiences of the general population.[12] Since the surveys also ask a range of other questions about respondents' background, experiences and so on, these questions have been correlated with crime victimization frequencies and, in turn, have been considered as proxies for causal antecedents, used to support, substantiate, or test various explanatory theories of crime victimization.

When the sampled count data of self-recalled crime victimization are arranged as a frequency distribution, they invariably display two characteristics: first, that crime victimization seems to be a *rare event* probability-wise—that is, the majority of the sampled population do not report victimization over the recall period; and that the population distribution is *over-dispersed*—that is, the sample variance exceeds the sample mean, for example, that there are more higher-frequency crime victims than would be expected (in comparison with an appropriate theoretical statistical distribution), or conversely, that the zero response observation is 'over-inflated'—again, that there are more non-victims (zeros) than would be expected. Frequency distributions of BCS data, illustrated in Table 3.3, show that these characteristics appear across a variety of types of crime and types of victim. Although these frequency rates differ between crime types—with property crime at one end of the spectrum and domestic violence at the other—the survey data nevertheless suggest a common pattern of multiple victimization, ranging from a fifth of victims of burglary to around three-quarters of victims of domestic violence. These similarities suggests that there might be a similar *data generating process* (DGP) underlying these different frequency distributions. The difficulty, however, lies in working out what are the actual social and behavioural processes that might be producing the observed frequency distributions. Essentially, that is a matter for theory and further empirical research, though comparing observed frequency distributions with theoretical statistical distributions (such as the Poisson or the Negative Binomial) can help to suggest clues for further investigation (see Hope, 2007a).

Table 3.3 Frequency distributions of self-reported crime victimization

Recalled-frequency crime distributions, previous 12 months—British Crime Survey (2002/03)
General adult population (percentages)

	Proportion of non-victims	Proportion of victims experiencing two or more incidents
Property		
Burglary—households	96.6	18
Vehicle-related theft—vehicle owning households	89.2	19
Violence		
Mugging	99.9	10
Stranger	98.4	21
Acquaintance	98.6	28
Domestic	99.4	45

Notes: Adults in the BCS are persons over 15 years of age.
Source: Simmons and Dodd (eds) HOSB 07/03

Table 3.3 *Continued*

Recalled-frequency domestic violence distributions, previous 12 months—British Crime Survey (2001) Adult women (percentages)

	Proportion of non-victims amongst adult women	Proportion of victims experiencing two or more incidents
Domestic violence— threat or force	95.8	72
Domestic force	96.6	68
—minor	97.4	63
—severe	98.4	73

Source: Walby and Allen (2004).
Taken from Hope (2007a).

REVIEW QUESTIONS

1 What is a frequency distribution?

2 What is 'over-dispersion' and how are crime victimization frequencies 'over-dispersed'?

The rate of crime victimization[13]

A *crime rate* is an attribute of a specific population (in Table 3.3 the populations are, respectively, all adults and adult women). Even so, the conventional idea of a crime rate—usually expressed as the number of crimes divided by the size of the population in the area in which the crimes were counted—may be misleading (Bottomley and Pease, 1986). While a population denominator may serve the useful purpose of comparing rates across jurisdictions of different population sizes (on the natural assumption that, other things being equal, the bigger the population the greater the number of crimes committed), this particular way of conceptualizing a crime rate may also mask other characteristics of the distribution of crime amongst populations. For instance, a programme of research work during the 1990s sought to 'unpack' other features of the crime victimization rate (Trickett *et al.*, 1995; Trickett *et al.*, 1992) by employing the heuristic idea of crime-flux (Hope, 1995). The simple idea behind the notion of crime-flux is that the commonplace crime rate—called the crime incidence rate—can be decomposed arithmetically into two distinct statistics that combine together. Thus:

(1) The crime *prevalence* rate = no. of victims (V) ÷ no. in population (P) = $V \div P$.

(2) The crime *concentration* rate = no. of victimization counts (C) ÷ no. of victims (V) = $C \div V$.

Therefore, the crime incidence rate = prevalence × concentration = (V ÷ P) × (C ÷ V).

This conceptual apparatus promised to provide a basis for understanding changes in crime rates. For instance, since statistical tests on data such as those illustrated in Table 3.3 suggests that there are fewer victims than would be expected if crime victimization was randomly distributed amongst the population, then it was supposed that concentrating effort on those fewer number of victims upon whom victimization appears to be concentrated—so-called 'repeat victims'—would produce a considerable efficiency gain relative to crime prevention effort (Farrell and Pease, 1993). So, it is possible that efforts to reduce crime victimization concentration rates would bring about reductions in the overall crime (incidence) rate. This possibility was so attractive to policy makers that the goal of reducing repeat victimization was developed by the Home Office as a key performance indicator for the police in England and Wales. Nevertheless, while the BCS shows that crime rates in England and Wales rose to a peak in the mid-1990s, and have fallen subsequently, Figure 3.1 suggests that changes in national crime rates—such as the volume crime of domestic burglary—may have been driven chiefly by changes in prevalence rates—that is, the number of victims in the population. During the period, the rate of crime concentration has remained relatively stable, apparently exerting a negligible influence on the trend in the burglary incidence rate.

It is possible that the two components of the crime incidence rate may be measuring different phenomena: as illustrated in Figure 3.1, while prevalence may measure the *rate*

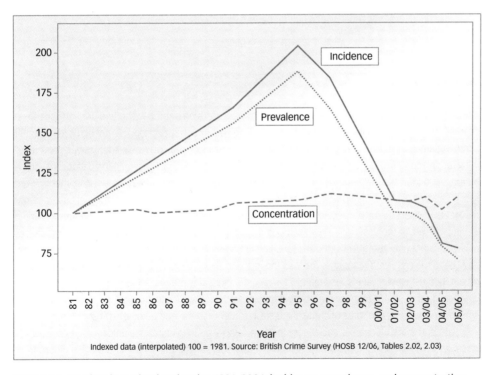

Figure 3.1 Burglary in England and Wales 1981–2006: incidence, prevalence, and concentration

Source: Hope (2007b)

of exposure to crime victimization amongst the general population, concentration may measure the *frequency rate* of crime victimization to those so exposed. Both rates are likely to be related in two ways: first, the arithmetic definition of the concentration rate (C/V) comprises both the total number of victims (the denominator V) as well as the number of victimizations (the numerator C). It follows that change in the rate of repeat victimization (as measured by the concentration rate) can be influenced both by changes in the prevalence of victims *as well as* by victimization frequency. Second, as is clear from Table 3.3, the proportion of repeat victims in the population is very rare. So, for the incidence rate to be determined by the concentration rate, a decline in the concentration rate would have to be very substantial indeed to overtake the effect of a reduction in the prevalence rate, since the latter may be simultaneously reducing the number of victims who would be exposed to further victimization. As there has been a reduction in the burglary incidence rate without a change in the concentration rate, the crime prevention benefits of targeting repeat victims may have turned out to have been less than policy makers had anticipated (Hope, 2007b).

REVIEW QUESTIONS

1 What is 'crime-flux'?

2 What are the two statistical components of the crime incidence rate?

3 Why might policy makers be attracted to reducing 'repeat victimization', and would they be justified in targeting these victims for crime prevention?

CONCLUSION

A final point can be made about crime statistics from the data presented in the two previous sections. That is, the statistical analyses presented here are still essentially *descriptive*. Although they suggest intriguing areas of research enquiry, and practical investigation, they do not in themselves prove anything much about the various social processes that might be producing these observed statistical distributions. To undertake that task requires, initially, the formulation of hypotheses, drawn from theory, from which can be constructed *hypothetical models* that can then be tested against empirical data, and the results used subsequently to revise our theoretical, explanatory models. There are obvious dangers in leaving matters at the descriptive level without enquiring further as to what social-statistical processes might be producing the observed distributions—not least in drawing the wrong conclusions, as may have been the case with respect to the idea that crime prevention gains could be achieved by targeting repeat victims. Nevertheless, as Figure 3.1 suggests, hindsight may also help in solving hypotheses, which is another justification for maintaining regular statistical series. In sum, the production of reliable counts, frequencies, and rates of crime is the start, rather than the end point, of statistical analysis.

To see crime statistics as a social construction in no way invalidates statistical research effort to investigate and explain them. The contemporary approach to the use of crime statistics differs from earlier uses. Rather than treat the statistics literally as an objective measure of a quantity called crime that exists as a social fact 'out there'—what was once called in textbooks the *positivist* approach—the role of statistical analysis is to develop and test explanations (models) that best represent the observed (or sampled) data and which take into account, or treat as an object of statistical study in its own right, the various social processes that lie behind them. Crime statistics are the product of a dialogue between reporter and recorder, between citizen and State. Thus, rather than being an unfortunate set of biases that need to be circumvented, analysis of the various social processes leading to those biases tells us about the dialectic at the heart of criminology—the relationship between deviance and its regulation.

QUESTIONS FOR DISCUSSION

1 Should a criminologist bother with crime statistics?

2 What does a comparison with either (a) police incident logs or (b) crime victimization surveys tell us about the reliability of official recorded crime statistics?

3 In what ways do contemporary policy makers' concerns reflect the way that crime statistics are collected and made available?

4 Do individual members of the public properly understand crime statistics, and should they care if they don't?

5 How representative and accurate are crime victimization surveys as a measure of crime; what are the principle sources of bias and inaccuracy in such surveys?

6 What does analysis of the frequency, and the rate, of crime victimization tell us about the distribution of crime?

GUIDE TO FURTHER READING

The following provide overviews of crime statistics and their relationship to criminology in Britain. They also contain information on other types of crime statistic not considered in this chapter:

Maguire, M. (2007) 'Crime data and statistics' in M. Maguire, R. Morgan, and R. Reiner (eds) *The Oxford Handbook of Criminology* (4th edn). Oxford: Oxford University Press.

Hough, M. and Maxfield, M. (2007). *Surveying Crime in the 21st Century: commemorating the 25th Anniversary of the British Crime Survey*. Crime Prevention Studies Vol. 2 22. Monsey, NY, USA: Criminal Justice Press/Cullompton, Devon, UK: Willan Publishing.

Statistics Commission (2006). *Crime Statistics: user perspectives*. Statistics Commission Report No. 30. London: Statistics Commission.

Bottomley, K. and Pease, K. (1986) *Crime and Punishment: Interpreting the Data*, Milton Keynes: Open University Press.

WEB LINKS

http://www.homeoffice.gov.uk/rds/soti
RDS statistics on the Internet. Up-to-date information on crime statistics in England and Wales from the Home Office.

Home Office Statistical Bulletins

Recent reports on criminal statistics and findings from the British Crime Survey. These are published periodically. (Previous reports on the BCS were published in the *Home Office Research Studies* series. Information on these sources can be obtained from the Home Office Research, Development and Statistics (RDS) Directorate at <http://www.homeoffice.gov.uk/rds>. Previously, crime statistics were published in the annual statistical series *Criminal Statistics*.)

http://www.ojp.usdoj.gov/bjs

Information on crime statistics for the USA from the Bureau of Justice Statistics, US Department of Justice.

http://www.europeansourcebook.org

Information on crime statistics for European countries from the Council of Europe *European Sourcebook of Crime and Criminal Justice Statistics*.

REFERENCES

Allen, J. (2007) 'Survey assessments of police performance in the British Crime Survey' in M. Hough and M. Maxfield (eds) *Surveying Crime in the 21st Century*. Monsey, NY, USA: Criminal Justice Press/ Cullompton: Devon: Willan.

Black, D. (1970) 'Production of Crime Rates'. *American Sociological Review*, 35: 733–48.

Black, D. (1980) *The Manners and Customs of the Police*. New York: Academic Press.

Bottomley, K. and Coleman, C. (1981) *Understanding Crime Rates*. Farnborough: Gower.

Bottomley, K. and Pease, K. (1986) *Crime and Punishment: Interpreting the data*. Milton Keynes: Open University Press.

Burrows, J.R., Tarling, R., Mackie, A., Lewis, R. and Taylor, G. (2000) *Review of Police Forces' Crime Recording Practices,* Home Office Research Study 204, London: Home Office.

Christie, N. (2004) *A Suitable Amount of Crime*. London and New York: Routledge.

Cicourel, A. (1968) *The Social Organisation of Juvenile Justice*. New York: Wiley.

Coleman, C. and Moynihan, J. (1996) *Understanding Crime Data: Haunted by the Dark Figure*. Buckingham: Open University Press.

Dorling, D. and Simpson, S. (1999) *Statistics in Society: the arithmetic of politics*. London: Arnold.

Durkheim, E. (1979) *Suicide: a study in Sociology*. London: Routledge and Kegan Paul.

Ericson, R.V. and Haggerty, K.D. (1997) *Policing the Risk Society*. Oxford: Clarendon Press.

Farrell, G. and K. Pease (1993). *Once Bitten, Twice Bitten: Repeat Victimisation and its Implications for Crime Prevention*. Crime Prevention Unit Paper 46. London: Home Office.

Farrington, D. and Dowds, E. (1985) 'Disentangling criminal behaviour and police reaction' in D. Farrington and J. Gunn (eds) *Reactions to Crime*. Chichester: John Wiley.

Foster, J. and Hope T. (1993) *Housing, Community and Crime: the impact of the Priority Estates Project*. Home Office Research Study No. 131. London: HMSO.

Fox, C., Hope, T., and Mackay, S. (2006). 'The independent review of crime statistics'. *Community Safety Journal*, 5 (4), 4–12.

HMIC, H.M. Inspectorate of Constabulary (2000). *On the Record*, Thematic Inspection Report on Police Crime recording, the Police National Computer and Phoenix Intelligence System Data Quality. HM Inspector Keith Povey, July 2000.

Home Office (1967). *Report of the Departmental Committee on Crime Statistics*. (The Perks Committee). London: Home Office.

Home Office (2000) *Review of Crime Statistics: a discussion document*. London: Home Office.

Home Office (2003) *The National Policing Plan, 2004–2007*, November 2003. London: Home Office.

Home Office (2006) *Crime Statistics: an independent review carried out for the Secretary of State for the Home Department*. November 2006. London: Home Office.

Hope, T. (1995) 'The Flux of Victimisation', *British Journal of Criminology*, 35 (3): 327–42.

Hope, T. (2007a). 'Theory and method: the social epidemiology of crime victims'. In S. Walklate (ed) *Handbook of Victims and Victimology*. Cullompton, Devon: Willan.

Hope, T. (2007b). 'The Distribution of Household Property Crime Victimisation: Insights from the British Crime Survey' in M.G. Maxfield and M. Hough (eds), *Surveying Crime in the 21st Century*. Crime Prevention Studies Vol. 22, Uffculme, Devon: Willan/New York: Criminal Justice Press.

Kershaw, C., Budd, T, Kinshott, G., Mattinson, J., Mayhew, P., and Myhill, A. (2000) *The 2000 British Crime Survey: England and Wales*. Home Office Statistical Bulletin 18/00. London: Home Office.

Kershaw, C., Chivite-Matthews, N., Thomas, C., and Aust, R. (2001) *The 2001 British Crime Survey: first results, England and Wales*. Home Office Statistical Bulletin 18/01. London: Home Office.

McCabe, S. and Sutcliffe, F. (1978) *Defining Crime: a Study of Police decisions*. Oxford: Blackwell.

MacDonald, Z. (2001) 'Revisiting the Dark Figure: a Microeconometric Analysis of the Under-reporting of Property Crime and its Implications', *British Journal of Criminology*, 41: 127–49.

Mayhew, P., Aye Maung N., and Mirrlees-Black, C. (1993) *The 1992 British Crime Survey*. Home Office Research Study No. 132. London: HMSO.

Pease, K. (1998) Repeat Victimisation: taking stock. Crime Detection and Prevention Series Paper 90. London: Home Office Police Research Group.

Reiner, R. (1992) 'Police research in the United Kingdom: a Critical Review', in M. Tonry and N. Morris (eds), *Modern Policing*. Crime and Justice: a review of research, Volume 15. Chicago: University of Chicago Press.

Reiss, A.J. (1971) *The Police and the Public*. New Haven, Conn.: Yale University Press.

Rose, N. (1999) *Powers of Freedom: Reframing Political Thought*. Cambridge: Cambridge University Press.

Simmons, J. and T. Dodd (2003). 'Crime in England and Wales 2002/03'. Home Office Statistical Bulletin, HOSB 07/03. London: Home Office.

Skogan, W.G. (1986) 'Methodological issues in the study of victimisation', in E. Fattah (ed) *From Crime Policy to Victim Policy*, Basingstoke, Hants: Macmillian.

Statistics Commission (2006). *Crime Statistics: user perspectives*. Statistics Commission Report No. 30. London: Statistics Commission.

Trickett, A., Ellingworth, D., Hope T., and Pease K. (1995) 'Crime Victimisation in the Eighties: Changes in Area and Regional Inequality', *British Journal of Criminology*, 35(3): 343–59.

Trickett, A., Osborn, D.R., Seymour, J., and Pease, K. (1992) 'What is Different About High Crime Areas?' *British Journal of Criminology*, 32: 81–9.

NOTES

1. <http://www.homeoffice.gov.uk/rds/recordedcrime1.html>.

2. <http://www.homeoffice.gov.uk/rds/recordedcrime1.html>.

3. Home Office (2000). *Review of Crime Statistics: a discussion document*. London: Home Office.

4. <http://www.homeoffice.gov.uk/rds/countrules.html>.

5. <http://www.crimestatistics.org.uk>.

6. The research reported here and in Table 3.2 was carried out as part of a study of 'The Relationship between Calls and Crimes: an areal analysis' supported by an Innovative Research Challenge Fund Grant from the Home Office, 2000–2001. Crown Copyright in the reproduction and presentation of findings and data is acknowledged.

7. The precise nature and scale of these disparities may have been peculiar to the police force in question, or have now changed as a result of Home Office effort to bring about consistent recording practice amongst police forces via the implementation (in April 2002) of the National Crime Recording Standard.

8. Although telephone ownership has greatly increased in Britain, poorer and more mobile households have tended not to have access to land-line telephones, at least until relatively recently; for this reason, the BCS has kept to face-to-face interviewing.

9. A good if somewhat dated guide to these methodological issues is Skogan (1986).

10. It is not clear from the wording of the question asked in the BCS whether this is a perception of police ineffectiveness *per se* or whether it is a perception restricted to the specific incident in question.

11. This section draws upon part of Hope (2007a).

12. Specifically, national victimization surveys such as the BCS sample representative adult populations of permanent residence. In the case of the BCS, respondents are aged 16 years or over and answer questions about themselves and their households. Respondents are selected using a complex multi-stage sample design and are interviewed in person using Computer Assisted Personal Interviewing (CAPI) techniques.

13. This section draws upon Hope (2007b).

4

Theoretical criminology: a starting point

Keith Hayward and Wayne Morrison[1]

INTRODUCTION

Theoretical criminology is a vast, sprawling subject that straddles more than two centuries of intellectual thought and a range of academic disciplines. It is not therefore something that readily lends itself to summary in a short stand-alone chapter. Instead, our aim here is to offer those new to the subject a 'starting point', a very general (and hopefully gentle) introduction to some of the main criminological theories that have sought to explain and account for crime and criminality in the modern age. If this chapter is a starting point, then our first task must be to point the way forward to those interested in theorizing crime in more detail.

The following textbooks each provide excellent introductions to the rudiments of criminological theory:

Theoretical Criminology by George Vold, Thomas Bernard, and Jeffrey Snipes (2002, Oxford: Oxford University Press).

Criminological Theory: Context and Consequences by Robert Lilly, Francis Cullen, and Richard Ball (2007, London: Sage).

Understanding Deviance by David Downes and Paul Rock (2007, Oxford: Oxford University Press).

Criminology: Theory and Context by John Tierney (2006, Harlow: Pearson Education).

Essential Criminology by Mark Lanier and Stuart Henry (2004, Boulder, CO: Westview Press).

An Introduction to Criminological Theory by Roger Hopkins-Burke (2005, Cullompton: Willan).

Criminology: A Textbook by Katherine S. Williams (2008, Oxford: Oxford University Press).

Criminological Theories: Traditional and Non-traditional Voices and Themes by Imogene Moyer (2001: Thousand Oaks, CA: Sage).

Theoretical Criminology: From Modernity to Postmodernism by Wayne Morrison (1995, London: Cavendish).

Theories of Crime and Punishment by Claire Valier (2001, London: Longman).

The recent collection *Fifty Key Thinkers in Criminology* by Keith Hayward, Shadd Maruna, and Jayne Mooney (2009, London: Routledge) is also an extremely useful resource in that it seeks to tell the story of criminological theory through the lives and times of the theorists themselves, whilst also setting the theories squarely against the historical and cultural backdrop in which they emerged. Cross reference the key names mentioned in each of the sections below with the relevant entries in *Fifty Key Thinkers in Criminology*—this will help to bring the theories 'alive' through biographical narrative.

If, after familiarizing yourself with some of these texts you feel you wish to explore the most up-to-date developments in the field of theoretical criminology, the following international journals provide some of the most exciting and cutting edge examples of contemporary criminological theory:

Theoretical Criminology: Creditably diverse in scope and content, *Theoretical Criminology* is a major interdisciplinary and international journal 'for the advancement of the theoretical aspects of criminological knowledge'.

Punishment and Society: A theoretical and empirical journal providing an 'interdisciplinary forum for research and scholarship dealing with punishment, penal institutions and penal control'.

Crime, Media, Culture: A cross-disciplinary journal that publishes research on the relationship between crime, criminal justice, media, and culture.

BACKGROUND

Perhaps the most important thing to highlight to those new to the subject is the overlapping nature of much criminological theorizing. Although our approach in this chapter is to break down theories into short, independent sections, it is important to recognize that criminological theory is not something that is easily compartmentalized. It is essential, therefore, to think critically about both the origins and the contemporary roles of criminological theories, rather than just repeating some learning of their basic outline/structure. One must also bear in mind that, whilst criminological theory is often viewed by many as an abstract, even esoteric enterprise (on this particular point see Valier, 2005), in reality its impact over the last century in areas such as crime control (see Chapters 21 and 22), juvenile justice (see Chapter 19), and public and penal policy (see Chapters 10, 26, and 27) has been profound and far-reaching. One need only think of the role played by criminological theory in such diverse policy initiatives as the 'welfarist' movement within youth justice during the 1970s, and the 'zero tolerance' policing phenomenon of the 1990s to recognize the influential, indeed potent, force of theory. In this sense, theoretical criminology should be seen as a vital, living subject, and not some historical or intellectual fancy. Finally, one should recognize that the collection of theoretical vignettes gathered together here is anything but exhaustive. A great number of other criminological theories abound from 'peacemaking' criminology (Quinney, 1991) to control-balance theory (Tittle, 1995), from routine activity theory (Felson 1998) to 'constitutive crimin-ology' (Henry and Milovanovic, 1996), all of which compete for attention against/with each other in the vibrant—if, at times, exasperating—world of criminological theory.

The theories—a beginner's guide

The founding doctrines

For much of modernity (roughly the last 200 years) social scientists believed that the problems of modern society would be overcome or at least managed by the careful, scientific pursuit of relevant knowledge and the application of this knowledge to a specific set of problems (for a good general introduction to the debates around mod-ernity see Bocock and Thompson, 1992; Hall and Gieben, 1992). The basket of differ-ing approaches that we may say collectively constitutes the discipline of criminology should thus be seen as part of this enterprise (see Beirne, 1993; Garland, 1994; Morrison, 2004). Certainly the discipline's two (contrasting) founding doctrines, the 'classical' and 'positivist' approaches to the study of crime, were fundamentally concerned with using the techniques and methods of enlightened science and philosophy to make good on their shared goal: the reduction and control of crime within modern, industrialized societies.

Classicism

The first sets of writings typically considered as criminology are labelled *classical criminology* and date from the late eighteenth century. It was a movement born of a combination of fear and optimism: fear of the breakdown of society, fear that there was no longer a God around which to centre things, and fear of the mob, the ragged, poverty-stricken masses that were increasingly drawn to the burgeoning cities of Western Europe; optimism in the sense of the steadfast belief that, as modernity unfolded, it would bestow social science with enlightened knowledge about the human condition. Classical scholars thus put their faith in these new 'sciences of man' in the belief that they would help create greater social stability.

Importantly, with classicism, the new intellectual instruments of modernity were employed not in a bid to understand the ultimate causes of human behaviour; rather the task was to find ways of controlling and directing behaviour by affecting *rational motivation*. In other words, the underlying social conditions of crime were unimportant. Instead the emphasis was on administration, ordered systems that would free society from arbitrary authority and open it up so that the basic true forms of the human condition would become visible. To this end, classical scholars set about reforming the system of investigation and punishing offences. A reasonably coherent, rational, intellectual structure was developed which legitimated the creation of a system of criminal justice based on equality and proportionality.

The central figure in classicism's development was the Italian, Cesare Beccaria (1738–94). In *On Crimes and Punishment* ([1764] 1963) Beccaria considered crime 'injurious to society'. It was this injury to society, rather than to the immediate individual(s) who experienced it (or for that matter the abstract sovereign), that was to direct and determine the degree of punishment. Beccaria claimed that criminal law should bind and guide society by laying out clear, rational rules. The rules are laid down by a legitimate body guided by a new science of decision making, namely *utilitarianism* (or the assumption that all social action should be guided by the goal of achieving the greatest happiness for the greatest number: see relatedly Hume [1739] 1978). From this viewpoint, the punishment of an individual for a crime was justified, and justifiable only, for its contribution to the prevention of future infringements on the happiness of others. Accordingly, Beccaria reasoned that, certain, transparent and quick, rather than severe, punishments would best accomplish these goals. Torture, execution, and other 'irrational' activities must be abolished. In their place there were to be quick and certain trials and, in the case of convictions, carefully calculated punishments determined strictly in accordance with the damage to society caused by the crime. Beccaria proposed that accused persons be treated humanely before trial, with every right and facility extended to enable them to bring evidence on their own behalf. (In Beccaria's time accused and convicted persons were detained in the same institutions, and subjected to the same punishments and conditions.)

Classicism was given further impetus by the British philosopher, Jeremy Bentham (1748–1832). Like Beccaria, Bentham insisted that prevention was the only justifiable purpose of punishment, and, furthermore, that punishment was too 'expensive' when it produced more evil than good, or when the same good could be obtained at the 'price' of less suffering. He recommended penalties be fixed so as to *impose an amount of pain in excess of pleasure that might be derived from the criminal act.* It was this calculation of pain compared to pleasure that Bentham believed would deter crime, it was his key for unlocking the functionality of human nature: 'Nature has placed mankind under the governance of two sovereign masters, pain and pleasure. It is for them alone to point out what we ought to do, as well as to determine what we shall do' (Bentham, [1789] 1982).

Famously, Bentham also attempted to radicalize imprisonment, an institution then used merely to hold persons awaiting trial or debtors. He spent much of his life trying to convince authorities that an institution of his design, called a 'Panopticon', would solve the problems of correction, of poverty, of idleness, and mental instability. There were three features to the panopticon. First, the architectural dimension; the panopticon was to be a circular building arranged so that every cell could be visible from a central point providing a hierarchy of continuous surveillance. The omniscient prison inspector would be kept from the sight of the prisoners by a system of 'blinds unless…he thinks fit to show himself'. Second, management by contract; the manager would employ the inmates in contract labour and he was to receive a share of the money earned by the inmates, but he was to be financially liable if inmates who were later released re-offended, or if an excess number of inmates died during imprisonment. Third, the panopticon was to be open to the inspection of the world. Bentham's panopticon idea was never fully implemented (although two prisons were built along his design in France and one in the US). The panopticon keeps its importance not for the institutions actually constructed, rather for the type of disciplinary rationality the scheme displays (on this point see Chapter 23). Indeed, in many ways, the panopticon remains the very embodiment of classicism.

In a bid to illustrate our earlier point that theoretical criminology is a vibrant, living subject, and not some historical fancy it is worth pointing out that many of the central ideas of classicism continue to endure within criminology today, not least the notion of rationality, which has been resuscitated in recent years by proponents of rational choice theory (see e.g. Clarke and Cornish, 1985; Roshier, 1989).

REVIEW QUESTIONS

1 What were the primary concerns of classical criminologists?

2 From where did classicism draw its ideas? In which areas of criminal justice did they hope to implement these ideas?

3 What has been the legacy of classicism within mainstream criminology?

Key readings

Beccaria, C. ([1764] 1963) *On Crimes and Punishments*. Indianapolis: Bobbs-Merrill.

Bentham, J. (1791) *Collected Works of Jeremy Bentham*. London: J. Bowring.

Clarke, R.V.G. and Cornish, D.B. (1986) *The Reasoning Criminal: Rational Choice Perspectives on Offending*. New York: Springer Verlag.

Roshier, B. (1989) *Controlling Crime: The Classical Perspective in Criminology*, Milton Keynes: Open University Press.

Textbook reading/secondary review

Lanier, M. and Henry, S., Chapter 4 ('Classical, Neoclassical and Rational Choice Theories') in *Essential Criminology* (1998). Boulder, CO: Westview Press.

Criminological positivism

While positivism is a broad term which includes a number of differing applications (see Morrison, 1995: chapters 6–9; Giddens, 1974), for the purposes of introducing criminological theory, we can say that it represents a field of criminological inquiry that emerged in the early nineteenth century which argued that criminality could be studied scientifically using methods derived from the natural sciences. Most famously, criminological positivism is associated with the Italian medical doctor, Cesare Lombroso (1835–1909). Lombroso laid claim to founding a new science—the 'science of criminology' that took as its focus not the criminal law or its related rational administrative practices (as with classicism), but the 'criminal (person)'. Thus, in sharp contrast to classicism, Lombroso's answer to the problems of criminal behaviour lay in *biology*, specifically a complex set of externally visible physiological variations that, he claimed, marked out certain individuals as predestined to commit crime. By observation and careful measurement of the bodily features of the criminal, Lombroso attempted to prove scientifically that those who broke the law were physically distinct from those who did not—this is the centrepiece of nineteenth-century criminological positivism.

Lombroso conducted thousands of post-mortem examinations and physiological studies of prison inmates and non-criminals. He concluded that the criminal existed, in the natural order of things, as a lower form of human evolution than the average man, with very distinct physical and mental characteristics (see editions of *L'Uomo delinquente*, first published in 1876). Lombroso proffered a four-fold classification:

(a) born criminal, those with true atavistic features;

(b) insane criminals, including idiots, imbeciles, and paranoiacs as well as epileptics and alcoholics;

(c) occasional criminals or criminaloids, whose crimes were explained largely by opportunity; and

(d) criminals of passion who commit crime because of honour, love, or anger. They are propelled by a (temporary) irresistible force.

Later, additional categories gave some allowance for the influence of social factors (on this particular point see the work of another Italian positivist, Enrico Ferri (1856–1929)) and he speculated somewhat as to the interaction of genetic and environmental influences (thus providing, to some extent, a precursor to socio-biological theories, see below). However, although Lombroso went some way to developing a multiple factor approach, he never really moved beyond the principle that the true 'born criminal' was responsible for a large amount of criminal behaviour.

Importantly, Lombroso was not alone in his search for the 'criminal type' (see also the work of the aforementioned Ferri and Raffaele Garofalo (1852–1934)—there has been, and indeed still is (see below), a number of scholars and research projects dedicated to reducing the problem of crime to the problem of the criminal. For this reason, one should be aware that positivist criminology does not begin and end with the Italian deterministic tradition (*scuola positiva*). It also extends to include various other early schools of criminological thought. For example, the work of early nineteenth-century 'social ecology' scholars such as the Frenchmen André-Michel Guerry and the Belgian Adolphe de Quételet is also typically described as positivist in the sense that it sought to unearth objective, 'law-like' scientific knowledge about crime (in their particular case, via the moral analysis of early crime statistics and how they might help us better understand what they described as 'the social mechanics of crime', see Beirne 1993 chapters 3 and 4).

REVIEW QUESTIONS

1 What were the main methods employed by the nineteenth-century positivists?

2 What value can we place on this form of criminology?

3 Is the positivists' ultimate aim of a purely 'scientific' form of criminology a valid one?

Key readings

Lombroso, C. (2006) *Criminal Man*. Trans. Gibson, M. and Rafter, N. Durham, NC: Duke University Press.

Ferri, E. (2003) 'Causes of Criminal Behaviour' in Muncie, J., McLaughlin, E., and Hughes, G. (eds) *Criminological Perspectives: A Reader*. London: Sage.

Beirne, P. (1993) *Inventing Criminology: Essays on the Rise of 'Homo Criminalis'*. Albany, New York: State University of New York Press. Chapter 6.

Gibson, M. (2002) *Born to Crime: Cesare Lombroso and the Origins of Biological Criminology*. Westport: Praeger.

Textbook reading/secondary source

Morrison, W., Chapter 6 ('Criminological Positivism 1: The Search for the Criminal Man, or the Problem of the Duck') in *Theoretical Criminology: From Modernity to Postmodernism* (1995) London: Cavendish.

Individual perspectives

Biological and genetic explanations of crime

Biological explanations of crime appear to offer the promise that, if humans were examined like other animals, the 'laws of nature' that govern 'human behaviour' could be established and accounted for. Under this perspective, human behaviour is determined by factors that, while universal to the species, reside to a greater or lesser extent in the constitution of the individual—individuals are therefore, to an extent, predetermined into a life of crime. In this sense, this line of work can be seen as extending from the Italian positivist school inspired by Lombroso. The following are a small selection of some of the better-known examples of the biological approach to the study of crime:

William Sheldon's 'body type' theory—Sheldon's famous (1942) study attempted to link body-build and personality. He famously divided humans into three body types, or 'somatotypes' (see, relatedly, the slightly earlier work of the English criminologist, Charles Goring (1913) and the Harvard anthropologist, A.E. Hooton (1939)):

(a) endomorphs: a heavy, soft or round build; relaxed, sociable, extrovert personality;

(b) mesomorphs: well-developed, muscular, athletic build; active, dynamic, aggressive (sometimes violent) personality;

(c) ectomorph: small, lean, delicate/weak build; hypersensitive, intellectual, sensitive, introverted personality.

Some individuals are 'pure types', while others are 'hybrids' incorporating elements from two, or even three of the builds in their physique. Sheldon argued that delinquents were characterized by a preponderance of mesomorphs, some indication of endomorphy, and a marked lack of ectomorphs. Sheldon concluded this pattern differed from that found in non-criminal populations, demonstrating that there were differences in the physiques of delinquent and non-delinquent males. More recent studies, of course, have concluded that no such link between body type and crime actually exists. But, even today, this does not deter those who are desperate to reinstate constitutional factors (for example, Cortes and Gatti's 1972 study that argued that crime was caused by an interaction between biological and social factors, hence the term 'biosocial perspective').

Genetic transmission theory—Throughout the twentieth century a series of studies have tried to ascertain the *hereditary* nature of crime. Simply stated, this is the idea that certain criminal tendencies are inherited—a criminal is born not made. For example:

- In the 1920s, the German physician Johannes Lange began the tradition of 'twin studies', where the criminal records of identical and fraternal twins were contrasted. Work continues in this area today.

- Raymond Crowe (1974) and Barry Hutchings and Sarnoff Mednick's (1975) work in the area of 'adoption studies'. Here the aim is to compare the criminal behaviour of adopted children with that of their biological parents. If the behaviour of the children more closely resembles the biological parents rather than the adoptive parents, then there is a strong case for genetic transmission theory.

There have been numerous other specific biological theories, such as:

- the attention given to the 'XYY Syndrome' in the 1960s (a chromosomal abnormality that was controversially linked to violent crime) (for example, Sandberg *et al.*, 1961).

- research into biochemical and hormonal imbalances and criminality in the 1920s and 1930s (for example, Berman 1921).

- the link between testosterone and aggression (for example, Moyer 1971).

- Kathy Dalton's (1961) work on the relationship between PMT and female criminality.

Today there are still those who continue to try and reinstate constitutional factors into the study of crime. In their controversial recent work *Crime and Human Nature* (1985) Wilson and Herrnstein devote several pages to reproducing diagrams and photography used by Sheldon, and conclude that 'wherever it has been examined, criminals on the average differ in physique from the population at large' (see 'Right Realism' below).

In conclusion, this body of work is inevitably plagued by the same problems encountered by the Italian positivists; specifically, it is constantly hampered by its inability to control for complex and interacting environmental and social influences. Thus, all informed scholars who claim that biology plays a strong role in criminality now no longer talk in terms of a dominating role; rather a picture is drawn of behaviour resulting from the *interaction* of the biological make-up of the organism with the physical and social environment.

REVIEW QUESTIONS

1 Can criminality be inherited?

2 If we accept that crime is not a natural phenomenon but is socially constructed, is it possible to explain crime in terms of individual pathology?

3 How much emphasis can criminology afford to place on questions of biology? What are the possible pitfalls of such an approach?

Key readings

Sheldon, W.H. (1942) *The Varieties of Temperament*. New York: Harper.

Ciba Foundation Symposium 194 (1996) *Genetics of Criminal and Antisocial Behaviour*. Chichester: Wiley.

Jeffrey, C.R. (1994) 'Biological and Neuropsychiatric Approaches to Criminal Behaviour' in Barak, G. (ed) *Varieties of Criminology: Readings From a Dynamic Discipline*. Westport, Connecticut: Praeger.

Wilson, J.Q. and Herrnstein, R. (1985) *Crime and Human Nature*. New York: Simon and Schuster.

Textbook reading/secondary source

Williams, K.S., Chapter 6 ('Influences of Physical Factors and Genetics on Criminality') in *Criminology: A Textbook* (2001) Oxford: Oxford University Press.

Psychological explanations of crime

The key psychological theories of crime and the relationship between psychology and criminology more generally are discussed in detail in Chapter 6 below ('Psychology and crime: understanding the interface' by Keith Hayward).

Early sociological perspectives

The term 'sociological perspective' is used here to refer to a specific segment of criminological approaches that deal with crime from a distinctly social perspective. Namely, those theories rooted in functionalism that find their origins with Emile Durkheim (although he never referred to his own theories in these terms) but have undergone many transformations (particularly in the hands of Robert Merton) and were dominant from the 1920s to the 1950s.

Functionalist theories see society as an integrated whole, where ultimately all parts or subsystems operate in an integrated ('organic') and coordinated way. A healthy society is one where balance is achieved—which (according to this theory) is the natural tendency of social functioning. Individuals are perceived to undergo a process of 'socialization', where they are taught appropriate role behaviours and values that contribute to the overall functioning of the system as a whole. It is conventional today, of course, to attack functionalism for its inherent conservatism and assumption of consensus.

The influence of Emile Durkheim (1858–1917)

Durkheim's original thesis still appears quite shocking: namely, that a certain level of crime is not only inevitable but also functional to society. He argues that because crime produces a social reaction (that is, rituals of sanction and punishment, whether repressive or restitutive) it serves to rebind the various parts of society and its members into a strengthened whole. Further, in a social order predicated on stabilizing mechanisms and conformity, sources of innovation and change are rare, so deviance is also valuable in challenging established moral values.

Durkheim argued that crime is normal in society because there is actually no extra social, or natural, dividing line between criminal activity and other more acceptable activities. The dividing line is an ongoing process of demarcation and labelling, which serves to differentiate between acceptable and unacceptable behaviour. The use of the concept of crime is merely the strongest labelling procedure which works to maintain social solidarity. Its effectiveness actually comes from the process of punishment and social emotions which are engendered within society. For by observing the punishment of people, and engaging in the feeling of moral and social outrage at the offence, individuals become bound to the common perception of the justified and unjustified, *the right and wrong*. Punishment becomes inevitable. Durkheim's thinking in this area is illustrated in the following much-quoted passage: 'Imagine a society of saints, a perfect cloister of exemplary individuals. Crimes, properly so-called, will there be unknown; but faults which appear venial to the layman will create there the same scandal that the ordinary offence does in ordinary consciousness. If, then, this society has the power to judge and punish, it will define these acts as criminal and will treat them as such' (Durkheim, 1965: 68).

He therefore calls upon us to consider that crime is actually a factor in public health, an integral part of social organization. That does not mean to say that there are not (socially) abnormal or pathological levels of crime, but that both the absence of crime and a surplus of crime are socially pathological. A society in which there is no crime would be a rigidly over-policed oppressive society. But a society which is experiencing too high a crime rate is a society in which the balance between regulation and individuality has broken down. Hence his conception of *anomie* (literally, the condition of normlessness), a condition in which individuals feel no identification with any system of values and thus have no reluctance to commit crime.

Durkheim argued that the economic structure of capitalism, with its strong emphasis on self-interested behaviour was itself a major cause of *anomie*. Likewise the forced division of labour associated with industrialized societies locates individuals in a structure of specialization and economic hierarchy where their position is not freely chosen but thrust upon each person by the accident of birth. As a result, many individuals find themselves estranged, resentful, and aspiring to social positions that are in fact arbitrarily closed off to them. Robert Merton was to call the reaction to this situation 'an anomie of injustice'.

REVIEW QUESTIONS

1 What does Durkheim mean when he says that crime serves an important social function?

2 What assumptions about human nature are contained in Durkheim's theories?

3 What social factors might underpin anomie today?

Key readings

Durkheim, E., Chapter 3 ('Rules for the distinction of the normal from the pathological') in *The Rules of Sociological Method* ([1895] 1982). New York: Free Press.

Durkheim, E. (1970) *Suicide: A Study of Sociology.* New York: The Free Press.

Taylor, I., Walton, P., and Young, J., Chapter 3 ('Durkheim and the break with analytical individualism') in *New Criminology: For a Social Theory of Deviance* (1973). London: Routledge and Kegan Paul.

Textbook reading/secondary source

Downes, D. and Rock, P., Chapter 4 ('Functionalism, deviance and control') in *Understanding Deviance* (2003) Oxford: Oxford University Press.

Wilkinson, I., 'Emile Durkheim' in Hayward, K., Maruna, S., and Mooney, J. (eds) *Fifty Key Thinkers in Criminology* (2009) London: Routledge.

Vold, G., Bernard, T., and Snipes J., Chapter 6 ('Durkheim, anomie, and modernization') in *Theoretical Criminology* (2002) Oxford: Oxford University Press.

Strain theory—the work of Robert Merton (1910–2003)

In the hands of Robert K. Merton, functionalism was radically amended (along with the meaning of *anomie*). Under the Mertonian rubric, it was not that individual criminals did not have the same goals and aspirations as non-criminals, but rather that they lacked legitimate means to achieve them. Thus, the typical problem in modern societies is the *gap* between the ideal of a truly meritocratic society and the arbitrary realities of one's determining birth position (class, gender, ethnicity, and so on) within the social structure. Ironically, the rise of literacy and the onset of institutions of universal education serves to make this situation worse, making promises about opportunities that the society is not able to deliver. Merton famously articulated this situation in terms of a *strain theory* of deviance (1938), that is, the variable response of individuals' adaptations (including criminal ones) to tensions between a highly stratified social structure and the mass of cultural messages present in contemporary life (for example, advertisements for products that purport to instil identity etc).

Merton's theorizing was a challenging moment because it considerably blurred the positivist boundary between 'them' (the criminal) and 'us' (the non-criminal). Following Merton, no longer was the criminal essentially different from the good citizen.

In turn, strain theory was taken a step further by Albert Cohen whose classic (1955) study, *Delinquent Boys*, included not only material goals but also social status, drawing on the idea of 'culture' as the realm of meaning as distinct from social structure. Culture, under this rubric, enables people to 'solve' problems created for them by the social structure by investing their lives—including their criminal activity—with an 'acceptable' meaning. For Cohen, for example, it allowed boys to lay claims to the great American value of achievement—if not at school, then in other (deviant) activities. Today the relevant value might be consumer culture, 'the fostering of the propensity to *consume* irrespective of the material possibilities of such a course' (Downes and Rock, 1988: 94; see also Hayward, 2004 chapter 5).

The final step in this journey was the idea of subcultures (see Chapter 7). For is there not a problem in the assumption that everyone is part of the one overarching system of norms and values (white, middle class, imbued with the Protestant ethic)? Rather—and still maintaining the key theme that deviant actors *share the values* of the dominant culture—was it not more appropriate for theory to explore the diversity of cultures within any one set of national boundaries? Throughout this body of work (see also Cloward and Ohlin (1960)), the issue of conflict was less at the individual level and more portrayed as a clash of cultures. Occasionally teetering on the brink of racism (it took an incredible interest in immigrant groups in the US), subcultural theory became a huge industry in the 1960s, applied primarily to areas such as youth culture and sexuality.

REVIEW QUESTIONS

1 What are the similarities and differences between the way Durkheim and Merton understand crime?

2 What is meant by the term 'subculture'?

3 List some contemporary examples of 'deviant' subcultures. How relevant is sub-cultural theory today?

Key readings

Merton, R.K. (1938) 'Social structure and anomie' *American Sociological Review* 3: 672–82.

Cohen, A. (1955) *Delinquent Boys: the Culture of the Gang.* New York: Free Press.

Cloward, R.A. and Ohlin, L., (1960) *Delinquency and Opportunity*, New York: The Free Press.

Agnew, R. (1992) 'Foundation for a general strain theory of crime and delinquency', *Criminology*, 30: 47–87.

Textbook reading/secondary source

Downes, D. and Rock, P., Chapter 5 ('Anomie') in *Understanding Deviance* (2003) Oxford: Oxford University Press.

Young, J., 'Robert King Merton' in *Fifty Key Thinkers in Criminology* (2009), edited by McLaughlin, E. and Murcie, J., London: Sage.

The Chicago School of Sociology

To understand the Chicago School it helps to know something of Chicago itself. By the 1930s, Chicago had expanded to a population of more than three million. One of the striking features of this phenomenal expansion was the extent to which the city had become home to a panoply of ethnic groups, both African-Americans escaping the rural poverty of the South and European immigrants.

The Chicago School's version of milieu—ecology—drew upon bio-ecological notions of plant adaptation and association that emphasized orderly spatial distribution as both enabling adaptation to the environment and maximizing the use of resources. Park (1925) postulated that human communities were closely akin to any natural environment in that their spatial organization and expansion was not the product of chance, but instead was patterned and could be understood in terms analogous to the basic natural processes that occur within any biotic organism. Thus, Park maintained that the city could be thought of as a *super-organism*; an amalgamation of a series of subpopulations, each unified at one level by race or income or business interests. Accordingly, each of these groups acted 'naturally' in that they were underpinned by a collective or organic unity. Furthermore, not only did each of these 'natural areas' have an integral role to play in the city as a whole, but each community or business area was interrelated in a series of 'symbiotic relationships'. Close observation of these relationships enabled Park to conclude that, just as is in any natural ecology, the sequence of 'invasion-dominance-succession' was also in operation within the modern city.

Such thinking was developed by Park's colleague Ernst Burgess (1925) in his concentric zone theory which contended that modern cities expanded radially from an inner-city core. Burgess identified five main concentric zones in Chicago—which in turn came to stand for all cities. At the centre was the business district (1), an area of low population and high property values. This, in turn, was encircled by the 'zone in transition' (2)—crucial from the crime point of view—characterized by run-down housing, high-speed immigration, and high rates of poverty and disease. Then followed the belts of: (3) working-class housing; (4) middle-class housing; and, ultimately, (5) the affluent suburbs.

The (unfortunately named) 'invasion' aspect arises because, once immigrants establish themselves, they seek to leave the zone in transition and live in a more prosperous zone (typically zone 3). This makes the zone in transition itself a great place of flux and restlessness, not exhibiting a proper 'biotic balance' with its (always temporary) inhabitants. Also, it is itself always subject to invasion from the expansion of the core, business, district (and, in anticipation, property speculators hence keep the rents low, and the buildings unrepaired). The Chicagoans used the term 'social disorganization' to characterize the unstructured and fluid ethos of this social space with its disturbed social equilibrium, and to account for its higher rate of crime.

One influential study by Shaw and McKay (1931, 1942) mapped out juvenile court referral rates and found that these correlated closely to the zones, with the highest level in socially disorganized areas and progressively diminishing in the other zones—*irrespective of demographic/ethnic composition*. This was a momentous breakthrough that did much to dispel earlier criminological theories that located the root cause of crime in the individual (or populist racist theories of criminal ethnic minorities). Instead it was now the neighbourhood, the area, and the immediate environment that was the key factor in promoting delinquent values, largely through youth culture (rather than parent–child relations). Having established this important position, Shaw and McKay went on to claim that socially disorganized neighbourhoods perpetuate a situation in which delinquent behaviour patterns are *culturally transmitted* 'down through successive generations of boys, in much the same way that language and other social forms are transmitted' (1942: 166). This observation, along with Edwin Sutherland's (1939) theory of *differential association*, was an important strand in subsequent criminological theories that attempted to account for crime by reference to deviant subcultures.

Strongly related to their substantive arguments, the other important feature of the Chicago School was their *method*. Unlike Shaw and McKay who relied (perhaps naively) on official statistics, the majority of the Chicago School took their lead from Robert Park, a former newspaper journalist, who proceeded from the premise that the best way to study crime was through the close observation of the social processes distinctive to the city. In this they were positivists to the extent that they sought first-level facts or data through which to get to some underlying level of social reality (which would provide the explanatory connections). But their key contribution was in the area of *qualitative* methods—*participant-observation* and the *focused interview*. Such techniques enabled the Chicagoans to 'enter the world of the deviant' and compile ethnographic data on everything from hobos to 'taxi-dancers', racketeers to street-gang members (see, for example, Thrasher, 1927; Cressey, 1932; Anderson, 1975). The influence of this method can clearly be seen in subsequent writers of the labelling perspective, such as Howard Becker (see below).

The work of the Chicago School was criticized primarily at the explanatory level—whether its theories about social organization and disorganization did not rely on unexplored assumptions about consensual values, and whether the claim about the effect of environment was too strong (the so-called 'ecological fallacy'). What has survived most strongly (apart from their contribution, already noted, to qualitative methods and the study of social actions from the deviant's perspective) has been the observational tradition of collecting data about the spatial organization and distribution of crime. In Britain a number of area studies combined (uneasily) 'mini-ethnographies' of primarily working-class areas with a positivist search for definitive factors in the turn to crime. More recently, under the banner of administrative and environmental criminology (see Bottoms 1994, 2007), the interest in area studies of the offender's *residence* has shifted to a concern with the location of criminal *offences*, and the notion of crime 'hot spots' (see Sherman *et al.*, 1989).

REVIEW QUESTIONS

1 Can locality itself be considered a causal factor in explaining crime and other social problems?

2 Was the ecological analogy useful or did it ignore some of the key forces that are present within city life?

3 What has been the legacy of the Chicago School within contemporary criminology?

Key readings

Park, R.E. 'The city: suggestions for the investigation of human behaviour in the urban environment' in Park, R.E., Burgess, E.W., and McKenzie, R.D. (eds), *The City* (1925) Chicago: Chicago University Press.

Shaw, C.R. and McKay, H.D. (1942) *Juvenile Delinquency and Urban Areas*. Chicago: University of Chicago Press.

Sutherland, E. (1942) *Principles of Criminology*, Philadelphia, J.P. Lippincott.

Anderson, N. (1975) *The Hobo: The Sociology of the Homeless Man*. Chicago: University of Chicago Press.

Textbook reading/secondary source

Vold, G., Bernard, T., and Snipes, J., Chapter 7 ('Neighbourhoods and crime') in *Theoretical Criminology* (2002) Oxford: Oxford University Press.

Hayward, K.J., 'The Chicago School' in *Sage Dictionary of Criminology* (2009), edited by Hayward, K. Maruna, S., and Mooney, J., London: Sage.

The 'labelling' perspective (including social interactionism)

'Labelling' is the term that the American sociologist Howard Becker, writing in the 1960s, used to describe the profound effect on a person of naming them as deviant. Such social 'proclamations' transform the doing of a deviant act into a core part of a person's identity—a symbolic reorganization of self—that, in a theatrical metaphor, 'pre-scripts' their future performances according to their new, conferred, role as deviant. Becker, and also Erving Goffman (1968), studied many examples of such roles, from 'becoming a marijuana user' to the 'sick role' involved in becoming a patient.

As a theoretical development, the labelling perspective proved devastating both to the whole positivist tradition of investigating the 'criminal', and to the established way in which criminology analysed the criminal justice system. These paradigms are challenged if we can no longer use words such as 'offender' or 'criminal or 'deviant'—all 'naming words'—simply as given, 'natural' categories describing the world as it just exists. What happens to these obvious vocabularies when we become aware of the social processing—the *work*, as Becker puts it—that has gone into creating the characterization of the person before us?

For Becker and fellow *symbolic/social interactionists*, the primary moments in this process was what was at stake in the labelling and the individual's way of dealing with this. Such analysis drew upon a mix of theoretical frameworks, including the philosophical pragmatism of George Herbert Mead ([1934]1962), and his distinction between the 'I' and the 'me' (I as observer/me as object of observation). For Mead, no (wo)man is an island; the self does not pre-exist interaction with others. Labelling as social or symbolic interactionism thus takes as its starting point the notion that people *lack* a strong sense of self—of who they are and what they can do—and rely on constant processes of social exchange.

Equally important was the role of linguistic and visual components in the construction—*and* interactive negotiation—of meaning. Deviance, like any action or mode of being, only becomes deviance when it enters social life by receiving a linguistic response. Social control is thus not so much an external force but embedded in the very meanings we confer on acting and being. By the same token, the use of language also provides individuals with resources for 'negating' blame—what David Matza called 'neutralization techniques' by which we tell ourselves, for example, that 'everybody does it' or 'she was asking for it' (Sykes and Matza, 1957). Labelling theory can thus lead to strong associations with subculture theory when attention is paid to the elaboration of deviant 'worlds' with a sympathetic 'audience'.

For mainstream criminologists, more directly interested in formal social control and the criminalization process, labelling theory could also be absorbed in a straightforward causal way as part of the aetiology of 'the criminal' (and the formation of a criminal 'career'). This meant turning sociological theories on their head: it was not that deviance produced social control as a reaction but, rather, that social control produced deviance.

Lemert (1951), for example, distinguished between 'primary deviance' (the original act—whose causes remained—were heuristically assumed to be unknown) and 'secondary deviance' (that is, deviance resulting from the labelling attached to the original act). Such re-incorporation of labelling theory reputedly caused Becker much distress, leading him to say that he wished that he had never invented the term. It must also be remembered that crime as such had not been the core focus of the theorizing but, rather, any mode that came to be seen as deviant. From this perspective, labelling theory leads away from the effects of criminalization on the individual and wonders instead what rules and labels tell us about society. Why do societies *react* the way they do, penalizing different particular acts and in different particular ways at different historical moments and parts of the world? (see Sumner, 1990; Cohen, 1972).

REVIEW QUESTIONS

1 How does the labelling perspective differ from both classicism and positivism?

2 Identify a significant 'label' by which you define yourself. How does that label condition how you act?

3 What is important about the distinction between deviant *acts* and deviant *people*?

Key readings

Becker, H.S. (1963) *Outsiders*. Free Press of Glencoe: Collier-Macmillan.

Goffman, E. (1968) *Stigma: Notes on the Management of a Spoiled Identity*. London: Penguin.

Matza, D. and Sykes, G. (1957) 'Techniques of neutralization: a theory of delinquency', *American Sociological Review*, 22 pp. 664–70.

Textbook reading/secondary source

Lilly, R., Cullen, F., and Ball, R., Chapter 5 ('The irony of state intervention: labelling theory') in *Criminological Theory: Context and Consequences* (2002) London: Sage.

Downes, D. and Rock, P., Chapter 6 ('Symbolic interactionism') in *Understanding Deviance* (2003) Oxford: Oxford University Press.

Marxist/radical criminology

The late 1960s and 1970s saw dramatic changes in the study of crime. Moving on from the soft libertarianism of theories of deviancy and labelling theory, the emphasis was now to be the *political economy* of crime. Political economy implied a basic commitment to the idea that capitalism was criminogenic. Broadly, this meant a recognition that society was fundamentally organized around class-based structural antagonisms. Where more traditional criminology operated around naive consensual assumptions about shared values and socially functional processes, Marxism saw conflict not as social or individual pathology but as the social norm. In Britain, this turn to a Marxist inspiration was announced in Taylor, Walton, and Young's groundbreaking work *The New Criminology* (1973).

At the explanatory level, focusing on the 'political economy' of capitalism as criminogenic meant potentially two different aspects of causation. The first (more classically Marxist) was that the causes of criminal activity were to be found in the structure and operation of market relations, including the commodification of human labour—and to be studied at the direct level of the economy. Typical concerns would be the relation between unemployment and crime (Box, 1987) or the claim that crime reduces surplus labour by providing a black economy (Chambliss, 1975). Such issues have been developed (particularly in the USA) to encompass the interplay of different power economies (not only class, but also race and gender) notably in the work of James Messerschmidt (1993), who offers a version of the 'kick the dog' syndrome as a basis of crime (loosely, you pick on the person who is lower than you in the hierarchies).

Second—and far more prominent in British theorizing (in turn reflecting the origins of this movement in deviancy and labelling theory) is the question of criminalization—what is criminalized and what forms does that criminalization take? This is where we find out what a society values as its core concerns and, more subtly (and this has to be acknowledged as a Durkheimian insight), what is also revealed by forms of social processing of infractions. Much of the most productive work on this theme looked at the past, partly inspired by the work of social historians such as E.P. Thompson (1975), Eric Hobsbawm (1972), and Marx's own great text on the criminalization of the theft of wood. The transition from feudalism to capitalism showed very dramatically how new social arrangements produced new criminalizations geared to the motor of a new economic system driven by the capitalist institution of private property as an alienable commodity (that is, that could—and must—only be bought and sold on the marketplace). As illustrated by the eighteenth-century introduction of legislation imposing capital punishment for poaching game, installing the new system and driving out the old one was simultaneously, (a) dramatically coercive on the part of the rising bourgeoisie; (b) complex in the mobilization of class resistance (with feudal aristocrats and 'their' peasants acting together in defence of the old way of life); and (c) subtle in its associated ways of disciplining the new factory workforce into an appreciation of the basic capitalist equation: time = money (see Thompson, 1968).

This kind of work in turn led in different directions. On the one hand, the conjunction of 'macro-power' (criminal law/coercion/death penalties) with 'micro-powers' was echoed in the work of Michel Foucault (1977) and Dario Melossi (1990) and to emphasize the continuities in disciplinary/policing mechanisms between prisons, factories, and schools (see Chapter 23). On the other hand, *The New Criminology*, reinforced by the tone of social historians' texts (such as Hobsbawm's *Bandits*) had an undeniable tendency to romanticize 'the criminal' as proto-revolutionary or at least social critic—in Marxist terms, implying a degree of class-conscious warfare.

Finally, at the political and professional level, what was involved was a fundamental self-examination in which criminologists were urged to become aware of and, ideally, disengage from, their professional collusion with the State. Criminologists must stop being useful 'problem solvers' and become *'problem-raisers'* (Nils Christie). An important background paper of this period was Stan Cohen's (1981) 'Footprints in the Sand', which linked State recognition (and funding!) with professional criminologists' positivist tendencies towards measurable indices, in turn necessarily oriented to potential points of individual intervention. The target was identified as 'correctionalism'—the ideology and very real practices of dealing with crime as a problem of the individual law-breaker seen as in need of alteration. Adapting Marx's *Theses on Feuerbach*, the slogan was: 'the point is not to change the individual—the "criminal"—but to change society'.

REVIEW QUESTIONS

1 Should certain types of law-breakers be seen as class warriors?

2 In what different ways can crime and criminalization be explained by reference to political economy?

3 Why were historical studies so important to Marxist-inspired criminology?

Key readings

Taylor, I., Walton, P., and Young, J. (1973) *New Criminology: For a Social Theory of Deviance*. London: Routledge and Kegan Paul.

Quinney, R. (1974) *Critique of the Legal Order: Crime Control in Capitalist Society*. Boston: Little Brown.

Box, S. (1983) *Crime, Power and Mystification*. London: Tavistock.

Chambliss, W. (1975) 'Toward a political economy of crime', *Theory and Society*, 2 pp. 149–70.

Textbook reading/secondary source

Jones, S., Chapter 10 ('Conflict, Marxist and Radical theories of crime') in *Criminology* (2001) London: Butterworths.

Lanier, M. and Henry, S., Chapter 11 ('Capitalism as a criminogenic society: conflict and radical theories of crime') in *Essential Criminology* (1998) Boulder, CO: Westview Press.

Gender and crime: the feminist perspective

Feminist-influenced writing started in criminology in earnest in the 1970s and has provided a fertile source of challenges and critiques to the mainstream criminological enterprise. Traditional and radical criminology stood accused not only of neglecting the study of women but falsely implying that the theories produced were theories of crime, rather than being what they actually were—theories of males committing crime. As a result, it was not surprising that women 'did not fit' the standard explanations. Even on the rare occasions when they have been considered, typically they have been portrayed in very stereotypical ways (for example, Lombroso, see below).

As a preliminary exercise, let us begin with 'the facts' as given by crime statistics. The most striking fact is that women have always featured to a much lesser extent than men. Typically, in the crime statistics for England and Wales, 80 per cent of crime is committed by men. Moreover, crimes committed by females tend to be less serious (for more on this point see Chapter 17 below). What implications, then, could be drawn from such analysis of statistics?

Traditional criminology dealt with these statistical facts in two different ways. On the one hand, it regarded them as fictional—a type of scepticism about statistics that identifies a huge reluctance on the part of men (whether as victims or criminal justice agents) to label women as criminals. While commentators such as Otto Pollak (1950) saw this as part of a system of oppression of women (an idealization that functions to keep them in their place, that is, the home), his deeply problematic depiction of women is itself 'backed up' with stereotypes about women as cunning deceivers excellent at concealing their true crime rate, especially in the home whose privacy provides many opportunities for abusing their families. On the other hand, the fact of women's non-delinquency was taken as correct; the key question about women being, why were they so conformist? (Lombroso). Here a further repertoire of stereotypes provided 'answers', concerning women's less individualized, non-achievement oriented natures. Consequently, those women who *did* commit crimes appeared as 'doubly deviant', departing from social and feminine norms—and often receiving explanations in terms of medical or psychological pathology.

This line of critique continued through the history of criminology up to the present day, documenting criminology's deficiencies writer by writer (for example, Heidensohn, 1968, 1996; Klein, 1973; Smart, 1976).

The question then was how should feminist criminology develop after critique? The dilemma posed was incorporation/assimilation or existing as a 'special topic'. On the one hand, should women be treated 'equally' and be subject to the same sorts of explanations as men? On the other hand, should there be special explanations relating to women's differences? Hence one dominant strand in feminist criminology unwittingly reproduced Lombroso's question (why are women so conformist?) while rejecting his (biologistic pseudo-evolutionary) answer. Posed in the language of social control theory, women's non-deviance was to be understood in terms of the internalization of social norms *and* the nature of external informal controls, largely through family responsibilities, applied throughout women's lives (see Heidensohn 1985; Cain 1989).

Other approaches tended to step sideways, sometimes querying why feminism, in an era of radical critique, was so anxious to 'sign up' to categories such as 'criminality': why reproduce the most criticized categories of criminological theory? Alternatively, much attention was focused on women as *victims* of crime, especially rape, including their 'second victimization' in the courtroom. Attention thus became more socio-legally oriented and also connected with campaigns to change criminal law or the law of (sexual character) evidence. Conventional victimology was also shown to be symptomatically deficient, especially, again in the area of rape.

One of the most vivid responses to the dilemma has been to argue that criminology was, in fact, correct all along to be studying men because men *are* the problem. But while past theories have been implicitly written from a male standpoint, they have not really confronted the issue of masculinity as such (see Messerschmidt 1993; Jefferson 1996; Collier 1998 for attempts to correct this lacunae; for more on this particular point see also Chapter 11 below). The subject of gender and crime is discussed in more detail in Chapter 17 ('Gender and crime') of this volume.

REVIEW QUESTIONS

1 Draw up a list of diverse crimes and account for how gender differences might account for different levels of involvement.

2 What have been the main achievements of feminist perspectives in criminology?

3 How has feminism transformed the discipline of criminology?

Key readings

Smart, C. (1976) *Women, Crime and Criminology*, London: Routledge.

Heidensohn, F. 'Gender and crime' in Maguire, M., Morgan, R., and Reiner, R. (eds) (1st edn) *The Oxford Handbook of Criminology* (1994) Oxford: Oxford University Press.

Gelsthorpe, L., 'Feminist methodologies in criminology: old wine in new bottles' in Gelsthorpe, L., and Morris, A., *Feminist Perspectives in Criminology* (1990) Milton Keynes: Open University Press.

Jefferson, T. 'Masculinities and crime' in Maguire, R., Morgan, M., and Reiner, R. (eds) (2nd edn), *The Oxford Handbook of Criminology* (1997) Oxford: Oxford University Press.

Textbook reading/secondary source

Hopkins-Burke, R., Chapter 10 ('Feminist perspectives') in *An Introduction to Criminological Theory* (2001) Willan: Cullompton.

Criminological realism

After the intellectual energy brought into the area by the labelling perspective, Marxism, and a host of other influences in the 1960s and 1970s, the mid-1980s saw a return to basics. Crime rates seemed to move upwards in the face of economic recession and the attempts of criminology to come up with workable theories designed to control/reduce crime. Writers from the political right, such as James Q. Wilson, asserted that the time had come to stop attempting to *explain crime* and simply concentrate instead on *controlling it* (a position that became known as right realism). At the same time, a 'nothing works' message came from several commentators who investigated the supposed success rates of penal measures and a general public perception surfaced in the US and UK that the criminal justice system had gone 'soft on the criminal'. Meanwhile, on the political left, many critical criminologists had become deeply disillusioned with the 'outdated' Marxism associated with radical criminology, not least its 'utopian' dreams of a revolutionary politics. In the face of an increasingly complex world, the desire for simplistic solutions reasserted itself—enter criminological 'realism'.

Right realism

Based largely around the work of James Q. Wilson (1985), right realism emerged in the United States during the 1970s, as a direct response to the aetiological crisis in criminology. Unlike left realists (see below), right realists accept *prima facie* that crime has risen dramatically in the post-war era and that, furthermore, if left unchecked will continue to rise, irrespective of improved social conditions, unless governments change their overall approach to the problem of crime. Consequently, right realists are interventionists primarily interested in the issue of societal order. As a consequence, they rarely flinch from deploying those two old stalwarts of the right—incapacitation and criminal law—as a general deterrence and as a means of protecting the propertied.

The central plank of Wilson's thesis is that, at a community level, crime begets crime. Or to use his favourite analogy, if a window is smashed in a building and not replaced, it indicates to the immediate community that no one cares about the property; consequently it will only be a matter of time before other windows are smashed and the building falls prey to more serious criminals (Wilson and Kelling, 1982). Wilson describes this as the 'developmental sequence' of crime and disorder. This being the case, it is essential that governments acknowledge this pattern and implement specific policy initiatives to address it. Wilson further argues that governments should finally wake up to the fact that they can do little to attack the root cause of crime, and should strive instead for more 'realistic goals' and instigate a series of measures that will have a real and quantifiable affect on both recorded crime and importantly, the *fear of crime*—the measures to which he refers primarily centre around a new and somewhat controversial role for the police.

Wilson asserts that if inroads are to be made in areas of high crime and urban decay, then police work needs to be based around 'order maintenance' and 'crime prevention'. In other words a shift in police practices from 'incident orientated policing' to 'community-orientated policing'. Briefly, this means expanding the practice of everyday police work to include certain social problems that he believes greatly affect levels of crime. In his own words: 'It means defining as a problem whatever a significant body of public opinion regards as a threat to community order. It means working with the good guys, and not just against the bad guys' (Wilson and Kelling, 1989). Effectively, then, the primary task for the police should be to establish order in problem areas by undertaking a systematic, hands-on, street level assault on anti-social behaviour—a policy referred to by some as 'zero tolerance policing'. Police officers are encouraged to 'sweep the streets of undesirables', and clamp down on behaviour like drunkenness, rowdiness, prostitution, begging, and vandalism. The theory behind this approach is that if significant inroads can be made in the level of lesser crimes in an area, then eventually more serious crimes will also 'cave-in' and neighbourhoods can begin to shed the skin of endemic criminality.

More controversial are views held by certain right realists concerning causality. While, originally, it was enough for right realists simply to refute the liberal orthodoxy that crime is a by-product of poor social conditions, more recently they have accounted for this by suggesting that criminality is in fact a complex composite of socio-environmental (especially familial), psychological, and contentiously biological factors. Drawing on the behaviourist psychology of Hans Eysenck (1970), Wilson and Herrnstein argue in *Crime and Human Nature* (1985) that certain personality traits—whether levels of intelligence or indeed levels of psychopathy—are the outcome of *genetic inheritance*. However, they are keen to point out that these traits do not in themselves result in criminal or deviant behaviour. What is of equal if not greater importance is the early 'social conditioning' and positive reinforcement that an individual experiences within key social environments (in this sense their ideas correspond with contemporary control theories, see below). The stress placed by Wilson on hereditary factors has resulted in this aspect of his work being decried as 'neo-positivism', and Wilson himself dismissed as an old-fashioned moral conservative. More controversial still was Herrnstein and Murray's 1994 book *The Bell Curve*, in which it was suggested that black people and Latinos are over-represented within the US 'underclass' because of lower IQ and a resulting lack of 'self-control'. Other features, such as the experience of unemployment or location in the social hierarchy, are regarded as spurious and seen simply as a direct consequence of individual-level differences which are either inherited or caused by family-school processes at an early age. Needless to say, such assertions were met with a considerable challenge by commentators from the political left.

REVIEW QUESTIONS

1 Why are right realists typically described as 'interventionists'?

2 What policing practices are associated with 'zero tolerance policing'? What is this approach to street crime hoping to achieve?

3 What mutual ground exists between right and left realists? (see below)

Key readings

Wilson, J.Q. (1985) *Thinking About Crime*. New York: Vintage Books.

Wilson, J.Q. and Kelling, G. (1982) 'Broken Windows' *Atlantic Monthly*, pp. 29–38.

Wilson, J.Q. and Herrnstein, R. (1985) *Crime and Human Nature*. New York: Simon and Schuster.

Herrnstein, R. and Murray, C. (1994) *The Bell Curve*, New York: The Free Press.

Textbook reading/secondary source

Lilly, R. Cullen, F., and Ball, R., Chapter 8 ('Conservative criminology: revitalizing individualistic theory') in *Criminological Theory: Context and Consequences* (1995) London: Sage.

Left realism

In the UK a movement called new left realism (owing its roots to the radical energies of the 1970s and a decline of utopian thinking), loosely grouped around members of Middlesex University, originated as a political platform with a message to the left to take crime seriously as a pressing practical problem. In many ways, the emergence of left realism can be seen as a response to both the rise of the 'neo-positivism' of right realism and the significant political and cultural transformations that took place in the 1980s and 1990s—not least, the continued hegemony of capitalism and the subsequent fall of communist Eastern Europe. Although it would be doing a disservice to imply that new left realism might simply be viewed as a way in which radical criminology sought to free itself from its limiting ideological roots, it is fair to state that left realism provided a more pragmatic, policy-oriented approach to the problem of crime than much previous critical criminology. Rather than the focus placed by radical criminology on macro political theory and in particular the crimes of the powerful, left realism views crime from both ends of the social structure.

The disenchantment with radical criminology (or left idealism as left realists preferred to call it) came about for several reasons. First, as mentioned above, several of the leading lights of radical criminology had grown tired of the inherent Marxist 'utopianism' that underpinned 1970s British radical/critical criminology. Second (and by the same token), the move to left realism was mediated by several positions adopted within radical criminology that were perceived by realists as being either morally ambiguous or just plainly too liberal, in particular, radical penology's attempts to abolish the prison system and certain liberal positions adopted concerning drug use. Third, left realists took issue with the view asserted by many radical criminologists that there had been no real increase in levels of crime in the post-war era. (Radical criminology had always dismissed the 'aetiological crisis', claiming that the continued rise in recorded crime was a fallacy and that statistical evidence to that effect could be explained by police preference and anomalies in the recording processes.) Fourth, and most fundamentally, many former radicals upheld the belief that left idealism was 'failing to take crime seriously'. Left realists argued that because of its lopsided concern with the crimes of the powerful, radical criminology had lost touch with the reality of 'normal crimes'. Traditionally, left idealism upheld the view that offenders themselves were victims of social inequality and racial and class biases. Consequently, many radicals dismissed (and on occasions even celebrated) lower-class crime as political (or indeed quasi-revolutionary) action. Left realists, however, have tended to shy away from this position. While the realist approach does not lose sight of the fact that the working classes are often the victims of the crimes of the powerful ('the working-class is a victim of crime from all directions...one sort of crime tends to compound another' Lea and Young 1984: 264), they now place a greater emphasis on those members of society who are the *victims* of (normal) crime. Thus we see a significant shift in criminological attention away from the *working-class law-breaker to the working-class victim*.

Following this line of thought, left realists look at the social and symbiotic relationship between the victim, the offender, and both formal and informal controls in a bid to better understand both the anxieties of victims (and 'the fear of crime' generally) and offender motivations. This more comprehensive approach has a twofold purpose:

(a) it enables left realists to wrest the 'law and order' initiative out of the hands of the conservative right; and

(b) it produces a less ideologically tainted picture of contemporary crime.

This picture is made considerably clearer by undertaking a widescale empirical enquiry into levels of crime within society. For left realists the official crime statistics collated by the Government are inaccurate indices that are not only highly subjective, but also corrupted by political and state agency bias. Instead, they favour (and indeed pioneered) the use of victim surveys and other types of localized crime surveys as a means of extracting more accurate data on the incidence of crime in a given locality (for example, Jones *et al.*, 1986).

As the name implies, left realism maintains that the best way to accomplish a reduction in crime is by developing common-sense policies that will have a quantifiable impact on crime and the fear of crime across all societal levels; but particularly among those most often victimized—the poor and the socially deprived. What is more, for maximum effectiveness, these 'realistic' initiatives should be implemented at local or 'community' level rather than nationally or regionally. As Lea and Young (1984: 267) explain: '[t]he organization of communities in an attempt to pre-empt crime is of the utmost importance'. In their emphasis on pragmatic community reform and crime prevention practices, left realists are very much reappropriating policies traditionally favoured by conservatives and right realists. Indeed, as noted earlier, many of the initiatives they advocate are often strikingly similar to those championed by right realists and administrative criminologists. However, left realists are keen to stress that these localized policies are infused by an underlying socialist ethos. This emphasis on community and the inclusion of marginalized and disenfranchised segments of society within localized crime-control initiatives is a central component of contemporary left realism (see Taylor *et al.*, 1996).

Needless to say, the main criticism of the left realist approach stems from the established radical and critical criminological tradition. For critical criminologists, the development of the left realist approach has been a major ideological step backwards.

REVIEW QUESTIONS

1 How does left realism differ from more traditional forms of Marxist criminology?

2 What are the key ideological differences between left realism and right realism?

3 What practical solutions might left realists employ in an effort to reduce crime on a troubled inner-city housing estate?

Key readings

Lea, J. and Young, J. (1984) *What is to be done about Law and Order?* Harmondsworth: Penguin.

Currie, E. (1985) *Confronting Crime*. New York: Pantheon.

Kinsey, R., Lea, J., and Young, J. (1986) *Losing the Fight Against Crime*. Oxford: Blackwell.

Young, J. (1992) 'Ten points of realism', in Young, J. and Matthews, R. *Rethinking Criminology: The Realist Debate* (1992) London: Sage.

Textbook reading/secondary source

Hopkins-Burke, R., Chapter 15 ('Left realism') in *An Introduction to Criminological Theory* (2001) Willan: Cullompton.

Control theory

American criminology, largely through the work of Travis Hirschi (1969), took up a reading of Durkheim's ideas and combined this with the assumption of classical criminology (that a tendency to crime is normal in any human being) to argue that criminal behaviour results from a failure of conventional social groups (family, school, social peers) to bind or bond with the individual. In other words, to maintain social order, society must teach the individual *not to offend*. Control theorists argue that we are all born with a natural proclivity to violate the rules of society; thus, delinquency is a logical consequence of one's failure to develop internalized prohibitions (controls) against lawbreaking behaviour.

In his early 'social bond theory', Hirschi focused on *how* conformity is achieved—this was a theory not of motivation, but of *constraint*. Put simply, *what is it that stops individuals from offending*? Hirschi outlined four major elements of the social bond:

(a) *Attachment*: the ties that exist between the individual and primary agents of socialization (parents, teachers, community leaders etc). It is a measure of the degree to which law-abiding persons serve as a source of positive reinforcement for the individual.

(b) *Commitment*: investment in conformity or conventional behaviour and a consideration of future goals which are incompatible with a delinquent lifestyle.

(c) *Involvement*: a measure of one's propensity to participate in conventional activities (sports, pastimes, work etc).

(d) *Belief*: acceptance of the moral validity of societal norms.

Delinquency was thus associated with weak attachments/bonds to conventional institutions and modes of conduct.

In 1990 social bond theory was considerably updated/augmented with the publication of Gottfredson and Hirschi's *A General Theory of Crime*. In this work, the emphasis shifts from external to *internal* controls. In other words, in proposing a theory of low *self*-control, Hirschi moved away from his classic *social* bonding formulation to present differential rates of self-control as a set of individual propensities that give differing propensities to refrain from, or to commit crime, at all ages, and under all circumstances. Gottfredson and Hirschi's theory states that individuals with high self-control will be 'substantially less likely at all periods of life to engage in criminal acts' (1990: 89); while those with low self-control are highly likely to commit crime.

The source of low self-control is seen as ineffective or incomplete socialization, especially ineffective childrearing. Parents who are attached to their children, supervise their children closely, recognize the lack of self-control in their children, and punish deviant acts, will help to socialize children into social control. Such children will generally not become delinquent as teenagers or engage in criminal acts as adults. The explicit disapproval of parents or others about whom one cares is the most important negative sanction. School and other social institutions contribute to socialization, but it is the family in which the most important socialization takes place. Consequently, unlike with social-bond theory, peer groups are relatively unimportant in the development of self-control and in the commission of delinquency or crime (the four key elements of social bonding theory—belief, attachment, commitment, and involvement—are virtually absent from Gottfredson and Hirschi's theory). Once formed in childhood, the amount of self-control that a person has acquired remains relatively stable throughout life.

The authors also spell out the policy implications of self-control. According to self-control theory, official actions taken to deter crime in adulthood are not likely to have much effect. Self-control, they contend, is already fixed, and therefore only preventative policies that take effect early in life and have a positive impact on families have much chance of reducing crime and delinquency.

These variants of control theory, however, have not gone uncriticized (see Morrison, 1995 for an extended critique of control theory). For example, commentators have pointed out the tautology in the self-control hypothesis; specifically, that propensity towards crime and low self-control appears to be one and the same. More accurately, Gottfredson and Hirschi do not identify operational measures of low self-control as separate from the very tendency to commit crimes that low self-control is supposed to explain. To avoid this tautological problem, conceptual definitions or operational measures of self-control must be developed that are separate from measures of crime or propensity towards crime. Unless that step is taken, this theory will remain untestable; much of the empirical work that picks up on the theory strives to develop indices of what self-control can be taken as.

REVIEW QUESTIONS

1 Describe what you consider is meant by the term 'self-control'. What are its constitutive elements?

2 Outline how control theories differ from other criminological theories you have studied.

3 What difficulties might be encountered when attempting to measure social control?

4 Control theory is predicated on a set of values—but whose values?

Key readings

Hirschi, T. (1969) *Causes of Delinquency*. Berkeley CA: University of California Press.

Gottfredson, M. and Hirschi, T. (1990) *A General Theory of Crime*. Stanford CA: Stanford University Press.

Reis, A.J. (1951) 'Delinquency as a failure of personal and social controls'. *American Sociological Review*, 16: 196–207.

Agnew, R. (1985) 'Social control theory and delinquency: a longitudinal test', *Criminology*, 23 pp. 47–61.

Textbook reading/secondary source

Vold, G., Bernard, T., and Snipes, J., Chapter 10 ('Control theories') in *Theoretical Criminology* (2002) Oxford: Oxford University Press.

Cultural criminology

Cultural criminology is a theoretical, methodological, and interventionist approach to the study of crime that places criminality and its control in the context of culture; that is, it views crime and the agencies and institutions of crime control as cultural products—as creative constructs. It emphasizes the centrality of meaning, representation and power in the contested construction of crime—whether crime is constructed as an everyday event or subcultural subversion, as social danger or state-sanctioned violence. From the perspective of cultural criminology, then, the subject matter of any useful and critical criminology must necessarily move beyond narrow notions of crime and criminal justice to incorporate symbolic displays of transgression and control, feelings and emotions that emerge within criminal events, and the ideological foundations of public and political campaigns designed to define (and delimit) both crime and its consequences. This wider focus allows for a new sort of criminology—a *cultural* criminology—better attuned to prevailing social conditions, and so more capable of conceptualizing and confronting contemporary crime and crime control. This cultural criminology seeks both to understand crime as an expressive human activity, and to critique the perceived wisdom surrounding the contemporary politics of crime and criminal justice.

Although cultural criminology is a fairly recent development (dating from the mid-1990s; see Ferrell and Sanders, 1995), it actually draws heavily on a rich tradition of sociologically-inspired criminological work, from the early sub-cultural and naturalistic ideas of the Chicago School, to the more politically-charged theoretical analyses associated with the critical criminology of the 1970s (see above). However, while it is undoubtedly the case that many of the key themes and ideas associated with cultural criminology have been voiced elsewhere in the criminological tradition (see Ferrell *et al.*, 2008: chapter 2), it is clear that this dynamic body of work offers something new—primarily in the way it seeks to reflect the peculiarities and particularities of the *late modern socio-cultural milieu.*

With its focus on situated meaning, youth culture, identity, space, style, and media culture, along with its commitment to understand and account for the ongoing transformations and fluctuations associated with hypercapitalism, cultural criminology is an attempt to create a 'post' or 'late' modern theory of crime. Here criminal behaviour is reinterpreted as a technique for resolving certain psychic and emotional conflicts that are in turn viewed as being indelibly linked to various features of contemporary life (see e.g. Hayward, 2004 on the relationship between consumerism and certain forms of 'expressive criminality'). In other words, cultural criminology seeks to fuse a 'phenomenology of transgression' (see e.g. Katz, 1988; Lyng, 1990) with a sociological analysis of late modern culture (see e.g. Young 1999, 2007).

Such complex foci require the utilization of a wide-ranging set of analytical tools. No surprise, then, that cultural criminology is stridently inter-disciplinary, interfacing not just with criminology, sociology, and criminal/youth justice studies, but with perspectives and methodologies drawn from *inter alia* cultural, media and urban studies, philosophy, postmodern critical theory, cultural geography, anthropology, social movement studies, and other 'action' research approaches. To quote Jeff Ferrell, cultural criminology's goal is to be 'less a definitive paradigm' than an 'array of diverse perspectives' (Ferrell, 1999: 396). The strength of the 'cultural approach', then, is the way it tackles the subject of crime and criminalization from a variety of new perspectives and academic disciplines. In effect, its remit is to keep 'turning the kaleidoscope' on the way we think about crime, and, importantly, the legal and societal responses to it. (Cultural criminology and the relationship between culture and crime more generally are discussed in more detail in Chapter 7, 'Crime and Culture' by Jeff Ferrell.)

REVIEW QUESTIONS

1 In what ways is deviance a cultural phenomenon?

2 Draw up a random list of crimes and identify the emotions that are integral to each. How does each crime differ in terms of specific emotions?

3 What does it mean when cultural criminologists suggest that much criminality can be understood as an 'array of reactions against mundane, secular, society'?

Key readings

Ferrell, J., Hayward, K., and Young, J. (2008) *Cultural Criminology: An Invitation*, London: Sage.

Ferrell, J., Hayward, K., Morrison, W., and Presdee, M. (2004) *Cultural Criminology Unleashed.* London: GlassHouse Press.

Ferrell, J. and Sanders, C.S. (1995) *Cultural Criminology*. Boston: Northeastern University Press.

Presdee, M. (2000) *Cultural Criminology and the Carnival of Crime*, London: Routledge.

Textbook reading/secondary source

Hayward, K. and Young, J. 'Cultural criminology' in Maguire, M. *et al. The Oxford Handbook of Criminology* (2007) Oxford: Oxford University Press.

Morrison, W., Chapter 13 ('Culture and crime in the postmodern condition') in *Theoretical Criminology: From Modernity to Postmodernism* (1995) London: Cavendish.

CONCLUSION

Trying to summarize 200 years of criminological thought in one short chapter was a difficult, daunting, and some might say rather foolhardy task. It was certainly very difficult deciding what to include and what to leave out. The trained criminological eye will inevitably point to certain gaps in the 'story', but we hope they will forgive us the broad sweep of our narrative. After all, as we state in the title, the chapter is meant purely as a 'starting point'. Moreover, much effort has been made to point the interested student to classic studies and further secondary readings for each of the chapter's ten theoretical themes. We hope, indeed urge, you to follow these signposts, and not to read this chapter in isolation. All theories need to be unpicked and deconstructed if we are to understand what lies behind them and thus fully comprehend the political and social forces that brought them into existence. We feel that this chapter represents a decent starting point from which you can begin your own personal theoretical journey.

WEB LINKS

http://www.crimetheory.com

'An educational resource for the learning, researching and teaching of theoretical criminology' maintained by Bruce Hoffman, Department of Sociology, Ohio University.

http://www.asc41.com

The website of The American Society of Criminology. The ASC is the pre-eminent organization of academic, theoretical, and applied criminology in the United States.

http://www.culturalcriminology.org

This site houses key papers and news about conferences and publications in the area of cultural criminology.

http://tcr.sagepub.com/

Theoretical criminology: An international journal for the advancement of the theoretical aspects of criminology.

http://pun.sagepub.com/

Punishment and Society: An interdisciplinary journal on punishment, penal institutions, and penal control.

http://cmc.sagepub.com/

Crime, Media, Culture: An international journal on the relationship between crime, criminal justice, media and culture.

http://www.crimeandjustice.org.uk/cjm.html

The website of the UK publication Criminal Justice Matters, which frequently publishes engaging and accessible articles debating theoretical matters within criminology.

REFERENCES

Anderson, N. (1975) *The Hobo: The Sociology of the Homeless Man*. Chicago: University of Chicago Press.

Beccaria, C. ([1764] 1963) *On Crimes and Punishments*. Indianapolis: Bobbs-Merrill.

Beirne, P. (1993) *Inventing Criminology: Essays on the Rise of 'Homo Criminalis'*. Albany, New York: State University of New York Press.

Bentham, J. ([1789] 1982) *A Fragment of Government and an Introduction to the Principles of Morals and Legislation*. London.

Berman, L. (1921) *The Glands Regulating Personality.* New York: Macmillan.

Bocock, R. and Thompson, K. (eds), (1992) *Social and Cultural Forms of Modernity*. Buckingham: Open University Press.

Bottoms, A.E. (1994) 'Environmental criminology' in M. Maguire, R. Morgan, and R. Reiner (eds), *The Oxford Handbook of Criminology*. Oxford: Oxford University Press.

Bottoms, A. E. (2007) 'Place, space, crime, and disorder' in M. Maguire, R. Morgan, and R. Reiner (eds), *The Oxford Handbook of Criminology*. Oxford: Oxford University Press.

Box, S. (1983) *Crime, Power and Mystification*. London: Tavistock. Box, S. (1987) *Recession, Crime and Punishment*. London: Macmillan.

Burgess, E.W. (1925) 'The growth of the city' in R.E. Park, E.W. Burgess, and R.D. McKenzie (eds), *The City*, Chicago: University of Chicago Press.

Cain, M. (1989) *Growing Up Good*. London: Sage.

Chambliss, W.J. (1975) 'Towards a Political Economy of Crime', *Theory and Society* 2, pp. 149–70.

Clarke, R.V.G. and Cornish, D.B. (1985) 'Modelling offenders' decisions: a framework for policy and research' in M. Tonry and N. Morris (eds) *Crime and Justice: An Annual Review of Research*, 6.

Cloward, R. and Ohlin, L. (1960) *Delinquency and Opportunity: A Theory of Delinquent Gangs*, New York: The Free Press.

Cohen, A. (1955) *Delinquent Boys: the Culture of the Gang*. New York: Free Press.

Cohen, S. (1972) *Folk Devils and Moral Panics*. London: MacGibbon and Kee.

Cohen, S. (1981) 'Footprints in the sand: a further report on criminology and the sociology of deviance in Britain' in M. Fitzgerald, G. McLennan and J. Pawson (eds) *Crime and Society: Readings in History and Theory*. London: Open University Press.

Collier, R. (1998) *Masculinities, Crime and Criminology*. Buckingham: Open University Press.

Cornish, D.G. and Clarke, R.V.G. (1986) *The Reasoning Criminal: Rational Choice Perspectives on Offending*. New York: Springer-Verlag.

Cortes, J.B., and Gatti, F.M. (1972) *Delinquency and Crime: A Bio-psychological Approach*. New York: Seminar Press.

Cressey, P. (1932) *The Taxi-Dance Hall*. Chicago: University of Chicago Press.

Crowe, R.A. (1974) 'An adoption study of anti-social personality', *Archives of General Psychiatry*, 31: 785–91.

Dalton, K. (1961) 'Menstruation and crime', *British Medical Journal*, 2 1752–53.

Downes, D. and Rock, P. (1988) *Understanding Deviance*, Oxford: Oxford University Press.

Durkheim, E. (1965) *The Rules of Sociological Method*, trans. Solovay and Mueller. New York: Free Press.

Eysenck, H. (1970) *Crime and Personality*. London: Paladin.

Felson, M. (1998) *Crime and Everyday Life*, Thousand Oaks, CA: Sage.

Ferrell, J. (1999) 'Cultural Criminology', *Annual Review of Sociology* 25: 395–418.

Ferrell, J. and Sanders, C.R. (eds), (1995) *Cultural Criminology.* Boston: Northeastern University Press.

Ferrell, J., Hayward, K.J., Morrison, W., and Presdee, M. (2004) *Cultural Criminology Unleashed.* London: GlassHouse.

Ferrell, J., Hayward, K.J., and Young, J. (2008) *Cultural Criminology: An Invitation,* London: Sage.

Ferri, E. (2003) 'Causes of Criminal Behaviour' in J. Muncie, E. McLaughlin, and G. Hughes, *Criminological Perspectives: A Reader.* London: Sage.

Foucault, M. (1977) *Discipline and Punish: The Birth of the Prison.* London: Penguin Books.

Garland, D. (1994) 'Of crime and criminals: the development of criminology in Britain' in M. Maguire, R. Morgan and R. Reiner (eds), *The Oxford Handbook of Criminology* Oxford: Oxford University Press.

Giddens, A. (1974) *Positivism and Sociology.* London: Heinemann.

Goffman, E. (1968) *Stigma: Notes on the Management of a Spoiled Identity.* London: Penguin.

Goring, G. (1913) *The English Convict.* London: Darling & Son.

Gottfredson, M. and Hirschi, T. (1990) *A General Theory of Crime.* Stanford CA: Stanford University Press.

Hall, S. and Gieben, B. (1992) *The Formations of Modernity.* Cambridge: Polity.

Hayward, K.J. (2004) *City Limits: Crime, Consumer Culture and the Urban Experience.* London: GlassHouse Press.

Hayward, K.J., and Morrison, W. (2002) 'Locating "Ground Zero": caught between the narratives of crime and war' in *Law After Ground Zero.* J. Strawson (ed). London: Cavendish.

Hayward, K.J. and Young, J. (2004) 'Cultural criminology: some notes on the script' Theoretical Criminology, 8(3): 259–73.

Heidensohn, F. (1968) 'The Deviance of Women: a Critique', *British Journal of Sociology,* 19.

Heidensohn, F. (1996) *Women and Crime.* London: Macmillan.

Henry, S. and Milovanovic, D. (1996) *Constitutive Criminology: Beyond Postmodernism.* London: Sage.

Herrnstein, R.J. and Murray, C. (1994) *The Bell Curve:* Intelligence *and Class Structure in American Life.* New York: The Free Press.

Hirschi, T. (1969) *Causes of Delinquency.* Berkeley CA: University of California Press.

Hobsbawm, E. (1972) *Bandits.* Harmondsworth: Penguin.

Hooton, E.A. (1939) *The American Criminal: An Anthropological Study.* Cambridge MA: Harvard University Press.

Hume, D. ([1739] 1978) *A Treatise on Human Nature.* Oxford: Oxford University Press.

Hutchings, B. and Mednick, S.A. (1975) 'Registered criminality in the adopted and biological parents of registered male criminal adoptees', in R.R. Fieve, D. Rosenthal, and H. Brill (eds) *Genetic research in Psychiatry,* Baltimore: Johns Hopkins University Press.

Jefferson, T. (1996) 'Introduction to the masculinities', Special edition of the *British Journal of Criminology,* 36.

Jones, T., MacLean, B., and Young, J. (1986) *The Islington Crime Survey.* Aldershot: Gower.

Katz, J. (1988) *The Seductions of Crime: Moral and Sensual Attractions in Doing Evil.* New York: Basic Book.

Kinsey, R., Lea, J., and Young, J. (1986) *Losing the Fight Against Crime.* Oxford: Blackwell.

Klein, D. (1973) 'The Etiology of Female Crime: a Review of the Literature', *Issues in Criminology,* 8.

Lea, J. and Young, J. (1984) *What is to be done about Law and Order?* Harmondsworth: Penguin.

Lemert, E.M. (1951) *Social Pathology.* New York: McGraw Hill.

Lombroso, C. (1876) *L'Uomo Delinquente.* Milan: Hoepli.

Lyng, S. (1990) 'Edgework: a Social Psychological Analysis of Voluntary Risk-Taking', *American Journal of Sociology* 95: 876–921.

McLaughlin, E. (2001) 'Functionalism' in E. McLaughlin and J. Muncie (eds), *The Sage Dictionary of Criminology.* London: Sage.

Matthews, R. and Young, J. (1992) *Issues in Realist Criminology.* London: Sage.

Mead, G.H. ([1934] 1962) *Mind, Self, and Society: From the Standpoint of a Social Behaviorist.* Chicago, IL: University of Chicago Press.

Melossi, D. (1990) *The State of Social Control.* Cambridge: Polity.

Merton, R.K. (1938) 'Social Structure and Anomie', *American Sociological Review* 3: 672–82.

Messerschmidt, J. (1993) *Masculinities and Crime.* Lanham MD: Rowman and Litchfield.

Morrison, W. (1995) *Theoretical Criminology: From Modernity to Post Modernism.* London: Cavendish.

Morrison, W. (2004) 'Lombroso and the Birth of Criminological Positivism: Scientific Mastery or Cultural Artifice?' in J. Ferrell *et al., Cultural Criminology Unleashed.* London: GlassHouse.

Moyer, K.E. (1971) 'The physiology of aggression and the implication for aggression control' in R.G. Green and E.I. Donnerstein (eds) *The Control of Aggression and Violence*. New York: Academic Press.

Park, R.E. (1925) 'The city: suggestions for the investigation of human behaviour in the urban environment' in R.E. Park, E.W. Burgess, and R.D. McKenzie (eds), *The City*. Chicago: Chicago University Press.

Pollak, O. (1950) *The Criminality of Women*. New York: A.S. Barnes.

Presdee, M. (2000) *Cultural Criminology and the Carnival of Crime*. London: Routledge. Quinney, R. (1991) *Criminology as Peacemaking*. Bloomington IN: Indiana University Press.

Roshier, B. (1989) *Controlling Crime*. Milton Keynes: Open University Press.

Sandberg, A.A., Koepf, G.F., Ishiara, T., and Hauschka, T.S. (1961) 'An XYY human male', *Lancet* 262: 488–9.

Shaw, C.R. and McKay, H.D. (1931) *Social Factors in Juvenile Delinquency*. Washington DC: Government Printing Office.

Shaw, C.R. and McKay, H.D. (1942) *Juvenile Delinquency and Urban Areas*, Chicago: University of Chicago Press.

Sheldon, W.H. (1942) *The Varieties of Temperament*. New York: Harper.

Sherman, L.W., Gartin, P.R., and Buerger, M.E. (1989) 'Hot spots of predatory crime: routine activities and the criminology of place'. *Criminology* 27: 27–55.

Smart, C. (1976) *Women, Crime and Criminology: A Feminist Critique*. London: Routledge.

Sumner, C. (1990) *Censure, Politics and Criminal Justice*. Milton Keynes: Open University Press.

Sutherland, E. (1942) *Principles of Criminology*. Philadelphia: J B Lippincott.

Sykes, G.M. and Matza, D. (1957) 'Techniques of neutralization'. *American Sociological Review* 22.

Taylor, I., Evans, K., and Fraser, P. (1996) *A Tale of Two Cities: Global Change, Local Feeling and Everyday Life in the North of England: A Study in Manchester and Sheffield*. London: Routledge.

Taylor, I. Walton, P., and Young, J. (1973) *New Criminology: For a Social Theory of Deviance*. London: Routledge and Kegan Paul.

Thompson, E.P. (1968) *The Making of the English Working Class*. Harmondsworth: Penguin.

Thompson, E.P. (1975) *Whigs and Hunters*. London: Allen Lane.

Thrasher, F.M. (1927) *The Gang: A Study of 1,313 Gangs in Chicago*. Chicago: Chicago University Press.

Tittle, C. (1995) *Control Balance: Toward a General Theory of Deviance*. Boulder CO: Westview Press.

Valier, C. (2005) 'Just theory: theory, crime and criminal justice' in C. Hale, K. Hayward, A. Wahidin, and E. Wincup, (eds) *Criminology*. Oxford: Oxford University Press.

Wilson, J.Q. (1985) *Thinking About Crime*. New York: Vintage Books. Wilson, J.Q. and Kelling, G. (1982) 'Broken windows', *Atlantic Monthly*, pp. 29–38.

Wilson, J.Q. and Herrnstein, R. (1985) *Crime and Human Nature*. New York: Simon and Schuster.

Young, J. (1999) *The Exclusive Society*, London: Sage.

Young, J. (2007) *The Vertigo of Late Modernity*, London: Sage.

NOTE

1. This chapter has been adapted from *Theoretical Criminology* (Hayward and Morrison, 2002), a subject guide used in connection with the University of London's External Laws Programme. Our thanks go to the External Programme for kindly allowing us to reproduce sections of that text here.

5 Researching crime and criminal justice

Emma Wincup

INTRODUCTION

Each chapter within *Criminology* draws upon the findings of criminological research. Collectively these studies draw upon a range of disciplines and theoretical traditions and utilize a variety of research designs and methods to gather both qualitative and quantitative data. Criminological knowledge is produced when these data are analysed and subsequently disseminated, typically through academic publications. To make effective use of this knowledge, students need to adopt a critical stance when interpreting it; one which appreciates both its strengths and its limitations. This requires them to evaluate the studies on which it is based. This chapter aims to provide students with the necessary skills to appraise the studies they read.

The chapter is divided into three main sections. The first outlines the range of options available to criminologists when researching crime and criminal justice. It identifies the key questions researchers need to ask when selecting a research design, outlines the different types of methods criminologists can select from, and explores the advantages and disadvantages of seeking to combine methods. In many respects, the discussion in the first section applies equally to social scientists interested in social phenomenon other than crime and criminal justice. In contrast, sections two and three have been written specifically with criminologists in mind. The second section seeks to identify some of the unique challenges faced by researchers interested in crime and criminal justice. It draws attention to the political nature of criminological research, the increased likelihood that criminologists will be exploring sensitive topics with consequent ethical implications, and the heightened need to manage risk during the research process. The final section draws attention to recent methodological developments, considers the opportunities they present for researching crime and criminal justice, and, where relevant, controversies surrounding their use.

BACKGROUND

This chapter focuses on the empirical research tradition within criminology, which can be defined as research based upon the analysis of data rather than conceptual analysis. It can be contrasted with theoretical research. Within criminology, there is a tendency for researchers to define themselves, or be defined by others, as either theorists or empirical researchers. As Bottoms (2007) argues, this form of specialization can be helpful in terms of building successful research careers; however, it tends to misrepresent the relationship between theory and data and fails to appreciate that criminologists cannot avoid theory. Empirical research needs to engage with theoretical debates so it can either test theory (for example, by testing hypotheses) or generate theory (for example, by generating concepts to make sense of the social world). Indeed, some of the most important theoretical insights within criminology have been derived from empirical studies; for example, Becker's (1963) study of marihuana users consolidated the development of the labelling perspective (see Chapter 4). Similarly, even if they do not conduct empirical research themselves, theorists still need to draw upon studies conducted by others.

The emergence of the empirical research tradition within criminology can be traced back to the nineteenth century when, as Garland (2002) argues, positivism rose to the fore and began to establish criminology as 'scientific' discipline. Positivism is explored in detail in Chapter 4 but is essentially concerned with emulating the approaches of the natural scientists in order to develop objective knowledge about crime and criminal justice. There is considerable variation in the work of criminologists associated with the positivist school. For example, early positivists included the 'moral statisticians' (for example, Quetelet) who made use of the newly published official crime statistics, and linked them to social, economic, and environmental factors to suggest that crime rates are regular and predictable. Those who adopted an experimental approach to search for a criminal 'type' (most famously Lombroso; see Chapter 4) by comparing the physiological characteristics of 'offenders' and 'non-offenders' can also be described as early positivists. Despite these differences, three common characteristics of the work of positivists are the search for cause and effect relationships, viewing crime in terms of either individual or social pathology, and a preference for quantitative (i.e. numerical) data.

Criminologists soon came to realize the inherent weaknesses of the positivist approach, particularly its inability to appreciate the complex nature of criminal behaviour. In the twentieth century, they took inspiration from the emergent interpretivist tradition and explored different approaches to understanding the social world in general, and crime and criminal justice in particular. Interpretivism can be defined as a theoretical approach which seeks to explore the subjective meanings through which individuals understand the social world. This tradition was influential in exposing criminologists to a wider variety of approaches and methods for researching the social world. In particular, the work of the Chicago School (see Chapter 4) from the 1920s onwards was highly influential in establishing the ethnographic tradition. Ethnography can be defined as:

> the study of groups of people in their natural setting, typically involving the researcher being present for extended periods of time in order to collect data systematically about their daily activities and the meanings they attach to them. (Noaks and Wincup, 2004: 93)

In general terms, this involves the collection and analysis of qualitative data (i.e. data which are not amendable to measurement and are textual, visual, or audio).

Making choices (1): choosing between research designs

The limited space available precludes a discussion of the development of the initial idea. Instead, readers are directed to King and Wincup (2007) which explores potential sources of inspiration; for example, the academic literature, personal experiences, and current policy concerns. They also discuss the process of turning initial ideas into researchable problems; a seemingly straightforward task which is surprisingly challenging and can be inordinately time-consuming. It involves thinking through what can realistically be done given the resources available and any requirements which must be fulfilled; for example, to obtain funding or an academic degree. It also requires imaginative thinking to develop a research question which contributes in some way, however modest, to criminological knowledge. As King and Wincup argue, both these stages of the research process involve interrogating the literature(s)—theoretical, methodological, substantive (i.e. focused on the topic of interest or closely related ones), and policy. In recent years, a number of texts have been published which explore the processes of searching and reviewing the literature. These are strongly recommended for novice researchers embarking on a task which can easily become unfocused and unmanageable (see Hart, 1998 and 2001).

Once they have selected their research topic and developed their research question(s), criminologists need to focus their attention on the choice of research design and methods. This can be a challenging task because of the range of possibilities offered, and the methodological literature tends to confuse more than clarify in a number of respects. First, the distinction between research design and methods is not always apparent and often the terms are used interchangeably. For example, ethnography—a strategy for conducting research defined above—is often conflated with participant observation—a research method defined later in this chapter. Second, the literature tends to focus more on specific research methods rather than more general issues of research design so that, as King and Wincup (2007: 23) argue, 'all too often new researchers make a serious mistake by moving straight from deciding the research question to choosing between methods' without thinking through how best to approach the study based upon both intellectual and pragmatic considerations. Third, whilst the methodological literature often presents neat typologies of research designs, in practice it can be difficult to attach a label to the chosen research design. Finally, the labels 'qualitative' and 'quantitative' are used to describe different research designs or methods rather than used more appropriately to characterize forms of data.

In a recently published chapter, King and Wincup (2007) outlined some of the key questions for consideration when choosing a research design. Essentially these questions require the researcher to reflect upon three, albeit interrelated, issues: the relationship between research and theory; the relationship between research and policy; and the type of data needed to answer the research questions(s). We will now explore each of these issues in turn.

Theory and criminological research

Theory provides the researcher with a conceptual framework to make sense of the data. It should not be conflated with theories of criminal behaviour such as those discussed in Chapter 4. It guides, or at least it should guide, all aspects of the research process. The relationship between research and theory is complex and it is impossible to do justice to its intricacies within the confines of one short chapter. It is, however, possible to make a distinction between research which is deductivist in its approach and aims to test theory, and research which is inductivist in its approach and aims to generate theory. In practice, this distinction over-simplifies the role theory plays in relation to criminological research (see Bottoms, 2007 for a more nuanced exploration of the relationship between theory and empirical observations in criminology). Nonetheless, the distinction helps us to draw out the implications for research design.

The starting point for deductivist research is to develop a theoretically informed hypothesis. A hypothesis is an 'untested assertion about the relationship between two or more variables' (Jupp, 2006: 137) and it is the task of the researcher to collect data which proves or disproves the hypothesis. Typically, this involves the collection of data from large samples using methods which form part of an experimental research design in order to assess the possibility of causality between independent (the 'cause') and dependent (the 'effect') variables. Emulating the approach of natural scientists, some criminologists have adopted such research designs, although they have usually made compromises and conducted 'quasi' rather than 'true' experiments. Both involve comparing and contrasting data (usually quantitative) gathered from 'experimental' and 'comparison' groups, but only the latter involves the random allocation of research participants to each group. For quasi-experiments, the comparison group may be the 'experimental' group prior to the intervention, allowing data to be collected before and after an intervention. Whilst 'true' experiments are the norm in many disciplines, for example, medical sciences, criminologists have seldom adopted this approach. However, as we will explore towards the end of this chapter, 'true' experiments are gaining in popularity to evaluate the effectiveness of criminal justice interventions despite their controversial nature. Experimental research designs are often viewed as more powerful than the alternatives due to perceived high levels of internal validity. Internal validity refers to the accuracy of any claims made, or indeed rejected, about causality between variables. 'True' experiments are viewed as the gold standard because the random allocation removes the possibility that similarities and differences between the 'experimental' and 'control' groups can be attributed to chance. This form of experiment also enables bold claims to be made about external validity, the ability of the research findings to be generalized beyond the group studied, because the sample achieved is a probability one (i.e. all in the target population have an equal chance of being selected).

In contrast, inductivist research is exploratory rather than experimental in its approach. Rather than attempting to imitate the approach of natural scientists, it aims to generate theory through careful analysis of data gathered from researching in detail one aspect of the social world. Glaser and Strauss (1967) describe the outcome of this process as 'grounded theory'. In many respects, research can never be characterized as wholly inductivist because theory may inform the early stages of the research process. Hypotheses may be formulated at the outset although when the chosen approach is to collect qualitative data, they are unlikely to be expressed in terms of cause and effect relationships. Exploratory research designs are often subject to harsh and unfair criticism by those who favour experimental approaches. Criteria used to assess the quality of experimental research are rooted in positivist approaches to researching the social world. Consequently, exploratory approaches, which tend to involve the collection and analysis of qualitative data from non-probability samples, are often described as weak in terms of internal and external validity. In recent years, there has been increasing recognition of the need to judge different forms of research in another way (see for example, Bryman *et al.*, 2008). Moving away from using quality criteria grounded in the positivist paradigm and using ones more appropriate to their interpretivist roots, we can appreciate that studies based upon exploratory research designs are of good quality if they can convey a high level of trust in the conclusions reached and contribute to the task of generalization through the development of theoretical concepts which merit exploration with other populations and/or within different settings.

The relationship between research and policy

The relationship between research and policy can take many forms and there is a long-standing history of social scientists trying to map out the range of possibilities (see Young *et al.*, 2002 for a recent five-fold typology of the relationship between research and policy). This relationship has been the subject of considerable academic debates during the past decade, fuelled in part by the apparent shift under New Labour—in rhetoric if not always in practice—towards evidence-based policy. For criminologists, this has had particular implications for research design, which have not been universally welcomed, and we will return to this issue later in the chapter. For now, we will consider the impact of the relationship at a more general level.

Policy-makers are often concerned with issues of effectiveness and therefore seek to commission evaluative rather than research studies. Research and evaluation are closely related but in some respects serve different purposes. It is important not to exaggerate the differences between research and evaluation: both involve choosing from the same 'menu' of research methods in order to collect and analyse data systematically. Evaluation can perhaps best be considered as a form of 'applied' research, which prioritizes solving practical problems over the generation of new knowledge (the core aim of 'basic' or 'blue-skies' research). Evaluative studies are most closely associated with experimental designs and the gathering of quantitative data. These data are collected as part of an attempt to measure 'what works' by considering inputs (for example, characteristics of participants), outputs (for example, proportion of participants completing the intervention), and outcomes (for example, the impact of the intervention on participants' behaviour). Qualitative data are sometimes gathered to provide an insight into processes, usually through interviews with the key stakeholders or observation of interventions.

For some researchers, the desire to influence policy takes the research design in a different direction, although there are some parallels with the approach explored above because both can be viewed as forms of applied research. Known as 'action research', it involves the identification of a 'problem', the introduction of a specific policy to address it, and the exploration of the effects of the policy on the 'problem'. The policy may be modified in response to the findings and further research conducted to consider whether it produces more positive outcomes. It is, essentially, a 'social experiment' (Payne and Payne, 2004: 9). This approach blurs the boundaries between researchers and policy makers and allows participants to become active collaborators in the research process. These two characteristics make it distinct from evaluation but make it vulnerable to criticisms about lack of objectivity because of the blurred boundaries between research and policy making. Proponents of action research may retort by arguing that most research designs rely upon the exploitation and alienation of research participants (see Newton, 2006).

Data considerations

Taking into account the type of data needed to answer the research questions posed is essential when choosing between research designs. In this respect, considerations about the relative balance between breadth and depth are paramount. The narrow focus of a 'case study' approach is compensated for by the rich and detailed data gathered. In contrast, the broader focus of a 'survey' approach balances the somewhat decontextualized and superficial data gathered.

The term 'case' refers to a social unit with clear boundaries which can be studied holistically (Payne and Payne, 2004). The approach taken is exploratory rather than experimental and is often combined, therefore, with an ethnographic approach. The methods used tend to prioritize the collection of qualitative data. As Keddie (2006) outlines, a case can be an individual (for example, an offender), an event (for example, an urban riot), a social activity (for example, an offending behaviour programme), an organization (for example, a penal reform charity), or an institution (for example, a prison). Traditionally understood as the study of a single case (see, for example, Payne and Payne, 2004), an increasingly common approach is to incorporate multiple case studies into the research design. This helps to allay concerns about the lack of external validity (i.e. the ability of the findings to be generalized beyond the particular case), particularly if care is taken to select a range of diverse cases. For example, a research study seeking to explore resettlement provision in prisons could make a stronger argument regarding generalizability if research design included institutions accommodating prisoners serving different sentence lengths and could offer an even more robust defence if a women's prison was included. This case is a 'critical' one in the sense that women make up only a small proportion of the total prison population (see Chapters 17 and 27).

Surveys are conflated with questionnaires, which is one of the main methods used by those who adopt a survey approach to collect predominantly quantitative data from a large, and ideally representative, sample. This sampling approach allows survey researchers to make bold claims about the generalizability of their findings if accompanied by a high response rate. It also enhances confidence in the results of any statistical techniques used to test hypotheses. Surveys can involve direct contact with research participants or indirect by using post, email, the Internet, and the telephone. They tend to adopt a structured and standardized approach so there is very limited flexibility once the survey is underway. Piloting of research instruments to ensure their reliability is essential. In the context of social research, reliability refers to consistency of measurement.

A further consideration when designing a research study is whether cross-sectional or longitudinal data are needed. Often the data gathered are cross-sectional and provide a snapshot of a particular point in time, and this may be the only option to the researcher given the resources available. There are common exceptions, for example, studies which involve an ethnographic approach. There are few criminological studies which have adopted a long-term view and followed up research participants over a substantial period. These have tended to focus, at least initially, on young people and their pathways into crime (see Chapter 19 for examples). One compromise is to renew contact with research participants a matter of months after the initial contact. However, even this can be extremely resource-intensive. Sustaining contact with research participants is highly demanding (see Wincup and Hucklesby's (2007) account of conducting follow-up interviews with ex-prisoners).

Making choices (2): choosing between research methods

Criminologists have two options available to them when they are making decisions about how to obtain the data they need to answer their research question(s). First, they can make use of existing datasets, both qualitative and quantitative. Many of these are held at the UK Data Archive (see the web links section at the end of the chapter) and at the time of writing (Autumn 2008), entering the term 'crime' into its search engine resulted in access to details of 648 studies. The archive includes large-scale studies, usually government funded. Criminologists can make use of specialist surveys such as the British Crime Survey (see Chapter 3 for a discussion of the coverage of this survey) or more generic surveys such as the General Household Survey which provide data on issues related to crime such as poverty, unemployment, and alcohol use rather than on crime itself. Some researchers, and it is usually a requirement if funded by the Economic and Social Research Council, deposit their datasets in the archive. This has promoted access to qualitative datasets suitable for secondary analysis. Using existing datasets has obvious advantages. They make accessible to researchers data which it would not normally be possible to collect because of the high financial costs involved and these can be accessed relatively quickly and easily. Once research has been completed, rarely have all the analytical possibilities been exhausted, which opens up new avenues for other researchers to explore. With the data already available in a form suitable for analysis, researchers can devote all the available resources to this task. Alongside these advantages are some important drawbacks. Most importantly there is a danger that the data cannot answer the research questions posed. Secondary analysis of qualitative datasets is still in its infancy, but there are particular issues here because reflexivity plays a key role when such data are gathered. Whilst depositors are required to provide detailed documentation to accompany their dataset, it is still difficult to reflect upon the context in which the data were gathered.

Second, criminologists can decide to collect their own (primary) data and there are four main research methods from which they can choose: questionnaires, interviews, focus groups, and observation. It is important to be clear that specific criminological research methods do not exist, although, as we will explore later in this chapter, when used to explore criminological issues each research method can present some unique challenges because of the subject matter. Criminologists therefore have to select from the same menu of research methods as their fellow social scientists and face similar constraints. Their chosen methods have to fit with the theoretical position and research design adopted, although researchers should resist rigid prescriptions about the incompatibility of particular methods with their chosen theoretical and methodological approach. Whilst researchers should not assume that 'anything goes', purist assertions, for example, that questionnaires cannot be used for exploratory research and that participant observation has no role to play in experimental research, are unhelpful. Other considerations include the resources available and the expertise and ethical stance of the researcher (see King and Wincup, 2007).

The term questionnaire describes a standardized research instrument used to collect data from respondents about a particular topic. This method relies on participants completing it themselves, although the term questionnaire is sometimes used to describe a highly structured interview schedule. Traditionally, administering questionnaires has required respondents to record their answer on 'paper' copies distributed directly by the researcher or indirectly via a third party or post. Increasingly questionnaires are distributed and completed electronically (see the example on page 120). Questions are normally closed in the sense that the respondent has to select from a list of possible answer, thus the data gathered are quantitative. Asking open questions can produce qualitative data but answers tend to lack detail and responses are normally placed in categories allowing the data to be quantified.

Suggested further reading: Oppenheim (2000)

Figure 5.1 Questionnaires

Questionnaires (see Figure 5.1) are particularly suited to studies which require relatively straightforward data to be gathered from a large number of respondents who have good levels of literacy. Whilst it is not impossible to use questionnaires for sensitive topics (for example, to research offending behaviour) or for groups with low levels of literacy (for example, prisoners), extra care needs to be taken in these circumstances. The key to their success is good questionnaire design. A well-designed questionnaire with clear instructions can help to boost response rates, minimize the likelihood of incomplete answers, and reduce the possibility that respondents will not complete the questionnaires as intended (for example, selecting multiple answers where only one is required). Getting the design right at the outset is important because questionnaires are an inflexible research method. Once the questionnaire has been distributed there is no scope to amend it, hence it is imperative to pilot (i.e. test) the questionnaire in advance with a small sample.

Criticisms of questionnaires as a research method are numerous but tend to coalesce around response rates and the nature of the data gathered. Response rates, particularly for self-completion approaches, can be notoriously low, raising concerns that those who complete questionnaires may be different in some way from those who do not, thus compromising the representativeness of the sample. There is a tension between the researcher's desire to boost response rates (i.e. by designing a short questionnaire) and the need to gather sufficient data to answer the research questions. Even if a large number of questions are asked the data in some respects are inevitably superficial because the researcher has imposed limits on the nature of answers which can be given. This leads some social scientists to conclude that questionnaires cannot provide a complete understanding of the issue being investigated.

Interviews (see Figure 5.2) are the favoured method of many social scientists including criminologists. Their relative strengths and weaknesses depend upon the type of interview conducted. Highly structured interviews share many of the same advantages and disadvantages as questionnaires. However, response rates tend to be higher and the data may be more complete, but these advantages come at a greater financial cost. Less structured interviews have different merits, particularly because they present

Interviews describe a data collection method based upon the posing of a series of questions, usually face-to-face but, as we will explore later in this chapter, technological developments now permit other forms of interaction. Interviews can be placed upon a continuum in terms of their degree of structure, ranging from highly structured interviews used in survey research to collect quantitative data using closed questions through to unstructured interviews most closely associated with ethnographic approaches which gather qualitative data through open questions. In between lie semi-structured interviews which combine the flexibility of more unstructured approaches with the standardization of more structured approaches. The data gathered using this type of interview are usually but not exclusively qualitative.

There are a number of techniques for recording interview data: interviewers may decide to take notes or record the discussion, allowing for the preparation of verbatim transcripts. The latter is often seen as the most desirable because it allows the interviewer to concentrate on the processes of listening and asking questions and facilitates analysis. However, transcribing is an extremely time-consuming task so interviewers need to assure themselves that that the benefits outweigh the costs,

Interviews normally involve only one participant but on some occasions it may be preferable to conduct group interviews, for example, if the interviewee requests that someone else is present. Group interviews are not synonymous with focus groups, discussed in Figure 5.3.

Suggested further reading: Arksey and Knight (1999)

Figure 5.2 Interviews

an opportunity for the interviewer to explore beyond the initial answers given. They also present possibilities to record non-verbal aspects which can either serve as data in their own right and/or be incorporated into a reflexive account of the research process. Unstructured interviews, in which the individual is treated as someone with a story to tell, provide the greatest prospect that new themes will emerge, making them ideally suited to exploratory research. However, the interviewer runs the risk that much of the data collected may not be relevant to the research questions and making sense of the data gathered can be difficult. Semi-structured approaches often emerge as the preferred option. They allow the interviewer to retain control over the interaction at the same time as responding to the interviewee by rephrasing questions, asking additional ones, or changing their order. This promotes some degree of consistency across transcripts, which simplifies the task of data analysis.

Focus groups (see Figure 5.3) are an increasingly popular way to gather data. They have the potential to provide an effective way of establishing a large and diverse sample and their participant-led nature makes them ideal for exploratory studies. Many of the drawbacks of focus groups relate to practical considerations: they can be difficult to arrange and manage but careful planning can minimize the likelihood of problems arising. Focus groups may not be the preferred method for all studies. If the topic is a sensitive one, the privacy and confidentiality which can be afforded to research participants in a one-to-one interview might be more appropriate. Moreover, whilst focus groups provide an opportunity to observe group dynamics, they do so in an artificial environment. Consequently, if the research questions require a more contextualized understanding of

Focus groups take advantage of the dynamic interaction of groups to collect largely qualitative data. The discussion is participant-centred and the researcher takes on the role of a moderator. They may be supported by an additional researcher with responsibility for recording data, a more challenging task in a group setting. Groups normally comprise of between six and eight participants: a sufficiently high number to generate discussion yet still providing opportunities for all to have a voice. To obtain the best data, groups need to gel quickly so participants are generally chosen because they are like the others in some way. Homogeneity of participants is especially important if sensitive topics are to be discussed (Morgan, 2006).

Suggested further reading: Bloor *et al.* (2001)

Figure 5.3 Focus groups

these dynamics, then there is little substitute for observing research participants in their natural setting.

Observation is a research method which involves watching and observing social activities. Often this takes place in a 'natural' setting although sometimes researchers seek to create situations which can be observed in the 'artificial' environment of a research setting. Criminological examples include observing the impact of media violence on children (see Chapter 8). Like interviews, observation can take many forms. Key sources of variation are the extent to which the observation is structured and the extent to which observers participate in the social setting they are observing. At the one extreme, observation can be highly structured, collecting largely quantitative data according to pre-specified criteria using a pro-forma. The observer in this instance takes on a detached role. At the other end of the spectrum, observers participate in the setting they are observing and record both their experiences and observations through compiling field-notes. The data gathered are typically qualitative.

Another key distinction between approaches to observation is the extent to which the observer takes on an overt or covert role. Strong objections to the latter are raised on ethical grounds, an issue we will return to later in this chapter. Unsurprisingly observation is usually carried out overtly.

Suggested further reading on participant observation, the favoured choice of criminologists: Spradley (1980)

Figure 5.4 Observation

As for the use of interviews, the relative strengths and weakness of the observation (see Figure 5.4) as a research method are highly dependent on the form selected. However, all forms allow researchers to observe directly what people do rather than rely on accounts of what people say they do. This can prove extremely resource-intensive, making it most appropriate for studies which deploy a case study design. The more structured and detached approaches are praised by some because they reduce researcher bias, encourage objectivity, and enhance the reliability of the data. For others, they unnecessarily restrict the data which can be recorded, resulting in a potential loss of some of the most interesting data. In contrast, less structured and more participative approaches provide the opportunity to collect rich and detailed data by allowing researchers to explore not only behaviours but the meanings attached to them. Unsurprisingly, participant observation is the favoured method of ethnographers, often coupled with unstructured interviews. The act of participation makes it vulnerable to criticism because it raises the issue of whether the presence of the research fundamentally changes the researcher setting. It has also led to concerns being raised about whether the research can maintain a sufficient degree of academic detachment to facilitate analysis as they become increasingly familiar with the research setting and the research participants.

The distinction between primary and secondary data is not always clear-cut and when conducting documentary research, it can be difficult to assess whether to treat the data as primary or secondary data. Documentary research involves using existing sources of information, but researchers need to invest considerable time and energy converting this information into the data they need to answer their research questions. Denscombe (2007) distinguishes between three categories of documents: those which are in the public domain; those whose access is restricted; and secret documents. Applying this typology to documents which may be of interest to criminologists, the former might include newspapers, publications produced by organizations which deliver criminal justice and those who monitor them (for example, the Independent Police Complaints Commission or HM Inspectorates), and parliamentary debates (published in Hansard). Increasingly, these documents can be accessed electronically. It is more difficult to think of criminological examples of secret documents for which access could ever be obtained, but personal correspondence and diaries would fall into this category. Often criminologists make use of documents which fall under the 'restricted access' heading, and they include records kept by criminal justice agencies and related organizations in the form of databases and individual files. The examples given above are numerical or textual in form, but documents may also include visual images.

Regardless of their form or their accessibility, the same criteria should be applied to documents to evaluate their utility as a source of data. Scott's (1990) four key criteria are the accepted started point for this task and involve asking questions about authenticity, credibility, representativeness, and meaning. Together they require researchers to adopt a reflexive approach and consider the social context in which the documents were originally produced (Noaks and Wincup, 2004). Of especial importance is recognizing that the documents were initially created for another purpose. Once this task has been completed the researcher can move on to use these documents as source of qualitative and/or quantitative data. Sometimes this decision is obvious. For example, documents which contain largely numerical data will provide little in the way of qualitative data. Sometimes it is less so. For example, newspaper articles can be used to collect both quantitative data on the proportion of space devoted to particular crimes and qualitative data on media representations of such crimes through a consideration of language, meaning, and so on (see Chapter 8 for a more detailed discussion).

Combining research methods

Increasingly criminologists combine methods when conducting research on crime and criminal justice. This practice is usually referred to as 'method' or 'technique' triangulation, although as Hoyle (2000) argues the term shrouds in mystery straightforward and sensible means of looking at the social world. A better term, which Walklate (2007: 325) advocates, is 'methodological pluralism'. The term 'triangulation' is based upon the belief that using different methods (or forms of data, theories, or researchers; see Noaks and Wincup (2004) for a more detailed discussion) can enhance the research findings. Before moving on to discuss the relative merits and demerits of combining methods, it is important to appreciate that at one level, all research is multi-method. For example, researchers interested in one aspect of the criminal justice process are likely to begin by conducting documentary research such as reading policy documents or other published material, although their study may be based upon observation.

Combining methods avoids the tendency for 'methodological pigeonholing' which Bottoms (2007: 81) describes as unhelpful. He warns against assuming that particular methods are incompatible with specific research designs. Such exclusionary practices, he argues, militate against the collection of the most appropriate data to answer the research questions posed. For instance, whilst a survey approach is typically accompanied by the use of methods which can collect quantitative data from a large sample; for example, using questionnaires, there are good reasons for considering additional research methods which can be used to collect qualitative data. For instance, focus groups could be arranged to develop the questionnaire or to discuss the emerging findings.

Within the methodological literature, a common theme is that a multi-method approach enhances the validity of the research findings. As previously discussed, validity has multiple meanings when used by social scientists, but essentially it refers to the credibility and plausibility of the conclusions reached. We need to be wary about equating triangulation with a search for 'truth' to be achieved through the use of multiple methods which can compensate for each others' weaknesses and reduce bias. Instead, we should use the different methods available to us (if it is meaningful and pragmatic for us to do so, as we will discuss below) and take advantage of the opportunity this creates to look out for contradictions as much as confirmation between the data sets gathered using different techniques. The role of the researcher then becomes one of explaining apparent inconsistencies or complementary findings rather than seeking to establish 'facts'. Researchers often find themselves with the challenge of making sense of multiple versions of reality because different methods produce different findings, particularly if two or more techniques were deliberately chosen to explore different dimensions of the same issues; for example, 'paper' justice as articulated in policy documents and 'real' justice as reported by those involved in its delivery or recipients of it.

Researchers should approach the question about whether to combine methods with 'healthy cynicism' (Noaks and Wincup, 2004: 10) and only do so if convinced that a multi-method approach adds value to the study by enhancing understanding of the criminological issue being researched. In some instances it may detract from it. Some combinations of methods may not complement each other because they are based upon different assumptions of the social world. For instance, it is difficult to see what might be gained by selecting a research design which incorporated unstructured interviews and a questionnaire. There may be practical reasons too for not using multiple methods. The resources available (time, human, financial) may make this unrealistic, and a better approach is to use one method well and outline the possibilities for extending the research in the publications produced. In sum, researchers should not keep adding research techniques with the blind hope that it will produce a better outcome.

REVIEW QUESTIONS

1 What are the most important considerations when choosing a research design?

2 What are the most important considerations when choosing a research method?

3 What are the advantages and disadvantages of combining different research methods? You might find it helpful to think about triangulation with reference to a particular criminological issue; for example, students' experiences of criminal victimization.

Unique challenges: politics, ethics, and managing risk

The politics of criminological research

Criminological research is political in a number of senses. The term 'political' does not have to be reserved for references to politics at the level of government, although there is no doubt that the politics of law and order discussed in Chapter 21 can shape the research process from initial conception of the research idea through to the publication and dissemination (or not as the case may be) of results, either directly because the Government is funding and/or conducting the research and/or indirectly because it shapes the context in which the research takes place. Wider political agendas such as New Labour's insistence that policy must be evidence-based can also be highly influential, and we will explore later in this chapter how this has determined which forms of research are acceptable. There are other ways in which criminological research can be viewed as a political endeavour. Research may be funded by other organizations such as research councils (principally the Economic and Social Research Council) and charitable foundations such as the Joseph Rowntree Foundation or Nuffield Foundation. Each has its own priorities and preferences in terms of the types of research designs they wish to fund and the substantive focus of potential research projects (see Morgan and Hough, 2007; Noaks and Wincup, 2004). Evaluating criminological knowledge therefore requires pertinent questions to be asked about the context in which the knowledge was produced.

The discussion above notes some of the factors which influence the extent to which criminological research may be characterized as political. Beyond funding arrangements and the timing of the research, it is important to note the influence of the theoretical framework selected and the chosen subject matter. For some criminologists, those which Bottoms (2007) describes as political-activist criminologists, research and knowledge are viewed as part of the political process. Critical and feminist criminologists (see Chapter 4) fit most neatly into this category. Their stance is at the other end of the continuum from the now largely discredited positivist position which maintains that research can be wholly objective and value-free. They challenge too the reluctant acceptance of many criminologists that political influences shape research by actively engaging in the pursuit of political goals through research. Their choice of subject matter is influential in this respect. At the heart of critical and feminist criminological work lies a desire to challenge structural inequalities through researching discrimination and oppression of the powerless.

There is a further sense in which criminological research can be considered political. Political influences, in this instance, operate at a micro-level, although they are not disconnected from the more macro-political agendas. Criminologists often need to collect data in a range of settings which require relationships with the key players to be negotiated carefully in order to understand their different, and, sometimes opposing, perspectives. Researchers may find themselves confronted with the question 'whose side are you on?' (see Becker's (1967) classic essay on the subject). In relation to prison research, Liebling (2001) maintains that it is possible to understand the perspective of more than one 'side' and to do so without alienating opposing groups. She argues that attempting to synthesize different or competing perspectives (for example, between prisoners and prison officers, or between prison officers and prison governors) enhances the end product by sharpening the analysis. At the same time, she appreciates that this places the researcher in a precarious position as they try to keep everyone happy to maintain access.

The ethics of criminological research

In recent years, the issue of research ethics has come to the fore. Almost all learned societies in the social sciences have their own ethical code (see the web links section for details of how to access those most relevant to criminological research). There is now a burgeoning academic literature on research ethics, including specialist journals such as *Research Ethics Review*, and a wide range of training courses on offer. To a greater extent than in the past, researchers are required to demonstrate that their research is ethically sound. Research proposals are subject to scrutiny by ethics committee at an early stage, certainly before the process of data collection commences, but sometimes before funding is sought. For criminologists working in academic institutions, this normally involves submitting the necessary documents to a committee operating at department, faculty, or university level. There are, however, exceptions, and criminologists seeking to collect data which requires contact with NHS patients (for example, prisoners receiving health care services) or vulnerable people (for example, young offenders) may need to gain ethical approval from an external NHS or social services committee.

Ethical codes typically describe the professional standards to which researchers should adhere to ensure that they produce research which is high quality and methodologically sound whilst fulfilling their obligations to those involved in the research as colleagues, sponsors, and participants. The term 'sponsors' refers not only to those who provide financial support, but also to those who provide support in other ways; for example, 'gatekeepers' who facilitate access. Codes of ethics can vary but all aim to strike a balance between providing sufficiently detailed guidance to assist researchers and avoiding rigid prescriptions of what should and should not be done.

Criminological research has the potential to produce ethical dilemmas which are distinct in many respects from those which emerge when researching topics other than crime and criminal justice. Much depends on the subject matter but there is a heightened likelihood that criminological research will require collecting data on sensitive issues (for example, offending behaviour or experiences of victimization) from individuals who might be described as 'vulnerable' in some way. These considerations have an impact on the researcher's ability to protect research participants from experiencing the research process as intrusive and a cause of harm. The current British Society of Criminology code of ethics argues that researchers should make every effort to respect the rights of those they study, their interests, sensitivities, and privacy. It also briefly outlines strategies for preventing this, including referring research participants to support services.

Researching 'vulnerable' groups raises challenges in terms of obtaining informed consent. This involves the researcher providing as much detail about the research as necessary in a manner which is accessible to the potential research participant to allow them to make a decision about whether to participate. Obtaining consent occurs at the outset, but it should be viewed as a process rather than a one-off event and the participants made aware that they can withdraw, either fully or partially (for example, by refusing to answer a question), at any point without adverse consequences. By virtue of their age (for example, children) or inability to understand the research process (for example, those with severe learning difficulties), sometimes consent needs to be obtained from an additional person (for example, parent or social worker) as well as from the individual. For some criminological studies, obtaining informed consent can be difficult. Particular issues arise when conducting participant observation where it is not practical to obtain consent from all those present and there is a debate whether it is necessary to do so if the setting is a public one. Deliberately seeking to avoid obtaining consent is another matter and covert observation is only seen as ethically sound in exceptional circumstances; for example, when the subject matter would make an overt strategy impossible.

The final ethical issue which can prove particularly challenging for criminologists relates to privacy and confidentiality because there is a heightened potential that research participants may disclose that they themselves are at risk or that they pose a risk to others. Promises of absolute confidentiality that may need to be broken are therefore unwise, and research participants should be informed at the outset of any limitations to confidentiality so it can feed into their decision about whether to give consent.

Managing risk

The climate in which criminologists conduct research is changing and universities are now introducing risk assessment and risk management procedures, predominantly but not exclusively for those engaged in empirical research. These procedures are closely associated with the promotion of health and safety in the working environment, but also relate to other workplace agendas. Those who develop such procedures may adopt a broad definition of 'risk' and include questions about both ethical and legal issues; for example, relating to data protection and the potential for an adverse impact on the reputation of the researcher, the university, or a third party (for example, members of an advisory body). Aside from ethical risks which were discussed in the previous section, the main issues for criminologists are risks to their own personal safety; theft, loss or damage to personal or university property; and the collection or processing of personal data. Unless the degree of risk is judged to be minimal, researchers are asked to provide further information about the nature and extent of the risk posed and to outline their strategies for protecting themselves, research participants, and the organizations involved (for example, their university or funding body) from harm.

In general terms, criminologists have paid more attention to promoting the health and safety of research participants than their own. The level and nature of risk, of course, varies from project to project and is dependent upon the subject matter, the extent to which it involves direct contact with research participants, and the setting in which it takes place. These factors all need to be taken into account and the comparative risks of different projects may not be as they first appear. For example, interviewing members of the public in their own homes might be considered more risky than interviewing offenders in prisons where there are multiple procedures in place to promote personal safety and offenders have been subject to risk assessments.

Despite criminologists' frequent exposure to risk, physical or emotional, there is surprisingly little attention paid in the criminological literature to the issue and a lack of guidance for criminologists to follow. It would be wrong, however, to deduce from this that criminologists are unaware of the risks or that they fail to take measures to protect themselves. They are and they do, but there may be considerable scope for improvement so that as far as possible the risks are fully appreciated in advance and strategies put in place to minimize them. When outlining the range of strategies they plan to adopt to ensure their own safety, in the absence of specific guidance, criminologists musts turn to general guidance for social researchers (for example, the Social Research Association's (2001) *Code of Practice for the Safety of Researchers*) or advice relating to personal safety in the workplace (for example, from the Suzy Lamplugh Trust, <http://www.suzylamplugh.org/>). There is an urgent need for criminological researchers to share good practice in relation to promoting their safety and to develop professional guidance.

REVIEW QUESTIONS

1 Can research on crime and criminal justice be anything other than political?

2 Is it ever desirable to compromise on ethical principles when conducting research on issues of crime and criminal justice?

3 Why is it important that criminologists conduct risk assessments prior to commencing data collection?

New methodological developments: innovation and controversy

Assessing the impact of technology on criminological research

Some of the most important methodological developments over the past two decades relate to the rapid expansion of technology. Most experienced researchers will be able to recount stories of how their research practices have been transformed in at least some respects by technological developments which have impacted upon all aspects of the research process. Most studies begin with a literature review, a task which is now much easier thanks to the advent of searchable databases such as *Criminal Justice Abstracts*, *ASSIA* (Applied Social Sciences Index and Abstracts), and *Web of Science*, and search engines which can be used to locate academic and policy literature plus statistics which are now increasingly available electronically via the Internet. Similarly the task of data analysis is now often more straightforward, particularly when large amounts of data are involved, due to the development of specialist software: usually *SPSS* (Statistical Package for the Social Sciences) for quantitative data and *NVivo* and *atlas.ti* for qualitative data. It is, however, important to emphasize that such software only facilitates the analysis of data and the process is only meaningful if guided appropriately by the researcher. Technology has also simplified the dissemination process making it far easier to reach the intended audience(s) using the Internet to publish reports online or by creating bespoke websites. This, of course, leads to the issue of 'technological exclusion' because the reliance on electronic forms of publications has the potential to exclude those who are unable to access them, for example, those living in poverty or older people. Arguably some of the most interesting technological developments relate to their potential to alter radically the data collection process. The remainder of the section explores these with specific reference to researching crime and criminal justice.

Writing in 2007, Williams argues that whilst criminologists have made effective use of the Internet to retrieve information, for example, to obtain statistics, few have taken the opportunity to collect primary data online, and he goes as far as to claim that their use of the Internet for research 'remains largely parochial' (2007a: 476). The Internet allows criminologists to use many of the 'traditional' methods in a different context. Using specialist websites, questionnaires can be designed and completed online (see the example on p. 120). Interviews, particularly the more unstructured forms, could be conducted using instant messaging, although researchers would need to assess carefully whether the advantages (for example, the ability to interview people from across the world) outweigh the disadvantages (for example, the lack of face-to-face interaction) and consider whether disadvantages could be partially overcome (for example, through the use of webcams). Using online methods is very appealing, not least because they offer the potential of easy access to participants at low-cost.

The development of social networking websites such as *Facebook* also opens up possibilities for building up a sample of individuals who can be invited to complete an online questionnaire. Using snowball sampling, a form of non-probability (or non-random) sampling, through which each individual contacted is asked to identify other participants, a large sample can be established in a short space of time with minimal effort. It works, therefore, in a similar way to a chain letter (Oliver, 2006). Of course, the achieved sample will not be representative of a particular population because, for example, young people are likely to be over-represented. However, it offers a solution when achieving a sample through other means would be extremely difficult and is most effective when combined with alternative means to secure a more diverse sample.

EXAMPLE: FASHION COUNTERFEITING

A PhD student at the Centre for Criminal Justice Studies at the University of Leeds is currently conducting a study of fashion counterfeiting. Part of her research involves a questionnaire which can be completed online (using *Survey Monkey*) or by completing a paper-based version. Whilst the research is still in its infancy, she has already begun to appreciate the advantages to using an online questionnaire. The software allows her to keep tabs on the number of respondents and their responses to each question. By adding questions on their demographic characteristics (for example, age, gender, and ethnicity), she can identify which groups are under-represented so they can be targeted. The problem of missing data is eradicated because participants are not allowed to move on to the next question before they have answered the current one. Finally, the facility to transfer the data electronically to *SPSS* avoids the time-consuming task of data entry.

One of her strategies for accessing a sample is to use *Facebook*. In this instance, accessing the general population is not as straightforward as it might appear. Building up a sample via the electoral roll and sending postal questionnaires would be extremely time-consuming and costly and likely to generate a poor response rate: rates of 25 per cent are not unusual (McLean, 2006). Approaching individuals in public settings might produce a better response rate but there are considerable risks involved for a lone female researcher.

The Internet also presents new opportunities to access virtual worlds and adapt 'traditional' methods to explore them. Williams (2007a, 2007b) used a 'virtual ethnographic' approach based heavily upon participant observation to research a graphical online community, associated newsgroups, webpages, and email distribution lists. He also conducted focus groups online with community members. Reflecting upon his experiences, he is eager to point out that transferring 'traditional' designs and methods to a virtual setting involves encountering new challenges; for example, in terms of ethical practices or data analysis, for which there is little or no guidance. It also required revisiting methodological debates that had previously been held in relation to their usage for researching the 'actual' rather than 'virtual' social world.

The growth of evidence-based policy and its implications for criminological research

Earlier in this chapter we noted that there has been a 'utilitarian turn' (Solesbury, 2001: 4 cited by Young *et al.*, 2002: 215) in the social sciences. In theory, this enhances the role that research can play in the policy-making process because it views research as a useful resource for answering questions about 'what works'. There are, however, dangers attached to this shift in thinking. Narrow instrumentalism, as Young *et al.* (2002) warn, not only limits the scope of research but glosses over the broader role research can play through the creation of new knowledge. Limiting its scope to questions of effectiveness in relation to issues defined by government agendas has multiple implications. It places unhelpful constraints on the development of academic disciplines and detracts from our understanding of key policy concerns.

New Labour's political commitment to evidence-based policy was initially welcomed by many criminologists. Taking the form of a Crime Reduction Programme, £400 million of public money over a ten-year period was earmarked to develop strategies which might provide effective, and indeed cost-effective, solutions to crime problems. A significant proportion of the budget (10 per cent of the original £250 million) was allocated for evaluating the 1,500 projects which were funded covering strategies as diverse as CCTV, targeted policing, the prevention of domestic burglary, and arrest referral schemes for drug users. The aspiration was that evaluations of these pilot projects would inform decisions about whether they should be implemented nationally.

The 'fairly short and unhappy life' (Morgan and Hough, 2007: 56) has been discussed at length elsewhere (see in particular the special issue of the journal *Criminal Justice* 4(3)). Briefly, it ran for a much shorter period of time than initially envisaged (three years from 1999) and was a 'triumph of hope over experience' (Morgan and Hough, 2007: 56). It was vulnerable to political expediency with pressures to spend the allocated funds resulting in undeveloped projects being subject to evaluation. Inevitably, these produced few conclusive claims of effectiveness and repeated accounts of implementation failure. Much of the research was not published. Our concern for the remainder of this section is the fallout of this, which impacted significantly on the type of research that the Government was willing to fund.

The largely negative experience of the Crime Reduction Programme from the perspective of research funders (Home Office) and research contractors (largely but not exclusively academics) opened up a debate about how best to study criminal justice initiatives. This was not contentious in its own right, only because the direction taken privileged particular forms of research over others. The result was a research programme in which evaluation was prioritized over other forms of research. This is understandable given the political assertions about the importance of evidence-based policy, but the experience of the Crime Reduction Programme illustrated the need for more exploratory research to be conducted which could feed into the development of new initiatives. The Home Office began to advocate that one particular form of evaluation could provide definitive answers to politicians' demand to know 'what works'. Influenced by the approaches of the Cochrane and Campbell collaborations which are associated with evaluating health care and criminal justice respectively, 'pure' experiments based upon randomized controlled trials were heralded in some parts of the Home Office as the panacea for answering questions relating to effectiveness.

Thus literature reviews which were commissioned were required to be 'systematic', referring not to the usual understanding of the term but to adherence to strict guidelines which researchers must follow. Systematic reviews aim to include only high quality and methodologically sound research, again not problematic in itself but potentially so when combined with an aspiration to conduct meta-analysis. This statistical technique brings together the results of several studies in order to calculate a common measure of effectiveness. To fulfil this aspiration, only studies based on randomized controlled trials can be included. Systematic reviews commissioned by the Home Office have had to make compromises because of the lack of UK randomized controlled trials on criminological topics. Nonetheless they have privileged experimental studies over others.

In practice, randomized controlled trials funded by the Home Office (and now the Ministry of Justice) have been few in number and other forms of research and evaluation still continue to be funded, not least because implementing such trials involves over-coming moral and ethical objections to their use as well as finding solutions to multiple practical problems. However, the shift of direction has had important implications for the status of qualitative data and methods used to generate such data. In some respects, qualitative data have been viewed as the 'poor relation' of quantitative data and judged harshly using criteria which are more applicable to assessing the quality of quantitative data such as generalizability. The result is a failure to appreciate fully what qualitative data can contribute to policy: not only can it inform the development of policy by giving a voice to potential stakeholders but it provides a vehicle to convey nuanced understand-ings of the complexities of the policy implementation process.

REVIEW QUESTIONS

1 Evaluate the impact of technological developments on the processes of data collection and analysis.

2 What implications has the 'utilitarian turn' had for criminological research?

3 How might criminologists whose preference is to collect qualitative data defend their work?

CONCLUSION

Like Chapter 4, which introduces students to criminological theory, this chapter is intended to be a start-ing point. Within the constraints of one short chapter, it has not been possible to do justice to the diver-sity of forms criminological research can take and the abundance of issues which arise throughout the research process. For instance, limited space has precluded a detailed discussion of core topics such as sampling (see Bryman, 2008; Chapter 7 for an introductory overview) and data analysis (see Coffey and Atkinson, 1996 for qualitative data; and Bryman and Cramer, 2008 for quantitative data). We hope students will consult the more detailed texts outlined in the guide to further reading at the end of this chapter. Read in conjunction with this chapter, students should become skilled and confident evalua-tors of the studies they read and begin the process of designing their own small-scale studies if they are required to complete a dissertation or undertake project work.

QUESTIONS FOR DISCUSSION

1 Look at articles published in one of the leading academic journals, for example, the *British Journal of Criminology*, and focus on the articles which report the findings of empirical research studies. What does it reveal about the research designs and methods most frequently utilized?

2 Look at the Home Office website—<http: //www.homeoffice.gov.uk>—and focus on the studies published by their Research, Development and Statistics section. Select a sample of them. Can you identify any patterns in terms of research design and methods?

3 Compare and contrast the codes of ethics produced by learned societies and professional associations which criminologists can draw upon. The web links section refers to some of the most important ones but you may wish to look at others, for example, the British Sociological Association, <http://www.britsoc.co.uk/>, or the British Psychological Society, <http://www.bps.org.uk/>.

4 Draw up a checklist of the main criteria you might use when evaluating a criminological study.

5 Select a criminological study, either a recent one or a classic, and use your checklist to evaluate its contribution to criminological knowledge. Repeat the activity by selecting a study which used either a contrasting research design or different methods.

GUIDE TO FURTHER READING

Bryman, A. (2008) (3rd edn) *Social Research Methods*. Oxford: Oxford University Press.

This leading textbook, and the companion website, explores in detail the main approaches and techniques in social research methods.

Jupp, V. (ed) (2006) *The SAGE Dictionary of Social Research Methods*. London: Sage.

This useful resource contains over 200 entries of key concepts associated with social research. For each, it provides a working definition, outlines its distinctive features, and evaluates the term. Links are made to other key concepts contained in the book, and readers are directed to key readings relating to the concept.

King, R. and Wincup, E. (eds) (2007) (2nd edn) *Doing Research on Crime and Justice*. Oxford: Oxford University Press.

This is one of the few texts which focus specifically on criminological research. Its main aim is to provide an honest account of the research process through the inclusion of chapters by established academics and new scholars.

Noaks, L. and Wincup, E. (2004) *Criminological Research: Understanding Qualitative Approaches*. London: Sage.

Focusing specifically on the collection and analysis of qualitative data on criminological topics, this textbook aims to provide a practically focused account of the research process.

May, T. (2004) (3rd edn) *Social Research: Issues, Methods and Processes*. Buckingham: Open University Press.

This popular textbook aims to provide students with an accessible introduction to the main social research methods and their philosophical underpinnings.

WEB LINKS

http://www.britsoccrim.org/

The British Society of Criminology is a learned society which aims to further the interests and knowledge of both academic and professional people who are engaged in any aspect of work or teaching, research, or public education about crime, criminal behaviour, and criminal justice in the United Kingdom. Its Code of Ethics for Researchers in the Field of Criminology can be found on its website, alongside details of academics that can be approached for guidance on ethical matters.

http://www.slsa.ac.uk/

The Socio-Legal Studies Association brings together socio-legal scholars working in social scientific and humanities disciplines. Its website includes its statement of principles for ethical research practice.

http://www.the-sra.org.uk/

The Social Research Association aims to advance the conduct, development, and application of social research. Its members include academics and researchers working in a range of applied settings. Its ethical guidelines, code of practice for the safety of social researchers, and details of the training courses it offers can be found on the website.

http://www.esrc.ac.uk

The Economic and Social Research Council (ESRC) is the UK's leading research funding and training agency addressing economic and social concerns. Its website contains a copy of its Research Ethics Framework plus funding opportunities for research training.

http://www.data-archive.ac.uk/

The UK Data Archive (UKDA) is a centre of expertise in data acquisition, preservation, dissemination, and promotion, and is curator of the largest collection of digital data in the social sciences and humanities in the UK. It holds both quantitative data suitable for secondary analysis (for example, the British Crime Survey) and qualitative data (for example, data from Cohen's (1972) classic study of Mods and Rockers).

REFERENCES

Arksey, H. and Knight, P. (1999) *Interviewing for Social Scientists: An Introductory Resource with Examples*. London: Sage.

Becker, H. (1963) *Outsiders: Studies in the Sociology of Deviance*. New York: Free Press.

Becker, H. (1967) 'Whose side are we on?' *Social Problems*, 14 (Winter): 239–47.

Bloor, M., Frankland, J., Thomas, M., and Robson, K. (2001) *Focus Groups in Social Research*. London: Sage.

Bottoms, A. (2007) 'The relationship between theory and empirical observations in criminology' in R. King and E. Wincup (eds) *Doing Research on Crime and Justice* (2nd edn). Oxford: Oxford University Press.

Bryman, A. (2008) (3rd edn) *Social Research Methods*. Oxford: Oxford University Press.

Bryman, A., Becker, S., and Sempik, J. (2008) 'Quality criteria for quantitative, qualitative and mixed methods research: a view from social policy' *International Journal of Social Science Research Methodology*, 11(4): 261–76.

Bryman, A. and Cramer, D. (2008) (3rd edn) *Quantitative Data Analysis with SPSS 14, 15 and 16: A Guide for Social Scientists*. London: Routledge.

Coffey, A. and Atkinson, P. (1996) *Making Sense of Qualitative Data*. London: Sage.

Cohen, S. (1972) *Folk Devils and Moral Panics: The Creation of a Moral Panic*. London: MacGibbon and Kee.

Denscombe, M. (2007) (3rd edn) *The Good Research Guide for Small-scale Social Research Projects*. Buckingham: Open University Press.

Garland, D. (2002) 'Of crimes and criminals: the development of criminology in Britain', in M. Maguire, R. Morgan, and R. Reiner (eds) *The Oxford Handbook of Criminology* (3rd edn). Oxford: Oxford University Press.

Glaser, B. and Strauss, A. (1967) *The Discovery of Grounded Theory*. Chicago: Aldine.

Hart, C. (1998) *Doing a Literature Review: Releasing the Social Science Research Imagination*. London: Sage.

Hart, C. (2001) *Doing a Literature Search: A Comprehensive Guide for the Social Sciences*. London: Sage.

Hoyle, C. (2000) 'Being a "nosy bloody cow": ethical and methodological issues in researching domestic violence' in R. King and E. Wincup (eds) (2nd edn) *Doing Research on Crime and Justice*. Oxford: Oxford University Press.

Jupp, V. (2006) 'Hypothesis' in V. Jupp (ed) *The SAGE Dictionary of Social Research Methods*. London: Sage.

Keddie, V. (2006) 'Case study method' in V. Jupp (ed) *The SAGE Dictionary of Social Research Methods*. London: Sage.

King, R. and Wincup, E. (2007) 'The process of criminological research' in R. King and E. Wincup (eds) (2nd edn) *Doing Research on Crime and Justice*. Oxford: Oxford University Press.

Liebling, A. (2001) 'Whose side are we on? Theory, practice and allegiance in prisons research', *British Journal of Criminology*, 41(3): 472–84.

McLean. C. (2006) 'Questionnaire' in V. Jupp (ed) *The SAGE Dictionary of Social Research Methods*. London: Sage.

Morgan, D. (2006) 'Focus group' in V. Jupp (ed) *The SAGE Dictionary of Social Research Methods*. London: Sage.

Morgan, R. and Hough, M. (2007) 'The politics of criminological research' in R. King and E. Wincup (eds) (2nd edn) *Doing Research on Crime and Justice*. Oxford: Oxford University Press.

Newton, J. (2006) 'Action research' in V. Jupp (ed) *The SAGE Dictionary of Social Research Methods*. London: Sage.

Noaks, L. and Wincup, E. (2004) *Criminological Research: Understanding Qualitative Methods*. London: Sage.

Oliver, P. (2006) 'Snowball sampling' in V. Jupp (ed) *The SAGE Dictionary of Social Research Methods*. London: Sage.

Oppenheim, A. (2000) (2nd edn) *Questionnaire Design*. London: Continuum International Publishing Group Limited.

Payne, G. and Payne, J. (2004) *Key Concepts in Social Research*. London: Sage.

Scott, J. (1990) *A Matter of Record*. Cambridge: Polity Press.

Social Research Association (2001) *Code of Practice for the Safety of Researchers*. London: Social Research Association.

Spradley, J. (1980) *Participant Observation*. USA: Wadsworth/Thomson Learning.

Stewart, K. and Williams, M. (2005) 'Researching Online Populations: The Use of Online Focus Groups for Social Research' *Qualitative Research*, 5(4): 395–416.

Walklate, S. (2007) 'Researching victims' in R. King and E. Wincup (eds) (2nd edn) *Doing Research on Crime and Justice*. Oxford: Oxford University Press.

Williams, M. (2007a) 'Cybercrime and online methodologies' in R. King and E. Williams, M. (2007b) 'Avatar watching: participant observation in graphical online environments' *Qualitative Research*, 7(1): 5–24.

Wincup (eds) (2nd edn) *Doing Research on Crime and Justice*. Oxford: Oxford University Press.

Wincup, E. and Hucklesby, A. (2007) 'Researching and evaluating resettlement' in A. Hucklesby and L. Hagley-Dickinson (eds) *Prisoner Resettlement: Policy and Practice*. Cullompton: Willan.

Young, K., Ashby, D., Boaz, A., and Grayson, L. (2002) 'Social science and evidence-based policy movement' *Social Policy and Society*, 1(3): 215–224.

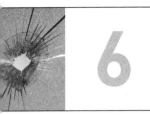

6 Psychology and crime: understanding the interface

Keith Hayward

INTRODUCTION

Many students new to academic criminology are often confused by exactly what role psychology plays in the contemporary criminological enterprise. Very often they have visions of a discipline preoccupied with offender profiling, forensic crime analysis, and the study of psychopathic or mentally impaired serial killers. This chapter aims to set the record straight by providing students with a brief introduction to some of the main points of interface between criminology and psychology. It combines a general review of some of the more prominent psychological explanations of criminal behaviour with some brief examples of how this work has come to be employed in criminological theory and practice. At various intervals, the chapter also adopts a more reflexive stance in a bid to develop some critical insights into the way that 'criminological psychology' is portrayed and perceived within the popular imagination. In this sense, the viewpoint taken here is very much that of a criminologist's perspective of psychology (for an opposite perspective see Hollin, 2007).

BACKGROUND

It has become a cliché to say that recent years have been marked by an increasing popular fascination with the subject of crime and criminality. Yet, in terms of understanding the ever-growing 'psychologistic preoccupation' among criminology students, it is worth pausing to consider some of the reasons behind this current 'fascination'. As Ian Taylor (1999: 2) pointed out, much of this interest is attributable to powerful cinematic and televisual representations of forensic or criminological psychology that serve both to popularize and legitimize various forms of 'analytically individualist criminology'. In Taylor's words, this 'is a form of common-sense criminology organized around "the criminal", and particularly "the criminal mind" as an "object of analysis", and also complicit in the task of identification, prevention and containment of the individual [psychologically distinct] criminal' (ibid.).

In these representations, criminal psychology is frequently portrayed in a very favourable light, almost as if it were a sort of 'secret science', its practitioners capable of feats of identification and detection that far exceed the laboured efforts of the police and other state agencies (Ainsworth, 2000: 1–3). Moreover, in these accounts, the mundane, prosaic aspects of crime rarely feature. Instead we are offered up a steady diet of crimes that contain a highly charged emotional (typically pathological) dimension—rape, child abduction, stalking, hate crimes, sexual homicides, and other forms of expressive violence.

The attraction of this type of fiction (and increasingly non-fiction; see e.g. the Channel Four documentary series *The Real Cracker* and the US A&E network's *Serial Killers: Profiling the Criminal Mind*) is that it suggests criminological psychology is capable of identifying and understanding 'uniqueness', of identifying whom we should trust and whom we should fear. Whether it is Robbie Coltrane's compelling portrayal of the forensic psychologist Fitz in the Granada Television series *Cracker*, or the mass of popular crime-psychology titles that occupy the shelves of the 'Real Crime' section in high street bookshops, the message is always the same: that crime is about *individual difference* and that psychology holds the key to understanding that difference. I would argue that the impact of such representations of crime has been far-reaching, not least in the way it has contributed to how crime and criminality are currently perceived and understood within the contemporary socio-cultural imagination (Furedi, 2004: 30). Today, the popular image of the criminal is no longer that of an 'economically marginalized' or 'socially under privileged' offender, but of an 'emotionally disturbed' or 'psychologically distinct' individual.

In stark contrast, criminology as an academic discipline has tended, in the main, to focus on wider questions concerning the complex relationship(s) that exist between crime, criminal justice, and society—something that should immediately be apparent from the diverse range of chapters that comprise this volume. This is not to suggest that sociological criminologists discount the many important gains made by psychologists in understanding a whole range of abnormal and extreme criminal behaviour, both in terms of individual and collective action (see Gadd and Jefferson's (2007) recent work in the field of 'psychosocial criminology') . Rather, simply to point out that, in the majority of cases, most academic criminologists approach the subject of crime and criminality from a much broader perspective that includes not just the 'causes of crime', but also questions about how crime is itself constructed (see Chapter 1), and how society and the State seek to both control and to respond to crime (see Chapters 21 and 22).

It should be obvious, then, even from this general introduction that, despite a shared interest in criminal behaviour, criminology and psychology have often made rather uneasy bedfellows. In the next section, as attention turns to the main psychological explanations of criminal behaviour, I will make some intermittent comments about how this relationship has ebbed and flowed over the last 100 years or so. In the meantime, however, in a bid to keep to my introductory remit and (more importantly perhaps in terms of disciplinary politics!) to illustrate a sense of even-handedness, I will conclude this section with the following passage from Putwain and Sammons' introduction to criminological psychology:

> The contribution that psychology can make to criminological issues tends to reflect the strengths and weaknesses of psychology as a discipline. On the positive side, psychologists undergo rigorous training in research methodology, and are therefore well placed to carry out their own investigations and experiments and to comment on and evaluate the work of others. On the negative side, psychology tends to emphasize *individual* factors at the expense of *social* factors. For example, psychological explanations of criminal behaviour tend to concentrate on why *individuals* become offenders by considering factors such as personality and brain function. In contrast sociological approaches tend to emphasize social factors such as poverty and social class...Neither approach is foolproof and each complements the other. When taken in isolation, each approach can only provide part of the whole picture, but when taken together they provide a more comprehensive understanding of crime. (Putwain and Sammons 2002: 2–3)

Key psychological explanations of criminal behaviour

Introduction

Some brief historical context

Generally speaking, psychology and criminology emerged as distinct disciplines at a very similar historical moment—the latter half of the nineteenth century. Typically, one associates the birth of modern criminology with the work of Cesare Lombroso

(1835–1909) and his fellow members of the Italian positivist school (*scuola positiva*; see Chapter 4, for a general introduction to positivism and other key moments in the historical development of criminology). At this point, of course, the nascent 'science of criminology' was still fundamentally preoccupied with matters relating to the individual actor, the so-called 'criminal person or type' (see Beirne, 1993: Chapters 2 and 3; Morrison, 2004 for recent commentaries). Only later would it broaden its horizons to include wider social and economic factors in accounts of crime. Psychology, meanwhile, had begun to coalesce around the early experimental research of the German, Wilhelm Wundt (1832–1920)—the first person to call himself a psychologist—and the American, William James (1842–1940). (Sigmund Freud, of course, began his career as a neurologist and thus his early work was very much rooted in biology. It was not until slightly later that criminal psychologists took up his psychodynamic theory of personality; see below.)

Such contemporaneous development is not surprising, for both disciplines should be seen as clear products of modernity's faith in enlightened science and philosophy. If modernity was about anything it was about the belief that society's failings would be overcome or at least managed (controlled) by the careful, scientific pursuit of relevant knowledge and the application of this knowledge to a specific set of problems. The then fledgling disciplines of criminology and psychology exemplified such ideals; protagonists of both 'sciences' steadfastly believing that rational scientific analysis could 'make sense' of human behaviour by identifying flaws and categorizing traits and types. No longer would there be talk of humans possessing a 'soul' or a 'spirit'—or indeed of 'good' and 'evil'. Instead, the psychologist and the criminologist would be the objective recorder of 'personality' and 'criminality' respectively—only later would these two sub-fields collide.

Some basic psychological 'distinctions' explained

Perhaps the most enduring (and over-simplified) controversy within psychology is the 'nature versus nurture debate'. In simple terms, the controversy revolves around the *origins* of individual human behaviour/personality. Carlson and Buskist neatly summarize the debate, whilst also pointing out that, as with various other aspects of psychology, what initially appear to be clear-cut distinctions are in fact rather blurred:

> 'Is it [personality] caused by biological or social factors?' 'Is it innate or learned?' 'Is it a result of hereditary or cultural influences?' 'Should we look for an explanation in the brain or in the environment?' Almost always, biology, innateness, heredity, and the brain are placed on the 'nature' side of the equation. Society, learning, culture, and the environment are placed on the 'nurture' side. Rarely, does anyone question whether these groups of items really form a true dichotomy...most modern psychologists consider the nature-nurture issue to be a relic of the past. That is, they believe that *all* behaviours, talents, and personality traits are the products of both types of factors: biological and social, hereditary and cultural, physiological and environmental. The task of the modern psychologist is not to find out which one of these factors is more important but to discover the particular roles played by each of them and to determine the ways in which they interact. (1997: 99–100)

Such is also the case with psychological understandings of criminality. While, countless criminological psychologists have, over the years, sought to identify a single biological (that is, 'nature') explanation of crime, such attempts have born little fruit (for a brief introduction to the some of the major biological and genetic explanations of crime—William Sheldon's 'body type' theory; genetic transmission theory; twin and adoptee studies etc.—see Chapter 4; see also Hollin, 1989: 23–34; Lanier and Henry, 1998: Chapter 5; Bartol, 2002: Chapter 3; and in more detail Jeffrey, 1994; Ciba Foundation, 1996). Indeed, the idea that human behaviour is determined by factors that, while universal to the species, reside to a greater or lesser extent in the *constitution of the individual*, is now distinctly unfashionable (cf. Mednick *et al.*, 1987; Raine, 1993 for more recent attempts to reassert the role of genetics in criminal behaviour). To put it more bluntly, few psychologists still cling to the idea that certain individuals are somehow predetermined into a life of crime. Instead, the 'nature-nurture' dichotomy is seen to be less an absolute distinction and more an interacting framework for thinking about causal factors in the commission of crime.

Another key definitional issue within criminological psychology, and one that often trips up students new to the subject, is the distinction between cognitive psychology and behavioural psychology. Once again, as the following quote makes clear, the two approaches are anything but mutually exclusive:

> Cognitive theories place the study of psychology in the *mind*; they see human action as the result of driving or compelling mental forces or to be the result of mental reasoning and beliefs. These theories take account of *internal feelings* such as anger, frustration, desire and despair. In fact, all activity is seen as the result of *internal mental processes*. In contrast, the behavioural theorists, whilst taking account of internal factors, place them in a *social context*. They see that internal mental processes can be affected and even altered by *certain factors in the environment which either reinforce or discourage the behaviour*. Clearly there is no strong dividing line between these two. *A degree of overlap is likely, whilst some psychological theories may not fit neatly into either school*. (Williams, 2004: 170 [emphases added])

I will return to these two psychological variants at certain points in the chapter. In the meantime, suffice it to say that criminological psychology is a multi-faceted discipline which, despite its overall goal of striving to understand, explain, and predict criminal behaviour, typically tends to shy away from making any major pronouncements about there being a single or universal cause/explanation for deviant action. That said, criminological psychology has made significant strides in applying 'psychological theory and investigation to understanding (and attempting to change) criminal behaviour' (Hollin, 2007: 43). Moreover, since its emergence as a significant sub-discipline in the early 1960s, criminological psychology (along with its 'sister' discipline, legal psychology (see Müller *et al.*, 1984; Bartol and Bartol, 1994; Kapardis, 1997; Gudjonsson and Hayward, 1998; Adler, 2004) has proven to be of considerable practical use, both in terms of police work and to those working within the legal profession (see below). Indeed, such has been the rise of criminological psychology as a disciplinary variant in its own right that recent years have seen the publication of a whole host of excellent textbooks aimed at introducing the reader to the subject (for example, Hollin, 1989, 1992; Blackburn, 1993; Feldman, 1993; Ainsworth, 2000; Putwain and Sammons, 2002; McGuire, 2004; Bartol and Bartol, 2005; Webber, 2008). Readers new to this area would do well to access one of these texts for a good general synopsis of the interface between psychology and criminology. Now, however, I wish to proceed by focusing on some of the main psychological theories of criminal behaviour. Again, I should point out that what follows is only the briefest of snapshots of some of the more prominent psychological explanations of crime.

Psychoanalytical theories of crime

Most readers will have some understanding of the term psychoanalysis and the work of the Austrian psychiatrist, Sigmund Freud (1856–1939). However, few will be aware of the considerable impact his thinking had on criminological psychology. Despite the fact that, in reality, Freud himself had very little to say about crime, his ideas served as the cornerstone for a whole host of theories that sought to understand crime and deviance by recourse to psychoanalytic techniques—even though many of these subsequent so-called 'psychoanalytical theories' of crime very often represented something of an adulteration (or more charitably, an augmentation) of classic Freudian psychoanalytic theory (see Freud, 1935; Kline, 1984). Let us start at the beginning, by introducing some of the central tenets of Freud's thinking.

Freud's great achievement was to highlight the way that innate desires and repressed emotions shape individual human behaviour. For example, according to Freudian thinking, violent, aggressive, or sexually deviant acts should be seen as expressions of buried internal (psychic) conflicts that are the result of traumas or deprivations experienced during childhood (see below). To fully appreciate this perspective one must first understand how Freud perceived the human mind. In simple terms, Freud argued that the mind was comprised of three provinces: the *ego*, the *id* and the *super-ego* (Figure 6.1).

First, the *id* represents the primitive, instinctive, animalistic portion of the 'unconscious mind'. It is here that the primeval human desires reside: that is, fundamental biological and physiological concerns such as innate sexual urges (*libido*); the 'life instinct' (*Eros*) or drive for life; the destructive 'death instinct' (*Thanatos*); and the desire to eat, sleep, and be comfortable and so on. The goal of the *id* is simple: to gratify instincts at all costs. According to Freud, the unconscious desires and urges that well up in the id

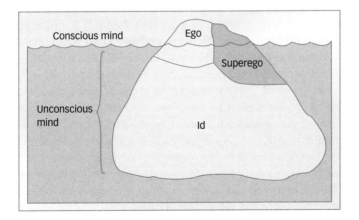

Figure 6.1 The 'pyramid' diagram of Freud's notion of the psyche

are wholly unresponsive to the demands of reality and are instead governed by what he termed 'the pleasure principle'. Needless to say, over the years, such drives have been of considerable interest to criminal psychologists (see, for example, the work of Lorenz, 1966; Storr, 1970). Second, the ego relates (primarily) to the 'conscious mind', and acts as a sort of 'mediating device' between the two opposing mental forces of the id and the super-ego. Because of the conscious recognition within the individual that 'every act has a consequence', Freud claimed that the ego was driven by the 'reality principle'. Finally, the (largely conscious) super-ego is the 'repository of moral values' and the seat of guilt within the individual. Perhaps the best way to perceive the super-ego is as a sort of internal 'nagging parent' or moral or ethical guardian. Importantly, especially for psychoanalytical theories of crime, the super-ego develops as a result of a series of early social experience(s) (and, for Freud at least, admonishments) that serve to engender in the individual an internal 'source of self-criticism based on the production of guilt'.

In crude terms, Freud maintained that human behaviour should be thought of as a 'struggle between the internalized psychic forces of the id and the super-ego'—with the ego constantly striving to maintain a suitable balance. It is this checking and controlling process that is of vital importance to Freudian psychoanalysis. Over time, and largely formed through learned behaviour, the ego strives to undertake a complex mental balancing act between the primeval desires of the id and the internalized conscience of the super-ego, whilst all the time seeking to work out the best way in which to actually 'serve' the id by meeting some of its requirements: 'A baby learns that it is fed only after crying, and a child learns to say "please" in order to obtain things. It learns that in some circumstances, giving into the id leads to punishment and unpleasantness, and so it may not follow its desires in order to avoid these consequences...Slowly, the ego develops and controls or tempers the id' (Williams, 2004: 172).

But what does all this mean in terms of understanding criminal behaviour? The key thing here is this process by which the super-ego is formed. As mentioned above, a well-developed super-ego is the result of early social interactions with parents (or with those acting *in loco parentis*). Consequently, for proponents of psychoanalytical criminology, criminal behaviour can be understood as an expression of buried internal (mental) conflicts that are the result of traumas or deprivations experienced during childhood.

The first to apply such psychoanalytical models to the study of crime was the former schoolteacher August Aichorn (1925). Aichorn postulated that traditional environmental factors (such as those being outlined by the Chicago School of Sociology at a similar time; see Chapter 4) were not sufficient in and of themselves to account for individual involvement in criminal activity. Instead he argued that many of the delinquent children he studied exhibited what he described as *latent delinquency*—an 'underlying predisposition' which psychologically conditions the child 'for a lifetime of crime'. In other words, a failure to establish productive early emotional relationships resulted in a breakdown in the *socialization process*, 'allowing the latent delinquency to become dominant: a state which Aichorn describes as "dissocial". The criminal behaviour is therefore the result of a failure of psychological development, thereby allowing the underlying, latent delinquency to govern the behaviour' (Hollin, 1989: 35). In even plainer terms, for Aichorn childhood delinquency is the product of a badly structured/supervised early childhood (whether as a result of parental neglect or over-indulgence). This being the case, his remedy was straightforward; delinquent children must be provided with a well-supervised, pleasant social environment that will encourage the type of emotional relationships which, in turn, will help develop a well-established *super-ego.*

Following Aichorn, the importance of early childhood development on behaviour was further emphasized by a whole host of psychoanalysts—including most famously, the work of Abrahamson (1944) and Alexander (Alexander and Staub, 1931; Alexander and Healy, 1935) on failure to control drives associated with the 'pleasure principle'; and Healey and Bronner's (1936) research into the Freudian concept of 'sublimation', or the way that 'unsatisfied instinctual desires' are often channelled into other forms of behaviour, including deviance. However, perhaps the most influential figure in this field was the British developmental psychologist, John Bowlby (1907–90). Bowlby's achievement was to solidify the link between *maternal deprivation* and antisocial behaviour (Bowlby, 1944; 1951). This commitment to understanding behaviour by recourse to early familial circumstances is made abundantly clear in the following quote:

> No variables have more far-reaching effects on personality development than a child's experiences within the family. Starting during his first months in his relation to both parents, he builds up working models of how attachment figures are likely to behave towards him in any of a variety of situations, and on all those models are based all his expectations, and therefore all his plans, for the rest of his life. (Bowlby, 1973: 369)

More specifically, what was important for Bowlby was the close, loving relationship between mother and child. Consequently, any rejection or separation between mother and child during early child development is likely to prove highly problematic. Indeed, according to Bowlby's sample groups, such ruptures in familial relations will be disproportionately represented in serious cases of delinquency in later life.

Bowlby's writings, along with other related research (for example, Little, 1965; Rutter, 1972), proved extremely effective in terms of influencing governments and generating policy initiatives. Not least, ideas about maternal deprivation and other later so-called 'broken home theories' were a central element in the rehabilitative 'welfarist' movement in youth justice of the 1960s and 1970s (see Chapter 19). However, these early forays into the psychology of the offender did not sit well with everyone. Many commentators objected strongly to the lack of scientific rigour associated with this early psychoanalytical criminology (specifically the '*tautological*' and 'untestable' nature of the intra-psychic Freudian approach). Others meanwhile questioned the extent to which the psychoanalytical approach relied upon the interpretative expertise of the analyst in teasing out the particular link between the criminal act and the hidden unconscious drive—a link that, for many, was simply too convoluted and contingent. That said, the psychoanalytical approach to deviance, and other subsequent theories derived from psychoanalysis (see below), went on to exert considerable influence within both psychology and criminology for many decades to come (see Garland, 1994: 42–60; Valier, 2006). Not least, its enduring legacy is the concrete link it cemented in the minds of many practitioners and caregivers between chaotic early child development and behavioural problems in later life.

Behavioural and social learning theories of crime

In contrast to theories of crime that suggest the root cause of deviance lies with primitive instinctive drives and internal psychodynamic struggles, behavioural and social learning theories—as the name clearly implies—assert instead that crime and deviance are *learned responses*. The starting point for this expansive body of work was Edwin Sutherland's (1883–1950) renowned sociological theory of 'differential association' (1947). For Sutherland, behaviour—including crime—is a social product, a result of different interactions and patterns of learning that occur in the intimate personal groups and surrounding social circumstances that encapsulate the individual. According to Sutherland, such groups teach 'definitions'—including special skills, motivations, norms, and beliefs—either 'unfavourable' or 'favourable' to the violation of the law (that is, in the latter case, the *association* of an individual with a group, or indeed a community, that is both ingrained with criminal traits and norms, and also isolated from more positive anti-criminal traits and attitudes). Despite criticisms of differential association (not least questions about why, under shared conditions, individuals still tend to behave very differently from each other) Sutherland's work was extremely influential, ushering in a whole host of subsequent theories that sought to prove that the determinants of behaviour reside *outside the individual.*

This line of thinking inevitably chimed loudly with the shift already underway within American psychology towards 'behaviourism' (see, for example, Watson, 1913 for an early example). But as Clive Hollin makes clear, rather than making for harmonious relations between psychology and criminology, this apparent convergence in thinking surrounding the role of *external stimulants* in the development of behaviour, instead heralded a parting of the ways for the disciplines, as behavioural psychologists continued to focus their attention exclusively on the *individual behaviour* rather than the wider external circumstances in which that behaviour was forged. Consequently, 'psychology failed to connect with criminology and the opportunity for a genuine academic alliance slipped away' (Hollin, 2007: 49). The uneven and, at times, strained relationship between psychology and criminology was underway.

Psychological developments in learning theory meanwhile drew further strength from the behavioural research of B.F. Skinner (1904–90), and especially his principles of 'operant learning' (1938, 1953). Crudely stated, operant learning suggests that 'behaviour is determined by the environmental consequences it produces for the individual concerned'. Put another way, behaviour that leads to 'awards' will increase (that is, is 'positively reinforced'); behaviour that produces an unpleasant stimulus (that is, is 'punished') is avoided: 'Any such behaviour, driving a car, writing a letter, talking to a friend, setting fire to a house, is *operant* behaviour. Behaviour does not occur at random; environmental cues signal when certain behaviours are liable to be reinforced or punished...the Antecedent conditions prompt the Behaviour which in turn produces the Consequences—the ABC of behavioural theory' (Hollin, 1989: 40).

Among the first to suggest that criminal behaviour could be understood in terms of operant learning was C.R. Jeffrey (1965) and his *theory of differential reinforcement* (see also more recently Akers, 1985). By combining the principles of Skinner's operant learning with Sutherland's differential association, Jeffrey maintained that, although criminal behaviour might well be the result of pervasive socio-cultural norms and attitudes within a given locality (à la Sutherland), it is also greatly affected by the particular consequences (or 'reinforcements' in Skinnerian terms) that deviance produces for the individual. For example, 'The majority of crimes are concerned with stealing where the consequences are clearly material and financial gain: the gains may therefore be seen as positively reinforcing the stealing' (Hollin, 1989: 41). Such an approach has the advantage of overcoming the main problem associated with differential association. By focusing on *individual learning histories* (that is, unique reward and punishment experiences), differential reinforcement theory explains how, despite shared environmental conditions, individual actors ultimately behave very differently.

While Skinner and Jeffrey did not wholly discount the role of internal mental processes in their particular brand of behaviourism, neither did they feature prominently in their analyses. The first to actively integrate 'internal processes' into learning theory was the psychologist Albert Bandura (1973, 1977; also Rotter, 1954). Bandura's 'social learning theory' hypothesis was an uncomplicated one: individual behaviour is something learnt at the *cognitive level* by observing and then imitating the actions of others. Most famously, Bandura conducted an experiment in which a group of infants watched a film depicting an adult violently attacking an inflatable rubber 'Bobo' doll (see Chapter 8, Figure 8.2). In subsequent tests, this group were significantly more likely to repeat the aggressive behaviour toward the doll than were the members of a control group who had not been exposed to the film—indeed, this second group behaved more passively throughout the whole experiment. Because of the emphasis Bandura placed on 'learnt aggression', his findings quickly found support within criminological psychology (for example, Nietzel 1979).

Such experiments suggested that, not only does social learning take place at the familial and sub-cultural level, but also via the observation of cultural symbols and media 'role models' (see Chapter 8). 'For example, a child may learn to shoot a gun by imitating television characters. He or she then rehearses and fine tunes this behavioural pattern by practicing with toy guns' (Bartol, 2002: 128). Naturally, just like other operant behaviour, cognitively learned behaviour is further 'reinforced' or 'punished' via the process of socialization ('The behaviour is likely to be maintained if peers also play with guns and reinforce one another for doing so', ibid.).

This interest in the relationship between wider social and cultural determinants and individual criminal behaviour could have heralded the onset of a productive, collaborative relationship between criminology and psychology. Not for the last time, however, this opportunity for disciplinary accord would be largely squandered. While behavioural and social learning theories continued to develop, by the end of the 1970s most criminal psychologists had turned their back on this approach, choosing instead to pursue a very different course based around theories of criminal behaviour concerned with the identification of individual *personality traits*.

Trait-based personality theories

The study of individual personality traits is nothing new in psychology (see, for example, Allport, 1937; Cattell, 1965). As we saw earlier, one could even view Freud's work as the study of personality development. Yet, while Freud saw abnormal behaviour as the product of unconscious desires and motivations, the new 'Trait-based personality theories' set out to identify and classify particular personality characteristics, and to empirically measure how these traits become assembled differently in different people. The central figure in this shift towards understanding human behaviour via 'psychometric' statistical testing was Hans Eysenck (1916–97). Eysenck's work is especially pertinent to the current discussion as his goal was the creation of a general psychological theory of crime (1977; Eysenck and Gudjonsson, 1989).

Eysenck had little time for the 'sociological turn' in the study of crime and deviance, something made abundantly clear in the following quote: 'In many ways we disagree with various sociological theories that have become so popular since World War II but which, we believe, are fundamentally erroneous and counter to the fact' (Eysenck and Gudjonsson, 1989: 1 cited in Bartol, 2002: 70). Instead Eysenck stressed the fundamental role of inherited genetic predispositions (especially in relation to the cortical and autonomic central nervous systems) in determining the way each individual responds to environmental conditioning. In other words, Eysenck subscribed to the view that an individual's personality—including those personality traits that he considered constitutive of the criminal personality—was largely the product of their genetic make-up. Yet, this was no simple return to biological determinism (see Chapter 4); rather Eysenck's theory was a fusion of biological, socio-environmental, and individual factors.

Because Eysenck spent much of his life's work constantly retesting and augmenting his theory of crime, his key assertions are not easily summarized; however, the following passages by Lanier and Henry provide a succinct general synopsis (for more detailed summaries see Eysenck, 1984; Bartol, 2002: 70–85; Hollin, 1989: 53–9):

> Eysenck claimed to show that human personalities are made up of clusters of traits. One cluster produces a sensitive, inhibited temperament that he called *introversion*. A second cluster produces an outward-focused, cheerful, expressive temperament that he called *extroversion*. A third dimension of personality, which forms emotional stability or instability, he labelled *neuroticism*; to this schema he subsequently added *psychoticism*, which is a predisposition to a psychotic breakdown. (Lanier and Henry, 1998: 119)

Eysenck plotted the personality traits of the individuals he studied on a very rudimentary graph that has since become one of the most famous diagrams in all psychology (Figure 6.2). Although something of an oversimplification, Eysenck concluded that most people in society would reside somewhere near the middle of the axis (that is, within the inner 'square'), but that what was important in terms of explaining criminal behaviour were those individuals who featured at the extremes of the diagram.

> Normal human personalities are emotionally stable, neither highly introvert or extrovert. In contrast, those who are highly neurotic, highly extroverted, and score high on a psychoticism scale have a greater predisposition toward crime, forming in the extreme the psychopathic personality. Eysenck explained that such personalities (sensation seekers) are less sensitive to excitation by stimuli, requiring more stimulation than normal, which they can achieve through crime, violence and drug taking. These people are impulsive, being emotionally unstable. They are also less easy to condition and have a higher threshold or tolerance to pain. Low IQ can [also] affect the ability of such personalities to learn rules, perceive punishment, or experience pain, as in biological theory. (ibid.)

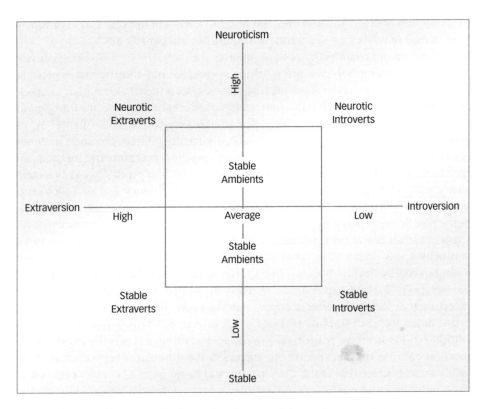

Figure 6.2 Eysenck's personality dimensions for neuroticism and extraversion

Taken at face value, Eysenck's theories seem convincing. Yet, a trawl through the mass of empirical research undertaken in an attempt to test his propositions reveals a more ambiguous picture—not least many of these studies point to a number of significant methodological and theoretical flaws. Crucially, whilst there is general support for his contention that offenders will score highly on both the psychoticism and neuroticism dimensions, there is little evidence to support the crime–extroversion connection. Furthermore, a common charge often labelled at the trait-based approach is that it is inherently tautological: 'Stealing may be taken as an indicator of impulsiveness and impulsiveness given as the reason for stealing. Thus a recurrent criticism of trait-based theories is that they represent correlational rather then causal connections' (ibid.: 121).

These and various other criticisms aside, the wider influence of the trait-based approach to deviance can be seen in the continued growth of psychometric questionnaires and other related diagnostic devices that have emerged out of this field of research. These include early examples of so-called 'personality inventories' such as the Minnesota Multiphasic Personality Inventory (MMPI) (first proposed in 1939) to British equivalents like the British Maudsley Personality Index (MPI) and Eysenck-inspired self-report questionnaires such as the Eysenck Personality Inventory (EPI) and its subsequent iterations (see relatedly Boyle et al., 2008). Basically, the idea here is that specific personality traits can be measured and assessed by asking the individual a battery of specially designed questions (or more recently by testing responses to a series of images). Such assessments are then used to predict, prevent, and treat future deviant behaviour.

Inevitably, many commentators have pointed out the intrinsic problems associated with statistical attempts to measure anything as complex and multifaceted as personality (see most famously, Taylor *et al.*, 1973: 44–61)—not least the all too familiar methodological pitfalls associated with self-report studies (for a criminology-specific introduction to the problems of self-reporting see Coleman and Moynihan 2002: Chapter 3). Yet, most of this type of psychology has proceeded virtually oblivious to such methodological criticism and has continued to embrace empirical psychometric methods and other forms of quantitative analysis. This unflinching faith in psychology as a positivist science, coupled with the continued emphasis placed by Eysenck and his followers on the importance of *biological factors* in the development of personality, served to drive a deep wedge between psychology and criminology. For almost at the same moment that Eysenck's influence was being felt most acutely in psychology (the late 1960s and 1970s), criminology was dramatically affected by a new wave of Marxist-inspired research, as announced by Taylor, Walton, and Young in the groundbreaking work *The New Criminology* (1973) (see Chapter 4: and relatedly the work of 'anti-psychiatry' movement writers such as Laing, Esterson, Cooper, and Szasz). As (the majority of) criminology turned down the road towards theories of crime couched firmly in sociological and political economic terms, mainstream psychology continued down the experimental, empirical path. As Hollin explains: 'To appreciate the differences between Taylor *et al.* and Eysenck, is to see that at the time, there could be no point of contact between the new criminology and mainstream psychology (of which Eysenck was a leading figure)' (2007: 55). Such disharmony between the disciplines would only intensify, as psychology embarked on its next theoretical stage.

Cognitive theories of crime

Such was the speed at which cognitive theory impacted on psychology its emergence on the scene is often described in terms of a 'cognitive revolution' (Baars, 1986). Drawing on the early work of the Swiss child psychologist, Jean Piaget (for example, 1954), and Lawrence Kohlberg's (1969) notion of 'progressive moral development', cognitive theory 'has as its major theme how mental thought processes are used to solve problems—to interpret, evaluate, and decide on the best of actions. These thought processes occur through mental pictures and conversations with ourselves' (Lanier and Henry, 1998: 126). More simply, it is an attempt to understand the way people think via investigations of such concepts as intelligence, memory structure, visual perception, and logical ability (see Eysenck and Keane, 1997; Lamberts and Goldstone, 2004; and Brown, 2006 for comprehensive overviews of mainstream cognitive psychology).

The first major cognitive study to make an impression on criminology was Yochelson and Samenow's infamous *The Criminal Personality* (1976; see Glueck and Glueck, 1950 for a precursor study). In an expansive three-volume work, Yocheslon and Samenow set themselves the ambitious task of 'mapping the criminal mind'. The positivist zeal with which they undertook this task is made clear in the following quote by Samenow:

I shall expose the myths about why criminals commit crimes, and I shall draw a picture for you of the personality of the criminal just as the police artist draws a picture of his face from the description. I shall describe how criminals think, how they defend their crimes to others, and how they exploit programs that are developed to help them. (Samenow, 1984: 5)

All this from a sample group of only 240 offenders, each one of whom had been adjudged 'not guilty by reason of insanity' and who, at the time of study, were institutionalized in a psychiatric hospital in Washington DC. After several thousands of hours of qualitative interviewing Yocheslon and Samenow identified '52 errors of criminal thinking' or 'problematic thinking styles' that, they claimed, taken together constituted 'the criminal personality'. These included *inter alia* 'chronic lying', irresponsible decision making, 'super optimism', 'distorted self-image', and a lack of empathy for others' (a trait that has since been made much of in contemporary cognitive-behavioural programmes for sex offenders; see below). According to Yochelson and Samenow, such 'cognitive distortions' ensure that '[C]riminals *think differently* from responsible people' and, moreover, that 'Crime resides *within the person* and is "caused" *by the way he thinks, not by his environment*' (Samenow, 1984: xiv, cited in Lanier and Henry, 1998: 127, emphases added). Naturally, such assertions have implications in terms of how one treats the offender. Indeed it is within the sphere of contemporary treatment programmes that the influence of cognitive theory has been greatest—I will thus return to this subject in more detail below. In the meantime, it is worth pausing to reflect on some of the much-voiced criticisms of Yochelson and Samenow's *The Criminal Personality*, as these critiques also serve to illustrate many of the problems associated with various other types of empirical psychology concerned with statistically measuring or 'mapping' the complexities of the human criminal personality.

To start with, little distinction is made between the various types of criminal studied. Thus, their assertion that all criminals share the same thought patterns/processes is highly problematic—does a violent offender, for example, share the same cognitive distortions as an embezzler? Second, by focusing so intently on internal thought process and dysfunctional cognitions, Yochelson and Samenow downplay the importance of both psychobiological *and* socio-environmental influences. Third, theories of crime that stress cognitive irregularities are seen as tautological in that certain behaviours are said to be indicative of cognitive processes, while these same cognitive processes are then used to explain away the behaviour. Fourth, and perhaps most obviously, Yochelson and Samenow's sample was comprised only of *incarcerated* offenders. Yet, while one cannot deny the existence of these and several other theoretical and methodological flaws, it is hard not to be drawn to some of their ideas about cognitive reasoning, especially in relation to interpersonal relationships. Unsurprising, then, that many other psychologists have chosen to pursue this line of inquiry and in so doing have developed a body of work that not only greatly augments Yocheslson and Samenow's research, but which has since gone on to be enthusiastically received by practitioners working in the treatment arena.

A central assumption of *The Criminal Personality* is that a criminal's erroneous thinking can be corrected if they are first taught to construct a 'moral inventory' of their everyday thoughts, and then, by working with a practitioner, to identify and ultimately eradicate any dysfunctional cognitions (Samenow, 1984: 6–7). Although something of an oversimplification, this is the rationale behind the majority of cognitive therapeutic interventions that seek to correct problems experienced by offenders in their everyday lives. For example, such programmes typically concentrate on cognitive considerations such as:

- insufficient levels of *self-control* (that is, impulsivity or the failure to delay gratification) (for more on the role of self-control more generally within criminological theory, see Chapter 4);

- an inability *to feel empathy for others*—especially victims;

- deficits in basic *social problem-solving skills*—the type of skills we all employ to negotiate interpersonal relationships and everyday struggles;

- problems in the interpretation of *visual and situational cues* (e.g. a great deal of research suggests that violent individuals not only perceive fewer social cues than non-violent people, but that they are also much more prone to interpret social cues in a hostile fashion) (see Crick and Dodge's 1994, 1996 work on social information processing);

- an inability to distinguish between which facets of personal life are subject to *internal control* (i.e. are governed by one's own actions) and those which are subject to *external control* (i.e. are governed by the actions of others).

Cognitively inspired treatment programmes are currently very popular within the UK criminal justice system, being employed in increasing numbers both within the prison setting and as an alternative to custody. However, while these correctional programmes have often proved successful at reducing certain forms of persistent offending, ultimately they remain fundamentally limited in scope—primarily in the sense that they never really offer a full and inclusive explanation of why someone becomes involved in criminality (or, for that matter, decides to stop; on this point see the interesting article by Shadd Maruna (2000) 'Criminology, desistance, and the psychology of the stranger'). That said, perhaps this is not really the point. These cognitively inspired programmes make little attempt to consider traditional criminological concerns such as the inequalities associated with class, race, gender, and socio-economic deprivation. Instead, the goal is the distillation of crime and criminality to rigid 'narratives of feeling' and formalized reductionist understandings of the social world. Only when this process is complete, it is asserted, will the individual offender then be in a position to assume responsibility for his or her actions. As Wayne Morrison points out, such psychotherapeutic practices represent the new wave of governmental and institutional weapons in the fight against crime, a discourse preoccupied solely with strategies of pacification and control (see Garland, 1997, 2001; O'Malley, 2004, 2008 for a more general introduction to criminological thinking in this area)—with the psychologist as independent arbiter of acceptable behaviour and intention:

> Psychology presents a variety of tools and knowledges: methods of awareness (which strive to make a self visible to the person)…The aim of these knowledges and methodologies is to visualize the healthy, and get rid of pathological aspects. The task is to change anxiety into

excitement through techniques of self-reflection and self-examination, and thereby to ensure that we become a reflexive self, more able to redirect our [internal] forces. Thus we can learn processes of control over ourselves which the behavioural manipulators claim they can exercise from without...We learn a language and a technique, a process which makes us governable, and yet offers us the possibilities of governing ourselves. This reflects the dialectics of modernity: control and autonomy, responsibility and inclusivity, civilization and citizenship. (Morrison, 1995 163–4)

REVIEW QUESTIONS

1 Outline the main differences and similarities that exist between the four psychological explanations of crime outlined above.

2 Draw up a list of diverse crimes that range in seriousness from petty street crime through to murder. Which of the above theories do you think best accounts for each type of crime?

3 Given what you have just read, how would you describe the historical relationship between the disciplines of psychology and criminology? What have been the main points of agreement and contestation?

Theory into practice: some examples of the way psychology is employed within criminal justice

The second half of this chapter will focus on some of the more prominent practical applications of psychology within the sphere of criminal justice (see Adler, 2004 for a general introduction). Students should recognize that, once again, what follows here is only an introduction and that, needless to say, countless other practical interfaces abound (see, for example, HM Prison Service and the National Probation Service, 2003; Towl, 2004).

Recent psychological developments in rehabilitation and treatment

The most obvious place to start is with psychological attempts at rehabilitation, as the various treatment programmes put forward by psychologists naturally draw heavily on many of the psychological theories and principles outlined above. The key point here is that psychologically based rehabilitation models operate on very different principles to traditional judicial sanctions such as imprisonment or fines. To start with they are less concerned with *punishing the offender* than with reducing the 'risk' of reoffending. Consequently, 'they are based on psychological theories of offending, rather then the (sometimes rather vague) notions of "human nature" on which judicial sanctions often seem to be based' (Putwain and Sammons, 2002: 147).

Since the 1980s numerous psychologically based treatment programmes have been pioneered, both within and outside the custodial setting. However, I have chosen here to concentrate on what are perhaps the two most common initiatives—*cognitive behavioural treatments for offending* based on cognitive and social learning theories of crime, and *token economies* based more specifically on operant conditioning theories.

As Anne Worrall makes clear in her chapter on offender management in this volume, the nature of probation intervention has changed radically in the past two decades. The disillusionment and pessimism encapsulated in Robert Martinson's infamous 1974 remark that 'nothing works' in penal interventions (see Chapter 26, this volume) epitomized the lack of confidence in the efficacy of established offender treatment/supervision modalities, heralding a 'crisis in confidence' both in the National Probation Service specifically and the 'welfarist' treatment paradigm more generally (see, for example, Bean, 1976; Hudson, 1987). This loss of confidence lasted until the early 1990s and the emergence (initially in North America) of cognitive behavioural programmes based in large part on a new wave of psychological research—or more accurately, a new spirit of collective endeavour and reciprocity between learning, behaviour, and cognition theorists (see McGuire, 1995 on the subsequent initiatives associated with the 'What Works?' conferences; and Raynor, 2002; Lipsey *et al.*, 2004 for recent commentaries on developments in this area).

As mentioned above, rather than attempting to change the whole personality or circumstances of an offender, cognitive behavioural programmes focus on specific unacceptable behaviours and seek to modify these by correcting distortions in the way offenders think about their crimes. The practitioner's primary goal, therefore, is to get the offender to 'face up' to their crimes and accept responsibility for their actions (instead of blaming the victim or their social circumstances). Likewise, treatment programmes also concentrate both on correcting problem behaviours (such as anger management, drunk driving, or deviant forms of sexual arousal), and the acquisition of new social and interpersonal skills that will help the offender better deal with certain situations that, previously, had triggered antisocial or criminal behaviour. Typically, these strategies are bundled together in the form of a treatment/correction 'programme', which in turn draws 'together a series of planned and sequential learning opportunities into a cumulative sequence, covering an appropriate curriculum of skills and allowing plenty of opportunity to reinforce learning through structured practice' (Raynor, 2002: 1185).

Since their emergence in the UK in the early 1990s, the use of such programmes has grown exponentially. Jill Peay, for example, estimates that, by 2001, 'over 100 prisons were running such programmes, with five specific programmes in prisons and nine in the probation service having been accredited' (2002: 775). The interesting thing to note here about such growth is the way that cognitive behavioural programmes are now employed as a 'mainstream application' within the contemporary probation system. No longer are they employed simply as a means of treatment for chronic offenders with various personality disorders, or as a way of assessing, managing, and ultimately *reducing the risk of re-offending* among sexual and violent offenders (see Kemshall, 2001; Jones, 2000: 151–6; and Kemshall, 2003 more generally). Increasingly, these programmes are offered to offenders involved in a much more general—dare I say it, even commonplace—range of so-called 'antisocial behaviours' (see McGuire, 2004: Chapter 6). Clearly, this is more evidence of the widening of what Wayne Morrison described above as the net of governmental structures of self-reflection and self-examination.

Leaving this more critical point aside, the incredible growth of cognitive behavioural treatment programmes have resulted in them being a somewhat difficult phenomenon to define accurately (see McGuire, 2000). Consequently, as Hollin explains, the relationship between theory and effective practice in this area has, on occasion, been a somewhat disjointed one:

> ...rather then the purist sequence of a theory leading to the design of an intervention, so producing outcome evidence by which to amend theory and practice, 'What Works' has started from a quite different position. The meta-analyses have brought together a disparate batch of treatment outcome studies and distilled their effective components. In an about turn, the position has been arrived at whereby positive treatment outcome data have outstripped theory. (Hollin, 2002: 167)

Inevitably, this situation throws up certain problems in terms of moving the field forward, yet it should not blind us to the fact that a significant number of these therapies have proven highly successful in the treatment of both adult and juvenile offenders (see Andrews *et al.*, 1990; Lipsey and Wilson, 1998; Redondo *et al.*, 1999). It is for this reason that many psychologists and practitioners are highly optimistic about the future potential of cognitive-behavioural rehabilitative strategies (Vennard and Hedderman, 1998), some even suggesting that work in this area offers the potential for establishing 'genuine cross-disciplinary collaboration' between psychological and criminological research (Hollin, 2002: 168). However, before we get carried away, we need also to consider the concerns of many criminological researchers that the current enthusiasm for cognitive behavioural practices could result in the further marginalization of 'traditional' programmes such as basic literacy and social skills. Moreover, commentators such as Pat Carlen have pointed to the problematic way in which many of the programmes that constitute the 'What works' movement are assessed and evaluated:

> The verity of the 'programmer's' claims to 'success' are often 'proven' by dubious self-report questionnaire evidence from prisoners that a programme 'works'—usually in terms of changing prisoners' understanding of their offending behaviour (Indeed, in view of all these 'programmers' and 'counsellors' claiming to have found the philosopher's stone in relation to changing offenders' behaviour, it is truly amazing that the prisons have not been emptied by now!). (Carlen, 2002: 120)

Another psychologically based treatment modality to have gathered momentum since the 1980s (although less so in the UK) is the idea of the *token economy*. Only feasible within the prison/institutional setting, the token economy is a system whereby, having complied with an agreed list of 'desirable behaviours' (for example, establishing courteous or positive relations with a member of staff, or completing a set of pre-arranged chores), offenders receive 'tokens' which they can then exchange for *reinforcers* such as confectionary, soft drinks, or visits home. The programmes are based on the basic principles of operant conditioning theory: that is, if all behaviour is learnt through 'reinforcement and punishment', then 'bad behaviour' can be 'unlearned' through 'lack of reinforcement', and good behaviour 'learned' via the process of 'positive reinforcement'. While early research into these schemes threw up some interesting findings (for example, Ayllon and Milan, 1979), subsequent research into the longer-term rehabilitative value of token economies has cast considerable doubt on the lasting benefits of this approach. Indeed, most studies concluded that token economies were only of real benefit when employed as a means of managing offenders within the institutional setting.

Psychology and police work

In the modern police force, psychology seems to play an ever-expanding role (see Reiser, 1973; Bull *et al.*, 1983; Ainsworth and Pease, 1987; Hollin, 1989: Chapter 5). For example, it is employed *inter alia* as a major tool in the following areas:

- the selection and training of police recruits;
- analysing the values, norms, and perceptive skills of police officers as they proceed through their careers;
- training and ultimately improving the way officers conduct interviews with witnesses (see for example, Geiselmen *et al.*, 1985 on the idea of the 'cognitive interview'; McGurk *et al.*, 1993);
- understanding the way police officers deal with work-related stressors such as complaints made against them by the public or being faced with a violent or dangerous confrontation (see, for example, Terry 1981);
- improving the ability of police officers to retrieve, recall, and interpret events that may have a bearing on a criminal investigation (see Clifford and Bull, 1978);
- improving interrogation techniques (Gudjonsson, 1992); conversational relations with uncooperative suspects (Mortimer and Shepherd, 1999); and the detection of lies and false statements (Vrij, 2008);
- understanding and improving officer decision-making in riot and firearm situations;
- and, of course, most famously (and perhaps most contentiously) as a key component in the construction of offender profiles.

Let us look briefly at some of these areas.

The complex and multifaceted nature of contemporary police work has ensured that many forces around the world increasingly rely upon the use of psychological testing in their selection processes. The goal behind using tests like the Minnesota Multiphasic Personality Inventory (MMPI) (see above) or other similar psychometric questionnaires is straightforward: either to 'screen out' candidates who exhibit unwanted characteristics such as deceitfulness or racism, or who by their responses to situational tests illustrate that they may be prone to high levels of stress or anxiety; or to 'screen in' candidates who exhibit desirable personality traits such as honesty or the ability to think calmly when confronted with potentially volatile situations (see Burbeck and Furnham, 1985; Yuille, 1986).

This type of psychological analysis of the personalities of police officers and their decision-making strategies does not stop at recruitment stage. The psychological scrutiny of police work has extended to virtually all aspects of policing—from the way officers negotiate their daily administrative duties, to how they cope with more challenging situations such as a hostage scenario or the violent death of a fellow officer (see for example, Fridell and Binder, 1992). Central to this field of study is the notion of the distinct 'police personality' (Evans *et al.*, 1992). This argument follows that, whether by 'predisposition' (that is, characteristics already present in the individual prior to joining the police), or via the process of 'socialization' (that is the compliance with and ultimate acceptance of the dominant norms and values already embedded within police culture), police officers hold a very different set of attitudes and values than the rest of the population. The psychological findings in this area are decidedly mixed. While there is some evidence to suggest that police officers in various countries do share higher than average instances of certain personality characteristics such as 'authoritarianism' (Colman and Gorman, 1982), 'conservatism' (Cook, 1977), and 'extraversion' (Gudjonsson and Adlam, 1983), there is no conclusive evidence to indicate whether or not these tendencies existed prior to joining the police or were subsequently learnt on the job. Consequently, psychologists conclude that there is thus much need for more detailed longitudinal studies to be carried out in this area.

Perhaps the most celebrated application of psychology within police work is the notion of the psychological *offender profile* (see Jackson and Bekerian, 1997; Ainsworth, 2001; Holmes and Holmes, 2002 for general introductions). Certainly the role of the 'offender profiler' has, over the last decade or so, become a major theme within the mass entertainment industry, featuring in a slurry of TV shows and hit movies such as *Manhunter* and *Red Dragon*. Consequently, the idea of the so-called 'mind hunter' now holds something of a fascination with both the general public, and a great many students new to academic criminology—a number of whom often labour under the misapprehension that an undergraduate degree in criminology could lead to a formal 'job' as an offender profiler. In reality, in the UK, there are currently only five full time 'profiling' positions, known as Behavioural Investigation Advisors (Webber, 2008; see also Gudjonsson and Copson (1997) for a guide to what profilers actually do):

> 'The best way to become a profiler is to become a chartered forensic psychologist or a chartered forensic psychiatrist, and then, after you've done that, wait ten years and then wait to be asked.' Dr Julian Boon, the British psychologist and offender profiler. (*The Real Cracker*, Channel 4 TV, 2001)

While definitions of profiling abound—each new book offering its own iteration—the following statement by Swanson *et al.* still stands as one of the clearest expositions:

> The purpose of the psychological assessment of a crime scene is to produce a profile, that is, to identify and interpret certain items of evidence at the crime scene which would be indicative of the personality type of the individual or individuals committing the crime. The goal of the profiler is to provide enough information to investigators to enable them to limit or better direct their investigations. (Swanson *et al.*, 1984: 700–1)

One of the key questions surrounding profiling concerns which crimes are suitable to be profiled (Pinizzotto, 1984; Stevens, 1995). While some maintain that profiling is only applicable in crimes that indicate a high degree of psychological abnormality (such as violent, sexual assaults or seemingly 'motiveless' murders), others claim that the practice could be extended to include a range of other crimes that do not necessarily involve personal contact or clinical disorders. Rider (1980), for example, has produced psychological profiles of the economic arsonist; Boon has applied profiling to various cases of extortion; while others have attempted to develop a profile of the political terrorist (see Strentz, 1988). This debate is interesting in the way that, to a certain degree, it mirrors the divide that exists more generally between the two major approaches to profiling: the crime scene analysis approach favoured by the FBI Investigative Support Unit (formerly the Behavioural Science Unit), and the 'investigative psychology' approach as favoured by the British psychologist David Canter and his various proponents (see Ainsworth, 2001; Chapters 6 and 7 for introductions to these different approaches).

Essentially, the FBI's approach is to cross reference crime scene evidence (such as levels of violence or mutilation, timing of the offence, body disposal/position, or levels of premeditation and so on) with established 'offender typologies' to determine a working personality profile of the perpetrator(s), thus enabling the authorities to better focus their investigations. However, whilst these typologies have considerable 'discriminatory power', they inevitably rely upon the 'subjective judgments' of the individual profiler (see Ressler and Shachtman, 1992). Such reliance upon individual intuition has led many to question the empirical value of this approach, with critics such as David Canter (1994) and Philip Jenkins (1994) asserting that individual hunches and rigid typologies based primarily on interviews with notoriously distrustful offenders are no basis for a systematic science.

The second approach is different in that it eschews the so-called informed speculation—or what David Canter has described as the 'flash of insight'—that is a key feature of the FBI approach. Instead it seeks to construct a situational/geographic profile of the offender(s) based on the assumption that the offender, like most people, acts consistently over time (the criminal consistency hypothesis). It is for this reason that the investigative psychology approach is not limited solely to crimes such as murder and rape, and that it can also be used to profile a whole range of more prosaic 'volume' crimes (see e.g. Canter and Alison, 2000). The goal of investigative psychology profiling, then, is to identify intelligible patterns between things like time and location of offence (Canter and Larkin, 1993; Canter and Gregory, 1994), factors surrounding victim selection and, if the victim survived (for example, non-homicidal rape cases), a close analysis of the offender's behaviour (Canter and Heritage, 1990), and speech patterns. Canter's goal, then, is the rigorous application of applied psychological principles to the study of offender profiling.

Canter's work was originally based on five aspects of the interaction between the victim and the offender—the five-factor model:

(1) *Interpersonal coherence* assumes that offenders will deal with their victims in a manner similar to the way they treat people in their day-to-day lives.

(2) *The significance of time and place* may provide analysts with clues about the offender's mobility and even his residence.

(3) *Criminal characteristics* are used by researchers and analysts to place offenders into broad categories, from which subcategories can be selected or developed.

(4) *Criminal career* is an assessment as to whether the offender may have engaged in criminal activity before and what type of activity it most likely was.

(5) *Forensic awareness* draws in part from Step 4 above, criminal career. It is an assessment of the scene and evidence to determine if the offender has any special knowledge of evidence gathering procedures used by the police.

Source: *Criminal Investigation* (Chapter 8) by Swanson, C.R., Chamelin, N.C., and Territo, I. (2002) New York: McGraw-Hill.

Despite optimistic noises about the growing 'scientific' rigour of offender profiling, significant doubts still remain about its empirical legitimacy—not least the problem of how one measures the accuracy and thus the ultimate value of profiles. Certainly it has proven difficult to establish reliable data on the overall effectiveness of personality profiles (see e.g. Alison *et al.*, 2003 and Alison and Kebbell, 2006), something due in no small part to the fact that there is considerable 'variability' in the way that profilers go about 'compiling' their profiles (Bekerian and Jackson, 1997: 212). Likewise, when a profile does appear to have been useful in facilitating an arrest, it can often prove difficult to ascertain exactly whether the success was due to the profile or was in fact simply the result of traditional police inquiries. Such scepticism, however, has done little to dampen down the popular appeal of offender profiling within the public's imagination. As Ainsworth suggests, the 'exclusive focus upon the type of profiling most often portrayed in the media is misleading and often unhelpful. The portrayal of "experts" with their intuitive minds and amazing powers of deduction may do little to educate the public as to the real role which profilers, or more correctly forensic psychologists, might play in crime investigation' (2001: 181).

Psychology and the courtroom

The last two decades have witnessed a growing mass of psychological research produced on various aspects of the legal process. A detailed account of what is often referred to as legal psychology is beyond the compass of this chapter. Instead I have chosen here to introduce three key areas of overlap between psychologists and those working in the legal profession: the pre-trial role of psychologists and psychiatrists in the assessment of mentally disordered offenders; the psychological research into eyewitness testimony; and the decision-making strategies and psycho-social dynamics of jurors/juries.

For more detailed summaries of the practical and theoretical work that constitutes the field of psycho-legal studies see Farrington *et al.* (1979); Lloyd-Bostock (1981); Müller *et al.* (1984); Losel *et al.* (1992); Bartol and Bartol (1994); Maguire *et al.* (2000); Kapardis (1997). For interesting commentaries on both the common ground and the various mutual problems that exist between psychology and law, see the review articles by Tapp (1976) and Monahan and Loftus (1982).

Mental disorder and criminal responsibility

The question of whether mentally abnormal—or, more accurately, 'mentally disordered'—offenders should be incarcerated in prisons and institutional facilities or cared for within the community is an incredibly complex and contentious one (see Peay, 2002 for an excellent summary). Such an extensively documented subject is not easily summarized, yet it would be remiss of me not to point out briefly the important, if at times indefinite (see Roberts, 1996), role played by psychiatric and psychological evidence in the legal processes surrounding mentally disordered offenders.

The key problem in this area is one of definition: mentally disordered offenders simply do not constitute a distinct group. As Jill Peay makes patently clear: ' "Mental disorder" ... is a term of acute terminological inexactitude. Definitions of mental disorder act like a concertina, expanding and contracting in order to accommodate different client groups with little or no coherence. Their mismatch frequently results in uncertainties and anomalies' (2002: 753). Inevitably, these definitional problems ensure that there is a ready need for the assessment expertise of the psychiatrist, not least in relation to *mens rea* (the notion of criminal intent) and the thorny question of whether or not the offender was in a sound psychological state of mind when committing the criminal act (Prins, 1986).

Such clinical testimony, along with various other courtroom roles played by the psychologist—such as the expert witness (see MacKay *et al.*, 1999) and the role of advisor to counsel—ensure 'that psychiatric and psychological evidence is increasingly prevalent and influential in criminal proceedings' (Peay, 2002: 766). Indeed, the wealth of empirical studies undertaken within psychology into abnormal behaviour (some of which have been discussed above), in tandem with the long history of predominantly medical diagnoses proffered by psychiatrists, have served as the catalyst for the modification of the law's approach to a number of issues concerning criminality and mental health—even to the point where forensic psychologists are occasionally asked to assist in making recommendations to Parliament.

The psychology of eyewitness memory

Many of us have witnessed an accident or a crime in the course of our daily round. Depending on its seriousness, we are often asked to recall the details of the event, whether by witness statement or police interview, or perhaps even via an artist's impression, photo-fit, or identity parade (Putwain and Sammons, 2002: 111–19). In every case, it is essential that the police and other authorities be provided with accurate and reliable information. To assist in this process, a body of work has emerged in recent years based on the psychology of eyewitness memory (and testimony) (see Clifford and Bull, 1978; Loftus, 1979; Gudjonsson, 1992; Ainsworth, 1998; Heaton-Armstrong *et al.*, 1999 for comprehensive overviews). The goal of these studies is to better understand the processes and problems associated with memory:

> Most people seem to think that our memory works passively like a video recorder. We can 'play back' information in exactly the same form that it was recorded, providing an accurate and objective record of the world. If our memory worked like this then eyewitness memory would not raise any issues. Witnesses would be able to provide accurate accounts of events with no loss of detail and identify suspects without any chance of error. Unfortunately, memory does not work like this. Witnesses can sometimes provide only hazy recollections of events, sometimes contradicting themselves and mistakenly identifying suspects. (Putwain and Sammons, 2002: 97)

By way of summary, one can state that the psychology of eyewitness memory focuses on three stages of the memory process: *acquisition*, *retention*, and *retrieval* (see Cohen, 1999):

(a) *Acquisition (or encoding) stage—the witnessing of the incident*: This stage can be affected by time factors like the length of time spent witnessing the event; the time of day when the event took place (studies show that witnesses recall more details about crimes that took place in daylight than at night); the nature of the incident witnessed (for example, the so-called 'weapon focus effect', where victims of gun-related crime often recall intimate details about the firearm, but very little about other aspects of the crime).

(b) *Retention (or storage) stage*: Research in this area has shown that this stage of the memory process can be affected by the duration of time that passes between witnessing a crime and the request to retrieve the details; and whether the witness discusses the events with others prior to giving evidence—the so-called contamination effect.

(c) *Retrieval stage—the process of giving evidence*: Studies around the retrieval of information have highlighted that memory can be affected by subtle changes in the way the questions are worded/inferred; or by the process of *expectation*, where witnesses often tend to report what they expected to see (on such points, see the large body of work by the psychologist, Elizabeth Loftus).

Psychology of the jury

As with other areas of the legal process, criminological psychology has had much to say about courtroom dynamics and, in particular, the way that juries arrive at their decisions (see Ainsworth, 2002: chapter 7 and Hollin, 1989: 161–71 for student-friendly introductions). Importantly, one should point out that because of the obvious inherent practical and ethical difficulties of studying actual jury decision-making strategies, much of the psychological research in this area is the product of experiments conducted on mock juries/trials. Summarized below are a few of the main research areas:

(a) *Eyewitness testimony*: research suggests that juries place considerable emphasis on eyewitness testimony when weighing their decisions—even when counsel has cast doubt on the veracity of the eyewitness (see Loftus, 1974).

(b) *The effects of pre-trial publicity on the jury*: experimental studies in this area have found clear evidence to suggest that juries are prejudicially affected by exposure to pre-trial publicity, a process that does not appear (in mock trials at least) to be offset by judicial instruction.

(c) *Levels of confidence displayed by witnesses*: perhaps unsurprisingly, research indicates that jurors tend to place most faith in witnesses who display a confident manner when testifying.

(d) *The extent to which jurors perceptions about defendant characteristics such as attractiveness, gender, race, age, status/qualifications and demeanour affect their decision-making* (see Fife-Schaw 1999).

(e) *Jury selection procedure*: In the United States the 'screening out' of jurors who counsel believe may have the 'wrong type of personality' to try a particular case has become a major area of psychological research (see Kassin and Wrightsman, 1983). Indeed, this practice of *voir dire* has become a specialism of certain trial lawyers— as illustrated most publicly in the trial of O.J. Simpson.

(f) *The social dynamics of how a group of 12 jurors arrive at their verdict.*

(g) *The problems associated with children's testimony.*

REVIEW QUESTIONS

1 What are the limitations of psychologically based rehabilitation programmes?
2 Is offender profiling a systematic science or just intuitive guesswork?
3 What psychological factors might affect eyewitness memory/testimony?

CONCLUSION

It is hoped that this chapter has provided the reader with a solid introduction to the various ways in which psychological research has contributed to our understanding of crime and the criminal justice system. On the way, I hope it has also helped to shatter some of the popular myths and 'media-created' assumptions about criminological psychology. In particular, my goal has been to dispel the erroneous conception of criminal psychology as a sort of 'secret science', wherein its practitioners are capable of identifying and detecting something as specific and observable as a psychologically distinct criminal mind or personality.

We have also seen that, despite the fact psychological research has frequently served as an important driver of change in society's attitudes and responses to crime, there still exists a slightly uneasy relationship between criminology and psychology. Certainly, we still find ourselves in a situation where researchers in one discipline are often working independently of those in the other. In part this is due to the disciplinary schisms that are an intrinsic part of the history of Western social sciences. That said, I have endeavoured to highlight some of the more productive interactions between these areas of ongoing research. It remains to be seen if a more conciliatory approach may lead to a greater consensus or convergence in 'scientific knowledge'.

QUESTIONS FOR DISCUSSION

1 What early behavioural characteristics/traits might be listed as predicators of violent crime? Do you agree with the statement that 'most psychological problems have their roots in some sort of trauma yet to be resolved'?

2 Think about some of your own characteristics, traits, and behaviours. To what extent have these behaviours been learned, either via 'positive reinforcement', 'differential association', or via the observation of cultural symbols and media 'role models'?

3 Is it really possible to empirically map something as complex as the human personality? Moreover, could you make the argument that psychology is not really a science?

4 What are the social and cultural factors behind the public's fascination with criminal psychology?

GUIDE TO FURTHER READING

Ainsworth, P. (2002) *Psychology and Policing*, Cullompton: Willan.
A good general introductory account of the way in which psychological principles and practices are applied to policing.

Bartol, C.R. and Bartol, A. M., (2005) *Criminal Behaviour: A Psychosocial Approach*, Upper Saddle River, NJ: Pearson Education.

An engaging and helpfully frequently updated introduction to the role of psychology in understanding criminal behaviour.

Blackburn, R. (1993) *The Psychology of Criminal Conduct: Theory, Research and Practice*. Chichester: Wiley.

A detailed and comprehensive account of many of the themes discussed in this chapter.

Hollin, C. R. (1989) *Psychology and Crime: An Introduction to Criminological Psychology*. London: Routledge.

Despite being over 15 years old, this book continues to provide the most comprehensive and accessible review of the literature on criminological psychology.

Kapardis, A. (1997) *Psychology and Law: A Critical Introduction*. Cambridge: Cambridge University Press.

A general introduction to psychology's various contributions to criminal justice and socio-legal studies.

Crighton, D. A. and Towl, G. J. (2008) *Psychology in Prisons,* Oxford: Blackwell.

'*Prison Psychology*' is a one-stop-shop for anyone interested in the application of psychological practice and theory within the prison setting.

Webber, C. (2008) *Psychology and Crime*. London: Sage.

Webber's *Psychology and Crime* provides a good overview of both these areas, as well as an analysis of the consequences of crime for victims, offenders, and wider society. It also includes a range of practical devices to support the learning process. The book is also useful in that it discusses some of the more thoughtful critiques of psychology by writers such as Nicholas Rose and Michel Foucault.

WEB LINKS

http://www.dialogical.net/psychology/notables.html

Link to the *Psychology World Wide Web Virtual Library*, a site that keeps track of psychology related websites.

http://www.psychology.org/

The Encyclopaedia of Psychology website.

http://www.psychologyinfo.com

A private US Internet resource run by Donald J. Franklin, Phd, that provides general and accessible information about the practice of psychology, see more specifically <http://www.psychologyinfo.com/forensic/>.

http://faculty.washington.edu/eloftus/

The homepage of Elizabeth Loftus, one of the leading researchers in eyewitness testimony and other aspects of legal psychology. The site has various links to her books and articles.

http://www.freudfile.org/

A website dedicated to the life and work of the psychoanalyst Sigmund Freud.

http://www.bps.org.uk/index.cfm

Website of the British Psychological Society.

REFERENCES

Abrahamson, D. (1944) *Crime and the Human Mind*. New York: Columbia University Press.

Adler, J.R. (2004) *Forensic Psychology: Concepts, Debates and Practice*, Cullompton: Willan.

Aichorn, A. (1925) *The Wayward Youth*. New York: Meridian Books.

Ainsworth, P.B. (1998) *Psychology, Law and Eyewitness Testimony*, Chichester: Wiley. Ainsworth, P.B. (2000) *Psychology and Crime: Myths and Realities*. London: Longman.

Ainsworth, P.B. (2001) *Offender Profiling and Crime Analysis*. Cullompton: Willan.

Ainsworth, P.B., and Pease, K. (1987) *Police Work*. London: Methuen.

Akers, R. (1985) *Deviant Behaviour: A Social Learning Approach*. Belmont, CA: Wadsworth.

Alexander, F., and Healy, W. (1935) *Roots of Crime*. New York: Knopf.

Alexander, F., and Staub, H. (1931) *The Criminal, The Judge and the Public*. New York: Macmillan.

Alison, L. and Kebbell, M. (2006) 'Offender profiling: limits and potential' in M. Kebbell and G. Davies, (eds) *Practical Psychology for Forensic Investigations and Prosecutions*. Chichester: Wiley.

Alison, L., Smith, M.D., and Morgan, K. (2003) 'Interpreting the accuracy of offender profiles', *Psychology, Crime and Law*, 9 (2) 185–95.

Allport, G.W. (1937) *Personality: A Psychological Explanation*. New York: Holt.

Andrews, D., Zinger, I., Hoge, R.D., Bonta, J., Gendreau, P., and Cullen, F.T. (1990) 'Does correctional treatment work? A clinically-relevant and psychologically informed meta-analysis', *Criminology* 28, 369–404.

Ayllon, T., and Milan, M. (1979) *Correctional Rehabilitation and Management: A Psychological Approach*. New York: Wiley.

Baars, B.J. (1986) *The Cognitive Revolution in Psychology*. New York: Guildford Press.

Bandura, A. (1973) *Aggression: A Social Learning Analysis*. Englewood Cliffs, NJ: Prentice Hall.

Bandura, A. (1977) *Social Learning Theory*. New York: Prentice Hall.

Bartol, C. R., (2002) *Criminal Behaviour: A Psychosocial Approach*, Upper Saddle River, NJ: Prentice hall.

Bartol, C.R. and Bartol, A.M. (1994) *Psychology and Law*. Pacific Grove, CA: Brooks/Cole.

Bartol, C.R. and Bartol, A. M., (2005) *Criminal Behaviour: A Psychosocial Approach*. Upper Saddle River, NJ: Pearson Education.

Bean, P. (1976) *Rehabilitation and Deviance*. London: Routledge.

Beirne, P. (1993) *Inventing Criminology*. Albany, NY: State University of New York Press.

Bekerain, D.A., and Jackson, J.L. (1997) 'Critical issues in offender profiling' in J.L. Jackson and D.A. Bekerian (eds) *Offender Profiling: Theory, Research and Practice*. Chichester: Wiley.

Blackburn, R. (1993) *The Psychology of Criminal Conduct: Theory, Research and Practice*. Chichester: Wiley.

Boon, J.C.W. (1997) 'The contribution of Personality Theories to psychological profiling' in J.L. Jackson and D.A. Bekerian (eds) *Offender Profiling: Theory, Research and Practice*. Chichester: Wiley.

Bowlby, J. (1944) 'Forty-four juvenile thieves: their characters and home life'. *International Journal of Psycho-Analysis*, 25: 19–52 and 107–27.

Bowlby, J. (1951) *Maternal Care and Mental Health*. World Health Organization: London: Her Majesty's Stationery Office.

Bowlby, J. (1973) *Separation: Anxiety and Anger. Volume 2 of Attachment and Loss*. London: Hogarth Press.

Boyle, G.J. Matthews, G., and Saklofske, D.H. (2008) *Handbook of Personality Measurement and Assessment* (Vols 1 and 2), Thousand Oaks, CA: Sage

Brown, C. (2006) *Cognitive Psychology*, London: Sage.

Bull, R.H.C., Bustin, B., Evans, P., and Gahagan, D. (1983) *Psychology for Police Officers*. Chichester: Wiley.

Burbeck, E., and Furnham, A. (1985) 'Police Officer Selection: a Critical Review of the Literature', *Journal of Police Science and Administration* 13: 58–69.

Canter, D. (1994) *Criminal Shadows*. London: Harper Collins.

Canter, D. and Alison, L. (2000) *Profiling Property Crimes*, Aldershot: Ashgate.

Canter, D., and Gregory, A. (1994) 'Identifying the Residential Location of Rapists' *Journal of the Forensic Science Society*, 34: 169–75.

Canter, D., and Heritage, R. (1990) 'A Multivariate Model of Sexual Offence Behaviour: Developments in Offender Profiling', *Journal of Forensic Psychiatry*, 1: 185–212.

Canter, D. and Larkin, P. (1993) 'The environmental range of serial rapists' *Journal of Environmental Psychology*, 13: 63–69.

Carlen, P. (2002) 'Carceral Clawback: The Case of Women's Imprisonment in Canada' (Review Essay) in *Punishment and Society*, 4:1 (January): 115–121.

Carlson, N.R. and Buskist, W. (1997) *Psychology: The Science of Behaviour*. Boston, Mass: Allyn and Bacon.

Cattell, R.B. (1965) *The Scientific Analysis of Personality*. Harmondsworth: Penguin.

Ciba Foundation (1996) *Ciba Foundation Symposium 194: Genetics of Criminal and Antisocial Behaviour*. Chichester: Wiley.

Clifford, B.R. and Bull, R. (1978) *The Psychology of Person Identification*. London: Routledge.

Cohen, G. (1999) 'Human memory in the real world' in A. Heaton-Armstrong, E. Shepherd and D. Wolchover (eds) *Analysing Witness Testimony*, London: Blackstone.

Coleman, C. and Moynihan, J. (2002) *Understanding Crime Data*. Buckingham: Open University Press.

Colman, A.M., and Gorman, L.P. (1982) 'Conservatism, dogmatism, and authoritarianism in British police officers', *Sociology* 16: 1–11.

Cook, P.M. (1977) 'Empirical survey of police attitudes', *Police Review* 85: 0142, 1078; 1114; 1140.

Copson, G. (1995) *Coals to Newcastle? Part 1: A Study of Offender Profiling*, London: Police Research Group Special Interest Series/Home Office.

Crick N.R., and Dodge, K.A. (1994) 'A review and reformulation of social information processing mechanisms in children's social adjustment', *Psychological Bulletin*, 115: 74–101.

Crick N.R. and Dodge, K.A. (1996) 'Social information processing in reactive and proactive aggression', *Child Development*, 67: 993–1002.

Evans, B.J., Coma, G.J. and Stanley, R.O. (1992) 'The police personality: Type A behaviour and trait anxiety', *Journal of Criminal Justice*, 20: 429–41.

Eysenck, H. (1977) *Crime and Personality*. London: Routledge.

Eysenck, H. (1984) 'Crime and Personality' in Müller, D.J. *et al.* (eds) *Psychology and Law*, Chichester: Wiley.

Eysenck, H. and Gudjonsson, G. (1989) *The Causes and Cures of Criminality* New York: Plenum Press.

Eysenck, M., and Keane, M. (1997) *Cognitive Psychology: A Student's Handbook*. Hove: Psychology Press.

Farrington, D.P., Hawkins, K., and Lyod-Bostock, S. (1979) *Psychology, Law and Legal Process*, London: Macmillan.

Feldman, P. (1993) *The Psychology of Crime*. Cambridge: Cambridge University Press.

Fife-Schaw, C. (1999) 'The influence of witness appearance and demeanour on witness credibility' in A. Heaton-Armstrong, E. Shepherd, and D. Wolchover, (eds) *Analysing Witness Testimony*. London: Blackstone.

Freud, S. (1935) *A General Introduction to Psychoanalysis*. New York: Liveright.

Fridel, L.A. and Binder, A. (1992) 'Police Officer Decision Making in Potentially Violent Confrontations', *Journal of Criminal Justice* 20: 385–99.

Furedi, F. (2004) *Therapy Culture*. London: Routledge.

Gadd, D., and Jefferson, T., (2007) *Psychosocial Criminology: an Introduction*, London: Sage.

Garland, D. (1994) 'Of crimes and criminals: the development of criminology in Britain' in M. Maguire, R. Morgan, and R. Reiner (eds), *The Oxford Handbook of Criminology*. Oxford: Oxford University Press.

Garland, D. (1997) '"Governmentality" and the Problem of Crime: Foucault, Criminology and Sociology' *Theoretical Criminology* 1(2): 173–214.

Garland, D. (2001) *The Culture of Control*. Oxford: Oxford University Press.

Geiselman, R.E., Fisher, R.P., MacKinnon, D.F., Holland, H.L. (1985) 'Eyewitness Memory Enhancement in Police Interview: Cognitive Retrieval Mnemonics Versus Hypnosis', *Journal of Applied Psychology* 70: 401–12.

Glueck, S., and Glueck, E. (1950) *Unravelling Juvenile Delinquency*, New York: Harper and Row.

Gudjonsson, G.H. (1992) *The Psychology of Interrogations, Confessions and Testimony*. Chichester: Wiley

Gudjonsson, G.H., and Adlam, K.R.C. (1983) 'Personality Patterns of British Police Officers' *Personality and Individual Differences* 4: 507–12.

Gudjonsson, G.H., and Copson, G. (1997) 'The role of the expert in criminal investigation' in J.L. Jackson and D.A. Bekerian (eds) *Offender Profiling: Theory, Research and Practice*. Chichester: Wiley.

Gudjonsson, G.H. and Hayward, L.R.C. (1998) *Forensic Psychology: A Guide to Practice*. London: Routledge.

Healy, W., and Bronner, A.F. (1936) *New Light on Delinquency and its Treatment*. New Haven, Conn: Yale University Press.

Heaton-Armstrong, A., Shepherd, E., and Wolchover, D. (eds) (1999) *Analysing Witness Testimony*. London: Blackstone.

HM Prison Service and the National Probation Service (2003) 'Driving Delivery: A strategic framework for psychological services in prisons and probation' HM Prison Service, NPS, London: Applied Psychology Group.

Hollin, C.R. (1989) *Psychology and Crime: An Introduction to Criminological Psychology*. London: Routledge.

Hollin, C.R. (1992) *Criminal Behaviour: A Psychological Approach to Explanation and Prevention*. London: Falmer Press.

Hollin, C.R. (2002) 'Criminological psychology' in M. Maguire *et al.* (eds) *The Oxford Handbook of Criminology* (3rd edn). Oxford: Oxford University Press.

Hollin, C.R. (2007) 'Criminological psychology' in M. Maguire *et al.* (eds) *The Oxford Handbook of Criminology* (4th edn). Oxford: Oxford University Press.

Holmes, R.M. and Holmes, S.T. (2002) *Profiling Violent Crimes: An Investigative Tool*. London: Sage.

Hudson, B. (1987) *Justice Through Punishment*. London: Macmillan.

Jackson, J.L. and Bekerian, D.A. (eds) (1997) *Offender Profiling: Theory, Research and Practice*. Chichester: Wiley.

Jeffrey, C.R. (1965) 'Criminal Behaviour and Learning Theory' *Journal of Criminal Law, Criminology, and Police Science*, 56: 294–300.

Jeffrey, C.R. (1994) 'Biological and Neuropsychiatric Approaches to Criminal Behaviour' in G. Barak (ed) *Varieties of Criminology: Readings from a Dynamic Discipline*. Westport, Connecticut: Praeger.

Jenkins, P. (1994) *Using Murder: The Social Construction of Serial Homicide*. New York: Aldine de Gruyter.

Jones, S. (2000) *Understanding Violent Crime*. Maidenhead: Open University Press.

Kapardis, A. (1997) *Psychology and Law: A Critical Introduction*. Cambridge: Cambridge University Press.

Kassin, S.M. and Wrightsman, L.S. (1983) 'The construction and validation of a juror bias scale', *Journal of Research in Personality*, 17, pp. 423–442.

Kemshall, H. (2001) *Risk Assessment and Management of Known Sexual and Violent Offenders: A Review of Current Issues*. Police Research Series Paper 140. HMSO.

Kemshall, H. (2003) *Understanding Risk in Criminal Justice*. Open University Press: Maidenhead.

Kline, P. (1984) *Psychology and Freudian Theory*. London: Methuen.

Kohlberg, L. (1969) 'Stage and sequence: the cognitive-developmental approach to socialization' in D.A. Gosling (ed) *Handbook of Socialization Theory and Research*. Chicago: Rand McNally.

Lamberts, K. and Goldstone, R. (2004) *Handbook of Cognition*, Thousand Oaks, CA: Sage.

Lanier, M., and Henry, S. (1998) *Essential Criminology*. Boulder, CO: Westview Press.

Lipsey, M.W., and Wilson, D.B. (1998) 'Effective intervention for serious youth offenders: a synthesis of research' in R. Loeber and D.P. Farrington (eds) *Serious and Violent Juvenile Offenders: Risk Factors and Successful Interventions*. Thousand Oaks, CA: Sage.

Lipsey, M.W., Landenberger, N.A., and Chapman, G.L. (2004) 'Rehabilitation: an assessment of theory and research' in C. Sumner, (ed.) *The Blackwell Companion to Criminology*, Oxford: Blackwell.

Little, A. (1965) 'Parental deprivation, separation and crime: a test on adolescent recidivists', *British Journal of Criminology* 5: 419–30.

Lloyd-Bostock, S. (1981) *Psychology in Legal Contexts: Applications and Limitations*. London: Macmillan.

Loftus, E.F. (1974) 'The Incredible Eyewitness', *Psychology Today*, December 117–19.

Loftus, E.F. (1979) *Eyewitness Testimony*. Cambridge: Harvard University Press.

Lorenz, K. (1966) *On Aggression*. New York: Harcourt Brace World.

Losel, F., Bender, D., and Bliesener, T. (eds) (1992) *Psychology and Law: International Perspectives*. Berlin: Walter de Gruyter.

McGuire, J. (1995) (ed) *What Works: Reducing Reoffending*. Chichester, John Wiley.

McGuire, J. (2000) *Cognitive Behavioural Approaches: An Introduction to Theory and Research*. London: HMSO.

McGuire, J. (2004) *Understanding Psychology and Crime*. Maidenhead: Open University Press.

McGuire, J., Mason, T., and O'Kane, A. (eds) (2000) *Behaviour, Crime and Legal Process: A Guide for Practitioners*, Chichester: John Wiley.

McGurk, B.J., Carr, M., and McGurk, D. (1993) *Investigative Interviewing Courses for Police Officers*, London: Home Office.

Mackay, R.D., Colman, A.M., and Thornton, P. (1999) 'The admissibility of expert psychological and psychiatric testimony' in A. Heaton-Armstrong, E. Shepherd, and D. Wolchover (eds) *Analysing Witness Testimony*, London: Blackstone.

Maruna, S., (2000) 'Criminology, desistance and the psychology of the stranger' in D. Canter and L. Alison (eds) *The Social Psychology of Crime: Groups, teams and Networks*, Aldershot: Ashgate.

Mednick, S.A., Moffitt, T.E., and Stack, S.A. (1987) *The Causes of Crime: New Biological Approaches*. Cambridge: Cambridge University Press.

Monahan, J., Loftus, E.R. (1982) 'The Psychology of Law', *Annual review of Psychology*, 33: 441–75.

Morrison, W. (1995) *Theoretical Criminology: from Modernity to Post-modernism*. London: Cavendish.

Morrison, W., (2004) 'Lombroso and the Birth of Criminological Positivism: Scientific Mastery or Cultural Artifice?' in J. Ferrell (*et al.*) *Cultural Criminology Unleashed*, London: GlassHouse.

Mortimer, A. and Shepherd, E. (1999) 'Frames of mind: schemata guiding cognition and conduct in the interviewing of suspected offenders', in A. Memon and R. Bull (eds) *Handbook of the Psychology of Interviewing*, Chichester: Wiley.

Müller, D.J., Blackman, D.E., and Chapman, A.J. (eds) (1984) *Psychology and Law*. Chichester: John Wiley and Sons.

Nietzel, M.T. (1979) *Crime and its Modification: A Social Learning Perspective*. New York: Pergamon.

O'Malley, P. (2004) *Risk, Uncertainty and Government*, London: GlassHouse.

O'Malley, P. (2008) 'Governmentality and risk' in J. O. Zinn (ed) *Social Theories of Risk and Uncertainty: An Introduction*, Oxford: Blackwell.

Peay, J. (2002) 'Mentally disordered offenders, mental health and crime' in M. Maguire *et al.* (eds) *The Oxford Handbook of Criminology* (3rd edn). Oxford: Oxford University Press.

Piaget, J. (1954) *The Construction of Reality in the Child*. New York: Basic Books.

Pinizzotto, A.J. (1984) 'Forensic psychology: criminal personality profiling' *Journal of Police Science and Administration*, 12: 32–40.

Prins, H. (1986) *Dangerous Behaviour, the Law and Mental Disorder*, London: Tavistock.

Putwain, D. and Sammons, A. (2002) *Psychology and Crime*. London: Routledge.

Raine, A. (1993) *The Psychopathology of Crime: Criminal Behaviour as a Clinical Disorder*. San Diego, CA: Academic Press.

Raynor, P. (2002) 'Community penalties: probation, punishment and "What Works"' in M. Maguire *et al.* (eds) *The Oxford Handbook of Criminology* (3rd edn). Oxford: Oxford University Press.

Redondo, S., Sanchez-Meca, J., and Garrido, V. (1999) 'The influence of treatment programmes on the recidivism of juvenile and adult offenders: a European meta-analytic review, *Psychology, Crime and Law*, 5: 251–78.

Reiser, M. (1973) *Practical Psychology for Police Officers*. Springfield, ILL: C.C. Thomas.

Ressler, R. and Shachtman, T. (1992) *Whoever Fights Monsters*. New York: St Martins.

Rider, A.O. (1980) 'The firesetter: a psychological profile', *FBI Law Enforcement Bulletin*, 49 (6): 6–13.

Roberts, P. (1996) 'Will you stand up in court? On the admissibility of psychiatric and psychological evidence', *Journal of Forensic Psychiatry* 7: 63–78.

Rotter, J.B., (1954) *Social Learning and Clinical Psychology*. Englewood Cliffs, NJ: Prentice Hall.

Rutter, M. (1972) *Maternal deprivation Reassessed*. Harmondsworth: Penguin.

Samenow, S.E. (1984) *Inside the Criminal Mind*. New York: Times Books.

Skinner, B.F. (1938) *The Behaviour of Organisms*. New York: Appleton.

Skinner, B.F. (1953) *Science and Human Behaviour*. New York: Macmillan.

Stevens, J.A. (1995) 'Offenders in profile' *Policing Today*, August.

Storr, A. (1970) *Human Aggression*, Harmondsworth: Penguin.

Strentz, T. (1988) 'A terrorist psychological profile', *Law Enforcement Bulletin*, 57: 11–18.

Sutherland, E. (1947) *Principles of Criminology*. Philadelphia: Lippincott.

Swanson, C.R., Chamelin, N.C., and Territo, L. (1984) *Criminal Investigation*. New York: McGraw-Hill.

Tapp, J.L. (1976) 'Psychology and law: an overture', *Annual review of Psychology*, 27: 359–404.

Taylor, I. (1999) *Crime in Context*. Cambridge: Polity.

Taylor, I., Walton, P. and Young, J. (1973) *The New Criminology*. London: Routledge.

Terry, W.C. (1981) 'Police Stress: the Empirical Evidence', *Journal of Police Science and Administration*, 9: 61–75.

Towl, G.J. (2004) 'Applied psychological services in Prisons and Probation' in J.R. Adler (ed) *Forensic Psychology*. Cullompton: Willan.

Valier, C. (2006) 'Psychoanalytic Criminology' in McLaughlin, E., and Muncie, J. (eds) *The Sage Dictionary of Criminology*. London: Sage.

Vennard, J., and Hedderman, C. (1998) 'Effective Interventions with offenders' in P. Goldblatt and C. Lewis (eds) *Reducing Offending: An Assessment of Research Evidence on Ways of Dealing with Offending Behaviour.* Home Office Research Study No. 187, London: Home Office.

Vrij, A. (2008) *Detecting Lies and Deceit: The Psychology of Lying and the Implications for Professional Practice,* Chichester: John Wiley and Sons.

Watson, J.B. (1913) 'Psychology as the behaviorist views it', *Psychological Review.*

Webber, C., (2008) *Psychology and Crime,* London: Sage.

Williams, K. (2004) Textbook on Criminology, Oxford: Oxford University Press.

Yochelson, S. and Samenow, S. (1976) *The Criminal Personality.* New York: Jason Aronson.

Yuille, J.C. (1986) 'Police Selection and Training: The Role of Psychology'. Dordrecht: Martinus Nijhoff.

7

Crime and culture

Jeff Ferrell

INTRODUCTION

In contemporary society, criminal practices and cultural dynamics intertwine within the experiences of everyday life. Many common forms of criminality emerge out of criminal and deviant subcultures that are themselves shaped by shared conventions of meaning, symbolism, and style. These subcultures in turn produce intensely collective experiences and emotions that define their members' identities and reinforce their members' marginal social status. At the same time those who undertake enterprises conventionally defined as 'cultural'—popular music, art photography, film, and television programmes— regularly confront public accusations of promoting criminal and delinquent behaviour, and at times face criminal justice actions ranging from police raids to obscenity trials. In today's society, all of these phenomena—criminal identities, popular controversies, crime control campaigns, experiences of crime victimization—are increasingly offered and displayed for public consumption. Moreover, all of these phenomena take shape within a larger mediated universe—a universe in which criminal subcultures appropriate popular images and create their own forms of mediated communication; political leaders launch public campaigns of criminalization and panic over crime and criminals; and everyday citizens go about consuming crime as news and entertainment. Because of this, criminologists today realize that a critical awareness of cultural dynamics is necessary if we are to understand even the most basic dimensions of crime and crime control.

BACKGROUND

Over the past few decades a number of criminologists have attempted to locate issues of crime and crime control within broader cultural dynamics. Generally speaking, culture refers to the shared symbolic environment in which the members of social groups operate—that is, their shared way of life within which everyday objects, practices, and interactions come to have meaning. In examining cultural dynamics, then, criminologists have investigated those features of everyday life that embody issues of symbolism and representation, and that therefore define the meaning of crime and crime control. During the 1970s, for example, the British 'Birmingham School' of cultural studies, and the radical theorists associated with the 'new criminology' (for example, Taylor *et al.*, 1973, see Chapter 4 above), began to examine the mass media's role in constructing understandings of criminal subcultures and in contributing to crime control. Stanley Cohen (2002 [1972/1980/1987]) documented the media's role in casting members of youth subcultures as folk devils who symbolize danger and threat, and allegedly embody larger social problems. Through this process, Cohen argued, the media and public officials are also able to construct moral panic around criminal events and identities, creating a sense among the public that a particular crime or criminal is in fact symptomatic of greater social harms. Similarly, Jock Young (1971) showed how the police, public officials, and the media operate in such a way as to 'amplify' the reality of a criminal problem, rather than to solve it; and others (Hall *et al.*, 1978) revealed how public officials and the mass media at times generate public concern over crimes and alleged crime patterns as a way of furthering their own political agendas.

During this same period, criminologists and sociologists in the United States began to investigate the dynamics of illicit subcultures, and to develop a criminological perspective that came to be known as labelling theory (see Chapter 4 in this volume, for more). In a groundbreaking book, Howard Becker (1963) demonstrated that the meaning of human activity is in large part defined by others' responses to it—in the case of crime and deviance, by the labelling of certain activities as criminal or deviant. Moreover, Becker showed, some groups and institutions hold far greater power than others to assign such labels; in many cases, it is the work of moral entrepreneurs—powerful individuals or groups pushing their own moral agenda—that results in activities being labelled criminal or deviant. Given this, Becker and others (Polsky, 1998 [1967]) argued, criminologists cannot simply rely on conventional, exterior understandings of groups labelled criminal or deviant; instead they must go inside the subcultures of such groups to explore the distinctive rituals, symbols, and practices that emerge there.

From the first, criminologists' attempts to account for the cultural context of crime and crime control have relied on a variety of disciplines. As the field of cultural studies emerged over the past few decades, so did criminologists' willingness to investigate often ignored dimensions of social life (popular culture, style and fashion, entertainment), and their understanding that these cultural dimensions were essential to the practice of crime and crime control. As criminologists developed labelling theory and similar perspectives on crime's contested meaning, they relied on the insights offered by sociology, and specifically on the sociological approach known as symbolic interactionism—an approach that understands social reality to be constructed out of ongoing, meaningful interaction among individuals and groups. In addition, criminologists interested in cultural dynamics came to see the essential role of the mass media in constructing everyday understandings of crime and crime control, and so borrowed perspectives from fields like media studies and film studies. In this sense, the study of crime and culture intertwines with subjects explored elsewhere in this volume—among them 'media images of crime', 'crime and everyday life', 'young people and crime', 'criminological theory', and 'surveillance'.

Today, criminological interest in the cultural dynamics animating crime and crime control is flourishing. In many criminological works, an inquiry into the traditional subject matter of criminology—crime, criminals, policing, courts—has now been recast as an inquiry into 'media images of' or 'representations of' these phenomena. Moreover, many criminologists have now moved beyond simply studying the mass media's role in creating images or accounts of crime, and to an understanding that crime, crime control, and the media are endlessly entangled in a series of mediated loops and spirals (Ferrell, Hayward, and Young, 2008; Manning, 1998) whereby each phenomenon reflects and embodies images of the other. Criminological understandings of criminal subcultures are also developing. Following the lead of early researchers (Hebdige, 1979), criminologists continue to explore style as the symbolic medium through which illicit subcultures define and display their identities, crime control agents respond to the subculture's public presence, and mass media institutions appropriate and portray subcultural images. Continuing to investigate also the internal meanings of these subcultures, criminologists embrace their own first-hand understanding of criminality, their own sense of criminological *verstehen* (see below, and Ferrell, 1997), as they attempt to penetrate the situated logic and emotion of these worlds. In this way, for example, they are able to make sense of moments of illicit edgework (Lyng, 1990) in which subcultural skills and values become manifest in the experience of extreme risk. In fact, current criminological interest in the cultural and subcultural dynamics of crime and crime control is such that a new form of criminological research and theory has now evolved: cultural criminology (Ferrell, Hayward, and Young, 2008; Ferrell and Sanders, 1995; Presdee, 2000; Ferrell *et al.*, 2004; Hayward and Young, 2004, 2007; also Chapter 4).

Crime and culture

Among the many intersections of culture and crime, five in particular offer significant insights into the complex cultural dynamics within which the practice of crime and crime control takes shape.

Subculture and style

Much of the illicit behaviour that criminologists study is organized and defined by criminal subcultures. Criminal subcultures provide repositories of skill from which subcultural members learn the techniques essential to successful criminal conduct, whether they be the skills needed for efficient automobile theft, surreptitious embezzlement, or effective violence. Perhaps more importantly, these subcultures create a collective ethos, a fluid set of values and orientations that define their members' criminal behaviour as appropriate, even honourable; in this way criminal subcultures also function as countercultures, ways of life that oppose and defy conventional understandings of legality, morality, and achievement. In most cases, these subcultural orientations come to be embodied in the subculture's distinctive style—subtle conventions of dress and comportment, distinctive linguistic codes often incomprehensible to the outsider, and everyday rituals designed to mark the boundaries of subcultural membership. Given this constellation of skills, attitudes, and styles, criminal subcultures operate as much more than proximities of personal association among their members. They become symbolic communities, communities of shared meaning that define for their members the nature of criminality perhaps more than does the criminal act itself.

Understood in this way, the powerful pull of criminal subcultures operates in ways that are as much cultural as interpersonal. Dressed in clothes that embody a host of illicit sartorial codes, fluent in the nuances of subcultural argot, wrapped in the defiant assurance of an 'outlaw' identity, a street gang member or race track hustler maintains subcultural membership even when no others are around; the subculture surrounds its members even when they wander from it. At the extreme, this cultural dynamic suggests to criminologists that criminal subcultures can operate effectively even when their members seldom if ever come face-to-face; this dynamic in turn suggests to those concerned with controlling criminal subcultures and their dissemination that the task will not be as simple as arresting one member or another.

In the US, for example, hip hop graffiti writers have for many decades operated within conventions of style so carefully constructed that writers could effectively communicate status and meaning by way of 'tags' and murals even when they had never met, and could therefore know and understand one another as members of a shared urban subculture even without direct association. More recently, transcontinental freight trains have emerged as the preferred medium for hip hop tags and murals, and with them an illicit subculture that now stretches from New York City to Los Angeles, communicating, solidifying—even recruiting—by means of dislocated subcultural symbolism (Ferrell,

Figure 7.1 Early hip hop graffiti: New York City subway train, c. 1970. The Crown above the COCO signifies Coco's claim to be a king in the emerging hip hop graffiti subculture

Source: © Hulton Archive

1998). At the other end of the technological spectrum from rusty freight trains and spray paint cans, illicit cyber-communities now operate within a welter of fabricated identities and stylized language practices that form powerful, encompassing associations among strangers around the world. In fact, it is just this symbolic construction of the subculture itself, this profound lack of face-to-face interaction, that keeps on-line communities of child pornographers or prostitutes so impenetrable to outside authorities (Jewkes, 2003; Jenkins, 2001).

And yet legal authorities themselves increasingly understand these cultural dynamics as well, and so turn to these very subcultural symbols and styles in their attempts to prevent or control criminal activity. Watching for the emergence of new linguistic or sartorial styles among marginal groups, instituting surveillance programmes based on subtleties of appearance or comportment, constructing official 'gang lists' on the basis of young people's sport shoes and tattoos, reading gang graffiti for signs of impending trouble, legal and political authorities contribute their own complex of meanings to these subculture styles and symbols, and so themselves come to participate in this ongoing cultural interplay. In doing so, they raise a host of troubling questions regarding definitions of crime and legitimate measures of crime control—questions that are essentially *cultural* in nature. Is it appropriate for probation officers to violate the probation of a juvenile offender on the basis of the juvenile's new 'gang' tattoo or choice of 'gang-related' attire (Miller, 1995)? Is 'racial profiling' or 'terrorist profiling' in the US and Great Britain an appropriate response to subtle displays of criminal affiliation, or a form of institutionalized racism based on unfair stereotypes? Most broadly, in their attempts to respond to the symbolism and style of marginal subcultures, do legal authorities in effect criminalize the lives and activities of those on the margins by defining their styles as de facto indicators of criminality?

However powerful—or appropriate—is the response of legal authorities to the styles of illicit subcultures, there is another external response that is likely to have a more powerful effect, and along the way to forge yet another link between crime and culture. Increasingly, clothing manufacturers, advertisers, and other member of the corporate economy recognize that the illicit styles of gang members, graffiti writers, street hustlers, pimps, and other 'outlaws' lend a degree of street legitimacy to fashion, music, and other commodities, especially when these commodities are designed for sale to young people (see Hayward, 2004: 166–73 for more on this 'commodification of transgression'). Because of this, corporations carefully appropriate the symbolism and style of illegal subcultures, blending these styles into new product lines, and incorporating these styles in sophisticated marketing campaigns designed to promote new products. Losing ground to Japanese motorcycles and on the brink of bankruptcy, Harley-Davidson Motorcycles, for example, reinvented its product line, building the previously illicit, after-market styles of the outlaw biker subculture into the motorcycles produced in the Harley-Davidson factory, and promoting these newly stylized motorcycles through corporate advertising campaigns; as a result, the company was reborn as a viable, profitable, and high-profile icon of leisure consumption (Lyng and Bracey, 1995). Similarly, as Heitor Alvelos (2004) has recently shown, corporate marketers in the UK and elsewhere have begun to copy the symbolism, style, and placement of street graffiti—to the point that the legal, street-level graffiti of corporate advertising campaigns is at times indistinguishable from the illegal, street-level graffiti of hip hop graffiti writers and other illicit artists (see also Snyder, 2009). In this way, corporate marketers, like legal authorities, add yet another layer of cultural meaning to the illicit codes of criminal subcultures—and in doing so, often do more to undermine the subcultural integrity of these codes, and to sanitize their illicit purpose, than the legal authorities themselves.

REVIEW QUESTIONS

1 By displaying illicit styles, do members of criminal subcultures 'invite' legal surveillance and control? Are legal authorities justified in using these styles as indicators of criminality? If so, in what circumstances, and with what limitations?

2 Is it appropriate for major corporations to market the styles of illegal subcultures to young people and others? Should parents or school authorities be concerned if young people begin wearing clothes, or using products, associated with criminal subcultures?

Edgework, adrenalin, and criminological *verstehen*

While the lives of those engaged in criminal activity are often shaped by their stylized subcultural identities, and by the response of others to these identities, a recent body of cultural criminological research has shown that they are often shaped by some-thing else as well: intensely emotional and intensely meaningful collective experiences (Katz, 1988; Lyng, 1990; Ferrell, 1996; Hayward, 2004 Chapter 5; Jackson-Jacobs, 2004). In investigating a wide range of criminal activities, from street fighting to fire setting, criminologists have found that criminals often embrace the extreme risk and danger that accompanies their criminal activity; rather than shying away from such risk, or see-ing it only as an unfortunate consequence of their illicit occupations, they come to enjoy it—to the point that they regularly report being 'addicted' to the dangerous experiences, the 'adrenalin rushes', of criminality.

Often outsiders misunderstand this enjoyment of extreme risk as embodying an out-of-control, haphazard orientation on the part of wildly violent criminals; others assume that this enjoyment of danger must constitute some sort of nihilistic death wish on the part of those disconnected from conventional morality. In fact, criminological research shows, it is neither. Instead of seeking death in these moments of extreme risk, criminals seem to be seeking a more vivid version of life itself, an experience that transcends the conventions of everyday living. And rather than simply being the by-products of out-of-control individual behaviour, these 'edgework' experiences seem clearly to embody the work of criminal subcultures, integrating as they do illicit subcultural skills with moments of meaningful danger. In fact, it is precisely these subcultural skills and atti-tudes that define the allure of edgework experiences; in such moments the countercul-tural values of the subcultural are confirmed at the level of existential experience, the value of the subculture's illicit skills now measured, and proven, against the risk of vio-lent failure. After all, a burglar's skills matter most when silently jemmying open a win-dow, a graffiti writer's most when spray painting a midnight alley wall. Likewise, BASE jumper's carefully honed subcultural skills matter most when they are executing the sort of illegal, low-level parachute jumps that define their subculture. 'It isn't a death wish like everybody thinks it is,' reports one young woman BASE jumper. 'You know you're alive when you do this, every sense is working...You want to live so you can do it again' (in Ferrell, 2002: 85).

The regularity with which members of illicit subcultures talk of 'adrenalin rushes' and dismiss notions of a 'death wish' suggests yet another cultural dimension of these experi-ences: their meaning is constructed not only out of shared subcultural skills, but out of shared subcultural language. As criminological researchers have found time and again, subcultural members define the nature and importance of these experiences by talk-ing about them—and by talking and thinking about them within a shared subcultural argot, or slang, that both defines particular experiences as unique to the subculture, and closes the meaning of these experiences to outsiders. In the seconds surrounding a moment of edgework, later in the evening over a pint, or years later as part of subcul-tural lore, the powerful meanings of edgework are constructed and reconstructed as they are negotiated within the linguistic structure of the subculture. As the criminologist Donald Cressey (1954) once argued in regard to 'compulsive' crimes, what appear to be ephemeral, individual experiences in this sense remain soundly collective and thor-oughly cultural, defined as they are within shared 'vocabularies of motive'. And as with subcultural style, the collective conceptualization of edgework experiences ensures that an individual caught up in a moment of illicit excitement operates within the dynamics of the subculture, even when no one is there to notice.

At the same time existentially invigorating and subculturally meaningful, these edge-work experiences provide further evidence for the powerful 'seductions' of crime (Katz, 1988); in them criminologists begin to glimpse a dynamic so powerful that criminals consistently characterize it as 'addictive'. The prevalence of these edgework experiences also suggests a significant critique of certain criminological theories. They cast doubt on 'rational choice' and 'routine activity' theories that presume a sort of mechanistic, acquisitive rationality underlying criminal acts and situations; instead, these edgework experiences reveal criminal acts animated by risk and excitement, and criminal situations sought after for their seductions (Young, 2003). More broadly, as Katz (1988) has argued, the vivid, seductive experiences of crime's 'foreground' call into question the usual assumption that criminological theories can account for crime by focusing primarily on 'background' or structural factors such as social class or ethnic inequality. While these background factors certainly remain interwoven with criminal acts, as do the existing codes and conventions of various criminal subcultures, they seem clearly to take on meaning inside the act itself, rather than simply 'causing' it in some exterior, deterministic fashion. Finally, the specific dynamics of these edgework experiences undermine—both conceptually and practically—crime control or crime deterrence models based on aggressive policing strategies. As the catalyst that brings these edgework experiences to life, risk is essential to their subcultural meaning and vitality—and so, as illicit edgeworkers regularly report, increased risk of legal apprehension or harassment generally amplifies, rather than diminishes, the adrenalin-fuelled seductions of the criminal experience.

To the extent that moments of edgework and subcultural excitement shape the reality of criminality, conventional criminological methods of research must be reconsidered as well. Methods that simply accumulate crime statistics or tabulate survey responses cannot penetrate the subcultural meanings of these vivid foreground experiences; instead, methods are needed that can situate criminologists as close as possible to the immediacy of criminal situations and events. Because of this, criminologists concerned with the dynamics of crime and culture, and especially those interested in investigating subcultural dynamics, often utilize field research or ethnographic methods that place criminologists, again as best as possible, inside the actual lives and experiences of criminals (see for example Ferrell and Hamm, 1998). Pushing this methodology further still, these criminologists often pursue the goal of achieving criminological *verstehen*—a deep, even emotional understanding of the dangerous experiences that define criminality—as a way of gaining criminological insight unavailable to others. Such a methodology of course challenges conventional notions of research 'objectivity', and of criminology as a 'social science' of crime and crime control; it also raises for criminologists difficult issues of morality and legality. Still, if the meaning of crime is largely constructed in the immediacy of its experience, how else are criminologists to investigate and understand it?

Culture as crime

If by 'culture' we mean the lived world of images and symbols, the complex symbolic environment of everyday life, then in contemporary society we can identify certain individuals and groups especially involved in constructing this cultural environment: artists, musicians, photographers, film makers, and television directors, for example. Some of these individuals and groups create forms of culture traditionally thought of as 'high culture', such as gallery and museum art, and fine art photography. Others produce television programmes, commercial films, popular music, and other cultural forms more commonly thought of as 'popular culture'. No matter what the cultural realm in which they operate, though, these individuals and groups remain vulnerable to having their cultural enterprises, and their cultural products, redefined as criminal. Time and again, fine art photographers whose work focuses on nude figures or sexually explicit subjects face accusations of producing not art, but obscenity and pornography. Musicians, producers, distributors, and retailers involved with musical forms as different as punk, heavy metal, and rap are regularly accused of disseminating obscene lyrics, and of influencing young listeners to commit assault, murder, or suicide. In the same way, television programmes, popular films, even animated cartoons are often blamed for inciting crime and delinquency, and for spinning off 'copy-cat crimes' in imitation of their content. In some cases these accusations of criminality simply circulate in the public realm; in other cases legal charges are brought, arrests made, and convictions gained. In either case, moral entrepreneurs and others work to reconstruct cultural enterprises as criminal endeavours, to reconceptualize culture as crime.

Two threads often run through theses cases, linking the criminalization of cultural forms as different as museum photography and rap music. First, those attempting to connect cultural products to crime often operate from a simplistic assumption: that cultural products directly induce imitative behaviour in those exposed to them, causing a 'copy-cat' reflex among listeners or viewers. In fact, cultural criminologists argue, this reductionist assumption is inadequate on two fronts: it mistakenly reduces the complex workings of the cultural milieu to some sort of simple triggering mechanism, and it likewise reduces the complexities of human perception to a model of robotic reaction. Certainly the swarm of mediated images that saturates everyday life shapes to some degree the frameworks of perception and understanding within which individuals operate; in contemporary society, the sheer breadth of the mediated environment all but ensures that it will play a part in individuals' efforts to make sense of the world around them. This very breadth, though, also ensures that individuals will sort and assemble a remarkable range of cultural influences in constructing their values and behaviours, rather than responding unthinkingly to a single image or lyric. In this sense, the meanings and effects of cultural products reside less in the products themselves than in the interactions that surround them; their potential links to crime and delinquency are less predetermined than they are negotiated. And, to the extent that these negotiations take place within various criminal and non-criminal subcultures, yet another layer of ambiguous cultural meaning is added to the world of mediated information.

That complexities of cultural meaning and perception would be ignored in debates over culture's criminal or criminogenic (that is, crime-causing) properties is not surprising in light of a second thread running through these debates: their role within heated 'culture wars' over morality, sexuality, and ethnicity. In the great majority of cases, accusations linking cultural products to crime have emerged within larger political battles and specifically as part of campaigns against cultural outsiders of one sort or another. This pattern becomes evident when one notices the identities of the accusers and of those accused. Cultural reactionaries, religious fundamentalists, and other conservative moral entrepreneurs regularly identify as obscene the works of gay photographers and of feminist, lesbian, and gay performance artists, and especially those works which allegedly embody anti-religious images. In both Great Britain and the US, producers and performers of politically progressive punk music face police raids, confiscation of records and promotional materials, and charges of obscenity and distribution of harmful materials to minors. Rap musicians and producers, even record store owners stocking rap records, confront arrests, obscenity convictions, and carefully organized police boycotts that in many ways reproduce racialized condemnations of 'race music' styles like jazz and rock 'n' roll in earlier decades. In all of these cases, accusations of criminality tend to emerge not from individual outrage, but as part of well-funded and highly publicized campaigns. And while some of these campaigns have in fact resulted in criminal charges and convictions, they in many ways succeed even when they do not. Publicizing allegations of criminality, publicly accusing artists and musicians of criminal conduct, these campaigns seem designed primarily to criminalize marginal groups at the level of image and perception, and thus to contribute to their ongoing cultural stigmatization.

Operating in this way, these campaigns of pointed criticism against particular cultural producers, these organized moral panics over the criminogenic effects of everyday culture, embody a revealing irony: they don't stand apart from everyday culture so much as they participate in it. Such campaigns are themselves cultural enterprises, occupying the same mediated terrain as those they critique. Artists, photographers, and musicians work to create one set of cultural meanings around their work, defining it in terms of aesthetics, enjoyment, or social progress; those who accuse them of criminal behaviour work to create an alternative set of meanings around issues of obscenity, crime, and delinquency. In this sense both groups contribute to the always-contested debate over crime and culture, and both groups do so through the same channels: press conferences and press releases, the distribution of evocative images, the organization of marketing campaigns and media coverage. Caught up in a series of self-reinforcing media loops and spirals, both groups construct their own images, and offer for public display images of the other's images, continually blurring as they do the boundaries separating culture from crime.

REVIEW QUESTIONS

1 If, in a court trial, the claim was made that the crimes of the accused had been caused by exposure to violent media images—that is, that the accused had simply committed a 'copy-cat' crime, and was therefore not personally culpable—what evidence could be presented to support this claim? What evidence could be presented to rebut this claim?

2 What guidelines might be developed to balance concerns for the potential harm of violent media imagery with concerns for freedom of speech and expression? Should mediated expression be limited by its potential harm?

Crime, culture, and public display

Producing and disseminating countless images of crime, criminal justice, and victimization, the mass media put crime issues on display for everyday public consumption. But this is not the only way in which crime issues are displayed in contemporary society; they are also displayed as part of everyday social activities and interactions, and as part of the built environment within which social life goes on.

While crime is conventionally thought of as a secretive activity conducted away from public view, residual indicators of criminality often remain available for public scrutiny. Abandoned automobiles stripped of their parts, broken locks and unhinged gates, gang or hip hop graffiti on city walls, tyre tracks across a village green—all suggest something of criminal activity, and so become symbols that various groups and individuals 'read' for signs of safety or threat. In fact, one of today's most prominent and politically influential perspectives on crime is based on an alleged understanding of this interplay between crime and public display. According to the model of 'broken windows' (Wilson and Kelling, 2003 [1982]), broken windows and other public displays of petty criminality signal a lack of surveillance or concern, in this way offering a symbolic invitation to more serious forms of criminality, and ultimately setting in motion a downward spiral of criminal disorder. Utilized as the justification for aggressive street policing strategies against beggars, homeless populations, graffiti writers, and others who commit minor but visible 'quality of life' crimes—so as to stop this downward spiral before it starts— this 'broken windows' thesis has significantly altered the politics and policing of the contemporary city.

From the perspective of cultural criminologists, however, the popularity of the 'broken windows' thesis far exceeds its usefulness as an accurate, scholarly understanding of crime and public display. Certainly 'law-and order' politicians have found it a convenient foundation for their focus on the alleged criminality of marginal urban populations—but in this same context, cultural criminologists have found 'broken windows' to be an inadequate and politically distorted analysis of crime and culture. Arbitrarily assigning a series of abstract meanings to public displays and to their imagined audiences, the 'broken windows' thesis in fact misses the complex nuances of meaning and perception that link culture and crime. Depending on a particular situational context, for example, a building's broken windows can offer, instead of an invitation to criminality, any number of alternative meanings to any number of audiences: evidence of a personal grudge, problems of absentee ownership, anticipated urban development, even

Figure 7.2 Hip hop graffiti mural, Vancouver, Canada, 2008
Source: © Jeff Ferrell, 2008

informal community accommodation of the homeless. Likewise, urban graffiti can suggest to various groups a remarkable range of meanings, among them pride in ethnic heritage, an informal demarcation of drug sale territories, even the substitution of a symbolic status system for interpersonal street violence. None of these symbolic meanings is self-evident or assured; each is negotiated day-to-day amidst the swirl of urban populations.

Because of this, accurately understanding public display as a key nexus between crime and culture would seem to require attentiveness and long-term emersion in everyday situations—not abstract generalizations about 'broken windows'.

Similarly complex issues emerge in considering public displays of crime control and crime prevention. Motivated by fear of crime, desperate to guard themselves against it, individuals at times display their fear for all to see, buffering their homes with 'No Trespassing' signs and their front gardens with displays of surveillance that coalesce into what Mike Davis (1992) has described, in a study of Southern California suburbia, as 'angry lawns'. Similarly, the sorts of 'target hardening' strategies often recommended as effective crime prevention sometimes operate as contradictory symbolic practices, with newly spiked fences, well-trained guard dogs, and expensive CCTV cameras suggesting that in this location there is indeed something worth protecting—and worth stealing. At a larger level, criminal justice agencies increasingly embrace the policing of public space through environmental design—that is, through the integration of symbolic control structures into public settings. Arguing that such structures can signal surveillance and control while at the same calming fear of crime, environmental designers utilize thorny bushes, CCTV cameras (whether activated or not), specially designed fences and park benches, and permanently elevated compartments (in which a police officer may or may not be hiding) to quite literally build displays of social control into the public environment. In doing so, of course, they at times transform policing from a process of human interaction into a display of symbolic control, and reconstruct open public space as significantly less open and public (Ferrell, 2002).

Perhaps the most evocative of contemporary public displays are those symbolizing the collective sorrow surrounding crime victimization and violence. The death of a celebrity often generates a broad and largely spontaneous public display of collective grief, with cascades of flowers, condolence notes, and photographs affixed to fences or piled in doorways; the massive accumulation of flowers in front of Kensington Palace following the death of Princess Diana stands as a particularly striking example. High-profile crime events and public tragedies likewise elicit countless public commemorations of loss and sorrow, as with the thousands of informal public shrines that emerged in Manhattan following the 9/11 bombings of the World Trade Center, or the informal memorials that filled London's Russell Square after the 7/7 bombings (Young, 2007). At other times, public memorials emerge in response to acts of victimization seen by the public as particularly egregious, or in the midst of moral panic over a perceived pattern of victimization; shrines and memorials dedicated to abducted or murdered children often develop in this context. Throughout the US, Mexico, Greece, Italy and other countries, friends and family members likewise build shrines to those lost to automotive violence; such shrines are often constructed at the location of a deadly automotive wreck, at times even incorporating pieces of the wreckage along with flowers, photographs, and personal memorabilia (Ferrell, 2003). In all of these cases, such public memorials forge yet another link between crime and culture as they help construct the collective meaning of crime victimization, begin to create new symbolic identities for the victims of crime, and organize opportunities for ongoing, shared public commemoration.

Faced with the proliferation of these public memorials, criminal justice agencies have developed a variety of responses. Some have moved to prohibit such memorials on the grounds that they encourage illegal public gatherings and pose a distracting danger to motorists and other members of the public. Other agencies have attempted to regulate and standardize the memorials, setting limits on their size, location, and temporal duration, and working to bring their construction and maintenance under the jurisdiction of the agencies themselves. Still other criminal justice and governmental agencies have enacted procedures to protect these informal public memorials on the grounds that they often embody significant cultural traditions, and offer important opportunities for the expression of collective grief. Yet as different as they are, all of these official responses affirm the importance of these memorials, and of other public displays, as components of the symbolic environment within which we makes sense of crime, victimization, and justice.

REVIEW QUESTIONS

1 As you move about your everyday environment, what symbols of crime, crime control, or crime victimization do you see? How do you interpret these in terms of your own sense of safety or vulnerability?

2 How might a person's interpretations of public displays associated with crime or crime control vary based on that person's gender, sexual orientation, social class, age, ethnic origin, or personal experiences?

Media, crime, and crime control

In contemporary society the mass media provide the preponderance of the public's information on crime and crime control (see also Chapter 8). In order to understand public support for particular crime control policies, or public concerns over everyday criminality, then, the various media of mass communication must be examined. When they are examined, a significant pattern emerges: the mass media transmit not only information, but emotion. In both news and entertainment programming, the mass media regularly overemphasize the threat posed by street-level crime in comparison to the harms of corporate criminality; focus on the criminal victimization of strangers rather than the dangerous intimacies of domestic or family conflict; and overplay violent criminality in comparison to more pervasive, non-violent property crime. While these particular patterns of sensationalism result in some part from political manipulation of the media, and from the media's reliance on official sources, they seem to be driven in large part by the media's ongoing desire to build television ratings, sell newspapers and magazines, and increase profits. Yet whatever their source, the cumulative effect of these distortions remains soundly political; they regularly amplify and misdirect public fears over crime, set inappropriately punitive public agendas regarding crime control, and ready the public for the next moral panic over crime and criminality.

In this sense contemporary media do not simply report, with greater or lesser accuracy, on existing crime and crime control issues; instead, the media actively participate in constructing the social reality of these very issues (see Hayward and Presdee, 2009).

Politicians and moral entrepreneurs utilize the media to deploy evocative crime imagery as they work to consolidate political power or criminalize marginal groups. Policing agencies increasingly coordinate their operations with those of existing media institutions, and develop their own channels of mediated communication and surveillance, in the interest of gaining public support, recruiting new members, and apprehending criminals. At the same time, everyday policing operations themselves become fodder for 'reality' television programming, with televised police chases and high-profile sting operations presented in the form of morally charged entertainment. All the while, commercial films, popular music, and nightly television programming offer a swarm of crime and crime control characterizations, by turns celebrating and condemning the activities of outlaws, police officers, and judges. In the end, this ongoing stream of dramatic imagery accumulates into a vast cultural stockpile, a complex of images, symbols, and meanings by which individuals and groups come to make sense of crime, violence, and crime control. In doing so, they participate in a looping, self-fulfilling process by which symbols of criminality or images of violence refer not so much to external experience as to other images and symbols, as each new mediated moment references earlier mediated meanings and understandings (Ferrell, Hayward, and Young, 2008).

Not surprisingly, those occupying criminal or criminalized worlds also participate in this endless process of mediated negotiation. Street gangs, skinheads, hip hop graffiti writers, and other groups maintain websites designed to present their own understandings of crime and society. Urban skateboarders shoot illicit videos as they defiantly trespass on private property or skate across the very physical barriers designed to control them. Outlaw BASE jumpers wear helmet-mounted video cameras to record their own illegal parachuting from bridges and buildings, circulating these videos within the BASE jumping underground, and often selling them to mass media outlets as a way of raising funds for the next illegal jump (Ferrell, Milovanovic, and Lyng, 2001). Within progressive political groups, videographers and 'camcordistas' play an increasingly important role, as they employ video cameras to document police misconduct during street protests and to create their own alternative news footage. In this sense, as McRobbie and Thornton (1995) have noted, illicit groups are not always passive victims of the moral panic constructed around them; with the emergence of new media technologies, they are at times able to create their own images of crime and crime control, to counter the construction of moral panic, and to turn mediated crime campaigns to their own ends. In this way both the mass media and the micromedia of marginal or criminal groups engage in an endless appropriation and reinvention of each other's images and understandings.

This investigation of mediated meaning as an essential component of crime and crime control continues the refinement of key concepts such as 'moral panic' and 'moral entrepreneurship'; it also expands the conceptual range of labelling theory. In the contemporary world, the labelling process—that is, the labelling of certain individuals, groups, and activities as criminal—can be seen operating not only among individuals and within institutions, but amidst an emergent mediated environment. As political leaders, policing agencies, mass media organizations, and illicit subcultures produce images of crime and crime control—and contested images of each other, and of each others' images—they engage the public in negotiating the meaning of crime itself. These public, mediated negotiations of crime's meaning offer us a sense of the labelling process writ large.

Yet despite these important conceptual advances, much scholarly work on media, crime, and crime control remains to be done. In particular, the many and varied audiences for these public negotiations require closer attention; unfortunately, the actual meanings and effects of mediated crime imagery in the daily lives of various groups and populations often remain more imagined than investigated.

REVIEW QUESTIONS

1 What can be done to correct the mass media's emotional distortion and over-dramatization of crime issues?

2 Is it appropriate for criminal or criminalized groups to produce their own websites and videos? Should there be limits on these sorts of illicit media?

3 How might we go about studying the audiences that consume mediated crime imagery, and its effects on them?

CONCLUSION

In the many confluences of crime and culture, certain patterns can be seen time and again. Subcultures organized around criminal or marginal behaviour emerge also as communities of shared symbolism and meaning, encoding common experience in counter-cultural values and expectations, inventing rituals that confirm and celebrate legal marginality, and indulging in nuances of alternative language, demeanour, and style. For their part, legal authorities attend to these symbolic displays in their efforts at surveillance and control, often policing the culture of crime as much as crime itself; corporate marketers work to appropriate such displays, hoping to capture something of their edgy currency; and the mass media utilize such symbolic displays as dramatic markers of criminality, drafting from them gross caricatures of criminality in the interest of constructing folk devils and moral panic. In this way, all the parties to crime and crime control operate within a common if contested cultural milieu, shaping the reality of crime through the medium of symbolism and style. In turn, these negotiations of meaning develop within larger cultural frames: a mediated environment already saturated by crime as news and entertainment, a political culture cut through by controversies linking art and music to crime and criminality, and a human landscape dotted with public displays of criminality, crime control, and crime victimization. Yet within this contested cultural vortex, members of criminal subcultures continue to find experiences of edgework and adrenalin—experiences of intense, situated affirmation—if only for a moment.

This ongoing cultural construction of crime and crime control intertwines with other areas of criminological concern as well, many of them considered in this volume. It is of course within this larger context of culture and crime that the importance of critically analysing 'media images of crime' (see Chapter 8) begins to make sense. In addition, the links between 'crime and everyday life' (see Chapter 9 below) can be seen to be as much cultural as experiential, constructed as they are out of culturally manufactured perceptions of crime's consequences, and from encounters given meaning within broader cultural frames of reference and interpretation. 'Young people and crime' (see Chapter 19) seem especially to be connected by way of illegal or marginal subcultures, stylized representations of illicit identity, and mediated images of criminality—and for young people and others, the experience of edgework and adrenalin offers one of many powerful links between 'psychology and crime' (see Chapter 6 above). As already seen, such stylized identities in turn provide opportunities for 'surveillance' on the part of legal authorities (see Chapter 23 below). In these ways the study of crime and culture has become an essential component in the larger practice of criminological inquiry—and yet it has also begun to take shape as a distinctly cultural criminology that today contributes to the pantheon of 'criminological theory' (see Chapter 4).

Perhaps most importantly, the connections between crime and culture continue always to evolve; crime and crime control can best be understood not as accomplished cultural facts, but as ongoing cultural processes. For this reason any attempt to document the subtleties of subcultural style or to catalogue the range of mediated crime representations becomes, at the moment of its writing, a cultural history—important in its own right, but already a step behind the emerging trajectory of crime and culture. And for this reason it is essential that students—those who are already becoming the next generation of criminological scholars—become involved in researching and analysing the connections between crime and culture. Existing scholarship, no matter what its merits, can never be enough; it can only offer a foundation from which to build new understandings of crime and culture.

This task takes on particular significance when the contemporary politics of crime and culture are considered. The intersection of culture and crime is today emerging as an essential domain of political and moral conflict; it is here that fundamental issues of human identity and social justice are being contested. The scope and effects of everyday surveillance and criminal profiling; the balancing of free expression with the potential for social harm; the negotiation of boundaries separating art from obscenity, or popular culture from pornography; the legitimacy and visibility of competing crime control agendas; the proper role of various media forms in the policing of contemporary society—all of these issues take shape in the interplay of crime and culture. Because of this, the critical analysis of crime and culture is no abstract intellectual exercise; it is, at its best, an exercise in engaged citizenship and informed activism.

QUESTIONS FOR DISCUSSION

1 Select a controversial issue having to do with crime or crime control—the legal rights of immigrants, for example, or the prevalence of domestic violence. Using only images culled from the mass media and popular culture; create a visual essay that presents your critical understanding of this issue.

2 Construct a set of guidelines for mass media coverage of everyday crime. Consider not only the fairness and accuracy of particular news reports, but ways to ensure that the cumulative effect of ongoing crime reporting is helpful to the public's understanding of larger crime issues.

3 If the possession and consumption of coffee were to be made illegal, what sort of illicit subculture might evolve among users of coffee? What sorts of subcultural values, styles, rituals, and experiences might emerge? Why?

4 If, upon the event of your death, your family and friends built a public memorial to you, what sorts of images and cultural references would you want included in it?

5   This chapter has discussed the styles, rituals, and practices of criminal subcultures. But what is the subculture of policing? In what ways is this police subculture similar to, or different from, the subcultures formed by criminal or marginalized groups?

GUIDE TO FURTHER READING

Ferrell, J., Hayward, K., and Young, J. (2008) *Cultural Criminology: An Invitation*. London: Sage.
Attempting to develop a relatively comprehensive account of crime, culture, and cultural criminology, this book considers not only topics like media, emotions, and everyday life, but the methods of cultural criminology, and its history and future.

Ferrell, J., Hayward, K., Morrison, W., and Presdee, M. (eds) (2004) *Cultural Criminology Unleashed*. London: GlassHouse Press.

This book expands the theoretical and substantive range of cultural criminology, and includes research into culture and crime across a variety of local, regional, and national settings.

Ferrell, J. and Sanders, C.R. (eds) (1995) *Cultural Criminology. Boston*: Northeastern University Press.

The first book to define the new criminological approach known as 'cultural criminology', this work builds from earlier British and American studies of crime and culture, and includes chapters on mass media, music, subcultures, and style.

Cohen, S. (2002 [1972, 1980, 1987]) *Folk Devils and Moral Panics* (3rd edn). London: Routledge.

Now in its third edition, this book remains a classic study in the intersections of culture and crime. The ongoing vitality and importance of Cohen's 'folk devil' and 'moral panic' concepts are highlighted in a new introduction to this third edition.

Presdee, M. (2000) *Cultural Criminology and the Carnival of Crime*. London: Routledge.

This book utilizes the lens of cultural criminology to examine a wide range of everyday practices—raving, joyriding, and sadomasochism, for example—and finds among them the shattered remains of human carnival.

Hayward, K. (2004) City Limits: *Crime, Consumer Culture and the Urban Experience*. London: GlassHouse Press.

This book offers the reader a series of unique cultural insights into the way that urban space is changing. Expanding the vision of criminology by drawing on cultural studies, social theory, urban studies, architectural theory and research into urban consumerism practices, Hayward argues that consumption is now central to understanding the crime-city relationship.

Crime, Media, *Culture: An International Journal*. London: SAGE.

This award-winning criminological journal provides a forum for international research into crime and culture. The journal includes articles on crime and media, and on the cultural dynamics of crime and criminal justice; it also includes photographs, photographic essays, drawings, and poems relating to crime and culture.

Silver, Tony, director (1983) *Style Wars*. New York: Plexifilm.

Produced by Henry Chalfant, this historic documentary traces the evolution of hip hop graffiti within the larger hip hop culture of music and dance.

Valdez, Luis, director (1982) *Zoot Suit*. Los Angeles: Universal Studios.

Based on the highly regarded stage play, this film examines the historical emergence of the stylized Latino Zoot Suiter in the United States (particularly Los Angeles), and explores the cultural politics of the 1940s 'zoot suit riots' in Los Angeles.

Daniel, Bill, director (2005) *Who Is Bozo Texino?* (http://www.billdaniel.net/who_is_bozo_texino/)
Daniel spent many years making—and living—this film, a rolling, hypnotic journey inside the illicit world of American railroad hobos and hobo freight train graffiti.

WEB LINKS

Cultural Criminology http://www.culturalcriminology.org/
This site includes key writings, biographies, photographs, films, event listings, and links, with special focus on cultural criminology at the University of Kent.

CultureX http://www.indiana.edu/~culturex/
Maintained by Professor Stephanie Kane, this site offers a guide to issues in culture, law, and crime.

StopViolence.Com http://stopviolence.com/ and Paul's Justice Page http://www.paulsjusticepage.com/
Maintained by Professor Paul Leighton, these two sites offer a variety of resources, essays, images, and links relating to contemporary crime and crime control issues.

REFERENCES

Alvelos, H. (2004) 'The Desert of Imagination in the City of Signs: Cultural Implications of Sponsored Transgression and Branded Graffiti' in J. Ferrell, K.J. Hayward, W. Morrison and M. Presdee (eds), *Cultural Criminology Unleashed*. London: GlassHouse Press.

Becker, Howard S. (1963) *Outsiders: Studies in the Sociology of Deviance*. New York: Free Press.

Cohen, Stanley (2002 [1972, 1980, 1987]) *Folk Devils and Moral Panics* (3rd edn). London: Routledge.

Cressey, Donald (1954) 'The Differential Association Theory and Compulsive Crime', *Journal of Criminal Law and Criminology* 45: 49–64.

Davis, M. (1992) *City of Quartz*. New York: Vintage.

Ferrell, J. (1996) *Crimes of Style: Urban Graffiti and the Politics of Criminality*. Boston: Northeastern University Press.

Ferrell, J. (1997) 'Criminological Verstehen: Inside the Immediacy of Crime', *Justice Quarterly* 14(1): 3–23.

Ferrell, J. (1998) 'Freight Train Graffiti: Subculture, Crime, Dislocation', *Justice Quarterly* 15(4): 587–608.

Ferrell, J. (2002) *Tearing Down the Streets: Adventures in Urban Anarchy*. New York: Palgrave/Macmillan.

Ferrell, J. (2003) 'Speed Kills' *Critical Criminology* 11(3): 185–98.

Ferrell, J. and Hamm, M. (eds) (1998) *Ethnography at the Edge: Crime, Deviance and Field Research*, Boston.

Ferrell, J. and Sanders, C.R. (eds) (1995) *Cultural Criminology*. Boston: Northeastern University Press.

Ferrell, J., Hayward, K.J., Morrison, W., and Presdee, M. (eds) (2004) *Cultural Criminology Unleashed*. London: GlassHouse Press.

Ferrell, J., Hayward, K., and Young, J. (2008) *Cultural Criminology: An Invitation*. London: SAGE.

Ferrell, J., Milovanovic, D., and Lyng, S. (2001) 'Edgework, Media Practices, and the Elongation of Meaning', *Theoretical Criminology* 5(2): 177–202.

Hall, S., Critcher, C., Jefferson, A., Clarke, J. and Roberts, B. (1978) *Policing the Crisis: Mugging, the State, and Law and Order*. London: Macmillan.

Hayward, K.J. (2004) *City Limits: Crime, Consumer Culture and the Urban Expression*. London: GlassHouse. Northeastern University Press.

Hayward, K.J. and Presdee, M. (2009) *Framing Crime: Cultural Criminology and the Image*, London: Routledge

Hayward, K.J. and Young, J. (2004) 'Cultural criminology: some notes on the script' *Theoretical Criminology*, 8: 3 pp. 259–85.

Hayward, K. J and Young, J. (2007) 'Cultural criminology' in M. Maguire, R. Morgan, and R. Reiner, (eds) *Oxford Handbook of Criminology* (4th edn) Oxford: Oxford University Press.

Hebdige, D. (1979) *Subculture: The Meaning of Style*. London: Methuen.

Jackson-Jacobs, C. (2004) 'Taking a Beating: Narrative Gratifications of Fighting as an Underdog' in J. Ferrell, K.J. Hayward, W. Morrison and M. Presdee (eds), *Cultural Criminology Unleashed*: 231–244. London: GlassHouse Press.

Jenkins, P. (2001) *Beyond Tolerance: Child Pornography on the Internet*. New York: New York University Press.

Jewkes, Y. (ed) (2003) *Dot.cons: Crime, Deviance and Identity on the Internet*. Devon, UK: Willan.

Katz, J. (1988) *Seductions of Crime: Moral and Sensual Attractions in Doing Evil*. New York: Basic Books.

Lyng, S. (1990) 'Edgework: A Social Psychological Analysis of Voluntary Risk Taking' *American Journal of Sociology* 95: 851–86.

Lyng, S. and Bracey, Jr., M.L. (1995) 'Squaring the One Percent: Biker Style and the Selling of Cultural Resistance' in J. Ferrell and C.R. Sanders (eds), *Cultural Criminology*: 235–76. Boston: Northeastern University Press.

Manning, P. (1998) 'Media Loops' in F. Bailey and D. Hale (eds) *Popular Culture, Crime, and Justice*: 25–39. Belmont CA: West/Wadsworth.

McRobbie, A. and Thornton, S.L. (1995) 'Rethinking "Moral Panic" for Multi-Mediated Social Worlds', *British Journal of Sociology* 46: 559–74.

Miller, J. (1995) 'Struggles Over the Symbolic: Gang Style and the Meanings of Social Control' in J. Ferrell and C.R. Sanders (eds), *Cultural Criminology*: 213–34. Boston: Northeastern University Press.

Polsky, N. (1998 [1967]) *Hustlers, Beats, and Others*. New York: Lyons Press.

Presdee, M. (2000) *Cultural Criminology and the Carnival of Crime*. London: Routledge.

Snyder, G. (2009) *Graffiti Lives*. New York: New York University Press.

Taylor, I., Walton, P. and Young, J. (1973) *The New Criminology*. New York: Harper & Row.

Wilson, J.Q. and Kelling, G.L. (2003 [1982]). 'Broken Windows: The Police and Neighborhood Safety' reprinted in E. McLaughlin, J. Muncie, and G. Hughes (eds). (2003) *Criminological Perspectives: Essential Readings* (2nd edn): 400–441. London: Sage.

Young, J. (1971) 'The Role of the Police as Amplifiers of Deviancy, Negotiators of Reality and Translators of Fantasy' in Stanley Cohen (ed), *Images of Deviance*, 27–61. Harmondsworth, UK: Penguin.

Young, J. (2003) 'Merton with Energy, Katz with Structure: The Sociology of Vindictiveness and the Criminology of Transgression', *Theoretical Criminology* 7(3): 389–414.

Young, A. (2007) 'Images in the Aftermath of Trauma' *Crime, Media, Culture* 3(1): 30–48.

8 Crime and media: understanding the connections

Chris Greer

INTRODUCTION

The contemporary era—whether we term it the information society, the network society, the image world, postmodernity, or late modernity—is a fundamentally 'mediatized' era. It is also an era in which high crime rates and high levels of concern about crime have become accepted as 'normal'. The rapid and relentless development of information and communication technologies (ICTs) over the past 100 years has shaped the modern age, transforming the relations between space, time, and identity. Where once 'news' used to travel by ship, it now hurtles across the globe at light speed and is available 24 hours-a-day at the push of a button. Where once cultures used to be more or less distinguishable in national or geographical terms, they now mix, intermingle, and converge in a constant global exchange of information. Where once a sense of community and belonging was derived primarily from established identities and local traditions, it may now also be found, and lost, in a virtual world of shared values, meanings, and interpretations. In short, media are not only inseparable from contemporary social life; they are, for many, its defining characteristic. Understanding the connections between crime and the media is central to understanding the cultural place that crime and media occupy in our social world.

This chapter is an introduction to the investigation of crime and media. My main aim is to present a summary of some of the major themes and debates which have shaped the research agenda. But I also want to sharpen the focus of investigation on some less well-rehearsed issues. The chapter is divided into four main sections. The first offers some background information and addresses the crucial question of why exploring media images of crime and control is important. The second section considers how scholars have gone about researching crime and media and presents an overview of the main findings. The third section critically discusses the dominant theoretical and conceptual tools which have been used to understand and explain media representations of crime. The fourth section considers evidence for the influence of media representations, both on criminal behaviour and on fear of crime. Finally, I will offer some tentative suggestions about useful areas for future research and investigation.

BACKGROUND

Fortunately, though sections of the popular press may suggest otherwise, most of us have little first-hand experience of serious criminal victimization. Our understanding of the crime problem—how much crime is out there, what types of crime are most prevalent, who is most at risk, what are the best responses—derives mostly from sources other than personal experience. Paramount among these are the media. The media, then, are key producers and purveyors of 'knowledge' about crime, disorder, and control. For this reason alone, media representations are worthy of in-depth investigation.

But precisely what kinds of knowledge do these representations generate, and to what effect? Below are some of the key questions which have perplexed students of crime and media:

- Is it possible to discern a coherent picture of 'the crime problem' from the media and, if so, does this picture bear any resemblance to what we may claim, however tentatively, to know of the 'reality' of crime and disorder?

- Do the media merely reflect, objectively and impartially, what happens in the world, or are they active agents in socially constructing 'mediated realities' in which certain values, interests, and beliefs are promoted, while others are downplayed, or even actively suppressed?

- Do the media reproduce and reinforce prejudice and the stereotyping of marginalized groups or actively challenge it?

- Do the media undermine or fortify the existing structures of power and authority?

- Does violence in the media make us more aggressive, more fearful, or both?

Concern about the pernicious influence of the media is perennial, and academic research exploring media representations of crime dates back to the early 1900s (Pearson, 1983; Bailey and Hale, 1997). Yet despite literally hundreds of studies, these key questions have generated few straight answers. It is important to be clear that media today cannot (if they ever could) be usefully thought of in the singular, like some monolithic, unified institution to be understood through generalized statements and assumptions. The media are a multiplicity of institutions, organizations, processes, and practices which are hugely diverse in composition, scope, and purpose (Briggs and Cobley, 2002). Currently there are more media forms (television, newspapers, magazines, radio, the Internet, mobile phone Wireless Application Protocol (WAP) technology) and greater levels of diversity within each individual form (satellite, cable, and digital television) than ever before. Understanding media, therefore, requires a critical and reflexive appreciation both of the diversity of forms and formats involved and of the complexity with which images, texts, messages, signs are produced, transmitted, and consumed.

One of the key points to grasp—and one of the issues I want to communicate most forcefully—is that we do not all use, interpret, and respond to media representations in the same way. Images of violent crime, for example, may repel some and attract others, disturb some and excite others, frighten some and anger others. I, along with the other contributors in this collection, am keen to encourage you to look beyond the instinctive desire to tackle complex dilemmas with simplified accounts and generalizations. The relationship between media images and the world around us is so fascinating precisely because it is complex and hard to pin down.

Researching crime and media

Research on crime and media covers three principal areas of interest: content, production, and consumption and influence. Each area has its own particular research methods and approaches (Greer, 2009). Media content analysis can be broadly split between studies which are primarily either quantitative or qualitative. Quantitative analyses are concerned first and foremost with measuring the amount of crime, violence, or control in the media—for example, the number of crime stories reported in a newspaper, or the number of violent incidents appearing in a television programme. The 'media picture' of crime is then usually compared and contrasted with the 'real world' picture, normally derived from official crime statistics. Quantitative approaches have predominated in research on media content. Qualitative content analyses, by contrast, are concerned primarily with investigating the nature of media representations of crime, violence, and control. Though they often incorporate some quantitative component, qualitative research is more interested in untangling the complex processes through which media images are produced, exchanged, and interpreted—for example, by exploring the use of language, the forces and constraints that shape media production, or the wider influence of the economic, political, moral, and cultural environment. Both quantitative and qualitative analyses may be equally concerned with media effects.

Each approach has its strengths and weaknesses, but some of the limitations of purely quantitative research are particularly noteworthy. Official statistics are a very poor indicator of crime rates and may reveal more about the reporting and recording practices of the public and the police than they do about actual levels of offending (Maguire, 2007). Quantitative claims about the relationship between media images and the statistical 'reality' of crime, therefore, need to be treated with caution. More fundamentally, because quantitative analyses cannot tackle the crucial issue of meaning, for many they can only ever provide a surface description of media representations of crime rather than a deeper understanding, which would generally be the favoured research outcome. Nevertheless, quantitative research can offer important insights into changing patterns and trends in the representation of crime, as well as generating useful data on which deeper qualitative investigations can be based.

Content analyses of media representations of crime—whether news, film, television drama, magazine articles, or Internet sites—are the key method of establishing 'how' various forms of media represent crime. Content analysis alone, however, cannot explain 'why' media images take the particular forms that they do. It is only through a focus on media production that representations can be explained. Research on media production is necessarily more qualitative in nature, since it is concerned with the 'social processes'—commercial, ideological, moral—that shape media content. These processes are too complex to be quantified or reduced to statistical data. The majority of criminological research has sought to understand media production 'at a distance' by analysing, for example, the 'news values' that determine which crimes are newsworthy and which are not, or the impact of the wider socio-political environment on the representation of crime and justice in film or television drama (Soothill and Walby, 1991; Sparks, 1992; Jenkins, 1992, 1994; Reiner *et al.*, 2000a, 2000b; Soothill *et al.*, 2002; Leishman and Mason, 2003; Peelo, 2006). A minority of researchers have sought to understand media production 'up close'. In addition to considering the structural determinants of media production and the wider socio-political environment, they have also employed interviews—with journalists, editors and producers, police and probation officers, and victims and offenders—and ethnography—immersing oneself in the natural environment of the research subjects (for example, exploring crime journalism through shadowing news reporters). The aim here is to gain a deeper, interpretive understanding (or *verstehen* in Weberian terms) of media production by engaging directly with those involved in the production process (see Chibnall, 1977; Ericson *et al.*, 1987, 1989, 1991; Schlesinger and Tumber, 1994; Kitzinger and Skidmore, 1995; Greer, 2003).

The third principal area of interest is media consumption and influence. Much media criminology is underpinned by an often implicit assumption of media influence: the media distortion of crime and deviance has a significant impact on society, and that this impact is somehow detrimental. On the political right, the concern has been that media glamourize crime and encourage criminality. On the political left, it has been that media increase fear of crime, encouraging political acquiescence to the status quo and strengthening support for authoritarian measures of control and containment. However, with the important exception of studies on media and fear of crime, criminologists have actually conducted very little research to 'evidence' the nature of media influence. Thus there is a fundamental tension within media criminology: much is assumed, but little is actually researched, still less comprehensively evidenced. What research does exist on media consumption and influence has, like content analysis, tended to be quantitative in nature. It has largely been situated not within sociological criminology, but within a psychological positivism which foregrounds classification and counting over a more nuanced, in-depth understanding of what media 'mean' to active consumers. The pros and cons of this type of research are discussed below, along with the emergence of more qualitative approaches to understanding media consumption and influence that are being championed from within media studies. Next, though, it is useful to consider in greater detail the content of media representations of crime and control.

The nature and extent of crime in the media

A virtually universal finding in the literature is that media representations exaggerate both the levels of serious interpersonal crime in society and the risk of becoming a crime victim (see also Ferrell, this volume). This is the case for studies of newspapers (Marsh, 1991), television (Gunter et al., 2003) and radio content (Cumberbatch et al., 1995), across both news and entertainment media (Reiner et al., 2000a), and literary crime fiction (Knight, 2004). The representation of crime is largely event-oriented in that it focuses on specific criminal cases and incidents rather than wider debates around causes, prevention, or policy (Rock, 1973; Naylor, 2001; Greer, 2003). All media forms focus overwhelmingly on violent or sexual offences.

Calculations of the proportion of news space devoted to crime vary considerably depending on the definition of 'crime' adopted, and the types of material included and excluded on that basis. Some studies, for example, may only include news reports of particular criminal events or court cases (Ditton and Duffy, 1983; Smith, 1984). Others, in addition to considering news reports, may also include feature items, editorial pieces, and letters to the editor (Hall et al., 1978; Ericson et al., 1987). Studies may also expand the definition of 'crime' to explore a wider range of deviant acts, such as corporate offending (Cavender and Mulcahy, 1998; Tombs and White, 2001; Knotterus et al., 2006), environmental crime (Lynch et al., 2000), and state violence (Cohen, 2001; Herman and Chomsky, 1994). 'Popular' (normally tabloid) news outlets are generally found to include a greater proportion of crime stories reported in a more sensational style than 'quality' (broadsheet) ones (Graber, 1980; Schlesinger and Tumber, 1994). Estimates of the proportion of crime in the UK news media have ranged from 4 per cent in one study (Roshier, 1973) to 13 per cent in another (Williams and Dickinson, 1993). A summary of

Figure 8.1 'A Sun Reader Writes' The Sun Newspaper front page—Monday 21 January 2008

Source: © News International Syndication, 2008

content analyses in the US found the proportion of crime news to range from just over 1 per cent, to more than 30 per cent (Marsh, 1991). In the entertainment media, an average of around 25 per cent of US and UK primetime television programming, and around 20 per cent of film releases are crime-centred (Allen *et al.*, 1997; Reiner *et al.*, 2000a).

Through a mixture of quantitative and qualitative research methods, Reiner *et al.* (2000a, b) identified changing trends and patterns in the representation of crime and justice between the 1940s and the 1990s. Both news and fictional representations of offenders changed relatively little over this time, though portrayals have become less sympathetic toward the structural influences on criminality and more condemnatory of what is perceived as individual evil. Images of the criminal justice system have become more complex and critical, with greater attention, for example, to police ineffectiveness, corruption within the criminal justice system, and conflict between institutions. The most significant change, however, relates to representations of the crime victim, who has 'moved from a shadowy and purely functional role in crime narratives to a pivotal position. Their suffering increasingly constitutes the subject position or the raison d'être of the story' (Reiner *et al.*, 2000b: 187). The increasing centrality of crime victims in the media reflects the 'discovery', growing concern about, and subsequent politicization of the victim within criminal justice systems (and criminology) throughout the 1980s (Davies *et al.*, 2007).

This section has provided a brief review of the research literature on the content of media representations of crime and control and drawn attention to some of the factors that may influence that content. The aim in the next section is to establish a clearer picture of the forces and influences that shape media representations of crime.

REVIEW QUESTIONS

1 Why is it both important and useful to study crime and the media?

2 What are the main differences between quantitative and qualitative methods of content analysis and what are their respective strengths and weaknesses?

3 Can a coherent picture of the crime problem be discerned from media representations? If so, what is it, and is it accurate?

Theorizing crime and media

Crime news is not simply plucked out of thin air; nor does it exist in a vacuum. It is the end result of a complex process of selection, processing, and prioritization, and is shaped by interactions between journalists, editors, their working conditions, the wider environment, and, crucially, news sources. News sources are those individuals, organizations, and institutions that provide the information on which journalists often base their stories. In relation to crime news, key sources include the police, probation, prison and court services, politicians, penal reform groups, victim organizations, and a host of other interested parties.

Reporting crime takes time, money, and effort. Editors and producers seek to maximize the efficiency and cost effectiveness of this process by concentrating limited resources around sources which can offer consistently reliable and reportable crime material within the rhythms of the news production process. Powerful criminal justice institutions like the police and the judiciary routinely produce a significant volume of reportable information, and are therefore extremely useful to crime reporters. For this reason, they enjoy what Hall *et al.* (1978) refer to as 'privileged access' in the media: that is, they find it easier than less powerful, or less useful (in news terms), organizations to have their views or version of events publicized. This 'privileged access' is further enhanced by the credibility and cultural authority—the 'expert status'—associated with official agencies on matters of crime and control (Ericson *et al.*, 1989, 1991). That journalists are to an extent reliant on powerful institutional sources is undeniable. The consequences of this reliance, however, and the wider implications for the democratic flow of information and the objectivity and impartiality of the news product, may be interpreted very differently depending on the theoretical approach adopted.

Media theory and crime news production

Traditional theorizations of news media production can be broadly distinguished according to two opposing positions: radical and liberal pluralist. Radical approaches are influenced by the theories of Karl Marx and Antonio Gramsci, among others, and stress the unequal distribution of economic and cultural power throughout society, and its impact on media production. Liberal pluralist interpretations are underpinned by the ideals of classical liberal theory, and emphasize the principles of freedom, choice, and democracy, and their impact on media production. There are numerous variations on each perspective, but in their simplest terms, radical readings see the mass media as controlling the people, while liberal pluralist readings see the mass media as serving the people. With the proliferation of media and the transformation of the information landscape in recent decades, these modernist theoretical approaches have come under fire for being too rigid and deterministic, incapable of capturing the fluidity and unpredictability of power and information flows in multi-mediated societies. For postmodernists in particular, in today's 24–7, hyper-mediatized environment, the grand theories and all-encompassing statements of media power and control that tended to characterize traditional approaches have become obsolete. Some of the most relevant examples of each position are outlined below.

At the radical extreme, the 'propaganda model' views the media as an extension of the State's apparatus of ideological control. Over three decades, Ed Herman and Noam Chomsky have argued that economic, political, military, and cultural elites conspire to control the content and flow of media information, filtering out or delegitimizing dissenting views to protect ruling class interests (Chomsky, 1989; Herman and Chomsky, 1994). Through analysing news coverage of 'terrorism' and the media's alleged collusion in the 'criminalization' of non-friendly regimes, the authors argue that the key actors in the news production process are not journalists, who are seen as largely powerless, but media owners, who share interests in common with other elite groups. In this critical materialist interpretation the function of the news media is to 'manufacture consent' around elite ideas in the name of the 'national interest' and, in so doing, to engender political compliance and acceptance of the established order.

A less conspiratorial approach is the 'hegemonic model', based on the neo-Marxist writings of Antonio Gramsci (1971). Here the media are viewed not as the direct mouthpieces of the powerful, but as sites of contestation on which alternative viewpoints actively compete for ideological dominance or hegemony. Due to their privileged access, however, criminal justice institutions are able to advance a 'primary definition' of crime-related issues, which frames the terms for any ensuing debate and subverts competing viewpoints, though these may still be heard, to marginal status (Hall *et al.*, 1978). Journalists may think they are autonomous, but in practice they are constrained to reproduce the elite 'ideas' of the dominant sources on which they rely, in turn helping to make these the 'ideas' of everyone. This is why, it is suggested, crime reporting tends to favour an elite (conservative) portrayal of the crime problem—an issue of working-class, minority ethnic youth offending (not white collar corruption or state violence), requiring greater punishment and control of particular groups (not government accountability and corporate regulation) (Fishman, 1978; Barlow *et al.*, 1995).

The radical perspective in its various guises contrasts with liberal pluralist media theory (Gans, 1980; Koss, 1984; Hetherington, 1985). Liberal pluralists concede that certain official interests are advantaged in the media but they insist that any significant source bias or pressure from media owners is offset by journalistic professionalism (in particular the requirements of objectivity and balance), the ideological and stylistic diversity of the media, and what is viewed as open and equal competition between a wide range of groups for media access and influence. Journalists insist upon, indeed pride themselves upon maintaining high levels of professional autonomy and are actively encouraged in this pursuit by colleagues who share the same system of values (Gans, 1980). Any pressure to follow a particular line, apply a particular 'spin', suppress a particular piece of information, or in some other way distort the 'truth status' of the news will be forcefully resisted.

Nor does the 'privileged access' of powerful institutions guarantee definitional control. Journalists and other social actors both can and do challenge the established order. This is clear, for example, when the high-profile exposure of scandal (political, sexual, economic) forces senior politicians to resign from office (Thompson, 2000), or the credibility of criminal justice agencies is undermined by media exposés evidencing corruption, incompetence, or institutional racism (Greer, 2007). In the liberal pluralist view, then, the media act as 'fourth estate'—exposing injustice and holding the powerful to account. They provide a voice for marginalized groups and, in so doing, defend the integrity of the democratic process (Blumler and Gurevitch, 1995).

In practice, the power relations between journalists and sources are more fluid than radical scholars have tended to argue but more constraining than liberal pluralists suggest (Greer, 2003). The radical position tends to overstate the dominance of official agencies and rather understates the ability both of journalists to challenge the status quo, and of other competing groups to enter and, sometimes with alarming effectiveness, reframe the terms of a given debate (Miller, 1993). The radical view also assumes, on some level, the existence of an 'elite consensus' which is then promoted by some unified constellation of ruling class interests (McNair, 1998, 1999). This interpretation overlooks the considerable levels of conflict and competition both between and within political and economic elites (the ongoing debates around a European Constitution, the continued military presence in Iraq, the extended detention of terror suspects without charge), and fails to recognize that access to the media changes over time. On the other hand, liberal pluralists understate the various influences within news agencies—for example, editorial pressures and the pursuit of promotion within a particular newsroom culture—which severely limit journalists' freedom to report objectively and impartially. Competition for media access and influence is clearly not equal. It is beyond doubt that criminal justice agencies maintain a clear definitional advantage, if not guaranteed definitional control, on issues of crime and justice. Less powerful or marginalized groups can, of course, gain access, but they generally need to work harder and more creatively to have their views heard. These constraints have real consequences for the production and dissemination of crime and justice knowledge, and cannot be disregarded on the basis of claims to professional autonomy, ideological diversity, and equal competition.

Sensitized to the complexities of understanding contemporary media forms and flows, postmodernist thinking maintains that there is no general explanation, still less some grand theory, capable of accounting for news production in all its diversity (Brown, 2003). Many postmodernists argue that in societies where images, signs, and codes are constantly recycled through the media, it is no longer possible to distinguish with any certainty between 'image' and 'reality', the 'represented' and the 'real' (Baudrillard, 1983; Poster, 1990); how crime policy is presented becomes more important than what the policy actually is. In an age of media proliferation, political spin, ubiquitous public relations operatives, and ever-more sophisticated media audiences, perceptions of credibility may shift from story to story, and the balance of definitional power becomes increasingly unstable and unpredictable.

One recent intervention that seeks to theorize this instability and unpredictability is Brian McNair's notion of 'cultural choas' (McNair, 2006a). For McNair, the early twenty-first-century news mediasphere is characterized by the intensified commodification of news and counter-culture, increasing market competition, a hyper-adversarial news media, and the rapid rise of 'mediated access' to public participation broadcasting (for example, Talk Radio and live television debates). These conditions, it is suggested, coalesce to create a post-Cold War media milieu in which ideological hegemony is replaced by ideological dissolution, and journalistic consensus around dominant ideas—whether manufactured in the radical sense, or organic in the liberal pluralist sense—is replaced by journalistic dissensus. The emergence of a highly diversified, widely accessible, and ultimately chaotic media environment has changed the terrain upon which struggles over media power and influence are played out. At the national level, for example, an already fragmented government struggles to control the crime news agenda, but is repeatedly beaten down by hostile journalists intent on taking the next big political scalp. Dissatisfied and increasingly vociferous victims and victim groups now routinely employ professional public relations advisers to make the public articulation of their cases more 'media-friendly', and therefore more widely disseminated. Media audiences, tired of the 'permanent crisis in criminal justice', are actively encouraged to participate in the news production process by emailing, texting, or phoning in their views and concerns. At the global level, the Coalition invasions and ongoing military presence in Afghanistan and Iraq continue to attract moral opprobrium from significant sections of the press and public, making discursive closure around the 'war on terror' an impossibility. Botched surveillance operations at home are reported alongside the mounting deaths of troops abroad. Photographs of US soldiers proudly posing beside Iraqi torture victims in Abu Ghraib prison are made globally accessible online, further undermining official efforts to maintain the moral high ground and portray Iraq as a 'just war' (Sontag, 2004; Hamm, 2007). Meanwhile, 'freelance gangs of insurgents can exploit the news values of global media and compel us to watch the Twin Towers collapse in real time, or the murder of school children unfold live in Beslan. Terrorist atrocities are not new to the 21st century, but the scale of their political and psychological impact is' (McNair, 2006b: 1). Cultural chaos is one of the few recent attempts to take full account of the relentless and frequently unpredictable contemporary, 24–7 globalized news media culture.

News values and newsworthiness

Only a tiny fraction of events, criminal or otherwise, are deemed sufficiently 'newsworthy' to merit media attention. News values are the criteria that determine 'newsworthiness'. They enable journalists and editors to decide which stories to run and which to drop, which are headliners and which are fillers, which are the most important details and which are the least. Having 'a good nose for a story', then, may equally be interpreted as having a well-honed appreciation of news values.

Table 8.1 outlines three different but overlapping interpretations of what it is that make events in general, and criminal events in particular, worthy of media attention.

News values help to explain the broad profile of media representations of crime and control (see above). Interpersonal crimes of sex and violence can be more easily presented as dramatic and titillating than non-violent crimes—for example, most property and white collar offences—particularly when they have high levels of proximity (spatial nearness and cultural meaningfulness) to the consumer. By focusing on people (as victims and offenders) and events rather than abstract issues and debates, crime reporting is individualized and simplified, which also contributes to the common association of crime with individual pathology rather than wider social, structural, and political influences. Crimes are more newsworthy if they involve famous or notable people. In an increasingly secular society, some suggest that the culture of celebrity is for many a more powerful source of social cohesion than religion (Rojek, 2001). Although names will generally be included where possible, one of the most compelling images in crime narratives is that of the 'unknown' predatory stranger. As the producers of reality crime shows like *Crimewatch UK* or *America's Most Wanted* and countless newspaper editors know only too well, few stories capture the public imagination as forcefully as the killer on the loose, especially when the (potential) victims are children. In addition to their inherent drama, individualization, violence, and proximity, such narratives possess an unnerving sense of immediacy and a palpable risk of further attacks. They have a clear capacity to fulfil that vital, commercially driven journalistic imperative; the requirement to shock (Greer, 2003).

This imperative is increasingly realized by capitalizing on the highly visual nature of contemporary culture. As the experience of crime and control has become more mediatized, so too has it become more image-oriented. Stories are more readily personalized and individualized, they more easily invoke empathy, disdain, shock, when they are accompanied by visual images. Today 'crime stories are increasingly selected and "produced" as media events on the basis of their visual (how they can be portrayed in images) as well as their lexical-verbal (how they can be portrayed in words) potential' (Greer,

Table 8.1 Criteria of newsworthiness

Galtung and Ruge (1965)	Chibnall (1977)	Jewkes (2004a)
Threshold (importance)		Threshold (importance)
Unexpectedness (novelty)	Novelty (unexpectedness)	
Negativity (violent, harmful, deviant, sad)		Violence
Unambiguity (clear and definite)	Simplification (removing shades of grey)	Simplification (removing shades of grey)
Dramatization (action)		
Frequency (timescale, fit within news cycle)	Immediacy (the present, fit within news cycle)	
Elite-centricity (powerful or famous nations or people)	Personalization (notable individuals, celebrities)	Celebrity or high-status (notable individuals)
	Structured access (experts, officials, authority)	
Composition (balance, fit with other news)		
Personification (individual focus or causality)	Individual pathology (individual causality)	Individualism (individual focus or causality)
Continuity (sustainability)		
		Children (young people)
	Graphic presentation	Spectacle or graphic imagery
	Visible/spectacular acts	
Meaningfulness (spatial and cultural relevance)	Proximity (spatial and cultural relevance)	
Consonance (fit with existing knowledge and expectations)	Conventionalism (hegemonicideology)	Predictability (expectedness)
	Titillation (exposes, scandal)	
		Risk (lasting danger)
	Sexual/political connotations	Sex
	Deterrence and repression	Conservative ideology or political diversion (deterrence, distraction from wider problems)

Sources: Galtung and Ruge (1965); Chibnall (1977); Jewkes (2004)

2007: 29). The availability of an image may determine whether or not a story is run or dropped. The availability of the right image can help elevate a crime victim or offender to national or even global iconic status.

The previous sections have reviewed the literature on the nature and extent of representations of crime and control in the media, and offered an overview of some of the main theoretical and conceptual tools used to understand why media representations take on the form that they do. The next section considers the evidence for media effects.

REVIEW QUESTIONS

1 What are the principal characteristics of the radical and liberal pluralist readings of news production? How does each reading view journalistic freedom and source power?

2 How useful are modernist approaches to understanding media in an age of media proliferation, diversification, and saturation?

3 What is it that makes some crimes so eminently reportable, whilst others are scarcely mentioned?

Problematizing crime and media

When toddler James Bulger was murdered by two ten-year-olds in 1993, enormous attention was directed at the film *Child's Play III*, and other 'video nasties', as a likely cause (Barker, 2001; Green, 2008). When two teenagers shot 12 classmates and one teacher in Columbine in 1999, before killing themselves, the music of Marilyn Manson, the Hollywood film *The Basketball Diaries*, and violent computer games were all cited as causal factors (Muzzatti, 2003). Two events in 2007 forced the world to reflect on the costs of a celebrity-obsessed media culture in which fame—like so many disposable consumer goods—is commoditized, widely accessible, and ephemeral. A shooting spree at the Virginia Tech University resulted in 32 deaths, many more woundings, and the suicide of the killer. Before embarking on the worst killing spree by a lone gunman in US history, the perpetrator sent a manifesto, photographs, and video tapes to NBC news, seeking global media coverage of the declaration that he would be remembered as the 'saviour of the oppressed'. When a troubled young man shot dead eight people and then himself in an Omaha mega-mall in 2007, the note he left behind claimed 'Now I'll be famous' (*The Times*, 6 December 2007).

Few today would suggest that media representations have no influence on their audiences. Rather, the debate is about the nature, extent, and significance of that influence. As noted above, the concern on the political right has been that media images glamorize crime and violence, undermining respect for authority and the rule of law, and encouraging criminality. On the left it has been that media images of crime and deviance increase public fears and anxieties, helping to win support for authoritarian measures of control and containment. The evidence for the criminogenic effects of the media will be considered first.

Media violence and the problem of 'effects'

Research on media effects has for decades sought to demonstrate a causal relationship between media violence and violent thoughts and behaviours in the real world. Typically, subjects (most often children) are exposed to some aggressive stimulus (say, a short violent film) within a controlled setting (frequently a laboratory or office), and then observed to see if they think or behave more aggressively than a control group not exposed to the aggressive stimulus. Myriad variations have been conducted on this 'stimulus-response' (SR) format, variously controlling for participant characteristics, type of violence shown, duration of exposure, and so on.

In a frequently quoted statistic, more than 70 per cent of studies claim to demonstrate that media violence does cause real life violence (Andison, 1977; Howitt, 1998). In the classic example, children exposed to a short film in which aggressive interaction with an inflatable 'Bobo doll' was rewarded performed more imitative aggression (for example, striking the Bobo doll with a mallet after having observed it in the film) than those who had viewed non-aggressive interactions, or interactions in which aggression was punished (Bandura *et al.*, 1961, 1963). The authors concluded that aggressive behaviour may result, to a significant extent, from 'social learning'. Furthermore, the effects of media violence, though typically small, appear to diminish over time, but not disappear entirely (Livingstone, 1996). Huesmann (1995) concluded after a 20-year follow-up study that children who watched more violent television at age eight had secured significantly more violent criminal convictions in adulthood, even after controlling for social class and intelligence levels. The relationship between childhood exposure to television violence and later criminality has been supported in a host of other studies (see Paik and Comstock, 1994; Wilson *et al.*, 1998).

Figure 8.2 Bandura's Bobo doll experiment

Source: © Albert Bandura

Such 'evidence' of criminogenic media effects is regularly cited by right-wing moral campaigners as justification for greater controls and censorship (Barker and Petley, 2001). But these claims should be treated with caution. Effects research has been heavily criticized on methodological, theoretical, and conceptual grounds. Gauntlett (2001) and others (Howitt, 1998; Murdock, 2001; Reiner, 2007; Carter and Weaver, 2003) have identified a number of problems with the 'effects model'. Some of the most pertinent are summarized below.

- Counting 'units' of violence in accordance with the pre-established definitions of the researcher ('this is violence, this is not'), ignores the different meanings that people attach to acts and behaviours and implicitly assumes not just that we all think the same way, but that we all think the same way as the researcher.

- It is dubious to suppose that how subjects behave in controlled laboratory or field experimental situations (where they know they are being observed), sometimes toward inanimate objects (for example, an inflatable doll), reflects how they will behave in the real world toward real people.

- There is an assumption that only certain types of person are susceptible to the influence of media violence—mostly children, who are considered helpless victims, but sometimes also 'uneducated' or 'working class' populations, who apparently lack the maturity and sense most people take for granted.

- Different forms of violence—for example, in cartoons, soap operas, and horror movies—are often conflated, treated as equal in weight, and reduced to statistical data lacking any sense of plot or context. Whether violence is rewarded or punished, realistic or humorous, perpetrated by a 'hero' or a 'villain', may influence its impact profoundly.

- A correlation—violent people enjoy violent media—is not the same as a causal relationship—people are violent because of violent media. Media representations may provide technical knowledge about committing violent crimes but that does not mean they also provide the motivation to use it.

- Whether intended or not, effects studies play into the hands of conservatives and right-wing moral campaigners who wish simplistically to blame the media for society's ills rather than addressing more intractable sources of crime like social inequality, prejudice and stereotyping.

- Media influence, short term or cumulative, can never be disaggregated entirely from other social, psychological and cultural influences, yet studies routinely search for a 'pure' (negative) media effect. Pro-social images, rarely considered, may be every bit as powerful as anti-social ones, and perhaps even more so.

While some critics have challenged the validity of the entire effects enterprise (Barker and Petley, 2001), others are less damning. Carter and Weaver (2003: 8), for example, recognize the limitations, but maintain that the effects tradition 'needs to be engaged with intelligently, rather than rejected out of hand as ill informed'. A growing body of work is using sophisticated methods of audience research to investigate the reception and interpretation of media images, not in isolation, but as part of an ongoing process of interaction, both with other media images and with the 'material and social realities of people's lives' (Kitzinger, 1999: 11; see also Buckingham, 1993, 2000; Philo, 1999). Gauntlett (1997), for example, has explored the influence of mass media on children by inviting young participants to make their own videos. Hunt (1997) has studied the complex ways in which 'raced subjectivity'—racial sense of identity and community—influences the viewing and interpretation of images of racial violence. Kitzinger (2004) has conducted in-depth interviews and focus groups with media practitioners, interest groups, and consumers to explore the role of media representations in shaping understanding of sex crime as a contemporary social problem.

Media and fear of crime

Fear of crime first registered on the policy agenda in the early 1980s, when the British Crime Survey suggested it was becoming as big a problem as crime itself (Hough and Mayhew, 1983). Its consequences may range from not walking home alone at night to withdrawing from society altogether and living in isolation (Ferraro, 1995). Given the centrality of fear of crime in the public and political imagination, understanding its origins is an important criminological undertaking. Fear of crime is influenced by a range of social and demographic variables—perceptions of risk and vulnerability, age, social class, geographical location, ethnicity, and experience of criminal victimization (Box *et al.*, 1988; Davis, 1994; Hale, 1996). Media representations, though enormously diverse, are only one possible influence among many. As such, their significance remains a matter for debate.

Probably the best known research in this area is the 'cultivation analysis' of Gerbner *et al.*, which over several decades has employed content analyses and survey questionnaires to assess quantitatively the influence of violence on prime-time US television (Gerbner and Gross, 1976; Gerbner *et al.*, 1994). The central finding is that 'heavy' television viewers (those who watch most TV—more than four hours per day in Gerbner's studies) cultivate a world view which more closely resembles the 'television message' than 'light' television viewers (those who watch less than two hours per day). Since television overstates both the seriousness and risk of criminal victimization, portraying the world as 'mean and scary', heavy viewing is said to cultivate higher fear of crime.

While supported in some studies (Hawkins and Pingree, 1980; Morgan, 1983), others have failed to replicate the cultivation effect (Gunter, 1987; Cumberbatch, 1989), and a number of empirical and theoretical weaknesses have been identified. It does not necessarily follow, for example, that people who watch the most television watch the most television violence. An exaggerated sense of the risk of crime is not the same as fear of crime, yet these distinct concepts are easily confused. Many of the limitations of quantitative content analyses more generally—the distinction between forms of violence, the subjective definition of what violence is, the direction of influence, the relative importance of non-media factors—apply equally to cultivation studies of fear of crime.

In an attempt to address these weaknesses, more recent studies, including revised work by Gerbner and colleagues, have paid greater attention to the nature, form, and context of crime and violence in the media. While earlier studies considered violent incidents as decontextualized units, recent work considers the complete scene, in which the consequences of violence are also shown, or the entire programme, in which the *overall* message may be one of restored order and reassurance, rather than dread and fear (Potter *et al.*, 1997). The extent to which images of crime and violence resonate with consumers' lives may be crucial to their impact. Schlesinger *et al.* (1992), for example, found that women may be particularly sensitive to images of interpersonal attacks. Partly on this basis, concerns have been expressed that the highly unrepresentative focus on 'real' violent and sexual interpersonal crimes in the BBC's long-running reality show *Crimewatch UK* may increase levels of fear in sections of the viewing audience (Schlesinger and Tumber, 1993; Jewkes, 2004).

The resonance of media images of crime and violence may also be influenced by their perceived proximity (spatial and cultural nearness). Research on US television news concluded that local crime coverage generates more fear than national coverage, particularly within individuals who have experienced victimization and perceive television accounts to be realistic (Chiricos *et al.*, 2000; see also Eschholz *et al.*, 2003; cf. Heath and Petraitis, 1987; Roberts, 2001). The purely quantitative approach limits any explanation of these findings, though they are supported in studies on US newspaper readership (Heath, 1984). In the UK, Ditton *et al.* have conducted a series of analyses which seek to advance the media-fear of crime debate in two substantive ways (Ditton *et al.*, 2004). Firstly, their quantitative data included variables relating to distant-past as well as immediate-past media consumption, since anxieties about crime and disorder may have been established long before participation in the study. Secondly, a sub-sample of the participants surveyed quantitatively was also interviewed qualitatively. The quantitative data reveal some fear of crime, but do not establish a connection between this fear and media consumption. In line with the 'reception analysis' work of media scholars, including Schlesinger *et al.* (1992) discussed above, the qualitative data indicate that it is not the 'objectively determined randomness, localness or sensationalism that is important, but rather the interpretation of media content as relevant to and by the consumer' (Ditton *et al.*, 2004: 607).

Aside from illustrating the contradictory nature of the research findings, these examples further demonstrate the usefulness of developing qualitative research approaches which consider the everyday contexts within which media images are consumed. Such approaches help not only to describe the relationships between media and fear of crime, but also to explain and understand them. While the relationship between media images and fear of crime remains difficult to demonstrate conclusively, it is beyond doubt that media can have a profound influence on sections of the population at certain times. It is with this in mind that the next section considers the sociological theory of moral panic.

Moral panics and multi-mediated societies

The term 'moral panic' refers to the disproportionate and hostile social reaction to a group or condition perceived as a threat to societal values. It involves sensational and stereotypical media coverage, public outcry, and demands for tougher controls. As the name suggests, the panic may subside as rapidly as it erupted (Goode and Ben-Yehuda, 1994; Murji, 2001; Garland, 2008). Moral panics have most often emerged around youth-related issues, particularly subcultural forms of youth expression and identity—for example, punk, acid house, rave, and the wider drugs culture—but football hooliganism, satanic child abuse, and the re-housing of child sex offenders in the community have also been the source of recent panic (Best, 1990; Jenkins, 1992; Silverman and Wilson, 2002; Cross, 2005).

In the original analysis, Cohen (1972) problematized the social reaction to the Mods and Rockers disturbances in 1964, when boredom and bad weather one Bank Holiday resulted in a few fights, lots of noise, and some windows being smashed. Though the damage was minor, the national press exaggerated and sensationalized the disturbances using phrases like 'day of terror' and 'hell-bent on destruction'. News reports predicted further violence, demanded tighter controls, and portrayed Mods and Rockers as 'folk devils'—a symbol not just of youth delinquency but of wider permissiveness and social decline. Cohen (1972) demonstrates how the labelling and marginalization of Mods and Rockers, and the emphasis on mutual antagonism, created a 'deviancy amplification spiral' in which future disturbances were virtually guaranteed. These disturbances seemed to justify initial fears, resulting in more media coverage, more public outcry, more policing, and thus the spiral of reaction and deviancy amplification continued. The moral panic occurred at a time of rapid social change. In particular, the increase in youth spending power and sexual freedom, defiantly flaunted and revelled in by so many young people, blurred moral and class boundaries and challenged the traditional ethics of hard work and sobriety, generating uncertainty and hostility among 'respectable society'. The 'creation' of Mods and Rockers, then, provided scapegoats or 'folk devils'—a deviant minority against whom the conforming (nostalgically reactionary, adult) majority could unite at a time of uncertainty, conflict, and change.

In a radical, Gramscian analysis of 'hegemonic crisis' at a time of economic recession, political decline, and class unrest in 1970s Britain, Hall *et al.* (1978) argue that the State orchestrated a moral panic around 'mugging', casting in the central role the image of the black street criminal. The creation of this 'folk devil', again against which all 'respectable citizens' could unite, tapped into escalating fears around crime, race, and social decline, and allowed the State to reassert and re-legitimate itself—'policing the crisis', crucially with the consent of the people, by stamping down hard on the problem from above (see *Crime, Media, Culture: An International Journal*, 4,1 for a special section on 'Policing the Crisis Thirty Years On').

Critics of moral panic theory have questioned the attribution of 'disproportionality' to social reaction because this assumes some superior knowledge of the objective reality of the issue against which the reaction can be measured, and a tacit assumption regarding what a 'proportionate' reaction would look like (Waddington, 1986). Left realists, in particular, have committed to 'take crime seriously' and insist that crime and fear of crime cannot simply be dismissed as groundless media-induced hysteria (Matthews and Young, 1992). Others have gone further, suggesting that in multi-mediated societies the concept of moral panic needs to be reformulated (McRobbie and Thornton, 1995; Ungar, 2001). While folk devils were once helpless against their demonization, they may now find themselves being supported vociferously in the same mass media that castigate them. In the chaotic 24–7 global mediasphere, they may also provide counter-definitions and explanations in any number of alternative media outlets. While moral panics were once rare, they are now commonplace, and even commercially desirable. One of the best ways of promoting (and selling) records, clothes, books, films—most popular cultural commodities, in fact—is actively to court controversy and generate a little 'panic'. Few things get in the way of commercial success, particularly of youth-oriented products, more than conventional approval.

REVIEW QUESTIONS

1 What does the 'effects' model propose? In what ways has effects research been criticized?

2 Compile a list of factors, other than media representations, which might influence fear of crime. Which of these do you think are most/least important?

3 Can you think of any recent moral panics? On what basis would you say that the term 'moral panic' is sociologically justified?

Contemporary dimensions in crime and media: Global terror, surveillance, and the cyber

Today, newsworthy crime and justice events are reported as they happen, high-profile 'celebrity' trials are broadcast live, and the growth in 'reality' programming continues to erode the boundaries between news and entertainment, fact and fiction (Fishman and Cavender, 1998; Brown, 2003; Valverde, 2006). This blurring of the boundaries between the represented and the real shapes our perceptions of the world in profound ways. As Sontag (1977: 161) noted some years ago: 'It is common now for people to insist about their experience of a violent event in which they were caught up—a plane crash, a shoot-out, a terrorist bombing—that "it seemed like a movie". This is said, other descriptions seeming insufficient, in order to explain how real it was.'

The destruction of New York's twin towers—the symbolic heart of Western capitalism—on 11 September 2001 was also an exercise in media politics. Across the world, live coverage of the horror served both as the ultimate humiliation of American imperial power and a calling to like-minded fundamentalists to join the struggle. During the subsequent invasions of Afghanistan and Iraq, the US military employed 'shock and awe' (Ullman and Wade, 1996), a strategy that seeks to achieve rapid dominance over adversaries by overloading their perceptions and understandings of events to the point of paralysing the will to carry on. Sheer and spectacular brute force is combined with rapidity of action and the near total control of information (and misinformation), including the relentless media broadcasting of the annihilation of enemy targets. Faced with this overwhelming military might, insurgents realize that the media are one of the most effective weapons with which to retaliate (Ferrell *et al.*, 2005). Alongside spectacular acts of mass destruction, carefully staged mujahideen executions of Western kidnap victims—featuring props, backdrops, scripts to be read aloud by the condemned—are cast live on the Internet, bringing violence of an extraordinary intensity into the living rooms of a global media audience. The contest of strike and counter-strike, claim and counter-claim, becomes hyper-mediatized in a manner unimaginable in the industrial

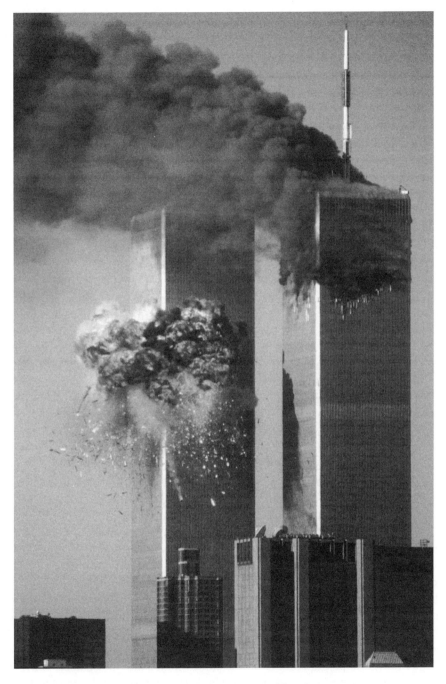

Figure 8.3 The 11 September 2001 attacks on New York's twin towers

Source: © Reuters/CORBIS

modern era. As Castells (2004: 139) argues: 'The media, local and global, are the means of communication through which the public mind is formed. Therefore, action has to be media-oriented, it has to be spectacular, provide good footage, so the whole world can see it: like a Hollywood movie because this is what has trained the human mind in our times.'

This process of hyper-mediatization extends to other spheres of crime and control, in turn looping back to connect again with defining twenty-first century fears and insecurities (Ferrell *et al.*, 2008). With more than four million operational surveillance cameras, the UK has the dubious distinction of containing the highest ratio of cameras to people anywhere in the world: the inner city citizen can be captured by more than 300 CCTV cameras every day (Home Office Affairs Committee, 2008). While some level of surveillance is necessary for the smooth running of any democracy—for example, an up-to-date record of every citizen's name and address is a requirement for postal services and electoral systems to function—the exponential increase in surveillance has generated concerns about the erosion of civil liberties and the boundaries between public and private in a 'surveillance society' (Lyon, 2001; Norris and Armstrong, 1999; McCahill, 2002; Smith, 2007). Considered alongside the massive growth in personal data gathering in the private and public sectors—travel, credit, store loyalty and identity cards, mobile phones, online banking, shopping and social networking facilities, the development of predictive customer profiling systems—the clear benefits of surveillance cannot eclipse its potential problems. Individuals are reduced to 'bits' of information, classified into particular categories or groups on the basis of their recorded, expected, or 'suspected' preferences or activities. There are real risks of data loss and abuse by those in power, the criminal appropriation of confidential personal information, and the demonization and stereotyping of whole sections of society (Coleman, 2005; Finch, 2006). Such stereotyping spans the full spectrum of deviance, from efforts to control everyday youthful transgression—such as banning hooded tops or 'hoodies' from shopping centres (Hayward and Yar, 2006)—to the ongoing 'war on terror'. For Mythen and Walklate (2006), intensified surveillance breeds a climate of fear that serves to secure tacit consent for the introduction of increasingly repressive legislation, simultaneously encouraging not only personal vigilance, but also suspicion and mistrust of potentially 'risky' situations and individuals. When combined with often simplistic and reductionist media representations of the non-white 'terrorist Other' (Greer and Jewkes, 2005), the impact on minority ethnic communities can be considerable. In the five weeks following the 7 July 2005 London bombings, there was a six-fold increase in religious hate crimes (Mythen and Walklate, 2006).

The massive expansion of the Internet generates unprecedented opportunities for social networking and establishing virtual communities (Greer, 2004), but also new forms of criminality and criminal victimization. The spread of hate sites (Franko Aas, 2006), cyberstalking (Wykes, 2007), viral victimization (Brown, 2003), and the 'grooming' of children and perpetration of online child sexual abuse (Martellozzo, forthcoming), have all come under the criminological gaze. In response, new forms of justice and control are likewise shaped by the cyber. In the US, following the 1994 murder of New Jersey seven-year-old Megan Kanka by a convicted paedophile, Megan's Law allows anyone with an Internet connection to access the names, photographs, and addresses of convicted sex offenders living in the community. Repackaged as some kind of reality entertainment, in *To Catch a Predator* millions of Americans watch weekly as hidden camera 'sting' investigations expose potential sex offenders arriving at meetings they believe to be with minors for sex. That the meetings are arranged online with adult volunteers posing as children and that the suspected predators are met first by camera crews, and then the police, muddies still further notions of responsibility, legal authority, and justice in a multi-mediated world. Across the 24–7 global mediasphere, the conceptualization, definition, and experience of crime and control are changing. The challenge is for media criminologists to keep up.

CONCLUSION

This chapter has provided an overview of some of the main issues and debates which continue to inform the scholarly investigation of crime and media. You should now have a sense of the nature and extent of crime, violence, and control in media content, an understanding of some of the dominant theoretical and conceptual tools used to explain and understand media representations, a working knowledge of the evidence for and against media effects, and an awareness of new developments in crime and media research. Equipped with this knowledge and insight, you can now explore in greater detail any issues which have challenged your assumptions, tested your critical faculties, or stimulated your imagination.

The themes developed in this chapter should not be considered in isolation, but as part of a much wider criminological enterprise which seeks to 'make sense' of our social world and to understand matters of crime, deviance, and control from a diversity of perspectives. Some of the chapters in this volume deal with the related matters of, for example, theory, youth, and policing. Others describe particular movements and orientations within criminology, borne out of the growing popular, political, and intellectual fascination with deviance and disorder. Cultural criminology, in particular, is highly sensitized to the significance of media, image, style, and representation to the processes of criminalization, control, resistance, and identity (see Chapter 6, also *Theoretical Criminology*, special issue on Cultural Criminology, 2004).

Today, image and representation penetrate all areas of social existence. Media tap into and reinforce social and political concerns. They help shape individual and collective identities, sensibilities, fears, anxieties, and appetites. They provoke public outcry and, at times, generate moral panics. They serve as ideological weapons in the ongoing struggle for hegemony. They impart important, but often mixed, messages about the nature and extent of 'the crime problem', how we should think and feel about it, who is most at risk, and what is to be done. They indicate, however inaccurately, the State of the nation. They also entertain. 'Crime talk' (Sasson, 1995), in whatever form, simultaneously elicits fear and fascination; it is a major source of concern, but also of distraction, resistance, escapism, and moral reassurance (Sparks, 1992; Ferrell, 1996, 2003; Greer and Jewkes, 2005). Crime sells. It always has.

Whether as news, fiction, or that expanding cultural form that lies somewhere in between, the sheer quantity of crime in the media illustrates that we have an insatiable appetite for narratives of deviance and control. And there is evidence to suggest we are growing hungrier (Reiner *et al.*, 2000a). Given the close inter-relationship between the political, commercial, and cultural significance of crime and disorder, it is small wonder it features so prominently across all media and markets. As the boundaries between fact and fiction (the represented and the real) become increasingly diffuse and uncertain, so the importance of understanding the connections between crime and the media becomes more concrete.

QUESTIONS FOR DISCUSSION

1 Design and conduct your own content analysis of newspaper crime reporting. Make sure you include both quantitative and qualitative considerations.

2 Compare coverage of the same crime or justice event in at least three different media forms (newspaper, Internet, television, radio). How and why does representation differ between media forms and organizations?

3 Watch an episode of your favourite crime drama or a recent film and note the portrayal of policing and criminal justice. Are the representations favourable or critical?

4 Keep a 'crime diary' for a week and record your thoughts and feelings about crime and personal safety. Do media representations have any impact on your fear of crime?

GUIDE TO FURTHER READING

Cohen, S. (2002) *Folk Devils and Moral Panics: The Creation of Mods and Rockers* (3rd edn). London: Routledge.

The book that launched a thousand studies, this classic text presents the original development of 'moral panic'—one of the most widely used (and often misused) concepts in the sociology of crime and social control.

Crime, Media, Culture: An International Journal. London: Sage.

This international journal provides a forum for the increasing number of researchers working at the interface between criminology, media studies and cultural studies. In addition to publishing more conventional scholarly articles, CMC includes photographic essays, international research think-pieces, and reviews of relevant crime-media material.

Greer, C. (2008) *Crime and Media: A Reader.* London: Routledge.

This book provides the only comprehensive collection of key and classic readings on crime and media in one volume, covering the key areas of: Understanding Media; Researching Media; Crime, Newsworthiness and News; Crime, Entertainment and Creativity; Effects, Influence and Moral Panics; and Cybercrime, Surveillance and Social Control.

Jewkes, Y. (2005) *Media and Crime,* London: Sage.

This highly accessible textbook offers a book length analysis of many of the issues discussed in the chapter you have just read.

Mason, P. (ed) (2003) *Criminal Visions: Representations of Crime and Justice.* Cullompton: Willan.

This edited collection presents a series of insightful analyses exploring the relationship between crime, control, and a wide range of media forms in late modernity.

WEB LINKS

http://www.lexisnexis.com

LexisNexis is a useful resource for conducting online searches of news and other print media from around the world. As noted in this chapter, however, beware that data are returned structure, style, and image free. Use LexisNexis to locate the coverage, then go get the original copy to research it!

http://www.spiked-online.com

Spiked is an independent online publication which offers an alternative and always critical take on the news stories of the day. Its self-stated priorities are liberty, enlightenment, experimentation, and excellence.

http://www.theory.org.uk

Theory.org.uk is a fun and accessible website maintained by David Gauntlett, which includes information on media effects, key social and cultural theorists, and plenty of links to other useful media-oriented sites.

http://www.ccms-infobase.com

The Communication, Cultural and Media Studies Infobase contains a wide range of salient links, definitions, and issues for debate—pitched at an introductory undergraduate level—which are easy to navigate.

REFERENCES

Allen, J., Livingstone, S., and Reiner, R. (1997) 'The Changing Generic Location of Crime in Film: A Content Analysis of Film Synopses', *Journal of Communication*, 47, 4: 89–101.

Andison, E. (1977) 'TV Violence and Viewer Aggression: A Cumulation of Study Results, 1956–1979', *Public Opinion Quarterly*, 41, 3: 314–31.

Bailey, F. and Hale, D. (1997) *Popular Culture, Crime and Justice*. Belmont, CA: West/Wadsworth.

Bandura, A., Ross, D., and Ross, S. (1961) 'Transmission of Aggression through Imitation of Aggressive Models', *Journal of Abnormal and Social Psychology*, 66, 3: 575–82.

Bandura, A., Ross, D. and Ross, S. (1963) 'Imitation of Film-Mediated Aggressive Models', *Journal of Abnormal and Social Psychology*, 66, 1: 3–11.

Barker, M. (2001) 'The Newson Report: A Case Study in Common Sense', in M. Barker and J. Petley (eds) (2001) *Ill Effects: The Media/Violence Debate* (2nd edn). London: Routledge.

Barker, M. and Petley, J. (eds)(2001) *Ill Effects: The Media/Violence Debate* (2nd edn). London: Routledge.

Barlow, M., Barlow, D., and Chiricos, T. (1995) 'Economic Conditions and Ideologies of Crime in the Media: A Content Analysis of Crime News', in *Crime and Delinquency*, 41, 1: 3–19.

Baudrillard, J. (1983) 'The Precession of the Simulacra', in T. Doherty (ed) *The Postmodern Reader*. Hemel Hempstead: Harvester Press.

Best, J. (1990) *Threatened Children*. Chicago: University of Chicago Press.

Blumler, J. and Gurevitch, L. (1995) *The Crisis of Public Communication*. London: Routledge.

Box, S., Hale, C., and Andrews, G. (1988) 'Explaining Fear of Crime', *British Journal of Criminology*, 28: 340–56.

Briggs, A. and Cobley, P. (eds) (2002) *The Media: An Introduction* (2nd edn). London: Longman.

Brown, S. (2003) *Crime and Law in Media Culture*. Buckingham: Open University Press.

Buckingham, D. (1993) *Children Talking Television: The Making of Television Literacy*. London: Falmer Press.

Buckingham, D. (2000) *The Making of Citizens: Young People, News and Politics*. London: Routledge.

Carter, C. and Weaver, C. (2003) *Violence and the Media*. Buckingham: Open University Press.

Castells, M. (2004) *The Power of Identity* (2nd edn). Oxford: Blackwell.

Cavender, G. and Mulcahy, A. (1998) 'Trial by Fire: Media Constructions of Corporate Deviance', in *Justice Quarterly*, 15, 4: 697–719.

Chibnall, S. (1977) *Law and Order News: An Analysis of Crime Reporting in the British Press*. London: Tavistock.

Chiricos, T., Padgett, K., and Gertz, M. (2000) 'Fear, TV News, and the Reality of Crime', in *Criminology*, 38, 3: 755–85.

Chomsky, N. (1989) *Necessary Illusions*. London: Pluto Press.

Cohen, S. (1972) *Folk Devils and Moral Panics: The Creation of the Mods and Rockers*. London: MacGibbon and Kee.

Cohen, S. (2001) *States of Denial: Knowing about Atrocities and Suffering*. Cambridge: Polity.

Coleman, R. (2005) 'Surveillance in the City: Primary Definition and Urban Spatial Order', *Crime, Media, Culture: An International Journal*, 1, 2: 131–148.

Cross, S. (2005) 'Paedophiles in the Community: Inter-Agency Conflict, News Leaks and the Local Press', *Crime, Media, Culture: An International Journal*, 1, 3: 284–300.

Cumberbatch, G. (1989) 'Violence in the Media: The Research Evidence', in G. Cumberbatch and D. Howitt (eds) *A Measure of Uncertainty: the Effects of the Mass Media*. London: John Libbey.

Cumberbatch, G., Woods, S., and Maguire, A. (1995) *Crime in the News: Television, Radio and Newspapers: A Report for BBC Broadcasting Research*. Birmingham: Aston University, Communications Research Group.

Davies, P., Francis, P., and Greer, C. (2007) *Victims, Crime and Society*. London: Sage.

Davis, M. (1994) 'Beyond Blade Runner: Urban Control. The Ecology of Fear', in E. McLaughlin, J. Muncie, and G. Hughes (eds) (2003) *Criminological Perspectives: Essential Readings* (2nd edn). London: Sage.

Ditton, J., Chadee, D., Farrall, S., Gilchrist, E. and Bannister, J. (2004), 'From Imitation to Intimidation: A Note on the Curious and Changing Relationship Between the Media, Crime and Fear of Crime', *British Journal of Criminology*, 44, 4: 595–610.

Ditton, J. and Duffy, J. (1983) 'Bias in the Newspaper Reporting of Crime', in *British Journal of Criminology*, 23, 2: 159–65.

Ericson, R., Baranek, P., and Chan, J. (1987) *Visualising Deviance: A Study of News Organisation*. Milton Keynes: Open University Press.

Ericson, R., Baranek, P., and Chan, J. (1989) *Negotiating Control: A Study of News Sources*. Milton Keynes: Open University Press.

Ericson, R., Baranek, P., and Chan, J. (1991) *Representing Order: Crime, Law and Justice in the News Media*. Milton Keynes: Open University Press.

Eschholz, S., Chiricos, T., and Gertz, M. (2003) 'Television and Fear of Crime: Programme Types, Audience Traits and the Mediating Effect of Perceived Neighbourhood Racial Composition', in *Social Problems*, 50, 3: 395–415.

Ferraro, K. (1995) *Fear of Crime: Interpreting Victimisation Risk*. New York: State University of New York, Albany.

Ferrell, J, (1996) *Crimes of Style: Urban Graffiti and the Politics of Criminalisation*, Northeastern University Press: University Press of New England.

Ferrell, J. (2003) 'Cultural criminology' in E. McLaughlin, J. Muncie, and G. Hughes (eds) *Criminological Perspectives; Essential Readings*. London, Sage.

Ferrell, J., Greer, C., and Jewkes, Y. (2005) 'Hip Hop Graffiti, Mexican Murals, and the War on Terror' in *Crime, Media, Culture: An International Journal*, 1, 1: 5–9.

Ferrell, J., Hayward, K., and Young. J. (2008) *Cultural Criminology: An Invitation*. London: Sage.

Finch, E. (2006) 'The Problem of Stolen Identity and the Internet', in Y. Jewkes (ed) *Crime Online*, Cullompton: Willan.

Fishman, M. (1978) 'Crime Waves as Ideology', *Social Problems*, 25, 5: 531–43.

Fishman, M. and Cavender, G. (eds) (1998) *Entertaining Crime: Television Reality Programmes* New York: Aldine de Gruyter.

Franko Aas, K. (2006) 'Governance and the Internet' in Y. Jewkes (ed) *Crime Online*, Cullompton: Willan.

Galtung, J. and Ruge, M. (1965) 'Structuring and selecting news', in S. Cohen and J. Young (eds) (1981) *The Manufacture of News: Deviance, Social Problems and the Mass Media* (rev. edn). London: Constable.

Gans, H. (1980) *Deciding What's News*. London: Constable.

Garland, D. (2008) 'On the Concept of Moral Panic', in *Crime, Media, Culture: An International Journal*, 4, 1: 9–30.

Gauntlett, D. (1997) *Video Critical: Children, the Environment and Media Power*. London: John Libbey.

Gauntlett, D. (2001) 'The Worrying Influence of "Media Effects" Studies', in M. Barker and J. Petley (eds) *Ill Effects: The Media/Violence Debate* (2nd edn). London: Routledge.

Gerbner, G. and Gross, L. (1976) 'Living with Television: the Violence Profile', in *Journal of Communication*, 26, 1: 173–99.

Gerbner, G., Gross, L., Morgan, M., and Signorielli, N. (1994) 'Growing up with Television; The Cultivation Perspective', in J. Bryant and D. Zillman (eds) *Media Effects*. Hillsdale, NJ: Lawrence Erlbaum.

Goode, E. and Ben-Yehuda, N. (1994) *Moral Panics: The Social Construction of Deviance*. Oxford: Blackwell.

Graber, D. (1980) *Crime, News and the Public*. New York: Prager.

Gramsci, A. (1971) *Selections from the Prison Notebooks*. London: Lawrence and Wishart.

Green, D. (2008) *When Children Kill Children: Penal Populism and Political Culture*. Oxford: Clarendon.

Greer, C. (2003) *Sex Crime and the Media: Sex Offending and the Press in a Divided Society*. Cullompton: Willan.

Greer, C. (2004) 'Crime, Media and Community: Grief and Virtual Engagement in Late Modernity', in J. Ferrell, K. Hayward, W. Morrison and M. Presdee (eds) *Cultural Criminology Unleashed*. London: Cavendish.

Greer, C. (2007) 'News Media, Victims and Crime', in P. Davies, P. Francis, and C. Greer (eds) *Victims, Crime and Society*. London: Sage.

Greer, C. (2009) *Crime and Media; A Reader.* London: Routledge.

Greer, C. and Jewkes, Y. (2005) 'Extremes of Otherness: Media Images of Social Exclusion' in *Social Justice (special edition on Emerging Imaginaries of Regulation, Control and Oppression).* 32, 1: 20–31.

Gunter, B. (1987) *Television and the Fear of Crime.* London: John Libbey.

Gunter, B., Harrison, J., and Wykes, M. (2003) *Violence on Television: Distribution, Form, Context and Themes.* London: Lawrence Erlbaum.

Hale, C. (1996) 'Fear of Crime: A Review of the Literature', *International Review of Victimology,* 4: 79–150.

Hall, S., Critcher, C., Jefferson, T., Clarke, J., and Roberts, B. (1978) *Policing the Crisis: Mugging, the State and Law and Order.* London: Macmillan.

Hamm, M. (2007) 'High Crimes and Misdemeanors: George Bush and the Sins of Abu Ghraib', in *Crime, Media, Culture: An International Journal,* 3, 3: 259–284.

Hawkins, R. and Pingree, S. (1980) 'Some Processes in the Cultivation Effect', *Communication Research,* 7, 2: 193–226.

Hayward, K. and Yar, M. (2006) 'The "Chav" Phenomenon: Consumption, Media and the Construction of a New Underclass', *Crime. Media, Culture: An International Journal,* 2, 1: 9–28.

Heath, L. (1984) 'Impact of Newspaper Crime Reports on Fear of Crime: Multi-Methodological Investigation', *Journal of Personality and Social Psychology,* 47, 2: 263–76.

Heath, L. and Petraitis, J. (1987) 'Television Viewing and Fear of Crime: Where is the Mean World?' *Basic and Applied Social Psychology,* 8, 1/2: 97–123.

Herman, E. and Chomsky, N. (1994) *Manufacturing Consent: The Political Economy of the Mass Media.* New York: Pantheon.

Hetherington, A. (1985) *News, Newspapers and Television.* London: Macmillan.

Home Office Affairs Committee (2008) *A Surveillance Society.* London: The Stationery Office.

Hough, M. and Mayhew, P. (1983) *The British Crime Survey,* Home Office Research Study 76. London: HMSO.

Howitt, D. (1998) *Crime, the Media and the Law.* London: Wiley.

Huesmann, A. (1995) *Screen Violence and Real Violence: Understanding the Link,* Auckland: Media Aware.

Hunt, D. (1997) *Screening the Los Angeles 'Riots',* New York: Cambridge University Press.

Jenkins, P. (1992) *Intimate Enemies: Moral Panics in Contemporary Great Britain.* Hawthorne, NY: Aldine de Gruyter.

Jenkins, P. (1994) *Using Murder: The Social Construction of Serial Homicide.* Hawthorne, NY: Aldine de Gruyter.

Jewkes, Y. (2004) *Media and Crime.* London: Sage.

Kitzinger, J. (1999a) 'A sociology of media power: key issues in audience reception research', in G. Philo (ed) *Message Received.* London: Longman.

Kitzinger, J. (2004) *Framing Abuse: Media Influence and Public Understanding of Sexual Violence Against Children,* London: Pluto.

Kitzinger, J. and Skidmore, P. (1995) 'Child Sexual Abuse and the Media', Summary Report to ESRC. Award no. R000233675. Report available from Glasgow Media Group.

Knight, S. (2004) *Crime Fiction 1800–2000.* Basingstoke: Palgrave Macmillan.

Knottnerus, D., Ulsperger, J., Cummins, S., and Osteen, E. (2006) 'Exposing Enron: Media Representations of Ritualised Deviance in Corporate Culture' in *Crime, Media, Culture: An International Journal,* 2, 2: 177–195.

Koss, S. (1984) *The Rise and Fall of the Political Press in Britain.* London: Hamish Hamilton.

Leishman, F. and Mason, P. (2003) *Policing and the Media: Facts, Fictions and Factions.* Cullompton: Willan.

Livingstone, S. (1996) 'On the Continuing Problem of Media Effects', in J. Curran and M. Gurevitch (eds) *Mass Media and Society.* London: Arnold.

Lynch, M., Stretesky, P., and Hammond, P. (2000) 'Media Coverage of Chemical Crimes, Hillsborough County, Florida, 1987–1997', in *British Journal of Criminology,* 40, 1: 112–26.

Lyon, D. (2001) *Surveillance Society: Monitoring Everyday Life.* Buckingham: Open University Press.

Maguire, M. (2007) 'Crime Data and Statistics', in M. Maguire, R. Morgan, and R. Reiner (eds) *The Oxford Handbook of Criminology* (4th edn). Oxford: Oxford University Press.

Marsh, H.L. (1991) 'A Comparative Analysis of Crime Coverage in Newspapers in the United States and Other Countries From 1960–1989: A Review of the Literature', in *Journal of Criminal Justice,* 19, 1: 67–80.

Martellozzo, E. (forthcoming) Policing Child Sexual Abuse Online, unpublished PhD Thesis., Kingston University.

Matthews, R. and Young, J. (1992) (eds) *Rethinking Criminology: the Realist Debate.* London: Sage.

McCahill, M. (2002) *The Surveillance Web: The Rise of Visual Surveillance in an English City.* Cullompton: Willan.

McNair, B. (1998) *The Sociology of Journalism*. London: Arnold.

McNair, B. (1999) *News and Journalism in the UK: A Text Book* (3rd edn). London: Routledge.

McNair, B. (2006a) *Cultural Chaos: Journalism, News and Power in a Globalised World*. London: Routledge.

McNair, B. (2006b) 'The Culture of Chaos', *The Guardian*, 1 May.

McRobbie, A. and Thornton, S. (1995) 'Rethinking "Moral Panic" for Multi-Mediated Social Worlds', *British Journal of Sociology*. 46, 4: 559–74.

Miller, D. (1993) 'Official Sources and "Primary Definition": The Case of Northern Ireland', *Media, Culture and Society*, 15, 3: 385–406.

Morgan, M. (1983) 'Symbolic Victimisation and Real World Fear', in *Human Communication Research*, 9, 2: 146–57.

Murdock, G. (2001) 'Reservoirs of dogma: an archaeology of popular anxieties' in M. Barker and J. Petley (eds) (2001) *Ill Effects: The Media/Violence Debate*, (2nd edn). London: Routledge.

Murji, K. (2001) 'Moral panics', in E. McLaughlin and J. Muncie (eds) *The Sage Dictionary of Criminology*. London: Sage.

Muzzatti, S. (2003) 'Criminalizing Marginality and Resistance: Marilyn Manson, Columbine and Cultural Criminology', paper presented at the American Society of Criminology Conference, Denver, Colorado, November 2003.

Mythen, G. and Walklate, S. (2006) 'Communicating the Terrorist Risk: Harnessing a Culture of Fear', in *Crime, Media, Culture: An International Journal*, 2, 2: 123–142.

Naylor, B. (2001) 'Reporting Violence in the British Print Media: Gendered Stories', in *Howard Journal of Criminal Justice*, 40, 2: 180–194.

Norris, C. and Armstrong, G. (1999) *The Maximum Surveillance Society: The Rise of CCTV*. London: Berg.

Paik, H. and Comstock, G. (1994) 'The Effects of Television Violence on Anti-Social Behaviour: A Meta-Analysis', in *Communication Research*, 21, 4: 516–46.

Pearson, G. (1983) *Hooligan: A History of Respectable Fears*. London: Macmillan.

Peelo, M. (2006) 'Framing Homicide Narratives in Newspapers: Mediated Witness and the Construction of Virtual Victimhood', *Crime, Media Culture: An International Journal*, 2, 2: 159–175.

Philo, G. (ed) (1999) *Message Received*. London: Longman.

Poster, M. (1990) *The Mode of Information: Poststructuralism and Social Context*. Cambridge: Polity Press.

Potter, W., Vaughan, M., Warren, R., Howley, K., Land, A., and Hagemeyer, J. (1997) 'Aggression in Television Entertainment: Profiles and Trends', *Communication Research Reports*, 14: 116–24.

Reiner, R. (2007) 'Media Made Criminality: The representation of crime in the mass media', in M. Maguire, R. Morgan and R. Reiner (eds) *The Oxford Handbook of Criminology* (4th edn). Oxford: Oxford University Press.

Reiner, R., Livingstone, S., and Allen, J. (2000a) 'Casino culture: media and crime in a winner-loser society' in K. Stenson and D. Cowell (eds) *Crime, Risk and Justice*. Cullompton: Willan.

Reiner, R., Livingstone, S., and Allen, J. (2000b) 'No more happy endings? The media and popular concern about crime since the Second World War', in T. Hope and R. Sparks (eds) *Crime, Risk and Insecurity*. London: Routledge.

Roberts, M. (2001) 'Just Noise? Newspaper Crime Reporting and the Fear of Crime', in *Criminal Justice Matters*, 43, Spring: 12–13.

Rock, P. (1973) 'News as eternal recurrence' in S. Cohen and J. Young (eds) (1981) *The Manufacture of News: Social Problems, Deviance and the Mass Media* (rev. edn). London: Constable.

Rojek, C. (2001) *Celebrity (FOCI)*. London: Reaktion Books.

Roshier, R. (1973) 'The Selection of Crime News by the Press', in S. Cohen and J. Young (eds) (1981) *The Manufacture of News: Deviance, Social Problems and the Mass Media* (rev. edn). London: Constable.

Sasson, T. (1995) *Crime Talk: How Citizens Construct Social Problems*. Howthorne, NY: Aldine de Gruyter.

Schlesinger, P., Dobash, R.E., Dobash, R., and Weaver, C.K. (1992) *Women Viewing Violence*. London: British Film Institute.

Schlesinger, P. and Tumber, H. (1993) 'Don't have Nightmares: Do Sleep Well', *Criminal Justice Matters*, 11: 4.

Schlesinger, P. and Tumber, H. (1994) *Reporting Crime: The Media Politics of Criminal Justice*. Oxford: Clarendon Press.

Silverman, J. and Wilson, D. (2002) *Innocence Betrayed: Paedophilia, the Media and Society*. Cambridge: Polity Press.

Smith, G. (2007) 'Exploring Relations Between Watchers and Watched in Control(led) Systems: Strategies and Tactics', *Surveillance and Society*, 4, 4: 280–313.

Smith, S. (1984) 'Crime in the News', in *British Journal of Criminology*, 24, 3: 289–95.

Sontag, S. (2004) Regarding the Torture of Others, *New York Times*, 23 May.

Soothill, K. and Walby, S. (1991) *Sex Crime in the News*. London: Routledge.

Soothill, K., Peelo, M., Francis, B., Pearson, J., and Ackerley, E. (2002) 'Homicide and the Media: Identifying the Top Cases in The Times', *Howard Journal of Criminal Justice*, 41, 5 401–421.

Sparks, R. (1992) *Television and the Drama of Crime: Moral Tales and the Place of Crime in Public Life*. Buckingham: Open University Press.

Thompson, J.B. (2000) *Political Scandal: Power and Visibility in the Media Age*. Cambridge: Polity.

Tombs, S. and White, D. (2001) 'Reporting Corporate Crime out of Existence', *Criminal Justice Matters*, 43: 22–24.

Ullman, H. and Wade, J. (1996) *Shock and Awe: Achieving Rapid Dominance*. Washington, DC: National Defence University.

Ungar, S. (2001) 'Moral Panics versus the Risk Society: The Implications of the Changing Sites of Social Anxiety', *British Journal of Sociology*, 52, 2: 271–91.

Valverde, M. (2006) *Law and Order: Images, Meanings, Myths*. Routledge: London.

Waddington (1986) 'Mugging as a Moral Panic: A Question of Proportion', *British Journal of Sociology*, 37, 2: 245–59.

Williams, P. and Dickinson, J. (1993) 'Fear of Crime; Read All About It; The Relationship Between Newspaper Crime Reporting and Fear of Crime', in *British Journal of Criminology*, 33, 1: 33–56.

Wilson, B.J., Donnerstein, E., Linz, D., Smith, S., Gray, T., Blumenthal, E., and Potter, W. (1998) 'Content analysis of entertainment television: the importance of context', in J. Hamilton (ed) *Television Violence and Public Policy*, Ann Arbor, Michigan: University of Michigan Press.

Wykes, M. (2007) 'Constructing Crime: Culture, Stalking, Celebrity and Cyber', *Crime, Media, Culture: An International Journal*, 3, 2: 158–174.

Part Two

FORMS OF CRIME

9 'Volume crime' and everyday life

Mike Presdee

INTRODUCTION

We all carry within us a view of crime that is partly created by personal experience and partly by what we read, view, and hear. Film, literature, and the media all tell a story of crime that we store away in our consciousness to be used when we make decisions in our everyday lives such as where we might walk at night, who we might fear or be wary of, who we might trust or not. In other words we all think we 'know' something about crime. What we think it is, where we think it takes place, and who the supposed criminals are—the what, where, and whom of crime. We read about 'true' crime that typically tends to be spectacular crime—great robberies, serial killers, gang leaders, or sexual predators (see Howitt, 1998; Reiner, 2002 for general introductions). The names come and go, entering the realm of popular culture, all the time adding to our collective understandings of crime (see Chapter 8 above). These acts need to be 'wicked', 'evil', or simply 'spectacular' before we categorize them within the collective conscience as crime, yet such crimes make up only a very small part of 'recorded' or 'reported' crimes in any given year. It remains the case that the vast majority of crime, is 'petty' by nature and often considered by us all to be unimportant or not really 'proper' crime at all. We might buy something cheap at a garage sale which we consider to be 'a good buy', or just remove something lying around that we assume is no longer wanted (Ferrell, 2005). We might 'fiddle' expenses; do some 'cash work' that we fail to declare to the Inland Revenue; 'spin' our CVs; pull a 'sicky' when we want a day off work; or take 'things' home from our place of business as a 'perk' of the job. In other words, we simply do not consider these acts to be crimes and ourselves criminals. They are simply a part of everyday life (Gabor, 1994). Yet it is here, located in the hustle and bustle of everyday life that the vast majority of reported crime—what increasingly is referred to as 'volume crime'—occurs, whether 'property' or 'behaviour' based. This sort of crime takes up 20 per cent of a patrol officer's time and is therefore extremely expensive, deflecting personnel away from other detection duties (ACPO 'Investigation of volume crime manual' 2002).

BACKGROUND

The use of the term 'volume crime' is a fairly new concept in criminological writing and arises out of what was previously described as the 'crimes of everyday life' or 'acquisitive crime.'(Felson, 1998; Carrabine *et al.*, 2002; see relatedly Baldwin and Bottoms, 1976; Cohen and Felson, 1979; Figlio *et al.*, 1986; Brantingham and Brantingham 1991, 1993). The aim of this body of work was to explore the ways in which the experiences of modern life make us all vulnerable to crime and criminality. In particular, it creatively examined the ways in which the minutiae of our lives lead us to be either offenders or victims of crime: the way we travel to work, to shop, to our leisure; where we live, how we live, and with whom we live; our age, our gender, our ethnicity; whether we work, study, or are unemployed; when we work and what we work at. All were seen, and are still seen, as a constitutive part of the dynamics of everyday crime.

As an obvious example of this thesis, consider the everyday life of the average university student. The annual British Crime Survey clearly shows that being both young and a student makes you more susceptible to being a victim of crime. You spend your days on a busy campus surrounded by lightly engaged strangers; your car is often left for long periods in an unattended car park; you live in mass accommodation blocks; you often party long and late; and very often have limited financial resources. All these factors make for what David Garland has described as a micro 'crime-prone society' (2001: 91); a set of spatial and temporal circumstances that frequently culminate in students becoming the victims of both property crimes and acts of so-called 'anti-social behaviour'. In such circumstances, students and occasionally staff are themselves often tempted to become involved in the criminal marketplace (Dodd *et al.*, 2004: 54; see also Fisher and Sloan, 1997 for a policy summary). Marcus Felson in *Crime and Everyday Life* (1998) talks of a university campus in this way:

> A college campus is a giant delivery system. It funnels students, faculty, staff, and various products into one general location and moves them from building to building to deliver education. It also delivers crime opportunities. Students and their property may play several roles in crime. University employees fit the same bill. The university itself owns many items worth stealing and provides many corners where illegal action can occur ... All crime is local—every offender goes from some local area to another. The minimal elements of crime converge locally. The physical and social processes generating crime therefore are intricately related. (Felson, 1998: 75; see relatedly Rengert *et al.*, 2001)

One should also be aware that the contemporary term 'volume crime' also evokes a much more managerial dimension than previous concepts which have sought to explain/define crime. By this I mean that it extrapolates from the crimes of everyday life those particular offences that are seen by the government, the police, and other criminal justice agencies as the most socially pressing and in need of attention. This redefinition should be seen as part of a wider ideology of late modern social control (a series of instrumental administrative and bureaucratic strategies solely concerned with the 'management of crime'; see Garland, 2001 for an overview, and Chapter 23 below). Inevitably this process has political as well as criminological connotations, with politicians now scrambling to define which offences are, or are not, on the political agenda. The result is the inclusion of a new discourse of 'anti-social behaviour' within the context of 'volume crime'. This now allows a much wider spectrum of behaviours to be defined as anti-social. For example, where drunkenness, substance abuse, begging, and other strictly illegal activities used to be the focus of state agency concern, now their remit has extended to behaviours that are more generally perceived as 'disorderly', such as 'fly-tipping, pestering people, bullying, games in inappropriate areas, loud music' and the like (Home Office Report 26, 2004: 4). Activities such as these (typically associated with young people) are all now increasingly classified as anti-social acts and subject to the criminalization process (see Squires, 2008).

What is or is not deemed to be volume crime is, as mentioned above, both defined and determined by politicians and criminal justice agencies alike. It is a fluid concept forever being redefined in line with political considerations, crime trends, and, importantly, changes in social and cultural aspects of everyday life (see Chapter 1 above). In this sense, then, and given the material and behavioural dimensions associated with volume crime, we must pay particular attention to changes in relation to both: (a) what we own, and how we protect it—as this inevitably impacts on levels and modalities of property crime; and (b) how we behave and interact with each other within social contexts. Consider, for example, the impact that late modern consumer culture has had both on the physical and structural nature of urban space and also at the level of individual subjective emotions—what Keith Hayward has described as 'the hidden patterns of behaviour and the new and distinct forms of subjectivity precipitated and engendered by a fast-paced consumer society' (2004: 1, for more on this point see below). Not only will changes in these areas affect what we buy, how we buy it, and how we protect what we buy, but it also brings about changes in our cultural lives. This of course is not class or even poverty related. The Centre for Crime and Justice Studies (CCJS) at King's College London reported on Monday 25 June 2007 that they had found that 'nearly two thirds of consumers regularly commit a range of offences against business, government and their employers' (CCJS, 2007). They found that '61% of their sample had committed one of various offences, including paying cash in hand to avoid taxation, keeping money when given too much change, wrongly using and swapping identity cards for their own gain and cheating in second-hand sales' (CCJS, 2007). Further findings show clearly the extent of petty crime considered by many to not be crime but the 'perks' of life. Five per cent claimed refunds they knew they weren't entitled to; 6 per cent asked a friend in bureaucracy to 'bend the rules'; 7 per cent padded an insurance claim; 11 per cent avoided paying their TV licence; 18 per cent had taken something from work; 31 per cent kept money when 'over-changed'. Most of these offenders came from the 'law abiding majority' and were middle class in background (CCJS, 2007). Ten years ago alcohol-related violence and general drunkenness were problems contained within the end of the working week. In contemporary society, changing social and leisure patterns mean that people can now 'party' seven days a week, irrespective of the time of day (Measham et al., 1998; Hobbs et al.; 2000, 2003; Hayward and Hobbs, 2007; Measham, 2008). As a consequence, noise and drunken behaviour become ever more visible social problems. From the State's perspective such behaviour also threatens to disrupt working life and thus is something that increasingly falls under the rubric of anti-social behaviour. In what follows, I will explore both property crime and anti-social behaviour in more detail and in direct relationship to our experiences of everyday life.

Property crime and everyday life

What is property crime?

Property crime is not just the single event of theft or robbery but concerns all the dimensions involved in the taking, distributing, and buying of stolen goods. In the latest *Crime in England and Wales 2006/2007* report published by the Home Office, data is interpreted from the British Crime Survey (BCS) to draw a statistical sketch that demonstrates the diversity and extent of property crimes in England and Wales. For example, it estimates there were 1,689,000 vehicle thefts which have remained stable since 2005/06. (Yet since the peak year of 1995 there has been a 61 per cent fall in vehicle thefts whilst at the same time the number of cars on the road has increased by 4 million.) At the same time there were 726,000 burglary offences; 574,000 thefts from the person; and 1,141,000 'other thefts of personal property' alongside of 482,000 bicycle thefts. Robbery and mugging offences (estimated at 399,000) are classified as crimes of violence rather than property crimes even though both involve the loss of property, including, for example, mobile phone theft (see Figure 9.1). Property crime also includes both the £1.8 billion of retail shop theft (often called shoplifting), as well as the £1.5 billion 'pilfered' from shops by employees (often described by employees as 'perks') (*Retail Express*, 28 September 2004). Whilst such statistical data is useful for criminologists in terms of identifying patterns and trends in particular types of crime (see Chapter 3 above), and even though much property crime is dropping there are still a great number of people of all ages, who are effected by property crime both in personal and emotional ways. In other words there are still millions of citizens who are victims of property crime. Statistical evidence and crime science tells us very little about the more complex social dimensions involved in the processes of property crime. For example, property crime happens not just in the street, but also at home, at work, even at school. It can happen when we are awake or asleep. How, then, can we explain the complex processes and dynamics associated with property crime? What are the social dimensions involved and how has it become so much a part of all our everyday lives?

Explanations

Markets

Above all else volume property crime is about the identification of markets and the dynamics associated with the production, distribution and consumption of commodities

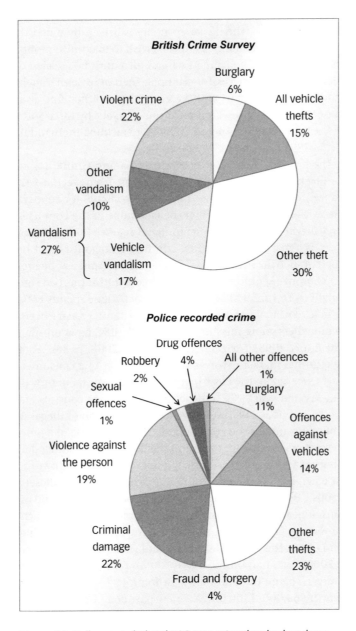

Figure 9.1 Police recorded and BCS property crime broken down by offence, 2006/07

Source: *Crime in England and Wales 2006/07*. Sian Nicholas, Chris Kershaw, and Alison Walker (London: HMSO: 2007), p. 74 <http://www.homeoffice.gov.uk/rds/pdfs07/hosb1107.pdf>.

(see Clarke, 1999; and Kock *et al.*, 1996 for an interesting analysis of the market for stolen electrical goods). In this sense, the illegal economy is driven by much the same basic dynamics as the formal legal economy. Producers wish to maximize profits, and need to distribute goods and services to consumers who in turn must be satisfied that they have received value for money. The successful criminal, then, must either identify a market and seek out goods to feed it, or start with a commodity and then find a suitable market for distribution (see the mass of research on 'crime markets' by Mike Sutton, especially his work on the Market Reduction Approach (MRA) to tackling theft and illegal trading, for example, Sutton 1995; Sutton *et al.*, 1998, 2001).

For example, the growing consumer boom in India and China has created a soaring demand for black market scrap metal of all types, from steel at £120 a ton, aluminium £600 a ton, £20,000 for bronze, and £4,000–£8,000 for copper, (making the copper in 2p pieces worth more at 3p than the face value of the coin itself). The result is a lucrative and illegal £360,000,000 scrap metal market (BBC news online 12 July 2008). Here, then, is a market identified by criminal protagonists that has resulted in the increased theft of such bizarre items as bronze plaques from war memorials, a Henry Moore £3,000,000 bronze sculpture, and a hundred aluminium road signs that disappeared in one night in Devon, whilst Newham council alone spends £60,000 a year in replacing 'man hole' covers. Even the Royal Yacht Britannia hasn't been spared, with two huge spare propellers going missing in June 2008 (BBC news online 12 July 2008, Telegraph online 8 July 2008, *The Daily Express* 3 July 2008, p. 38). Another example of an emerging criminal market involves the end product of a consumer society—the disposal of waste. Once again, the costs involved in the disposal of unwanted products have risen in the last ten years as a result of more and more controls and regulations over waste disposal practices. The result has been the creation of illegal waste disposal services that dump unwanted goods throughout the countryside in a process known as 'fly-tipping'. The cost of cleaning up the countryside of such consumer detritus is in the end, of course, borne by local communities. But in the present 'credit crunch' other new markets are just emerging. As the price of fuel increases so petrol, diesel, and oil theft begin to re-establish itself. Farmers are claiming thousands of pounds from insurers as whole tankfuls of heating oil are stolen. Other farmers are suffering the theft of red diesel with one women farmer collapsing and dying after pursuing thieves who had just targeted her farm in the North East of England (*The Times* 21 January 2008, Times online 10 June 2008, Guardian online 3 May 2008). Farmers are of course, not unlike students, easy targets, being rural and difficult to protect so it is no wonder that even their tractors worth £63,000–£100,000 are now part of a criminal marketplace worth over £3,000,000 (*The Times* 21 January 2008).

However we all need to be reminded that markets go down as well as up and in line with this, specific crimes begin to fall whilst others remain stable or are rising. In the new financial climate of recession criminals search for more lucrative criminal market places. For example the scrap metal market has collapsed mirrored by an equally dramatic fall in scrap metal crime. Within the last 12 months of deepening recession there has been a spectacular 95 per cent drop in church metal thefts whilst only 12 months previously there were six thefts from churches a day! (*The Times* 15 January 2009).

Table 9.1 Theft and stages of the product life cycle

	Product innovation	Product growth	Product in mass market	Product saturation
Product users	Few and special	Growing and general	Many and universal	Nearly everyone
Ease of product use	Difficult to use	A bit easy to use	Some are easy to use	Wide range of usability
Ease of product transportation	Difficult to carry	A bit difficult to carry	Easy to carry	Easy to carry
Price	Prohibitive price	Price coming down	Wide price range	Low price
Theft risk	Not often stolen	Thefts accelerate	Epidemic of thefts	Declining thefts

Source: Felson, M. (1998) *Crime and Everyday Life*. Sage: Thousand Oaks, CA, p. 187.

Financial changes within market places begin to restructure the nature of crime itself. Some theft will increase whilst other more violent crimes may rise as the social stress of living in poverty begins to bite. A new generation of 'law breakers' is created by financial policies and transgression becomes endemic. This we may call *'Recession Crime'* and must be taken into account when we study criminal market places.

The products of criminal activities need, of course, to be acquired in the first place, either from individual people or from legal businesses. Most consumer items have a 'life' of their own which determines their desirability and value. Felson, for example, identifies in grid form these connections between theft and the 'stages of a product's life' (see Table 9.1) that clearly shows the rise and fall of property theft during the life of particular mass commodities. However, there are also 'specialist' markets that do not necessarily follow these rules. The markets in stolen artworks and stamps, for example, are especially lucrative. There even exists a specialist stolen pedigree dog market, with certain breeds attracting up to £3,000 per dog, whilst the 'chipping' of all dogs is now recommended for all dog owners.

Once a market has been established and a 'product' stolen then the next element of the process, that of distribution, comes into play. Without an efficient distribution network, theft remains small scale, for personal use and consumption only. The ability to distribute stolen goods is therefore an essential element of property crime.

Distribution

There is, then, a need for criminal producers to identify and seek out both a population of people that make up a particular market place, and a means of safely distributing and delivering stolen property to those consumers (see Sutton *et al.*, 2001: 15–18). This process takes many forms. Professional 'garage' sales, weekly car boot sales, and market places, including antique markets and auction houses, provide easy outlets for stolen goods, as do electronic market places such as 'eBay'. There are few controls over these activities, and goods circulate quickly and are difficult to trace back to the original seller. Likewise, friendship and family groups quickly become distribution 'networks' for stolen goods. Even motorway service areas often emerge as convenient sites for the distribution of stolen goods. These areas are like crowded local market places made up of a transitory population where within hours both seller and buyer are many hundreds of miles away and most likely impossible to trace. Lastly, in impoverished rundown urban areas, second-hand shops often provide an outlet for stolen goods. Normally, property sold here is in poor condition and overpriced but still allows a segment of the population to consume like other members of the population and as such becomes part of the local economy. With few questions asked, and even fewer answers given, everyone appears happy—except of course the original owner or legitimate producer of the property. Marcus Felson once again neatly sums up the living, organic, criminal aspects of everyday crime when he writes:

> Crime feeds off the physical form of local life, whether in a village, town, city, suburb, or university campus. That form is organized by how people and things move about in everyday life. In the ways that they move around, people often prevent crime, whether they are aware of it or not, and both people and things sometimes contribute to crime in their presences or absences. People are sometimes offenders or combatants, sometimes targets or guardians, sometimes buyers or sellers of illegal goods. As they move through time and space, people also come into contact with products, some of which are stolen, some of which are sold as illegal goods or used for illegal acts. Everyday life thus sets the stage for people to break laws, hurt each other, and even hurt themselves. (Felson 1998: 75)

Consumers

In the past criminology has too often concentrated on the 'producer' of criminal goods (the thief) or the sales staff (the dealers) and even occasionally the CEOs or top managers (the crime 'Barons'), rather than analysing the role of the consumers of criminal commodities. What is it, then, that makes us become consumers of other people's stolen property? Why is it that millions of normally law-abiding citizens come to act no differently to common criminals? What dynamics are at work that are so powerful as to lead such large numbers of people into the processes of crime? How many of us have been tempted to buy what we know are stolen goods? A cheap mobile phone, phone cards, clothes, CDs and DVDs, bikes and bits of bikes, tools, TVs, computers and computer games. The bargains are there as long as we can put out of our mind the fact that we are partaking in a criminal activity. But do we only consider price or are there deeper and more personal dynamics that lead us into the cycle of property crime? To fully understand the suspension of reality that takes place when we buy stolen property we must take a moment to understand the motivations behind such purposes.

Property crime offences, both estimated and recorded, make up the majority of criminal acts (notwithstanding the fact that most property crimes have shown a decrease in recent years). This demonstrates that one of the central defining dynamics of personal identity in contemporary society—that is the conspicuous ownership and consumption of commodities—is permanently under threat of violation. If our personal identity becomes reliant on what we consume and own, then property crime often becomes an act of *personal* violence, a violation felt deeply by the individual (rather than society as a whole) and thus closely connected to what we as individuals desire, need, or want at any given time. The whole notion of property crime therefore comes to rest on our insatiable need to consume as a central activity within society (see Lury, 1996; Miles, 1998; Edwards, 2000 for general introductions to the subject of consumer culture). We now live in a consumer society where 'to have is to be'; where 'we are what we consume'; or, as Eric Fromm so brilliantly expressed it:

> In a culture in which the supreme goal is to have … and to have more and more … and in which one can speak of someone as 'being worth a million dollars', how can there be an alternative between having and being? On the contrary, it would seem that the very essence of being is having; that if one has nothing, one is nothing. (Fromm, 1976: 3)

The very act of consuming and 'becoming' involves both deeply desiring a commodity and obtaining access to it through legal or illegal markets. Everyday items that make us what we want to 'be' are imbued with such social status that often many of us will acquire them by whatever means necessary. It is through this dynamic of desire and wanting that we become both victim and offender. Commodities such as mobile phones, jeans, watches, hand bags, music CDs, and film DVDs are all highly desirable items. Indeed this desirability is unlikely to be affected just because these goods are now being sold in illegal markets. Consider, for example, the healthy market in counterfeit—or 'knock off'—products, from unlicensed generic prescription drugs to 'designer label' clothing.

In this way property crime is defined through the very process of the coming together of culture and economics that creates through its social dynamics criminal market places. That is property crime becomes an integral part of the fabric of everyday life. Out of this fabric arise such seemingly bizarre or abstract criminal markets as the illegal wild fish market, and even a large market in stolen caravans (*The Times*, 16 August 2004), each reflecting the personal identities and everyday lives of particular groups as they go about affirming their identities through the consumption of stolen goods.

We cannot escape the premise that criminal markets and the culture of consumption go together. Illegal crime markets and criminal consumption are thus at the very heart of volume property crime, something which in turn is driven by the overwhelming desire to 'have' in order to 'be'. As I have said elsewhere, these desires:

> [no] longer respect the limits and cultural boundaries produced in the past to protect the institution of ownership. This new and all encompassing consumer culture creates a confused consumer psyche where anxiety and its social antidotes are themselves producing much so called 'social disorder' and 'transgression', as groups and individuals attempt to make sense of a life increasingly mediated through the new and distinct processes associated with late modern consumerism. The search for the thwarted promise of happiness through consumption leads many to hedonism and seemingly irrational acts. (Presdee, 2000: 279)

Everyday cultural processes, then, inextricably link culture with crime, investing commodities with cultural meanings and understandings. The mobile phone industry, for example, is a site of production where sheer desirability and technological style are seductively woven together, creating a continuing demand for the 'latest models'. By employing a 'seduction of the new', each new marketing campaign encourages us to be ashamed of our current phone. Indeed many communications companies play on the theme of personal embarrassment through the use of an outdated handset, too few pixels, the wrong ring tone etc. In such a highly personalized and therefore pressurized market place both criminal acquisition and criminal consumption are seemingly inevitable. Under these circumstances is it any surprise that mobile phone theft is still such a major part of property crime in most countries?

REVIEW QUESTIONS

1 Try and identify the various criminal markets that you might come across in your everyday life.

2 By examining the emotions of consumption, analyse the image and identity you are seeking through your own consumption strategies.

Anti-social behaviour and the politics of control

The emergence of anti-social behaviour

As Prime Minister in the mid 1990s, John Major introduced a high profile 'back to basics' campaign. His goal was to highlight the importance of family values, moral fortitude, and discipline at school and work in an attempt to counteract the ever growing, and increasingly visible 'anti-social' activities of the new so-called 'yob culture'. The campaign made much of the threat posed by anti-social behaviour to the lives and well being of 'ordinary' citizens. According to John Major and his fellow Conservatives, young people were out of control, laziness was rife, and infidelities within families were destroying the British way of life. At the time, the Labour opposition leader, Tony Blair, viewed such an approach to crime and deviance as a cheap electioneering stunt, and gained considerable political capital when eventually the campaign collapsed under the weight of 'Tory Sleaze', including a series of sensational sex scandals involving Conservative MPs. However, once in power, the current Labour Government quickly took up the 'battle cry' again, only this time the 'back to basics' rubric was replaced with a war on anti-social behaviour. The mythical 'yob' was once again cast as a threat to 'decent' citizens, a sort of enemy within, eating away at order through disorder, creating a generalized feeling of insecurity throughout the population.

This puritanical approach defines that which interrupts the processes of organized production as 'anti-social', and identifies a perceived general lack of discipline for work and social order as the major ill confronting contemporary societies. Worklessness and 'bad behaviour' become a social and moral weakness to be controlled and criminalized. As a result anti-social citizens must be considered 'disturbed' or 'depraved' or 'dangerous' or all three and in need of precise definition to enable legislation to be enacted that would control such undesirable behaviour. Now on the tenth anniversary of the

Anti-Social Behaviour Order (ASBO) legislation through the Crime and Disorder Act of 1998, the use of the issuing of ASBOs as both a controlling and punishment tool is being 'run down'. The breaching of ASBOs has risen to 61 per cent, resulting in the number of orders actually being given falling 34 per cent from 2005 so that the total numbers of ASBOs have declined from 4,123 in 2005 to 2,706 in 2006, a trend that has continued over the last 12 months (Guardian online 9 May 2008). Under the new leadership of Prime Minister Gordon Brown's Children's Minister, Ed Balls, a more diverse set of preventative measures are being deployed by the Home Secretary Jacqui Smith that includes parenting orders, acceptable behaviour contracts, and support orders (Guardian online 9 May 2008). Whilst the trend is now moving away from a single form of sanction, namely the ASBO, some police forces along with local councils continue to pursue draconian measures. On 11 July 2008 police and councils in Cardiff announced a proposed application for a ten-year ASBO to be served on six young people aged from their late teens to their early twenties that would prohibit them from going to Canton Park in Cardiff. It is possible, then, that some of these young men would be in their thirties and fathers and yet be unable to take their own children to this particular park, thereby making their children the victims of a punishment that was given before they were born (Wales online 12 July 2008). At the same time more young people are being imprisoned for breaches of an ASBO. Almost 1,000 'children' (under the Children's Act) were sent to prison for breaching an ASBO between 2000 and 2006 with 42 per cent of all children breaching an ASBO being given an average prison sentence of 6.4 months. This has resulted in the number of children in prison in April 2008 being 3,012, up from 2,643 in July 1997, an increase of 14 per cent since Labour came to power (<http://Publicpolitics.net> 7 July 2008).

The defining process

The present Labour Government began the 'defining' process in September 2003 by identifying through its Anti-social Behaviour Unit's 'one day snapshot' of anti-social behaviour, over 60,000 anti-social reports within a 24-hour period (Home Office, 2003). They further identified another 250,000 neighbourhood disputes that were reported to local authorities and environmental agencies in one year alone.

Reflecting the present Government's concerns regarding anti-social behaviour, the Home Office produced its report *Defining and Measuring Anti-Social Behaviour* (2004) which in turn built on the 2003 White Paper 'Respect and Responsibility: Taking a stand against anti-social behaviour'. These publications served to set out a working definition of what anti-social behaviour is and how community practitioners might apply that definition to particular communities. However, right from the outset there was considerable concern about definitional boundaries. They begin by saying:

> People's understanding of what constitutes anti-social behaviour is determined by a series of factors including context, location, community tolerance and quality of life expectations. As a result, what may be considered anti-social behaviour to one person can be seen as acceptable behaviour to another. The subjective nature of the concept makes it difficult to identify a single definition of anti-social behaviour. (Home Office, 2004: 3)

They also recognized the shortcomings of the definition set down by the Crime and Disorder Act (1998) that defined the anti-social as: 'Acting in a manner that caused or was likely to cause harassment, alarm or distress, to one or more persons not of the same household as the defendant.' This definition defines the anti-social not through what it is, but by examining the effect that so-called anti-social behaviour has on people and society. However, in order to bring more precision and focus to the defining process, the Home Office have continued their attempts to proscribe a particular range of social actions as being anti-social. Again they tried to avoid 'demonizing' or 'excluding' specific groups such as young people, or socially excluded sections of the population like the homeless, or those involved in drug rehabilitation programmes. Even so, a number of respondents felt that a specific 'youth nuisance' category should be added to the typology, recognizing that groups of young people are often perceived as a problem. (The BCS 2006/07 showed that 33 per cent of the public perceived 'teenagers hanging around' as the biggest anti-social behaviour problem in their local area—up from 25 per cent on the 2002/03 figure.)

Ultimately, however, the decision was taken not to include a youth category in the typology, as it was felt that anti-social behaviour should be defined by the nature of the activity not the age of the perpetrator (Home Office, 2004: 5).

Instead, the Government embarked on a much more subtle strategy. As Table 9.2 makes clear, the Home Office typology of anti-social behaviour includes a whole host of activities primarily associated with young people, such as the playing of loud music, joyriding, graffiti, hooliganism, playing games in inappropriate places, and skateboarding and

Figure 9.2 Proportion of people perceiving anti-social behaviour to be a problem in their area, 2006/07 BCS.

Source: Home Office, Crime in England and Wales 2006/07, a summary of the main figures (HMSO: 2007) p. 15 <http://www.homeoffice.gov.uk/rds/pdfs07/crime0607summ.pdf>.

Table 9.2 RDS typology of anti-social behaviour

Misuse of public space	Disregard for community/ personal well-being	Acts directed at people	Environmental damage
Drug/substance misuse & dealing	Noise	**Intimidation/ harassment**	**Criminal damage/ vandalism**
Taking drugs	Noisy neighbours	Groups or individuals making threats	Graffiti
Sniffing volatile substances	Noisy cars/motorbikes	Verbal abuse	Damage to bus shelters
Discarding needles/drug paraphernalia	Loud music	Bullying	Damage to phone kiosks
Crack houses	Alarms (persistent ringing/ malfunction)	Following people	Damage to street furniture
Presence of dealers or users	Noise from pubs/clubs	Pestering people	Damage to buildings
Street drinking	Noise from business/ industry	Voyeurism	Damage to trees/plants/ hedges
Begging	**Rowdy behaviour**	Sending nasty/ offensive letters	**Litter/ rubbish**
Prostitution	Shouting & swearing	Obscene/nuisance phone calls	Dropping litter
Soliciting	Fighting	Menacing gestures	Dumping rubbish
Cards in phone boxes	Drunken behaviour	*Can be on the grounds of:*	Fly-tipping
Discarded condoms	Hooliganism/loutish behaviour	Race	Fly-posting
Kerb crawling	**Nuisance behaviour**	Sexual orientation	
Loitering	Urinating in public	Gender	
Pestering residents	Setting fires (not directed at specific persons or property)	Religion	
Sexual acts	Inappropriate use of fireworks	Disability	
Inappropriate sexual conduct	Throwing missiles	Age	
Indecent exposure	Climbing on buildings		
Abandoned cars	Impeding access to communal areas		
Vehicle-related nuisance & inappropriate vehicle use	Games in restricted/ inappropriate areas		
Inconvenient/illegal parking	Misuse of air guns		

Table 9.2 *Continued*

Misuse of public space	Disregard for community/ personal well-being	Acts directed at people	Environmental damage
Car repairs on the street/in gardens	Letting down tyres		
Setting vehicles alight	**Hoax calls**		
Joyriding	False calls to emergency services		
Racing cars	**Animal-related problems**		
Off-road motorcycling	Uncontrolled animal		
Cycling/skate boarding in pedestrian areas/ footpaths			

Source: Research Development and Statistics Directorate.

cycling in pedestrianized areas. This defining process ensures that it is young people rather than adults who become trapped by the rubric of anti-social behaviour, further adding to what has been described as the 'creeping criminalization and control of youth' (see Jeffs and Smith, 1996; Hayward, 2002).

It is quite clear, then, that the present Government, like governments before it, have little understanding about the realities of everyday life for young people in contemporary society, in particular, their search for fun, excitement, and an escape from the boredom of everyday routines. As I have said elsewhere:

> Excitement, even ecstasy (the abandonment of reason and rationale), is the goal ... the quest for excitement is directly related to the breaking of boundaries, of confronting parameters and playing at the margins of social life in the challenging of controllers and their control mechanisms...It is the realm of resentment and irrationality par excellence and also the realm of much crime. It is that part of social life that is unknowable to those in power and which therefore stands outside of their consciousness and their understanding. They cannot understand it or indeed even 'read' it as real life, but only as immoral, uncivilized, obscene and unfathomable social behaviour. (Presdee, 2000: 7–8)

Or in the context of the present chapter, 'unfathomable social behaviour' becomes defined as anti-social behaviour and rendered understandable, knowable, and therefore preventable through control mechanisms.

The Government has further extended the binary social/anti-social categorization of social behaviour by attempting to identify particular behaviours that are most likely to cause 'alarm', 'distress', and 'harassment' within specific communities. Take, for example, the recent furore over binge drinking and the way it has been cast as the number one social problem within certain urban locations (see Measham, 1996, 2005, 2008). In post-industrial cities, urban regeneration has resulted in the rapid development of the night time economy as cities have re-invented themselves as sites of consumption and leisure (Hobbs *et al.*, 2002, 2003; Measham, 2004). Often the regeneration and re-zoning of these urban spaces is accompanied by the relaxation of local licensing laws enabling people to drink into the early hours of the morning. In turn this is blamed for the rapid growth of anti-social behaviour, creating both a fear of inner city areas and a demand for more controls over perceived rises in alcohol related crime (see the following chapter by Emma Wincup). Both the user and the seller of alcohol are seen here as anti-social, with licensees being controlled through legal frameworks, leaving consumers to be controlled by the criminal justice system or by local social control programmes. For example, in Sunderland, the local authority saw fit to employ a 'drink reduction officer' to assist in controlling and changing the perceived anti-social recreational behaviour of local people (*Sunderland Echo*, 16 March 2004; see also Winlow 2001 for a more general discussion of alcohol related crime in a North-East city). This example illustrates the increasing criminalization of everyday leisure activities.

Everyday 'order' and the anti-social

In his book *Understanding Social Control* Martin Innes discusses the notion that in contemporary society there is a growing sense of insecurity that feeds the need for ever more controls over certain sections of the community. He goes on to state that:

> We are living through a period of history where the control apparatus is being reconfigured. It is evident that the conduct of social control in late-modern societies is very complex, involving a range of state and non-state agencies, using an array of layered and interlocking technologies, strategies and ideas...There is an accompanying sense that the reach of social control is extending and the social control network is expanding...it seems as if more and more people are subject to some form of control. (Innes, 2003: 144)

This reconfiguring involves not just the control of individuals through behaviour orders, but also the control of segments of society such as 'youth' or the 'homeless' or the 'poor'. For example, young people have been barred from particular areas at particular times through the use of generalized curfews enacted for no other reason than they may be at risk of committing anti-social behaviour in the future. Such was the reasoning for the suggested ban on under 16-year-olds from the 'West End' of London after 9 p.m. in the evening and the barring of young people in Rossendale, Lancashire, from 'playgrounds' after 6 p.m. in winter and 9 p.m. in summer (Presdee, 2000: 111). As Jeffs and Smith remark this approach is problematic because it criminalizes 'perfectly legal and acceptable behaviour on the grounds of age ... to select young people and criminalize them for doing what the rest of the population can freely do is doubly discriminating' (Jeffs and Smith, 1996: 11).

A collection of government acts including the Anti-social Behaviour Act 2003, the Police Reform Act 2002, and the Criminal Justice and Police Act 2001, have combined to create a considerable raft of social control measures to direct social behaviour and punish those who transgress through the issue of on-the-spot Fixed Penalty Notices (FPNs) (a number of which are now being issued on a trial basis to children as young as ten). These 'on-the-spot' fines can be issued by the Police, community support officers, or anyone

Table 9.3 Current fixed penalty notices for disorder (Criminal Justice and Police Act 2001)

Wasting police time	£80
Knowingly giving a false alarm to the fire brigade	£80
Knowingly giving a false alarm to a person acting on behalf of the fire brigade	£80
Causing harassment, alarm, or distress	£80
Using a public electronic communication system to cause alarm or distress	£80
Drunk and disorderly	£80
Sale of alcohol to a person under 18	£80
Buying alcohol for a person under 18	£80
Delivering, or allowing delivery of, alcohol to a person under 18	£80
Throwing fireworks in a thoroughfare	£80
Contravention of firework regulations and giving false statements	£80
Theft	£80
Destroying or damaging property	£80
Trespass on a railway	£50
Throwing stones on a railway	£50
Drunk on a highway	£50
Drinking in a designated public area	£50
Consuming, or allowing the consumption of alcohol under 18	£50
Depositing and leaving litter	£50

Source: The Penalties for Disorderly Behaviour (Amount of Penalty) (Amendment No. 2) Order 2004 No. 2468.

else accredited by the Chief Constable of a particular region. Such fines serve to bring an immediacy to punishment that is aimed at reinforcing the unacceptable and anti-social nature of a particular range of behaviours. At the present time fines are issued as set out in Table 9.3.

This ratcheting up of everyday techniques of social control does not stop with the issuing of FPNs. The range of anti-social behaviours now identified under various statutes is stunning in its comprehensiveness, including everything from:

- controls over gardening (the banning of high hedges over two metres);
- graffiti removal orders against those whose properties have been targeted;
- holding 'raves' and other such unauthorized gatherings indoors as well as outside;
- cycling on footpaths;
- selling spray paint;
- using airguns under 17;
- two or more young people on the street after 9 p.m. and before 6 a.m.;
- selling fireworks to under 18s;

- throwing fireworks;

- begging.

These contemporary forms of social control are mechanisms and responses to what Stan Cohen identified, with typical foresight, as:

[c]rime, delinquency and allied forms of deviant and/or socially problematic behaviour (i.e. *Anti-social behaviours*) which are actually conceived of as such, whether in the reactive sense (after the putative act has taken place, or the actor has been identified) or in the proactive sense (to prevent the act). (Cohen, 1985: 3)

What Cohen described in the 1980s as 'socially problematic behaviour' is now commonly referred to as anti-social behaviour and is seen by Government as a threat to the flimsy and fragile existence of social order. The idea that social controls should be instituted as a form of situational crime prevention comes alongside the idea of social control as a form of protection against 'yob culture' and other perceived threats to social order, thereby allowing the State to increase its powers to intervene in everyday social life.

In many ways, this approach can be seen as a consequence of a general and identifiable loss of confidence and patience in the ability of family structures to ensure everyday order (see Wilson, 1985; Taylor, 1999: 42–50 for criminological introductions to this point). As Innes remarks:

Over the past two decades, there has been a particular focus upon the family as an object of control because of the popular concerns relating to physical and sexual abuse...but also, due to fears that the family's effectiveness as a mechanism of informal social control is waning. The dramatic rises in recorded crime between the 1960s and mid-1990s were causally attributed to the increase in number of single mothers and families without fathers, by politicians who, for ideological reasons, found this a more palatable explanation, than to look at the structural inequalities caused by their liberalization of free market mechanisms (Mooney, 1998). (Innes, 2003: 57)

For the State, the identified rise in anti-social behaviour, is a result of bad parenting rather than, for example, in the case of alcohol-related crime and disorder, due to changes in the alcohol industry and the changing social and spatial dynamics associated with the late modern night-time economy (see Children's Minister Ed Balls' 'Youth Crime, Action plan' 15 July 2008). By defining anti-social behaviour so widely both in what it is and who commits it the present Government has ensured that it has become the new 'volume crime', thus allowing more political and practical attention to be concentrated on it. This cycle creates a new crime agenda that legitimates government actions on social control. All this can be seen as part of the ongoing surveillance of civil society. I think we are quite safe to propose that young people are more controlled, more regulated, more surveilled than at any time in the history of youth. With an ever growing number of legal regulations held over and against them it is not absurd to suggest that the criminalization of the social life of young people is now a reality in contemporary Britain. In true Cromwellian style, control of nihilism and hedonism has become the new law and order 'project'. Over the last 10 years government initiatives have been introduced to ensure that young people go to school; don't get pregnant; don't drink; don't play loud music; don't leave their neighbourhoods; don't stay up too late; don't play with fireworks; don't protest; don't wear hoods; don't see 'So Solid Crew'; don't use the 'F' word. We now have controls over where young people are; who they associate with and when; what they wear and what they say—the who, what, where, and when of the everyday social life of young people. This has resulted in young people and their social and cultural behaviour becoming, in itself, volume crime.

REVIEW QUESTIONS

1 Make a list of all the social behaviours you and your friends regard as anti-social. Which do you think are the most important and how might they best be tackled?

2 Who currently has the power to identify particular behaviour as acceptable or not?

CONCLUSION

In this chapter we have identified the major elements of volume crime, both in terms of property crime and anti-social behaviour. We have discussed the underlying dynamics of property crime as being connected to the acquisition, distribution, and consumption of stolen goods that make up what we call criminal markets. For each element we have teased out how the internal dynamics of the market are reliant on each other and make up the process of property crime. We have shown the importance of the identification of a market in the setting-up of the process of property crime; that there must also be distribution networks to enable goods to be offered for sale and consumers to ensure the process is successfully completed. We have examined closely the tensions involved in the social act of consumption and the way that the emotions of consumption interplay with the process of the formation of personal identity. We have suggested, therefore, that it is important to recognize that property crime is not just about the 'thief' but also involves those who handle stolen goods and those who consume them. In this way we expand our criminological concerns to include all those who are involved and play a part (no matter how seemingly insignificant) in the process of crime. In doing so, we suggest, they become an inescapable and integral part of the crime process itself.

In the second half of the chapter we positioned the concept of anti-social behaviour as volume crime. We identified how the activities of young people, the poor, and the socially excluded are increasingly being targeted as 'anti-social' and perceived by the State as a product of the breakdown in social order. We showed how at the heart of the anti-social behaviour debate is a desire by the State and Government to increase its controlling mechanisms over the everyday lives of increasing numbers of its citizens. In doing so we suggested that anti-social behaviour legislation and regulation subjects a greater proportion of people to the realms of the criminal justice system.

QUESTIONS FOR DISCUSSION

1 By examining both national and local newspapers, especially court roundups in local presses, examine the approaches they take to everyday crime. What do they include, who do they include, and what is absent from these accounts?

2 Discuss the question whether 'bad parenting' is responsible for most crime and the perceived breakdown in order.

3 Can legislation create 'good' behaviour?

4 Is it ever possible to isolate oneself from the everyday happenings of a consumer society?

GUIDE TO FURTHER READING

Criminal Justice Matters, Issue 57, Autumn 2004, 'Whose Justice'.
A series of accessible articles on anti-social behaviour written by academics and practitioners.

Felson, M., Crime and Everyday Life. Thousand Oaks, CA: Sage.
An interesting book concerned with examining how society encourages or inhibits crime in the routine activities of everyday life.

Hayward, K. and Hobbs, D. (2007) 'Beyond the Binge in Booze' *The British Journal of Sociology* 58; 3: 438–456.
An excellent discussion concerning young people and drinking.

Innes, M., *Understanding Social Control*. Maidenhead: Open University Press.
An interesting theoretical introduction to the way societies respond to a variety of forms of deviant behaviour.

Squires, P. (2008) (ed) *ASBO Nation: the Criminalisation of Nuisance*. London: Policy Press.
An excellent all round and up-to-date collection of essays concerning anti-social behaviour.

Sutton, M. 'Supply by theft: does the market for second-hand goods play a role in keeping crime figures high?' *The British Journal of Criminology*, 35 No. 3, 400–16.
A useful academic analysis of the way crime markets function.

Chapter 1 ('Youth crime: representations, discourse and data') in John Muncie's *Youth and Crime* (2nd edn). London: Sage.
A clear, concise introduction to some of the key issues surrounding contemporary youth crime.

WEB LINKS

http://www.statistics.gov.uk/CCI/nscl.asp?ID=5004
The 'crime and justice' page of the National Statistics Online web page. These pages provide a whole host of statistical information about such things as Police Cautions and other sentencing data.

http://www.guardian.co.uk/Archive/0,,,00.html
This is the 'archive' page of the UK daily newspaper *The Guardian*. Search under 'anti-social behaviour' for a plethora of articles, many of which adopt a very similar critical line to the one set down in this chapter.

http://www.homeoffice.gov.uk/anti-social-behaviour/
The 'Anti-social behaviour' page on the Home Office's website.

http://www.homeoffice.gov.uk/crime-victims/reducing-crime/alcohol-related-crime/
The 'Alcohol related' crime page on the Home Office's website.

http://www.hmso.gov.uk/acts/acts1998/19980037.htm

A full digital version of the 1988 Crime and Disorder Act. Check out the various sections on anti-social behaviour.

http://www.youth-justice-board.gov.uk/YouthJusticeBoard/

The website of the Youth Justice Board, including information on everything from Youth Offending Teams to Pre Court Orders.

REFERENCES

Baldwin, J. and Bottoms, A.E. (1976) *The Urban Criminal*. London: Tavistock.

Brantingham, P.J. and Brantingham, P.L. (1991) *Environmental Criminology*. Prospect Heights, Ill: Waveland.

Brantingham, P.J. and Brantingham, P.L. (1993) 'Environment, routine and situation: toward a pattern theory of crime' in R.V. Clarke and M. Felson (eds). *Routine Activity and Rational Choice: Advances in Criminological Theory 5*, New Brunswick, NJ: Transaction Books.

(CCJS) Centre for Crime and Justice Studies (2007) bulletin, 25 June 2007.

Carrabine, E., Cox, P., Lee, M., and South, N. (2002) *Crime in Modern Britain*. Oxford: Oxford University Press.

Cohen, L. and Felson, M. (1979) 'Social Change and Crime Rates: a Routine Activity Approach' *American Sociological Review* 44: 588–608.

Cohen, S., (1985) *Visions of Social Control: Crime, Punishment and Classification*. Blackwell: New York.

Clarke, R.V. (1999) *Hot Products: Understanding, Anticipating and Reducing Demand for Stolen Goods*, Police Research Series paper 112. London: HMSO.

Dodd, T., Nicholas, S., Povey, D., and Walker, A. (2004) *Crime in England and Wales 2003/4*. London: Home Office.

Edwards, T. (2000) *Contradictions of Consumption: Concepts, Practices and Politics in Consumer Society*. Buckingham: Open University Press.

Felson, M. (1998) *Crime and Everyday Life* (2nd edn). London: Pine Forge Press.

Ferrell, J. (2005) *Empire of Scrounge*. New York: New York University Press.

Figlio, R.M., Hakim, S., and Rengert, G.F. (1986) *Metropolitan Crime Patterns*, Monsey, New York: Willow Tree Press.

Fisher, B. and Sloan, J.J. (1997) *Campus Crime: Legal, Social and Policy Perspectives*. Springfield, Ill: Charles C Thomas Publishers.

Fromm, E. (1976) *To Have or To Be*. London: Harper Collins.

Gabor, T. (1994) *Everybody Does It! Crime by the Public*. Toronto: University of Toronto Press.

Garland, D. (2001) *The Culture of Control*. Oxford: Oxford University Press.

Hayward, K. (2002) 'The vilification and pleasures of youthful transgression' in J. Muncie, E. Hughes and E. McLaughlin, (eds), *Youth Justice: Critical Readings*. London: Sage.

Hayward, K. (2004) *City Limits: Crime, Consumer Culture and the Urban Experience*. London: Cavendish.

Hayward, K. and Hobbs, D. (2007), 'Beyond the Binge in Booze Britain', *British Journal of Sociology* 58 (3):437–456.

Hobbs, D. *et al* (2002) 'Door Lore: The Art and Economies of Intimidation.' in *BJC* vol. 42, issue 2, pp 352–70.

Hobbs, D., Lister, S., Hadfield, P., Winlow, S., and Hall, S. (2000) 'Receiving Shadows: Governance and Liminality in the Nighttime Economy', *British Journal of Sociology* 51 (4): 701–17.

Hobbs, D., Hadfield, P., Lister, S., and Winlow, S. (2003) *Bouncers: Violence and Governance in the Night-time Economy*. Oxford: Oxford University Press.

Home Office (2003) *Respect and Responsibility: taking a stand against anti-social behaviour*.

Home Office Development and Practice Report 26 (2004), *Defining and measuring anti-social behaviour*.

Howitt, D. (1998) *Crime, the Media and the Law*. Chichester: Wiley.

Innes, M. (2003) *Understanding social control: Deviance, Crime and Social Order*. Maidenhead: Open University Press.

Jeffs, T. and Smith, M. (1996) 'Getting the dirt bags off the street-curfews and other solutions to juvenile crime', *Youth and Policy*, no. 53: 1–14

Karstedt, S. and Farrall, S. (2007) 'Law-abiding majority? The everyday crimes of the middle classes.' Centre for Crime and Justice Studies 2007.

Kock, E., Kemp, T., and Rix, B. (1996) *Disrupting the Distribution of Stolen Electrical Goods*, Crime Detection and Prevention Series, paper 69, London: HMSO.

Lury, C. (1996) *Consumer Culture*. Cambridge: Polity.

Measham, F. (1996), 'The "Big Bang" approach to sessional drinking: Changing patterns of alcohol consumption amongst young people in north west England', *Addiction Research*, Volume 4, No. 3: 283–99.

Measham, F., Parker, H., and Aldridge, J. (1998) 'The Teenage Transition: From adolescent recreational drug use to the young adult dance culture in Britain in the mid-1990s', in R. Power (ed), *Journal of Drug Issues*, Special Edition, Contemporary Issues Concerning Illicit Drug Use in the British Isles, Volume 28, No. 1: 9–32.

Measham, F. (2004), 'Play Space: Historical and socio-cultural reflections on drugs, licensed leisure locations, commercialisation and control', *International Journal of Drug Policy*, Special Edition: Social theory in drug research and harm reduction, forthcoming.

Measham, F. (2005), 'The Decline of Ecstasy, the Rise of "Binge Drinking" and the Persistence of Pleasure', *Probation Journal*, Special Edition: Rethinking Drugs and Crime, forthcoming.

Measham, F. (2008) 'Binge Drinking: British Alcohol Policy and the New Culture of Intoxication', *Crime Media Culture*, 1 April 2008.

Miles, S. (1998) *Consumerism as a Way of Life*. London: Sage.

Mooney, J (1998) 'Moral Panics and the new right: single mothers and feckless fathers—is this really the key to the crime problem?' in P. Walton and J. Young (eds) *The New Criminology Re-visited*. London: Macmillan.

Muncie, J., Hughes, G., and McLaughlin, E. (2002) *Youth Justice: Critical Readings*. London: Sage.

Muncie, J. (2004) *Youth and Crime* (2nd edn). London: Sage.

Presdee, M. (2000) *Cultural Criminology and the Carnival of Crime*. London: Routledge.

Reiner, R. (2002) 'Media made criminality: the representation of crime in the mass media' in M. Maguire, R. Morgan, and R. Reiner (eds), *The Oxford Handbook of Criminology* (3rd edn). Oxford: Oxford University Press.

Rengert, G.F., Mattson, M.T., and Henderson, K.D. (2001) *Campus Security: Situational Crime Prevention in High Density Environments*. Monsey, New York: Willow Tree Press.

Squires, P. (2008) (ed) *ASBO Nation: The Criminalisation of Nuisance*. London: Policy Press

Squires, P. and Stephens, D.E. (2005) *Rougher Justice: Anti-social Behaviour and Young People*. Cullompton: Willan Publishing.

Sutton, M. (1995) 'Supply by theft: does the market for second-hand goods play a role in keeping crime figures high?' *The British Journal of Criminology*, 35 No. 3: 400–416.

Sutton, M., Johnston, K., and Lockwood, H. (1998) *Handling Stolen Goods and Theft: A Market Reduction Approach*, Home Office Research Study 178. London: HMSO.

Sutton, M., Schneider, J., and Hetherington, S. (2001) *Tackling Theft with the Market Reduction Approach*, Crime Reduction Research Series Paper 8. London: HMSO.

Taylor, I. (1999) *Crime in Context: a Critical Criminology of Market Societies*. Cambridge: Polity.

Wilson, J.Q. (1985) *Thinking About Crime*. New York: Vintage Books.

Winlow, S. (2001) *Badfellos: Crime, Tradition and New Masculinities*. Oxford: New York.

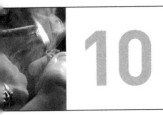

10 Drugs, alcohol, and crime

Emma Wincup and Peter Traynor

INTRODUCTION

Drug and alcohol use are frequently offered as explanations for crime. The use of so-called 'hard' drugs such as heroin and crack cocaine is cited as one of the causes of a range of crimes, particularly acquisitive crimes; excessive alcohol use is perceived as closely connected with anti-social and violent behaviour. For many members of the general public and the media, the relationship between drug or alcohol use and criminal activity is clear and the solutions straightforward. This contrasts sharply with the findings of research studies which identify the need for a more complex understanding and consequently, a multi-faceted response.

This chapter is divided into two main parts. The first part focuses on drug use and addresses three key issues: (a) the nature and extent of drug use; (b) the relationship between drug use and crime; and (c) strategies for reducing drug-related crime. In the second part, we explore the same issues in relation to alcohol use. Exploring the relationship between drugs, alcohol, and crime is a huge task and it is necessary to impose some editorial boundaries. First, we will be concentrating predominantly on England and Wales. Second, space precludes a detailed consideration of organized crime relating to drug and contraband alcohol markets or the policing of these markets. For introductory overviews of these topics, readers are directed to Barton (2003), Bean (2008), and Pearson (2007).

Part one: Drugs and crime

BACKGROUND

Attempts to control drug use date back to the Pharmacy Act 1868 which confined the sale of opium to pharmacists. Prior to that there was little external regulation of drug markets which operated on the principles of free enterprise (Shiner, 2006). Throughout the twentieth century, other statutes were passed in a piecemeal fashion to strengthen the laws regulating drug use, including a succession of Dangerous Drugs Acts. The 1971 Misuse of Drugs Act consolidated earlier statutes and laid the foundations for existing and future controls on the import, export, possession, use, manufacture, and distribution of 'controlled' drugs (Jason-Lloyd, 2007). We should pause for a moment and reflect upon the language utilized within the legislation because it is revealing about the ideological assumptions underpinning the Acts and offers an insight into shifting conceptions of

Table 10.1 The 1971 Misuse of Drugs Act	
Category	**Examples of controlled drugs**
Class A (judged to be the most harmful)	Cocaine (crack and powder), ecstasy, hallucinogens (LSD, magic mushrooms), Opiates (heroin, methadone),
Class B	Amphetamines (unless in injectable form, then Class A), cannabis (in all forms),
Class C (judged to be the least harmful)	Anabolic steroids, ketamine, minor tranquillisers

drug use across time. By 1971, the language of danger, with its moralistic overtones, had been replaced by the language of control which emphasized the need to control drugs by preventing their inappropriate use at the same time as permitting their correct use in medical contexts. The 1971 Act divided controlled drugs into three categories (see Table 10.1) according to official perceptions of their relative harmfulness when misused. The level of control is expected to be proportionate to official definitions of harmfulness.

Although a series of statutes have been passed since, the 1971 Act continues to be 'the major stepping-stone in the modern regulation of controlled drugs' (Jason-Lloyd, 2003, p. 1: 4). An independent inquiry into the Act (Police Foundation, 2000) outlined a comprehensive reform programme, advocating a less punitive approach to possession offences and a more punitive approach to supply ones. Whilst many of its recommendations have not been implemented, cannabis was downgraded from a Class B to a Class C drug in 2004, and in most instances possession of cannabis is no longer an arrestable offence (see May *et al.*, 2007 for a more detailed discussion). This move was supported by research findings (May *et al.*, 2002) which suggested that reclassification could potentially allow police officers to respond more effectively to other demands on their time and remove a source of friction between the police, individuals, and communities. In practice, research has found that the reclassification of cannabis had a smaller impact than advocates of the changes hoped and opponents feared (May *et al.*, 2007).

Legislation is based upon official perceptions of the harm caused by drugs, which may not be shared by all members of society. This is illustrated vividly by the debate about whether cannabis should be reclassified as a Class B drug. In May 2008, the Home Secretary, Jacqui Smith, announced that she had taken the decision to upgrade the legal status of cannabis (subsequently done in January 2009). Her decision was largely based upon a concern that skunk, a strong version of cannabis, now dominates drug markets. Smith's action contradicted the findings of a public consultation which found strongest support for leaving the legal status of cannabis unchanged (Ipsos MORI, 2008) and went against the advice of the Advisory Council of the Misuse of Drugs which reached a majority decision against reclassification (Advisory Council of the Misuse of Drugs, 2008).

A number of classic criminological studies illustrate vividly the plurality of perceptions of the harmfulness of illegal drugs (Becker, 1963; Young, 1971). These qualitative studies were shaped by symbolic interactionism (see Chapter 4) and focused on cannabis use. They emphasized the plurality of societal norms and values and identified the processes by which drug use was socially constructed as a 'deviant' act and drug users portrayed as belonging to a counter-culture. More recently, criminological work has drawn attention to the 'normalization' of drug use, or more accurately of recreational drug use (defined in the next section). Its strongest advocates, Howard Parker and his colleagues (Parker *et al.*, 1998), argue that drug use is no longer confined to atypical subcultural groups. Instead it forms part and parcel of growing up in contemporary Britain and is one of a number of ordinary, unremarkable activities (see also Coffield and Gofton, 1994; South, 1999). They argue that drugs are widely available and are accommodated within youth culture; levels of drug trying are high (although few people will engage in long-term use); young people are open-minded about their future drug use; and their knowledge of drugs is extensive. The 'normalization thesis' (see Manning, 2007 for a collection of readings on this topic) has been criticized for being simplistic (Shildrick, 2002) and exaggerating the extent of drug use by young people (Shiner and Newburn, 1997; 1999). Nonetheless it usefully draws attention to the plurality of norms and values which continue to surround illegal drugs.

The drug 'problem' has been officially defined as a law and order, social, medical, and public health 'problem'. These different interpretations have, at different times, influenced the development of UK drug policy. During the 1980s and most of the 1990s, the UK adopted a public health approach to drug policy, initially concerned with reducing the risk drug users pose to themselves and later with risks to wider society (Harman and Paylor, 2002). The public health approach was a response to the realization that unsafe injecting practices could transmit HIV. As the new millennium drew close, a new approach to drug policy was adopted: problem drug use and offending became increasingly interlinked. *Tackling Drugs to Build a Better Britain* (President of the Council, 1998), a ten-year strategy launched in 1998, included reducing crime and anti-social behaviour among its four overarching aims. Critics of the shift in policy emphasis are numerous, and it has been described as a 'war on drug users' (Buchanan and Young, 2000: 409). An updated drug strategy published in 2002 (Home Office, 2002) brought about a further strategic orientation through accelerating the introduction of criminal justice interventions, all with the aim of channelling and coercing drug-using offenders to undergo treatment in the hope it would promote desistance from crime. The 2008 drugs strategy (discussed later in this chapter) promises to consolidate this approach.

The nature and extent of drug use

Commonly used terms to describe drug use include experimental, recreational, and problem, but these are based more on individual opinion than accepted definitions (Health Advisory Service, 2001). In one sense, all drug use is problematic due to the health risks involved and because it can lead to contact with criminal justice agencies.

The difficulties of defining categories of use adequately have been commented on elsewhere (Barton, 2003); however, we offer some working definitions here. Recreational drug use is characteristically centred on the use of cannabis and 'dance drugs' (for example, ecstasy), and whilst these drugs may be used frequently on a recreational basis, unlike problem drug use, recreational use does not involve dependency, regular excessive use, or use which exposes users to serious health (for example, through injecting) or other risks (social, psychological, physical, or legal). Problem drug use typically involves consuming Class A drugs and has the strongest links with offending behaviour.

Estimating the extent of illegal drug use is extremely difficult and there is no comprehensive data source. Criminologists seeking to understand the nature and extent of drug use have to piece together data from official statistics, self-report studies, and academic studies.

Official statistics

The Home Office publishes data on the number of offenders charged with drug offences that come to the attention of the police or HM Customs and Excise who are subsequently cautioned, convicted, or dealt with in some other way. In 2004, 89,820 people were dealt with for 105,570 drug offences (Mwenda, 2005). The number of drug offenders was 25 per cent less than the previous year, which can be explained by the reclassification of cannabis in January 2004. Unlawful possession of controlled drugs was the most common offence (85 per cent of all drug offences) and despite changes to the legal status of cannabis (see page 230), over half of possession offences related to this drug. The typical offender was young (one-third were aged under 21) and male (88 per cent). The majority of episodes of drug use form part of the 'dark figure' of undetected crime; hence drug offender statistics provide little insight into the nature and extent of drug use. An alternative data source is national data on the number of drug users seeking drug treatment. The latest data demonstrate that just over 195,000 individuals received drug treatment in England between April 2006 and March 2007 (National Treatment Agency for Substance Misuse, 2007). This is likely to represent the 'tip of the iceberg'. It excludes drug users who were unable to, did not wish to, or did not need to access treatment. Given these limitations, researchers have developed elaborate models to estimate the prevalence of problem drug use using data gathered from various agencies that problem drug users are likely to make contact with; for example, criminal justice agencies, GP surgeries, and hospital accident and emergency departments (see Singleton *et al.*, 2006 for an overview). The latest estimate is that in 2005/06 there were approximately 330,000 problem drug users (defined as those using opiates, crack cocaine, and/ or injecting) in England (Hay *et al.*, 2007). Their estimate reveals that the typical problem user is male (comprising approximately three-quarters of problem drug users) and aged between 25 and 34, and, in comparison with figures for 2004/05, the problem drug user population remains similar in size. Data on other forms of drug use are best obtained via self-report studies.

Self-report studies

Self-report studies have become the most commonly used means of assessing how many people use, or have used, drugs. However, criticisms of this method are numerous (see Coleman and Moynihan, 1996 for an overview). The two main studies which provide data on drug use for England and Wales are the British Crime Survey and the Offending, Crime and Justice Survey. Both are conducted by the Home Office.

The British Crime Survey (BCS) was established in 1982 as a large survey of adults living in a representative cross-section of private households in England and Wales. Whilst the main focus of the survey is on experiences of crime, data have been collected on drug use since 1994. Respondents enter their answers directly into a laptop computer so that sensitive information can be kept confidential and refusal rates kept to a minimum. The 2006/07 BCS (Murphy and Roe, 2007) estimated that 36 per cent of 16- to 59-year-olds have used one or more illicit drugs in their lifetime, and 14 per cent have used a Class A drug at least once. Levels of drug use within the past year were lower with only 10 per cent of all 16- to 59-year-olds admitting to taking an illicit drug and 3 per cent to using a Class A drug. Levels of drug use within the past month are lower still, and this is illustrated in Table 10.2. The data show that usage varied tremendously between drug types and provide further evidence of the strong relationship between drug use and age. Comparing patterns of drug use over the past decade reveals that, with the exception of a growth in the use of cocaine powder, drug use is relatively stable (Murphy and Roe, 2007).

The BCS does have its limitations as a survey of drug use. In addition to the limitations described in Chapter 3, it is important to note that the BCS is a household survey, and therefore excludes some of the groups most likely to be involved in drug use such as homeless people (Fountain and Howes, 2002; Wincup et al., 2003). Nor does it include young people aged under 16, although there are plans to interview children aged between 10 and 15 in selected households (Home Office, 2008a). Surveys

Table 10.2 Prevalence of drug use in the last month by age group

Type of drug	% used (16- to 24-year-olds)	% used (16- to 59-year-olds)
Cannabis	12.0	4.8
Ecstasy	3.2	0.8
Cocaine (powder or crack)	2.5	1.3
Amphetamines ('speed')	1.2	0.5
Amyl nitrate ('poppers')	1.7	0.5
Any Class A drug	4.3	1.7
Any illicit drug	14.3	5.9

Source: British Crime Survey 2006/7 (Murphy and Roe, 2007).

of young people's (aged 11 to 15) use of drugs (plus alcohol and tobacco) are commissioned by the Department of Health. The 2007 survey (Clemens *et al.*, 2008) was in accordance with the results of previous years and reported a decline in the prevalence of drug use. Drug use was largely confined to cannabis or sniffing glue, gas, aerosols, and solvents.

The Offending, Crime and Justice Survey (OCJS) was established in 2003 and is a nationally representative, longitudinal, self-report survey of people's attitudes towards and experiences of offending. Like the BCS, the OCJS uses Computer-Assisted Personal Interviewing (CAPI). Whilst it collects data on drug use, to date this has not been made publicly available on a routine basis. The sole exception is data from the 2003 sweep. This identified five groups of young people which were vulnerable to drug use: those who had ever been in care; those who had ever been homeless; truants; those excluded from school; and serious offenders (admitting to serious offences such as burglary, robbery, car theft, assault with injury, or dealing Class A drugs) or repeat offenders (admitting to at least six offences) (Becker and Roe, 2005). This mirrors the findings of mostly small-scale academic studies.

Academic studies

Academic studies have captured the diversity of the drug-using population by exploring different populations, such as homeless people (Wincup *et al.*, 2003); care leavers (Ward *et al.*, 2003); young offenders (Hammersley *et al.*, 2003); clubbers (Measham *et al.*, 2001); and sex workers (Cusick *et al.*, 2004). These studies identify that levels of drug use are far more prevalent among these groups. For example, Wincup *et al.*'s (2003) research on young homeless people aged between 16 and 25 found that almost all (95 per cent) of their sample had tried illegal drugs compared to approximately half of young people of the same age participating in the 2000 BCS. In the year prior to interview 89 per cent of the homeless sample had used illegal drugs compared to 28 per cent of the equivalent BCS sample. The studies also highlight that levels of problem drug use among these groups are high. Wincup *et al.*'s (2003) research categorized 27 out of 160 young people as problem drug users and a further 23 as former problem users. Together these studies support the conclusion that certain groups are more vulnerable to becoming problem drug users and that it is important to understand the risk factors associated with the onset of problem drug use to develop effective approaches to drug prevention (Lloyd, 1998).

Academic research has also drawn attention to the link between social divisions and drug use. Both theoretical work (Ettore, 1992, 2007) and empirical research (for example, Taylor, 1993) has pioneered the development of a feminist understanding of women's drug use and argued for the development of gender-sensitive policy responses (Harding, 2006). Research on the links between ethnicity and crime is undeveloped which has hindered the attempts of drug treatment agencies to respond to the diverse needs of the minority ethnic population (Fountain *et al.*, 2003). The available evidence from Britain (see Bennett and Holloway, 2007 for a review) suggests that there are clear ethnic differences in patterns of drug use, with the white population reporting the highest levels of drug use. There is a growing literature on the interconnections between social exclusion and problem drug use, which recognizes that whilst drug experimentation is widespread, problem drug use is largely confined to the most disadvantaged sectors of the population requiring multi-faceted policy responses to tackle the range of problems they face (Foster, 2000; Neale, 2006).

REVIEW QUESTIONS

1 What are the main sources of data on drug use?

2 What are the strengths and weaknesses of the main data sources?

3 How might we capture data on the drug use of those groups currently excluded from household surveys?

Exploring the links between drug use and crime

There have been multiple attempts to conceptualize the links between drug use and crime. This is a complex task because both drug use and crime encompass a wide range of behaviours. Unsurprisingly, therefore, some academics have restricted their analysis to particular forms of crime and/or drug use. For example, Goldstein (1985) focused on the relationship between drug use and violence. Seddon (2000) concentrated on the links between 'non-recreational' (i.e. problem) drug use and acquisitive crime (theft, burglary, robbery, shoplifting, fraud, and deception).

Essentially the literature consists of a number of typologies which have been developed to make sense of the relationship between drug use and crime (Bean, 2008; Bennett and Holloway, 2005, 2007; Hammersley, 2008; Hughes and Anthony, 2006; McSweeney *et al.*, 2007). The number of categories within them varies but, broadly speaking, all begin by exploring initially whether a clear relationship between drug use and crime exists and if so, which behaviour is the cause and which is the effect. From this starting point, two ways of understanding drug-crime connections emerge. The first is that drug use leads to crime. Taking this further, Bennett and Holloway (2005) outline psychopharmalogical, economic and lifestyle explanations for this link. Drug use can be criminogenic due to the impact of drugs on the behaviour of drug users, due to drug users' needs to generate income to support their drug use, or due to the crime being embedded in drug networks. At their most basic, these explanations are deterministic and suggest that crime is an inevitable consequence of drug use. More sophisticated analyses acknowledge the role of mediating and moderating factors. They also recognize the need to explore evidence which challenges accepted wisdom; for example, that drug use can prevent or reduce other forms of offending or that drug use is linked with victimization.

The second main way of understanding drug-crime connections is to explore the counter view that crime causes drug use. Bennett and Holloway (2005) propose that the three types of explanations described above can be used to understand how involvement in crime can lead to the development of a drug-using career. Psychopharmalogical explanations propose that drugs may be used to celebrate offending or used to facilitate committing an offence (through the provision of 'dutch courage'). Economic explanations identify that surplus proceeds from crime allow drugs to be purchased, whilst lifestyle explanations argue that drug use is a systemic part of a criminal lifestyle.

Whilst the two main ways of understanding durg-crime connections described above helpfully draw out the different ways in which drug use and crime are connected, neither are satisfactory in isolation. Consequently, academics have attempted to identify alternative ways to conceptualize the links between drug use and crime. Most discussions are accompanied by a warning that explanations are often undeveloped and in need of further research. Nonetheless, they have shifted thinking away from direct, causal understandings of the relationship between drug use and crime. These conceptualizations are described below.

- Interactive (or reciprocal) approach: the relationship between crime and drug use is bi-directional as criminal and drug-using careers develop in parallel.

- Shared (or common) cause approach: crime and drug use are both caused by a single reinforcing factor, which may be psychological, social, or environmental (see Bennett and Holloway, 2005).

- Multivariate approach: both crime and drug use are linked to a complex set of macro and micro factors which may be socio-economic, cultural, or individual (see Seddon, 2000).

- Spurious (or coincidence) approach: involvement in crime and drug use are unconnected and are merely behaviours which occur simultaneously.

Each model has its strengths and weakness. None of them are satisfactory in their own right. Crucially it is important to recognize that for many drug users, especially those engaged solely in recreational drug use, their involvement in crime is largely restricted to possession and use of a controlled drug.

Reviewing the available evidence

Offering a comprehensive review of the available literature, which may or may not offer support for these models, is beyond the scope of this chapter. More comprehensive overviews can be found elsewhere (for example, Bennett and Holloway, 2005, 2007). Instead, we will focus on some of the key studies which have been published in the past decade.

One major piece of research is the Home Office Arrestee Survey. Covering England and Wales, this nationally representative study provides data on patterns of drug use and criminal activity for arrestees aged 17 and over. The 2003–04 survey collected data from 7,535 individuals across 60 custody suites (Boreham et al., 2006). Typically, the arrestees were male (86 per cent), aged under 35 (71 per cent), and white (84 per cent). Assault and shoplifting were the most common reasons for being arrested (16 per cent and 12 per cent respectively), and over half (55 per cent) had been arrested on at least one further occasion in the year prior to interview. Levels of drug use in the past four weeks were high with over half (57 per cent) reporting use of one or more drugs. Most commonly this was cannabis (46 per cent) but small yet significant proportions admitted to using heroin

(18 per cent) or crack (15 per cent). Despite high levels of drug use in the previous month, relatively few arrestees (15 per cent) admitted to committing offences to buy or obtain drugs. Those that did tended to be users of heroin, crack, or cocaine: 28 per cent of the sample admitting to using these drugs in the previous four weeks. This allows us to conclude (although we should treat self-report data with care) that drug use (and even Class A drug use) does not inevitably lead to involvement in other forms of crime. Committing drug-related crime is most likely among those drug users who are dependent drug users. The survey found the greatest evidence of dependency among heroin users and revealed that a minority of the sample (13 per cent) reported using heroin at least five times a week. This group were the most likely to become involved in drug-related crime.

Data gathered at different points within the criminal justice process also suggest high levels of problem drug use among offenders. OASys (Offender Assessment System), a risk/needs assessment tool used for adult offenders in England and Wales, provides an insight into drug use and its links with crime from the perspective of the criminal justice professional conducting the assessment and the offender subject to it. Analysis of the self-assessment questionnaires completed by over 100,000 prisoners and offenders on probation (from January 2003 to May 2006) found that whilst 24 per cent said that drugs were a problem for them, only 16 per cent said their drug use was linked to their offending (Moore, 2007). Professional assessments identified a closer relationship between drug use and offending for a greater proportion of offenders. Howard's (2006) assessments completed whilst OASys was being piloted (from November 1999 to April 2000) found that 31 per cent of offenders were judged to have 'drug misuse' as a criminogenic need (i.e. an attribute linked to offending). This group was made up disproportionately of offenders convicted of acquisitive crimes and drug offences. Reconviction rates for 757 offenders (which must be treated cautiously, see Lloyd *et al.* 1994; Mair *et al.* 1997) were substantially higher for offenders assessed with this criminogenic need (74 per cent had been convicted for at least one offence two years after being discharged from prison or commencing a community order compared to 41 per cent).

Bringing together the findings of the studies discussed above allows us to conclude that for a small proportion of drug users there appears to be a close relationship between their involvement in (problem) drug use and (prolific) offending. Nonetheless it is problematic to assume that the relationship is unidirectional or causal because the studies tell us little about the interaction between criminal and drug-using careers. Pudney's (2002) study helps to shed light on this. He analysed Youth Lifestyle Survey data in order to explore the timing of young people's initiation into drug use and offending. Analysing this self-report data from almost 5,000 young people aged between 12 and 30 from across England and Wales, he found that crime tends to precede drug use. The average age of onset for crime was 14.5 compared to 16.2 for drugs. Interpreting the findings is challenging because the onset of both offending behaviour and drug use are best viewed as processes rather than one-off events. For example, a drug 'career' may commence with experimenting with alcohol, tobacco, glues, and solvents around the age of 14, moving on to take cannabis and 'poppers' aged 16, and heroin and crack cocaine aged 17 or 18. We cannot conclude from Pudney's research that crime causes drug use. The situation is more complex than this. The relationship between problem drug use and crime can best be viewed as 'dynamic or interactive' (Edmunds *et al.*, 1998: 10) because drug and criminal careers tend to develop in parallel. For instance, acquisitive crime or sex work can provide people with sufficient money to become involved in drug use, and if the drug use becomes problematic they may become locked into involvement in crime. Additionally, as Pudney concludes, social, economic, and family circumstances are key influences on young people's risk of becoming involved in both crime and drug use.

Lloyd (1998) reviewed studies which have sought to identify the risk factors associated with problem drug use. Lloyd concluded that risk factors can relate to the family (for example, parental or sibling drug use, family disruption, poor attachment or communication with parents and child abuse); school (for example, poor educational performance, exclusion); involvement in crime and other conduct disorders (for example, truancy); mental disorder; social deprivation; and young age of onset for drug use. He suggests that these factors are highly connected and best viewed as a 'web of causation' (p. 217). More recently, a systematic literature review explored factors predictive of illicit drug use among young people (Frisher *et al.*, 2007). In contrast to Lloyd, they explored all forms of drug use and it is questionable whether it is appropriate to try to predict behaviour as widespread as drug experimentation and recreational drug use. Frisher *et al.* found that the most extensive and consistent evidence for predicting drug use related to young people's relationship with their families. Parental discipline, family cohesion, and parental monitoring were judged to be key predictors, but they concluded, albeit very tentatively, that the balance between factors which make young people vulnerable to drug use (risk factors) and those which insulate young people from engaging in drug use (protective factors) may be more important than any individual factor in predicting drug use among young people. Unusually for a systematic review which tend to focus on quantitative studies, the authors explored the findings of qualitative studies, which led them to the conclusion that the context in which young people experience drug use (for example, drug availability, peer drug use, individual motives) is crucial for understanding how risk and protective factors operate in relation to drug use. The importance of looking at drug careers in context, both in term of geography and socio-economic status, is vividly illustrated in a series of ethnographic studies on the lives of young people growing up in Britain's poor neighbourhoods (MacDonald and Marsh, 2005)

REVIEW QUESTIONS

1 Critically evaluate the different ways in which the relationship between drug use and crime has been understood.

2 Consider the following policies. Which approaches to understanding the relationship between drug use and crime are they linked to?

- Drug treatment for offenders
- Tackling social exclusion
- Prevention programmes for young people at risk of offending
- More intensive policing of drug markets

3 Refer to Chapter 19. How similar are the risk factors for problem drug use and youth crime?

Breaking the links

In Spring 2008, the UK Government launched *Drugs: Protecting Families and Communities* (HM Government, 2008), a ten-year cross-governmental initiative involving the Home Office, the Department for Children, Schools and Families, the Department of Health, and a variety of other departments and agencies. This long-term strategy focuses on England. The devolved administrations of Scotland, Wales, and Northern Ireland were tasked with developing strategies which both mirror and complement the UK drugs strategy whilst being tailored to the particular circumstances of each country. At the time of writing (Summer 2008), only Scotland has published its new strategy (The Scottish Government, 2008).

As Fraser and Padel (2002) note, attempts to tackle drugs have traditionally operated in three spheres: prevention, treatment, and enforcement. All strategies across the UK focus on this trio of interventions. The aims of *Drugs: Protecting Families and Communities* are listed below:

1. protecting communities through robust enforcement to tackle drug supply, drug-related crime, and anti-social behaviour;

2. preventing harm to children, young people, and families affected by drug misuse;

3. delivering new approaches to drug treatment and social re-integration; and

4. public information campaigns, communications, and community engagement.

Like its predecessors, the 2008 strategy places special emphasis on breaking the links between drug use and crime through the provision of treatment via criminal justice agencies. The criminal justice process is viewed as ideally placed for targeted interventions because of the large number of problem drug users that come into contact with it and because treatment opportunities exist from the point of arrest through to release from prison (Kothari *et al.*, 2002). These interventions are co-ordinated through the Drug Interventions Programme (DIP). Launched in April 2003 in England (and later Wales), DIP aims to provide an integrated approach for adult users of Class A drugs from the point of arrest through to beyond sentencing. Explicitly focused on reducing reoffending through the provision of treatment, DIP involves police forces, the criminal courts, probation areas, and prisons working in partnership with providers of drug treatment and social support (for example, housing). Since 2003, over £500 million has been invested in the programme (Home Office, 2008b).

Broadly speaking criminal justice interventions involve drug testing, drug treatment, or both. At the pre-trial stage, individuals arrested for 'trigger' offences (i.e. those often deemed to be drug-related such as forms of acquisitive crime) are required to undergo testing following the introduction of the Drugs Act 2005. Testing on arrest is currently operational in all DIP-intensive areas (i.e. those with the greatest levels of problem drug use) in England (see <http://www.nta.nhs.uk/areas/criminal_justice/DIP_areas.aspx> for a list) and supplements police powers to test upon charge which were introduced in April 2003. Those testing positive for heroin, crack, and cocaine are required to undergo an initial and follow-up assessment. Failure to comply, without good cause, is a criminal offence. Test results are also used to inform court decisions. For example, since the restriction on bail provision was introduced in March 2006, defendants who test positive in police custody and whose offence is judged to be linked to drug use face an increased risk of being refused bail unless they are engaged in drug treatment (see Hucklesby *et al.*, 2007 for an evaluation of this provision). Similarly the police can use the information for their own purposes; for example, they can attach a drug rehabilitative condition to a caution (for adults only). Failure to comply in this instance can lead to an individual being prosecuted for the original offence.

At the sentencing stage, courts now have access to tailored sentences for drug-using offenders. Courts, in this instance, refers mainly to Magistrates' and Crown Courts, although dedicated drug courts are currently being piloted in England and Wales and already exist in Scotland (see McIvor, forthcoming). The introduction of the Drug Treatment and Testing Order across the UK following the Crime and Disorder Act 1998 paved the way in this respect. Drug Treatment and Testing Orders were replaced following the introduction of the Criminal Justice Act 2003 in 2005 (in England and Wales and Northern Ireland but not Scotland) by drug rehabilitation requirements attached to a generic community order (see Chapter 26). They continue to be used widely, typically in combination with supervision by a probation officer and sometimes in conjunction with attendance at an accredited offending behaviour programme; for example, *Addressing Substance-Related Offending* (Ministry of Justice, 2007). Only relatively rarely is drug treatment included as the sole requirement. Overall, 11,749 offenders (6 per cent of all offenders sentenced to community orders) were required to undergo drug treatment in 2006. Thirty per cent of these offenders were female, more than twice the overall proportion of women sentenced to community orders (14 per cent). The pattern of using drug rehabilitation requirements in conjunction with additional requirements is mirrored for suspended sentence orders. Overall, 2,728 offenders (5 per cent of all offenders given suspended sentence orders) were required to undergo drug treatment in 2006. Again, women were over-represented. Almost two-fifths (38 per cent) of these offenders were female, over three times the overall proportion of women in receipt of such sentences (12 per cent).

Those sentenced to custody are also afforded opportunities to seek treatment for their drug use through Counselling, Assessment, Referral, Advice and Treatment (CARAT) schemes. However, offering treatment alongside measures such as mandatory drug testing and increased security measures to prevent circulation of drugs and drug paraphernalia within prisons is fraught with contradictions (Duke, 2003). At present, liberal responses (for example, the issuing of sterilizing tablets to prisoners who inject) operate alongside punitive responses. Drug policy within prison remains centred on 'control', 'order', and 'punishment' rather than harm minimization and treatment. Additionally the vision to provide continuity of treatment for drug-using prisoners is not always realized in practice, especially for short-sentence prisoners (Paylor and Wilson, forthcoming). For some prisoners, control will extend beyond the prison gate as the Criminal Justice and Court Services Act 2000 permitted a drug testing requirement to form part of a condition of release from prison.

Whilst drug users are required to take part in some of these interventions, principally those limited to drug testing, others are voluntary. However, drug users are 'coerced' into participating in the sense that failing to comply results in less favourable outcomes; for example, it could lead to being remanded in custody rather than being granted bail or being given a custodial sentence rather than a community penalty. The notion of 'coerced treatment' no longer attracts the controversy it did a decade ago when the introduction of the Drug Treatment and Testing Order was met with considerable resistance. Prior to this it was possible to attach a condition that an offender attended treatment to a probation order (now referred to as supervision, see Chapter 26), but in practice this was rarely used because probation officers were concerned about the effectiveness of coerced treatment and drug agencies were reluctant to work with drug users who may not be fully motivated to change (Bean, 2008). The debate is now focused on whether coerced drug treatment is effective, which as Seddon (2007) argues is premature and misleading.

Whilst evidence on the impact of criminal justice interventions on drug-using and offending behaviour is far from unequivocal, it is certainly the case that the number of drug users receiving treatment has increased rapidly in recent years. Figures for England report that between 1998/99 and 2005/06, the number of drug users entering treatment more than doubled (National Treatment Agency for Substance Misuse, 2007). Whilst this has undoubtedly had a positive impact on drug users, families, and potential victims of crime, Reuter and Stevens (2007) argue that this is unlikely to have a substantial and measurable impact on overall levels of problem drug use and crime. They note that many problem drug users do not engage in treatment, treatment programmes vary in terms of their effectiveness, and rates of relapse are high plus new problem drug users replace those who have abstained (Reuter and Stevens, 2007).

REVIEW QUESTIONS

1 Why does tackling drug-related crime require the co-operation of a range of government departments and agencies?

2 What assumptions underpin the introduction of coerced drug treatment for offenders?

3 What impact can the provision of drug treatment have on crime rates?

Part two: Alcohol and crime

BACKGROUND

Attempts to restrict alcohol use date back to the nineteenth century. Beginning with the 1872 Licensing Act, legislation has been introduced periodically to prevent or reduce the problems associated with excessive alcohol consumption. Most recently, the Licensing Act 2003 represented an ambitious attempt by the Government to simplify, rationalize, and build upon the accumulated legislation. This was a challenging task because alcohol occupies an ambiguous position in contemporary Britain, associated with pleasure but also individual and social harms (Newburn and Shiner, 2001). Britain is often described as having a 'wet' culture; in other words, drinking alcohol is widespread and socially accepted as a legitimate and pleasurable activity (Newburn and Shiner, 2001). At the same time, concerns have been expressed about the health and public order implications of problem drinking (Academy of Medical Sciences, 2004; Mistral *et al.*, 2006). Furthermore, alcohol and related industries are seen as important in economic terms: they play an important role in regenerating urban centres, provide employment, and serve as a source of government revenue.

We referred above to 'problem drinking'. In policy documents, three 'types' of drinking are defined: sensible, harmful, and binge drinking; and the notion of 'problem drinking' captures the latter two. Of course, these definitions are open to debate and notions of what constitutes sensible drinking or otherwise have changed over time. The current alcohol strategy defines sensible drinking as 'drinking in a way that is unlikely to cause yourself or others significant risk of harm' (HM Government, 2007: 3). The Government advice is that women should not regularly drink more than two to three units of alcohol a day and men should not regularly drink more than three to four units per day (HM Government, 2007). Harmful drinking refers to long-term consumption at levels that lead to significant harm to the physical and mental health of the individual but which can also affect families, communities, and wider society. Binge drinking refers to excessive intake over shorter periods of time (over six units per day for women and eight for men) and can lead to both long- and short-term problems, principally through drunkenness, which among other things includes an increased likelihood of committing an offence, being involved in an assault or accident, or contracting a sexually transmitted disease.

Reviews of the literature from criminological perspectives have explored how problem drinking can lead to domestic violence (in all its forms), drink-driving and violence, from minor assaults through to homicide (Deehan, 1999; Finney, 2004a, 2004b, 2004c). Academic, political, and media attention has focused in particular on the extent of alcohol-related violence and disorder in urban centres (Academy of Medical Sciences, 2004; Finney, 2004a; Hobbs *et al.*, 2003; Mistral *et al.*, 2006). In post-industrial cities, urban regeneration has resulted in the rapid development of the night-time economy as cities have re-invented themselves as sites of consumption and leisure (Hobbs, 2003). Binge drinking in particular places heavy demands on the resources of criminal justice agencies, although policing is increasingly pluralized and the night-time economy is now 'policed' by both public and private personnel (Hobbs *et al.*, 2003).

The nature and extent of alcohol use

Ninety per cent of adults in England consume alcohol and most confine their drinking to reasonable levels (HM Government, 2007). Data on alcohol consumption can be obtained from a variety of sources. The General Household Survey (GHS) provides data annually on alcohol use for those aged 16 and over based upon face-to-face interviews with individuals from over 13,000 households. Analysis of the 2006 survey (Goddard,

2007) used two measures of daily consumption to estimate levels of problem drinking. The first asks whether people have exceeded the recommended weekly benchmarks to capture harmful drinking, and the second measure explores whether people have engaged in binge drinking by questioning them about the maximum amount drunk on any one day in the week prior to being interviewed. For the first time, this took into account the number of units that people drank, reflecting the fact that alcohol is now often stronger than it was in the past and that measures of alcohol, especially wine, are more generous than in the past. Despite this methodological improvement, the author warns that the data need to be treated with caution because increasing social pressures to drink sensibly may lead to under-reporting of alcohol consumption. This new approach revealed that levels of weekly alcohol consumption were considerably higher than previously assumed, particularly for women. Despite this finding, like its predecessors, the 2006 study noted the persistence of significant gender differences. Men remain more likely than women to have engaged in both harmful and binge drinking, although the gender difference is less marked for the 16 to 24 age group. Overall, the proportion of the public who report either harmful and/or binge drinking has fallen during the past decade but there is still cause for concern. Whilst on average individuals consume 13.5 units (18.7 for men and 9.0 for women), 31 per cent of men and 20 per cent of women drink more than the recommended weekly limit. Similarly whilst the majority of women and men do not binge drink, in the week prior to interview 40 per cent of men and 33 per cent of women did. The data reveal that involvement in problem drinking is not restricted to the younger age groups, although those aged 65 and over were far more likely to drink sensibly. This contrasts with media images which focus on the drinking of young people. The context in which the different age groups drink may be significant here with binge drinking in public space, predominantly by young people, being more visible than the same behaviour by older age groups within the private sphere.

The annual school-based survey for England provides data on alcohol use for young people aged between 11 and 15. Analysis of the 2007 data (Clemens *et al.*, 2008) found that girls and boys were equally likely to have drunk alcohol in the last seven days but that boys tended to drink more than girls. One in five (20 per cent) had drunk alcohol in the previous week, maintaining the decline in the prevalence of drinking recorded in recent years. Despite this decline, the average weekly consumption among pupils who drank in the last week is high at 12.7 units, close to the level recorded for adults by the General Household Survey.

The Offending, Crime and Justice Survey also includes questions on alcohol consumption. Findings from the 2004 survey (Matthews *et al.*, 2006) reveal that underage drinking is widespread: over half (56 per cent) of all 10- to 17-year-olds reported having had an alcoholic drink in the previous year. Whilst this is of some concern, frequency of use was relatively low, particularly among the younger age groups. In addition, almost half said they obtained alcohol from their parents, implying that in some cases at least their use of alcohol was supervised. The findings suggest that underage drinking by a small proportion of interviewees is the most problematic. This group includes those who drink frequently and/or consume sufficient alcohol to feel drunk. It includes both males and females but is made up disproportionately of those aged 16 and 17. As we will discuss in the next section, frequency of drinking was related, albeit not causally, to involvement in crime including drug use.

REVIEW QUESTIONS

1 What are the main strengths and weakness of the different data sources?

2 How can we explain higher levels of alcohol consumption among men? (You might find it helpful to refer to Chapter 17)

3 What are the possible implications of young people's patterns of alcohol use?

Exploring the links between alcohol use and crime

The link between alcohol use and crime has been explored extensively. Collins (1982) concluded that there was sufficient evidence to justify the inference that alcohol is sometimes causally implicated in the occurrence of serious crime, although this conclusion has been the source of considerable debate. Numerous attempts have been made to develop typologies for understanding the relationship between the drinking and offending behaviour, and whilst these vary, all agree that the link between alcohol and crime is multi-faceted. A useful starting point is offered by Hayes (1993) who suggests that the relationship can be characterized in three ways. First, the relationship may be causal because an offender has committed an alcohol-defined offence, an alcohol-induced offence (for example, assaulting someone when drunk), or an alcohol-inspired offence (for example, shoplifting to obtain alcohol). Second, the relationship between alcohol and crime may be contributory: alcohol provides 'dutch courage' to commit an offence, acts as a catalyst, or is offered later as an excuse for offending behaviour. Finally, there may be no relationship between alcohol and crime, with the two behaviours simply co-existing as separate activities.

Similarly, Purser (1995) developed a functional model of the alcohol and crime relationship, distinguishing between the different roles alcohol plays in the offence. His five categories are listed below:

(a) offences which specifically mention alcohol;

(b) offences against the licensing law;

(c) offences committed while under the disinhibiting effects of alcohol where alcohol has affected the person's self-control or judgement;

(d) offences resulting from an alcohol problem where alcohol need not have been consumed immediately prior to the offences being committed;

(e) offences where alcohol is used as an excuse.

Both approaches are helpful but tend to oversimplify the relationship between alcohol and crime. Hayes' typology runs the risk of attributing causality more readily than appropriate, whilst Purser's model tends to assume that alcohol and crime are always related, even if alcohol is not always a causal factor in crime. Research on the relationship between alcohol and crime is voluminous and difficult to interpret. A number of researchers have reviewed the available literature (Deehan, 1999; Newburn and Shiner,

2001; Ramsay, 1996; Sumner and Parker, 1995). Rather than repeat their efforts, we will focus here on the most recent studies.

The British Crime Survey explores among other things alcohol-related violence, which it categorizes as woundings, assaults with minor injury, assaults with no injury, and robberies where the offender was thought to be under the influence of alcohol. According to analysis of the 2007/08 data (Hoare and Povey, 2008), victims of violence believed the offender or offenders to be under the influence of alcohol in 45 per cent of all violent incidents. The offender was judged to be under the influence in almost three-fifths (58 per cent) of incidents of violence between strangers; almost half (48 per cent) of incidents of violence between acquaintances; almost two-fifths (37 per cent) of domestic violence; and one-sixth (17 per cent) of muggings. These findings reveal the co-existence of alcohol use (but not necessarily drunkenness) and crime, but cannot provide an insight into whether alcohol was a contributory factor. However, when coupled with the accounts of offenders they enhance our understanding of the relationship between alcohol and crime.

The 2004 Offending, Crime and Justice Survey (Matthews *et al.*, 2006) begins to illustrate the complex relationship between alcohol use and youth offending. Among 10- to 17-year-olds, those who drank at least once a month committed offences more often than those who drank less frequently or not at all. This applied to all offences but particularly to violent offences. Similarly, 10- to 17-year-olds who drank at least once a week (14 per cent of respondents) were responsible for a disproportionate amount of crimes (37 per cent of all offences) committed by this age group. Those who drank at least once a week or more frequently were more likely to admit involvement in crime and/or disorder during or after drinking, especially arguments, fights, and criminal damage. They were also more likely to engage in other forms of risky or illegal behaviour, including smoking and drug use. Analysis of the 2003 survey data (Matthews and Richardson, 2005) for an older age group (those aged 18 to 65) similarly revealed a close relationship between binge drinking and involvement in criminal and/or anti-social behaviour, particularly for males aged between 18 and 24.

The majority of the crimes reported to the Offending, Crime and Justice Survey did not lead to offenders having contact with criminal justice agencies. Information about the alcohol use of those who do can add to our understanding gleaned from household surveys and relates to individuals at different stages of the criminal justice process. The Arrestee Survey (Boreham *et al.*, 2006) used the Fast Alcohol Screening Test to calculate the proportion of arrestees whose alcohol use could be considered hazardous. Almost three-fifths of arrestees (57 per cent) of all ages were judged to be alcohol 'misusers', with the proportion of women only slightly lower than the proportion of men (51 per cent compared to 58 per cent). The data are also revealing about the links between drug and alcohol use. Especially for 17- to 24-year-olds, there appeared to be a relationship between the use of cocaine (in its powder form) and alcohol use.

Whilst data gathered from surveys of households and arrestees imply close links between heavy drinking and involvement in crime, the accounts of convicted offenders provide a different perspective. Self-assessment data gathered using OASys (Moore, 2007) reveals that only one-quarter of offenders reported that drinking too much alcohol was a problem for them and a smaller proportion (19 per cent) stated that it was linked to their offending. OASys assessments by criminal justice professionals (Howard, 2006) point to a greater degree of fit between alcohol use and crime with almost one-third (31 per cent) of offenders judged to have 'alcohol misuse' as a criminogenic need, a group which comprised in particular those convicted of violent offences and criminal damage. In contrast to drug misuse, alcohol misuse was not a good predictor of the likelihood of further offending.

So far our discussion has drawn upon the findings of surveys which have collected quantitative data. Whilst these shed light on the links between alcohol use and crime, they fail to reveal its complexity. In this respect, studies which have collected qualitative data are especially valuable. Engineer et al. (2003) explored binge drinking and disorderly behaviour through 16 focus groups with young people aged between 18 and 24 from across England and Wales. They found that drinking was an integral part of the social scene for many young people and that few felt that their drinking habits were something that they should change, even if they had been involved in various forms of risk or disorder as a consequence. One of the main conclusions was that the boundaries between 'risking', 'offending', and becoming a 'victim' while drunk are easily crossed. The majority of the young people had experienced more than one of these things while drinking, and many all three.

Focusing more narrowly on persistent offenders, Parker (1996) conducted in-depth interviews with 66 young people aged between 18 and 25 subject to probation supervision. The majority (52) were current drinkers and just under half of these (24) stated their use of alcohol caused problems, typically relating to involvement with crime and contact with the police. The entire sample felt alcohol was sometimes part of the explanation for their offending but even the heavy drinkers did not perceive alcohol as central to their explanations of their own offending behaviour. Parker argued that the search for a simple correlation between alcohol use and offending is not 'good criminology' (Parker, 1996: 291). He found that through analysis of their qualitative motivational accounts, other variables emerged relating to illegal drug use and the desire to pursue a preferred lifestyle; thus attempts to isolate alcohol use as a key variable are misguided. Parker concluded that for persistent young adult offenders alcohol is both an accessory to crime and to a lawful good time, and in the latter respect they are no different to law-abiding young adults as the accounts of young people who participated in Engineer et al.'s study (discussed above) reveal.

REVIEW QUESTIONS

1 What are the difficulties of relying upon victims' perceptions of whether the offence was alcohol-related?

2 What can be concluded from the different surveys about the relationship between alcohol use and crime?

3 Do the qualitative studies challenge these conclusions? If so, in what ways?

Breaking the links

Concerns about alcohol-related crime and disorder have moved up the political and public agendas in recent years, heightened by media stories about lawless urban centres, and binge drinking, and more recently 'feral' teenagers. The Labour Government has responded with a range of initiatives. The Licensing Act 2003 represented a significant 'shake up' of existing legislation and set out new priorities in tackling alcohol-related problems. The Act defined four key objectives for local authorities:

1. the prevention of crime and disorder;
2. public safety;
3. the prevention of public nuisance; and
4. the protection of children from harm.

A number of new measures were introduced, including the controversial extension of drinking hours, which drew criticism from an array of sources including the media, the public and the medical profession. The stated aim of this change was to reduce alcohol-related violence by staggering closing times. In practice, whilst alcohol-related violence has reduced at what were the traditional closing times (11 p.m. for pubs and 2 a.m. for clubs), overall some studies have found that alcohol-related violence has increased and is spread more widely throughout the night (Newton *et al.*, 2007).

The new legislation accompanied the launch of a much awaited strategic approach to tackling problem drinking and its effects. In 2004, the *Alcohol Harm Reduction Strategy for England* was published (Prime Minister's Strategy Unit, 2004) and set out the broad framework in which local authorities and partners were obliged to work together to tackle problem alcohol use. It identified a range of harms arising from alcohol use, including harms to the health of individuals and harms to public order. A key priority was tackling alcohol-related crime and disorder, particularly in town and city centres 'blighted by alcohol misuse at weekends' (2004: 5). *Safe, Sensible, Social—Next Steps in the National Alcohol Strategy* (HM Government, 2007) was published three years after the original strategy. This acknowledged that more needed to be done to tackle alcohol-related offending. It recognized that despite a major fall in violent crime since the mid-1990s, the public perception is that such crime has actually increased and that a small yet significant proportion of violence is committed around pubs and clubs (17 per cent in 2005/06). *Next Steps* built on the original strategy and set out three key objectives:

1. to ensure laws and licensing powers are being used widely and effectively to crack down on crime and disorder, bear down on irresponsible management of licensed premises and to protect young people;
2. to sharpen the focus on the minority of drinkers who cause or experience the most harm to themselves and their communities and their families (underage drinkers, 18- to 24-year-old binge drinkers, harmful drinkers); and
3. to work together to shape an environment that actively promotes sensible drinking.

It remains to be seen how effective this will be but some commentators are heartened by what they see as a tougher approach to industry practices than in the original strategy Calls for a tougher approach have increased with the recent publication of an independent review of social responsibility within the drinks industry which found considerable evidence of 'inducements to people to drink more and faster, and to allow under-age people entry to premises, and blatantly serving intoxicated people' (Home Office/KPMG, 2008: 10).

It would be inappropriate to give the impression that, prior to the launch of the strategy, there were few attempts to reduce levels of crime related to problem drinking. A wide range of interventions are described by Alcohol Concern (1999), Deehan (1999), and Felson (2002), with most being attempts to change the environment in which drinking takes place through a variety of situational crime prevention (SCP) measures. These are 'directed at highly specific forms of crime which involve the management, design or implementation of the immediate environment in which these crimes occur...so as to reduce the opportunities for these crimes' (Hough *et al.*, 1980: 1). They include the use of plastic glasses, serving food with alcoholic drinks, reduced prices for low- and non-alcohol drinks, and the abolition of happy hours. Local Community Safety Partnerships are increasingly using such measures as part of a growing toolkit to tackle alcohol-related disorder. Recent innovations include sophisticated data analysis which allows disorder 'hotspots' to be identified, taxi marshalling schemes to prevent crime and disorder and promote public safety, and online CCTV in a number of city centres to enhance surveillance. Whilst SCP approaches offer a potentially effective means of reducing alcohol-related harm, they are only part of the solution. Criminologists have been urged by Hayward (2004) to adopt a cultural perspective and ask why the majority of violent assaults in the UK involve the use of alcohol in one form or another.

Alongside SCP measures, there are opportunities to work with offenders as they progress through the criminal justice process. The Drug Intervention Programme, described earlier in this chapter, currently focuses on problem drug use but there is support for it to be tailored to work with those whose offending is judged to be related to problem alcohol use. Opportunities are more developed for convicted offenders. Following the implementation of the Criminal Justice Act 2003 in 2005, the criminal courts in England and Wales can now require adult offenders to undergo alcohol treatment as part of a community order or suspended sentence order. In 2006, 3,163 offenders were required to attend alcohol treatment; in three-quarters of cases as a condition of their community order rather than a suspended sentence order (Ministry of Justice, 2007). In contrast to the condition to undergo drug treatment, women were not over-represented and the proportions were as expected given the gender breakdown of the National Probation Service caseload. The requirement to engage with alcohol treatment was typically combined with supervision, and less frequently with attendance at an accredited offending behaviour programme. The notion of coerced alcohol treatment remains in its infancy. Leaving aside the issue of the appropriateness of coerced treatment (see Part One of this chapter), questions need to be asked about whether there are sufficient services available given recent reports about its scarcity (HM Inspectorate of Probation, 2006).

REVIEW QUESTIONS

1 What impact has the 2003 Licensing Act had on levels of crime and disorder?

2 What are the strengths and weaknesses of using situational crime prevention measures as a means to tackle alcohol-related crime and disorder?

3 What might a cultural perspective add to our understanding of how best to reduce alcohol-related crime? (You may find it helpful to refer to Chapter 7)

CONCLUSION

In this chapter, we have pieced together the available evidence, and acknowledged its limitations, to present a picture of drug and alcohol use in England and Wales. We have noted that alcohol use and, to a lesser extent, drug use is widespread but problem use is confined to a minority. Males, especially young males, are most likely to be engaged in problem drug or alcohol use and therefore more likely to come into contact with criminal justice agencies.

Reviewing the available evidence suggests that current knowledge about the relationship between drugs, alcohol, and crime remains patchy and prone to misinterpretation. We have explored the dangers of relying upon deterministic explanations and suggested that 'chicken and egg' arguments about whether drug (or alcohol) use leads to crime or vice versa are both simplistic and unhelpful. Instead, we have argued for a more complex understanding of the relationship between drugs, alcohol, and crime which locates it within its social, economic, political, and cultural context.

Finally, it is important to note that the material on drugs and alcohol has been presented separately to aid understanding of a challenging criminological issue. Whilst this mirrors policy responses (with the exception of Wales which has an integrated strategy (National Assembly for Wales, 2000)), this approach runs the risk of glossing over the fact that both the causes and effects of problem drug and alcohol use may be similar, and that alcohol is often a common element in polydrug use among offenders (Boreham *et al.*, 2006)

QUESTIONS FOR DISCUSSION

1 Look at newspaper reporting of crime. To what extent are drug and alcohol use offered as explanations for offending?

2 Is it possible to obtain an accurate figure of the nature and extent of drug and alcohol use?

3 How can we respond to the commonly held view that the relationship between drugs (or alcohol) and crime is straightforward?

4 What are the main differences between policy responses to drugs and alcohol?

5 Is more legislation likely to reduce levels of drug-related and alcohol-related crime?

GUIDE TO FURTHER READING

Bennett, T. and Holloway, K. (2005) *Understanding Drugs, Alcohol and Crime.* Buckingham: Open University Press.

This text provides a succinct overview of current theory and research on the links between drugs, alcohol, and crime.

Dingwall, G. (2006) *Alcohol and Crime.* Cullompton: Willan Publishing.

This text seeks to understand the nature of the connection between alcohol and crime, and the way criminal justice system responds to the problem.

Hammersley, R. (2008) *Drugs & Crime.* Cambridge: Polity Press.

Challenging simplistic and misguided thinking about drugs and crime, this text argues that the relationship between drug problems and crime needs to be examined in their complex social and psychological contexts.

Simpson, M., Shildrick, T., and MacDonald, R. (eds) (2007) *Drugs in Britain: Supply, Consumption and Control.* Basingstoke: Palgrave Macmillan.

An edited collection which explores the distribution and consumption of illicit drugs and debates surround the policing of drugs and the care and control of drug users.

South, N. (2007) 'Drugs, Alcohol and Crime' in M. Maguire, R. Morgan, and R. Reiner (eds) *The Oxford Handbook of Criminology* (4th edn). Oxford: Oxford University Press.

This chapter covers similar ground to the chapter you have just read, but offers a more detailed discussion of trends in drug and alcohol use and strategies to tackle both the demand for, and supply of, drugs.

WEB LINKS

http://www.drugscope.org.uk

DrugScope is an independent centre of information and expertise on drugs and aims to inform policy development and reduce drug-related harms. Its website provides authoritative and reliable information on all aspects of drugs and the harms they cause.

http://www.alcoholconcern.org.uk

Alcohol Concern is the national voluntary agency on alcohol misuse, acting as an umbrella body for 500 local agencies tackling alcohol-related harm. Its website is a vital part of its aim to act as the principal source of information on alcohol to the general public, the media, and professionals (including government officials).

http://www.ukdpc.org.uk

The UK Drug Policy Commission is an independent body providing objective analysis of UK drug policy. It aims to improve political, media, and public understanding to develop a rational and effective response to problems caused by illegal drugs.

http://www.drugs.homeoffice.gov.uk

Aimed at professionals, this site offers the latest news and guidance from the Government about the drugs strategy.

http://www.dh.gov.uk

The Department of Health website includes details of the Government's health policies on alcohol misuse and access to a wide range of statistical information on alcohol use (prevalence, consumption patterns, health-related issues, alcohol-related harm, and expenditure), mainly for England.

REFERENCES

Academy of Medical Sciences (2004) *Calling Time: The Nation's Drinking as a Major Health Issue*. London: Academy of Medical Sciences.

Advisory Council on the Misuse of Drugs (2008) *Cannabis: Classification and Public Health*. London: Home Office.

Alcohol Concern (1999) *Proposal for a National Alcohol Strategy for England*. London: Alcohol Concern.

Barton, A. (2003) *Illicit Drugs: Use and Control*. London: Routledge.

Bean, P. (2008) *Drugs and Crime* (3rd edn). Cullompton: Willan Publishing.

Becker, H. (1963) *Outsiders: Studies in the Sociology of Deviance*. New York: Free Press.

Becker, J. and Roe, S. (2005) *Drug Use among Vulnerable Groups of Young People: Findings from the 2003 Crime and Justice Survey*, Findings 254. London: Home Office.

Bennett, T. and Holloway, K. (2005) *Understanding Drugs, Alcohol and Crime*. Buckingham: Open University Press.

Bennett, T. and Holloway, K. (2007) *Drug-Crime Connections*. Cambridge: Cambridge University Press.

Boreham, R., Fuller, E., Hills, A., and Pudney, S. (2006) *The Arrestee Survey Annual Report: Oct 2003–Sept 2004 England and Wales*, Home Office Statistical Bulletin 04/06. London: Home Office.

Buchanan, J. and Young, L. (2000) 'The War on Drugs—A War on Drug Users', *Drugs: Education, Prevention and Policy*, 7 (4): 409–22.

Clemens, S., Jotangia, D., Lynch, S., Nicholson, S., and Pigott, S. (2008) *Drug Use, Smoking and Drinking among Young People in England 2007*. London: The NHS Information Centre for Health and Social Care.

Coffield, F. and Gofton, L. (1994) *Drugs and Young People*. London: Institute for Public Policy Research.

Coleman, C. and Moynihan, J. (1996) *Understanding Crime Data: Haunted by the Dark Figure*. Buckingham: Open University Press.

Collins, J. (1982) *Drinking and Crime; Perspectives on the Relationship between Alcohol Consumption and Criminal Behaviour*. London: Tavistock.

Cusick, L., Martin, A., and May, T. (2003) *Vulnerability and Involvement in Drug Use and Sex Work*. Findings 207. London: Home Office.

Deehan, A. (1999) *Alcohol and Crime: Taking Stock*, Crime Reduction Research Series Paper 3. London: Home Office.

Duke, K. (2003) *Drugs, Prisons and Policy-Making*. Basingstoke: Palgrave Macmillan.

Edmunds, M., May, T., Hearnden, I., and Hough, M. (1998) *Arrest Referral: Emerging Lessons form Research*, Drug Prevention Initiative Paper 23. London: Home Office.

Engineer, R., Phillips, A., Thompson, J., and Nicholls, J. (2003) *Drunk and Disorderly: A Qualitative Study of Binge Drinking among 18- to 24-year olds*. Home Office Online Report 262/03. London; Home Office.

Ettore, E. (1992) *Women and Substance Use*. Basingstoke: Macmillan.

Ettore, E. (2007) *Revisioning Women and Drug Use: Gender, Power and the Body*. Basingstoke: Palgrave Macmillan.

Felson, M. (2002) *Crime and Everyday Life*. Thousand Oaks, CA.: Sage.

Finney, A. (2004a) *Violence in the Night-time Economy: Key Findings from the Research*, Findings 214. London: Home Office.

Finney, A. (2004b) *Alcohol and Sexual Violence: Key Findings from the Research*. Findings 215. London: Home Office.

Finney, A. (2004c) *Alcohol and Intimate Partner Violence: Key Findings from the Research*, Findings 216. London: Home Office.

Foster, J. (2000) 'Social Exclusion, Crime and Drugs', *Drugs: Education, Prevention and Policy*, 7 (4): 317–30.

Fountain, J., Bashford, J., Winters, M., and Patel, K. (2003) *Black and Minority Ethnic Communities in England: A Review of the Literature on Drug Use and Related Service Provision*. London/Preston: National Treatment Agency for Substance Misuse/Centre for Ethnicity and Health.

Fountain, J. and Howes, S. (2002) *Home and Dry? Homelessness and Substance Use*. London: Crisis.

Fraser, P. and Padel, U. (2002) 'Editorial', *Criminal Justice Matters*, 47: 3.

Frisher, M., Crome, I., Macleod, J., Bloor, R., and Hickman, M. (2007) *Predictive Factors for Illicit Drug Use among Young People*, Home Office Online Report 05/07. London: Home Office.

Goddard, E. (2007) *Smoking and Drinking among Adults 2006*. London: Office for National Statistics.

Goldstein, P. (1985) 'The Drugs/Violence Nexus: A Tripartite Conceptual Framework', *Journal of Drug Issues*, Fall, 493–506.

Hammersley, R. (2008) *Drugs and Crime*. Cambridge: Polity Press.

Hammersley, R., Marsland, L., and Reid, M. (2003) *Substance Use by Young Offenders: The Impact of the Normalisation in the Early Years of the 21st Century*, Home Office Research Study 261. London: Home Office.

Harman, K. and Paylor, I. (2002) 'A Shift in Strategy', *Criminal Justice Matters*, 47: 8–9.

Hayes, P. (1993) 'A View from the Probation Service', in J. Russell (ed) *Alcohol and Crime: Proceedings of a Mental Health Foundation Conference*. London: Mental Health Foundation.

Hay, G., Gannon, M., MacDougall, J., Millar, T., Eastwood, C., and McKeganey, N. (2007) *National and Regional Estimates of the Prevalence of Opiate Use and/or Crack Cocaine Use 2005/06: A Summary of Key Findings*, Home Office Online Report 21/07. London: Home Office.

Hayward, K. (2004) *City Limits: Crime, Consumer Culture and the Urban Experience*. London: GlassHouse Press.

Harding, T. (2006) 'Gender, drugs and policy', in R. Hughes, R. Lart, and P. Higate (eds) *Drugs: Policy and Politics*. London: Longman.

Health Advisory Service (2001) *The Substance of Young Need*. London: Health Advisory Service.

HM Government (2007) *Safe, Sensible, Social: Next Steps in the National Alcohol Strategy*. London: HM Government.

HM Government (2008) *Drugs; Protecting Families and Communities: The 2008 Drug Strategy*. London: HM Government.

HM Inspectorate of Probation (2006) *Half Full, Half Empty: An Inspection of the National Probation Service's Work with Offenders*. London: HM Inspectorate of Probation.

Hoare, J. and Povey, D. (2008) 'Violent and sexual crime' in C. Kershaw, S. Nicholas, and A. Walker (eds) *Crime in England and Wales 2007/08: Findings from the British Crime Survey and Police Recorded Crime*, Home Office Statistical Bulletin 07/08. London: Home Office.

Hobbs, D. (2003) *The Night-Time Economy*, Alcohol Concern Research Forum Papers. London: Alcohol Concern.

Hobbs, D., Hadfield, P., Lister, S. and Winlow, S. (2003) *Bouncers: Violence and Governance in the Night-time Economy*. Oxford: Oxford University Press.

Home Office (2002) *Updated Drug Strategy 2002*. London: Home Office.

Home Office (2008a) *Consultation of the British Crime Survey Extension to Cover under 16s*. London: Home Office.

Home Office (2008b) Drug Interventions Programme. Available at <http://drugs.homeoffice.gov.uk/drug-interventions-programme/strategy/?version=1> (accessed 1 September 2008).

Home Office/KPMG (2008) Review of the Social Responsibility Standards for the Production and Sale of Alcoholic Drinks, Volume 1. London: Home Office.

Hough, M., Clarke, R., and Mayhew, P. (1980) 'Introduction' in R. Clarke and P. Mayhew (eds) *Designing Out Crime*. London: Home Office.

Howard, P. (2006) *The Offender Assessment System: An Evaluation of the Second Pilot*, Findings 278. London: Home Office.

Hucklesby, A., Eastwood, C., Seddon, T., and Spriggs, A. (2007) *The Evaluation of the Restriction on Bail Pilot; Final Report*, Home Office Online Report 06/07. London: Home Office.

Hughes, R. and Anthony, N. (2006) 'Drugs, crime and criminal justice', in R. Hughes, R. Lart, and P. Higate (eds) *Drugs: Policy and Politics*. London: Longman.

Ipsos MORI (2008) *Drugs: Our Community, Your Say: A Report on the 2008 Drug Strategy Consultation: Views on Reclassifying Cannabis to a Class B Drug*. London: Ipsos MORI.

Jason-Lloyd, L. (2003) *Drugs, Addiction and the Law*. Huntingdon: Elm Publishing.

Jason-Lloyd, L. (2007) *Misuse of Drugs*. Winchester: Waterside Press.

Kothari, G., Marsden, J., and Strang, J. (2002) 'Opportunities and Obstacles for Effective Treatment of Drug Misusers in the Criminal Justice System in England and Wales', *British Journal of Criminology*, 42 (2): 412–32.

Lloyd, C. (1998) 'Risk Factors for Problem Drug Use: Identifying Vulnerable Groups', *Drugs: Education, Prevention and Policy*, 5 (3) 217–32.

Lloyd, C., Mair, G., and Hough, M. (1994) *Explaining Reconviction Rates: A Critical Analysis*, Home Office Research Study 136. London: Home Office.

MacDonald, R. and Marsh, J. (2005) *Disconnected Youth? Growing up in Britain's Poor Neighbourhoods*. London: Palgrave Macmillan.

Mair, G., Lloyd, C., and Hough, M. (1997) 'The limitations of reconviction rates', in G. Mair (ed) *Evaluating the Effectiveness of Community Penalties*. Aldershot: Ashgate.

Manning, P. (2007) *Drugs and Popular Culture: Drugs, Media and Identity in Contemporary Culture*. Cullompton: Willan Publishing.

Matthews, S. and Richardson A. (2005) *Findings from the 2003 Offending, Crime and Justice Survey: Alcohol-related Crime and Disorder*, Findings 261. London: Home Office.

Matthews, S., Brasnett, L., and Smith, J. (2006) *Underage Drinking: Findings from the 2004 Offending, Crime and Justice Survey*, Findings 277. London: Home Office.

May, T., Warburton, H., Turnbull, P., and Hough, M. (2002) *Times they are A-changing: The Policing of Cannabis*. York: Joseph Rowntree Foundation.

May, T., Duffy, M., Warburton, H., and Hough, M. (2007) *Policing Cannabis as a Class C Drug: An Arresting Change?* York: Joseph Rowntree Foundation.

McIvor, G. (forthcoming) 'Drug courts: lessons from the UK and beyond', in A. Hucklesby and E. Wincup (eds) *Drug Interventions and Criminal Justice*, Buckingham: Open University Press.

McSweeney, T., Hough, M., and Turnbull, P. (2007) 'Drugs and crime: explaining the links', in M. Simpson, T. Shildrick, and R. MacDonald (eds) *Drugs In Britain: Supply, Consumption and Control*. Basingtoke: Palgrave Macmillan.

Measham, F., Aldridge, J., and Parker, H. (2001) *Dancing on Drugs: Risk, Health and Hedonism in the British Club Scene*. London: Free Association Press.

Ministry of Justice (2007) *Offender Management Caseload Statistics 2006*, London: Ministry of Justice.

Mistral, W., Velleman, R., Templeton, L., and Mastache, C. (2006) 'Local action to prevent alcohol problems: is the UK Community Alcohol Prevention Programme the best solution?' *International Journal of Drug Policy.* 17(4): 278–84.

Moore, R. (2007) *Adult Offenders' Perceptions of their Underlying Problems: Findings from the OASys Self-assessment Questionnaire*, Findings 284. London: Home Office.

Murphy, R. and Roe, S. (2007) *Drug Misuse Declared: Findings from the British Crime Survey*, Home Office Statistical Bulletin 18/07. London: Home Office.

Mwenda, L. (2005) *Drug Offenders in England and Wales*, Home Office Statistical Bulletin 23/05. London: Home Office.

National Assembly for Wales (2000) *Tackling Substance Misuse in Wales: A Partnership Approach*. Cardiff: National Assembly for Wales.

National Treatment Agency for Substance Misuse (2007) *Statistics for Drug Treatment Activity in England 2006/07: National Drug Treatment Monitoring System*. London: National Treatment Agency for Substance Misuse.

Neale, J. (2006) 'Social exclusion, drugs and policy', in R. Hughes, R. Lart, and P. Higate (eds) *Drugs: Policy and Politics*. London: Longman.

Newburn, T. and Shiner, M. (2001) *Teenage Kicks? Young People and Alcohol: A Review of the Literature*. York: Joseph Rowntree Foundation.

Newton, A., Sarker, S., Pahal, G, van den Bergh, E., and Young, C. (2007) 'Impact of the new licensing law on emergency hospital attendances: a cohort study', *Emergency Medical Journal*, 24(8): 532–34.

Paylor, I. and Wilson, A. (forthcoming) 'Drug' in A. Hucklesby and E. Wincup (eds) *Drug Interventions and Criminal Justice*, Buckingham: Open University Press.

Parker, H. (1996) 'Young Adult Offenders, Alcohol and Criminological Cul-de-sacs', *British Journal of Criminology*, 36(2): 282–98.

Parker, H., Aldridge, J., and Measham, F. (1998) *Illegal Leisure: The Normalization of Adolescent Recreational Drug Use*. London: Routledge.

Pearson, G. (2007) 'Drug markets and dealing: from "street dealer" to Mr Big', in M. Simpson, T. Shildrick, and R. MacDonald (eds) *Drugs In Britain: Supply, Consumption and Control*. Basingstoke: Palgrave Macmillan.

Police Foundation (2000) *Drugs and the Law: Report of the Independent Inquiry into the Misuse of Drugs Act 1971*. London: Police Foundation.

President of the Council (1998) *Tackling Drugs to Build a Better Britain: The Government's Ten Year Strategy for Tackling Drug Misuse*. London: The Stationery Office.

Prime Minister's Strategy Unit (2003) *Alcohol Harm Reduction Project: Interim Analytical Report*. London: Cabinet Office.

Prime Minister's Strategy Unit (2004) *Alcohol Harm Reduction Strategy*. London: Cabinet Office.

Pudney, S. (2002) *The Road to Ruin? Sequences of Initiation into Drug Use and Offending by Young People in Britain*, Home Office Research Study 253. London: Home Office.

Purser, R. (1995) *Alcohol and Crime*, Submission to the All Party Group on Alcohol Misuse.

Ramsay, M. (1996) 'The relationship between alcohol and crime' in C. Bryon (ed) *Home Office Research and Statistics Directorate Research Bulletin No. 38*. London: Home Office.

Reuter, P. and Stevens, A. (2007) *An Analysis of UK Drug Policy*. London: UK Drug Policy Commission.

Seddon, T. (2000) 'Explaining the Drug-Crime Link: Theoretical, Policy and Research Issues', *Journal of Social Policy*, 29 (1): 95–107.

Seddon, T. (2007) 'Coerced drug treatment in the criminal justice system: conceptual, ethical and criminological issues', *Criminology and Criminal Justice*, 7(3): 269–86.

Shildrick. T. (2002) 'Young People, Illicit Drug Use and Questions of Normalization', *Journal of Youth Studies*, 5 (1): 35–48.

Shiner, M. (2006) 'Drugs, law and the regulation of harm', in R. Hughes, R. Lart, and P. Higate (eds) *Drugs: Policy and Politics*. London: Longman.

Shiner, M. and Newburn, T. (1997) 'Definitely, Maybe Not: The Normalisation of Recreational Drug Use amongst Young People', *Sociology*, 31(3): 1–19.

Shiner, M. and Newburn, T. (1999) 'Taking tea with Noel: the place and meaning of drug use in everyday life', in N. South (ed) *Drugs: Cultures, Controls and Everyday Life*. London: Sage.

Singleton, N., Murray, R., and Tinsley, L. (eds) (2006) *Measuring Different Aspects of Problem Drug Use: Methodological Developments* (2nd edn). Home Office Online Report 16/06. London: Home Office.

South, N. (1999) 'Debating Drugs and Everyday Life: Normalisation, Prohibition and "Otherness"', in N. South (ed) *Drugs: Cultures, Controls and Everyday Life*. London: Sage.

Sumner, M. and Parker, H. (1995) *Low in Alcohol: A Review of the International Research into Alcohol's Role in Crime Causation*. London: The Portman Group.

Taylor, A. (1993) *Women Drug Users: An Ethnography of a Female Injecting Community*. Oxford: Clarendon Press.

The Scottish Government (2008) *The Road to Recovery: A New Approach to Tackling Scotland's Drug Problem*. Edinburgh: The Scottish Government.

Ward, J., Henderson, Z., and Pearson, G. (2003) *One Problem Among Many: Drug Use among Care Leavers in Transition to Independent Living*, Home Office Research Study 260. London: Home Office.

Wincup, E., Buckland, G., and Bayliss, R. (2003) *Youth Homelessness and Substance Use: Report to the Drugs and Alcohol Research Unit*, Home Office Research Study 258. London: Home Office.

Young, J. (1971) *The Drugtakers*. London: Paladin.

11 Violent crime

Larry Ray

INTRODUCTION

This chapter is an introduction to criminological and sociological analysis of violence that will provide you with an overview of some of the main debates and issues along with suggestions for further reading. It begins by raising the question 'what is violence?' which is itself subject to debate. It then examines a key theoretical approach to violence developed by the sociologist Norbert Elias that has placed the understanding of violence in historical context as well as provided a theory accounting for the gradual but uneven diminution of interpersonal violence in modern societies. The chapter then presents summary data on the prevalence of violence in the UK based largely on information from the British Crime Survey (BCS). Next it examines specific issues—aggression and masculinity, violence in the private sphere, racist violence, and homicides. For each type of violence a summary of the data, its prevalence, and discussion of some key explanatory frameworks is given. The chapter ends with some general questions for discussion and a guide to further reading and Internet sources.

BACKGROUND

What is violence? There is no simple answer to this question. The sociological analysis of violence has focused on criminal forms—especially homicide, assault, child abuse, sexual violence, and intimate violence—with the result that a research literature has developed that is specialized but lacks overall theoretical coherence (Jackman, 2002). Except for specialist studies of war, revolution, and social movements, the sociology of violence tends to focus on interpersonal rather than collective or State violence, and works within a criminal justice framework. 'Violence' tends to be separated from 'legitimate force' so that the killing of a police officer by a civilian is considered 'homicide' (that is, violence), whereas the killing of a civilian by a police officer 'in the line of duty' is generally not. Similarly, the exposure of workers to hazardous working conditions that result in death or injury is not considered violence, either because the hazard level is within the law or because the motives of the corporation cannot be verified within legal notions of premeditated intent. Indeed, the definition of violence is contested and this dispute itself is part of the process of identifying ways of resisting violence and the structures that give rise to it (Hearn, 1998). We could say that violence is behaviour that intentionally threatens or does physical harm, and more generally 'involves the infliction of emotional, psychological, sexual, physical and material damage' (Stanko, 1994: 38). Kelly's (1987) famous definition, developed in the context of domestic violence, is a continuum of verbal, emotional, and sexual abuses of power. This definition extends violence to include abusive behaviour that might not inflict direct physical harm but ties the concept to 'abuse of power', which is a theme that will be discussed here. For many writers violence forms a continuum of types of threatening and harmful behaviour including name-calling, stalking, vandalism, and intimidation. On the other hand, for Collins (2008) it is essential to separate violence as physical harm from situations of confrontation and threat, the majority of which do *not* lead to actual violence, because in his view violence is difficult and requires overcoming deep aversion grounded in an evolutionary-psychological desire to form social bonds. There are quite different approaches here to the definition of violence.

Like any other behaviour, violence is embedded in complex ways in social relations and values. Although violence is often described as 'meaningless', and violent offenders are imagined to be 'out-of-control' and psychologically disturbed, violence is virtually never without purpose and often takes place between people who know each other. Violence is generally embedded in social relations where its use has meaning to victims and perpetrators. For example one of the common triggers for a violent incident can be a situation where someone responds to taunts and harassment in an unexpected way—by rejecting a subordinate role and resisting. Finally, it is mainly men who perpetrate violence. Most offenders in England and Wales are male (accounting for about 90 per cent of stranger attacks) and in 66 per cent of attacks on women the assailant is male. 'More than anything else', says Oliver James, 'violence is caused by not being female' (James, 1995: 75).

REVIEW QUESTIONS

1 What is violence?

2 Try to list as many forms of harm as you can and decide whether they would be considered to be 'violence' or not? Why?

3 Why is violence enacted by the State likely to be judged differently from violence against the State?

4 Should injuries that result from poor health and safety regulations be considered 'violence'?

Violence, the body, and the civilizing process

Violence is about relationships to and around the body and more particularly about pain, emotions, control, and discipline. As such it is an intensely emotional experience, variously invoking, among other things, hatred, pleasure, fear, and threat. Hence understanding emotions and their social consequences is central to the process of management and control of violence on interpersonal and wider levels. Recently there has been increased attention to the importance of emotion, and in particular shame, in social life, in opposition to the dominant cognitive focus in the human sciences (for example, Scheff and Retzinger, 2001), and such concern echoes earlier sociological theories such as those of Simmel, Goffman, and Elias. It is beyond the scope of this introductory chapter to do this, but there is a need for broader conceptualizing of various forms of hurt, injury, and threat within a common theoretical framework.

Norbert Elias (1897–1990), whose work is currently receiving increased attention in sociology and criminology, famously proposed the thesis of a 'civilizing process'. This occurred during the transition between European medieval and modern societies during which complex social, cultural, and psychological changes occurred that resulted in a reduction in interpersonal violence. This thesis aimed to reverse the view that industrialization and urbanization are inseparable from *rising* violence. Elias claims that the growth of increasingly mannered social interaction was accompanied by increased public intolerance of violence and cruelty. Repugnance towards physical violence increased with advancing thresholds of shame and embarrassment surrounding the body—acts once performed publicly, such as defecation and sexual intercourse, become intensely private. Most people now regard carnivals of violence, such as public executions, or the torture of animals, as deeply repugnant. Underlying this cultural and psychological shift there is a deepening and widening of interdependencies between people which Elias calls 'figurations'.

In medieval society war is the normal state of society and pleasure is derived from cruelty, destruction, and torment evidenced, for example, in the mutilation of prisoners of war, burning heretics, public torture, and executions. In modern societies there is a concentration of the means of violence in the State such that 'If in this or that region the power of central authority grows, if over a larger or smaller area people are forced to live at peace with one another, the moulding of affects and the standards of the economy of instincts are gradually changed as well' (Elias, 1994 [1939], 1: 201). Elias argued that with the centralization of State power there was a growth in personal restraint and mannered conduct, initially in court society, gradually spreading more widely along with the expansion of trade, urban life, a more complex division of labour, and the formation of 'civil society'. The longer and denser were networks of interdependence, the more people were obliged to attune their action to those of others and the less their interactions will be marked by overt violence. Stephen Mennell (1995) offers one example of these changes, pointing to the difference between a medieval and modern journey. A medieval journey was a difficult and dangerous undertaking, along muddy roads on which there were few other travellers and risk of collision was low. However, the medieval traveller had to be alert to dangers posed by animals, other travellers, and bandits. This state of alertness required a volatile temperament and eager readiness to fight and a personality that would be impulsive and resort quickly to violence. On the other hand on modern roads the danger of physical attack is low but the risk of collision high. In this context (typical of the interconnected and complex nature of modern society) the development of control systems based on self-regulation, constant vigilance, foresight, and self-control is crucial. These require personalities that are not impulsive but rational, calculating, technically competent.

However, in modern society people still feel the need for excitement—which is provided by institutionalized and regulated activities such as sport, in which rules reduce the risk of injury but gratify need for excitement. Sport institutionalizes calculated violence (such as the professional foul) without loss of self-control, while spectators have the opportunity to vicariously enjoy the excitement of contest without the actual violence of earlier spectacles such as gladiatorial struggle. This analysis does raise the issue, though, of how to explain actual violence among rival spectators, which has become a major topic of research pursued particularly by followers of Elias such as Dunning *et al.* (1987). Their work points to factors such as a change in social composition of spectators and decontrolling emotional controls in explaining spectator violence.

Elias argues that over several hundred years there developed increased sensitivity and repugnance towards violence. Is there any evidence for this? Trends can be viewed across several time-scales. Looked at over a scale of millennia, some archaeological anthropologists such as Lawrence Keeley argue that in prehistoric societies violence was more deadly, more frequent, and more ruthless than in recent periods (Keeley, 1997), although there is much debate about this. On the time scale of centuries there is again some evidence, such as that collected by Eisner (2001), for a declining rate of homicide between the thirteenth and twentieth centuries (illustrated in Figure 11.1).

These observations are consistent with the view that with modernization came a long-term decline in interpersonal violence, although many factors might produce short-term fluctuations such as the rising rates of violent crime in particular years or decades. However, long-range data should be interpreted with caution because of the inadequacy of records over much of this period, changes in key juridical concepts such as *mens rea*, changing rules of evidence and so on. There is evidence that although Britain, for example, became less violent during the first half of the twentieth century than it had

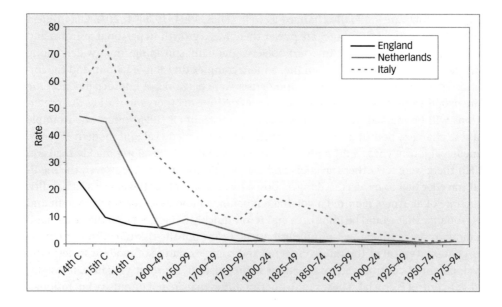

Figure 11.1 Long-term trends in homicide rates for selected countries (per 100,000 of population)

Source: Eisner (2001).

been in the nineteenth, levels of interpersonal violence rose again in the latter half, and serious violent assaults rose steeply between 1975 and 1996 (see Figure 11.2). Moreover, the pacification of society does not preclude the continued existence of a 'culture of violent solutions' in which its use is commonplace. While Elias acknowledged this, he has been criticized for ignoring the extent to which much violence is hidden, 'private', and endured in silence, and most is kept away from the criminal justice system. This notably applies to domestic violence, which is considered below. However, Cooney (2003) argues that Elias' theory accurately predicts both a decline in public violence and a (proportionate) increase in intimate violence which is consistent with more general privatization and individualization of social relationships.

Elias' thesis has been influential and offers insight into the formation of the modern self through regulation of violence, in ways that for Smith (1999) parallels Michel Foucault's work on similar themes. Elias describes the formation of a personality structure governed by self-control and foresight combined with feelings of shame, repugnance, and embarrassment towards our own and others' behaviour. The pressures of surviving within highly interdependent social networks lead us to treat others and ourselves as a 'danger zone'—we feel anxiety about our vulnerability to other's behaviour and to our own inner drives (Elias, 1994 [1939], 1: 445). The experience of these tensions has two consequences in particular. First, modern human beings draw tight boundaries between themselves and whatever is 'outside', to the point of doubting the 'reality' of our perceptions of the outside world. Second, there is the tendency to see ourselves as free and unique sovereign individuals and deny that we are shaped

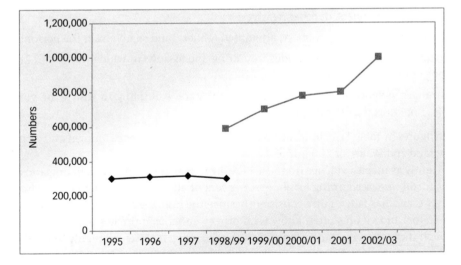

Figure 11.2 Trends in violent crime in England and Wales

Source: Research Development and Statistics (RDS), Home Office. (In 1998/99, the chart shows a break because police were asked to start recording certain new offences—such as 'Common assault', 'Assault on a constable', 'Harassment', and 'Possession of a weapon'.)

by the figurations into which we are born. Thus, renunciation of violence forms the modern self as individuated and subject to internal and external techniques of control. This in turn has structured how violence tends to be viewed in sociological and criminological literature as a threat arising in some sense from 'outside'—either from somewhere spatially separate, such as transitory spaces (deserted trains, subways, night metro stations) or from 'below' (the threat to social order from the dispossessed and dark places of our inner psyche). However, one theme in recent studies of violence has been to suggest its routine or habitual nature such that its origins lie within, not outside, and nowhere is safe.

REVIEW QUESTIONS

1 What is the 'civilizing process'?

2 Why is there less interpersonal violence in modern than medieval societies?

3 Is it true that the modern person feels repugnance at public displays of violence?

4 Does the appearance of virtually created violence contradict Elias' argument?

Patterns of violence

Violent crime measured by the British Crime Survey[1] is subdivided into a typology of four groupings based broadly on the relationship between suspect and victim:

- domestic violence—including all violent incidents involving partners, ex-partners, household members, or other relatives;

- mugging—comprising robbery, attempted robbery, and snatch from the person;

- acquaintance violence—includes wounding and assaults in which the victim knew one or more of the offenders, at least by sight;

- stranger violence—includes common assaults and wounding in which the victim did not know the offenders in any way.

The figures in Table 11.1 show the breakdown of types of violence for men and women in England and Wales for 2006/07.

Currently available evidence from the BCS suggests that violent crime in England and Wales is still rare (accounting for about 4 per cent of all crimes), although it rose during the 1980s and has fallen fairly consistently since the mid-1990s. According to the BCS, perpetrators and victims often know each other—either as intimates or acquaintances, although the pattern is clearly gendered, with men being represented highly in incidents of stranger violence and women in domestic violence. Victims are most often men aged 16 to 24 (15.1 per cent of that group in the past 12 months), single people living alone (8.9 per cent), single parents (8 per cent), people living in private rented accommodation

Table 11.1 Violent incidents by type and gender

	All (000s)	Percentage of all violent incidents	Percentage against men within violence type	Percentage against women within violence type
All violence	2,471	100	62	38
Domestic	407	16	23	77
Mugging	392	16	55	45
Stranger	894	36	76	24
Acquaintance	845	34	68	32

Source: BCS 2006/07.

(7.4 per cent), those living in 'disordered areas' (7.3 per cent), and women between the ages of 16 and 25 (6.9 per cent). Moreover, ethnic minorities—especially Afro-Caribbean and Pakistani British—have twice the risk of being victims of violent crimes than other Britons.

Fear of violence generally exceeds its statistical risk (Croall, 1998: 93–5) and is likely to give rise to anger about threats of crime (Ditton *et al.*, 1999). Yet young men, who are most at risk from assault, express least worry about it, while the elderly (who are least at risk) worry most (Croall, 1998: 93–5). There are problems, however, with these kinds of risk assessments. Questions about fear of crime in the BCS do not relate people's answers to their locality, which, for example, may have higher than average crime. On the other hand the possibility of risk factors being compounded (for example, if many single parents also live in 'disordered areas', or if many men aged 16 to 24 are single) is not addressed in these surveys.

Where does violence take place? Violence takes place in all settings although different types are predicted by their location, often in unsurprising ways. Masculine confrontation violence is most common in public leisure areas (such as pubs and clubs) and in the workplace. In fact 25 per cent of reported incidents in England and Wales occur at work and of these, 75 per cent are perpetrated by members of the public on practitioners and service providers (ESRC, 2002). High-risk professions include the police, public transport, medical, public transport, bouncers, and teachers. Domestic violence takes place largely in the home, where it is probably still under-reported—for example the BCS for 2006–07 found reported prevalence rates for domestic violence around five times higher in self-completion modules (where the respondent completes an electronic questionnaire) than in face-to-face interviews (Home Office, 2007: 61). This suggests a continuing reluctance amongst victims to report experience of violence directly to other people.

Aggression and masculinity

As shown in Table 11.2 there is a marked gender difference among victims and perpetrators of violence with an excess of prosecutions of men for violent offences in England and Wales:

This gender patterning of crime is not a new trend—males have been over-represented in all major violent crime categories since the collection of crime statistics began and the same pattern is found in all countries. In the USA, for example, men committed 83 per cent of crimes in 1996, and there are similar figures in France and Germany (Croall, 1998: 136). There is a slightly rising trend of convictions for women in the UK—in 1992 only 8.7 per cent of convictions for violence against the person were women while in 2002 this had risen to 10 per cent. In the teenage years the gap between girls and boys in delinquency, broadly defined, is relatively small, although the gap in more serious offending is considerably wider (Smith *et al.*, 2001).

Explaining male violence

While it is often taken for granted that (especially young) men do more crime than women, recent work has undertaken more complex analysis of the nature of masculinity and its relationship with violent crime. A division has appeared between bio-social, evolutionary approaches on the one hand and sociological explanations on the other.

Table 11.2 Ratio of male and female prosecutions by type of offence

	Ratio (M:F)
Sexual offences	71:1
Homicide	11:1
Criminal damage	10:1
Offences against the person	7:1

Source: Calculated from Chen Y.-F. and Lewis, C. (2007).

Evolutionary lag

Evolutionary explanations point out that for 99 per cent of our history humans have lived in small hunting groups in which violence was natural rather than pathological since it aided survival. Masculine violence aided hunting success and maximized food supply while men competed with one another for reproductive mates. However, this violence would be balanced by a need to preserve the size of the group, thus cultural norms of reciprocity and reconciliation emerged to limit violence (Hatty, 2000: 50). However, in modern societies violence has become dysfunctional and is no longer restrained by environmental pressures. Steven Pinker (2004) claims that aggressiveness is largely genetically coded, although increased social complexity and learned social influences have led to long term diminution of violence. Nonetheless, he says:

> Many scientific organizations have endorsed the slogan 'violence is learned behavior,' and even biologically oriented scientists tend to treat violence as a public health problem like malnutrition or infectious disease. Unmentioned is the possibility that the strategic use of violence could have been selected for in human evolution, as it has been in the evolution of other primate species. (Pinker, 2004)

These views are widely shared by evolutionary psychologists but it is problematic to suggest that human aggressiveness is a kind of biosocial lag from an earlier developmental state. In a wide-ranging comparative study of violence among humans and other primates, Eric Fromm (1979) argued that human violence has become pathological (detached from self-defence and hunting) and that 'man is the only mass murderer'. Evolutionary theory attempts to explain aggressiveness in terms of a *continuation* of primal tendencies, when in fact humans display *more* destructive violence than other primates do. Evolutionary accounts pay little regard to the symbolic and culturally mediated forms that violence can take (for example in rituals) and cannot easily explain why rates of violence vary among locales and countries. If there is an underlying biological tendency towards masculine violence this should manifest similarly in different cultures and places, which it clearly does not. Further, James (2002) has taken issue with evolutionary theories of human aggression arguing that family influences are critical. He claims that children born to violent parents but raised in peaceable households are no more likely to have violent criminal records than those born to non-violent parents.

Social theories and 'hegemonic masculinities'

There are many social and cultural theories of violent behaviour, stressing social learning, youth sub-cultures, economic inequality (for example, Hearn, 1998; Newburn and Stanko, 1994) and the potential thrill and enjoyment of violence (see Katz, 1988; Ferrell, Chapter 7, and Presdee, 2000). Through the process of gender socialization (how we learn the attributes of 'masculine' and 'feminine' behaviour) violence may acquire different meanings for men and women. Through violence men may attempt to affirm a positive self-concept, enhance self-esteem and reclaim personal power, while women on the other hand may see violence as a failure of self-control. Further Campbell (1993) suggests that men tend to engage in justifications for violence that minimize their use of violence while women are more likely to express guilt. Justifications for violence are learned speech acts that prepare ground for violence and deploy wider available narratives in society.

In these terms excess male violence reflects patterns of socialization in which the male role involves greater readiness to use violence as a means of control and assertion of power. In Connell's (1995) and Messerschmidt's (1993 and 1997) theory of 'hegemonic masculinities' masculinity is viewed as a crucial point of intersection of different sources and forms of power, stratification, desire, and identity.[2] Unlike socialization theories Connell and Messerschmidt emphasize performance and choice rather than passively learnt behaviour. Violent behaviour is *chosen* while calling upon dominant discourses of masculinity for support and legitimation. Connell thus sees crime as a way of 'doing gender'; which manifests differently in social situations structured by the influences of race, class, and age. Violence is a resource that men can call upon based in prevailing idealized cultural conceptions involving the dominance of women, heterosexuality, the pursuit of sexual gratification, independence.

Criminal behaviour is seen here as a resource for 'masculine validation'. For example, white, middle class boys can achieve masculinity through moderate academic success, sports, and preparation for a career. But schools are repressive and authoritarian so these boys will deviate outside of school through, for example, vandalism, drinking, and petty theft. This is 'opposition masculinity' that demonstrates to peers dominance, control, and aggressiveness. White, working class boys, on the other hand, tend to demonstrate opposition masculinity outside of school, but also in school, through fighting, vandalism, and so on. They do still have opportunities in the labour market, however, whereas disadvantaged (racial minority and lower class) boys have even fewer conventional opportunities to accomplish gender (they perceive no future in schooling or good job prospects in the real world), and are more likely to use illegal means like robbery and crimes of violence to demonstrate their masculinity. They are more likely then to engage in serious crime in and out of school.

How useful is the concept of hegemonic masculinity for explaining the predominance of men in violent crime figures? This approach has the advantage of avoiding reification of 'masculine' and 'feminine' traits and emphasizing the active process of 'doing gender'. But one limitation is that it does not explain the meaning of crime perpetrated by women, while at the same time 'over-predicting' male criminality (see Miller, 2002). There are problems with specifying what performance of masculinity is hegemonic since these will vary by class, ethnicity and generation (Demetriou, 2001). Connell and Messerschmidt (2005) respond to these and other critiques but present a reformulated concept of hegemonic masculinity that is explicitly ambiguous. Further, there is not a great deal of empirical support for the theory. One exception is Krienert (2003) who undertook a study of 704 offenders in Nebraska and found that masculine traits alone failed to predict violent events. But men with very high 'masculine' traits and few acceptable outlets to assert masculinity (such as education, marital status, children, employment, and income) *were* more likely to have been involved in violent incidents. Even so, the theory lacks a subjective or motivational account of the meanings of violence for perpetrators, and Messerschmidt cannot show why some men are violent and (most) others are not. Like many theories of crime, it over-predicts incidence since if the theory were straightforwardly true then the incidence of violent behaviour would be much higher than it is.

'Crisis of masculinity'

Dominant forms of masculinity are at various historical periods thrown into crisis, a process also related to violent behaviour. Suzanne Hatty (2000: 6) comments, 'Violence is the prerogative of the youthful male especially when confronted by the contradictions and paradoxes of thwarted desire and personal and social disempowerment.' This account suggests that unemployment and decline of traditional working class male occupations combined with increasing women's equality provokes a 'crisis of masculinity'. Whereas the fathers and grandfathers of today's young men spent their lives in male spaces of manual work and associated leisure activities, young working class men are often unemployed and spend time at home or on the street. However, home is still a female space, whereas the street offers opportunities for alternative experiences of dominance and risk-taking—joyriding, theft, burglary, competition, and 'business'—drugs and organized crime. At the same time youth cultures emerge that emphasize and exaggerate features of traditional white working class masculine appearance and behaviour. Nayak (1999) argues that skinhead culture, for example, represents a consolidation of masculinity, sexuality, and white ethnicity in working class culture. Similarly Hebdige (1987) regarded skinheads as expressing a nostalgic exaggeration of white working class characteristics and 'mime of awkward masculinity' that was a macho, working class, white (often racist) 'geometry of menace'. The uniform—boots, braces, and cropped hair—represented a caricature of the traditional dress mode of a working man.

Phillipe Bourgeois's (1996) study of Puerto Rican migrants to the US exemplifies this argument. This is an ethnographic study of street-level drug dealers in East Harlem (USA) who had found that the work they had migrated to do was disappearing but they would not take work in the service sector, which was regarded as 'women's work'. However, their wives did take this work and gained more financial independence than they had previously had, thereby threatening the basis of male dominance in the household. The men often took refuge in drug economy where there were very violent norms of gang rape, sexual conquest, abandonment of families, and 'real manhood' based on devotion to group membership. Thus, the crisis of masculinity is more acute at lower socio-economic locations where violence is a way of confirming status in a street culture. Moreover, this is more consistent with the dynamics of shame and violence described by Scheff and Retzinger (2001) than an outcome of the confidence of enjoying 'hegemonic' power.

Rich insight into changing cultural representations of masculinity and violence can be found in popular culture and especially the film. Post-World War II masculine heroes showed little emotional sensitivity and were prone to impulsivity and anger. War was 'what good men do' and its portrayal was unproblematic, especially since in the war zone sexual differentiation was reaffirmed. In the later genre of 'hard body' films such as *Rambo First Blood Part Two* (1985) and *Die Hard* (1988) violence and single-handed rescue fantasy is unproblematic and unchallenging but also exaggerated, suggesting uncertainty about real life masculine roles. Hard masculine body cinematic representations of combat—robotic masculinity of *Robocop* and *Judge Dread*—concealed a growing crisis in masculinity, in which an alienated individual experiences potency through experiencing and inflicting pain. This idea becomes thematic in later films and is often related to violence. For example in *Falling Down* (1993) a middle class man, 'D-Fens' (Michael Douglas), divorced and unemployed, unable to visit his children engages in an escalating spree of violence that ends with his own demise. Playing to the theme of compromised masculinity, D-Fens is successfully pursued by Detective Prendergast of the LAPD (Robert DuVall) who took a 'safe' desk job some years back to placate his 'bossy' wife. The denouement in which D-Fens is shot while carrying only a toy gun compounds the sense of masculine aggression as impotent rage. David Fincher's *Fight Club* (1999) offers a more complex exploration of the crisis of masculinity and violence. Though sometimes regarded as an overtly masculine film, the powerful white masculinity of the 1980s and hard body films of 1990s is absent. It features Jack (the narrator) and Tyler Durden, his destructive alter ego whom we find first in a support group for men recovering from testicular cancer ('remaining men together') where, following chemotherapy, one character, Bob, has lost his testicles and grown breasts, symbolizing masculinity's demise. Jack's addiction to self-help groups has replaced his addiction to consumerism (again 'feminized' activity), which is then replaced by a search for authentic masculinity in the self-inflicted violence of the fight club. But the sole woman character Marla Singer (Helen Bonham-Carter) is dominant in the unfolding plot and enables Jack to renounce violence. However, when the film looks as though it has reverted to a familiar hero-rescue fantasy Jack is unable to prevent the terrorists of Project Mayhem from blowing up large commercial buildings, their falling symbolizing the failure of the masculine corporate world. Multiple cultural representations of masculinity and femininity are then available and these can be deployed in various ways—but one contemporary theme is that violence may be an outcome of a perceived *failure* to perform traditional masculine roles rather than necessarily an emanation of power. These kinds of filmic representations resonate with analysts who suggest that violence is a manifestation of (perceived) powerlessness rather than of power.

REVIEW QUESTIONS

1 Why is violent crime predominantly 'masculine'?

2 What do you understand by 'hegemonic masculinities'?

3 Is there a 'crisis of masculinity'? If so, why should it manifest in violence?

Violence in the private sphere

Closely related to masculinity and violence is the issue of violence against women and children within the family, which can take many different forms, including physical assault, rape and sexual violence, psychological or emotional violence, torture, financial abuse including dowry-related violence, and control of movement and of social contacts. For centuries domestic violence was not considered a serious problem. For example, it is sometimes claimed that in 1782 the English Judge Francis Buller ruled it permissible to beat a wife with a stick no wider than a thumb. There is some doubt as to whether the ruling was ever given, but English Common Law sanctioned violence against women and it is only recently, from the 1980s, that the police have seriously begun to pursue offenders. This change in perceptions of the seriousness of domestic violence arose from at least four developments (Pahl *et al.*, 2004):

- feminist activism in the 1970s identified this as an issue that would give practical expression to their more general concern about the position of women;

- the opening of women's refuges made visible what had previously been hidden;

- the growth of Women's Aid, as a coordinating body for the growing number of refuges, brought the activists together to share ideas and experience and to work for increased political visibility for their analysis;

- feminist scholars and activists were energetic in researching the issue and in pressing for more effective and appropriate action by relevant agencies.

How extensive is domestic violence? BCS data records experience of domestic violence both during the past 12 months and during a lifetime. In answer to the question 'have you experienced domestic violence during the past 12 months', 4.2 per cent of women *and* men experienced assault, although twice as many women as men had been injured, suffered repeated violence and frightening threats. Although this may create the impression that men and women experience domestic violence roughly equally, victimization takes two distinct patterns. One, accounting for about 10 per cent of cases, which both women and men perpetrate, is marked by occasional anger and aggression; the other, which is more likely to be 'male', is characterized by severe escalating violence and terrorization (Mirrlees-Black, 1999). This second type is more widespread. When asked about lifetime prevalence, a ratio of 1:4 women report being assaulted by a male partner, 1:8 women having been assaulted repeatedly; while 1:6 men reported occasional assault and 1:20 repeated assaults. Further, domestic violence typically escalates so that previous violence is a predictor of further violence—35 per cent of second incidents occur within five weeks of the first, and domestic violence has the highest rate of repeat victimization of any violent crime (Metropolitan Police Service, 2003).

Reported domestic violence varies considerably worldwide (ranging between 10–69 per cent of violent offences in different countries) and definitions vary considerably too, along with levels of culturally accepted violence. Statistics alone offer only limited insight into the issue. Questions such as 'have you ever been abused?' or even behaviourally specific questions might fail to take account of the atmosphere of terror in violent relationships and its effects on children. Some men may enjoy inflicting violence. One of the women interviewed by Hanmer (2000: 12) reported that 'the more violence he did to me the happier he would be... After he had hit me, he would say "Sit there in front of me, if I see any tears in your eyes then see what happens".' At the same time men may blame women for provoking violence and adopt the posture of victims (Glasser, 1998), which is a common feature of other violent offenders (Ray *et al.*, 2003). Some estimates suggest that many fathers in violent families also abuse children in the home and even those who do not suffer abuse will be witnesses to violence. Such children are likely to suffer from confused and torn loyalties; they may feel ashamed, guilty, isolated, and alone; they may respond by trying to protect their mothers, by phoning the police, or most dangerously, by trying to restrain their fathers (Krug *et al.*, 2002).

The World Health Organization indicates that the triggers for domestic violence are remarkably consistent across all countries and cultures (Krug *et al.*, 2002: 120). These include:

- 'not obeying the husband';
- 'arguing back';
- 'not having food ready on time';
- 'not caring adequately for children or home';
- 'questioning about money and girlfriends';
- 'going out without permission';
- 'refusing sex';
- pregnancy.[3]

One of the conclusions that can be drawn from this is that domestic violence is primarily about the exercise of power and a response to perceived challenges to male power. Even so, domestic violence occurs more in some settings and places than others and this patterning still requires more specific explanation.

Explanations

Many explanations of domestic violence follow the patterns of explanations of violence in general. There are explanations that focus on individual pathologies (for example, paranoid or narcissistic disorders), socialization (many abusers have come from dysfunctional and violent families), and social structural (for example, poor education, unemployment, low-income, and so on). There is an association between domestic violence and low socio-economic status (as there is for violence in general) and Finney (2004/05: 9) found that 'indicators of socio-economic status such as household income, vehicle ownership, tenure type and council/non-council areas, suggest fairly consistently that higher prevalence rates of intimate abuse are associated with relatively lower levels of socioeconomic status'. It is true that these accounts do not explain middle class domestic violence (for example, Pahl *et al.*, 2004), and feminist researchers suggest that rather than look for specific pathologies amongst perpetrators we should recognize that domestic violence is ubiquitous and a routine means of maintaining patriarchal power and authority. Feminist researchers emphasize factors such as:

- the historically subordinate position of women within marriage;
- women's responsibility for childcare (and consequent exclusion from the labour market and weak economic position in the household);
- patriarchy that reproduces male power/female dependence at all levels—social, cultural, and economic;
- machismo cultures and the tacit or explicit approval of male violence.

However, one weakness of these explanations is that, like the theory of hegemonic masculinities, they encounter the problem of over-prediction. If violence were routinely inscribed into intimate heterosexual relations then we would expect to find a higher incidence than we do, even allowing for significant under-reporting. A broader approach that incorporates feminist analysis would be a more multi-factorial one that estimates the risk of domestic violence across a number of dimensions. The model set out in Table 11.3 based on the WHO report on violence and health (Krug *et al.*, 2002: 98) attempts to combine individual, relationship, community, and societal levels of analysis while identifying markers of risk, rather than causes of violence. In this model poverty causes stress, inadequacy, a 'crisis of masculinity', while making it more difficult for women to leave abusive relationships. Social capital refers to social trust that facilitates coordination and cooperation for mutual benefit, so that people believe that a benefit granted now will be repaid indirectly within a community in the future. While this model may explain why some societies and individuals are more violent than others, we do not know the specific and relative weights to give the factors nor how they operate on different levels. However, these factors suggest that the dynamics of power and powerlessness in domestic violence might be complex and as Schrock and Padavic (2007) argue, 'men who harm women often do so when their sense of traditional manhood—such as being a breadwinner or having women meet their often-unspoken needs—is threatened'.

REVIEW QUESTIONS

1 How widespread is domestic violence?

2 Why might official figures under-represent its actual prevalence?

3 What are the causes of domestic violence?

Table 11.3 Risk factors in domestic violence

LEVEL	Individual	Relationship	Community	Societal
FACTOR	• Young	• Conflict	• Weak community sanctions	• Traditional gender norms
	• Alcohol abuse	• Marital instability	• Poverty	• Social norms supportive of violence 'machocultures'
	• Depression Personality disorder	• Economic stress	• Low social capital	
	• Low educational attainment	• Dysfunctional families		

Source: Krug *et al.* (2002: 98).

Racist violence

Racist violence in the UK came under sharp public scrutiny following the murder of a black teenager, Stephen Lawrence, by a gang of racist white youths in 1993 and the subsequent public inquiry that reported in 1999 (Macpherson, 1999). Criticism of the police investigation and wider suggestion that the police were 'institutionally racist' resulted in widespread scrutiny of institutional practices in the police and other public organizations of ways in which racism might be inscribed in routine practices and beliefs.[4] Among the UK police it resulted in the creation of many new practices, training, and requirements to report, record, and act on allegations of racist harassment and assault. Moreover, the targeting of racist violence, along with domestic and homophobic violence, is part of a wider social and legal agenda to tackle 'hate' or bias crimes where the victim is selected on the grounds of their social status. Partly as a result of this, the numbers of recorded racist incidents in England and Wales has risen from 15,000 in 1988 to 25,000 in 1999, and 57,902 in 2006 (see Figure 11.3).

However, the dramatic increase in reporting of racist incidents (within which increasing proportions are serious assaults) was not matched by increases in convictions, representing 5 to 6 per cent of reported incidents. Against this trend, however, it should be noted that the 2000 BCS reports *lower* estimated rates of racially motivated offences (about half of them actual attacks) than in the 1995 survey (280,000 against 390,000). This discrepancy between the BCS and police figures can be explained by greater willingness on the part of victims to report incidents to the police and better recording by

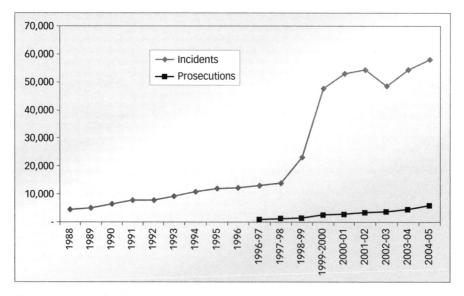

Figure 11.3 Racist incidents reported to the police in England and Wales

Source: Home Office Racist Incident Reports and CPS Reports 1997–2006.

the police of incidents reported to them. But the relationship between incidents, reporting and official statistics remains complex.

Explaining racist violence

The existing data provides several causal models of racist violence. These are generally multivariate models although there is again little attempt to weight the various factors cited and they are all usually assumed to be relevant.

Cognitive psychological models

Much of the research in this area follows hypotheses developed in the early 1990s, which in turn drew on classical models of authoritarianism and racism. For example, Heitmeyer (1994) argues that hostility towards foreigners is based on an identifiable process by which feelings of perceived threat develop into racist violence. First, feelings of 'estrangement' appear which are expressed as 'an attitude of distance' and 'contempt'. Second, this fear of foreigners becomes overshadowed by a 'competitive stance fuelled by economic and/or cultural considerations'. Third, tolerance disappears and 'complete hatred of foreigners' arises resulting in hostile 'offensive struggle' (Heitmeyer, 1994: 17). Bjørgo and Witte (1994) focuses on patterns and motives of violence towards immigrants and refugees in Scandinavia where youth gangs often with criminal records perpetrate the majority of racist incidents. Though not necessarily members of extreme right groups, they have been exposed to their propaganda and methods. The majority of cases are planned and/or carried out under the influence of alcohol, although it is generally recognized that this is most likely to be an aggravating rather than causal factor. Beck (2000) claims that pro-violent attitudes towards black and Asian people stem from an archaic belief in inferiority of other races and women that are perpetuated by allegiance to wider cultural group experience. These models regard the racist offender as having a distinctive personality that predisposes them to both racism and violence. Violent racism arises from poor and problematic moral reasoning, cognitive defects, inability to accept the impact of violence on the victim, a predisposition to resort to violence, and a 'distorted worldview'. These explanatory models inform many current intervention programmes in the UK probation service.

Social process models

There is considerable evidence that perpetrators' racist views are shared by the communities to which they belong and provide a source of reinforcement and justification of their behaviour, at least by not condemning it (for example, Sibbitt, 1997 and Ray *et al.*, 2003). This illustrates how human behaviour is not simply 'caused' but is embedded in systems of belief, legitimation, and justification within which it appears to be acceptable. Sibbitt (1997) argues that prejudice permeates whole communities that have entrenched problems of socioeconomic deprivation and crime and 'spawn' violent perpetrators through mutually supportive relationships between the perpetrator and the wider community (1997: 101). Hence she speaks of 'perpetrator communities' that scapegoat their problems onto visible minorities who serve to provide an external focus for their dissatisfaction, frustration, and alienation. Sibbitt developed a typology of different groups, stratified by generational experiences:

- the pensioners—long-term residents who feel that the area has been 'invaded';
- the 'people next door'—insecure adults who latch onto their parents' racialization of problems;
- the 'problem family'—with poor mental or physical health, who behave abusively towards children who in turn are low achievers and learn racist abusive behaviour;
- racist and anti-social behaviour is then transmitted to younger age groups who, although they will have black friends at school, learn to participate in racist violence and bullying.

Ray *et al.* (2003) further found that racist offenders tended to scapegoat South Asians for community problems of unemployment, the decline of local manufacturing, and (somewhat paradoxically) for the rise in local crime. There was evidence here of the kind of 'crisis in masculinity', noted elsewhere in this chapter. Ray *et al.* (2003) found a contrast between the global city image of central Manchester and the isolated and deprived life on outer-city housing estates from which many racially motivated offenders came. The latter expressed hostility at exclusion that was projected onto South Asians as symbols of an apparently cosmopolitan culture.

A conclusion of these studies is that there are links between deprivation, social and personal disorganization, and racist violence. Similar themes arise in the inquiry reports into the disturbances in English towns in 2001, which identify a territorial mentality, residential segregation, and the deep fracturing of communities on racial, generational, and religious lines. The Home Office reports into the disturbances put considerable weight on residential segregation, which is in turn symptomatic of several underlying structural conditions (Home Office, 2002: 12). These include:

- systematic disadvantage in that many members of ethnic minorities can only afford cheaper housing;
- higher unemployment than in the majority community, especially in Bangladeshi and Pakistani communities;
- cultural cohesion and choice amongst minority communities, which is possibly linked to fear of racist attacks and hostility from the surrounding areas;
- discrimination in council housing allocation that has been a major cause of residential segregation.

Cultural factors

Racism is not confined to areas of deprivation—it also affects rural, suburban, and prosperous areas as well as blighted inner city locales (Bowling and Phillips, 2002: 115). It can increase during periods of higher consumption, as it did during the 1990s. In addition to deprivation as a cause of racist violence, there are cultural logics in which deeply rooted fears and beliefs about 'contamination' by other cultures are crucial. One study of racist Internet chat rooms found no reliable connections between unemployment and racist hate, but did find a correlation with politicized mobilization, which was associated with fears of threats to integrity and in particular of interracial marriage (Glasser *et al.*, 2002). Again Back (2002) found that white supremacist Internet sites were preoccupied with fears of cultural 'pollution' manifest in 'White Singles' dating pages. These cultural fears are in turn rooted in the colonial past of European nations and a belief in the cultural and 'civilizational' inferiority of ethnic minorities that paradoxically pose a threat because of their supposed global power. Such views are of course part of articulated racist worldviews and other evidence indicates that these are relatively rare even amongst racist offenders (Ray *et al.*, 2003). Nonetheless, these assumptions and fears may be part of the cultural background of racism even when they are not explicitly articulated.

REVIEW QUESTIONS

1 Why did recorded racist incidents in the UK rise during the late 1990s and 2000s?

2 How do you explain racist violence?

3 Are there links between 'hegemonic masculinity' and racism?

Homicides

The most extreme form of violence is homicide. This is rare in the UK and in most other developed countries—generally ranging between 10 and 20 per million of the population per annum (slightly less in the UK at nine per million) (United Nations, 1996). There is a strong statistical association between homicide rates and rates of poverty and inequality. Men are more likely to be both victims and offenders than are women, and men are more likely to be killed by strangers—the highest risk of victimization in the UK is among Afro-Caribbean men aged between 21 and 25. Women are more at risk from spouses or former spouses with 20 per cent of all murders occurring among spouses (Metropolitan Police Service, 2003). Key factors in explaining homicide rates have been shown to include multiple deprivation, low social mobility, income inequality, a high proportion of 19- to 29-year-olds in a locality, and a high correlation between inequality measured by the Gini coefficient and homicide.[5] The relationship between income inequality and homicide rates is remarkably consistent cross-nationally (Daly *et al.*, 2001), although it is unlikely to be sufficient to explain variations in the rate, and other factors will be relevant.

Messner's (1989) now famous study claimed that there was a close relationship between inequality and homicide rates. Savolainen (2000) argues (using anomie theory) that the effect of economic inequality on the level of lethal violence is limited to nations characterized by relatively weak collective institutions of social protection (such as welfare states). He tests this hypothesis with two cross-national data sets drawn from Finland and Mexico. Both settings suggest that the effects of income inequality on homicide can be mitigated by the strength of the welfare state. Nations that protect their citizens from the vicissitudes of market forces appear to be immune to the homicidal effects of economic inequality. This suggests that it is the social disorganization caused by sharp inequality rather than the inequality itself that is the determining factor. Similarly, Kawachi *et al.* (1999) argue that the degree of cohesiveness in social relations among citizens, measured, for instance, by indicators of 'social capital', affect the level of violent crimes, including homicides, that were 'consistently associated with relative deprivation (income inequality) and indicators of low social capital'. Social capital here refers to the extent of voluntary groups, involvement in the community, social networks, and levels of social trust. The process that is suggested by studies like these is that relative poverty causes feelings of stress, inadequacy, 'crisis of masculinity', and undermines social capital. This in turn creates a context conducive to risk taking, criminality, and increasingly violent competition for resources such as street business and dominance. However, other factors will be relevant too. Messner (1989) pointed out that in addition to inequality, an aggravating factor would be the mechanism by which inequality was reproduced—so that, for example, inequality based on racist exclusion would result in high levels of diffuse hostility and a high homicide rate. It is worth noting in this context that South Africa, where there is a long and bitter history of apartheid, has one of the highest homicide rates in world at 600 per million per annum (United Nations, 1996) These factors may also be compounded by cultural attitudes towards violence. Commenting on higher rates of homicide in southern as opposed to northern states in the US, Cohen and Nisbett (1997) argue that southerners articulate and transmit attitudes that legitimate and encourage violence, especially violence in defence of personal and familial honour.

REVIEW QUESTIONS

1 How is the homicide rate related to inequality?

2 Who is most at risk from homicide?

3 How relevant are cultural factors in explaining the homicide rate?

CONCLUSION

One consequence of the civilizing process is an increased sensitivity to and fear of violence, which constitutes a threat to the integrity of the controlled and individualized self. There is evidence for a gradual diminution of interpersonal violence in modern societies, and social and political agendas around the control of violent emotions, such as hate crime legislation, illustrates how the civilizing process has increased repugnance towards violence and its causes. At the same time violence and its threat is a routine part of everyday life for large numbers of people in settings of the street, home, neighbourhood, workplace, and leisure activities. A great deal of research focuses on interpersonal violence and is accompanied by theoretical explanations that address the circumstances of individual perpetrators. Clearly, however, violence has multiple manifestations—and most of the theories discussed here point at least implicitly towards wider societal issues. In each type of violent behaviour examined here, explanations raise issues of power and dominance, but also powerlessness and inequality, the effects of which are mediated by broader cultural contexts. In order to develop a more comprehensive theory of violence we need to elaborate the ways in which power and exclusion, and the consequences of increasingly complex patterns of inequality intersect with emotional life and forms of socialization (See Ferrell, Chapter 7). There is clearly an important issue around masculinities and violence that is receiving increasing attention in the literature along with recognition that 'masculinity' cannot (any more than 'femininity') be viewed as a simple construction, but has multiple cultural and psychosocial manifestations. Once we begin to unravel the complex links between social, economic, and cultural reproduction, gender socialization, and the intersecting dimensions of identity and class, we may begin to understand how violence is embedded in everyday life.

QUESTIONS FOR DISCUSSION

1   What is violence and how are definitions linked to power? Consider different forms of harm to people and whether these would be considered 'violence' or not. Why?

2   What do you understand by the 'civilizing process'? Is Elias right? How would you decide?

3   How do you explain violence in society? Consider social as opposed to biological explanations.

4   Why do you think violent crime increased in the UK and many other countries in the later twentieth century? Do explanations of violence outlined here account for this?

5   What is the relationship between masculinity and violence? Is there a 'crisis of masculinity' and how might this be connected with violent behaviour?

GUIDE TO FURTHER READING

Bowling, B. (1998) *Violent Racism: Victimisation, Policing and Social Context*. Oxford, Clarendon Press.
This is a detailed analysis of official documents and historical origins of racist violence. Bowling uses a case study to analyse the language of white supremacy and the experience of racist victimization.

Collins, R. (2008) *Violence—A Macro-Sociological Theory*. Oxford: Princeton University Press.
This is a major study of the microdynamics of aggression and violence with detailed case studies that aims to develop a general theory of violence as a situational process. His core thesis is that violence is difficult and its enactment has to overcome deep inhibitions—the interaction processes of which are the main focus of the book.

Jackman, M.R. (2002) 'Violence in social life' *Annual Review of Sociology* 28: 387–415.
A good overview and critique of current sociological theories of violence and develops a programme for a new approach.

Messerschmidt, J. (1993) *Masculinities and Crime*. Rowman & Littlefield.
This has become a key text in theorizing the relationship between masculinities and crime and uses the theory of 'hegemonic masculinities'.

Scheff, T.J. (2000) 'Shame and the social bond: A sociological theory' *Sociological Theory* 18 (1): 84–99.

Develops a theory of the links between social solidarity, emotions, anger, and violence. Links with work inspired by John Braithwaite on shame and reintegrative shaming.

Stanko, E.A. (ed) (2003) *The Meanings of Violence*. London: Routledge.

A recent collection of chapters based on projects in the ESRC's Violence Research Programme. Offers new insights and data on violent crime.

WEB LINKS

http://www.worldbank.org/poverty/inequal/abstracts/violence.htm

World Bank Poverty Net website. This is a portal into articles, discussions and other material on the relationship between inequality and violence.

http://www.who.int/violence_injury_prevention/violence/world_report/en/

World Health Organization. World report on violence and health.

http://www.homeoffice.gov.uk/rds/bcs1.html

Home Office Research Development Statistics. Provides access to the British Crime Survey.

http://www1.rhbnc.ac.uk/sociopolitical-science/vrp/RESOURCE/TAKING_STOCK_2002.pdf

Report from the ESRC Violence Research Programme.

http://www.norberteliasfoundation.nl/

The Norbert Elias Foundation. Access to Figurations an online journal with discussions and reviews and other Elias related material.

http://www.disastercenter.com/crime/

United States crime statistics 1960–2006.

REFERENCES

Back, L. (2002) 'Aryans Reading Adorno: Cyber-culture and twenty-first century racism', *Ethnic and Racial Studies* 25, 4: 628–651.

Beck, A. (2000) *Prisoners of Hate* New York: Harper Collins.

Bjørgo T. and Witte, R. (eds) (1994) *Racist Violence in Europe*. London: St Martins Press.

Bourgeois P. (1996) *In Search of Respect*. Cambridge: Cambridge University Press.

Bowling, B. and Phillips C. (2002) *Racism, Crime and Justice*. London: Longman.

Campbell B. (1993) *Men, Women, Aggression*. London: Basic Books.

Chen, Y-F. and Lewis, C. (2007) 'Equality and Diversity Impact Assessment of CPS Statutory Charging: England and Wales: For the Period Ending March 2006' *Institute of Criminal Justice Studies* <http://www.cps.gov.uk/publications/docs/edia.pdf>.

Cohen D. and Nisbett, R.E. (1997) 'Field experiments examining the culture of honor: The role of institutions perpetuating norms about violence', *Personality and Social Psychology Bulletin* 23 (11): 1188–99.

Collins, R. (2008) *Violence—A Macro-Sociological Theory*. Oxford: Princeton University Press.

Connell, R. (1995) *Masculinities*. Cambridge: Polity Press.

Connell, R. and Messerschmidt, J. (2005) *Gender and Society* 19, 6: 829–59.

Cooney, M. (2003) 'The Privatization of Violence' *Criminology* 41, 4: 1337–1406.

Croall, H. (1998) *Crime and Society in Britain*. London: Pearson.

Daly, M., Wilson, M., and Vasdev, S. (2001) 'Income Inequality and Homicide rates in Canada', *Canadian Journal of Criminology* 43: 219–36.

Demetriou, D.Z. (2001) 'Connell's concept of hegemonic masculinity: a critique' *Theory and Society* 30, 3: 337–61.

Ditton, J., Farrall, S., Bannister, J., Gilchrist, E., and Pease, K. (1999) 'Reactions to Victimisation: Why Has Anger Been Ignored?' *Crime Prevention and Community Safety: an International Journal*, 1, 3: 37–54.

Dunning, E., Murphy, P., and Williams, J. (1987) *The Roots of Football Hooliganism*. London: Routledge.

Eisner M. (2001) 'Modernization, Self-control and Lethal violence. The Long-term Dynamics of European Homicide Rates in Theoretical Perspective', *British Journal of Criminology* 41 (4): 618–38.

Elias, N. (1994) *The Civilizing Process*. Oxford: Blackwells, vol. I.

ESRC (2002) *ESRC Violence Research Programme—Taking Stock*. Royal Holloway: HMSO.

Finney, A (2004/05) *Domestic Violence, sexual assault and stalking: findings from the British Crime Survey*. Home Office Online Report 12/06 <http://www.homeoffice.gov.uk/rds/pdfs06/rdsolr1206.pdf>.

Fromm, E. (1979), *Anatomy of Human Destructiveness*. London: Cape.

Glasser, J., Dixit, J., and Green, D.P. (2002) 'Studying Hate Crime with the Internet: What Makes Racists Advocate Racial Violence?' *Journal of Social Issues* 58(1): 177–93.

Glasser, M. (1998) 'On Violence: a Preliminary Communication', *International Journal of Psycho-Analysis* 79, 5: 887–902.

Hanmer, J. (2000) 'Domestic violence and gender relations: contexts and connections' in J. Hanmer and C. Itzin (eds) *Home Truths About Domestic Violence*. London: Routledge. pp. 9–23.

Hatty, S. (2000) *Masculinities, Violence and Culture*. London: Sage Publications.

Hearn, J. (1998) *The Violences of Men*. London: Sage.

Hebdige, D. (1987) *Subculture—Meaning of Style*. London: Methuen.

Heitmeyer, W. (1994) 'Hostility and violence towards foreigners in Germany' in Børgo and Witte. *Racist Violence in Europe*. pp. 17–28.

Home Office (2002) *A Report of the Independent Review Team Chaired by Ted Cantle*. London: Home Office.

Home Office (2007) *Crime in England and Wales* eds S. Nicholas, C. Kershaw, and A. Walker <http://www.homeoffice.gov.uk/rds/pdfs07/hosb1107.pdf>.

Jackman, M.R. (2002) 'Violence in Social Life', *Annual Review of Sociology* 28:387–415.

James, O. (1995) *Juvenile Violence in a Winner-Loser Culture*. London, Free Association Books.

James, O. (2002) *They F*** You Up*. London: Bloomsbury.

Katz, J. (1988) *Seductions of Crime—moral and sensual attractions in doing evil*. NY: Basic Books.

Kawachi I., Kennedy B.P., and Wilkinson R.G. (1999) 'Crime: Social Disorganization and Relative Deprivation', *Social Science and Medicine* 48 (6): 719–7.

Keeley, L. (1997) *War Before Civilization*. Oxford: Oxford University Press.

Kelly, L. (1987) *Surviving Sexual Violence*. Cambridge: Polity.

Kersten, J. (1996) 'Culture, Masculinities and Violence Against Women', *The British Journal of Criminology* 36: 381–95.

Krienert, J.L. (2003) 'Masculinity and Crime: A Quantitative Exploration of Messerschmidt's Hypothesis', *Electronic Journal of Sociology* <http://www.sociology.org/content/vol7.2/01_krienert.html>.

Krug E.G., Dahlberg, L.L., Mercy, J.A., Zwi A.B., and Lozano, A. (eds) (2002) 'World report on violence and health', Geneva, World Health Organization; http://www.who.int/violence_injury_prevention/violence/world_report/en/index.html.

Macpherson, W. (1999) *The Stephen Lawrence Inquiry. Report of an Inquiry by Sir William Macpherson of Cluny* (Cm 4262). London: The Stationery Office <http://www.archive.official-documents.co.uk/document/cm42/4262/4262.htm>.

Mennell, S. (1995) 'Civilisation and Decivilisation, Civil society and Violence' *Irish Journal of Sociology*, Vol. 5, pp.1–21.

Messerschmidt, J. (1993) *Masculinities and Crime*. Lanham, Md.: Rowman & Littlefield.

Messerschmidt, J. (1997) *Crime as Structured Action*. London: Sage.

Messner, S. (1989) 'Economic Distribution and Homicide Rates: Further Evidence on the Cost of Inequality', *American Sociological Review*, 54, 4, 597–612.

Miller, J (2002) 'The strengths and limits of "doing gender" for understanding street crime' *Theoretical Criminology* 6(4):433–60.

Mirrlees-Black, C. (1999) *Domestic Violence—Findings from a new BCS self-completion questionnaire*. Home Office: RDS.

Metropolitan Police Service (2003) *Findings from the Multi-Agency Domestic Violence Murder Reviews in London*. London: Metropolitan Police Service.

Nayak, A. (1999) '"Pale warriors": skinhead culture and the embodiment of white masculinities' in A. Brah, M. Hickman, and M. Mac an Ghaill *Thinking Identities*. London: Macmillan. pp. 71–99.

Newburn, T. and Stanko, E.A. (eds) (1994) *Just Boys Doing Business? Men, Masculinities and Crime*. London. Routledge.

Pahl, J., Hasanbegovic, C., and Yu, M-K. (2004) 'Globalisation and Family Violence', in George, V. and Page, R. (eds), *Global Social Problems and Global Social Policy*. Cambridge: Polity Press.

Pinker, S. (2004) 'Why nature & nurture won't go away' *Dædalus* Fall. pp. 1–13.

Presdee, M. (2000) *Cultural Criminology and the Carnival of Crime*. London: Routledge.

Ray, L., Smith, D., Wastell, L. (2003) 'Understanding racist violence' in E. Stanko (ed) *The Meanings of Violence*. London: Routledge. pp. 112–29.

Savolainen, J. (2000) 'Inequality, welfare state, and homicide: Further support for the institutional anomie theory', *Criminology* 38(4): 1021–42.

Scheff T.S. and Retzinger, S.M. (2001) *Emotions and Violence—Shame and Rage in Destructive Conflicts*. Lincoln NE: Backprint.

Schrock, D.P. and Padavic, I. (2007) 'Negotiating hegemonic masculinity in a batterer intervention program' *Gender & Society* 21, 5: 625–649.

Sibbitt, R. (1997) *The Perpetrators of Racial Harassment and Racial Violence*. London: Home Office.

Smith, D. (1999) 'The Civilizing Process and the History of Sexuality: Comparing Norbert Elias and Michel Foucault', *Theory and Society* 28, 1: 79–100.

Smith, D. J., McVie, S., Woodward, R., Shute, J., Flint, J., and McAra, J. (2001) 'The Edinburgh Study of Youth Transitions and Crime' <http://www.law.ed.ac.uk/cls/esytc/findings/digest14.pdf >.

Stanko, E. (1994) *Perspectives on Violence*. London: Quartet Books.

United Nations (1996) *Demographic Yearbook*. New York: United Nations.

NOTES

1. The British Crime Survey published by the Research Development Statistics branch of the UK Home Office, asks people about crimes they have experienced in the last year and about a range of other crime-related topics. The BCS is a large sample survey, now carried out annually, designed to collect information on the extent and nature of crime and on other crime related issues. See <http://www.homeoffice.gov.uk/rds/bcs1.html>.

2. 'Hegemony' refers to the ways in which the dominance of a group is sustained through culture. Hegemonic masculinity refers to cultural representations of dominant cultural ideals of masculinity that reinforce the subordination of women and marginal masculinities such as gay and racialized minorities (Connell, 1995: 77ff).

3. The ESRC's Violence Research Programme found that 2.5 per cent of pregnant women had suffered assault in the last 12 months and lifetime prevalence was 13.4 per cent. Women were ten times more likely to be assaulted in pregnancy if they had experienced violence in the last 12 months (ESRC 2002).

4. The report defined institutional racism as: 'the collective failure of an organisation to provide an appropriate and professional service to people because of their colour, culture or ethnic origin. It can be seen or detected in processes, attitudes and behaviour which amount to discrimination through unwitting prejudice, ignorance, thoughtlessness, and racist stereotyping which disadvantage minority ethnic people.'

5. The Gini coefficient measures the percentage difference between a hypothetical model of perfect equality (the Lorenz curve) and actual income inequality—so higher Gini coefficients indicate greater income inequality.

12 Sex crime

Terry Thomas

INTRODUCTION

As a category of criminal activity, sexual offending has long been seen as somehow 'different' to other crimes. Crimes of a sexual nature are particularly invasive and exploitative and accompanied by a latent or manifest violence. The victims are usually women or children and the offenders invariably men. Even within the prison community there has been a history of other offenders regarding the sex offender as 'different' and 'by tradition "nonces" are expected to know their place and keep out of the way of "straight cons"' (Sparks *et al.*, 1996: 179).

In the UK and North America the 'problem' of the sex offender has moved inexorably up the political agenda in the last decade. Sexual offending has become increasingly unacceptable and a range of adjustments have been made within the criminal justice system to improve the investigation of sexual offending, and the prosecution of sex offenders. More punitive sentences have been introduced and new civil measures, such as the sex offender 'register', have been developed to better protect the community.

This chapter examines the nature of sex offending and the forms it takes as well as the enhanced social response made to sex offending over the last ten years.

BACKGROUND

The sexual activities of individuals is usually a matter for them alone, but the very fact that sexual offending has become such a matter of public and political concern demonstrates that not all sexual activities can be just left to the participants.

The reasons for the increased public political attention to sexual offending are many and varied. The feminist movement of the 1970s highlighted the plight of women as victims of male violence and sexual offending. In the 1980s social workers and paediatricians focused on the sexual abuse of children and raised the question of what should happen to the adult perpetrators of these crimes. The 'law and order' lobby of the 1990s generally wanted more punitive punishments for a range of offenders and achieved a degree of success in this direction, encouraged by a rampant tabloid press and—in the case of sex offenders—even street demonstrations that led to vigilantism against identified offenders. In a world beset by changing values, there was some security to be had in knowing that, whatever else may change, the commission of sexual crimes against children was always going to be a constant 'wrong' and action against them would be needed. The 'paedophile' became the 'folk-devil' of our times.

'Folk devils' are those figures in society we are encouraged to dislike and avoid. In the past they have included young offenders, including football hooligans, muggers, punk rockers, and those mods and rockers who fought seaside battles in the 1960s. The phenomenon was originally examined by Cohen in his study of mods and rockers and the way in which their activities were exaggerated and distorted by the social reaction in terms of law enforcement, court judgments, and media reaction and then the interreaction between those responding agencies. The offenders take on a symbolic significance and the action and re-action that takes place duly spirals into what Cohen called a 'moral panic' (Cohen, 1973).

Sexual activity usually takes place between individuals freely consenting to that activity. Sexual offending only enters the picture when that consent is absent. Consent may also be imagined as a continuum from 'true' consent at one end through to reluctant acquiescence and submission at the other end. It is not an easy stand-alone concept to cover all circumstances. Some consensual activities may still be prohibited by law (see below). The actual activities engaged in may otherwise be as broadly defined as the parties in which they are involved are willing to agree.

In 2000, the UK Home Office published the final report of its comprehensive review of sexual offences and gave it the title 'Setting the Boundaries'; but even with such a title the Home Office was clear that the review's 'guiding principle was that the criminal law should not intrude unnecessarily into the private life of adults' (Home Office, 2000: para. 0.7).

Consent or free agreement

Consenting, or giving free agreement, to sexual activities is usually premised on the idea that we are talking about mature adults who know the full consequences of what they are doing and are under no duress and subject to no deceptions as to what they are agreeing to; we use the phrase 'consenting adults'. Consent may be impaired when the person giving it lacks the capacity to know the full consequences of what they are doing because they are, for example, an adult with intellectual impairments, or they are too affected by alcohol or drugs to give free agreement. Children are said to lack an adult capacity to consent.

We talk of an 'age of consent' which in the UK is set at 16 years. Children below the age of 16 may give a consent but the younger the child the more likely that consent is flawed and ultimately negatived by the child's absence of understanding the full physical and emotional consequences of what they are agreeing to; at such point sexual offending is taking place, and particular laws may be needed to protect children from predatory adults.

The problem of under-age consent is further confused when children under 16 have engaged in prostitution within the commercial sex industry. The UK still has laws allowing for the prosecution of such children for activities associated with prostitution even though some would say their 'invalid' consent makes them the victims of crime rather than the perpetrators (see below).

The actual 'age of consent' varies over time and from place to place. In England and Wales it was moved up from 13 to 16 years in 1885 for heterosexual activities, and remains at 16 to this day; in Northern Ireland it is 17. In Germany it is fixed at 14 and in Denmark at 15. When it comes to homosexual activities, the age of consent in England and Wales dropped from 21 to 18 in 1994 and dropped again to 16 in 2000.

Consent when applied to heterosexual activities is also very much a gender-specific concept. It is the woman who consents and not the man. Such a conceptualization implies that the man 'always' wants sex and the idea of him consenting to sexual activities is almost risible. The term 'free-agreement' in place of 'consent' has been suggested as going some way towards correcting this imbalance (Home Office, 2000: para. 2.10.5), but the current law still uses the word consent.

Even when consent has been present, the UK criminal law may still be invoked with a view to determining the presence of sexual offending. Certain relationships may be declared 'prohibited', such as that between a father and daughter or brother and sister (incest), regardless of whether there was consent. Governments have also seen it as proper to intervene in the interests of protecting public health, as the UK did in prosecuting a group of adult men under the Offences Against the Persons Act 1861 for indulging in sexual activities they had all consented to; the European Court of Human Rights upheld the prosecution (*Laskey, Jaggard and Brown v UK* (1997), 24 EHRR 39).

Teachers are prohibited from having sexual relations with their pupils even if those pupils are over the age of 16 and have consented. The criminal law considers this to be the offence of 'abuse of trust' which covers anyone working with young people in schools, children's homes, or similar settings (Sexual Offences Act 2003, ss. 16–24).

In making a retrospective attempt to unravel whether consent was present or absent at a particular incident, the picture is further confused by the range of complex messages— many of them non-verbal—used by adults to convey agreement or consent. Add to that the fact that sexual activities invariably take place in private and with no evidential witnesses and that external confusion on the truth of the matter is only exacerbated.

Forms of sexual offending

A definitive list of exactly what is and is not a sexual offence is probably impossible to draw up. We might be clear that lack of consent results in rape or indecent assault, and that those entering into a 'prohibited relationship' commit an offence of 'familial child sexual abuse', but as we develop the range of possible sexual offences the outer limits are less clear. When the UK sex offender 'register' was first proposed in a 1996 Consultation Paper, a total of 33 offences were suggested as possibly leading to registration in England and Wales; the Consultation paper completely overlooked the fact that two different lists would be needed for Scotland and Northern Ireland where the law was different (Home Office, 1996: Annex A). When the register was later enacted in law, this figure for England and Wales had dropped to just 12 (Sex Offender Act 1997, Schedule One, para. 1) and more recently there have been proposals to raise the number again (Scottish Executive, 2001: Chapter 4). Scotland and Northern Ireland had lists of 20 and 15 respectively (Sex Offender Act 1997, Schedule One, paras 2 and 3).

The categorization of a sexual offence can change with a simple change in law. In this way homosexual activities have been decriminalized (Sexual Offences Act 1967), and the rape of a man by another male has been recognized when previously it was not (Criminal

Justice and Public Order Act 1994, s. 143). At one time it was presumed a man could not be prosecuted for raping his own wife, but this was changed by court ruling in 1991 and statutory law in 1994 (Criminal Justice and Public Order Act 1994, s. 142). In similar vein boys under 14 were once assumed incapable of the act of rape, but since 1993 they can be prosecuted over the age of ten (Sexual Offences Act 1993; now in the Sexual Offences Act 2003, s. 1). Suggestions have been made that the purchase of sexual services (usually by men paying money to women) should become a new offence (Morris, 2007).

In general terms sexual crimes are committed by two groups of people; those who know their victims and those who do not. In the past, rapes, for example, have sometimes been categorized as 'acquaintance rapes' and 'stranger rapes', and the conventional wisdom has long held that children are far more at risk of sexual crime within their families than they are outside of it (although research still suggests we should not underestimate the risk children might be subject to outside of the family (Gallagher et al., 2002)).

Some adults who persistently target children for sexual activities may be described as 'paedophiles'. As such they have entered the lexicon of hatred for our times and been demonized by the press and popular opinion (Silverman and Wilson, 2002). Adult men who have sexually offended against children in schools, children's homes, and even the church have been the cause of numerous safeguards now put into place to prevent them ever getting such work giving them access to children (Thomas, 2007 esp. chapters six and seven). At the other extreme a 17-year-old boy having 'under-age' sex with a 15-year-old girl may receive only muted criticism, albeit committing the same offences by the letter of the law.

The commercial sexual exploitation of children through under-age prostitution has been tackled by a new focus on the organizers and purchasers of children as the criminals and the introduction of 'exit' strategies for the children now seen as the victims of abuse (Department of Health et al., 2000; Brown and Barrett, 2003).

Some men, including those described as 'paedophiles', have been known to travel across international boundaries specifically for purposes of having sex with children. This travel is premised on the idea that some countries have more relaxed laws and that even when laws are in place they are not enforced with any rigour. This form of abuse is invariably commercial in nature as family poverty in places like Thailand, the Philippines, and parts of Eastern Europe drives children into prostitution. The men travelling to avail themselves of these 'services' have become known as 'sex tourists' (Kane, 1998).

Although 'sex tourism' throws up problems for the destination countries, it has also received attention at home—the sending country—as measures have been put in place to restrict the levels of travel involved. People on the UK sex offender 'register' now have to notify the police when going abroad. The ultimate answer is to ensure an equivalence of law and law enforcement in all countries to remove any 'havens' that might exist.

The production, dissemination, and ownership of pornography has been considered a sexual offence and especially when that pornography has featured children. The rise of the Internet in the late 1990s meant it became a favoured medium for the dissemination of such material across international borders (Carr, 2004). The UK Government responded with its police High Tech Crime Unit to combat Internet crime, and international exercises such as Operation Ore followed. Operation Ore was an FBI-led operation from the USA which discovered some 7,000 people in the UK alone—including the rock star Pete Townshend—had subscribed to an illegal child pornography website ('How British police officer set trap for paedophiles', *The Observer*, 19 January 2003). Sometimes the difference between 'art' and 'child pornography' was hard to distinguish (Brooke, 2007) but mostly the difference was clear. The High Tech Crime Unit in turn became the Child Exploitation and Online Protection Unit or CEOP; the actor Chris Langham became another high profile offender to make the headlines.

The point is made that any photographs or film of a child being abused are images of a crime having taken place, even though the ultimate viewer may be far removed from that crime; the demand for child pornography has helped 'cause' the crime. In Sweden researchers have tried to track the children so abused in order to help them, and not least to help them with the emotional impact when they know their image has been disseminated (Svedin and Back, 1996).

Criminal processes

The criminal justice system processes sexual offenders just as it processes all offenders. A police investigation is followed by a decision to prosecute, a court hearing, and, on a finding of guilt, an appropriate punishment is imposed. The criminal justice system may be conceived of as a series of sub-systems wherein decisions are made concerning the offender; we start by considering the initial police investigation.

Investigating sexual offences

Sexual crimes have not always been readily reported to the police for investigation. As we have noted, sexual activity, whether of a consensual or a criminal nature, usually takes place in private. This in itself may lead to a reluctance to report because from the outset it may be just one person's word against another with no corroborating evidence. Add to this the possible shame or stigma experienced by the victim and the phenomena of 'under reporting' begins to take shape.

Further disincentives to report have in the past arisen from police attitudes to receiving reports of sexual crime. Negative attitudes of disbelief and incredulity from police officers and the nature of the investigative questioning have led rape victims in particular, to not bother reporting in the first place. In 1982 the UK's Thames Valley Police featured in a notorious 'fly-on-the-wall' documentary which showed two male officers dismissing a woman's report as nothing less than 'fairy tales' to cover up a consensual sexual experience. In such a climate a crime could often be recorded as 'no-crime' by the police.

Throughout the 1980s and into the 1990s the police—prompted by the Home Office—improved their investigative interviewing and techniques. Realizing that sexual crime takes place in private, they have taken victims' statements more seriously, made efforts to improve the reception of victims, and opened special medical suites to ensure that medical evidence can be taken without causing additional distress. Police officer training in this area has been improved and specialist teams of officers created to develop expertise; in Northern Ireland, for example, the Child Abuse and Rape Enquiry Unit—or CARE team—carry out the necessary investigations.

As the police slowly changed their attitudes, women victims became more willing to come forward. What had once been an area of crime 'under reported' now saw the 'reporting figures' start to rise. Research confirmed that the reporting of rape increased threefold between 1985 and 1996 (Harris and Grace, 1999). When the police became custodians of the sex offender 'register' in 1997 and later started partaking in Multi-Agency Public Protection Panels (see below), sexual offending was beginning to move from the margins of police thinking toward the centre. All of this, however, did not stop the Home Office in 2003 still referring to 'sexual offenders (being) significantly under-reported to the authorities' (Home Office, 2003a: p. 82).

Prosecuting sexual offenders

If the problem of sexual crime being 'under-reported' had been partially addressed, there still remained difficulties with the prosecution of alleged sex offenders. At the end of a police investigation, the case information has to be tied up and passed to the Crown Prosecution Service (CPS) for their analysis and decision on whether to take the accused to court. Guided by their own Code of Practice, the CPS needs to decide on the possibilities of winning the case and whether or not prosecution is in the public interest. If the evidence was not sufficient or contained irregularities or the case was, for some reason, not worth bringing to court in the public interest, the CPS would not proceed—or in their language the case would be 'discontinued'.

The Home Office sexual offences review noted a significant fall in the prosecutions for unlawful sexual intercourse with children and confessed 'we do not know why the numbers of prosecutions for USI have fallen so significantly' (Home Office, 2000: para. 3.2.10). A joint report of the Crown Prosecution Service and HM Inspectorate of Constabulary has further reported a fall in the number of prosecutions and 'a marked decline' in the percentage of successful prosecutions for rape offences.

> ... the rate of conviction for rape, after trial, has decreased from one in three cases reported (33 per cent) in 1977 to one in 13 (7.5 per cent) in 1999. Furthermore only one in five (20 per cent) reported cases currently reaches the trial stage.
>
> (CPSI/HMIC 2002: para. 1.3)

Evidential difficulties for the CPS with respect to sexual offending include:

- victims who are vulnerable in terms of age or learning disabilities;
- the victim's previous sexual history;
- a prior relationship between victim and offender which can test the victim's willingness to give evidence;
- when the case turns on the issue of 'consent', it is often one person's word against another.

> (Harris and Grace, 1999: 26)

In 2005 more research commissioned by the Home Office still found a poor level of prosecutions compared to the number of reports the police were getting. The number of reports was rising, but the number of prosecutions remained the same resulting in the proportion of convictions falling (Kelly *et al.*, 2005). The Government responded with a consultation exercise looking at what was going wrong (OCJR, 2006) and some proposals on ways forward looking in particular at:

- whether we needed a new law clarifying the capacity to consent when drink or drugs was involved;
- whether we should allow general expert evidence on the psychological impact of rape on victims to be put before a court;
- whether we should allow all evidence regardless of time before the alleged incident; and
- whether we should allow adult victims to give evidence by pre-recorded video. (OCJR 2007)

A fair hearing in court

A person accused of a sexual crime has the same rights as any other defendant in a criminal court to defend themselves whilst receiving a fair trial. The particular nature of sexual crime, however, has led to the introduction of special measures to help victims give sensitive evidence in what can be the intimidating environment of the court. In the interests of justice these special measures have to be balanced against the defendant's right to a fair trial.

In the late 1980s laws were passed to enable a child victim of sexual crime to give their evidence in court through a live video link to save them having to go into the court itself. These measures were soon followed by laws to allow children to give their evidence by means of a pre-recorded video tape, although they might still have to later make themselves available for cross examination by counsel. These arrangements are still in place and governed by revised Home Office guidelines (Home Office, 2002(a)).

Adult women victims of sexual crime have also been given forms of protection in court. In 1976 rape victims were allowed anonymity and this was extended to victims of other sexual offences in 1992. The same 1976 law—the Sexual Offences (Amendment) Act—also gave anonymity to defendants but this was withdrawn by a later law in 1988.

Since 1976, women victims of rape have had the additional protection of limits being placed on the degree to which their past sexual histories could be referred to in court. It was a common form of defence for the defendant to demonstrate, say, a past history of consensual sex between the two parties or a history of promiscuous sexual activity by the woman. Restrictions on these references to past sexual history were at the discretion of the judge and were meant to save the woman from irrelevant 'smearing' and 'innuendo' which made some women feel they were being 'abused' or even 'raped' again by the court process. In practice, however, the restrictions did not work very well and judges were seemingly far too willing to lift them. In 1999 new laws were introduced to strengthen them in the interests of the victim.

The Youth Justice and Criminal Evidence Act 1999, s. 41 strengthened the restrictions on evidence about the sexual behaviour of the victim which could only be given by leave of the court in specified circumstances. This was referred to as 'the rape shield'. Almost the first time the courts came up against the new s. 41, an appeal was made that it prevented the defendant getting a fair trial. The matter was referred to the House of Lords where the appeal was dismissed (*R v A (Respondent) (On Appeal from the Court of Appeal (Criminal Division)* 17 May 2001 [2001] UKHL 25).

The Youth Justice and Criminal Evidence Act also introduced other measures to help sexual offence complainants give evidence if the court believed fear and distress would diminish the quality of that evidence. Screens may be brought in to shield them from the defendant, and the court may even be cleared so the public are not present during the giving of evidence. The arrangements for live video links and pre-recorded video testimony were extended from children to adults who were particularly vulnerable (see Home Office, 2002a for full details).

Despite these measures the conviction rate for rape in particular remained low with some estimates putting it at less than 6 per cent of those incidents reported to the police (Kelly *et al.*, 2005; OCJR, 2006); proposals on ways forward continue to be discussed (see above and OCJR, 2007)

Punishing the sex offender

Over the last 15 years the punishments available to courts sentencing sex offenders have been increased in severity. In its 1990 White Paper the Government was unequivocal that it wished to give courts the power 'to give custodial sentences longer than would be justified by the seriousness of the offence to persistent violent and sexual offenders, if this is necessary to protect the public from serious harm' (Home Office, 1990: para. 3.13); the new sentences were introduced by the Criminal Justice Act 1991, s. 2(2) (b).

Subsequent laws have gone in the same direction. An automatic life sentence is now mandatory for a person committing a second serious offence; a serious offence includes rape, attempted rape, and intercourse with a girl under 13 (Crime (Sentences) Act 1997). The same Act (s. 52) increased the maximum sentence for gross indecency with a child under 14 from two years to ten years. Sentences for a sexual offence were lengthened again by the Crime and Disorder Act 1998, ss. 58–9; the lengthening applied to any part of a sentence that involved licence in the community and which followed the custodial element of the sentence. In future that period of supervision in the community under licence could be for as long as ten years.

The Criminal Justice Act 2003 introduced another new punishment that could be used for sex offenders. The worry was that some sex offenders had been imprisoned for a determinate period, had not availed themselves of treatment programmes, and were being discharged from custody just as dangerous as when they went in. The idea now was to manage that release and only allow it when the offender was no longer a risk to the public. The Criminal Justice Act 2003, s.225 provides for 'imprisonment for public protection (IPP) for serious offences' for offenders who are assessed as 'dangerous' (s. 229) having committed a specified violent or sexual offence. Imprisonment is for a determinate period followed by a 'reviewable' period during which the Parole Board will decided on release. IPP proved more popular with the courts than expected, but when some prisoners found they were not necessarily getting any help or treatment that might reduce the risk they posed, and help them demonstrate their readiness for release, they sought further legal clarification. The Appeal Court agreed with them and ruled the Secretary of State for Justice to have acted 'unlawfully' in not allowing prisoners subject to IPP to be able to demonstrate that they were no longer a danger to anyone (R (Walker(David)) v Secretary of State for Justice Regina (James (Brett)) v same Times Law Report 6 February 2008).

Measures to help with the rehabilitation of offenders back into the community were denied to people who had committed sex offences. In January 1999, a scheme was started whereby prisoners were released early from prison subject to wearing an electronic tag for the last 60 days of their formal custodial period; this was extended to 90 days in October 2002. This Home Detention Curfew, as it is known, is not available for sex offenders (Criminal Justice and Court Services Act 2000, s. 65).

Offenders who were on the sex offender 'register' and, therefore had obligations to report any change of address to the police as custodians of the 'register' (see below) also found their punishments increased if they failed to comply with their obligations. The Criminal Justice and Court Services Act 2000 increased the possible fine and the maximum term of imprisonment despite the fact that the reported compliance rate was actually running at some 94 per cent (Plotnikoff and Wilson, 2000: 6).

This toughening up of sentences imposed on sex offenders has not stopped the UK prison service ensuring that comprehensive Sex Offender Treatment Programmes are in place throughout the prison estate. Sex offenders are encouraged to take part in these Programmes, and results have been encouraging (Beech et al., 1998). The problem is that no '100 per cent cure' can be guaranteed and there is always the lurking fear that these offenders will remain a danger.

REVIEW QUESTIONS

1 What are the difficulties in investigating sexual offences?

2 How can we ensure victims get a fair hearing in court?

3 Are longer sentences the best way to protect the public from convicted sex offenders?

Civil measures

At the same time as the UK has brought in new criminal procedures and punishments to deal with the sex offender, there have been parallel moves to introduce a range of civil measures to reduce the risk of re-offending by those sex offenders we know about. The most high profile of these civil measures has been the sex offender register introduced in 1997. The 'register' concept recognizes that many sex offenders have ended their formal period of community or custodial punishment but may continue to pose a risk of re-offending. The idea that these offenders are 'untreatable' and therefore unlikely to change is an idea that dies hard. The conclusion is, therefore, that we need to know just where they are in the community at any one time, and we need to have surveillance and screening measures in place to prevent them engaging in particular work or travel arrangements that might enable them to re-offend.

These civil measures are essentially exercises in risk assessment and risk management. They are dependent on high quality information about the offender and his circumstances being made available to various professionals and practitioners—as well as the courts—charged with this risk reduction task. The decisions they make on receipt of this information should improve aggregate levels of community safety or be more specific decisions leading to individual child protection or the protection of a former victim.

The concept of risk has become all important when considering interventions against people who commit sexual offences, or, indeed, other forms of violent offending. The concept has been with us for a long time and in essence it is about trying to predict a person's future behaviour. Scientists, engineers, and insurance officers have refined the idea of risk and its calculation in order to reduce the negative aspects of risk and make the future more manageable.

Practitioners (especially those involved with Multi Agency Public Protection Arrangements—see below) now collate information about sexual and violent offenders, and their social environment to make risk assessments on the likelihood of future offending. Various 'instruments' have been designed to assist the practitioners in this task of collating and then weighing this information in order to improve the accuracy of risk assessment. Just how accurate risk assessment can ever be is a matter of contention.

In general terms risk assessment may be divided into an actuarial and a clinical form. Actuarial risk assessment is a statistical calculation borrowed from the world of insurance, looks at types of offenders, and makes a probability estimate of future (re)offending. Clinical risk assessment is more focused on the individual and uses the knowledge and wisdom of practitioners who work with them; clinical assessment can even include the idea of 'gut-feelings'. A lot of practitioners would seek to combine the two forms in their work. The Criminal Justice Act 2003, s. 325 made it mandatory for Multi-Agency Public Protection Arrangements (MAPPA) workers in the UK to carry out risk assessments on those they worked with (Hewitt, 2004).

Policy and practice based on risk assessment is inevitably problematic. Predicting the future is always going to be an imprecise science and the accuracy of risk assessment is always open to doubt. Even robust instruments designed to help may be fallible when implemented quickly by practitioners under pressure. It may even be said to be unethical to take action against people who may offend in the future—but who also may not (see, for example, Feeley and Simon, 1994; Garland, 2001).

Registering the whereabouts of sex offenders

The UK sex offender register is maintained by the police. It is not a discrete 'register' as such but simply a sub-category of the complete national criminal record collection maintained by the police on the Police National Computer. The Republic of Ireland and France are the only other European countries to have registers (Hansard House of Commons Debates, 10 January 2007, col. 292).

The idea for a register came about in the mid-1990s when various parts of the media picked up on the concept from the USA where federal legislation in 1994 had required all 50 states to have a register in place. More focused research from the University of Manchester supported the register idea (Hughes *et al.*, 1996) and a Home Office Consultation Document formally tabled it in 1996, saying, somewhat tentatively, 'it would help police identify suspects after a crime; it *could* help prevent crimes; and it *might* act as a deterrent' (Home Office, 1996: para. 43, emphasis added). The 1997 Sex Offender Act created the register; today its provisions are in the Sexual Offences Act 2003, ss. 80–96.

The unique feature of the register when it came into operation on 1 September 1997 was that offenders currently in the system or committing designated sexual offences after that date, would be required—in future—to notify the police every time they changed their name or address. In this way the police would have an up-to-date and more accurate picture of where all these known offenders lived. The exact length of time each offender would have to continue notifying the police was dependent on the severity of the original sentence—the most serious would have to register for life. Failure to register would be an offence in itself and punishable by a fine or imprisonment (for further details see Thomas, 2004).

From the outset the 'register' was criticized for not being retrospective and thereby missing out on an estimated 110,000 sex offenders in the community who had offended *before* the register came into existence (Marshall, 1997). It was also criticized for being too narrowly focused on its designated 12 sex offences (for England and Wales) listed in Schedule One to the 1997 Act. Some people wanted individuals to register even when there had been *no* conviction but, for example, where care proceedings had been taken on a 'substantiated' case of child sexual abuse in a family, but where insufficient evidence existed for a prosecution (see Thomas, 2000, chapter 7). The Government felt unable to act on these criticisms.

In 2000 the Home Office published its first evaluation of the 'register'. Some 94 per cent of those required to register were found to be complying with their obligations and to that extent the 'register' was working well. The police also reported that the 'register' had led to improved working relationships with other agencies like the probation service, who sometimes shared the information on the 'register' (see below). The one thing the evaluation could not say, however, was whether or not the 'register' was making communities any safer and it lamented the fact that 'no single measure of effectiveness emerged from this study as suitable for performance measurement' (Plotnikoff and Woolfson, 2000: 50).

A year later the Home Office published a further consultation paper on the sex offender 'register'. By this time various changes had been made to the 'register' by the Criminal Justice and Court Services Act 2000, including an increase in the punishment for non-compliance, but the consultation paper now proposed yet more changes. New Home Secretary David Blunkett, in an introduction to the paper, claimed the 'register' 'had proved a valuable tool in helping protect the public', even though there was no evidence to support this claim. He did, nonetheless, feel that 'experience in implementing it has suggested that aspects could be strengthened' (Scottish Executive, 2001: 1). The compliance rate was now set at 97 per cent and the numbers on the register totalled 'about 15,000' (ibid.: 11–12).

On the basis of the response to the consultation paper the new changes to the 'register' were announced in 2002. In future, offenders would have to report in person annually to the police to verify their details, changes had to be notified within three days (previously it was 14) and changes of addresses of more than seven days had to be notified (previously that was also 14). The police got more powers to photograph and fingerprint at each annual visit and more offences were proposed that would lead to registration (for example, serious violent offences where there was evidence that they presented a risk of causing serious sexual harm) (Home Office, 2002b: Chapter 1). All of these changes required new legislation, and the sex offender register slowly evolved in its own set direction (Thomas, 2008).

Multi-agency public protection panels

Once the sex offender 'register' had been implemented, the Home Office was anxious that it should not become a passive list of names that simply gathered dust on the metaphorical shelf. It wanted the list to be interactive and dynamic and something that made an active contribution to community safety. Some voices were heard calling for the register to be open to the public, so the community would know where these offenders lived. Home Secretaries have always resisted that call (see below).

In North Wales a test case on police disclosure of information to the public ruled that such 'controlled disclosures' were in order if they were in the interests of public safety and crime prevention. The disclosures were not to be routine or 'blanket' in nature but should only be where a particularly high risk of re-offending had been noted (*R v Chief Constable of North Wales Police ex p Thorpe* (1998) *The Times* 23 March). This begged the question of how you decided who on the register was high-risk, and who would actually make the decision?

The police as custodians of the sex offender 'register' realized that this was going to be their decision to make and to make effective risk assessments they needed the help of others like the probation service. When the register was implemented meetings between the police and probation service started to take place in varying degrees of formality, to consider the risk assessment and risk management of those on the register. Sometimes other agencies such as the local Social Services Department would be co-opted into the discussions.

These initial ad hoc arrangements made in the wake of the register's implementation were knocked into a more formal shape by the Criminal Justice and Court Services Act 2000 (ss. 67–8). In future these meetings would be called Multi-Agency Public Protection Panels or MAPPPs, and the arrangements known as Multi-Agency Public Protection Arrangements (MAPPA); although the police and probation services would take the lead, other agencies such as social services, housing, or health care professionals could be formally co-opted. MAPPPs would look at three layers of offenders:

(a) those on the register;

(b) violent and other sex offenders imprisoned for more than 12 months;

(c) any other offenders considered to pose a risk to the community.

The local MAPPPs would publish an annual report on their work and the Home Office would produce an annual national review of their work; neither report would name individual offenders. These arrangements were started on 1 April 2001 (see Bryan and Doyle, 2003).

First reports suggested that the MAPPPs were not very standardized in their work despite their new statutory status, and although the Home Office were pleased with the new structures they did not offer any additional resources to the police or probation to support the MAPPPs.

In 2002 pilot schemes were started to include lay members of the public on the MAPPPs for them to have a say in the risk assessment work that was being carried out. The plan was to include lay members in all areas of the country during 2004. They were not allowed to divulge confidential information on individuals that they might hear at the meetings. This inclusion of lay members may have been an attempt to avoid having to give public access to the register (see below) and it continues to be somewhat problematic and a role in need of clearer definition (Home Office, 2007: 16)

Managing the 'unregistered' sex offender

The sex offender register was not retrospective. Sex offenders who committed offences before the register's implementation (1 September 1997) were under no obligations to report their whereabouts. An early calculation suggested there were some 110,000 of them in this position (see above). As long as they were not re-offending they were not a problem, but perhaps something was needed if they looked as though they were about to re-offend. The civil measure of the Sex Offender Order was introduced to try and address this problem.

Sex Offender Orders were applied for by the police, on people known to have convictions that would normally have put them on the sex offender register, and who were now believed to be acting in a suspicious way as though they were intent on re-offending and there was, therefore, 'reasonable cause to believe that an order...is necessary to protect the public from serious harm' (Crime and Disorder Act 1998, s. 2, as amended by the Police Reform Act 2002).

If magistrates allowed the police application, a Sex Offender Order brought the offender on to the register and also imposed various 'negative' requirements on them to stop the activities that had been interpreted as suspicious by the police. Failure to comply resulted in criminal proceedings (Knock, 2002). The Sexual Offences Act 2003 later replaced the Sex Offender Order with the Sexual Offences Prevention Order (see below).

Restraining the sex offender

Restraining Orders were introduced by the Criminal Justice and Court Services Act 2000 (s. 66 and Schedule 5) which again amended the Sex Offenders Act 1997. The Restraining Order was made on a sex offender at the point of sentencing at the discretion of the court; no one had to specifically apply for it. The court had to be satisfied that the Order was needed to prevent risk of serious harm to the general public or to an individual; the latter would most likely be the victim of the crime. As with Sex Offender Orders the Restraining Order could only make 'negative' requirements for an offender to desist from certain activities and not 'positive' requirements that they do something. The Order could be for a specific time or for an indefinite period, and breach of the Order would be dealt with as a criminal matter with sanctions of imprisonment or fines. Like the Sex Offender Order, the Restraining Order was replaced by the Sexual Offences Prevention Order.

Sexual offences prevention orders

The Sexual Offences Act 2003 (ss. 104–13) replaced both the Sex Offender Order and the Restraining Order by combining them in the Sexual Offences Prevention Order (SOPO). The SOPO contains the two distinct strands of the former Orders with an Order by application or an Order added to a criminal sentence and has similar sanctions for breach of the Order. The SOPO is, however, expanded in scope to cover offences of violence where there is also a sexual component.

Sex offenders who travel abroad

The 'sex tourist' is the person who travels the world intent on having sexual encounters with children. As we have already noted, their travel is premised on the notion that some countries have less rigorous laws and less rigorous law enforcement. Mostly these travellers are seeking commercial sex from children acting as prostitutes (Kane, 1998; Barrett, 2000).

In 1997 civil provisions were implemented to allow prosecutions in this country of sexual crimes committed abroad; these measures were contained in the Sex Offenders Act 1997 Part II, and the provisions were first used against a man who had offended in France ('Camp site owner jailed for sex assaults on girls', *Independent*, 22 January 2000).

For those on the sex offender register further restrictions were imposed in 2000 with new requirements for registrants to notify the police if they went abroad for more than eight days. The idea was that the police could then notify their counterparts in the destination country who could choose whether they kept an eye on the traveller or not. These provisions were originally in the Criminal Justice and Court Services Act 2000 and are now in the Sexual Offences Act 2003.

Although the registered sex offender now had obligations to notify the police about his proposed foreign travel, the police had no powers to actually stop him going. Proposals to introduce such a power emerged during discussions on the Sexual Offences Bill in March 2003. The Home Office produced a short paper proposing a Foreign Travel Banning Order that the police could apply to the court for. A case would have to be made out to the effect that the person concerned already had offences against children, had subsequently acted in a way indicative of re-offending, and there were no realistic alternatives to the Banning Order (Home Office, 2003b). These Orders were renamed as Foreign Travel Orders when introduced by the Sexual Offences Act 2003, ss. 114–22.

The same Home Office paper also proposed adding to the 'register' all those who had offended and been convicted whilst abroad. This requirement was to be for both UK and foreign nationals now resident here (ibid.) and was formalized in the Notification Order that could be applied for when knowledge of such offences was available (Sexual Offences Act 2003, ss. 97–103).

Laws against 'grooming'

One troubling aspect of sexual offending for legislators was the practice of 'grooming' a child for sexual activity by lengthy befriending and often deception. Sex offenders had long been thought to do this, but the use of the Internet and 'chat-rooms' whereby adult men could anonymously pretend to be of the same age as their intended victims made the problem more urgent. The proposed answer was the Risk of Sexual Harm Order (RSHO) introduced by the Sexual Offences Act 2003 (ss. 123–29). The police can apply for these Orders if they see a pattern developing and there is an identifiable sexual component to the behaviour. Fines or imprisonment can be imposed for breach of the Order.

REVIEW QUESTIONS

1 Does the registration of sex offenders make communities safer?

2 Are civil measures to 'contain' sex offenders in danger of breaching their human rights?

3 Can we ever fully prevent adults from 'grooming' children for sexual purposes?

Public access to the 'register'?

A disputed aspect of the 'register' has been the debate as to whether the public should have access to it. To put it another way—should residents be told when a convicted sex offender moves into their street so that they can better protect themselves and their families? At present—as we noted above—the UK Government has always resisted such demands; in the USA the Government has taken an opposite tack and passed federal law (known as Megan's Law) requiring all states to give open access to their registers (Thomas, 2003).

The first attempts to get open access to the UK register were during the 1997 parliamentary debate on the Sex Offenders Bill (Thomas, 2000: 111–2). At one point the Home Secretary at the time looked set to concede open access ('Howard set to name sex offenders', *Guardian*, 12 February 1997), but in the end he did not. Later he would say that it had never been his intention to do so 'as it would be tantamount to inviting vigilante activity' (quoted in Silverman and Wilson, 2002: 162). The fear of vigilante activity and of driving offenders 'underground' has remained the primary argument against notifying communities when a sex offender has moved in.

In the summer of 2000, the 'News of the World' newspaper revived the argument for open access following the abduction and murder of eight-year-old Sarah Payne in Sussex.

Calling for a 'Sarah's Law' to reflect the US 'Megan's Law', the newspaper started publishing the names and photographs of the sex offenders it was aware of, and continued to do so for several weeks ('Named, Shamed', *News of the World*, 23 July 2000). A frisson of 'paedophile panic' went round the country and not least in Paulsgrove, an estate outside Portsmouth, where demonstrations and vigilante activity lasted a week (Silverman and Wilson, 2002, Chapter 8).

When the furore died down, the Government still held the line against public access, but it did make amendments to strengthen the 'register' with amendments to the Criminal Justice and Court Services Bill, then going through Parliament. The Home Secretary attributed these changes directly to the Sarah Payne murder, saying 'we have I believe, recognized the very strong public concern which her murder has evoked' (Home Office, 2000).

The Home Office will allow what it calls 'controlled disclosure' or 'discretionary disclosure' of 'register' information as opposed to public access in accordance with the North Wales Police judgment (see above). The police—as custodians of the register—decide when and where information might be disclosed. Often this is to a school or housing department, and occasionally to members of the public with a direct need to know (Cann, 2007). It was to help the police make these 'controlled disclosure' decisions that meetings began with the probation service and led on to the creation of MAPPPs. New laws in 2008 have firmed up these disclosure arrangements (see below)

At the time of writing (Autumn, 2008) the Home Office still continues to deny public access to the 'register', and indeed what evidence there is on the effectiveness of public access in the USA shows it to be policy that is limited (Fitch, 2006; see also Power, 2003).

REVIEW QUESTIONS

1 Who should know where convicted sex offenders live?

2 Would communities be safer if they knew where sex offenders live?

3 Is vigilantism a justified response to sex offenders?

The 'possibly' dangerous

In the normal course of events any loss of liberty imposed on an individual citizen is carried out by the criminal justice process sentencing that person to a period in custody. Some secondary forms of incarceration take place under the umbrella of mental health legislation taking people compulsorily into hospital. The last and most far-reaching measure proposed to reduce the risk of sex offending has been the idea of indeterminate sentences.

The idea that the behaviour of certain people can be described as 'dangerous' has—like the concept of risk—been with us for a long time. The Victorians referred to whole sections of society as the 'dangerous classes', and more recently there has been a 'rediscovery' of the dangerous person (Bottoms, 1977); invariably the dangerous person is the would-be sexual or violent offender. In the past we have incarcerated the dangerous person or transported them to the other side of the world. Today we may still imprison the most dangerous, but we also believe in community sentences and policies of decarceration and integration back into the community. This presents us with the problem of ensuring a degree of community safety or public protection for the community (see Nash, 2006).

Dangerousness as an adjective describing behaviour has become inextricably linked to 'risk assessment' and 'risk management'. In some senses the word dangerous has moved from being an adjective to being a noun and we now talk of the dangerous person as having dangerous attributes we can identify and isolate as part of a risk assessment. The shortcomings of risk assessment have already been referred to.

The problem with the sex offender is that: (a) he—or more rarely she—may be perceived as 'dangerous' before he has actually offended; and (b) he may not necessarily be mentally disordered. In these circumstances neither the criminal justice process or mental health provisions can be brought to bear, and the argument has been made that some new system of indeterminate sentence is needed on those few people assessed as 'dangerous', likely to offend, yet not mentally disordered.

In the USA a number of states have introduced such a 'third way' with their laws on civil commitment that permit the civil detention of people categorized as sexually dangerous predators. Such people can be removed from the community or—more likely—simply re-categorized as they come near to their release date from prison and further detained under these civil measures when they thought they were going home. A risk assessment has to be made and confirmed by the courts in the form of the civil commitment detention (Janus, 2000). Appeals to the Supreme Court that such further detention is 'unconstitutional' have been unsuccessful (*Kansas v Hendricks* (1997) 117 S. Ct. 2072) (see Janus, 2006 for a critique of the American systems).

In the UK the Home Office has proposed its own form of civil commitment, which it called 'indeterminate sentences' (Home Office, 1999). Since that first proposal there has been much discussion on the topic of 'personality disorders'—which includes sex offenders—and legislative proposals have bounced between the civil and the criminal law. Central to the debate is whether or not the sex offender, now classed as having a 'dangerous severe personality disorder', can ever be treated, and if not, what is the point of detention if not a form of custodial sentence from the criminal courts? As we have seen, the Criminal Justice Act 2003 introduced powers of 'imprisonment for public protection' (IPP) to keep convicted 'dangerous' people in prison for indeterminate periods beyond their original sentence and until such times as they were no longer a risk to the community.

Attempts to broaden the scope of mental health legislation to include those with dangerous severe personality disorders—even having committed no offence—have been long and protracted. The conundrum was whether or not such people were 'treatable' and just what was 'treatment'? The existing law (Mental Health Act 1983) required detention for purposes of treatment. People with severe personality disorders had been turned away by psychiatrists as 'untreatable'. A new Mental Health Act received Royal Assent in July 2007. The Act amends the 1983 Act in various ways including the introduction of a new 'appropriate medical treatment test' that sought to include those people with personality disorders previously excluded. Implementation was due in October 2008.

CONCLUSION

One of the most marked features of the social response to sexual offending has been the recourse to civil measures to complement the criminal arrangements that have been put in place. The investigation of sexual offending has been improved and the punishments in the criminal courts have been made more severe. The civil measures, however, appear to be of a new character and future proposals regarding children in particular now include such ideas as:

- allowing parents to request details of possible sex offenders;
- considering more disclosure of criminal records on child sex offenders;
- reviewing the use of satellite tracking to monitor high-risk sex offenders;
- using more drug treatments of offenders;
- using polygraphs ('lie-detectors') on offenders; requiring more information from those on the register;
- promoting community awareness campaigns. (Home Office 2007)

The law changed in early 2008 to allow some parents to request information on possible sex offenders (Criminal Justice and Immigration Act 2008, s. 140) but the Home Office started pilot schemes in four areas before implementing the law.

For the time being the sex offender 'register' and its attendant Multi-Agency Public Protection Panels form the mainstay of the UK's civil arrangements for greater public protection from sex offenders in the community. The requirements and obligations placed on those who must register have been slowly tightened since the 'register' came on line in September 1997. This tightening and strengthening of the register has caused the Home Office to issue a word of warning and a reminder that a civil measure like the register is *not* a criminal punishment from the courts but is only an administrative measure to improve community safety; the fear is that the two separate entities might get confused:

> It (the register) is a measure aimed at helping to protect the community from sex offenders not an additional penalty for the offender. (Scottish Executive, 2001: 11)
>
> Were the registration requirement to become more onerous, there could come a point at which the Act could no longer be seen as an administrative requirement. (ibid.: 13)

In effect the register as a civil measure could start becoming a punishment (Thomas, 2008).

Elsewhere other civil orders like the Sexual Offences Prevention Order or the Risk of Sexual Harm Order have been designed to transform into criminal proceedings should the subject of the Order breach its requirements. Already the House of Lords has ruled that the court must stop using civil procedures in deciding an original application and use criminal procedures (see above).

It is as though we believe the criminal sanctions we have are insufficient, but instead of increasing them we prefer to take the parallel course of civil measures. The fear is that the two may get inextricably muddled as the civil measures come in to fill the 'incapacitation gap' (Janus, 2000).

If the overall aim is to have sex offenders either excluded from society or where we can see them (registers, Sexual Offences Prevention Orders, and so on), there is also the possibility that we are only establishing them as 'others' against which we—the community—can identify and maintain our separate identities which we never have to question. In turn this leads to the danger of a 'jurisprudence of difference' whereby sex offenders become simply second class citizens, entitled to fewer rights than the rest of us, not just because they are offenders but because their 'bad behaviour flows inexorably from a being who is essentially different from the norm' (Janus, 2000).

QUESTIONS FOR DISCUSSION

1   Why is there so much concern about sex offending today compared to 20 years ago?

2   What forms does sexual offending take?

3   Why are we apparently prosecuting fewer and fewer sex offenders?

4   Should we punish or treat the sex offender?

5   How can we increase public protection from the sex offender?

GUIDE TO FURTHER READING

Brown, M. and Pratt, J. (eds) (2000) *Dangerous Offenders: Punishment and Social Order*. London and New York: Routledge.
A collection of essays with an international flavour looking at various aspects of 'managing' the dangerous offender, including sex offenders.

Kemshall, H. and McIvor, G. (eds) (2004) *Managing Sex Offender Risk*. London: Jessica Kingsley Publishers.
A collection of essays with a UK focus looking at various angles on protecting the public from sex offending in the community.

Janus, E. (2006) *Failure to Protect: Americas Sexual Predator Laws and the Rise of the Preventive State*. New York: Cornell University Press, Ithaca.
A critique of the American policies on sex offender registers, community notification, and civil commitments which has clear lessons and implications for UK policies.

Silverman, J. and Wilson, D. (2002) *Innocence Betrayed: Paedophilia, the Media and Society*. Cambridge: Polity.
Written by a journalist and an academic it is an easy to read account of contemporary social responses to sexual offending; particularly good on the politics, public opinion, and press side of the story.

Temkin, J. (2002) *Rape and the Legal Process* (2nd edn). Oxford: Oxford University Press.

Although written by a lawyer and with a clear legal perspective, this is an accessible book to the non-legal reader and presents a wider picture to contextualize the law in terms of contemporary society.

Thomas, T. (2005) *Sex Crime: Sex Offending and Society* (2nd edn). Cullompton, Devon: Willan Publishing.

A general history and descriptive account of penal and social responses to sex offending; contains detailed account of the parliamentary discussion on the proposals for a sex offender register.

WEB LINKS

http://www.nota.co.uk/

National Organisation for the Treatment of Abusers (NOTA). A UK-based organization for practitioners in a variety of professions working with sex offenders: contains policy papers, links to other organizations, and conferences.

http://www.stopitnow.org.uk/

Stop it Now! An organization that sees sexual crime as a preventable public health problem and encourages offenders to come forward for treatment. It started in the USA and has now come to the UK.

http://www.atsa.com/

Association for the Treatment of Sexual Abusers (ATSA). The US equivalent of NOTA; an organization for practitioners in a variety of professions working with sex offenders; has details of publications, conferences etc.

http://www.iatso.org

International Association for the Treatment of Sexual Offenders (IATSO). Takes a comparative view of global developments in working with sex offenders.

http://www.csom.org/

Center for Sex Offender Management (CSOM). A US-based centre supported by the Department of Justice which started in 1997. Wealth of publications available on all aspects of sex offender management plus useful links.

REFERENCES

Barrett, D. (ed) (2000) *Youth Prostitution in the New Europe.* Lyme Regis, Dorset. Russell House Publishing.

Beech, A., Fisher, D., Beckett, R., and Scott-Fordham, A. (1998) An evaluation of the Prison Sex Offender Treatment Programme, Research Findings No. 79, Research, Development and Statistics Directorate. London: Home Office.

Bottoms, A.E. (1977) 'Reflections on the Renaissance of Dangerousness', *Howard Journal of Criminal Justice*, 16: 70–96.

Brooke C (2007) 'Child-porn police "seize picture from Elton art collection"', *Daily Mail* 26 September.

Brown, A. and Barrett, D. (2003) *Knowledge of Evil: Child Prostitution and Child Sexual Abuse in Twentieth Century England.* Cullompton: Willan Publishing.

Brown, M. and Pratt, J. (eds) (2000) *Dangerous Offenders: Punishment and Social Order.* London and New York: Routledge.

Bryan, T. and Doyle, P. (2003) *Developing Multi-Agency Public Protection Arrangements,* in A. Matravers (ed) *Sex Offenders in the Community,* Cullompton: Willan Publishing.

Cann, J. (2007) Assessing the Extent of Discretionary Disclosure under the Multi-Agency Public Protection Arrangements, Online Report no. 13/07 (accessible at <http://www.homeoffice.gov.uk/rds/pdfs07/rdsolr1307.pdf>).

Carr, J. (2004) *Child Abuse, Child Pornography and the Internet.* London: NCH.

Cohen, S. (1973) *Folk Devils and Moral Panics.* St Albans: Paladin.

(CPSI) Crown Prosecution Service Inspectorate and (HMIC) HM Inspectorate of Constabulary (2002) A Report on the Joint Inspection into the Investigation and Prosecution of Cases Involving Allegations of Rape. London.

Department of Health, Home Office, Department for Education and Employment, National Assembly for Wales (2000) Safeguarding Children involved in Prostitution. London.

Feeley, M. and Simon, J. (1994) *Actuarial Justice: the Emerging New Criminal Law*, in Nelkin D. (ed) *The Future of Criminology*. London: Sage.

Fitch, K. (2006) *Megan's Law: does it protect children? (2)* London: NSPCC.

Gallagher, B., Bradford, M., and Pease, K. (2002) 'The Sexual Abuse of Children by Strangers: its Extent, Nature and Victims' Characteristics', *Children and Society* 16: 346–59.

Garland, D. (2001) *The Culture of Control: Crime and Social Order in Contemporary Society*. Oxford: Oxford University Press.

Harris, J. and Grace, S. (1999) A Question of Evidence: Investigating and Prosecuting Rape in the 1990s. Home Office Research Study 196. London.

Hewitt, D. (2004) 'An added duty of risk assessment'. *New Law Journal* 23 January: 87–8.

Home Office (1990) Crime, Justice and Protecting the Public, Cm. 965. London: HMSO.

Home Office (1996) Sentencing and Supervision of Sex Offenders: a consultation document, Cm. 3304. London.

Home Office (1999) Managing Dangerous People with Severe Personality Disorder, July. London.

Home Office (2000) Setting the Boundaries: reforming the law on sex offences, July. London.

Home Office (2002a) Achieving Best Evidence in Criminal Proceedings: guidance for vulnerable or intimidated witnesses, including children. London.

Home Office (2002b) Protecting the Public: strengthening protection against sex offenders and reforming the law on sexual offences, Cm. 5668. London.

Home Office (2003a) Crime in England and Wales 2002/3. London.

Home Office (2003b) Government Proposals on the Issue of Sex Offenders who Travel Abroad. London.

Home Office, (2007) Review of the Protection of Children from Sex Offenders. London.

Hughes, B., Parker, H., and Gallagher, B. (1996) Policing Child Sexual Abuse: the View from Police Practitioners, Police Research Group, Home Office. London.

Janus, E. (2000) 'Civil Commitment as Social Control: managing the risk of sexual violence', in M. Brown and J. Pratt (eds) *Dangerous Offenders: Punishment and Social Order*. London and New York: Routledge.

Janus, E (2006) *Failure to Protect: Americas Sexual Predator Laws and the Rise of the Preventive State*. New York: Cornell University Press, Ithaca.

Kane, J. (1998) *Sold for Sex*. Aldershot: Arena.

Kelly L., Lovett, J., and Regan, L. (2005) A Gap or a Chasm? Attrition in reported rape cases, Home Office Research Study 293. London

Knock, K. (2002) The Police Perspective on Sex Offender Orders: a preliminary review of policy and practice, Police Research Series, Paper 155. London: Home Office.

Marshall, P. (1997) The prevalence of Convictions for Sexual Offending, Research Finding No. 55, Research and Statistics Directorate. London: Home Office.

Matravers, A. (ed) (2003) *Sex Offenders in the Community*. Cullompton: Willan Publishing.

Morris, N. (2007) 'Paying for sex could be made illegal', *The Independent* 21 December.

Nash, M. (2006) *Public Protection and the Criminal Justice Process*. Oxford: Oxford University Press.

Nelkin D, (ed) (1994) *The Futures of Criminology*. London: Sage.

OCJR (Office of Criminal Justice Reform) (2006) Convicting Rapists and Protecting Victims: justice for victims of rape, a consultation paper. London.

OCJR (Office of Criminal Justice Reform) (2007) Convicting Rapists and Protecting Victims: justice for victims of rape—response to consultation, Attorney Generals Office. London

Plotnikoff, J. and Woolfson, R. (2000) Where Are They Now?: an evaluation of sex offender registration in England and Wales, Police Research Series, Paper 126. London: Home Office.

Power, H. (2003) Disclosing Information on Sex Offenders: the human rights implications, in A. Matravers (ed) *Sex Offenders in the Community*. Cullompton: Willan Publishing.

Scottish Executive (2001) Consultation Paper on the Review of Part I of the Sex Offenders Act 1997, July. London.

Silverman, J. and Wilson, D. (2002) *Innocence Betrayed: Paedophilia, the Media and Society*. Cambridge: Polity.

Sparks, R., Bottoms, A., and Hay, W. (1996) *Prisons and the Problem of Order*. Oxford: Clarendon Press.

Svedin, C.G. and Back, K. (1996) *Children Who Don't Speak Out*. Stockholm: Radda Barnen.

Temkin, J. (2002) *Rape and the Legal Process* (2nd edn). Oxford: Oxford University Press.

Thomas, T. (2000) *Sex Crime: Sex Offending and Society*. Cullompton: Willan Publishing.

Thomas, T. (2003). 'Sex Offender Community Notification: the American Experience' *Howard Journal of Criminal Justice* 42(3): 217–228.

Thomas, T. (2004) 'Sex Offender Registers and Monitoring', in H. Kemshall and G. McIvor (eds) *Managing Sex Offender Risk*. London: Jessica Kingsley Publishing.

Thomas, T. (2007) *Criminal Records: a database for the criminal justice system and beyond*. London: Palgrave Macmillan.

Thomas, T. (2008) 'The Sex Offender Register: a case study in function creep' *Howard Journal of Criminal Justice* 47 (3): 227–237, July.

13 Corporate crime

Steve Tombs

INTRODUCTION

If you were to stop one hundred people in the street and ask them to list, in their opinion, the five most serious crimes in Britain today, it is a very safe bet that in the vast majority of responses no form of corporate crime would feature. Similarly, check today's newspapers for reports of political discussions or Home Office statements on law and order: again, corporate crime will be absent. Now scour those newspapers more thoroughly, and try to find corporate crime stories—corporate crime may be covered, but is unlikely to be given prominence, nor discussed in the language reserved for 'real' crime. Check your TV guide for today's viewing, and search for corporate crime coverage amongst what will no doubt be a great deal of fictional, real-life, and documentary programmes on crime—and it would be a surprise to find much, if any. Open up your favourite (or most used!) criminology reader or textbook and look for corporate crime in the contents or even the index—and there is a chance you will not find it in either.

The substance of this chapter is determined significantly by this relative invisibility of corporate crime from popular and academic views. It begins by examining the emergence of the concept of corporate crime, discussing what this term means, and then reviewing the extent to which corporate crime represents a crime problem. The main body of the chapter considers various dimensions of corporate crime, paying particular attention to issues of visibility, causation, and control. The central aim of this chapter is to mark out corporate crime as a legitimate area of criminological concern.

BACKGROUND

In his famous Presidential Address to the American Sociological Association in 1939, and in various publications through the following decade, Edwin Sutherland (1940, 1945, 1983) introduced the idea of 'white-collar crime'—'a crime committed by a person of respectability and high social status in the course of his occupation' (Sutherland, 1983: 7). He thus challenged the stereotypical view of the criminal as lower class since 'powerful business and professional men' also routinely commit crimes. The main difference between the crimes of the upper and lower classes was in the implementation of the criminal laws that apply to them: 'upper class' criminals often operate undetected; if detected they may not be prosecuted; and if prosecuted they tend to receive relatively lenient (and overwhelmingly financial) penalties.

Sutherland's 'clarion call' to criminologists to focus upon such crimes fell largely upon deaf ears—notwithstanding notable exceptions (for example, some of the work of Geis through the 1960s, notably Geis, 1967, 1968). It was not until the end of the

1960s/beginning of the 1970s that there occurred a re-emergence of interest in corporate crime as one aspect of a more general proliferation of both an academic concern with 'white-collar' crime and a popular and political concern with the socially harmful effects of corporate activity. More recently, however, some commentators, notably Snider (2000), have argued that this concern had diminished dramatically by the end of the twentieth century, as the social credibility of business had increased with the rise of right-leaning political regimes and commitments to market economics. However, as the global economic crisis unfolds and its roots in corporate activity and poor regulatory oversight are exposed, this concern may receive a far higher priority.

In the UK, the level of academic attention to corporate crime has never reached that of some historical periods in the US. While there may be many reasons for this, one contributory factor has surely been the greater popular and political suspicion of 'big business' in the US. Yet there are signs, particularly with the emergence of post-privatization discourses around 'fat cats', demands for processes to ensure better accountability, probity, and openness in organizational conduct ('corporate governance'), the sheer ineptitude of some privatized companies, as well as a series of national and international corporate 'scandals', that questions of corporate crime, or least the more effective regulation of corporate activities, may be re-emerging within political, social, and even academic agendas.

Certainly one obstacle to the academic study of corporate crime can be traced back to Sutherland's path-breaking work. For, important as Sutherland's highlighting of 'white-collar' crime was, it generated significant theoretical and conceptual confusion, not least because having defined it in terms of people, Sutherland proceeded to study corporations (Cressey, 1989). To date, there remains considerable disagreement as to how to define this area of study (Friedrichs, 1992).

For the purposes of this chapter, corporate crime is viewed as 'illegal acts or omissions, punishable by the State under administrative, civil or criminal law, which are the result of deliberate decision making or culpable negligence within a legitimate formal organisation' (Pearce and Tombs, 1998, 107–10, following Box, 1983; Schrager and Short, 1977). Several aspects of this definition are worth emphasis. First, the term 'corporation' is used in its UK sense, so that this covers all companies registered under the Companies Acts, from the smallest limited liability company such as John Barr and Sons (the butchers involved in the E-Coli outbreak, below) to the largest multinationals such as ICI or BP. Second, while this definition may formally exclude some other kinds of organizations involved in the production of illegality—such as public sector bodies which carry out functions on behalf of the State (for example, health trusts or universities)—to the extent that these are involved in commercial activities then the modes of analysis set out below (notably in the section on causation) are mostly perfectly applicable to understanding illegalities produced by these. Third, through referring to 'legitimate formal organization', the definition marks off corporate crime from organized crime, even if the two phenomena share some key characteristics (Ruggiero, 1996; Rawlinson, Chapter 14 below). Lastly, it incorporates Sutherland's insight that the distinctions between different forms of illegalities—that is, whether these are classed as criminal, civil, administrative—to a great extent reflect the ability of the powerful, including corporations, to have activities in which they may be implicated classified as less serious (Pearce and Tombs, 2003).

Dimensions of corporate crime

Corporate crime is a wide-ranging term, covering a vast range of offences of omission and commission with differing types of modus operandi, perpetrators, effects, and victims. For example, some crimes—such as the financial accounting offences associated with Enron (the subject of much academic and popular writing, as well as Gibney's stunning 2005 documentary film, *Enron—the Smartest Guys in the Room*, see <http://www.imdb.com/title/tt1016268/>)—can only emerge as a result of intentional, well-planned, and systematic deception, not least on a scale amounting to widespread conspiracy; they are rendered possible by the multinational structure of the company; and have both a wide range and large number of victims, including employees (loss of jobs), governments (loss of taxation revenue), and investors (loss of returns). In contrast, a breach of the Health and Safety at Work Act, a criminal offence, may emerge from somewhat different origins. At times, this may be caused by the prioritization of profit, which, though clearly very conscious, does not have as its intention the production of death, injury, or illness; at other times, such a crime may lack intention, and occur more as the result of a complex chain of negligence and carelessness. Although either form of offence may end in large-scale disaster—such as the gas leak at Bhopal, India, which killed tens of thousands; see Pearce and Tombs, 1998: 194–219) or a multiple fatality train crash (Woolmar, 2001: 155–79)—more often the consequences of such an offence are very localized, if often tragic (such as the death of Simon Jones, a 24-year-old student who died within hours of his first day at work at Shoreham docks; see <http://www.simonjones.org.uk>). Because 'corporate crime' refers to a wide range of events and processes, it is useful to seek to group its different types. Amongst various categorizations, four are used most frequently: financial offences; offences against consumers; crimes against employees and employment protection; and environmental offences.[1]

A number of academic studies have focused upon a range of financial crimes, including: illegal share dealings, mergers, and takeovers; various forms of tax evasion; bribery; and other forms of illegal accounting. Enron is the classic example of the latter and has joined a list of offenders—including Guinness (involved in illegal share dealings in the 1980s; see Punch, 1996: 167–80) and BCCI, a global bank which was systematically involved in fraud, money laundering, and bribery (ibid.: 9–15)[2]—as symbols of what we mean by the term 'financial crime'.

A second general area of corporate crimes is those committed directly against consumers. Examples include illegal sales/marketing practices; the sale of unfit goods, such as adulterated food; conspiracies to fix prices and/or carve up market share amongst different companies, false/illegal labelling or information; and the fraudulent safety testing of products. A classic example of the last category was the outbreak of E-Coli amongst Lanarkshire residents in November 1996, resulting in 18 deaths and almost 500 people ill. The poisoning was traced back to a local butcher's which was eventually fined £2,500 for failing to ensure equipment was kept clean and that food was protected against contamination.

Third, we can identify crimes arising out of the employment relationship. These include cases of sexual and racial discrimination and other offences against employment law (including equal opportunities legislation); violations of wage laws; violations against rights to organize and take industrial action; and a whole range of offences against employee occupational health and safety. Such offences are widespread. For example, as Whyte (2004) has reported, it is estimated that there are up to two million school age children working in the UK (more than a quarter in food preparation and sales); around 75 per cent are thought to be employed illegally—employed without permits, in dangerous work, or in breach of working hours regulations.

The final category of offence, crimes against the environment, includes illegal emissions to air, water, and land; the failure to provide, or the provision of false, information; hazardous waste dumping; and illegal manufacturing practices. In 2006, industry accounted for over half—almost 500—of the pollution incidents classified as 'serious' by the Environment Agency. Prosecutions against companies produced a total of fines in excess of £3.5 million, averaging £11,800 per business; 29 company directors were also prosecuted, two of whom received custodial sentences totalling 14 months (ibid.). This is an Agency hardly known for a prosecutorial ethos, indeed explicitly noting that 'prosecutions are our last resort' (Environment Agency, 2006: 10). For example, a 2001 Greenpeace report calculated that between 1999 and 2001 there were 533 *known* breaches of licences by the ten municipal waste incinerators operating in England. Most were likely to be emissions of dioxins, highly toxic, known cancer-causing substances— but only one of these breaches had been prosecuted (Brown, 2001; Whyte, 2004).

Beyond identifying the range of offences that fall within the general rubric of 'corporate crime', there are several observations, based on the available research evidence, which we can state with confidence regarding its impact and prevalence.

Corporate crime has economic, physical, and social costs. Governments, taxpayers, consumers, workers, and other companies incur economic costs. Many forms of corporate crimes have physical costs—deaths, injuries, ill-health—arising out of dangerous workplaces, polluted environments, unsafe goods and services, and so on. Corporate crimes also have social effects. The economic and physical costs in general fall upon those in society who are already relatively disadvantaged: low paid workers are most likely to work in dangerous workplaces; poorer people are least able to relocate from polluted neighbourhoods; those on the tightest budgets are most vulnerable to purchasing goods and services which may lead them to be victims of corporate crime, such as the cheaper cuts of 'fresh' or processed meat, or cut-price electrical items. A further social cost of corporate crime is a diminution of social trust in the corporations upon whom we rely for the food we eat, the clothes we wear, the services we use and so on, and, by implication, the lack of trust in governments for their failure to regulate effectively the activities of these corporations.

Even if we confine ourselves to considering the economic costs of corporate offending, the best available evidence indicates that these far outweigh those associated with 'conventional' or 'street' offending. This conclusion is difficult to contest even whilst recognizing the difficulty faced by attempts to estimate the 'costs' of any form of crime. Even studies of 'single' examples or groups of corporate crime—such as the losses associated with the collapse of Farepak, estimated to have cost savers up to a total of £50m (Spalek, 2007)—are enough to support this general conclusion.

Finally, the range of work that now exists around corporate crime, such as case-studies either of particular offences or categories of offences by type or industry, as well as the more limited efforts at quantifying the scale and ubiquitousness of such crimes, indicates clearly that such offending is not a peripheral activity carried out by a marginal group of individuals and organizations, the so-called 'bad apples' of the business world. Rather, it is endemic within economic activity: corporate crimes are not simply widespread, they are routine and pervasive (Slapper and Tombs, 1999: 36–84).

REVIEW QUESTIONS

1 Can you think of examples (other than those given in this section) of the different categories of corporate crimes identified above?

2 What evidence exists to indicate that corporate crime is widespread and pervasive?

3 In what ways might corporate crimes be said to disproportionately victimize the poorer and more marginalized members of society? What exceptions are there to this general statement?

The invisibility of corporate crime

Given its consequences, why is corporate crime almost entirely absent from 'crime, law and order' agendas? To address this question we need to recognize that there are many social processes that contribute to removing such offences from dominant definitions of 'crime, law and order' (Slapper and Tombs, 1999).

Both formal politics and the law play crucial roles in the production and maintenance of definitions that exclude corporate crime.

At the political level, both in particular policy decisions—such as resource allocations for various enforcement agencies—and in the political rhetoric of crime, law, and order, corporate crimes are largely marginalized. Notice how 'zero tolerance', 'three strikes and you're out', mandatory sentences, being 'tough on crime and tough on the causes of crime', 'short sharp shocks', and protecting and furthering the rights of victims have all been deployed in the context of street or traditional crimes (Hale, Chapter 21) but not to corporate offending—even though they are perfectly applicable here as well (Etzioni, 1993; Geis, 1996; Lofquist, 1993).

Turning to the application of law and legal regulation, we find that, at every stage of the legal process, law tends to operate quite differently with respect to corporate crimes than in the context of 'conventional' crimes. Thus, in the very framing of the substance and parameters of legal regulation, its enforcement, the ways in which potential offences and offenders are investigated, the prosecution of offences, and the use of sanctions following successful prosecution, most forms of corporate and organizational offences are relatively decriminalized.

Related to the political and legal invisibility afforded to corporate crime is the poverty and paucity of official corporate crime data. Measures used to indicate the scale of the crime problem do not include corporate offences. Even a cursory examination of the notifiable offences for England and Wales reveals the extent to which they focus upon conventional as opposed to corporate crimes. If, as Maguire notes, 'a salient feature of almost all modern forms of discourse about crime is the emphasis placed upon terms associated with its quantification and measurement' (Maguire, 1994: 236), then it is hardly surprising that corporate crimes 'do not feature in…debates about the "crime problem"'(Nelken, 1994: 355; Green, 1990: 27).

Further, it is revealing that the Home Office's responses to problems in the official recording of conventional crimes, notably the sponsoring of the annual British Crime Survey (see Hope, Chapter 3), are not matched by any comparable energy to uncover the hidden figure of corporate crime. By contrast, it has, in recent years, been a key mover in developing a flourishing research area around crimes *against* business (Hopkins, 2002).

This latter point indicates the significance of ideologies surrounding business and the difficulties these pose for naming corporations as (potential) offenders (see Lacey, 1995: 21). Corporations are viewed differently to the objects of 'traditional' crime concerns; 'conventional criminals' tend to be represented as a burden upon society in a way that corporations will not be. Further, where business organizations engage in criminal activity, this is represented as an aberration from their routine, legitimate activities, while such offending tends to be cast as involving technical infringements of law, rather than real crimes.

These assumptions, and the general contrast with 'real' crime and 'real' criminals are reflected in and reinforced by the media. Whether we survey fictional or documentary-style treatments of crime on TV, or newspaper and other print media coverage of the issues, we find that while there may be some attention to corporate crime, representations of crime converge to produce 'blanket' conceptualizations regarding 'law-and-order' that reinforce dominant stereotypes of crime and the criminal (Chibnall, 1977). Thus, where corporate crime is covered, its presence is vastly outweighed by treatments of conventional crime; it is treated in lesser profile outlets or formats, and is often represented in the rather sanitizing language of scandals, disasters, abuses, and accidents rather than as criminal activity (Tombs and Whyte, 2001).

For many of us, then, corporate crime is far removed from our immediate experience. This is also partly an effect of the relationship between the offender and the victim in many corporate offences. In most forms of traditional crime there is, or must at some point be, a degree of proximity between offender and victim. By contrast, with corporate crimes, there are frequently enormous distances between offender and victim, in terms of both space and time. This has important implications in terms of awareness of, and then 'proving', victimization (Tombs and Williams, 2007).

First, many victims of corporate crimes may never be aware of their status as victims (Croall, 1989; Meier and Short, 1995). That is, if we overpay for goods because of price-fixing between leading retailers in the market, or are duped into buying inappropriate pensions or mortgages due to illegal selling, we may never realize that we have been victimized. Even if people *are* aware of their status as victims, acting upon this awareness is often extremely difficult (Croall, 1989)—we may recognize that our health and those of neighbours is declining, but not be able to pinpoint the exact source of illegal pollution; or, if we can identify a factory or industrial process, we may feel they are too big, or that we lack support from public bodies (such as the Environment Agency) to make it worth our while acting upon this recognition.

None of the various mechanisms whereby corporate crimes are rendered relatively invisible are particularly remarkable in isolation. What is crucial, however, is *their mutually reinforcing nature*—that is, they all work in the same direction and to the same effect, removing corporate crime from 'crime, law, and order' agendas.

> **REVIEW QUESTIONS**
>
> **1** In what ways is the absence of corporate crimes from official statistics an important factor in their invisibility?
>
> **2** In what ways do various media contribute to the invisibility of corporate crime?

The 'causes' of corporate crime

One group to whom we might turn in order to bring to light issues which are rendered invisible through political and social processes are academic researchers. Yet one of the most intriguing characteristics of criminology is that it has focused relatively little energy upon bringing to light corporate crimes—historically, and to this day, the vast majority of criminological teaching and research tends simply to assume 'crime' as an activity engaged in by *individual* men (and sometimes women). Quite remarkably for a social science, one key feature of criminology is that it has taken the social construction of crime as its starting point![3] This applies to criminological theorizing with particular force (Cressey, 1989).

For example, classicism (on this and other criminological theories referred to below, see Hayward, Chapter 4, this volume) sought to develop a rational, just system of penality, albeit one aimed exclusively at conventional crimes. Its key claim was that the criminal is rational—s/he chooses, more or less freely, to commit crime. This choice is influenced through a form of calculative reasoning, a reasoning paying particular attention to the benefits of a criminal act on the one hand, and the costs (likelihood of detection and consequences of detection) of that crime on the other.

Now, if it is unlikely that most individuals are in a position to calculate rationally the benefits and costs of offending, this might be much closer to what corporations, or their directors and managers, actually do. For a corporation is an organization that claims to act rationally, to calculate, and to predict external responses to its actions in order to maximize its long run profits. To then add to this tendency to calculate the existence of relatively weak regulation (see below) produces exactly the combination of factors that, according to classicist logic, provides a fertile ground for criminality. There is genuine scope for considering the application of classicist forms of reasoning to the area of corporate crime control. This might entail, for example, a theoretical and empirical exploration of the potential for deterrent-based strategies for controlling corporate crime, even if such approaches have manifestly failed with respect to 'traditional' offenders (Pearce and Tombs, 1998: 292–305).

If we turn to the emergence of individual positivisms within criminology, here we find attempts to identify the abnormalities that either propel individuals into crime, or ensure that they are more predisposed to committing crime than the general population. To include corporate crime within these considerations would be illuminating, if only to undermine the very basis of individual positivism—for one of the most interesting features about individuals involved in corporate offending is their normality, there being an almost total lack of meaningful differences between these and non-offenders (Snider, 1993: 61; see also Virta, 1999; Waring and Weisburd, 2001). By contrast, where corporate offenders appear not to be 'normal', they are still unlikely to be cast negatively, in terms of pathology. Rather, their 'abnormality' is cast as a form of distinctiveness as they are held up as the type of individuals that we might all aspire to be—as successful, wealthy, hard-working, innovative, well-respected and connected, pillars of their local community, and so on—figures precisely such as Kenneth Lay, the extremely well-connected Chief Executive Officer of the now-defunct global energy giant Enron.

There have been some attempts to apply an individual positivist type analysis to corporate crime, though these have been marginal to criminology, conducted mostly within business or management studies. These have sought to identify those 'personality' factors associated with people who succeed in private companies, and have tended to highlight features such as being innovative, ambitious, shrewd, aggressive, impatient, and possessing a 'moral flexibility' (see Snider, 1993). It is clear why such qualities are likely to be valued within the corporate world; but it is also clear how such individuals may be more likely to be involved in corporate illegalities, either as leading figures or as individuals prepared to turn a blind eye.[4] And this latter observation tells us something about how we might explain many forms of corporate crime—if corporations seek to recruit people with these characteristics, and if the higher one goes in the corporate hierarchy the more likely are these to be accentuated, then we need to know something about the culture and functioning of the corporation itself, as well as the environments within which it operates, to understand how its employees, from the most senior downwards, act, think, and rationalize. We shall return to this issue below.

If individual positivism failed to turn its attention to corporate offenders, then so too did the form of criminology that has dominated theorizing since the 1930s, namely sociological positivism. However, here there are some notable exceptions to this general failure to include corporate crime within theoretical frameworks.

As a member of the Chicago School, Sutherland himself attempted to develop a general, sociological, theory of crime causation, claiming that 'differential association' could explain both upper-class and lower-class crimes: crime arises from an excess of definitions favourable to law violation over definitions unfavourable to law violation. Criminal activity—motivations, *post hoc* rationalizations, and actual techniques of commission—is, like all behaviour, learnt. This learning, and exposure to different definitions regarding the appropriateness or otherwise of certain behaviours, emerges out of our various associations—and these associations vary by frequency, duration, priority, and intensity.

This does seem to have some validity for understanding the willingness of individuals to engage in crime within and on behalf of corporations. Even with the demise of the so-called job-for-life in most western economies, it remains the case that our associations with individuals within a corporation are hardly fleeting; we spend a significant part of our week at work, and are likely to spend years working for the same company or in the same kind of industry. Further, most of us invest our work with significance—either instrumentally, seeing work as sheer necessity or (for the lucky few) more expressively, as a means of realizing some ability or desire we possess.

Moreover, we know, either by experience or indeed by intuition, that within certain corporations or even industries, certain forms of activity are prevalent, both in terms of knowing how to engage in them and knowing why one must engage in them. Presumably, if this holds for legal activity, it holds for illegal activity too. For example, within the retail butchering trade it is common knowledge that frozen poultry can be defrosted in a particular way to make it resemble fresh poultry so that it can be sold at a higher price, as if fresh, thereby defrauding the consumer. Further, there may also be generalized knowledge that 'everyone' in the trade is doing it—which not only provides a motivation, since not to do it is to place one's own shop or company at a competitive disadvantage, but also that to do it is so generalized that it is acceptable, not really criminal.[5]

Differential association has been subjected to stringent criticism (Taylor *et al.*, 1973: 125–30). It is of interest, however, precisely because it attempted to incorporate corporate crime within a general theory of crime. Other variants of sociological positivism have not sought to do so in such an explicit manner, yet some aspects may be utilized to explain corporate crime. Notable here is Mertonian strain theory and its central concept, anomie. Merton linked deviant behaviour to the disjunction between institutionalized aspirations and the availability of legitimate opportunity structures—albeit in terms of lower class crime. But Passas has argued that there is no compelling reason why anomie cannot apply to corporate deviance:

> As the meaning and content of success goals vary from one part of the social structure to another, similar difficulties in attaining diversely defined goals may be faced by people in the upper social reaches too; they are, therefore, far from immune to pressures towards deviance. (Passas, 1990: 158)

The pressures to succeed exist for business and organizations in terms of maximization of profit, growth, and efficiency. These goals may have to be obtained *by all* or *any means* particularly when the continuation of the corporation is at stake and the corporate actors realize that the attainment of their own ends depends largely on the prosperity of the firm. Structural pressures and strains may be applied both to those at the top as well as employees, and the use of deviant methods may seem to be the only possible way of dealing with problematic situations (see Box, 1983).

Finally, those forms of criminology that have sought to place an understanding of power at the heart of their theorizing have also produced, or have the potential to produce, insights regarding the nature and incidence of corporate offending. Corporate crimes are, after all, made possible on the basis of relative power, or committed by the relatively powerful. Ironically, the labelling perspective, while it sought to examine how processes of criminalization operated with respect to individuals from certain social groups, failed to ask very obvious converse questions: why are certain kinds of crime *not* subject to social opprobrium, and why are certain kinds of offenders able successfully and consistently to resist the processes of criminalization to which lower-class offenders seem highly vulnerable? (Nelken, 1994)

Various forms of critical and radical criminologies—including Marxisms and feminisms—have made important contributions to our knowledge of corporate crime causation. Notable here are: *Crimes of the Powerful* (Pearce, 1976), where it is argued that corporations, with the connivance of the American State, act systematically to control the markets within which they operate; Stuart Hills' edited collection on *Corporate Violence* (Hills, 1987), which consists of a series of empirical and theoretical case studies of the ways in which injury and death are produced systematically by the drive for profit; and Szockyj and Fox's (1996) anthology of analyses of the myriad ways in which corporations exploit constructions of gender to victimize female consumers, workers, and recipients of health care.

Now, whilst there are clear differences between the labelling perspective, Marxisms, and feminisms, one characteristic these share is the theoretical commitment to move beyond the narrowest confines of criminology, in particular to deconstruct dominant categories of crime and to view these constructions, and the criminal justice systems based upon them, as both an effect of and also a means of reproducing power.

From the preceding, it is becoming clear that to understand corporate crime causation we must take into account a series of factors ranging from the individual through to the structural. These will be set out here—albeit very briefly—in four analytically (though not of course empirically) distinct 'levels'.

At the level of the individual, we need to take account of individual personality and characteristics, not least in terms of the kinds of personalities that are recruited or encouraged within the organization, as well as 'individual' factors that are socially constructed as relevant, such as rank/position within hierarchy, age, gender, and ethnicity. For example it is relevant to enquire whether an organization is one where being female diminishes one's social power, or in which time served adds authority.

Moving to the level of the immediate work-group or sub-unit within the organization, we must take account of inter-personal dynamics, the culture of the work-group (and the extent to which this coheres or clashes with the culture of the wider organization), and its location within the overall organization, both structurally and geographically—that is, is it relatively autonomous or highly supervised, is it part of one large organizational complex, or is it geographically isolated?

There are also key sets of issues to be raised in relation to the organization itself. We need to understand something of its structure, its internal lines of decision-making and accountability, its geographical scope of operations, and the nature, volume, and complexity of internal transactions. Issues of organizational culture must also be addressed: is the organization risk-taking or risk-averse; is it gendered; is it authoritarian; and is it one where a blame culture predominates? Of further relevance is to examine the very products or services that are the focus of the organization: are these opaque or transparent, are they sold to consumers or other organizations, is their production labour- or capital-intensive? Finally, and perhaps most obviously, we need to know something of the economic 'health' of the company, and of the organizational units within it, as well as the time-scale at which profitability is calculated.

Lastly, there are key sets of questions to be broached regarding the wider economic, political, and social environments within which the organization operates. Amongst these extra-organizational features are: the nature of the market structure; the size and scope of the market; the material and ideological state of regulation; the more general nature of state-business relationships; the dominant form of political economy; and concomitant societal values, including the nature and degree of pro- or anti-business sentiment. Lastly, key information is to be gleaned in any understanding of the general 'health' of the economies in which the corporation operates.

This is only to summarize briefly what is an extensive, and complexly interrelated, set of factors. But the urgency of developing such a wide-ranging integrated explanatory framework has been raised by some commentators on corporate crime (Coleman, 1987; Punch, 2000; Vaughan, 1992). In truth, however, theoretical development here remains at an early stage, although there are now a number of book-length studies which attempt to use some of this range of factors. These include studies of safety crimes generally (Tombs and Whyte, 2007), and specifically in the offshore oil industry (Whyte, 1999; Woolfson *et al.*, 1996), corporate crime in the asbestos (Tweedale, 2000), chemicals (Pearce and Tombs, 1998), and pharmaceutical (Braithwaite, 1984) industries, attempts to prosecute for corporate manslaughter (Slapper, 2000), corporate and state illegalities associated with the fateful launch of the Challenger space shuttle (Vaughan, 1996), and a national case study in the micro/macro control of 'economic' crime (Alvesalo, 2003).

REVIEW QUESTIONS

1 How might we apply both classicism and individual positivism to an understanding of corporate crime causation?

2 What forms of sociological positivism have been turned towards the explanation of corporate crime?

3 What factors need to be incorporated into an adequate explanation of corporate crime?

'Controlling' corporate crime

Understandings of how corporate crime is caused inevitably influence claims regarding how it is to be controlled. And it is in the area of regulation that there is perhaps the most significant body of academic research around corporate crime. There are a number of studies—mostly nationally based, though with some useful cross-national comparative work—examining the practices of a whole range of regulatory bodies (for a review, see, for example, Clarke, 2000: 136–61). These allow several broad generalizations to be made about the practices and effects of regulatory enforcement agencies: non-enforcement is the most frequently found characteristic; enforcement activity tends to focus upon the smallest and weakest individuals and organizations; and sanctions following regulatory activity are light (Snider, 1993: 120–24).[6]

The most common finding of studies of regulatory enforcement, across business sectors and discrete areas of legislation, is that a cooperative regulatory approach is dominant. In short, regulators seek to enforce through persuasion—they advise, educate, and bargain, negotiate and reach compromise with the regulated (see Pearce and Tombs, 1998: 223–46). When violations become known to inspectors, they engage in a dialogue with management, prioritizing compliance with laws being violated in some areas (the most serious offences), usually on the basis of an agreed timetable, whilst accepting that others, deemed less serious, may take much longer to put right. This dialogue clearly takes into account the priorities of the inspectorate along with the commitment, motivation, and resources of the regulated (see Hawkins, 2002).

There are, of course, important variations within this body of work, not least about whether, or the point at which, compliance approaches should be abandoned and more punitive forms of regulation are invoked. This combination of cooperation and punitiveness is captured by the phrase 'the regulatory mix'. The most sophisticated discussions of the appropriate 'regulatory mix' have been developed by John Braithwaite and colleagues. Their starting point is a consideration of the potential of self-regulation, on the basis that state regulators will never have the resources to enforce regulatory law effectively, and that internal regulators enjoy certain technical and social advantages over those on the outside (Braithwaite and Fisse, 1987). Self-regulation is described (and prescribed) on a 'carrot and stick' basis: where self-regulation proves ineffective, the next preferred regulatory tactic is to move to 'enforced self-regulation', this requiring a company to develop a tailored set of rules by which it intends to comply with law which, once approved by external regulators, would then be 'enforced' internally; where evidence of non-compliance emerges, the potential of punitive external intervention remains (Braithwaite, 2000: *passim*; Ayres and Braithwaite, 1992: 102–16; see also Gunnigham and Johnstone, 1999, on 'twin-track' and 'smart' regulation).

Strategies of enforcement are thus conceived of in terms of a pyramid, where non-compliance leads to the invoking of ever more interventionist or punitive modes of enforcement on the part of regulators (see, for example, Braithwaite, 2000: 78–82, 99–105). In essence, this is an incrementalist and compliance-oriented strategy based on the principle of deterrence.

By contrast there is a body of work that seeks to posit alternatives to cooperative approaches. This advocates a more punitive approach to enforcement—though not suggesting that each and every violation of law by corporations be prosecuted. A key argument of this work is that corporate crime becomes defined as *real* crime, and thus is subject to more adversarial, punitive, and interventionist forms of regulation (Pearce and Tombs, 1998: 280–316). Such an approach *may* appear unproven and idealistic. However, there is evidence of the success of this type of approach where it has been attempted in specific instances (Pearce and Tombs, 1990; Pearce and Tombs, 1998: 286–92). Moreover, under very specific social, political, and economic conditions, it remains possible that such an approach towards the regulation of corporations can be generalized (Alvesalo, 2003).

In any case, it is incorrect to view cooperative and punitive approaches to regulation as alternative strategies: in practice, all forms of regulation reflect a mix of each approach, so that actual enforcement strategies are understood as lying somewhere on a continuum between these two ideal-typical polar opposites (see Figure 13.1).

However, what is at issue between the proponents of variants of 'cooperative models' of regulation and those who argue for a more adversarial strategy are a series of disputes which revolve around the extent to which corporate entities can and do act morally;

Figure 13.1 The regulatory continuum

can and do operate on the basis of some sense of social responsibility; can and do act upon some concern for their reputation, in the absence of bottom-line considerations. To answer such questions in the positive ultimately requires us to overlook the legal duties owed by managements to shareholders to maximize profits, to disregard the short-term horizons of those who own and control corporations and the realities of the stock market pressures upon them, and to under-estimate the intimate relationships between corporations and States.

Notwithstanding these disputes, a key issue remains—namely, that of sanctions that can be imposed once a violation has been taken to court and proven there.

By far the most common sanction is the monetary fine. Only in cases investigated by the Serious Fraud Office (SFO), unique amongst regulatory bodies in the UK in being established as part of criminal justice legislation, is imprisonment of individuals likely to be an outcome. But even here caution is needed. Thus, Fooks (2003) has noted that, after a short period in which a small number of financial crimes were subject to criminalization, the SFO has in recent years experienced retrenchment, with an increasing role being taken by the Financial Services Authority, which has an explicitly cooperative approach to regulatory enforcement (Spalek, 2001). Even during the 1990s, when the SFO received criticism for over-zealousness in terms of prosecution, it was taking an average of just fifteen cases to court per year (Fooks, 1999). Further, since the victims of serious fraud tend to be other corporations (banks and institutional investors), regulation in this sphere has been termed regulation *for* rather than *of* the City (Fooks, 2003).

More generally, following successful prosecution for corporate crime, fines are levelled at companies—and these are almost uniformly low. The average fine for all Health and Safety Executive health and safety convictions for 2005/06 when the distorting effects of a few large fines—13 over £100,000 in 2005/06, for example—was £6,219. But even the few larger fines appear insignificant when set against a company's annual profits or turnover. The record fine for a health and safety offence in the UK was £15 million, levied on Transco Plc in August 2005; this amounted to less than 2 per cent of the previous year's after-tax profit, and just 0.16 per cent of turnover for 2004—the equivalent of a fine of £36 for someone earning £25,000 a year (Tombs and Whyte, 2007: 174–8). Such sanctions hardly appear significant, a conclusion reinforced when we turn to sentencing following environmental offences. In 2003, Barbara Young, the Chief Executive of the Environment Agency, criticized the 'weak' sentencing following environmental crime: 'Fines for environmental offences have struggled slowly upwards over five years, but still rarely exceed £20,000…with irreparable environmental damage or serious risk to public health, penalties often fail to match up to the costs avoided' (cited in Brown, 2003). As noted above, fines following successful prosecution for environmental offences averaged £11,800 per business in 2006.

Of course, at times large fines are imposed upon offending companies. For example, in February 2003, retailers Argos and Littlewoods were fined record amounts of £17.3 million and £5.4 million respectively by the Office of Fair Trading; they had, with manufacturer Hasbro, entered into agreements to fix the prices of Hasbro toys and games between 1999 and 2001, breaching competition rules. (Hasbro had its potential fine of £15.6 million waived for providing key evidence to the investigation.) However, the very fact that such large fines attract publicity is itself an indicator that they are the exception rather than the norm. Moreover, when these monetary sums are set against the annual turnover of companies, then they appear much less significant—often being the equivalent of 'small change'.

Whilst fines following successful prosecutions are low, it might be argued that, were they to be raised to sufficiently high levels to have a deterrent effect, this might be counter-productive: the company may pass the costs on to workers, consumers, or both, rather than to shareholders, who are the legitimate object of the sanction. Indeed, ultimately, fines that do impact too much upon a company may lead to its closure, thus affecting the innocent again—notably employees, but also other organizations (which, for example, may supply goods or services to the offending company) or consumers, who might find themselves buying goods or services in a less competitive market.

Of course, none of these are reasons why large fines should not be used in principle. Such factors do, however, indicate that fines need to be used sensitively—and also that they may take forms other than a direct monetary penalty, such as, for example, the use of an equity fine, which involves the confiscation of a block of shares by the Government or a local authority (see Tombs and Whyte, 2007: 179–192). Moreover, even if we accept that there are problems with the use of monetary sanctions, sentencing of corporations and/or individuals involved in corporate crime is an area in which there now exists a range of imaginative proposals, some of which have been introduced in limited fashion, others of which remain at the proposal stage. Amongst these are:

- disqualification of individual directors, a sanction used in the case of financial crimes, but rarely beyond this context;
- the withdrawal of licences to operate and the barring of convicted companies from bidding for government-related contracts;
- the use of community service or restitution orders, whereby a convicted company is required to make good damage caused, or to use its resources and expertise to provide goods and services to a victimized community;
- the use of probation and rehabilitation orders, whereby a company is required to hire outside 'experts' to reform, for example, safety training or financial reporting systems;
- the use of adverse publicity and 'shaming', requiring a company to name itself, or be named, as an offender in appropriate media outlets.

All of these potential sanctions have their drawbacks, none is a panacea, and each is more or less appropriate for particular types of corporation and following specific forms of offence (Slapper and Tombs, 1999). Ultimately while there are clearly enormous difficulties in developing effective sanctions in the case of corporate crime these tend to be political rather than technical (Lofquist, 1993; Etzioni, 1993). Again, the key issue is the political refusal to treat corporate crime as real crime.

REVIEW QUESTIONS

1 What are the main problems associated with the use of fines as a sanction against corporations following conviction?

2 What are the strengths and weaknesses of alternative forms of sanctions?

CONCLUSION

The central aim of this chapter has been to mark out corporate crime as a legitimate area of criminological concern. To do this, it began by examining the emergence of the concept of corporate crime, before highlighting the extent to which it represents a (largely invisible) crime problem. The chapter then examined various dimensions of corporate crime, paying particular attention to issues of causation and control.

The fact that this chapter repeats a demand made by Sutherland over half a century ago—that corporate crime be given greater attention within the discipline of criminology—indicates the significance of the economic, political and social, obstacles to the task of taking corporate crime seriously. What is at issue here is power—for exposing corporate crime means exposing crimes associated with what are relatively powerful organizations, moreover organizations with which states (local, regional, national) have increasingly intimate relationships (Tombs and Whyte, 2003).

There has, of course, been progress within criminology since Sutherland's 'clarion call'—even if, as this chapter has indicated, this has been rather faltering. The very existence of this chapter in an introductory undergraduate text is, perhaps, one small manifestation of that progress. Yet, somewhat analogous to the demands made by feminist academics from the 1970s onwards, namely that issues of gender must be considered through all social science concerns rather than separated off for discrete consideration, the aim must be not for separate chapters or course units on corporate crime—rather, when academics speak of crime, whether they are seeking to measure, describe, explain, or consider how to control more effectively this phenomenon, they need to recognize that the label 'crime' covers a range of acts and omissions beyond those associated with the relatively powerless individuals.

Corporate crime remains a problematic and contested area of inquiry. Notwithstanding the definitional, conceptual, methodological, and theoretical disagreement and problems, it speaks to phenomena which on almost any criterion one chooses—the nature and extent of economic, physical, and social harms—are significant crime and social problems. Clearly, we need more research on corporate crime, not least because of a number of contemporary, pressing factors, including: the spread of the corporate form, as privatization has been championed across nation-states; diversification in the nature of corporate structures and organization; the increasingly international nature of much corporate activity; and associated claims regarding the growing power of corporations vis-à-vis national governments and their populations.

But corporate crime research—as research on the relatively powerful—faces enormous methodological difficulties, may be relatively unattractive to the funders of research, and is unlikely to produce immediately utilizable policy proposals, all of which may further explain its relative omission from dominant criminological agendas (Tombs and Whyte, 2003). And the force of these pressures changes over time. Thus, in the current era, corporate crime research may be more difficult, even if it is more pressing, not least because of the increasing valorization of business activity alongside the power of corporations to seek, via their political allies, the decriminalization of their activities through the introduction of various forms of self-regulation or through simple deregulation, each of which appear to be significant trends in contemporary capitalist nation-states (Snider, 2000).

Lastly, and taking us back to the discipline of criminology, corporate crime research remains worthwhile simply because it can perform an important role for the discipline. It encourages criminological reflexivity: a focus upon corporate crime entails continual scrutiny of the coverage and omissions of legal categories, the presences and absences within legal discourses, the social constructions of these categories and discourses, their underpinning of, treatment within, and development through criminal justice systems, the ways in which particular laws are enforced (or not enforced), interpreted, challenged, and, of no little significance, the contours of the discipline of criminology itself. If the criminological imagination can shed important light upon corporate crime (White, 2003), then there is no doubting that the study of corporate crime is itself one means of reinvigorating that same criminological imagination (Alvesalo *et al.*, 2006).

QUESTIONS FOR DISCUSSION

1   The (in)visibility of corporate crime? Select one broadsheet and one tabloid newspaper from the same day, then:
   - find all stories related to: (a) conventional crime; and (b) corporate crime, and cut or photocopy;
   - 'count' the stories devoted to 'conventional crime' and those devoted to 'corporate' crime;
   - note the page (and/or section) of the newspaper on which they are found;
   - list the titles of the corporate crime stories, and give a brief indication of, the 'corporate crime' stories;
   - record any observations you have on the tone/nature of the corporate crime stories when compared with the conventional crime stories.

2   Explaining corporate crime?

   Select a case study of corporate crime.

   How might we apply the following criminological perspectives to understand the genesis and nature of this case?
   - classicism;
   - individual positivism;
   - sociological positivism;
   - labelling;

- Marxist/critical criminologies.

In what ways do the following factors help to understand the genesis of this case?

- individual/personality factors;
- organizational structure of the company/companies in question;
- organizational culture of the company/companies in question;
- wider political, social, and cultural contexts within which the company/companies in question operated;
- the nature and level of regulation to which the company/companies were subject.

3 Compliance-oriented enforcement?

One of the arguments proposed on behalf of cooperative enforcement vis-à-vis business organizations is that to attempt to enforce the law strictly and punitively will lead to the 'stimulation of opposition and the destruction of cooperation' (Kagan and Scholz, 1984: 73).

Is it likely that business organization will react to strict and punitive enforcement in this way?

If it is likely, what weight does it carry as an argument against strict and punitive enforcement and in favour of cooperative enforcement vis-à-vis business organizations?

4 Sanctioning corporate offenders?

What are the advantages and disadvantages of the monetary fine as a sanction applied against convicted corporations and individuals?

What other sanctions might be applied?

What are the strengths and weaknesses of these other sanctions?

GUIDE TO FURTHER READING

Academic texts

Alvesalo, A. (2003) *The Dynamics of Economic Crime Control*. Espoo, Finland: the Police College of Finland.

Exploring the nature and interaction of the macro- and micro-processes and forces that characterize corporate crime control, using Finland as an empirical case, this book includes unique ethnographic and interview-based material on how corporate crime work is incorporated into police work.

Box, S. (1983) 'Corporate Crime', in S. Box, *Power, Crime and Mystification*. London: Tavistock, chapter 2.

Over 60-plus pages, Box's classic introduction to this area of study explores the scale of corporate crime, its invisibility, ways in which it must be explained, and issues of regulation and control.

Pearce, F. and Snider, L. (eds) (1995) *Corporate Crime: contemporary debates*. Toronto: University of Toronto Press.

Across 19 articles, this edited text covers a range of theoretical and empirical issues related to the incidence, nature, and regulation of corporate crime, including contributions by most of the leading corporate crime scholars across the English-speaking world.

Szockyi, E. and Fox, J.G. (eds) (1996) *Corporate Victimisation of Women*. Boston, Mass.: Northeastern University Press.

The eight articles here take a gendered view of corporate crime, covering theoretical debates around corporate crime, case studies of particular industries and forms of crime, and discussing the nature of regulation as well as prospects for regulatory reform.

Tweedale, G. (2000) Magic Mineral to Killer Dust. Turner & Newall and the Asbestos Hazard. Oxford: Oxford University Press.

Tweedale meticulously documents the asbestos scandal and the central role of Turner & Newall as its largest producer, highlighting the socially constructed boundaries between legality and illegality and the lengths to which corporations will go to evade their legal and moral obligations at the expense of thousands of lives.

Other material

Class Action (Director: Michael Apted, 1990)

Based upon one of the most infamous of all corporate crimes, the sale of the Ford Pinto, the movie follows legal efforts to secure compensation from a multinational car manufacturer for the victims of car 'accidents'.

Enron—the Smartest Guys in the Room (Alex Gibney, 2005)

A 2005 documentary following the rise, demise, and pursuit through the criminal justice system of Enron, itself based upon a 2004 book by Bethany McLean and Peter Elkind.

Glengarry Glen Ross (James Foley, 1992)

A searing critique of the real estate industry in Reagan's America, this film examines the personal traumas and interpersonal conflicts generated by working in a business where lying, cheating, and stealing all are in a day's work.

The Insider (Michael Mann, 1991)

Based on a true story, this revolves around a former tobacco scientist violating contractual agreements to expose his ex-employer's inclusion of addictive ingredients in cigarettes, while a journalist struggles to report the story via the national media.

Moore, M. (1998) *Adventures in a TV Nation. The stories behind America's most outrageous TV show.* London: Boxtree.

The story behind the show TV Nation, axed after 17 episodes by the US TV network Fox, there is extensive coverage of corporate crime in this witty but savage indictment of American corporate politics, including the classic tale of 'Crackers, the Corporate Crime-Fighting Chicken'.

The Corporation (M. Achbar, 2004)

An award winning documentary which provides a detailed diagnosis of the modern corporation as psychopathic, to be viewed alongside a read of Joel Bakan's (2004) *The Corporation. The pathological pursuit of profit and power, New York: the Free Press.*

Wall Street (Oliver Stone, 1987)

A big budget Hollywood production with a predictably unrealistic ending, this is excellent at conveying the culture that surrounded the financial markets on both sides of the Atlantic during the 1980s, a culture captured in Gordon Gecko's catchphrase, 'Greed is Good'.

WEB LINKS

http://www.open.gov.uk/
The Open Government website, which contains links to all regulatory bodies in England and Wales.

http://www.corporatewatch.org/

A campaigning site, bringing together the work of activists and researchers seeking both to expose illegal and unethical corporate activity and to explore business-government relations in general.

http://www.essential.org/monitor/monitor.html

Documents unethical and illegal corporate activity, especially in the Third World, focusing particularly on public, worker, and environmental health and safety issues.

http://www.corporatepredators.org

Here you will find the US-based 'Focus on the Corporation', a weekly column on illegal and unethical corporate activity.

http://paulsjusticepage.com/elite-deviance.htm

An excellent source of corporate crime material, and many links, maintained by Paul Leighton, co-author of Jeffrey Reiman's *The Rich Get Richer the Poor Get Prison*.

REFERENCES

Alvesalo, A. (2003) *The Dynamics of Economic Crime Control*. Espoo, Finland: the Police College of Finland.

Alvesalo, A., Tombs, S., Virta, E., and Whyte, D. (2006) 'Re-Imagining Crime Prevention: controlling corporate crime?' *Crime, Law and Social Change*, 45, 1–25.

Ayres, I. and Braithwaite, J. (1992) *Responsive Regulation. Transcending the Deregulation Debate*. Oxford: Oxford University Press.

Box, S. (1983) *Power, Crime and Mystification*. London: Tavistock.

Braithwaite, J. (1984) *Corporate Crime in the Pharmaceutical Industry*. London: Routledge and Kegan Paul.

Braithwaite, J. (2000) *Regulation, Crime and Freedom*. Aldershot: Ashgate.

Braithwaite, J. and Fisse, B. (1987) 'Self-Regulation and the control of corporate crime' in C.D. Shearing and P.C. Stenning (eds), *Private Policing*. Beverly Hills: Sage, pp. 221–46.

Brown, P. (2001) 'Incinerator Breaches Go Unpunished. Poisonous chemicals pumped into atmosphere, report reveals' *The Guardian*, 22 May.

Brown, P. (2003) 'Pollution still pays as firms shrug off fine' *The Guardian*, 31 July.

Chibnall, S. (1977) *Law-and-Order News. An Analysis of Crime Reporting in the British Press*. London: Tavistock.

Clarke, M. (2000) *Regulation. The Social Control of Business Between Law and Politics*. London: Macmillan.

Cressey, D. (1989) 'The poverty of theory in corporate crime research' in F. Adler and W.S. Laufer (eds), *Advances in Criminological Theory*. New Brunswick, NJ: Transaction, pp. 31–55.

Coleman, J.S. (1987) 'Toward an Integrated Theory of White-Collar Crime', *American Journal of Sociology* 93: 406–39.

Croall, H. (1989) 'Who Is the White-Collar Criminal?' *British Journal of Criminology*, 29, (2); 157–75.

Environment Agency (2006) *Spotlight on Business. Environmental performance in 2006*, <http://publications.environment-agency.gov.uk/pdf/GEHO0707BMMX-e-e.pdf>.

Etzioni, A. (1993) 'The US Sentencing Commission on Corporate Crime: a critique' in G. Geis and P. Jesliow (eds), *White-Collar Crime. Special Issue of the Annals of the American Academy of Political and Social Science*. 525, January. Newbury Park, Ca: Sage.

Fooks, G. (1999) 'The Serious Fraud Office: policing the City or policing for the City?' paper presented to the British Criminology Conference, Liverpool.

Fooks, G. (2003) 'Contrasts in Tolerance: the Peculiar Case of Financial Regulation', *Contemporary Politics*, 9, (2): 127–42.

Friedrichs, D.O. (1992) 'White-Collar Crime and the Definitional Quagmire: a Provisional Solution', *Journal of Human Justice*, 3, (2): 5–21.

Geis, G. (1967) 'White-collar crime: the heavy electrical equipment anti-trust cases' in M. Clinard and R. Quinney (eds), *Criminal Behaviour Systems*. New York: Holt, Rinehart & Winston.

Geis, G. (1968) *White Collar Criminal: The Offender in Business and the Professions*. New York: Atherton Press.

Geis, G. (1996) 'A base on balls for white collar criminals' in D. Shichor and D.K. Sechrest (eds), *Three Strikes and You're Out. Vengeance as Public Policy*. Thousand Oaks, Ca: Sage.

Green, G.S. (1990) *Occupational Crime*. Chicago: Nelson Hall.

Gunningham, N. and Johnstone, R. (1999) *Regulating Workplace Safety. Systems and Sanctions*. Oxford: Oxford University Press.

Hawkins, K. (2002) *Law as Last Resort. Prosecution Decision-making in a Regulatory Agency*. Oxford: Oxford University Press.

Hills, S. (ed) (1987) *Corporate Violence. Injury and death for profit*. Totowa, NJ: Rowman & Littlefield.

Hopkins, M. (2002) 'Crimes Against Businesses: The Way Forward for Future Research', *British Journal of Criminology* 42, (4), 782–97.

Kagan, R. and Scholz, J. (1984) 'The Criminology of the Corporation and Regulatory Enforcement Strategies' in K. Hawkins and J. Thomas (eds), *Enforcing Regulation*. Boston: Kluwer-Nijhoff.

Lacey, N. (1995) 'Contingency and criminalisation' in I. Loveland (ed), *Frontiers of Criminality*. London: Sweet and Maxwell, pp. 1–27.

Lofquist, W.S. (1993) 'Organisational Probation and the US Sentencing Commission' in G. Geis and P. Jesilow (eds), *White Collar Crime. Special Issue of the Annals of the American Academy of Political and Social Science*. 525, January. Newbury Park, Ca: Sage.

Maguire, M. (1994) 'Crime Statistics, Patterns, and Trends: changing perceptions and their implications' in M. Maguire *et al.*, (eds), *The Oxford Handbook of Criminology*, pp. 233–91.

Meier, R.F. and Short, J.F. Jnr. (1995) 'The consequences of white-collar crime' in G. Geis *et al.* (eds), *White-Collar Crime. Classic and Contemporary Views* (3rd edn). New York: The Free Press, pp. 80–104.

Nelken, D. (1994) 'White-Collar Crime' in D. Nelken (ed), *White-Collar Crime*. Aldershot: Dartmouth.

Passas, N. (1990) 'Anomie and Corporate Deviance', *Contemporary Crises* 14: 157–78.

Pearce, F. (1976) *Crimes of the Powerful: Marxism, Crime and Deviance*. London: Pluto.

Pearce, F. and Tombs, S. (1990) 'Ideology, Hegemony and Empiricism: Compliance Theories of Regulation', *British Journal of Criminology* 30, (4): 423–43.

Pearce, F. and Tombs, S. (1998) *Toxic capitalism: corporate crime and the chemical industry*. Aldershot: Dartmouth.

Pearce, F. and Tombs, S. (2003) 'Multinational corporations, power and "crime"' in C. Sumner (ed) *The Blackwell Companion to Criminology*. Oxford: Blackwell, pp. 359–76.

Punch, M. (1996) *Dirty Business. Exploring Corporate Misconduct. Analysis and Cases*. London: Sage.

Punch, M. (2000) 'Suite Violence: Why Managers Murder and Corporations Kill', *Crime, Law and Social Change*, 33, 243–80.

Ruggiero, V. (1996) *Organized and Corporate Crime in Europe. Offers that can't be refused*. Aldershot: Dartmouth.

Schrager, L.S. and Short, J.F. (1977) 'Towards a Sociology of Organisational Crime', *Social Problems*, 25: 407–19.

Slapper, G. (2000) *Blood in the Bank. Social and Legal Aspects of Death at Work*. Aldershot: Ashgate.

Slapper, G. and Tombs, S. (1999) *Corporate Crime*. London: Longman.

Snider, L. (1991) 'The Regulatory Dance: Understanding Reform Processes in Corporate Crime', *International Journal of the Sociology of Law*, 19: 209–36.

Snider, L. (1993) *Bad Business. Corporate Crime in Canada*. Toronto: University of Toronto Press.

Snider, L. (2000) 'The Sociology of Corporate Crime: an Obituary. (Or, Whose Knowledge Claims Have Legs?)', *Theoretical Criminology*, 4, (2); 169–206.

Spalek, B. (2001) 'Policing the UK Financial System: the Creation of the "New" Financial Services Authority and its Approach to Regulation', *International Journal of the Sociology of Law*, 29, (1); 75–87.

Spalek, B. (2007) *Farepak Victims Speak Out: an exploration of the harms caused by the collapse of Farepak*. Centre for Crime and Justice Studies/Unison.

Sumner, C. (ed), *The Blackwell Companion to Criminology*. Oxford: Blackwell.

Sutherland, E. (1940) 'White-Collar Criminality', *American Sociological Review*, 5: 1–12.

Sutherland, E. (1945) 'Is "White-Collar Crime" Crime?' *American Sociological Review*, 10, 132–39.

Sutherland, E. (1983) *White-Collar Crime. The Uncut Version*, New Haven: Yale University Press.

Szockyj, E. and Fox, J.G. (eds) (1996) *Corporate Victimisation of Women*. Boston, Mass.: Northeastern University Press.

Taylor, I., Walton, P., and Young, J. (1973) *The New Criminology. For a Social Theory of Deviance*. London: RKP.

Tombs, S. (2002) 'Understanding Regulation? A Review Essay', *Social & Legal Studies*. 11, (1); 111–31.

Tombs, S. and Whyte, D. (2001) 'Media Reporting of Crime: Defining Corporate Crime Out of Existence?' *Criminal Justice Matters*, 43, Spring: 22–23.

Tombs, S. and Whyte, D. (eds) (2003) *Unmasking the Crimes of the Powerful: scrutinizing states ands corporations*. New York: Peter Lang.

Tombs, S. and Whyte, D. (2007) *Safety Crimes*. Cullompton: Willan.

Tombs, S. and Williams, B. (2007) 'Corporate Crime and its Victims' in B. Stout, J. Yates, and B. Williams, (eds), *Applied Criminology*. London: Sage.

Tweedale, G. (2000) *Magic Mineral to Killer Dust. Turner & Newall and the Asbestos Hazard*. Oxford: Oxford University Press.

Unison/Centre for Corporate Accountability (2002) *Safety Last? The Under-Enforcement of Health and Safety Law*. London: Unison/Centre for Corporate Accountability.

Vaughan, D. (1992) 'The Macro-Micro Connection in White-Collar Crime Theory' in K. Schlegel, and D. Weisburd (eds) *White-Collar Crime Reconsidered*. Boston: Northeastern University Press, pp. 124–145.

Vaughan, D. (1996) *The Challenger Launch Decision. Risky Technology, Culture, and Deviance at NASA*. Chicago: Chicago University Press.

Virta, E. (1999) 'A thief is a criminal who has not had enough time to start a company' in A. Laitinen and V. Olgiati (eds), *Crime-Risk-Security*. Turku: University of Turku, pp. 91–128.

Waring, D. and Weisburd, E., with Chayet, E.F. (2001) *White-Collar Crime and Criminal Careers*. Cambridge: Cambridge University Press.

White, R. (2003) 'Environmental Issues and the Criminological Imagination', *Theoretical Criminology*, 7, (4), 483–506.

Whyte, D. (1999) *Power, Ideology and the Management of Safety in the UK Offshore Oil Industry*. Unpublished PhD Thesis, Liverpool John Moores University.

Whyte, D. (2004) 'Regulation and Corporate Crime' in J. Muncie and D. Wilson (eds), *Student Handbook of Criminal Justice*. London: Cavendish.

Woolfson, C., Foster, J., and Beck, M. (1996) *Paying for the Piper: Capital and Labour in Britain's Offshore Oil Industry*, London: Mansell.

Woolmar, C. (2001) *Broken Rails. How Privatisation Wrecked Britain's Railways*. London: Aurum Press.

NOTES

1. Most work on corporate crime continues to emanate from the US, and many textbooks in this area understandably reflect this. This chapter aims to prioritize examples and work that derive from the UK.

2. See also 'BCCI's Criminality', section 4 of *The BCCI Affair. A Report to the Committee on Foreign Relations, United States Senate*, by Senator John Kerry and Senator Hank Brown (December 1992, 102d Congress 2d Session Senate Print 102–40), available at <http://fas.org/irp/congress/1992_rpt/bcci/04crime.htm>. This document further alleges: BCCI's support of terrorism, arms trafficking, and the sale of nuclear technologies; its management of prostitution; its commission and facilitation of income tax evasion, smuggling, and illegal immigration; and its illicit purchases of banks and real estate.

3. There are, of course, qualifications to this general observation. Notable exceptions are to be found within critical or radical criminologies. Further, one of the key contributions of feminist criminologies has been precisely to make more visible the myriad ways in which social institutions in general, and both the criminal justice system and 'malestream' criminologies in particular, obscure the peculiar experiences of women. Criminologically, this has particularly raised understandings of the peculiar (and often private) victimization of women, and the differential treatment of women through the criminal justice system. Feminist criminologies have had important impacts upon criminological theorizing and criminal justice practice.

4. *Wall Street* illustrates how the personality traits that helped to make Gecko a success were the same characteristics that allowed him, through a combination of intention and negligence, to break the law.

5. This is also one example of 'techniques of neutralization', which are crucial to understanding motivation in the context of corporate crime: see Box, 1983: 54–7; Slapper and Tombs, 1999: 118–23.

6. These are, of course, generalizations: there are important national differences in enforcement strategies (Pearce and Tombs, 1998: 229–45) and important differences in enforcement strategies across different spheres of regulatory activity (Snider, 1991).

14 Understanding organized crime

Paddy Rawlinson

INTRODUCTION

Over the past decade, the topic of organized crime has become an increasingly popular addition to criminology courses in the UK, previously attracting little more than a passing reference. Its growing recognition as a subject for serious academic discussion has, in part, been provoked by a growing awareness of organized crime on an international scale, what is sometimes referred to as 'transnational' organized crime (TOC). Despite the so-called 'sexy' nature of the topic, organized crime is a complex and thought-provoking phenomenon, which too often finds itself subject to exaggeration and over-simplification. The chapter addresses some of the problems of understanding organized crime. It examines the major debates on definition and the role played by the media in influencing the public's perception of a form of crime rarely encountered directly. The chapter also includes a brief history of organized crime in the US, the country which has arguably exerted the greatest impact on crime-fighting strategies worldwide. The section on transnational organized crime considers how global changes, such as the collapse of communism, have affected the nature of organized crime and the way policy makers and law enforcement respond to it. Finally, the section on theory and methods discusses the various criminological explanations of organized crime and the different ways in which data are collected on a particularly elusive form of offending.

BACKGROUND

There can be few subjects, which provoke so much excitement and debate as that of organized crime. On the one hand there are the popular media representations American gangsters, epitomized by the Corleone family of *The Godfather* trilogy or the angst-ridden mobster, Tony Soprano, of the award-winning TV series, and on the other the 'evil' figures behind human smuggling, drug trafficking, and international crime rings, which according to official discourse threaten the national security of civilized countries. The hugely diverse perceptions of organized crime make it difficult to get a handle on the reality of its operations, its structure, and the actual threat it poses.

In such an environment sound academic research takes on a highly significant role. However, criminologists who study organized crime are faced with problems less apparent or even absent from other areas of criminology. For obvious reasons data collection can prove difficult, although there are a growing number of ethnographies on the subject which serve to complement the more usual source of police records and media reports (Hobbs, 1988; Polsky, 1969; Rawlinson, 2007). Nor is it easy to define what exactly is meant by 'organized crime', a term which has become synonymous with other expressions such as mafia, criminal cartels, gangsters, the mob, to name but a few. Further complications arise when ethnic designations are used, for example, La Cosa Nostra, the Russian Mafia, the Yakuza, Triads, Yardies. These difficulties aside, the diverse activities conducted by organized crime provide a broad field of enquiry, some of which is relatively under-researched. These activities include illegal arms and drugs trafficking, people smuggling, the sex trade, protection rackets, contraband, the human organ trade, vehicle theft, loan sharking, fraud, and money-laundering. These sundry activities have broadened the study of organized crime beyond a criminological framework, often demanding a multidisciplinary approach. Collaborative research can involve political scientists, historians, economists, as well as security analysts, and even former Cold War specialists. The definitional ambiguities of the term 'organized crime' (see section below) also encourage an intra-disciplinary approach, incorporating other areas of criminology such as corporate crime (see Chapter 13), white-collar crime, state crime (see Chapter 1), and terrorism (see Chapter 15).

Against such a varied and contentious background the promise by policy makers to target organized crime primarily requires a greater effort in understanding the nature of this particularly elusive beast. The slow response by the academic community to engage in the study of organized crime prompted the comment by two American criminologists that: 'the field remains essentially in a state of intellectual atrophy ...' (Rogovin and Martens, 1997: 36). Whether this statement still remains the case is debatable. The recent participation of a new generation of academics, especially those indigenous to the so-called hot-spots of organized crime, particularly in Eastern Europe and Russia, would suggest the emergence of a renewed intellectual energy in understanding organized crime and its role in society (Markina, 1998; Backman, 1998). Cross-cultural collaborations also promise significant advances in the field. The recent surge of interest in organized crime, especially given its current high profile political status, provides greater opportunities for research. However this should not blind those who study organized crime to the possible constraints of officially funded projects which demand tangible policy outcomes in favour of, as opposed to alongside, more critically oriented independent research. As the rest of the chapter explains, the study of organized crime has raised as many questions as it has provided answers, not just in terms of the subject itself but as a critique of these so-called 'experts' who study and work with it: academics, officials, and practitioners alike.

What is this 'thing' called organized crime?

Legal definitions

Organized crime is broadly regarded as economically motivated offending involving more than two people. Unlike legally defined crimes or predicate offences such as murder, drug trafficking, money-laundering, and so on which refer quite clearly to specific proscribed *acts*, any legal description of organized crime tends to be confined to its *structures* and *relationships* and the general nature of the crimes committed by such associations.

Article 2 of the United Nations Convention Against Transnational Organized Crime states that an organized criminal group must have at least three members operating in concert to commit a serious crime as part of an internally structured organization which has been in existence over a period of time preceding and subsequent to the commission of the criminal act (United Nations, 2000). Such a definition, while it provides a general framework of understanding, can in practice undermine effective law enforcement responses. According to this definition an organized crime group can include anything from a four-person, low-level racketeering outfit to highly complex, international networks engaged in human smuggling or money laundering. Different criminal configurations will place varying pressures on police time and resources even though all are categorized as organized crime, leaving the police to prioritize cases according to the perceived threat at their local level, priorities which need not coincide with those of governments. The Netherlands-based 'Fijnaut Group' contests the notion of stable structures and instead provides a working definition, which accounts for fluid networks in what it terms 'criminal 'co-operatives'. This revision of orthodox definitions was prompted by years of failing crime control strategies, which had pursued organized crime groups according to non-existent hierarchical structures (Klerks, 2003).

Criminologists disunited

While there is a general consensus that organized crime involves a *multiplicity of actors*, the nature of its structures and operations, its relationship with legitimate bodies, and the extent of its impact on society are just some of the fiercely debated issues in academic circles, particularly in the US. The subject of terrorism, society's current other *bête noir*, displays similar difficulties in terms of definition and understanding (see Chapter 15). Certain interpretations, however, have dominated the official view. Alien conspiracy theory, which sees organized crime as an ethnically defined phenomenon, and comprising hierarchical, monolithic structures, was given its first official airing in the early 1950s by the Kefauver Committee (see below). The findings of the committee were to make the term 'organized crime' and 'Mafia' synonymous and set the tone for US crime control strategies for decades. Its oversimplification of the organized crime problem through focusing on particular ethnic groups, a practice which has continued beyond the labelling of American-Italians and now includes Mexicans, Russians, the Chinese, and so on, helped to maintain the authority of the dominant values of American society by locating organized criminality *outside* the mainstream, that is, as alien elements conspiring to attack these values. This interpretation was largely endorsed by Donald Cressey (1969) whose *Theft of a Nation* was to provide academic credibility for Mafia-based theories.

It is hardly surprising that many counter this view. The criticisms levelled at alien conspiracy theory reflect the diversity of opinion on how to define organized crime per se. Some see this as a convenient political smokescreen used by governments as a means of detracting from failing policies or flawed ideologies (Smith, 1975; Albanese, 1989). Albini writes that 'rather than blame themselves for their desire to use drugs in the 1960s, Americans found it easier and more exciting to blame those foreigners from Sicily who brought the Mafia to America and addicted a drug-virgin country' (Albini, 1997a: 69). Others argue that capitalism helps to deflect attention away from corrupt political and economic institutions, some of which willingly collaborate with organized crime (Block, 1993; Chambliss, 1988; Woodiwiss, 1993). The hierarchical, monolithic structure attributed to Mafia organizations are also frequently refuted. Ianni and Ianni's (1972) study found the mafia to be family-based networks, active both in illegal and legal business. Gambetta's work on the protection industry, the major focus of the Sicilian (Mafia?), identifies the protagonist(s) as 'a single person or a network of more or less organized agents' (1993: 17). Even if one acknowledges the predominance of minority ethnic members of organized crime groups, particularly in a multicultural society such as the US, some critics of alien conspiracy argue that it is not ethnic origin or nationality which determines criminality, but the socio-economic exclusion that immigrants often face because of their unfamiliarity with the dominant language and culture. As legal access to opportunities is blocked or made more difficult, organized crime, described famously by Bell (1962) as 'the queer ladder of social mobility', provides an alternative means to success and integration. In other words, organized crime can be an alternative means of acquiring the requisite pecuniary success that is often required to get on and move up socially for those who do not have access to conventional means.

Business as usual

Organized crime is 'the ongoing activities of those collectively engaged in production, supply and financing for illegal markets in goods and services' (Gill, 2002: 198). While an obvious generalization, the essential motivation of those engaged in organized crime is clear: business. Business takes many forms and involves different actors, but irrespective of which side of the legal divide it lies, its main preoccupation is seeking profit-making opportunities, in other words, enterprise. Even when organized crime is engaged in more politically motivated activities, such as the corruption of government officials, these relationships are underscored by entrepreneurial goals. However, academic opinion tends to be divided on the impact of these goals for society as a whole, and on whether the legal-illegal divide is too simplistic a way of representing a fluid, and often legally ambiguous world of commercial relations which link licit business and the underworld (Naylor, 1997).

As a provider of illegal goods and services, including drugs, a range of contraband, child pornography, human trafficking to name but a few, organized crime can be argued as primarily a *reactive* phenomenon, exploiting gaps in a diverse and lucrative market. Its clientele are, for the most part, 'ordinary' folk who seek, or are forced to seek, alternative routes to satisfying needs unmet or proscribed by the legislatures of the countries they inhabit or pass through (Caiden, 1985). In many cases clients are also victims, obliged or enticed into cooperation, as in the trafficking of women and children (Goodey, 2002). In areas of economic decline and acute social inequality organized crime can provide alternative employment and a reinstatement of status, a situation currently common in former communist states (Varese, 2001; Rawlinson, 2001). However, this tends to assume that organized crime is confined in its reach to the lower socio-economic stratum of society and that poverty is the major impetus for participation and victimization. Edwin Sutherland's famous study of white collar crime, looked at offences committed by those in employment, thus refuting the notion that crime was primarily caused by poverty, going as far as to describe crimes committed by corporations as being synonymous with organized crime (Sutherland, 1983). It was not just corporate crime he labelled in this way, but also professional theft, which he regarded as 'organized in the sense that it is a system in which informal unity and reciprocity may be found' (Sutherland, 1937: 209). Despite refocusing the debate onto crimes of the powerful, Sutherland has justifiably been accused of theoretical and definitional ambiguity, which can sometimes serve to undermine the importance of his work.

More recently, some studies have argued that even some *legal* corporate activity should be regarded as organized crime insofar as its social and economic impact is as harmful, if not more, than that of organized crime (Slapper and Tombs, 1999; Pearce, 1976). These approaches focus attention away from the legal definition of criminality and instead regard the actions of corporate business according to the harm they inflict, such as the impoverishment or marginalization of vulnerable communities, particularly in Third World countries. Ruggiero's work locates criminality, including that of an organized nature, in any economic environment, but more importantly, it emphasizes that different environments provide different motivations for illegal acts. What he terms 'causality of contraries' explains why organized crime can thrive at any level of society, from the boardroom to the ghetto, that is, wherever opportunities exist. Importantly, he recognizes that opportunities for illicit behaviour more frequently arise for high-level legal business. While at one level of organized crime 'the absence of the State encourages the development of enterprise type criminality' on another level 'access to the political and business financial elite has determined, rather than discouraged, the development of organized crime' (Ruggiero, 2000: 9).

The following brief history of organized crime in America, the country which has undoubtedly exerted (and continues to) the greatest influence on worldwide perceptions of organized crime and whose crime-fighting policies are being exported as enthusiastically as its Hollywood imagery, demonstrates the dangerous ambiguities and political minefields of a much misunderstood and misrepresented criminological genre.

REVIEW QUESTIONS

1 Why is organized crime so difficult to define?

2 How far is the ethnic label useful in our understanding of the term 'mafia'?

3 Discuss some of the similarities and differences between licit business and organized crime.

Organized crime in the USA

When America, home of legendary crime bosses Al Capone and John Gotti, and films such as *Scarface*, *The Godfather*, *Carlito's Way*, and *Goodfellas* pronounces on organized crime, the world listens. The USA can boast over a hundred years of documented and colourful history of organized crime, a cornucopia of resources available to the English-speaking world. These resources and the story they tell reveal not just the American experience of organized crime, but also, as Alan Block notes, 'the social history of the US', of which 'organized crime is but a part'. (1994: 57). Official and fictional representations of organized crime provide an insight into the political, social, and economic climate of the country, its insecurities, real and imagined.

Arguably the origins of organized crime in America began in the pioneer days of the market, as a brutal form of capitalism conducted by nineteenth-century so-called 'robber barons', speculators, and railroad owners such as Drew and Vanderbilt, who with little regard for the law, ruthlessly pursued the creation of their business empires. Organized crime as gangsterism was especially prevalent in the mid-1800s with the political gangster antics of the Tammany Hall bosses who offered protection to Irish immigrants in return for votes. As we have seen above, how we define has an impact on perception, and in this case historical location. However, few would dispute that, while by no means the first instance of organized crime, it was the famous Volstead Act of 1919, more commonly known as Prohibition, that became the defining moment of the emergence of organized crime in America. In this new black market for illegal alcohol, Italian immigrants were able to employ their winemaking skills to satisfy the unquenchable thirst of 'dry' America. This lucrative industry eventually shifted the balance of underworld power, placing ethnic Italians at the centre of organized criminal activity during, and for many years after, the Prohibition years.

The profusion of criminal activity in cities such as Chicago was to provide material for some of the first ethnographic studies of organized crime in the US, most notably Thrasher's *The Gang* (1927) and Landesco's *Organized Crime in Chicago* (1968). This burgeoning of criminal entrepreneurship elicited sober and restrained official responses which recognized the source of much of the problem and genuinely desired to address an actual rather than imagined problem. The Wickersham Commission, set up by President Herbert Hoover to look at, amongst other things, the proliferation of organized crime, concluded in 1931 that the Volstead Act was unenforceable and largely responsible for the criminogenic environment. Significantly, it revealed misconduct in the criminal justice system across the country, political corruption, and, as far as illicit entrepreneurship was concerned, 'bound the businessman-gone-wrong and gangsters into a single category of organized crime' (Smith, 1991). Two years later the Volstead Act was repealed. The Commission's findings were to have little or no impact on future official investigations.

The Kefauver Committee, formed two decades later to look into interstate gambling, could hardly have been more different in tone and content. It concluded that there existed a national and centrally run crime syndicate of Italian origin (Kefauver, 1951). Published during the height of the McCarthy anti-communist drive, the findings sat easily with a nation already fearful of Soviet communism. It was the McClellan hearings of 1963, which developed the Mafia theory further and provided the material for Cressey's (1969) highly influential *Theft of a Nation*. Central to the hearings (which were televised) was the confession of small-time gangster Joseph Valacchi who spoke of La Cosa Nostra (Our Thing) as bureaucratically structured crime families, run by a central organization known as the Commission. This interpretation became inculcated into policy responses to organized crime despite the methodologically unsound basis of giving such disproportionate credence to the testimony of one man (Block, 1994; Albini, 1997b). In 1970 the Racketeer Influenced and Corrupt Organizations Act, known as RICO, became the major legislative tool in fighting organized crime, owing much to Cressey's work. It made provision for prosecutors to try in one courtroom a number of defendants and their crimes, gave longer sentences for organized crime offences, and allowed the seizure of the accused's assets. While it can boast trophies such as crime bosses Tony Salerno and John Gotti, RICO's general effectiveness as a deterrent against organized crime is debatable. Nevertheless, it has become a global model for legislation against organized crime.

In the 1980s the US Government focused its attention more narrowly on organized crime and the illicit drugs business. The 'war' on drugs was to synthesize domestic and foreign policies and change the balance of power in the American underworld. The drugs war became a politically expedient means of engaging in an invasive foreign policy, under the guise of anti-drug-trafficking operations, in Central and South America (Bullington, 1993). It also allowed the US to export its law enforcement policies on drugs, organized crime, and other related areas to less experienced countries, thus creating a pan-American global police force (see below, Transnational Organized Crime). As far as the American Mafia, or so-called La Cosa Nostra, were concerned, the growing drugs trade was rapidly sidelining it as other crime groups indigenous to drug-producing countries were able to carve out their own business networks in the US. 'By the later 1980s' writes Peter Reuter, 'the traditional circuitous route for South-east Asian heroin, through Sicily, southern Italy or France, had primarily been replaced by direct importation, via the West coast, by Chinese and Vietnamese entrepreneurs. The Mafia proved helpless to deal with any of these incursions on its traditional territories' (1995: 91). Thus, crime control needed to refocus away from the traditional hierarchy image to complex international networks if it was to have any impact on the illegal drugs trade. The appropriate response was tardy. For too long US policies towards organized crime had been entrenched in the Kefauver-Cressey model. With the final collapse of communism in 1991 and the rapid dispersal of Russian-speaking crime groups beyond their hitherto confined national borders, the US found itself a new but ideologically familiar candidate for alien conspiracy theory, and with that stepped back into the limited horizons of the 1950s (Finckenauer and Waring, 1998).

Despite this, the impact of US policies towards organized crime has never been stronger. As new democracies emerge in Eastern Europe, crime control agencies, formerly the strong arm of the State, have been forced to confront soaring levels of organized crime and corruption, while lacking the proper resources, strategies, and expertise. Under communism it was not possible to officially acknowledge the existence of organized crime, designated as it was 'capitalist crime'. Years of 'turning a blind eye' together with the negative social consequences of the rapid transition to the free market mean that struggling law enforcement agencies are grateful for any form of support. The US recognized this need and was generous in its financial support and willingness to provide the necessary training. However, the vital questions concerning the success rate of US policies domestically and whether these policies are appropriate for transition states have hardly been asked, never mind answered.

REVIEW QUESTIONS

1 What impact did prohibition have on organized crime in the US?

2 What do the different findings of the Wickersham Commission and the Kefauver Committee tell us about political attitudes to organized crime?

Transnational organized crime

With the rapid advance of technology, the extension of the so-called 'free market', and the seismic political shifts which marked the end of the Cold War, national boundaries began to lose their significance. For example, the supranational state of the European Union, which is forever expanding, has provided a visa-free 'Schengen space' to allow the free movement of people and goods across a vast 'common' territory of member states. This world of shrinking frontiers, known as 'globalization' has had a huge impact on organized crime, providing opportunities for the expansion of cross-border criminal activity. Popularly referred to as 'transnational organized crime' (TOC) the notion of 'crime without frontiers' provides a challenge not only to crime control and policy institutions but, on a less tangible basis, challenges a number of preconceived ideas on legitimacy, victimization, security, human rights, and so on (Edwards and Gill, 2003).

Once again, the question of definition must be briefly examined, this time with the emphasis on the term 'transnational'. Meaning literally 'across nations', the term 'transnational' refers to crimes committed across a number of jurisdictions. But when looking at TOC in action and how it is policed, in contrast to that which we describe simply as 'organized crime', it has less credibility as a distinctive term. As Dick Hobbs (1998) points out, organized crime is 'local at all points', even when it involves international collaborations and operations. The execution of a crime, the demand for its goods and services, the victims, the benefactors, all these components exist in local space and not in a 'transnational' space. Even money laundering occurs at a series of 'local' points, albeit using 'virtual' means. So, too, is policing more likely to occur at a local level. Peter Stelfox, Head of Crime Investigation for Greater Manchester Police, is quite clear about the nature and response to so-called TOC:

> The fact remains, though, that most organized crime known about in England and Wales is not occurring in some virtual transnational domain, which remains un-policed in the absence of the sort of international treaties, legal instruments, data sharing protocols and cross-border policing structures … It is occurring, and being policed, locally. (Stelfox, 2003: 119)

In other words, while organized crime is increasingly exploiting opportunities offered on an international scale, such as drugs and human trafficking, these activities and the actors involved are locally based and will be affected by local conditions. The growing tragic trade in human trafficking, particularly involving women and children sold for sex, has arisen largely because of the increase in unemployment and poverty in certain parts of the world, and the rising demand for unprotected and underage sex in others (Hughes, 2002). Effective responses to this trade would include improving local socio-economic conditions as well as law enforcement strategies at the supply end.

The problem with TOC, even as an accepted concept, is that within its broad remit it throws up arbitrary designations of labels such as 'victim', or 'threat' which, in particular contexts, are reassigned contradicting meanings. A typical example of this is the issue of asylum seekers. The somewhat hysterical news coverage of so called large 'flows' of asylum seekers to Britain castigates a whole group of people who become threat rather than threatened. Further, because the majority of them have been forced to accept the services of organized crime as a means of escaping the often dire and dangerous conditions of their homeland, they form part of the broad TOC criminal picture, leaving them, as Goodey points out, in 'a "no man's land" between criminal and victim status' (2003: 168).

Policing TOC is now a major concern for many Western governments, especially in this post-September 11 era, experiencing, as it is, a greater convergence between international and national security interests. The intensification of collaboration between organized crime and terrorism, and indeed the suspected merging of these activities, has refocused attention onto centrally dispensed and intelligence-led policing. In the United Kingdom, the creation of the Serious and Organised Crime Agency (SOCA) in 2006, not only brought together various law enforcement bodies under a central umbrella, but demonstrates a trend in greater collaboration between the police and security services. There is concern, however, over the ambiguous status of such an organization which has clearly broken away from the traditions of transparency and accountability associated with policing in Britain (Harfield, 2006) as well as what appears to be 'the overall lack of fit between the new policing architecture and the reality it seeks to police' (Sheptycki, 2007: 59). Also in assessing the threat of TOC, the results of which will have a political impact as far as budgetary priorities are concerned, there are no standard methodologies for data collection (Burnham, 2003; Gregory, 2003). Different criminal codes, how and what types of crime are recorded and at what level all affect statistical outcomes and subsequent policy responses. And, of course, underlying all this is the ability and willingness of law enforcement agencies in the different jurisdictions to actually share intelligence and cooperate operationally.

The global environment of myriad cultures, different markets (regulated and unregulated), and numerous languages also requires structural adjustments by organized crime. Traditional hierarchies and centrally managed structures, if they ever existed, cannot survive in these conditions. The international market demands flexibility, short-term but effective collaborations, more complex forms of communication and safeguards against successful police operations, and the engagement of an increasing number of different actors in different locations. Networks are therefore less likely to attract attention and can be disassembled and reconstructed quickly and in different forms. The most powerful position is no longer the head or leader of a structure, but with those who occupy certain 'nodal' points within the networks which give them the greater overall knowledge of an operation or series of operations. For this reason social network analysis is becoming an important methodological tool amongst law enforcement agencies, allowing them to identify who liaises with whom and the status of these interactions in terms of inflicting the greatest damage on the criminal networks (Coles, 2001; Klerks, 2003).

None of this, however, explains why organized crime has become such a global phenomenon, or what and whom exactly it threatens. Piling more resources into law enforcement and creating more punitive legislation historically has had little or no effect on the growth of organized crime and, in some cases, has had the adverse consequence of impinging on human rights. Locating some of the causes, or explanations for the proliferation of organized crime, requires a more self-critical assessment of the values and ideologies, which dominate the global society we inhabit. Different motivations assume different standpoints; how we explain, in other words, will be coloured by what Dwight Smith (1991) refers to as 'the entry point' of our discussion or investigation. The following section presents some of these explanations.

REVIEW QUESTIONS

1 To what extent do you think that perceptions of and responses to terrorism are simply an extension of those employed to organized crime? You might find it helpful to consult Chapter 15.

2 What might the proliferation of organized crime on an international scale tell us about the development of 'global society'?

3 Is TOC a threat? If so, whom does it threaten and how?

Theories and methods

The varied nature of organized crime, reflecting as it does the different environments in which it operates, opens up a broad field of theoretical approaches. Alien conspiracy theory, which as we have seen provided a popular ground of understanding, has been widely criticized for its inherent prejudices and ideological slant. It has the useful political function, however, of creating cohesion amongst disparate groups in its ability to locate threat and danger in a distinctive 'other'. This serves the purpose of reinforcing and further legitimizing the dominant culture. Underlying this approach is the notion that those involved in organized crime have freely chosen this career path and are fully conscious of the nature and effects of their actions (although it could be argued that this approach takes a more positivist line by attributing higher rates of crime to among certain social-cultural groups). This typical classical approach to criminal behaviour, as with the majority of crime, sees solutions to the problem in punitive-based measures doled out by the State such as greater investment in crime control and harsher sentencing.

As a social phenomenon organized crime can also be explained in terms of a variety of relationships that the individual forges, or not, with society. Sutherland (1983) explains his white-collar criminal as one who has learned his deviant behaviour because it becomes more favourable to violate the law than to uphold it. What he terms differential association describes a learning process where individuals are 'socialized' into deviant behaviour through their contact with or observation of role models, or influential figures in their immediate or close environment. A person is more likely to join an organized crime group if members of his/her family or friends live and work in a criminal milieu. What this explanation does not shed light on is the origins of this association, that is, what type of conditions encourage criminal behaviour in the first place in the absence of role models to emulate. Strain theory looks more at the 'why' than the 'how'. Developed from the work of Robert Merton, strain theory explains criminal behaviour as a way of resolving the tension between achieving the dominant goals of society and the obstacles that prevent certain individuals and groups from achieving these goals legitimately. 'Crime and vice constitute a "normal" response to a situation where cultural emphasis upon pecuniary success has been absorbed, but where there is little access to conventional and legitimate means for becoming successful' (Merton, 1968: 198). Organized crime opens up possibilities for 'pecuniary success', particularly for those whose circumstances do not provide opportunities, such as education, good connections, employment and so on, to 'get on' in the world. This explains why marginalized sections of society, such as minority ethnic groups, might be more likely to engage in criminal enterprise (see Chapters 16 and 18).

Strain theorists stop short of criticizing the ideology of a society that places so much emphasis on wealth acquisition, the central feature of the Marxist critique. While Marx himself commented little on crime, Marxist criminologists recognize the underlying assumptions that there exists 'a relationship between economic conditions and the amount of crime' and that its manifestation is in fact a '"false consciousness", an adjustment to the society rather than an articulate striving to overcome it' (Taylor, Walton, and Young, 1973: 218). Marxist theory offers explanations for different levels of organized criminal activity, whether involving the working classes or the powerful elites. Pearce (1976) in *Crimes of the Powerful* notes that gangs in the US helped to contain trade union activity, operating at the behest of employers who wanted to keep wages low and work conditions basic. This is organized crime as servant rather than partner, he concludes. Taylor's analysis of Merton's work describes the very system of capitalism as criminogenic: 'The enormous value placed on money as a value itself—without regard to the intrinsic value of the activity through which pecuniary success had been realized—was accompanied by no moral or legal qualification on such success' (Taylor, 1994: 478). In other words, in a capitalist society the law and morality are subservient to the pursuit of wealth acquisition, a viewpoint echoed by the famous gangster Al Capone in his alleged comment to a journalist on the State of corruption of American society, 'Lady, no-one's on the legit'.

The functionalist view would regard the increase in organized crime as an indication of emerging pathologies within those societies in which it is seen to be a problem. While describing the existence of crime as normal to society, it was the level of crime (too much or too less) which Durkheim (see Chapter 4), the founding father of functionalism, regarded as the barometer for social cohesion and stability. The proliferation of organized crime in Russia after the break up of communism in 1991 was a classic indication of what Durkheim termed anomie, a state of lawlessness arising from the breakdown of social norms and the institutions that sustain them. The dramatic changes, such as the overnight move from a quasi-centralized to laissez-faire market and the collapse of communist state structures, left power vacuums which organized crime was quick to exploit, a pattern repeated in other transition states including South Africa, those in Eastern Europe, and those which were formerly part of the Soviet Union. Taking the functionalist paradigm a step further, there have been instances when organized crime has been seen to be an essential component of economic development. Echoing the role organized crime played in the containment of US trade unions, Luttwak attributes the success of much of Japan's building programme to the Yakuza (Japanese criminal groups) who employed 'their colourful repertoire of threats and vandalism' to encourage inert householders to sell their economically impractical plots of land (1995: 7). And in their report on the chaotic state of the Russian economy in the 1990s, the Organization for Economic Cooperation and Development (1995) wrote that 'a degree of criminal activity ... "could in a certain sense be thought of as providing a necessary service to business"'. This practical role of organized crime is, of course, only possible if, as Pearce observed, it remains subservient to the dominant structures.

Explaining organized crime is one thing, researching it is entirely another. Research into any areas of criminology is challenging, and even more so into the hidden and sometimes hazardous world of organized crime. A brief foray into how this research is carried out should simultaneously enlighten and dishearten.

REVIEW QUESTIONS

1 In your opinion which criminological theory best explains organized crime? Give reasons for your choice.

2 Discuss the differences between the functionalist approach to organized crime and the Marxist approach.

Madness in their methods

There are a number of ways of gathering information on organized crime: the most popular being media reports, police files, and ethnographic research. The quality of media reporting can vary enormously, from well researched articles and documentaries based on balanced interviews and all round impartiality, and occasionally, at the cost of a journalist's life, to hearsay and the frenzied hysteria so often found in the tabloids. Police reports can afford a valuable insight into the type of offences and persons involved in organized crime, though as Anderson warns, the remit of law enforcement agencies 'is to identify and prosecute violations of the law, rather than to provide data banks for social scientists' (1979: 147). This leaves us with the ethnographic approach, going out into the field and observing first hand. For the student of criminology, ethnographic research into organized crime makes interesting reading although, as with any methodology, this type of research has its flaws.

Ethnographic research (see Chapter 5) involves 'going out and seeing it for yourself'; in other words, leaving the comfort of the study or library and acquiring information from inside the group or community being researched. As a method of inquiry it has its origins in cultural anthropology but was adopted as a serious form of sociological research by the Chicago School in the 1920s and 1930s under Robert Park. Urban sociology, as it is referred to, is qualitative research combining theory and fieldwork. It is especially favoured when researching the social relationships of deviant groups (Hobbs and May, 1993). There are obvious potential pitfalls, however, in researching sensitive subjects, not least the responsibility of the researcher to those they are investigating (Lee, 1993) as well as the ethical considerations when the researcher has the option of becoming engaged in deviant activities as a means of continuing investigations (Whyte, 1943).

There is a growing literature on this type of research into organized crime. Landesco's (1968) study of organized crime in Chicago, Polsky's (1969) close encounters with pool-room hustlers, Ianni and Ianni's (1972) inclusion in the inner circle of the Lupollo crime family's social circle are all noteworthy examples of how first hand experience of the closed world of organized criminality can produce invaluable material. Nor has the subject matter deterred subsequent researchers. Hobbs' (1988) study of illegal entrepreneurship in London's East End, Rawlinson's (2001) work on organized crime in Moscow and St Petersburg, and Varese's (2001) study of protection rackets in Perm continue the tradition of ethnographic research across different time zones and varied geographies. 'Is it dangerous?' is a common and understandable, question. Hobbs refers to the murder of one researcher, Ken Pryce, who was looking into organized crime in the West Indian community in Britain (2000: 165). This fortunately is very much the exception. Collecting data on organized crime must have as top priority the security of the researcher and all of their contacts. Albini's work on organized crime in America led him to conclude that 'organized criminals, including my informants, couldn't care less what type of data academics usually collect' (1997a: 18). Academics are not out to expose organized criminals, and when they do get access to the underworld it tends to be on the conditions laid out by the criminals themselves. Does this colour the information received, the experiences observed? Undoubtedly, it must, thus emphasizing an important caveat for participant observers, that what you see is usually what you are allowed to get, unless of course, as some researchers have done, you do not reveal your academic identity, at which point the level of risk can increase dramatically.

So why engage in this type of research? Paradoxically, for the very reason that puts many people off: the inaccessibility of the topic and the abuses to which second- and third-hand data are subjected. Despite the possibility of unreliability and subjectivity, a danger in all types of research, there is arguably no better way of grasping the motivations and nuances of criminal society than 'being there'. Discussing the world of the illegal entrepreneur with its inhabitants in a London restaurant over a good meal and bottle of wine, as Ruggiero (2000) did for his work on this subject, can open doors to information and contacts that no official records or media reports ever could, even if it does put a strain on the liver and the wallet. While answers to our questions might not be forthcoming, more importantly we are provided with other questions, ones we might never have realized needed to be asked. And in the ambiguous arena of organized crime, this has to be an important part of developing a more realistic understanding of it.

CONCLUSION

Organized crime as a serious component of criminology courses is long overdue, as too is its inclusion in current academic debates within, and beyond, the discipline of criminology. It deserves particular attention at the beginning of the twenty-first century, not just because of its recent proliferation, but because its very presence challenges the values of the societies in which it finds so many opportunities for exploitation. There can be few areas of criminology in which the debate on definition is so enduring and which, even now, shows no sign of reaching an adequate consensus. This, in itself, should alert us to the dangers of simplistic explanations and categorizations, to the problems of ring fencing activities and labelling them 'good' or 'bad' according to who is conducting them. Organized crime, we could argue, effectively reflects back on society the inadequacies and ills contained with it. Organized crime is not the pathology itself, but a symptom of it.

The definition debate also indicates how amorphous are the boundaries within which we surround other areas of criminology which are the subject of separate chapters in this edited collection. Organized crime shares common ground with terrorism, violent crime, corporate crime; its huge inclusive remit embraces drugs and alcohol, 'race' and ethnicity; it feeds off social exclusion and marginalization and has been influential in setting the agenda for a whole range of responses to crime. And yet despite this mutability it expresses features that are exclusive to this type of offending, most notably the economic drive underlying the actions of a number of people who have come together, whether as a clearly structured group or a complex, flexible network, to exploit and profit from discovered opportunities. In some cases, it can even create these opportunities itself.

Organized crime has had a rich history particularly in the US, which continues to exert a strong influence, not just on perceptions of organized crime but also on crime control strategies to contain it. Since the end of the Cold War the assumed status of the US as 'global policeman' has intensified this authoritative stance. Unfortunately, the predilection of a number of US administrations towards, what Hofstadter (1966) refers to as 'the paranoid style of American politics', has evolved a conspiratorial slant on organized crime. A number of successful Hollywood films have been made on the back of this monolithic, hierarchically structured, ethnic Italian Mafia image of organized crime, guaranteeing a large audience for this particular version. Not surprisingly, many criminologists have countered this view, and while there is no consensus on the definition of organized crime, there is general agreement that the alien conspiracy image is not appropriate and that greater emphasis should be placed on its entrepreneurial nature. The diverse aspects of organized crime as business have brought into focus, especially from a critical criminological perspective, the relationships between licit and illicit enterprise. The mutual benefits evident in some of these collaborations call into question the nature of legal business and demand a deeper critique of the economic status quo.

Operating across countries, on a transnational level, organized crime is able to exploit inequalities and injustices, which are increasingly in evidence as negative fall-out from globalization. Despite the ability of organized criminals to extend their links internationally, the actual implementation of their activities is at the local level. To effectively respond to organized crime, therefore, law enforcement should operate on a number of levels and not rely overly on intelligence-led centralized forms of policing. Further, crime control agencies have not been able to adapt at the same speed, finding themselves caught up in political and financial straitjackets, as well as being hindered by traditional notions of what constitutes organized crime, though the latter is less of an issue as law enforcement adopts a broader and more realistic understanding of the problem.

Organized crime offers a challenge to practitioner and academic alike. For the student of criminology it demands a relinquishing of commonplace notions of crime and a willingness to think 'outside the box'. In some cases this will involve engaging in debates over the values and systems that have become integral to the way we live, an exercise that can be as disquieting as it can prove groundbreaking. For if, indeed, organized crime is but symptomatic of more entrenched problems in society at large it requires those who study it to look behind and beyond the symptom. Judge Falcone, Italy's most famous investigator into the Mafia's distinct brand of organized crime wrote: '... if we want to fight the Mafia organization efficiently, we must not transform it into a monster or think of it as an octopus or cancer. We must recognize that it resembles us' (1993: 70). It pays to take heed of a man who had first-hand experience of organized crime, and was determined to bring a genuine understanding to the criminal phenomenon he dedicated his life to and died confronting.

QUESTIONS FOR DISCUSSION

1 Why do you think organized crime is so difficult to police? What new approaches could you suggest to address the problem?

2 Describe the character of any fictional mobster you might have read about or seen in films or on television. Why do you think the author/director created them in this particular way?

3 What are the advantages and disadvantages of transferring perceptions of organized crime and crime control strategies across cultures?

4 Should the actions of corporate business be compared to those of organized crime if, as a consequence of legal corporate activity, social or other harms result?

5 In the chapter much of the discussion has been dedicated to exploring how to define organized crime. Why, if at all, is it important to try and provide an appropriate definition?

GUIDE TO FURTHER READING

Ryan, P.J. and Rush, G.E. (eds) (1997) *Understanding Organized Crime in Global Perspective: A Reader.* California: Sage Publications.

This is a perfect introduction to American perceptions of organized crime and includes wide ranging debates about the nature of organized crime and how different American administrations have responded to it. Its contributors include some of the leading US specialists on organized crime.

Edwards, A. and Gill, P. (eds) (2003) *Transnational Organized Crime: Perspectives on Global Security*. London: Routledge.

One of the first books published in Britain dedicated solely to transnational organized crime. Its importance lies in the fact that it contains contributions from practitioners as well as academics from a number of different specialist backgrounds.

Hobbs, D. (1988) *Doing the Business*. Oxford: Clarendon Press.

One of the classic texts on professional crime in the UK based on ethnographic research into illegal business in the East End. Hobbs not only provides a unique insight into the penumbral world of business and informal relations between the police and the criminal fraternity, but describes the rewards and problems (the latter sometimes with wry humour) of ethnographic research.

Howard Journal of Criminal Justice (Special Edition on Organized Crime), edited by Michael Levi. 37/4, 1998.

This special edition brings together a variety of perspectives on organized crime, including money-laundering, fraud, police strategies, media representations, and geographies written by academics and practitioners.

Ruggiero, V. (2000) *Crime and Markets: Essays in Anti-Criminology*. Oxford: Oxford University Press.

Ruggiero's essays look at criminal activities within licit and illicit markets in a number of European countries. He discusses the 'causality of contraries', the notion that this type of crime is motivated by different causes involving a whole range of actors. This is an essential text for a critical perspective on the amorphous world of 'organized crime'.

Wright, A. (2006) *Organised Crime*, Cullompton: Willan

This is an excellent text for anyone wishing to read in greater depth many of the themes touched on in this chapter. Wright tackles a wide range of issues, from the thorny problem of definition to policing, the political economy of organized crime, its transnational dimensions and a chapter on the history and perceptions of organized crime in Britain. Probably the best 'first stop' text around for the British reader.

WEB LINKS

http://www.iasoc.net

International Association for the Study of Organized Crime. This is aimed at academics and professionals. It includes the latest news on organized crime issues, reviews of publications on the subject, and a members' list with their areas of expertise.

http://www.organized-crime.de

Run by Klaus von Lampe, an academic based in the US, this website provides a wealth of information on organized crime, including academic and official definitions and other links to organized crime topics. It also alerts the user to recent publications on the subject, the latest conferences, and book reviews.

http://www.soca.gov.uk

This website provides up-to-date information on the work of the UK Serious and Organised Crime Agency. Its annual threat assessment provides a detailed description of the perceived scale and responses to different criminal issues, including the latest statistics and definitions of activities related to organized crime.

http://www.unodc.org/unodc/en/organized-crime/index.html

The official UN website for organized crime, policing, and other related areas. It provides a global view of strategies to fight transnational organized crime and is a useful starting point for investigating linked activities such as human and drug trafficking.

http://www.yorku.ca/nathanson

The Nathanson Centre for the Study of Organized Crime and Corruption is one of the leading research centres for this subject. It provides a wide range of perspectives on organized crime and related subjects.

OTHER RECOMMENDED SOURCES

The following is a list of personal favourites, media depictions of the criminal underworld that do not succumb to the usual over-dramatization of many Hollywood blockbusters. The strength of each is the social and personal context in which the main protagonists are placed.

The Sopranos HBO.

Shown on Channel 4. A hugely successful television series, which tells the story of Tony Soprano, a middle-aged crime boss, who struggles to manage family traumas, work problems, and his own neuroses.

Carlito's Way (1993) Director, Brian de Palma. Universal Studios.

A former drug-dealer, Carlito Brigante, attempts to go straight on his release from prison, but finds himself getting dragged deeper back into the only life he has ever known.

A Bronx Tale (1993) Director, Robert de Niro, HBO.

Narrated by the adult Calogero Anello, he tells of his childhood and adolescence as an Italian-American in the Bronx during the 1960s, and the effect that his father and the boss of the local mob had on his life.

Goodfellas (1990) Director, Martin Scorsese, Warner Studios.

Based on the novel *Wiseguys* by Nicolas Pileggi, the film tells the story of real-life gangster, Henry Hill, whose increasing cocaine dependency leads him from successful 'entrepreneur' to desperation and a life-saving Witness Protection Programme.

REFERENCES

Albanese, J. (1989) *Organized Crime in America* (2nd edn). Cincinnati: Anderson.

Albini, J. (1997a) 'The Mafia and the Devil' in P. Ryan G. and Rush (eds) *Understanding Organized Crime in Global Perspective: A Reader*. California. Sage Publications.

Albini, J. (1997b) Donald Cressey's contributions to the study of organized crime: an evaluation, in P. Ryan and G. Rush (eds) *Understanding Organized Crime: in Global Perspective: A Reader*. California: Sage Publications.

Anderson, A. (1979) *The Business of Organized Crime: a Cosa Nostra Family*. Stanford: Hoover Institution Press.

Backman J. (1998) *The Inflation of Crime in Russia: Paradoxes of a Threat Around the Baltic Sea*. Paper given at a seminar organized by the Scandinavian Research Council for Criminology. Espoo, Finland (no pages given).

Bell, D. (1962) *The End of Ideology*. New York: P.F. Collier.

Block, A. (1993) 'Defending the mountaintop: a campaign against environmental crime' in F. Pearce and M. Woodiwiss (eds) *Global Crime Connections*. Basingstoke: MacMillan.

Block, A. (1994) *Space, Time and Organized Crime*. New Brunswick: Transaction.

Bullington, B. (1993) 'All about Eve: the many faces of US drug policy' in F. Pearce and M. Woodiwiss (eds) *Global Crime Connections*. Basingstoke: MacMillan.

Burnham, B. (2003) 'Measuring transnational organized crime' in A. Edwards and P. Gill (eds) *Transnational Organized Crime: Perspectives on Global Security*. London: Routledge.

Caiden, G. (1985) 'Perspectives on organized crime' in H. Alexander and G. Caiden (eds) *The Politics of Organized Crime*. Massachusetts, Lexington.

Chambliss, W. (1988) *On the Take: From Petty Crooks to Presidents*. Bloomington: Indiana University Press.

Coles, N. (2001) 'It's Not What You Know—It's Who You Know That Counts: Analysing Serious Crime Groups as Social Networks', *British Journal of Criminology*, 41.

Cressey, D. (1969) *Theft of the Nation: The Structure and Operations of Organized Crime in America*. New York: Harper & Row.

Edwards, A. and Gill, P. (eds) (2003) *Transnational Organized Crime: Perspectives on Global Security*. London: Routledge.

Falcone, G. (1993) *The Truth about the Mafia*. London: Warner Books.

Finckenauer, J. and Waring, E. (1998) *Russian Mafia in America*. Boston: Northeastern University Press.

Gambetta, D. (1993) *The Sicilian Mafia: The Business of Private Protection*. Massachusetts: Harvard University Press.

Gill, P. (2002) 'Organized crime' in E. McLaughlin and J. Muncie (eds) *The Sage Dictionary of Criminology*. London: Sage.

Goodey, J. (2002) 'Whose insecurity? organized crime, its victims and the EU' in A. Crawford *Crime and Insecurity*. Cullompton: Willan Publishing.

Goodey, J. (2003) 'Recognising organized crime's victims: The case of sex trafficking in the EU' in A. Edwards and P. Gill (eds) *Transnational Organized Crime: Perspectives on Global Security*. London: Routledge.

Gregory, F. (2003) 'Classify, report and measure: The UK Organized Crime Notification Scheme' in A. Edwards and P. Gill (eds) *Transnational Organized Crime: Perspectives on Global Security*. London: Routledge.

Harfield, C. (2006) 'Soca: A Paradigm Shift in British Policing', *British Journal of Criminology*, 46, (4): 743–761.

Hobbs, D. (1988) *Doing the Business*. Oxford: Clarendon Press.

Hobbs D. (1998) 'Going down the Glocal: The Local Context of Organized Crime', *Howard Journal*, 37/4, 407–22.

Hobbs, D. (2000) Researching serious crime in R. King and E. Wincup (eds) *Doing Research on Crime and Justice*. Oxford: Oxford University Press.

Hobbs, D. and May, T. (eds) (1993) *Interpreting the Field-Accounts of Ethnography*. Oxford: Oxford University Press.

Hofstadter, R. (1966) *The Paranoid Style in American Politics and Other Essays*. London: Cape.

Hughes, D. (2002) *Trafficking for Sexual Exploitation: The Case of the Russian Federation*. IOM International Organization for Migration, Migration Research Series, No. 7.

Ianni, F. and Ianni, E. (1972) *A Family Business: Kinship and Social Control in Organized Crime*. London: Routledge & Kegan Paul.

Kefauver, E. (1951) *Crime in America*. New York: Doubleday.

Klerks, P. (2003) 'The network paradigm applied to criminal organizations: theoretical nitpicking or a relevant doctrine for investigators? Recent developments in the Netherlands' in A. Edwards and P. Gill (eds) *Transnational Organized Crime: Perspectives on Global Security*. London: Routledge.

Landesco, J. (1968) *Organized Crime in Chicago*. Chicago: University of Chicago Press.

Lee, R. (1993) *Doing Research on Sensitive Topics*. London: Sage.

Luttwak, E. (1995) 'Does the Russian mafia deserve the Nobel prize for economics?' *London Review of Books*, 3 August.

Markina, A. (1998) 'Organized crime in Estonia: a national and international issue' in K. Aromaa (ed) *The Baltic Region: Insights in Crime and Control*, Scandinavian Studies in Criminology, Vol. 15. Oslo: Pax Forlag A/S.

Merton, R. (1968) *Social Theory and Social Structure*. New York: Free Press.

Naylor, R.T. (1997) 'Mafias, Myths, and Markets: On the Theory and Practice of Enterprise Crime', *Transnational Organized Crime*, 3/3: 1–45.

Organisation for Economic Cooperation and Development (1995) 'Russian economy in line for boom' in *The European* 5–11, October.

Pearce, F. (1976) *Crimes of the Powerful*. London: Pluto Press.

Polsky, N. (1969) *Hustlers, Beats and Others*. New York: Anchor Books.

Rawlinson, P. (2001) 'Russian Organized Crime and the Baltic States: Assessing the Threat' Working Paper 38/01, ESRC Research programme 'One Europe or Several'.

Rawlinson, P. (2007) Researching Serious Crime' in R. King and E. Wincup (eds) *Doing Research on Crime and Justice* (2nd edn). Oxford: Oxford University Press.

Reuter, P. (1995) 'The Decline of the American Mafia', *The Public Interest*, 120, Summer: 89–99.

Rogovin, C. and Martens, F. (1997) 'The evil that men do' in P. Ryan and G. Rush (eds) *Understanding Organized Crime in Global Perspective: A Reader*. California: Sage Publications.

Ruggiero, V. (2000) *Crime and Markets: Essays in Anti-Criminology*. Oxford: Oxford University Press.

Sheptycki, J. (2007) 'Police Ethnography in the House of Serious and Organized Crime' in A. Henry and D. Smith (eds) *Transformations of Policing*. Aldershot, Ashgate.

Slapper, G. and Tombs, S. (1999) *Corporate Crime*. Harlow: Longman.

Smith, D. (1975) *The Mafia Mystique*. New York: Basic Books.

Smith, D. (1991) 'Wickersham to Sutherland to Katzenbach: Evolving an "Official" Definition of Organized Crime', *Crime, Law and Social Change*. 16(2): 134–54.

Stelfox, P. (2003) 'Transnational organized crime: a police perspective' in A. Edwards and P. Gill (eds) *Transnational Organized Crime: Perspectives on Global Security*. London: Routledge.

Sutherland, E. (1937) *The Professional Thief*. Chicago, Ill: Chicago University Press.

Sutherland, E. (1983) *White Collar Crime: The Uncut Version*. New Haven: Yale University Press.

Taylor, I. (1994) 'The political economy of crime' in M. Maguire, R. Morgan, and R. Reiner (eds) *The Oxford Handbook of Criminology*. Oxford: Oxford University Press.

Taylor, I., Walton, P., and Young, J. (1973) *The New Criminology: For a Social Theory of Deviance*. London: Routledge & Kegan.

Thrasher, F. (1927) *The Gang*. Chicago: University of Chicago Press.

United Nations (2000) *Summary of the United Nations Convention Against Organized Crime and Protocols Thereto*. New York: United Nations.

Woodiwiss, M. (1993) 'Crime's Global Reach' in F. Pearce and M. Woodiwiss (eds) *Global Crime Connections*. Basingstoke: MacMillan.

Varese, F. (2001) *The Russian Mafia: Private Protection in a New Market Economy*. Oxford: Oxford University Press.

Whyte, W. (1943) *Street Corner Society: The Structure of an Italian Slum*. Chicago; University of Chicago Press.

15 Terrorism and the politics of fear

Frank Furedi

INTRODUCTION

Since the destruction of the World Trade Center in September 2001, terrorism has become one of the defining issues of the twenty-first century. Billions of dollars have been devoted to the so-called 'War Against Terrorism'. New technologies and laws have been created to assist the crackdown of what according to official accounts constitutes the gravest risk to our existence. Unfortunately, in the discussion of terrorism, what divides fact from fiction and information from propaganda is inexact. This chapter attempts to address this problem. It starts by casting doubt on simple, typically very narrow, definitions of terrorism, before then going on to deconstruct the climate of fear currently surrounding the majority of research in this area. Finally, the chapter casts a critical eye on current counter-terrorism measures and recently invoked anti-terrorist legislation, arguing that, if governments continue to adopt a cavalier attitude towards civil liberties, they will surely face the risk of playing into the very hands of those who promote and perpetrate political violence.

BACKGROUND

The inexplicable behaviour of apparently irrational terrorists is often tenuously linked to events whose causes are not known. Incomprehensible events are readily presented as the consequence of the actions of agents we do not understand. As Jenkins (2003) observes, even with the best will in the world, government officials are not in the position to inform the public of all the facts. When it comes to terrorism, official agencies 'have a powerful vested interest in not revealing the full extent of the information available to them'. Indeed, transmitting misinformation is part of the job description of anti-terrorist agencies. 'Since so much official action involves clandestine methods or sources, even the most reputable and responsible agencies will on occasion present less than the full truth, or actively give false information in order to protect their methods or sources', writes Philip Jenkins (2003: 6).

Of course, official statements that are designed to provide misleading information are not confined to the crime of terrorism. Information about crime statistics and specific crimes is often conveyed through statements that seek to gain political advantage through manipulating the facts. However, when it comes to conventional crimes, the questioning academic researcher is often in a position to demystify the official version of events and offer a plausible alternative. Matters are much more complicated when it comes to analysing terrorism. As Jenkins (ibid.) argues, it is easy to know when a particular act constitutes a crime such as robbing a bank. It is much more difficult to be certain that a particular deed is an act of terrorism. For often, it is not the deed but the motives that inspired it that turns a particular event into an act of terrorism. A random shooting may be the act of a psychopath or of a politically motivated activist; as Jenkins remarks, 'before we know whether the act falls within the scope of terrorism, we have to know both who did it, and why they did it' (ibid.: 6). These are very difficult questions to answer and unless we have direct access to the individual accused of a terrorist crime it is difficult to offer an alternative to the official version of events.

Interpreting terrorism

'Traditionalist' versus 'social constructionist' conceptions of terrorism

Although the terms 'terrorism' and 'terrorist' are widely used, it is far from evident what these words actually mean. Until recently, terrorism tended to be associated with the tactics of individuals or organizations who were waging unconventional warfare against legitimate authority through targeting non-combatants and spreading fear through the populace (Wilson, 2003: 119). Since the turn of the century, the term terrorism is often used to connote a distinct identity or ideology of an individual or organization. Thus, the widely used phrase 'war on terrorism' suggests that there is more to this problem than the violent tactics carried out by illegitimate clandestine organizations. Implicit in this phrase is the idea that terrorism represents a way of life, a political outlook as well as a physical and military threat.

The unusual degree of controversy that surrounds the discussion on terrorism stems from the fact that acts of political violence encourage people to take sides. The vocabulary used to express acts of political violence is continually contested. It is not simply the case that 'one person's freedom fighter is another one's terrorist'. Are members of organizations like Hamas or ETA, militants, guerrillas, or terrorists? And are they fighting a war or committing crimes? Most of the time the answers to these questions are influenced by one's attitude to the particular conflict. Whether or not an act of political violence is represented as a crime is linked to beliefs about its legitimacy.

The literature on terrorism is sharply divided between the 'traditionalists' who perceive it as a distinct form of violence that can be understood in its own terms and those who perceive it as the product of social construction. Paul Wilkinson's classic traditionalist account, *Political Terrorism*, is devoted to the task of elaborating the fundamental features of this crime. According to Wilkinson the 'key characteristics common to all forms of political terror' are 'indiscriminateness, unpredictability, arbitrariness, ruthless destructiveness and the implicitly amoral antinomian nature of a terrorist's challenge' (Wilkinson, 1976: 17). Most supporters of the idea that terrorism is a distinct form of crime argue that its essential feature is the pursuit of violence for political ends. 'What distinguishes terrorism from both vandalism and non-political crime is the motivated violence for political ends', writes Crozier (1974). Political motivation, randomness, and the targeting of innocent non-combatants are the characteristics most often cited by contributors who seek to represent terrorism as a distinct form of violence (for a useful overview of these definitions see Thackrah, 2004: 66–71).

The main alternative to the project of representing terrorism as a distinct form of political violence that can be understood in its own terms is the social constructionist approach. This approach is oriented towards exploring how terrorism is constructed as a problem. As Jenkins argues, a social constructionist perspective does not necessarily imply that terrorism does not exist and that it is an invented problem. Nor does it imply a particular political stance towards the question (Jenkins, 2003: 14–15). However, by suggesting that terrorism is not a self-evident concept most constructionist contributors tend to question the dominant consensus and representation of this subject.

Some constructionists claim that the attempt to portray terrorism as a distinct form of political violence represents an attempt to objectify it. Oliverio argues that 'terrorism as a construct is given an objective formation because it is accepted by most scholars as a special form of political violence' (1998: 27). According to Oliverio the objectification of the terrorist construct is inextricably associated with the imperative of legitimizing the authority of the State. She claims that the 'construct of terrorism is typically adopted discursively by the State to represent threats against its sovereignty' (ibid.). Many constructionists regard the problematization of terrorism as a self-serving attempt by the State to consolidate its power. For example, Tomis Kapitan appears to be more concerned with deconstructing the official rhetoric on terrorism than with the phenomenon of political violence itself. From this perspective it is difficult to avoid the conclusion that the promotion of the rhetoric of terrorism constitutes a problem that is at least as significant as the acts of political violence by those labelled as terrorist.

Problem of definition

Terrorism is an unusually controversial concept. Most leading contributions in this field recognize the difficulty that social scientists have had in defining this concept (see for example Gurr, 1979: 24, or Wilkinson, 1977: 52). One study reviewed 109 definitions of terrorism that covered 22 definitional elements (Schmid and Jongman, 1988: 5–6). Walter Laqueur, a well known expert on the subject, has counted over 100 definitions. He has concluded that the only 'general characteristic generally agreed upon is that terrorism involves violence and the threat of violence' (Laqueur, 1999: 6). But of course the use and threat of violence is not confined to terrorism. The deployment and the threat of violence is also practised by institutions that are deemed to be legitimate—particularly those of the State.

One reason why there may be so much confusion surrounding the definition of this term is due to the fact that it is not simply an objective analytical concept but also a moral statement on the behaviour of the terrorist. 'Thus in attempting to determine whether a specific action (or series of actions) is terroristic or not, the scholar should be aware that he is making a value judgement about the perpetrators of the alleged act, and about the circumstances of their actions', writes Wilkinson in his classic account of the subject (1974: 21). The normative dimension of this concept is evident in the political controversies that surround the issue of terrorism. Since so often debates about terrorism are linked to taking sides, the controversy that surrounds it is likely to be far more inflated than the kind of arguments that occur around other forms of deviant behaviour in the social sciences. The moral and political concerns that surround discussion on this subject mean that the concept is rarely used consistently and objectively.

The term terrorist is a loaded one—highly subjective, with aggressive connotations. It has acquired extremely negative associations. In the West, only the crime of paedophilia can compete with the act of the terrorist as a symbol of evil (Filler, 2003). The terrorist label serves as a health warning; it suggests that those to whom it is attached are morally inferior individuals. 'To identify someone as a terrorist is to render judgement on them, not simply to make a discovery' writes Claudia Card (2003: 178). Frequently, the attempt to represent an individual or a movement as terrorist is part of a propaganda war designed to discredit opponents. Not surprisingly, academic discussion of terrorism is not entirely detached from the propaganda battle for hearts and minds.

Often the definition of terrorism that is adopted is self-consciously designed to undermine the legitimacy of those promoting political violence. According to the RAND Corporation, the aim of its definition is to criminalize the acts it deems to be terrorist. 'In separating terrorist tactics from their political context, the intent clearly was to criminalize a certain mode of political expression' (Jackson, 1999: v). Not surprisingly, when a definition serves in part as a political statement it is likely to become a focus for controversy.

Most serious contributions on the subject acknowledge that they have difficulty in defining terrorism. Often this difficult problem is side-stepped through attempting to enumerate a list of features that distinguish this form of crime. However, the attempt to construct a list of characteristics that are specific to terrorism is undermined by the fact that they can be found in other areas of violent activities. For example Wilkinson (1974: 13) claimed that 'a major characteristic of political terror is its indiscriminate nature'. The insistence that the indiscriminate quality of terrorist violence is one of this phenomenon's distinct features is accepted by many specialists on the subject. Images of the Washington snipers terrorizing passers-by during their killing sprees in the summer of 2002 or of pedestrians blown to bits in Tel Aviv by a hidden bomb lend weight to the argument that this form of violence is distinguished by its indiscriminate character. However, as the American sociologist Joel Best (1999) argues in his *Random Violence*, many of today's high-profile crimes have a capacity to scare the public precisely because they are perceived to be carried out indiscriminately. It is random violence that characterizes the acts of the serial killer, the perpetrator of road rage, or the paedophile preying on innocent children. Indiscriminate violence is not the sole property of terrorism. Indeed it is associated with many of the high-profile crimes that excite the public's imagination.

The claim that terrorism is premeditated, politically motivated violence that targets innocent non-combatants is widely accepted by specialists as important features of this phenomenon. Those who object to this definition raise questions about the nature of political motivation or of the meaning of innocence. 'This definition, however, begs the question of who is innocent and by what standards is innocence determined' notes Record (2003). Record and others contend that innocent non-combatants are frequently the victims of State-sponsored violence. He points to the firebombing of Japanese cities in 1945 and to the terrified inhabitants who were not involved in the war effort.

Many critics of conventional definitions of terrorism believe that its emphasis on the actions of non-State actors obscures the role of the State in promoting acts of political violence. In some cases, critics tend to represent political violence exercised by the State as another form of terrorism. Writing in this vein, Sterba (2003: 24) condemns the past misdeeds of the US and argues that 'the United States surely needs to take steps to radically correct its own wrongdoing if it is to respond justly to the related wrongdoing of Bin Laden and his followers. Likewise, Record criticizes the traditional definitions because 'they exclude state terrorism, which since the French Revolution has claimed far more victims—in terms of millions—than terrorism perpetrated by non-state actors' (Record, 2003: 7).

Whatever definition one supports it is difficult to make a fundamental distinction between the violence and attributes of terrorism and the acts of others. For example, the objective of terrorizing the enemy is widely practised by conventional military forces. 'Shock and Awe' was the term used by the Bush administration to describe its massive hi-tech air strike against the Iraqis during the Second Gulf War. Its aim was clearly to strike terror in the minds of the enemy population. But those who supported this campaign did not regard it as an act of terror for the simple reason that they believed that this was a legitimate operation against a legitimate opponent. Definitions of terrorism involve the making of judgements of value. They also involve an element of selection. (Furedi, 2007: xxvii–xxxi).

Definitions of terrorism are fluid because ideas are continually changing about what forms of acts are legitimate or illegitimate. For example, violence against abortion clinics in the US was not considered as an act of terrorism until 1994.

In the 1980s, Americans tended to view terrorism as a Middle Eastern phenomenon, whereas in the 1990s the threat was perceived 'at least as much domestic as foreign' (Jenkins, 2003: 57; see also Hamm, 2002; 2004a). In recent years there has been a tendency on the part of Western governments and institutions to widen the definition of terrorism. In Britain, until recently the official definition was based on the one contained in the 1989 Prevention of Terrorism (Temporary Provisions) Act. According to this Act, terrorism 'means the use of violence for political ends and includes any use of violence for the purpose of putting the public or any section of the public in fear'. A review of terrorism legislation, carried out by Lord Lloyd in 1996, claimed that this definition was far too narrow since it did not encompass acts carried out by promoters of religious and single issue causes. The definition adopted in s. 1 of the Terrorism Act 2000 reflected these concerns and includes action that involves the 'use or threat of action' designed to 'influence the government or to intimidate the public or section of the public'. Violent acts committed against scientists conducting experiments on animals or in association with a hate crime are thus now frequently described as forms of terrorism.

Since 9/11 there has been a radical re-conceptualization of the meaning of terrorism. Official anxiety about the growing threat of home-grown extremism represents a radical departure from the way that terrorism was conceptualized in the past. Today terrorism is understood as not merely a physical threat. It is not simply the capacity of the terrorist to wreak mass destruction that worries society. Terrorism is also endowed with moral and ideological power that it is able to exercise over significant sections of the domestic population. The influence that the cause of the terrorist is able to exercise over the minds of sections of the public endows this threat with unparalleled danger. Sir David Omand, the former UK Security and Intelligence Coordinator goes as far as to state that the 'most effective weapon of the terrorist at present is their ideology'. (Cited in Furedi, 2007: 90) The model of a terrorist as an effective purveyor of ideas represents a significant departure from the way this threat was perceived in the past. Indeed the idea that a terrorist can appeal to people's heart and minds and not just merely scare the public is fundamentally inconsistent with traditional definitions of this threat. Until recent times the danger of terrorism was interpreted through its capacity to inflict fear on its target population. It is only in recent times that terrorism is conceptualized as an effective ideological competitor.

State terrorism

One of the most frequent criticisms made against the mainstream definitions of terrorism is that by focusing on non-State actors it overlooks the far more important problem of State-sponsored violence. Critics argue that the focus on the violence of the individual overlooks the fact that the real threat to humanity is destructive acts of State institutions. Gearty argues that the language of terrorism has become 'the rhetorical servant of the established order, whatever and however heinous its own activities are' (2002: 36–37). According to this perspective, the term terrorist is a label that the powerful use to stigmatize the activities of the powerless. 'It is easy for the politically satisfied and militarily powerful to pronounce all terrorism evil regardless of circumstance, but, like it or not, those at the other end of the spectrum are bound to see things differently' argues one critic (Record, 2003: 8). The belief that the promotion of the ideology of terrorism has helped minimize the crimes of the powerful has led many to insist that the political violence exercised by the State should be viewed as another form of terrorism. Some contributors to the debate emphasize the association of terrorism with the State because they believe that this powerful institution is responsible for far more violence than what has been perpetrated by non-State actors (see Morrison, 2004; and relatedly Cohen, 2001). According to one account 'state terrorism' should be given 'pride of place' because it 'has been responsible for more killings, more tortures, and more disappearances than all other forms' of crime (Williams, 2004: 499).

Historically, the terms terror and terrorism have been associated with both individuals and States. Regimes such as those of revolutionary France, Stalinist Soviet Union, or Nazi Germany are just some of the States associated with terrorism. In more recent times Western government adopted the term 'State-sponsored terrorism' to denounce regimes deemed to be responsible for supporting and promoting terrorist activities. Nevertheless, in recent decades 'the anti-state sense of the term has become paramount' (Thackrah, 2004). Today, the terrorist threat is predominantly associated with non-State networks of activists.

Although the problem of State violence is an important issue requiring serious analysis and deliberation, it does not follow that it should be characterized by the same label as the one that is used to describe the bombing of a nightclub in Bali in October 2002 or the indiscriminate killing of railway commuters in Madrid in March 2004. There are problems in using a single concept of terrorism to account for all forms of politically influenced violence or threat of violence.

State violence is of course widespread and is a subject in its own right (see Hagan, 1997 for a general criminological introduction). However, its context and social dynamics make it a very different type of activity to those pursued by non-State actors. States possess a monopoly over the means of coercion and apply force and violence against some of their citizens as well as those from other societies. Historically the right of the State to exercise force has rarely been questioned. In all societies a distinction is usually made between the use of violence by the State and by others. Unlike civilians, in certain circumstances police and military personnel are allowed to shoot and kill. Some may have ethical objections to this double standard regarding the application of violence. But it is worth remembering that this double standard is integral to the institutionalization of authority in the modern nation state.

Approaching the problem

The downside of conceptualizing terror as a form of violence associated with non-State actors is that it can easily be absorbed into an ideology that criminalizes individuals or groups who may have a legitimate cause to promote. However, the frequent manipulation of the terrorist label requires that we exercise care when we discuss the problem. Given the value-laden and subjective character of the construction of the problem of terrorism, it is tempting to avoid using the term altogether. This was the conclusion drawn by the BBC's World Service, when in the aftermath of 9/11 it decided not to use the word terrorist since to do so implied an 'improper value judgement' (cited in Jenkins, 2003: 18). Yet the problems that lead to the conceptualization of terrorism ought not to be defined out of existence. Yes, there is a problem with the label terrorist—it is often used to mystify rather than clarify. But nevertheless there are a range of disturbing practices that need to be conceptualized through a distinct category. Twenty-first century terrorism has distinct features which will be discussed in the rest of this chapter.

Whilst any definition is unlikely to solve the problem of how to distinguish this form of political violence from others, it is possible to outline some of the significant features that are associated with contemporary terrorism. As many official and non-official definitions of this subject suggest, contemporary terrorism is self-consciously directed at non-combatants. These individuals are not hurt or killed by accident but are intentionally targeted. It is violence that is randomly directed at civilians. However, those who are killed are not the targets of terrorism. As Jackson notes, 'the identities of the actual targets or victims of the attack often were secondary or irrelevant to the terrorist objective of spreading fear and alarm or gaining concessions' (Lesser et al., 1999: v). This form of violence is directed at civilians in order to create fear in others.

Contemporary terrorism

Understanding the threat

Political violence has been around throughout most of history. Although often condemned, politically motivated violence is not always considered to be a crime. The right to armed resistance against oppressive and coercive regimes is recognized by most political traditions. The case for a morally justifiable resort to political violence against a tyrannical regime is acknowledged within both the Christian and Western legal tradition and also within the Islamic worldview. Terrorism is a form of political violence that does not enjoy this legitimacy. Although terrorist tactics are sometimes linked to revolt and resistance, terrorism is generally regarded as a violation of prevailing moral norms. As Fred Halliday (2004) remarks, the stigma attached to terrorism has been 'remarkably resilient and universal'. He notes that 'the killings of women and children, of prisoners, or of groups of civilians are actions widely recognized in all cultures, religions and contexts as invalid in principle' (ibid. 6).

While non-State terrorist movements have been active since the nineteenth century, it is only in the recent period that they have been perceived as a significant if not principal threat to global stability. Since the end of the 1980s, the process of globalization has been experienced as one that encourages uncertainty, instability and the promotion of destructive forces. According to some accounts, global change has led to the disintegration of previously stable countries and State systems. This development has stimulated the rise of religious, ethnic, and other forms of internal conflicts, which in turn have helped consolidate a climate of global instability (Staten, 1999: 8). The fragmentation of the structural integrity of many societies has been linked to the rise of a variety of transnational or non-State actors and to the emergence of a new breed of international terrorists. It has been suggested that this new breed of 'postmodern' terrorists is particularly dangerous because for the first time such malcontents are able and are likely to access weapons of mass destruction (WMD) (see Laquer, 1996). The British House of Commons Select Committee on Defence has also expressed the view that society faces a new kind of terrorist. It noted that:

> while the UK may be regarded as well geared up to deal with traditional terrorist threats in general, new forms of terrorism and other aspects of asymmetrical warfare such as the use of hostages, environmental degradation, cyberwar, black propaganda etc, may find us rather less well prepared. (Select Committee on Defence 2001, para. 74)

The releasing of the nerve agent *sarin* in the Tokyo underground system in March 1995 marks an important watershed in the conceptualization of the global terrorist. After

Tokyo, terrorism 'was said to have made a qualitative leap' since for the first time a terrorist organization was prepared to discharge materials of mass destruction (Zanders, 1999). Yet, the impact of this experience on the conceptualization of asymmetric threat pales into insignificance in comparison to the way in which the events of 11 September have come to define the problem. The tragic events of 11 September have served to lend credence to the claim that terrorist threats represent the major challenge to global stability. As Delpech (2002) noted; 'to think that the leading world power would have found itself in the extraordinary position of needing to mobilize four aircraft carriers and 400 planes to oppose a non-State actor is astonishing' (Delpech, 2002).

There is a substantial body of opinion that equates the threat of terrorism with WMDs, particularly chemical and biological weapons (CBWs). This diagnosis of the problem clearly has an anticipatory character. The experience until now provides little evidence that non-State actors have the capability to deploy WMDs. It is in the sphere of information technology that new forms of techno-terrorism have been most successful. Although the significance of cyber-terrorism is often exaggerated, a variety of radical organizations have been successful in manipulating and destroying their opponents' information systems. More importantly, the easy availability of information technology has facilitated the mobility of networks devoted to the pursuit of political violence. 'The latest communications technologies are thus enabling terrorists to operate from almost any country in the world, provided they have access to the necessary IT infrastructure' argues an authoritative contribution on this subject (Zanini and Edwards, 2001: 38).

Figure 15.1 Fire trucks amid the rubble of World Trade Center
Source: © Reuters/CORBIS.

Is there a new terrorism?

There is a substantial literature that insists that terrorism today is fundamentally different to the way it worked in previous times and that society is confronted with a new species of terrorism. (Laqueur, 1999). However there is very little that is genuinely 'new' about terrorism. Those devoted to the pursuit of political violence have always sought to use the latest technologies in order to maximize the destructive impact of their operation. More than three decades ago in 1972 a group of terrorists belonging to a right-wing sect called the Order of the Rising Sun were arrested after they were found to be in possession of a large quantity of epidemic typhus pathogens with which they wanted to poison the water supplies of cities in the Mid West of the US. Nor is there anything new about official concern about the proliferation of WMDs. For almost a half a century officials have been discussing how to deal with a catastrophic terrorist attack. In all this time there is little empirical evidence of a qualitative transformation of this threat.

The one event that promoters of the new terrorism constantly allude to as proof of the arrival of a new era of terrorism was the attempt by members of the Japanese cult Aum Shinrikyo to launch a sarin attack on the Tokyo subway in March 1995. Although this millenarian sect sought to inflict mass casualties on Tokyo commuters, fortunately due to its inability to design an effective delivery system only 12 passengers lost their lives. In one sense the failure of the release of the nerve agent sarin to cause mass casualties can be interpreted as a good news story. It points to 'the difficulties in developing, producing and deploying biological agents' (Durodie, 2004: 1). It is worth noting that although Aum was a relatively sophisticated organization with access to scientific expertise and significant financial resources it still failed to realize its objectives. One important assessment of this experience concluded that 'the probability of a major biological attack by either a state or a sophisticated terrorist group seems remote' (Parachini, 2001: 5).

The evidence so far indicates that those oriented towards inflicting violence on civilians appear to choose conventional weapons to create mass casualties. Superficially the experience of 9/11 can be interpreted as confirmation of the catastrophic terrorism thesis. Yet one of the principal defining features of the new terrorism—the use of WMDs—was conspicuously absent during this event.

In retrospect it is evident that the destruction of the World Trade Center was the consequence of tactics that have been deployed by terrorists for a very long time. As Gearson observes, 'instead of technologically sophisticated weapons of mass destruction, the superterrorists of 11 September utilised the long-established terrorist approach of careful planning, simple tactics and operational surprises to effect the most stunning terrorist "spectacular" in history' (Gearson, 2002: 7).

One of the most persuasive arguments used to distinguish the new from the traditional form of terrorism is the claim that today it is far more brutal, destructive, and indiscriminate in its attitude to human life. Specialists on this subject frequently counterpose the traditional terrorist who was relatively selective in choosing targets to today's perpetrator of catastrophic acts of mass casualty. However, this argument has been repeatedly restated since at least the 1970s. Acts of apparently indiscriminate violence have a long history. This trend is illustrated by examples such as the simultaneous bombings of the US and French barracks in Lebanon in 1983 which resulted in the deaths of 367 people, the destruction of Pan Am Flight 103 over Lockerbie that killed 270 people, and the bombing of an Air India plane by a Sikh group that resulted in 329 deaths. Another characteristic attributed to new terrorism is the motive of religious fanaticism. Yet from Sicarii of the Jewish Zealot movement of biblical times there have been numerous violent sects who were inspired by religious and millenarian impulses.

At first sight it is far from evident what has changed about terrorism. Virtually every characteristic that is associated with this new breed of destructive behaviour has been linked with terrorism in the past. However, the very fact that contemporary terrorism is perceived as very new, uniquely dangerous and the greatest threat to global stability renders it a distinct phenomenon. What is important about terrorism as a social phenomenon is how society responds to it. And the more dangerous that terrorism is perceived the more dangerous it becomes. It is the normalization of the expectation of catastrophic mass casualty events that transforms perceptions of terrorism into a global threat of unprecedented magnitude.

The one dimension of terrorism that is genuinely 'new' is the way it is conceptualized. On the one hand this is very much the case of reinterpreting old concerns and re-branding them as existential threat. On the other hand the meaning of terrorism has expanded and is used to account for a variety of threats. In recent decades a growing range of global threats have been assimilated into a narrative of new terrorism. The conceptual inflation of terrorism has been noted in an important study by Crelinsten who remarked that the 'tendency to place disparate phenomena into the same security basket' is 'reflected in recent analyses of terrorism' (Crenlisten, 1998: 390). A key development in this conceptual inflation was the shift from perceiving terrorism as a specific local phenomenon to one that was globally connected and therefore constituted a world-wide threat. During the 1970s a variety of disparate terrorist incidents in the West and in the Third World were interpreted as an integral part of a common global threat. 'All these events were increasingly incorporated into a single overarching narrative of "international terrorism"' notes Carr (2006: 198). One consequence of the perception of terrorism as an international phenomenon is that it becomes uprooted from any historical, cultural, and social context. As an international phenomenon it exists in its own right and terrorism can be readily interpreted as a stand-alone problem of apocalyptic dimensions.

The characteristic feature of non-State terrorists

Although terrorist organizations are the product of a wide variety of circumstances and exist throughout the world, it is the Middle Eastern variety that appears to personify the problem. Frequently the threat posed by terrorism is ascribed to the power of religious ideology, especially that of Islam. 'Islamic fundamentalism represents a deep and coherent ideology stretching back fourteen centuries, and that is interiorized into the souls of millions of people' (Phillips, 2003: 101–102). The success of many Islamist movements notwithstanding, it is important not to interpret terrorism as an essentially religious phenomenon. As Halliday (2004) notes, the politics of terrorism has its roots in 'modern secular politics' and not in the distant past. It is both a product of and a revolt against modernity.

Unfortunately, the discussion and analyses of non-State actors is relatively underdeveloped and constitutes a weak link in the conceptualization of the problem. Many commentators cannot resist the temptation of using essentially moral or highly subjective categories to make sense of these individuals. Steele (1998) writes that 'when all is said and done, most men, and especially men from non-western cultures and less-developed areas, are capable of taking great pleasure in great evil' (ibid.: 79) Many other observers adopt the perspective of regarding 'them' as our moral opposites. Dunlap claims that 'likely future adversaries will be unlike ourselves'. He characterizes opponents as members of 'The New Warrior Class' 'who have acquired a taste for killing, who do not behave rationally, who are capable of atrocities that challenge the descriptive powers of language, and who will sacrifice their own kind in order to survive' (Dunlap, 1996: 2). Numerous observers promote the view that terrorists are behaving irrationally. For example it has been suggested that the great practitioners of terror—Stalin, Hitler, Pol Pot, Osama Bin Laden, what Robins and Post (1998) call charismatic terrorists—suffer from a personality disorder. Apparently they have low self-esteem and end up blaming others.

It is difficult to ascribe a single cause or motive that can account for the pursuit of political violence. These acts are committed by a wide variety of individuals who often have very specific and sometimes very individual reasons for adopting this course of action. It is worth noting that that empirical research carried out on terrorists and suicide bombers does not support the idea that they are mentally unstable and irrational people. Scott Atran's (2003) research on the phenomenon of suicide bombers provides powerful evidence that suggests that these individuals are not irrational crazed people, but are frequently well-educated and stable members of their community.

From the previous analysis it should be evident that the abstract counterposition drawn between rational and irrational can lead to a mis-assessment of the dynamic of global terrorism. Even suicide bombing—which many in the West find incomprehensible—is motivated by the rational calculation that such tactics are likely to weaken the morale of the target population. As Sprinzak (2000) argues 'the perception that terrorists are undeterrable fanatics who are willing to kill millions indiscriminately just to sow fear and chaos belies the reality that they are cold, rational killers who employ violence to achieve specific political objectives' (ibid.: 4). Labelling such individuals as zealots and fanatics can lead to an underestimation or at least a misunderstanding of the problem. Sprinzak notes that the experience of 11 September indicates that 'some of the best and the brightest among the enemy would rather sacrifice themselves' for their cause. According to Sprinzak (2001) the people responsible for 9/11 can be seen as 'innovators' and 'developers' who are 'incessantly looking for original ways to surprise and devastate the enemy'.

One reason why the demonization of individuals engaged in political violence is counterproductive is that it helps transform them into omnipotent and unstoppable threats. Such an approach transforms them into a far more frightening and dangerous threat than is warranted by their capabilities. One possible consequence of this approach is to inflate public anxieties and thereby indirectly empower them.

Too great an emphasis on cultural differences—religion, value systems, morality—fails to take account of the fact that many individuals drawn towards terrorism are products of modern technologically advanced societies or have had considerable contact with life in western cultures. To take a few examples: members of the Rajneeshee cult, who employed biological agents to incapacitate many of the inhabitants of a small town in Oregon in 1984, were often American university-educated individuals; the *sarin* attack on the Tokyo underground in 1995 was carried out by a Japanese sect, whose members possessed considerable scientific and technological expertise; likewise, some of the individuals involved in the first terrorist attack on the World Trade Center were beneficiaries of American university education. Individual terrorists such as the 'Oklahoma bomber' Timothy McVeigh, an American Gulf War hero turned mass murderer, was no less prepared to inflict indiscriminate terror than his counterparts from different cultures. Similarly, the notorious 'una bomber', Theodore Kaczynski, is a former university lecturer. Neither the British nail-bomber, David Copeland, nor his fellow citizen, Richard Reid, the alleged Al-Qaeda operative, were brought up as members of a 'New Warrior Class'.

The problem of terrorism today is constituted through actors who are products of important changes within the global and domestic environment. One of the characteristic features of the so-called new terrorists is that they appear to be free of many of the constraints that curbed similar acts of violence in the past. The weakening of systems of State structures, the erosion of legitimate institutions and of shared values have played a significant role in the shaping of asymmetric threat. The process of globalization has provided new opportunities for non-State actors to develop powerful networks to sustain their operations. Halliday (2004) is right to draw attention to the fact that terrorism has emerged in 'rich and poor countries alike, as part of a transnational model of political engagement'. The global networks that underpin some of the terrorist organizations serve to enhance their influence. Hoffman claims that the problem is no longer confined to small groups of isolated individuals. The network associated with Osama Bin Laden can mobilize 4,000–5,000 individuals scattered throughout the globe. He believes that 'the appearance of these different types of adversaries—in some instances with new motivations and different capabilities—accounts largely for terrorism's lethality in recent years' (Hoffman, 1999: 9).

Campbell (1997) believes that one of the distinguishing features of 'post-modern' terrorists is that they are 'free of constraints provided by sponsoring nation-states'. Many associated terrorist organizations have the character of free agents, whose activities transcend national boundaries and cultures. They are often mobile members of diasporic organizations who are unconnected to any formal State institutions. As a result they are freed from the geopolitical calculations that State actors are forced to make. These actors are not only less connected to formal institutions—they are often freed from accountability to a community and other forms of conventional networks. The erosion of a consensus around fundamental values about life also diminishes communal restraint. Throughout the world—and especially in the West—there has been a weakening of the prevailing value systems (see Hayward and Morrison, 2002: 146–50 for an account of this process in relation to contemporary terrorist activity). This has undermined many societies' ability to integrate and socialize its members. As a result many individuals drawn towards political violence are less restrained by such values and are therefore less accountable to conventional forms of behaviour than was the case in the past. The wider social and cultural disagreements about values actually free potential activists from having to justify their actions according to a specific ethos accepted by their community.

At a time of weakening State systems, the erosion of a sense of community and shared values, it makes little sense to attempt to label terrorists according to conventional political labels. In the past terrorist organizations could be labelled along ideological lines—conservative, revolutionary, religious, or nationalist. Since the 1990s, as Sprinzak (2001) argues, this typology has been rendered obsolete. Although these groups are 'not politically blind—they remain apolitical'. Since the end of the Cold War, the erosion of the distinction between left and right has rendered ideologically driven politics problematic. Tucker (2001) insists that because today's 'most pernicious terrorists are not motivated by political ideology on the far left or right' they are 'more likely to be extremists on the fringe of traditional religions or idiosyncratic cults with an apocalyptic mindset'. This shift of focus from political objectives is also stressed by Carter (2002). He argues that 'not in all cases, but at least in some important cases, the motivation for mass terror is a vengeful or messianic one, rather than a politically purposeful one'. As a result the actions of many radical movements has become less predictable and less oriented towards seeking political change. Instead of ideology, some movements have adopted a morally sanctioned worldview where ideas of evil and salvation influence behaviour. Such forms of behaviour often characterize movements involved in the so-called 'culture wars'. It also affects contemporary violent protest movements, for example, animal rights campaigners. What unites Western bred-individuals like Timothy McVeigh and David Copeland with Islamic militants is the belief that their cause cannot be subject to conventional forms of restraint. As Tucker (2001) notes, today's terrorists 'experience fewer constraints on the use of violence to inflict indiscriminate casualties'. 'In these instances, the weakening of social capital lends individual grievances a cultural form.'

From research carried out by social psychologists, we know that individuals 'acting under the auspices of a group may feel that their personal accountability for the group's violent actions is diminished'. It is also suggested that, as a result, this diminished responsibility may lower individual thresholds of acceptability for violent behaviour (Pynchon and Borum, 1999: 345–6). What distinguishes some members of violent protest organizations from those of the past is that individual thresholds of acceptability for violent behaviour may become even lower in circumstances that prevail today (on this specific point see Chapter 11). With the intensification of social, institutional, and community fragmentation, the actions of militants are less contained by conventional norms and sanctions. This reduction in accountability is particularly the case for mobile transnational diasporic actors.

Finally, it is important to point out that the process of social fragmentation also encourages that of *individuation*. The general loosening of restraints also effects individual behaviour and may stimulate individual resentment to acquire a wider moral form. This may endow contemporary individual terrorism with a potentially more violent dimension. Developments in information technology help connect such individuals with one another and provide them with access to resources and ideas about how to conduct their affairs (see relatedly Chapter 8).

Conceptualizing the global problem of terrorism as the product of an estrangement from and rejection of modernity helps link this phenomenon to the wider social dynamic at work. The causes of individual cases of political violence are too numerous to be explained by a single set of variables. But it is not the existence of terrorism that represents a unique feature of the early twenty-first century. Rather it is its ability to significantly destabilize individual societies and the prevailing global order that constitutes the nub of the problem. And that is not merely the result of the actions of the terrorist but of the powerful forces of globalization that work to diminish the sense of common purpose in many societies.

REVIEW QUESTIONS

1 How do we account for the significance that contemporary society attaches to the problem of terrorism?

2 Discuss the concept of a 'post-modern' terrorist.

3 Is terrorism just politics pursued by other means?

4 Is State-sanctioned violence just another form of terrorism?

CONCLUSION

The relationship between political violence and the criminal justice system has always been an uneasy one. It is important to note that not every form of political violence is criminalized and certainly not to the same extent. An analysis of the US media noted that the Irish Republican Army got a better press than the Puerto Rican FALN (Hewitt, 2003: 112). And while the Reagan Administration refused to describe anti-abortionist violence as terrorist, the Clinton one did. It is only in the past decade that the terrorist label has been applied to violent single-issue campaigns such as the targeting of laboratories conducting animal experimentation or abortion clinics

Since terrorism is such a highly charged politicized concept there are considerable difficulties in treating it as a crime. Certainly, it is rarely treated as an ordinary crime. Since it is perceived as representing a threat to the security of society and the authority of the State, it is usually dealt with under special emergency powers. The official response to terrorism often exists in a state of tension between treating it as a crime—that is, as a normal law and order problem—or responding to this threat in a more militaristic fashion through the application of special anti-terrorist legislation (see Hamm, 2004b for a recent critique of this approach in relation to the US Patriot Act). In fact almost every violent act associated with terrorism could be prosecuted through the normal laws of the criminal justice system. Since the stated aim of these laws is to protect the public from harm, it stands to reason that they ought to be applied in all circumstances. However, advocates of special anti-terrorist legislation claim that extraordinary powers are necessary for dealing with the unique threat posed by terrorism. But, it can be argued that the very act of treating terrorism as a special, unique, and formidable threat serves to empower the terrorist as someone that cannot be dealt with through the normal institutions of society. It can also be argued that the use of special legislation serves to affirm the claim of those who argue that they are being persecuted for their beliefs rather than for their acts.

Although most governments and societies represent terrorism as a crime, they treat it as a problem that is quite distinct and one that requires special measures. Unlike a criminal who is seen to represent a threat to the wellbeing of the public, terrorism is perceived as a unique danger that threatens the very fabric of society. As a result, organizations that are deemed dangerous are formally banned and membership in them is considered to be a criminal offence. For example, in February 2001, 21 international organizations were banned under the UK Terrorism Act 2000. These include organizations such as Al-Qaeda, The Kurdistan Workers Party, and Palestinian Islamic Jihad. One of the objectives of terrorist legislation is to curb the international activities of terrorists, particularly acts that transcend national boundaries. A variety of such acts—inciting terrorism abroad, financing terrorists overseas—are now prosecuted under special legislation on both sides of the Atlantic. Such legislation is frequently justified on the ground that the domestic criminal justice system is inappropriate for dealing with global threats to the functioning of society.

Anti-terrorist legislation is different to normal criminal legislation in that it actively seeks to pre-empt and not simply catch the perpetrators of a terrorist act. As a result such laws can turn into criminal offences people's beliefs, organizational affiliation, possession of certain literature and otherwise legal substances. Anti-terrorist legislation also allows authorities to detain and interrogate suspects in circumstances that are very different to what is acceptable under the criminal justice system. While such unusual powers appear to be necessitated by the extraordinary threat represented by the terrorist, the application of special anti-terrorist measures can be seen to represent a threat to civil liberties. Numerous commentators have pointed to the problem of enacting laws that have the potential for undermining the established liberties of a democratic society in the name of protecting freedom. As Wilkinson (1974: 109) noted:

> if the government is provoked into introducing emergency powers, suspending habeas corpus, or invoking martial law, it confronts the paradox of suspending democracy in order to defend it. There is always the risk that by using heavy repression to crush the terrorist campaign the authorities may alienate the innocent mass of citizens caught up in the procedures of house-to-house searches and interrogations.

There is also the danger that a heavy-handed anti-terrorist policy could also end up repressing legitimate forms of dissent. Most governments have found it difficult to resist the temptation of adopting special powers to pre-empt and contain terrorism. Yet if governments adopt a cavalier attitude towards civil liberties they will surely play into the very hands of those who promote and perpetrate political violence.

QUESTIONS FOR DISCUSSION

1 Discuss the statement that 'Terrorism is in the eyes of the beholder'. Does the label terrorist necessarily represent a judgement of value?

2 How do we distinguish terrorism from other forms of violent crime?

3 What are the distinct features of twenty-first-century terrorism?

4 Provide your definition of terrorism and explain the reasons for your choice.

5 Why and how could government over-reaction play into the hands of the terrorist?

GUIDE TO FURTHER READING

The following texts each provide interesting accounts of the debates and issues surrounding contemporary terrorism. They also, to varying degrees, attempt to confront the rhetoric and politics of fear that often surround these debates:

Arquilla, J. and Ronfeldt, D. (2001) *Networks and Netwars; The Future of Terror, Crime, and Militancy.* Santa Monica, CA: RAND.

Carter, A. Deutch, J. and Zelikow, P. (1998) 'Catastrophic Terrorism; Tackling the New Danger', *Foreign Affairs,* November/December.

Filler, D.M. (2003) 'Terrorism, Panic, and Pedophilia', *Journal of Social Policy and the Law,* Spring.

Furedi, F. (2007) *Invitation To Terror: The Expanding Empire of the Unknown*: London: Continuum Press.

Hewitt, C. (2003) *Understanding Terrorism in America; From The Klan To Al Qaeda.* London: Routledge.

Jenkins, P. (2003) *Images of Terror: What We Can and Can't Know about Terrorism.* New York: Aldine de Gruyter.

Laqueur, W. (1999) *The New Terrorism: Fanaticism and the Arms of Mass Destruction.* New York: Oxford University Press.

Wilkinson, P. (1974) *Political Terrorism.* New York: Macmillan.

WEB LINKS

http://www.security.homeoffice.gov.uk
The Home Office counter-terrorism website: these pages provide information for the public on the threat from international terrorism and accounts of what the Government is doing to protect, prevent, and prepare for terrorist attacks.

http://www.terrorism.com
Website of the Terrorist Research Center

http://www.usinfo.state.gov/topical/pol/terror
US Department of State: Countering Terrorism.

http://www.hri.org/docs/USSD-Terror
US Department of State: Patterns of Global Terrorism Reports.

REFERENCES

Atran, S. (2003) 'Genesis of Suicide Terrorism', *Science* 299. March 7.

Best, J. (1999) *Random Violence; How we Talk about New Crimes and new Victims.* University of California Press: Berkeley.

Campbell, J. (1997) *Weapons of Mass Destruction—Terrorism.* New York: Interpact press.

Card, C. (2003) 'Making War on Terrorism in Response to 9/11' in J.P. Sterba (2003) (ed) *Terrorism and International Justice*. New York: Oxford University Press, p.178.

Carr, M. (2006) *Unknown Soldiers: How Terrorism Transformed the Modern World.* Profile Books: London.

Carter, A. (2002) in 'Understanding Terrorism; A Harvard Magazine Roundtable', *Harvard Magazine* January–February 2002.

Cohen, S. (2001) *States of Denial: Knowing About Atrocities and Suffering*. Oxford: Polity.

Crelinsten, R. (1998) 'The Discourse and Practice of Counter-Terrorism in Liberal democracies'. *Australian Journal of Politics and History*, Vol. 44, no. 1.

Crozier, B. (1974) *A Theory of Conflict*. London: Hamish Macmillan.

Delpech, T. (2002) 'The Imbalance of Terror', *The Washington Quarterly*, Winter 2002.

Dunlap, C. (1996) 'Sometimes The Dragon Wins; A Perspective on Information-Age Warfare' http://www.intowar.com/MIL_C4I/DRAGON.html-ssi.

Durodie, B. (2004) 'Facing the possibility of Bioterrorism', *Current Opinion in Biotechnology*, Vol. 15.

Filler, D.M. (2003) 'Terrorism, Panic, and Pedophilia', *Journal of Social Policy and the Law*, Spring issue.

Furedi, F. (2007) *Invitation To Terror; The Expanding Empire Of The Unknown*. London: Continuum Press.

Gearson, J. (2002) 'The Nature of Modern Terrorism', *The Political Quarterly*.

Gearty, C. (2002) 'Terrorism and Morality', *European Human Rights Law Review*.

Gurr, T. (1979) *Violence in America*. New York: Sage Publications.

Hagan, F.E. (1997) *Political Crime*. Needham Heights, MA: Allyn and Bacon.

Halliday, F. (2004) 'Terrorism in historical perspective', *Open Democracy*, 22 April.

Hamm, M. (2002) *In Bad Company: America's Terrorist Underground*. Boston: Northeastern University.

Hamm, M. (2004a) 'Apocalyptic violence: the seductions of terrorist subcultures' *Theoretical Criminology* 8 (3) Special Edition: Cultural Criminology.

Hamm, M. (2004b) 'The US Patriot Act and the politics of fear' in J. Ferrell, K. Hayward, W. Morrison, and M. Presdee (eds) *Cultural Criminology Unleashed*. London: GlassHouse.

Hayward, K.J. and Morrison, W. (2002) 'Locating Ground Zero: caught between the narratives of crime and war' in J. Strawson (ed), *Law After Ground Zero*. London: Cavendish Press.

Hewitt, C. (2003) *Understanding Terrorism in America; From The Klan To Al Qaeda*. Routledge: London.

Hoffman, B. (1999) 'Introduction' in I.O. Lesser, B. Hoffman, J. Arquilla, D. Ronfeldt, M. Zanini, and B. Jenkins (1999) *Countering The New Terrorism*. Santa Monica, Ca: RAND, MR–989.

Jackson, B.M. (1999) 'Foreword' in I.O. Lesser, B. Hoffman, J. Arquilla, D. Ronfeldt, M. Zanini, and B. Jenkins (1999) *Countering The New Terrorism*. Santa Monica, Ca: RAND, MR–989.

Jenkins, P. (2003) *Images of Terror: What We Can and Can't Know about Terrorism*. New York: Aldine de Gruyter.

Laqueur, W. (1996) 'Postmodern Terrorism', *Foreign Affairs*, Sept–October.

Laqueur, W. (1999) *The New Terrorism: Fanaticism and the Arms of Mass Destruction*. New York: Oxford University Press.

Lesser, I.O., Hoffman, B., Arquilla, J., Ronfeldt, D., Zanini, M., and Jenkins, B. (1999) *Countering The New Terrorism*. Santa Monica, CA: RAND.

Morrison, W. (2004) 'Criminology, genocide and modernity' in C. Sumner (ed) *The Blackwell Companion to Criminology*. Oxford: Blackwell.

Oliverio, A. (1998) *The State of Terror*. Albany, NY: State University of New York Press.

Parachini, J. (2001) *Combatting Terrorism: Assessing The Threat Of Biological Terrorism. Before the House Subcommittee on National Security, Veteran Affairs and International relations, Committee on Government Reform, US House of Representatives*, 12 October, Washington, D.C.

Phillips, R.L. (2003) 'The war against pluralism' in J.L. Sterba (ed) *Terrorism and International Justice*. Oxford: Oxford University Press.

Pynchon, M.R. and Borum, R. (1999) 'Assessing Threats of Targeted Group Violence: Contributions from Social psychology', *Behavioral Sciences and the Law*, Vol. 17.

Record, J. (2003) *Bounding The Global War On Terrorism*. Carlisle, PA: Strategic Studies Institute, available on <http://www.carlisle.army.mil>.

Robins, R.S. and Post, J.M. (1998) *Political Paranoia: The Psychopolitics of Hatred*. New Haven, CO: Yale University Press.

Schmid, A. and Jongman, A. (1988) *Political Terrorism: A New Guide to Actors, Authors, Concepts, Data bases, Theories, and Literature*. New Brunswick, NJ: Transaction Books.

Select Committee on Defence (2001) *Eight-Report*, para. 74. London: HMSO.

Sprinzak, E. (2000) 'Rational Fanatics', *Foreign Policy*, September/October.

Sprinzak (2001) 'The Lone Gunmen', *Foreign Policy*, November.

Staten, C.L. (1999) 'Asymmetric Warfare, the Evolution and Devolution of Terrorism: The Coming Challenge for Emergency and National Security Forces'. *Journal of Counter-Terrorism and Security International*. vol.5 no 4, p.8.

Sterba, J.L. (ed) (2003) *Terrorism and International Justice*. Oxford: Oxford University Press.

Steele, R.D. (1998) 'The Asymmetric Threat to the Nation,' Defence Daily Network (www.defensedaily.com/reports/takedown.htm). 22 June.

Thackrah, J.R. (2004) *Dictionary of Terrorism*. London: Routledge.

Tucker, J. (2001) 'The proliferation of Chemical and Biological Weapons Materials and Technologies to State and Sub-State Actors'. *Testimony before the Subcommitte on International Security, Proliferation, and Federal Services of the U.S. Senate Committee on Governmental Affairs*. 7 November 2001.

Williams, K.S. (2004) *Textbook on Criminology*. Oxford: Oxford University Press.

Wilkinson, P. (1974) *Political Terrorism*. New York: Macmillan.

Wilkinson, P. (1976) 'Terrorism versus Democracy: The Problem of Response', *Conflict Studies*, no. 76.

Wilkinson, P. (1977) *Terrorism and the Liberal State*. London: Macmillan.

Wilson N.B. (2003) 'Bibliographical Essay on Fear', *The Hedgehog Review*, Fall, Vol. 5, no. 3: 119.

Zanders, J.P. (1999) 'Assessing the Risk of Chemical and Biological Weapons Proliferation to Terrorists', *The Nonproliferation Review*, Fall.

Zanini, M. and Edwards, S. (2001) 'The Networking of Terror in the Information Age', in J. Arquilla, and D. Ronfeldt (eds) (2001) *Networks and Netwars: The Future of terror, crime, and militancy*. Santa Monica, CA: RAND.

Part Three
SOCIAL DIMENSIONS OF CRIME

16 Economic marginalization, social exclusion, and crime

Chris Hale

INTRODUCTION

This chapter looks at a long-standing debate within criminology about the relationships between the economy, poverty, and crime. Beginning with a review of what criminologists and others have to say about these factors, it then considers the research evidence for links between unemployment, and, more fruitfully the broader labour market, and crime. A more focused discussion of the links between poverty and crime follows, examining concepts such as the underclass and social exclusion. This will raise political issues of how to deal with these problems. For New Labour, integrating people into work is central to combating social exclusion and this links back to the discussion of the relations between the labour market and crime. At the centre of this debate lie not only matters of power and inequality, but also the need to question the nature of paid work and the position it takes within capitalist society.

BACKGROUND

The devil makes work for idle hands.
Poverty is the mother of crime.

These proverbs capture two strands of thought about the relationships between economic circumstances and crime. As with all folklore they contain a kernel of truth, but as with much 'common sense' they need interpreting with care.

The first suggests that work, gainful employment, is important in preventing crime. One take on this is that those who do not have jobs, the idle hands, are more likely to become involved in criminal pursuits, partly perhaps to provide resources for their daily needs and partly because they lack the discipline and structure going to work provides. As will be seen below, the relationship between unemployment and crime has been the site of much debate amongst criminologists. However, this is not the complete picture since it ignores the 'idle rich' and few suggest that they might benefit from the discipline of the workplace!

The second maxim suggests that poverty causes crime—that the poor will be more likely to be criminal. Again this seems sensible—those lacking in material resources may be forced into illegal behaviour to provide their daily bread, and further may have less to lose than the better off and so be less afraid of the consequences if their offending is discovered. Again it is silent about the crimes of the rich and the powerful where surely greed rather than need is more relevant. Space precludes examining the relationship between the economy and crimes of the powerful, but the interested reader is referred to Box (1987) and Tombs (Chapter 13 above).

So while this chapter will focus primarily on the debate around economic hardship and crimes such as burglary, vehicle theft, and robbery, it should not be forgotten that this debate is a product of ideological emphasis on those types of crime that are more likely to be committed by the powerless than by the powerful.

There are theoretical arguments and empirical evidence to support the hypothesis that crime and the economy are related. Some, but not all, studies of the relationship between unemployment and crime have found a link. Other studies show that the poor and unemployed form a significant proportion of known offender populations. More broadly, work linking crime with wider economic changes in the structure of economy can be cited.

Critics of these positions will object that this is to label all the poor and unemployed as criminals, whereas most are upright law-abiding citizens. Further, they will suggest that during the economic depression of the 1930s, when poverty was widespread and severe, crime was much lower than it has been throughout the period since 1945 when the standards of living of everyone in industrialized countries have improved considerably. Against this could be set the massive increase in recorded crimes in England and Wales during the severe recession between 1989 and 1992 and the fact that since 1992, and until the recent global economic downturn, the UK has had an unprecedented period of steady economic growth accompanied by a steady decline in crime whether measured by police statistics or the British Crime Survey. This signals the danger of seeking a single explanation for crime. Social relationships are historically contingent; what may hold in one period may not in another because of broader social and cultural changes. In particular how problems related to economic hardship are dealt with, both formally and informally, how inequality and wealth are viewed will affect the relationship between crime and economic conditions.

REVIEW QUESTIONS

1 In what ways might being unemployed or poor increase the likelihood of engaging in crime?

2 In what ways might being in work or rich increase the likelihood of engaging in crime?

3 What were the differences between the 1930s and the 1960s in terms of crime and unemployment?

Why might economic conditions affect the level of crime?

What does social theory have to say about the relationship between economic conditions and crime? Despite being nearly 20 years old, Box (1987) still remains an excellent review of this area, so his approach is summarized and developed below. (See also Hayward and Morrison, Chapter 4 above for a wider discussion of the theories considered here.) As Box notes, many theories can be read in a way that predicts more crime when unemployment increases and income inequalities widen. What follows is a brief and selective look, at what some have had to say.

Strain theory

Strain theory tackles the question of motivation—why would anyone want to commit a crime? It argues people would conform to prevailing norms and laws were it not for stresses and contradictions in their lives. Two variations are identified, anomie leading to 'thwarted ambition', and relative deprivation caused by material inequalities in wealth.

Durkheim's concept of *anomie* (Durkheim, 1893 (1985)) describes a situation in society where rules are breaking down, or are blurred and confused so that people do not know what to expect of each other. This produces a feeling of isolation and a sense of meaninglessness in life. Durkheim was writing in the late nineteenth century after the massive upheavals of the Industrial Revolution that transformed predominantly rural agricultural societies into urban communities where manufacturing industry dominated. He was concerned with the problems of modernity and how society adapts to the increasing individualism accompanying it. For Durkheim, anomie—a state of normlessness—arises during periods of rapid social change and leads to dissatisfaction, conflict, and deviance. Clearly this will happen during economic recessions, but it can also occur during periods of great prosperity. Many observers see changes in the late twentieth century, where industrialized countries have seen declining manufacturing industries and concomitant rises in the service sector as producing similar effects.

Robert Merton adapted anomie as the basis of his strain theory (Merton, 1938). Unlike Durkheim, he does not argue the problem is sudden social change. Instead crime is one possible response to the strains produced by the unequal opportunities available for achieving success. Where the dominant culture values success in terms of material goods and economic status, crime would be expected to increase whenever legitimate opportunities to achieve such success are restricted. In a supposedly meritocratic society the major way for attaining material success is through education and hard work. During an economic recession, when unemployment rises and inequality widens, more people will experience a sense of failure to achieve these culturally defined goals and will be more likely to resort to illegal activities to achieve their aims. Note, however, that crime, termed by Merton as an innovative approach, is one of five possible responses to strain (see Hayward and Morrison, Chapter 4). Strain theory is a structural theory that posits disjuncture between culturally prescribed goals of success and the opportunity structure. There is a lack of fit between cultural goals and the means available to achieve them. More generally the theory would suggest crime would be a lower class phenomenon since they will have similar goals as middle and upper classes, but will lack the means to achieve them.

Relative deprivation is related to, but distinct from strain. As the name suggests it refers to relative, rather than absolute poverty, hence to the distribution of wealth and income across society. Wealth and income can be increasing for all individuals, but relative deprivation will also increase if the gap between rich and poor increases. For example, one objective measure often used is to compare the income of the top 10 per cent income earners with that of the lowest 10 per cent. To take an artificial example, if the income of the top decile triples while that of the bottom only doubles, then inequality has increased.[1] Clearly the UK is a richer society today than it was 100 years ago and that applies not just to economic wealth but also in matters such as health and education. However, whether or not it is a more equal society is a different matter. At an individual level it is possible to be well off and still feel relatively deprived. For example, I feel poor when I compare myself to Bill Gates but rich when I look at the homeless in my local town. As well as the objective situation, an awareness of one's position is also important. In modern society people are continually bombarded by media images and definitions of what constitutes the 'good life'. This usually involves consumption adding to the sense of unfairness of those unable to afford designer labels and expensive holidays. Similarly in urban areas the stratification of neighbourhoods is less marked than it used to be with the process of gentrification that follows the move of the middle classes into poorer neighbourhoods. Relative deprivation has become a popular explanation for crime, because for long periods in the second half of the twentieth century—in the industrialized economies at least—rising living standards have been accompanied by rising crime. Note that, unlike strain theory, relative deprivation does not necessarily suggest that crime is a lower class phenomenon, amongst societies' 'losers' since it accepts that discontent '...can be felt anywhere in the class structure where people perceive their rewards to be unfair compared to those with similar attributes' (Young, 2001). Nevertheless, a sense of relative deprivation is likely to be more pronounced for those whose economic position is least secure especially during periods of economic recession when unemployment increases and wage levels are likely to be depressed.

Social disorganization theory—The Chicago School

The Chicago School is famous for the links it established between environmental factors and crime (see Hayward and Morrison, Chapter 4 and Hayward, 2001 for more detail). An important part of this work is the idea of a zone of transition within cities, characterized by run-down housing, high residential mobility, and high levels of poverty and poor health. It is the first home for immigrants who remain only long enough to become economically established before moving to more prosperous neighbourhoods. So the 'zone of transition' is a place of constant change, where communal ties are difficult to establish and most relationships impersonal. Such neighbourhoods were described as socially disorganized and as a consequence were likely to be low in informal methods of social control and high in crime. In Chicago, Shaw and McKay (1942) tested this hypothesis and found that delinquency rates were '...at their highest in run-down inner city areas and progressively declined the further one moved into the prosperous suburbs' (Hayward, 2001: 31). Generalizing these ideas, it seems a logical step to posit that in times and neighbourhoods where unemployment is high or economic prospects are poor it will be difficult to muster the necessary resources to combat social disorganization and maintain informal social control. Hence, again an argument suggests deteriorating economic conditions will lead to increasing levels of crime.

Economic theory: rational economic (wo)man

The economic model of crime posits individuals who choose between crime and legitimate work depending on the opportunities, rewards, and costs of each. Thus, individuals choose to work or to commit a crime depending on the chances of getting a job and the wages in the legitimate market compared with opportunities for illegal earnings, the risk of being caught, and the probability and severity of punishment if they undertake criminal activity (for an alternative to this calculating approach to crime that emphasizes its expressive attraction, see Ferrell, Chapter 7 above). Whilst originally this was posited as choice between legitimate and illegitimate work (Becker, 1968; Erhlich, 1973) more recently it has been extended to allow for individuals to engage in both crime and legitimate work during the same period of time. It will be argued below that this is particularly important in periods when many jobs are part-time, low quality, have little or no security, and are poorly paid. Again this theory suggests that as economic returns from paid employment deteriorate or disappear, crime will increase.

Control theory

Control theory avoids implicating social structure, its focus on individual responsibility appealing to those of a conservative political leaning. It asks not why do people commit crime, but rather how they are constrained not to offend, seeing offending as a natural human instinct. Individuals and their internalization of moral rules and codes become a key focus. One variant, Hirschi's social bond theory (Hirschi, 1969), emphasizes how social bonds to family, school, work, everyday activities, and beliefs insulate people against deviant behaviour. The theory argues that those who:

- are high in *attachment*, with close emotional links to others;
- have a strong *commitment* to the future in that they believe conventional behaviour will lead to immediate or long-term rewards;
- have *involvement* so that they are kept busy in conventional activities such as school or work;
- hold the 'right' *beliefs* about what is permissible or not, that is beliefs that coincide with conventional rules and norms,

are less likely to be involved in deviant or unlawful behaviour. At first sight this does not look hopeful for those seeking theoretical arguments relating unemployment and poverty to crime.

However, as Box (1987) argues, economic recession and unemployment might be expected to weaken social bonds and hence lead to increased levels of crime. Consider first *attachment*. Unemployment and increasing inequality are not likely to improve family relationships. Rather they will produce increased tension, anger, and sullenness against society that may be transferred onto the family leading to its breakdown. This fracture of attachment within the family may lead some to become involved in crime as they care less about what others think of them. Turning to *commitment*, Box (1987: 45) suggests that unemployment 'casts a long shadow' over institutions that are supposed to prepare people for employment. Here he has in mind particularly schools, that risk being delegitimized if their role in preparing pupils for the discipline of work seems redundant as prospects of future employment appear reduced. Next he argues that individual *beliefs* in the legitimacy of conformity will weaken as recession undermines families and schools and this will damage the ability of one generation to impress its values on the next. Alert readers will have spotted that *involvement* has been skipped over. Surprisingly, Box does not consider this factor in his discussion, although it seems straightforward to integrate it in his approach. With more unemployment, shorter working hours, and more part-time work, people will have less involvement in conventional activity and social bond theory would suggest that crime would increase.

Later work by Hirschi developed, or many would argue restricted, control theory, most notably in his 1990 collaboration with Gottfredson under the rather grand title of

A General Theory of Crime (Gottfredson and Hirschi, 1990). This rejected social bond theory conceiving of control instead as '...a permanent internal state' (Lilly *et al.*, 2002). As these authors note, this was part of a broader trend during the 1980s to prioritize individual, rather than structural, explanations of social problems. According to Gottfredson and Hirschi self-control, developed during early childhood, is the key factor that restrains people from engaging in crime. For them self-control depends on the quality of parenting during a child's early years. Ineffectual and neglectful parents will raise children who '... tend to be impulsive, insensitive, physical (as opposed to mental), risk-taking, shortsighted and nonverbal, and they will tend therefore to be engage in criminal and analogous acts' (Gottfredson and Hirshi, 1990). This somewhat depressing picture suggests that nothing can be done to correct traits already set firm in early years. And what of unemployment and recession? Harriet Wilson's work on socially deprived families in inner Birmingham (Wilson, 1980) looked at the degree of 'chaperonage' parents gave to their children. She found a:

> ... very close association between lax parenting methods (and) severe social stress. Lax parenting methods are often the result of chronic stress, situations arising *from frequent or prolonged spells of unemployment* (emphasis added), physical or mental disabilities among members of the family and an often permanent condition of poverty... It is the position of the most disadvantaged groups in society, and not the individual which needs improvement in the first place.

So again, control theory is combined with a strong structural analysis. But the implications for the relationship between unemployment and crime are different. Parenting might be expected to deteriorate in times of recession. However, the effect on crime would not be immediate. Rather it would impact in perhaps eight to ten years time. Dealing with today's crime problems would have required action a decade ago.

Opportunity and routine activity theory

These argue that, in order for a crime to occur, three things are needed—a motivated offender, a suitable target, and a lack of guardianship (see Hayward and Morrison, Chapter 4). Cantor and Land (1985) suggest rising unemployment will have two effects tending to increase the numbers of motivated offenders and the level of guardianship. The reasons behind the first effect have already been rehearsed. According to Cantor and Land (1985: 350) the second arises because the increased numbers of unemployed means that more individuals will remain at home and hence both reduce the risks of their property being burgled and provide more informal social control within neighbourhoods. At the same time, the fact that the unemployed are not involved in daily travel to and from work may reduce their risk of becoming victims of street crime. Hence they argue unemployment has two opposite effects on crime. On one hand crime will tend rise as unemployment potentially causes the numbers of motivated offenders to rise. On the other hand, more unemployed will mean increased levels of guardianship that will tend to cause crime to fall.

Having swiftly reviewed theories that suggest crime is related to economic conditions—mainly the level of unemployment—the next step is to consider what, if any, evidence exists to support or refute the hypothesis.

REVIEW QUESTIONS

1 What is meant by anomie?

2 What are the differences between relative and absolute deprivation?

3 Why might crime fall as unemployment increases?

What is the evidence for a relationship between crime and the economy?

It is worth beginning with some observations of Radzinowicz. In two classic papers looking at the economy and crime (Radzinowicz, 1939; 1971) he suggests that the more multi-faceted the economic structure of society becomes, the harder it is to measure cycles of depression or prosperity. While relatively straightforward in a simple agricultural community, in a complex industrial society measuring economic change is more complicated and relating these changes to trends in crime a more demanding task. Hence it will be necessary to use multiple economic indices rather than relying on single measures such as unemployment. Radzinowicz counsels that economic change may not influence crime at once but at some time in the future—there will be a lagged effect. Further, he makes the important point that economic conditions appear to affect certain types of crime more than others. He suggests property crime is the most sensitive and likely to decrease in times of prosperity. Conversely, crimes against the person seem to go up in times of economic growth.

Unemployment and crime

It has proved difficult to reach anything approaching a consensus on the unemployment-crime (U-C) relationship. As well as reviewing the evidence it is hoped to persuade the reader that a broader view of economic influences than just unemployment is needed. Others factors, including the quality of employment, wage rates, and the precariousness of employment, also need considering.

Two major surveys of the statistical work on unemployment and crime are Chiricos (1987) and Box (1987). Both concluded that, while not consistent, the evidence was slightly in favour of there being a positive relationship: as unemployment increases crime will rise. However, as Chiricos comments, the period covered by most of the studies were dominated by the years up to the 1970s when unemployment was much lower than during the following two decades. Further, he also noted that the evidence for a positive relationship was stronger in studies that focused on property crimes.

As noted above, Cantor and Land (1985) use opportunity theory to explain why negative relationships may arise as unemployment leads to increased guardianship. Positive U-C relationships can be explained by the increased motivation to offend as unemployment grows. Hence in any particular study crime may rise, remain constant, or fall as unemployment rises depending on the relative strengths of the two effects. Whatever the merits[2] of their argument, Cantor and Land alert us to the need to take a more nuanced approach to unemployment and crime.

More recently, studies have questioned the focus on the U-C link when examining the relationship between the economy and crime. Pyle and Deadman (1994) argue that unemployment may not be the best indicator of the state of the economy. At a practical level the definition of unemployment and its measurement underwent numerous revisions during the 1980s making it difficult to construct a consistent data series over a long period of time. (Unsurprisingly, the changes always reduced the numbers of unemployed entitled to benefit.) Further, they argue unemployment lags behind the business cycle by between six and twelve months. An economic recession will affect the labour market first through reduced overtime, more part-time work, and falling wages. Unemployment will begin to rise only after the recession has been underway for some time. However if property crime increases in response to worsening economic conditions, to falling standards of living brought about by the aforementioned reduced overtime and so on, the time lag before unemployment rises suggests it may not capture the observed effect. Instead Pyle and Deadman suggest using other economic indicators that more closely track the business cycle, such as Gross Domestic Product (GDP) or Consumers' Expenditure.

Other approaches to the relationship between the economy and crime

Field (1990) in a classic study found consumer expenditure was the best economic indicator for explaining crime. Twelve different categories of crime were examined using annual time series data for England and Wales. As well as economic variables, Field controlled for a wide range of demographic, criminal justice, and environmental effects using multivariate statistical techniques. He concluded that economic factors have a major influence on the trends in both property crime (including burglary, theft, robbery, vehicle crime, criminal damage, and fraud) and personal crime (including violence against the person, thefts from the person (excluding robbery), and sexual offences).

For property crime and consumption he found two opposite effects. In the short term, year-on-year changes in consumption were negatively, or inversely, related to changes in crime. Field ascribes this to a motivational effect where individuals will switch in and out of criminal activity as their economic fortunes decline or improve. In the long term, over a period of several years he found a positive or direct relationship between crime and the rate of growth of consumption. This he interpreted as an opportunity effect since in a growing economy there will be more goods and money available to steal.

Field's statistical models found that personal crime behaved quite differently from property crime. In both the short and the long term he found that personal crime is positively related to consumer expenditure. He suggests this is because increasing consumption leads to an increase in the amount of time spent outside the home and so increases the likelihood of being the victim of a personal attack. This is (probably) also linked to increased alcohol consumption as incomes rise (see Wincup and Traynor, Chapter 10 above). Again care must be taken in interpreting these findings. In particular it might be asked whether domestic violence is likely to follow this pattern. Are decreasing incomes and increasing unemployment likely to lead to less spouse abuse?

Pyle and Deadman (1994) and Hale (1998), while improving on Field's statistical techniques, confirmed his findings of short-term linkages between the economy and property crime: other things being equal it increases as economy declines. This held whether GDP, personal consumption, or unemployment was used as the economic indicator. Moreover, for burglary and theft they found positive long-term relationships between crime and economic growth, indicating that for the period under consideration (1950–91), the growing economy led to increased crime.

Notwithstanding the mixed results on the U-C relationship it would seem foolish to ignore unemployment or more generally economic inactivity when attempting to explain crime. One issue that needs more consideration is how to measure unemployment. Aside from the problems of definitional and measurement change noted above, it is not clear that a single measure is appropriate. Chamlin and Cochran (2000) discuss various alternatives but argue that for property crime long-term or permanent unemployment is the best measure. Using UK data, Carmichael and Ward (2000) find that youth unemployment is positively related to criminal damage and robbery while adult unemployment is linked to theft. Their research found burglary to be positively related to both youth and adult unemployment.

The conclusion to which we are tentatively moving is that while the U-C relationship is likely to be important in many circumstances it is important to look at broader economic factors than unemployment.

Crime and the changing labour market

Hale (1999) uses data from England and Wales to explore the impact of broader labour market changes as well as unemployment on crime between 1946 and 1994. He argues that the UK economy, and particularly its labour market, has undergone fundamental changes in this period. There has been:

- a shift in employment from the manufacturing to the service sector;
- an increase in part-time employment and an accompanying increase in numbers employed in temporary and untenured jobs;
- a shift in the patterns of employment from men to women.

A dual labour market has developed with a primary or core sector and a secondary or peripheral sector. The primary sector consists of skilled workers usually working full-time for large organizations with good employment and benefit rights. On the other hand, those in the secondary sector are either unemployed or have a high propensity to be unemployed at some time. They have low skills, and, when working, low wages. They are more likely to be employed part-time and have few rights to benefits with regard to sickness, holiday, or pensions. The secondary sector is characterized by high labour turnover among the least skilled workers. For those at the margins:

Employment in the 1990s has become far more unstable. The penalties attached to job loss, jobless duration, and the reduced wages on return have risen. Hence, the secondary labour market has become far riskier. However this new insecurity has been concentrated on a minority for whom jobs for life will become the stuff of legends. (Gregg *et al.*, 1999: 89)

In his empirical analysis Hale (1999) concentrated on de-industrialization, the shift from manufacturing to service sector jobs. This general approach was linked to the work of Allen and Steffensmeier (1989), on the relationship of youth crime to the quality of jobs available, and to that of Carlson and Michalowski (1994) which focuses on de-industrialization and crime. Allen and Steffensmeier show that for juveniles it is the availability of employment that matters, whereas for young adults it is the quality of employment that is important: part-time work with low pay leads to higher rates of property crime. Braithwaite *et al.* (1992)[3] looked at the impact of the increased participation of women in the labour market[4] on crime in Australia. They contend that increased female employment may lead to increased crime in a patriarchal society if appropriate measures are not introduced to '..."take up the slack" in the traditional female role of guardianship' (Triggs, 1997). The mechanisms they identify for this link between crime and female employment include:

- supervision—women in traditional roles: (a) guard their own homes and those of neighbours during the day; (b) look after children who, if unsupervised, are more likely to be both offenders and victims;

- opportunity and motivation—women in the labour force may have more opportunity to commit crime; conversely of course their motivation might decrease. Victimization of working women might increase if they are out more or if domestic tensions increase. Conversely of course domestic tensions might decrease if the household economic situation improves via female wage contribution.

Similar results using US data may be found in Witt and Witte (1998) and for the UK Hale (1999). Hansen (2003) argues that increased female participation in the labour market is likely to have had two effects. First, increasing the supply of labour will tend to lower wages rates. Second, given that the increased employment of women is mainly in part-time unskilled work, this increased supply is likely to increase male unemployment. This will particularly be the case amongst young, less well-educated men most likely to commit property offences. Using cross-section data from England and Wales, she shows that areas with higher rates of female labour force participation are likely to have higher levels of recorded crime.

Crime and inequality

These changes in the labour market interact with broader household changes and have contributed to the growth in income inequality (McRae, 1997).[5] During the past three decades inequality in the UK grew more rapidly than in any other industrialized nation (Atkinson and Micklewright, 1992; Rowntree Report, 1995). This process accelerated during the 1980s. Since 1979, the lowest income groups have not benefited from economic growth and the proportion of the population receiving less than half the average income trebled (Rowntree Report, 1995). There was also a rapid growth in the numbers living in low-income families with children. Hale (1999) used two separate measures for inequality. The first was the Gini coefficient, which captures the level of income inequality in the whole population, and the second the ratio of the share of income going to the highest 10 per cent of earners with that going to the lowest 10 per cent. He found that the second measure was positively related to growth in burglary.[6]

The growing polarization between 'work rich' and 'work poor' households has reinforced patterns of poverty and inequality. For example, while employment is as plentiful as it was 30 years ago, the numbers of workless households has roughly quadrupled (Gregg *et al.* (1999)).[7] One in five children in Britain are growing up in workless households.

Wage inequality in the UK reached record highs for the twentieth century at the beginning of the 1990s. A key factor in this increased inequality was the rapid deterioration in the labour market position of less skilled workers at the bottom end of the wage distribution. The economic model of crime argues that individuals will choose between legal and illegal work on the basis of their relative rewards. Many individuals find that, whilst in work, their jobs are insecure, low-paid, and low-skilled. Often they are in part-time or temporary work and they are on the economic and social margins. Many of the theoretical arguments presented above for why unemployment and crime might be related apply equally well to that between low wage, low-skill employment. The importance of exploring these issues in any model of crime is underlined by the results of analyses by Reilly and Witt (1996), Witt, *et al.* (1998, 1999), Hansen and Machin (2004), and Machin and Meghir (2004). Witt *et al.* (1998) find a positive relationship between widening (male) wage inequality and crime (see also Borooah and Collins, 1995).

Recent work using US data has looked at the statistical relationship between crime and low wages. Gould *et al.* (2002) find significant negative relationships across areas between changes in wages and changes in recorded burglary, aggravated assault, and robbery. Grogger (1998) shows that falling wages explain not only rising youth crime, but also age and ethnic differences. For England and Wales, Machin and Meghir (2003) analyse property crime (burglary plus theft and handling) at the police force area level from 1975 to 1996. They show that over this period falls in the wages of unskilled workers lead to increases in property crime.

In a similar vein Hansen and Machin (2004) examined the impact of the introduction of the minimum wage in England and Wales in April 1999. This gave a pay increase to an estimated two million low paid workers. Within an economic model of crime this would decrease the relative benefits of criminal as opposed to legal activity and so might be expected to persuade those on the margins not to engage in criminal activity and hence to reduce crime. Police force areas that gained most were those with the highest proportions of workers paid less than the new minimum prior to April 1999.[8] Hansen and Machin examined crime rates before and after its introduction. They looked at total crime, property crime, vehicle crime,[9] and violent crime (violence against the person) and found that, on average, areas that benefited most from the minimum wage saw the greatest decreases in crime.

As well as wages, social security benefits might be expected to have an impact on crime levels by mediating the effects of unemployment and economic recession. If welfare payments are cut, or their eligibility criteria tightened, then the economic benefits from crime would increase. Machin and Marie (2004) consider the impact of the introduction of the Jobseekers Allowance (JSA) in Britain in October 1996. Replacing both unemployment benefit and income support, it brought about major changes in benefit entitlement. The period of non-means tested contributory benefits was reduced from twelve months to six and the requirements for job seeking tightened by stopping benefit where an individual was judged not to be actively seeking work. Although the idea behind the JSA is to persuade people back to work, Machin and Marie point out unemployment may fall not by getting people back to work (or into education or training), but because they move off benefits and suffer an income cut. In such circumstances they are likely to find crime more attractive. They present evidence that crime rose by more in the areas more affected by JSA. Hence they argue that the benefits sanctions may have caused individuals previously on the margins to turn to crime.

Crime, the underclass, and social exclusion

Crime and its relationship to poverty reappeared in the last decades of the twentieth century as part of a politically right-wing response to the perceived failings of the welfare state. Cushioned by the welfare state so that they become 'welfare dependent', many were unable to stand on their own two feet.

Right realism saw crime and other social problems as the product of individual characteristics rather than the result of any structural factors. Criminality was voluntaristic, committed by individuals with no self-control who choose crime as well as unemployment and poverty.

Particularly relevant here is the work of Charles Murray (1984, 1990), who used the notion of the underclass.[10] For Murray the important distinguishing characteristic of the underclass is not that they are poor, although that is one characteristic, but that they are not respectable. 'Their homes were littered and unkempt. The men in the family were unable to hold a job for more than a few weeks at a time. Drunkenness was common. The children grew up ill-schooled and ill-behaved...' (Murray, 1990: 1).

For Murray, the underclass has three main characteristics: illegitimacy; violent crime; and economic inactivity. Murray essentially sees a segregated society. On the one hand are those sectors upholding traditional values of hard work, sobriety, and family; on the other the morally weak underclass who are unemployed, involved in crime and drug addiction, and have illegitimate children raised by single mothers living on welfare. For Murray this is a matter of choice and hence the solution is to reduce welfare payments for unmarried mothers to encourage the avoidance of pregnancy without working supportive fathers and the reduction of unemployment benefits to encourage those capable of work to seek employment. The problem of crime in Murray's view is that increasing numbers of young men are being brought up without positive male role models and are avoiding the civilizing institutions of marriage, family, and work, preferring to live on welfare or illegal activities.

Murray sees the habitual criminal as a classic member of the underclass living off the mainstream society without contributing to it. Indeed the definitive sign that an underclass has developed is that '...large numbers of young healthy, low income males *choose* not to take job' (Murray, 1990: 17) [italics added]. The key word here is of course 'choose' as Murray believes that, as well as unemployed workers who are actively seeking work, there is a large group of 'economically inactive' people, some of whom have opted not to work.

The notion of the underclass is not unique to Murray and indeed under another name 'socially excluded' is prominent in the writings of those of the left and indeed central to much of New Labour thinking. The terms are different, but the people who Murray would include in his underclass are the same as those who are regarded as socially excluded. Social exclusion covers not just poverty but also political and spatial exclusion and the notion that the excluded are denied access to '…information, medical provision, housing, policing, security etc' (Young, 2002: 457). These factors interact and reinforce each other to the extent that those who experience the exclusion are denied the chance to participate fully as citizens. Whilst the symptoms of the underclass and the socially excluded are similar, the latter implies the issue is a structural problem rather than the fault of the individual. Hence there are here two variants of social exclusion: the weak and the strong (Veit-Wilson, 1998; Bryne, 1999). The 'weak' version, following Murray, emphasizes individual weaknesses that prevent full participation in society. The dysfunctional members of the underclass have chosen their lot and must be 'encouraged' to participate in the low wage labour market of poor quality work by attacking the dependency culture encouraged by the welfare state. The 'strong' version sees the problems at the structural level, driven by economic globalization that has led to the rapid changes in the labour markets of industrialized countries driven by the decline in manufacturing and the rise of precarious employment in the service sector discussed above. Young (2002) sees two approaches within explanations that see social exclusion as a result of structural problems. He distinguishes between on the one hand a 'passive' and active version. The first, most notably in the work of William Julius Wilson (Wilson, 1987; 1996) sees the problems resulting from the failure of the system to provide jobs leading to '…"social isolation" wherein people lose not so much the motive to work but the capacity to find work because of lack of positive role models coupled with a spatial isolation from job opportunities' (Young, 2002: 458). The second emphasizes the active rejection of the underclass by society. In a story that should by now be familiar, it stresses the '…downsizing of industry, the stigmatization of the workless and the stereotyping of the underclass as criminogenic and drug-ridden with images that are frequently racialized and prejudiced' (Young, 2002: 458).

These distinctions are important when looking at the policies of New Labour. Whilst accepting the arguments that social exclusion is a structural problem, it has nevertheless adopted policies that blame the victim by locating solutions at the individual level. The Social Exclusion Unit (SEU) was set up in 1997 and has looked to tackle a wide range of issues including deprived neighbourhoods, unemployment, drug use, teenage pregnancy, truancy, school exclusion—a list of the classic symptoms of social exclusion. To stress the interconnectedness of the problems and hence the need for 'joined-up' solutions it works across government departments and is the responsibility of the Deputy Prime Minister. The SEU is clear that social exclusion is a major factor in both crime and fear of crime, and that in turn these are part of the interlinked facets of the problem (Social Exclusion Unit, 2001). Whilst acknowledging the (global) economic and social changes that have taken place, they see the problem of crime and social exclusion as related to issues of socialization and lack of control in young people related to poor parenting and inadequate schooling together with drug and alcohol abuse. Having first identified the problems at a structural level, the emphasis, as Matthews and Young (2003) point out, shifts to an implicit control theory. Central to New Labour's strategy of combating social exclusion, and hence being tough on the causes of crime, is entry into work. Any work is better than no work, and of course unpaid work is not proper work. So the focus has been persuading the unemployed and excluded back to work by threatening to cut benefits and offering re-training programmes. Evidence that suggested work per se is not the answer; that poorly paid work or part-time work with little security and sense of worth does not reduce crime in the long run was reviewed above (Hale and FitzGerald, 2007). As Currie (1998) has shown, inclusionary policies that focus on work as the mechanism where work involves long and inflexible hours serve to undermine the family and community and hence weaken rather than strengthen social control. As explored in Hale and FitzGerald (Chapter 21 below), this has been coupled with a political emphasis on being tough on crime that has increased rather decreased social exclusion by pushing crime and disorder to the margins of society (see the references below to Trickett *et al.*).

Victims, inequality, and crime

Thus far the focus has been on the economic circumstances of offenders and the relationship between crime and the business cycle. What of the economic situation of victims? In England and Wales the best sources of information on this are the somewhat inappropriately named British Crime Surveys (BCS).[11]

The most recent information comes from the 2002/03 BCS (Simmons and Dodd, 2003). This examines how crime victimization risk varies according to neighbourhood. The highest risk areas for burglary are: (a) town and city areas whose residents are well off professional singles and couples; and (b) council estates with, elderly, lone parent, or unemployed residents. For both the risk is 5 per cent compared to 3 per cent across households in England and Wales as a whole. Within the second group, households on estates with the greatest hardship have a burglary victimization risk of 6.9 per cent—over twice the national risk. For vehicle-related thefts, while 11 per cent of all vehicle-owning households were victims, this rose to 21 per cent in the highest risk areas, described as multi-ethnic low-income neighbourhoods. Again the highest risk of violence, at 7 per cent, was to adults in multi-ethnic low income areas compared to the overall average of 4 per cent.

More generally the risk of crime victimization is unequally spread across society and follows the pattern suggested by Ulrich Beck in his book *The Risk Society*:

> The history of risk distribution shows that, like wealth, risks adhere to the class pattern, only inversely; wealth accumulates at the top, risks at the bottom. To that extent, risks seem to strengthen, not to abolish the class society. Poverty attracts an unfortunate abundance of risks. By contrast, the wealthy (in income, power or education) can purchase safety and freedom from risk. (Beck, 1992: 35)

In a series of papers researchers from the University of Manchester Quantitative Criminology Group have analysed the unequal distribution of victimization across neighbourhoods. Their work, combining BCS and Census data, shows that around a fifth of the victims of household property crime in England and Wales live in the 10 per cent of residential areas with the highest crime rates and account for over a third[12] of the total of household property crime (see, for example, Hope, 2003; 2000). Twenty per cent of communities in England and Wales have over a third of all property crime victims and suffer over half of all property offences. At the other end of this crime spectrum, the least victimized 50 per cent areas suffer only 15 per cent of the crime and contain just 25 per cent of the victims. Moreover, when Census data on income and deprivation are considered a stark picture emerges of crime risk increasing markedly with area deprivation. Crime adds to the disadvantage suffered by the least well off groups in society and adds to their social exclusion. What is more, Trickett *et al.* (1995) show that during the 1980s, a decade when the long-term trend to greater equality of wealth, income, and opportunity was rapidly reversed, inequality of victimization also became more marked.

This redistribution of crime victimization can also be seen in the regional figures. The North-South divide in terms of economic and demographic trends—with economic and population growth in the latter at the expense of the former, exacerbated by de-industrialization—was again inversely reflected in patterns of crime victimization. During the 1980s the North's disproportionate share of property crime increased relative to the South and to Greater London in particular (Trickett *et al.*, 1995: 353). Hence, crime contributes to the very inequality and social exclusion that are seen as its causes.

REVIEW QUESTIONS

1 Why might an increase in female employment cause crime to rise?

2 What are the differences between the concepts of the 'underclass' and 'social exclusion'?

3 Will creating more part-time, low paid jobs necessarily reduce crime?

CONCLUSION

This chapter has considered the impact of economic conditions on crime. Inevitably some topics of importance have been ignored. As noted earlier, the focus has been on crimes such as burglary and theft rather than those that might be described as corporate and white collar. That is not to imply that in times of economic downturn these will not also increase as competitive pressures increase the incentives for individuals and businesses to cut corners and bend and break the law in order to survive (see Tombs, Chapter 13 above). Indeed the notion that market economies based on competition and rewarding risk taking might encourage criminality has not been developed. Finally, violent crime might also have been considered, but for constraints on space. Again the evidence suggests that the long-term trend has been for violence to decline as countries' economies develop. Broadly speaking, comparative analysis suggests that rates of violence in industrialized countries are lower than in less wealthy economies. However, in the short run it seems that economic booms lead to increased levels of violence fuelled at least in part by increased alcohol consumption (see Ray, Chapter 11; Wincup and Traynor, Chapter 10).

Turning to work, on balance both the theoretical arguments and the empirical evidence reviewed support the hypothesis that deteriorating economic circumstances will lead to increased property crime. Unemployment, poverty, inequality, and low wages have all been found to be related to property crime in one study or another. Other work suggests that the quality of work available may also be key.

The growth in the secondary labour markets, with precarious employment in low paid, part-time work, that have been the consequence of the process of globalization and economic restructuring over the last 30 years have had an impact on crime similar to that of the nineteenth century when the Industrial Revolution caused major ruptures in the established structures of society. However, the work reviewed here also questions whether strategies to combat social exclusion based on encouraging people back to paid employment will necessarily succeed, since it is not work per se that is important but its quality and the satisfaction it provides.

QUESTIONS FOR DISCUSSION

1 What do the main criminological theories have to say about the relationship between crime and the economy?

2 Compare and contrast the policy approaches of the New Right to the underclass with those of New Labour to social exclusion.

3 Is unemployment the main factor to consider when examining the relationship between crime and the economy?

4 Why might corporate crime increase during economic recessions?

GUIDE TO FURTHER READING

Box, S. (1987) *Recession, Crime and Punishment*. London: Macmillan.
This is as good a place as any to find a review of this field.

Gregg, P. and Wadsworth, J. (eds) (1999) *The State of Working Britain. Manchester*: Manchester University Press.
Provides a very useful discussion of labour market changes in the UK.

Hale, C. and FitzGerald, M. (2007) 'Social Exclusion and Crime' in D. Abrams, J. Christian, and D. Gordon (eds) *The Multidisciplinary Handbook of Social Exclusion Research*. Chichester: John Wiley and Sons.

Hagan, J. and Peterson, R.D. (eds) (1995) *Crime and Inequality*. Stanford: Stanford University Press.
Another book that provides an overview of a wide range of issues.

Reiner, R. (2007a) *Law and Order; An Honest Citizen's Guide to Crime Control*. Cambridge: Polity Press.

Reiner, R. (2007b) 'Political Economy, Crime and Criminal Justice', Chapter 12 in M. Maguire, R. Morgan, and R. Reiner (eds) *The Oxford Handbook of Criminology* (4th edn). Oxford: Oxford University Press.
The two works by Reiner provide an excellent review of broader political economy approaches to crime and punishment.

Taylor, I. (1995) Crime in Context: *A Critical Criminology of Market Societies*. Cambridge: Polity Press.

Provides an excellent discussion of broader issues of crime in market economies.

Young, J. (2002) 'Crime and social exclusion' in M. Maguire, M. Morgan, and R. Reiner (eds), *The Oxford Handbook of Criminology* (3rd edn). Oxford: Oxford University Press.

Jock Young's chapter is a good introduction to social exclusion.

WEB LINKS

http://www.jrf.org.uk/home.asp

The website for the Joseph Rowntree Foundation. This contains useful information.

http://www.poverty.org.uk/intro/index.htm

The Joseph Rowntree Foundation also supports this New Policy Institute site dedicated to monitoring poverty and social exclusion.

http://www.ifs.org.uk/

The site of the Institute of Fiscal Affairs. It has good reports on poverty and inequality and more generally on the economy.

http://www.tuc.org.uk

This is the website of the Trades Union Congress. It provides links to recent research and has discussion of labour market trends.

REFERENCES

Allen, E.A. and Steffensmeier, D.J. (1989) 'Youth, Underemployment, and Property Crime: Effects of the Quantity and Quality of Job Opportunities on Juvenile and Young Adult Arrest Rates', *American Sociological Review*, 54: 107–23.

Atkinson, A.B. and Micklewright, B. (1992) *Economic Transformation in Eastern Europe and the Distribution of Income*. Cambridge: Cambridge University Press.

Beck, U. (1992) *Risk Society, Towards a New Modernity*, London, Sage.

Becker, G. (1968) 'Crime and Punishment: An Economic Approach', *Journal of Political Economy*, 76: 175–209.

Borooah, V.K. and Collins, G. (1995) 'Unemployment and crime in the regions of Britain: a theoretical and empirical analysis', mimeo. University of Ulster: Ulster.

Box, S. (1987) *Recession Crime and Punishment*. London: Macmillan.

Braithwaite, J., Chapman, B., and Kapuscinski, C.A. (1992) 'Unemployment and crime: resolving the paradox', mimeo, *American Bar Foundation Working Paper 9201*. Chicago: Illinois.

Bruegel, I. (2000) 'No more Jobs for the Boys? Gender and Class in the Restructuring of the British Economy', *Capital and Class*, 71, 79–102.

Bryne, D. (1999) *Social Exclusion*. Buckingham: Open University Press.

Cantor, D. and Land, K.C. (1985) 'Unemployment and Crime Rates in Post World War II United States: a Theoretical and Empirical Analysis', *American Sociological Review*, 50, 317–32.

Carlson, S.M. and Michalowski, R.J. (1994) 'Structural change in the economy, economic marginality, and crime', mimeo. Western Michigan University.

Carmichael, F. and Ward, R. (2000) 'Youth Unemployment and Crime in the English Regions and Wales', *Applied Economics*, 32, 559–571.

Chamlin, M.B. and Cochran, J. (2000) 'Unemployment, Economic Theory, and Property Crime: A Note on Measurement', *Journal of Quantitative Criminology*, 16, 443–455.

Chiricos, T.G. (1987) 'Rates of Crime and Unemployment: An Analysis of Aggregate Research Evidence', *Social Problems*, 34, 187–211.

Cohen, L.E. (1981) 'Modelling Trends in Crime: a Criminal Opportunity Perspective', *Journal of Research in Crime and Delinquency*, 18, 138–164.

Cohen, L.E. and Felson, M. (1979) 'Social Change and Crime Rate Trends: A Routine Activities Approach', *American Sociological Review*, 44, 588–608.

Currie, E. (1998) *Crime and Punishment in America*. New York: Metropolitan Books.

Durkheim, E. (1893) *The Division of Labour in Society*, 1984 edition translated by W.D. Halls, with an introduction by Lewis Coser. Basingstoke: Macmillan.

Ehrlich, I. (1973) 'Participation in Illegitimate Activities: a Theoretical and Empirical Investigation', *Journal of Political Economy*, 81, 521–63.

Felson, M. and Cohen, L.E. (1980) 'Human Ecology and Crime: A Routine Activities Approach', *Human Ecology*, 8, 389–406.

Field, S. (1990), 'Trends in Crime and their Interpretation: A Study of Recorded Crime in Post-war England and Wales', *Home Office Research Study No. 119*, Home Office, London.

Gogger, J. (1998) 'Market Wages and Youth Crime', *Journal of Labour Economics*, 16: 756–91.

Gottfredson, M. and Hirschi, T. (1990) *A General Theory of Crime*. Stanford: Stanford University Press.

Gould, D., Mustard, D.B., and Weinberg, B.A. (2002) 'Crime Rates and Local Labor Market opportunities in the United States: 1979–1997', *Review of Economics and Statistics*, 84, 45–61.

Greenberg, D.F. (2001) 'Time Series Analysis of Crime Rates', *Journal of Quantitative Criminology*, 17, 291–327.

Gregg, P., Hansen, K., and Wadsworth, J. (1999) 'Workless households', Chapter 5 in P. Gregg and J. Wadsworth (eds) *The State of Working Britain*. Manchester: Manchester University Press.

Grogger, J. (1998) 'Market Wages and Youth Crime', *Journal of Labor Economics*, 16 (4), 756–91.

Hagan, J. and Peterson, R.D. (eds) (1995) *Crime and Inequality*. Stanford: Stanford University Press.

Hale, C. (1998) 'Crime and the Business Cycle in Post-war Britain Revisited', *British Journal of Criminology*, 38 (4), 681–98.

Hale, C. (1999) 'The labour market and post-war crime trends in England and Wales' in P. Carlen and R. Morgan (eds) *Crime Unlimited: Questions for the 21st Century*. Basingstoke: Macmillan.

Hale, C. and FitzGerald, M. (2007) 'Social Exclusion and Crime' in Abrams, D., Christian, J., and Gordon, D. (eds) *The Multidisciplinary Handbook of Social Exclusion Research*. Chichester: John Wiley and Sons.

Hale, C. and Sabbagh, D. (1989) 'Testing the Relationship between Unemployment and Crime: A Methodological Comment and Empirical Analysis using Time Series data from England and Wales', *Journal of Research into Crime and Delinquency*, 28: 400–417.

Hansen, K. (2003) 'The Impact of Increasing female Labour Force Participation on Male Property Crime' Paper presented at the British Society of Criminology Conference, Bangor, July.

Hansen, K. and Machin, S. (2004) 'Crime and the Minimum Wage', *Journal of Quantitative Criminology*.

Hayward, K. (2001) 'Chicago School of Sociology' in E. McLaughlin and J. Muncie (eds) *The Sage Dictionary of Criminology*. London: Sage.

Hirschi, T. (1969) *The Causes of Delinquency*. Berkeley: University of California Press.

Hope, T. (2000) 'Inequality and the Clubbing of Society' in T. Hope and R. Sparks (eds) *Crime, Risk and Insecurity*. London: Routledge.

Hope, T. (2003) 'Private Security and Crime Victimisation in Risk Society' Paper delivered at the conference *Per Una Società Più Sicura: il contributo conoscitivo dell.informazione statistica*, ISTAT, Rome, Italy, 3–5 December 2003.

Kapuscinski, C.A., Braithwaite, J., and Chapman, B. (1998) 'Unemployment and crime: resolving the paradox', *Journal of Quantitative Criminology*, 14: 215–44.

Lilly, J.R., Cullen, F.T., and Ball, R.A. (2002) *Criminological Theory: Context and Consequences* (3rd edn). London: Sage.

Machin, S. (1999) 'Wage Inequality in the 1970s, 1980s and 1990s', chapter 11 in P. Gregg and J. Wadsworth (eds) *The State of Working Britain*. Manchester: Manchester University Press.

Machin, S. and Marie, O. (2004) 'Crime and Benefit Cuts', Paper presented to the Annual Conference of the Royal Economic Society, Swansea, April.

Machin, S. and Meghir, C. (2004) 'Crime and Economic Incentives', *Journal of Human Resources*.

Matthews, R. and Young, J. (2003) *The New Politics of Crime and Punishment*. Cullompton, Willan.

McRae, S. (1997) 'Household and Labour Market Change: Implications for the Growth of Inequality in Britain', *British Journal of Sociology*, 48, 384–405.

Merton, R. (1938) 'Social Structure and "Anomie"', *American Sociological Review*, 3: 672–82.

Murray, C. (1984) *Losing Ground*. New York: Basic Books.

Murray, C. (1990) *The Emerging British Underclass*. London Institute of Economic Affairs.

Pyle, D. and Deadman, D. (1994) 'Crime and the Business Cycle in Post-war Britain', *British Journal of Criminology*, 34, 339–357

Radzinowicz, L. (1939), 'The Influence of Economic Conditions on Crime' *Sociological Review*, 33, 139–53.

Radzinowicz, L. (1971), 'Economic Pressures', chapter 34 in L. Radzinowicz and M.E. Wolgang, *Crime and Justice Volume 1: The Criminal in Society*. New York: Basic Books.

Reilly, B. and Witt, R. (1996) 'Crime, Deterrence and Unemployment in England and Wales: an Empirical Analysis', *Bulletin of Economic Research*, 48: 137–59.

Reiner, R. (2007a) *Law and Order; An Honest Citizen's Guide to Crime Control*. Cambridge: Polity Press.

Reiner, R. (2007b) 'Political Economy, Crime and Criminal Justice', chapter 12 in M. Maguire, R. Morgan, and Reiner, R. (eds) *The Oxford Handbook of Criminology* (4th edn). Oxford: Oxford University Press.

Rowntree Report (1995) *Inquiry into Income and Wealth*. Joseph Rowntree Foundation: York.

Shaw, C.R. and McKay, H.D. (1942) *Juvenile Delinquency and Urban Areas*. Chicago: University of Chicago Press.

Simmons, J. and Dodd, T. (2003) *Crime in England and Wales 2002/2003*. Home Office: London.

Social Exclusion Unit (2001) *Preventing Social Exclusion*. London: Stationery Office.

Taylor, I. (1995) *Crime in Context: A Critical Criminology of Market Societies*. Cambridge: Polity Press.

Trickett A., Ellingworth, D., Hope, T., and Pease, K. (1995) 'Crime Victimisation in the Eighties', *British Journal of Criminology*, 35, 343–59.

Triggs, S. (1997) *Interpreting Trends in Recorded Crime in New Zealand* <http://www.justice.govt.nz/pubs/reports/1997/crime>, New Zealand Ministry of Justice. Veit-Wilson, J. (1998) *Setting Adequacy Standards*. London: Policy Press.

Wilson, H. (1980) 'Parental Supervision: A Neglected Aspect of Delinquency', *British Journal of Criminology*, 20.

Wilson, W.J. (1987) *The Truly Disadvantaged*. Chicago: Chicago University Press.

Wilson, W.J. (1996) *When Work Disappears*. New York: Knopf.

Witt, R., Clarke, A., and Fielding, N. (1998) 'Crime, Earnings Inequality and Unemployment in England and Wales', *Applied Economics Letters*, 5: 265–67.

Witt, R., Clarke, A., and Fielding, N. (1999) 'Crime and Economic Activity: a Panel Data Approach', *British Journal of Criminology*, 39: 391–400.

Witt, R. and Witte, A.D. (1998), 'Crime, Imprisonment and Female Labour Force Participation: A Time Series Approach', *Journal of Quantitative Criminology*, 16: 69–86.

Young, J. (2001) 'Relative Deprivation' in E. McLaughlin and J. Muncie (eds) *The Sage Dictionary of Criminology*. London: Sage.

Young, J. (2002) 'Crime and Social Exclusion' in M. Maguire, M. Morgan, and R. Reiner (eds) *The Oxford Handbook of Criminology* (3rd edn). Oxford: Oxford University Press.

NOTES

1. The definition of poverty used in UK policy refers to the numbers of families who earn less than 60 per cent of median income. Hence poverty here is a relative concept and tackling it requires reducing inequality as well as increasing low incomes.

2. See Hale and Sabbagh (1989) and Greenberg (2001) for methodological critiques of their statistical approach.

3. Published as Kapuscinski *et al.* (1998). This idea may be traced at least back to the papers of Cohen (1981), Cohen and Felson (1979), and Felson and Cohen (1980) who use a 'residential population density ratio' in their statistical work. This variable is defined as the sum of female labour force participants with husbands present plus the number of households that are non-husband-wife households divided by the total number of households. This ratio will increase as either of the terms in the numerator gets larger. A higher ratio in terms of the approach of these authors implies less 'guardianship' and hence is likely to lead to increased crime. On a technical note, the numerator is strange in that it adds individuals to households and hence is not bounded by 1.

4. The research was originally published as Braithwaite *et al.* (1992).

5. See also Breugel (2000) for a discussion of the feminization of employment in Britain.

6. See also amongst others Machin (1999) and the data and sources on wage inequality given therein.

7. Family Expenditure Survey estimates give 4 per cent of households workless in 1968, 6.2 per cent workless in 1975, and 17.4 per cent workless in 1996. The Labour Force Survey estimates are comparable with 6.5 per cent workless in 1975 and 17.9 per cent workless in 1998 (Table 5.1, Gregg *et al.* (1999).

8. To take two (imaginary) extremes, in areas where everyone was paid more than the minimum wage to begin with, then no one would be better off when it was introduced. Conversely in areas where all workers earn less than the new minimum, then all will benefit.

9. Theft of a vehicle, theft from a vehicle, aggravated vehicle taking, vehicle interference, and criminal damage to a vehicle.

10. As he himself pointed it was not a new idea. The Marxist notion of the lumpen proletariat is similar, but of course from a different political provenance. It also has resonance with Victorian notions of respectable and unrespectable, the deserving and undeserving poor—those who would try to help themselves and tried to maintain moral standards and those who did nothing to help and abandoned themselves to dissolution.

11. Similar information for Scotland can be obtained from the Scottish Crime Surveys (SCS).

12. The point being that some households are victimized more than once. See Hope, Chapter 3 above for a discussion of area crime incidence (the number of crimes per head of population), area prevalence rate (the proportion of victims in the population), and area crime concentration (the number of victimizations per victim).

Gender and crime

Catrin Smith and Emma Wincup

INTRODUCTION

Crime is largely a male activity. Studies consistently show that males commit more crimes than females and their offences tend to be more serious and violent in nature. However, the 'maleness' of crime was, until the 1970s, largely taken for granted. Since then feminists have done much to make visible the experiences of women as offenders and victims and to highlight the gendered practices of the criminal justice process in relation to women but the important relationship between men, masculinity, and crime has been somewhat neglected. The purpose of this chapter is to provide an overview of the issues around sex, gender, and crime. It considers the contribution of feminist perspectives to the study of crime and criminal justice before providing an overview of the patterning of criminal behaviour and victimization according to sex. This leads to an analysis of the kinds of crimes men and women are involved in and the relationship between masculinity(ies), femininity(ies), and crime. The chapter then explores gendered differences in criminal justice at various stages within the process as well as the ways age, ethnicity, and class may affect how males and females experience the criminal justice system. The chapter concludes with a consideration of the implications of a 'gender agenda' for the discipline of criminology and for the criminal justice process.

BACKGROUND

The terms 'sex' and 'gender' are often used interchangeably as ways of categorizing the seemingly straightforward biological distinction between female and male. However, understanding the difference between sex and gender informs us that most differences between males and females are the result of complex social processes rather than biologically determined.

Sex differences are those based on biological criteria for classifying persons as male or female, including genital and hormonal differences and variations in reproductive capacity. In contrast, gender differences are ascribed by society and relate to expectations about appropriate social roles. Sex differences may determine an individual's ability to become pregnant, but gendered *assumptions* suggest that, because women have the reproductive capacity to bear children, it is women who should carry the burden of childcare responsibilities. Most differences between men and women in terms of social roles, expectations, and identities are gender not sex differences. They are often assumed to be 'natural', yet they are learnt during the process of socialization where cultural definitions of 'masculinity' and 'femininity' and what it means to be a 'man' or a 'woman' are passed on. Gendered constructions are historically diverse and different societies code 'manhood' and 'womanhood' in very different ways (Oakley, 1972). Moreover, there are differences not only between masculinity and femininity but also within them, and diversity among men and masculinities and among women and femininities exist on the basis of various aspects of social experience (Connell, 1987). However, in most forms of societal organization some versions of masculinity and femininity are valued over others. In late modern societies the dominant form of masculinity, or what Connell (1987) defines as 'hegemonic masculinity', is possessed by those males who are instrumentally active, tough, risk-takers, breadwinners, who show no fear and emotion, and who give expression to 'normative heterosexuality'. In contrast, what society codes as feminine involves an expressive capacity for emotion, care, compassion, passivity, and subservience. In such a system, 'successful' masculinity and 'successful' femininity depend upon the extent to which one adopts the deeds and actions associated with the idea of being male (but not female) or female (but not male). Central to an understanding of the distinction between sex and gender is an understanding of the ways in which social value systems construct and legitimate differences between males and females and give tacit primacy to some definitions of masculinity and femininity over others.

To understand the current debates concerning sex, gender, crime, and justice, it is first necessary to comprehend something of the relevant historical development of the discipline of criminology and the context into which feminist perspectives on crime and justice emerged. Criminology is a diverse and fragmented discipline (see Chapter 4). In all its guises, however, historically academic criminology has tended to ignore females as both victims and offenders. Where they have been included they have often been misrepresented in sexist and stereotypical ways. The work of Lombroso and Ferrero (1895), Thomas (1923), and Pollak (1961), for example, while different in certain ways, all expressed accepted views about female criminality, viewing females as 'driven' to crime because of biological and/or socio-sexual influences. In the main, however, female crime was seen as neither interesting nor important and, up until the 1970s, criminologists consistently left females out of their research, questions, and samples. For as long as systematic data on crime have been collated, males have far outnumbered females among known offenders, law-makers, and law enforcers. Similarly, criminology as a discipline has been dominated by men and male perspectives. As Hearn (2003) points out, the history of criminology has been largely a history of men but one in which the 'maleness' of crime, crime control, and crime analysis has been so taken for granted as to be rendered invisible.

The exclusion of females in criminological theorizing and empirical inquiry formed a key part of the critique developed by feminist writers, influenced by the growth of 'second wave' feminism and the women's movement (see Heidensohn, 1968; Smart, 1976). This work did much to expose the male dominance yet 'gender-blindness' of criminology and was formative in the development of what has become termed loosely as 'feminist criminology'. Contrary to popular opinion, not all feminists think alike and, as in criminology, there are many different feminist perspectives (see Walklate, 2001 for an overview). Despite the different stances, feminist theory is concerned generally with 'a woman-centred description and explanation of human experience and the social world' (Danner, 1989: 51). It asserts that gender and gender relations order social life and social institutions and it is directed towards social change and, in particular, towards negating the neglect and subordination of women. Inherent to many strains of feminist thought are the concepts of sexism and patriarchy. Sexism refers to oppressive attitudes and behaviours directed towards either sex but, in particular, the concept has been used to refer to discriminatory practices aimed primarily at women. Patriarchy, on the other hand, refers to a system of social structures and practices in which men dominate.

The influence of feminist thinking is evident in the large body of writing on the subject of women, gender, and crime. While there is no one set of perspectives which define 'feminist criminology', the main contributions to knowledge include:

- a more central focus on women as offenders and victims;
- a critique of earlier (male) criminological studies of, and theories about, (male) crime and the advancement of more rigorous research methodologies and theory-building around gender and crime;

- the deconstruction of the sexist and stereotypical images of female offenders and victims within much criminological theorizing;

- the identification of institutionalized sexism not only within academic criminology, but also within criminal justice policy and practice;

- an understanding of the effect of gender constructs on the propensity for women to offend and a recognition that inequalities between the sexes can differentially shape male and female experiences and behaviours, including criminality;

- an insight into the interrelationship between prior victimization and offending; and

- an increasing concern with examining how constructs of class, ethnicity, and sexuality affect the gender dimension of crime.

In making the 'woman question' central, feminist work has been accused of partiality and has been criticized for not including considerations of gender in relation to male crime. However, it is wrong to assume that feminist work has ignored men and masculinity. Rather, feminist theories have examined masculinity and men's lives in order to more fully understand women's, especially in relation to acts of force and violence committed *against* women. More recently, feminist research has also influenced the development of critical studies of male criminality and has helped understand similarity and difference in terms of risk factors for offending by males and females. The discipline of criminology has also benefited from more gender-specific crime modules, books, and journals, and through the academic production of more feminist scholars (women and men). Moreover, feminist thinking has also had an influence on criminal justice policy and practice. For instance, legal reform (especially in relation to sexual and domestic violence) and developments in crime prevention (especially in relation to women's safety) have resulted from a feminist focus on women and crime. In summing up the achievements of feminists working within criminology, Naffine (1997: 29) argues that feminist criminologies have helped us to 'see crime differently'. Many aspects of feminists' thinking will be developed throughout the sections to follow.

Sex and crime

Students of criminology and criminal justice will learn at an early stage to be critical of the main sources of data on crime—recorded statistics, self-report studies, and victim surveys (see Chapter 3). Despite their limitations, each source includes information on sex differences and, as such, is worthy of consideration.

Recorded statistics

The most commonly referred to sources of information on offending are the 'official statistics' on known offenders. These statistics are compiled annually in England and Wales by the Ministry of Justice and offer us the following picture of male and female offending in 2006 (Ministry of Justice, 2007a).

- Seventy-nine per cent of known offenders were male.

- The peak age of known offending for the most serious (i.e. indictable offences) was 17 for males and 15 for females.

- Between 82 and 93 per cent of offenders found guilty of, or cautioned for, burglary, robbery, drug offences, criminal damage, or violence against the person were male.

- Ninety-seven per cent of people found guilty of, or cautioned for, sexual offences were male.

- For indictable offences, 50 per cent of female offenders were found guilty of, or cautioned for, theft and handling stolen goods compared with 30 per cent of male offenders.

- In the ten years between 1996 and 2006, the numbers of female offenders found guilty or cautioned for indictable offences increased by 16 per cent whilst the number of male offenders found guilty or cautioned for indictable offences remained at a similar level.

- Between 2005 and 2006, offences of violence against the person rose by 9 per cent for males and 3 per cent for females; burglary offences rose by 15 per cent for males but remain unchanged for females; robbery offences rose by 1 per cent for males and 11 per cent for females; drug offences rose by 5 per cent for males and 4 per cent for females.

- In 2006, the proportionate use of immediate custody for males aged 21 or over was 30 per cent. This compares with 26 per cent in 1996. For females in this age group, the proportionate use of immediate custody was 17 per cent. It was 12 per cent in 1996 (Ministry of Justice, 2007b).

These statistics paint a somewhat complex picture. First, they suggest that crime is a 'male problem'. Males seem to commit more crime than females and are typically prosecuted for more serious offences. However, the statistics also indicate that female criminality is rising more rapidly than male criminality. Second, it appears that 'youth' is the most criminogenic age for both males and females (see Chapter 19). Third, they reveal that in comparison to males females tend to commit less crime and their offences are, in the main, less serious, the use of immediate custody for women has increased substantially. Indeed, the number of women in prison has risen steadily since the early 1990s. At that point in time, the average female prison population stood at approximately 1,500 (Howard League for Penal Reform, 2006). On 8 August 2008, there were 4,433 women in prison, representing just over 5 per cent of the total prison population in England and Wales (National Offender Management Service, 2008)).

Self-report studies

Most self-report studies suggest that offending is far more widespread than the official statistics would imply and that the sex gap in relation to offending is narrower. Muncie (2004) notes that the gap is narrowest in the teenage years, but whilst female offending is short-lived, males take much longer to 'grow out of' crime. The best source of data on the self-report offending of men and women of all ages is the Offending, Crime and Justice Survey (see Chapter 19 for a discussion of surveys which focus exclusively on young people). Conducted by the Home Office, the survey uses a sample of 12,000 people aged between 10 and 65 living in private households in England and Wales. The 2003 sweep

(Budd *et al.*, 2005) found that males were more likely than females to admit to committing one of 20 core offences during their lifetime: the respective figures were 52 per cent and 30 per cent. Males were more likely to be involved than females in a wider range of offences and were more likely to be serious or prolific offenders. Self-report data must be treated with caution. It relies upon interviewees providing accurate and truthful answers to questions about their involvement in crime and there may be gender differences in terms of willingness to confess to involvement in crime. Nonetheless, these studies provide evidence that women's contribution to crime is greater than the official statistics suggest.

Victim surveys

Victimization surveys such as the British Crime Survey (BCS) have been conducted since the early 1980s and have revealed that the extent of crime may be much greater than that detailed in the official statistics. In 2007/08, for instance, only 42 per cent of crimes were reported to the police (Kershaw *et al.*, 2008). In terms of sex differences, the BCS has also revealed that:

- men are almost twice as likely as women to experience violent crime in the year prior to interview, although the risk for both sexes is very low;
- males and females in the 16 to 24 age group are most at risk from violent crime and risk then decreases with age;
- domestic violence is the only category of violence where the risks for women are higher than for men;
- one-third of violence experienced by women can be classified as domestic violence, approximately eight times the proportion experienced by men;
- risk of stranger violence is substantially greater for men than for women;
- being female is associated with high levels of worry about burglary and violence; and
- fear of crime is more likely to have a high or moderate impact on the quality of life of females.

Women, femininity(ies), and crime

There is now a large body of work on women, femininity(ies), and crime and this section provides an overview of the main debates.

Female conformity

The relative lack of offending by females has been explained in various ways. Some writers suggest that the observable differences in the extent and nature of offending between males and females (and unquestioned by many criminological theories) are non-existent. Pollak (1961), for instance, maintained that women commit as many crimes as men, but rarely find their way into the official statistics.

Other writers point to the socially constructed nature of official statistics to account for the relationship between sex and offending. Crime statistics represent the end product of a series of decisions, including whether or not to report a crime and, if so, whether it is recorded as such. Moreover, changes in policing priorities and changes in legal definitions of what counts as crime will affect statistical representations. For example, sexual assault and domestic violence are both examples of events whose measurement has been susceptible both to changing cultural norms and measurement methods. Murgatroyd (2000) argues that official statistics are not gender-neutral. She suggests that, in areas such as crime, while the statistics include information on sex, there may be a tendency for the gender dimension to be hidden through measurement and/or conceptual difficulties, leading to gaps in information. Such gaps may result from cultural norms and assumptions regarding male and female characteristics and behaviours. This view leads to the suggestion that it is the *perception* of crime as a male activity that may affect the overall picture of men and women as perpetrators of crime. This perception may lead to female offending going unreported to the police and, where reported, not recorded; allowing females to evade the formal criminalization processes.

Heidensohn (1996) suggests that data on female offending may also be complicated by gender assumptions about what is 'typically' female crime. She argues that stereotypical assumptions about women's lives affect assumptions about the crimes they commit. For example, because stereotypes link women with shopping, shoplifting is viewed as an extension to women's 'normal' role (Morris, 1987). Hence, shoplifting is regarded typically as the female crime, despite the evidence that males still account for the vast majority of arrests and convictions for this type of offence. Similarly, prostitution, in law and in practice, has been traditionally constructed as a 'typically' female crime (see Walkowitz, 1980). Here, stereotypes which view sex work as an extension of the female role (to service male sexual desire) may serve to render male offenders invisible whilst sanctioning female prostitutes more rigorously than their clients, who are typically male. This suggests official statistics reflect not patterns of offending but a double standard in the construction and enforcement of the law.

Naffine (2003) suggests that the criminal law and its enforcement is about male patterns of behaviour and about male standards of acceptable conduct. She points to the construction of laws on violence which are significantly about men and what men do. Similarly, McIntosh (1978) suggests that there are more laws concerning male behaviour than female behaviour and that this explains why men are convicted of more crimes than women. She argues that female behaviour tends to be 'policed' in other contexts by informal, non-criminalizing means. This theme is picked up by Heidensohn (2002) who argues that in order to understand female conformity—what it is about women that makes them more law-abiding—it is important to understand something of the social construction of femininity and of the disciplinary forces that act upon women at various levels.

- *The media*: where cultural representations of 'appropriate' female appearance and behaviour serve to objectify the female body and exhort women to identify with, and mould their bodies into, a state of 'feminine excellence' (Dines and Humez, 1995).

- *The domestic sphere*: where women are constrained by, on the one hand, the responsibilities of motherhood and home-making (Oakley, 1981) and, on the other hand, through the exercise of male power (Carlen, 1983).

- *In public*: where fear of crime and of reputation damage effectively constrain women's public behaviour (especially after dark), relegating women to the context in which they are, in fact, most at risk: the home (Stanko, 1990).

- *In education and the workplace*: where ideas about the physical and emotional frailty of women have historically kept women uneducated and unemployed and where women are still constrained through social hierarchies and sexual discrimination (Benjamin *et al.*, 2003).

- *In medicine and psychiatry*: where illness labels may reflect social ideas about women's bodies (as more naturally unstable than men's) and where various aspects of women's lives have become defined as problematic requiring intervention and control (Reissman, 1998).

- *In legislation*: where models of femininity inform welfare policies restricting the choices open to women (Heidensohn, 1996).

Such approaches imply that the techniques of control and surveillance may be different for males and females. Heidensohn (2002) suggests that this provides some explanation for sex differences in offending and may help to explain why, in similar circumstances, women are less likely to offend than their male counterparts. This is not to suggest, however, that Heidensohn (2002) sees women as the passive recipients of informal control directives. On the contrary, she describes a complex process in which the 'norms of femininity' serve as a form of social control and where women themselves, often contradictorily, learn to discipline their own bodies and police themselves. Not all women, however, and not all the time, and, despite the seeming success of the system of gender imperatives, *some* women are unable or unwilling to conform.

Gender convergence

There has been much political and popular debate in recent years in relation to the perceived increase in female crime and, in particular, female violence. Batchelor (2002), for instance, points to news stories of so-called 'girl gangs' who have been associated with a 'rising tide' of lawlessness. Such stories have been bolstered by wider concerns about, for example, binge drinking and the increase in female alcohol consumption generally. Female offending, it seems, has achieved not only greater visibility as a women's issue, but also status as a social problem.

Heidensohn (1996: 154) points out that moral panics about female offending are not new and have been linked recurrently to concerns about female emancipation and liberation. She cites the work of Pike (1876) and Bishop (1931) who both argued that female criminality was linked to rising sexual equality. Pollak (1961), similarly, drew parallels between increased female offending and the progressive emancipation of women. However, it was in the 1970s that the patterns of female offending rates over time received increased attention with the advent of Adler's (1975) and Simon's (1975) so-called 'liberation hypothesis'. Adler (1975) and Simon (1975) both made links between the women's 'liberation' movement and the female crime rate, arguing that as women become more equal to men, offending rates will converge.

While liberation theories have been heavily criticized (Smart, 1982; Box and Hale, 1983; 1984), the main crime data sources provide some evidence in support of convergence. The official statistics, for instance, point to a change in the ratio between male and female crime over time. They also suggest an upward shift in the pattern of convictions of women for robbery, burglary, drug and violent offences (Ministry of Justice, 2007a). The dramatic and unprecedented increase in the female prison population in England and Wales in recent years also lends some support to a narrowing of the gap between male and female offending.

On closer examination, however, the hypothesis that women's crime rates are catching up with men's is questionable. Numerically, males far outnumber females in almost all offence categories and percentage rises for female crime, therefore, represent small increases to low base numbers. Furthermore, the largest numerical increases tend to be in less serious offence categories. With regard to violent crime, the proportional increases, tend to be in the less serious offence categories such as common assault rather than serious assault or homicide (Burman, 2003). Females account for a small percentage of violent crime and most research has found that it has, in fact, remained relatively stable (Burman, 2003) and violence remains a predominantly male activity. Discussions over whether female crime is increasing (or indeed decreasing) are, of course, complicated by changes in criminalization processes such as police recording procedures and priorities and the general patterns of sentencing over time.

Overall, there is limited evidence for convergence theses and most researchers agree that women's crime rates have more or less stayed the same. Where gender convergence seems to exist it may be understood in terms of inflation in the small number of women's crimes, changes in data collection methods and in law enforcement processes (see, for example, Smart, 1982; Belknap, 2001). Males still make up the majority of known offenders, even for those offences where there seems to be a convergence.

Female criminality

Most discussions of female criminality are grounded in the context of women violating socially prescribed gender roles as well as criminal laws; what has become known as 'double deviance'. While it is clear that some women offend and, indeed, women can be found in all offence categories from the most serious to the least serious, male and female criminal behaviour tends to be interpreted differently. For men, it is more likely to be viewed as 'normal' behaviour or as a rational response to such factors as boredom, peer pressure, necessity, greed, and so forth. In contrast, female offenders are so few so as to present something of an anomaly, in need of explanation. Female offending challenges the dominant scripts of femininity and, hence, is commonly explained, on the one hand, as a consequence of individual women failing to conform to their innate biological tendencies (masculinized, sexualized, pathologized) or, on the other hand, it is redefined as evidence of what Showalter (1987) refers to as the 'female malady' (irrationality, psychological instability). Positioning women's criminal behaviour in such a way effectively dismisses it. It removes any element of agency from the woman herself and any onus on society to reflect upon why it occurred.

Modern analyses of women and crime have done much to challenge stereotypical assumptions about female motivation and have highlighted the rational and purposeful nature of much female offending. Carlen (1985, 1988), for example, has argued that female criminality involves conscious decision-making processes and can, often, be understood in terms of women's socio-economic circumstances. Similarly, studies of girl gangs and of females charged with robberies and aggravated assault have found few differences in the motivations between males and females. Crimes of violence were most often committed to get money for material goods and/or to support drug use (Miller, 1998, 2001; Sommers and Baskin, 1993).

There is, of course, no monolithic female experience and female motivations for crime are likely to depend upon a number of factors. As we have seen, criminological theories have tended to be sex-blind, either ignoring females or viewing them in a stereotypical manner that usually distorts real-life experiences. Any analysis of gender must avoid a similarly restricted view by accounting for difference among females. Here, it is important to consider the ways in which sex interacts with other variables such as age, ethnicity, and class.

REVIEW QUESTIONS

1 Are women more law-abiding than men?

2 Are women becoming more criminal?

3 Do women commit crimes for the same reasons as men?

Men, masculinity(ies), and crime

If, as Heidensohn (1996) suggests, a central question for criminology concerns female conformity, then the issue of male criminality should be equally, if not more, pressing. All the available evidence suggests that men outnumber women among offender (and victim) populations. Men are more likely than women to be repeat offenders and more likely than women to engage in the most serious offence categories. So what is it about men that makes them so much more predisposed to criminality?

The 'man question' in relation to crime has, until relatively recently, been overlooked by criminologists. Historically, (male-dominated) criminology has focused attention on men and male offending without tackling the issue of masculinity head on (Winlow, 2004). The 'maleness' of crime has been so taken-for-granted as to be rendered invisible. As Sim (1994) suggests, studies have tended to be on men as offenders rather than offenders as men. However, the relationship between men, masculinity, and crime has been the focus of increased academic attention since the early 1990s, influenced, not least, by feminist criminological work, but also by scholars in gender and gay studies, and in critical, pro-feminist studies of men as gendered subjects (see, for example, Connell, 1987; Morgan, 1992).

Analyses of masculine identity and masculinity became increasingly important within criminology during the 1990s with a number of critical studies focusing specifically on men and crime (see, for example, Newburn and Stanko, 1994; Bowker, 1998; Messerschmidt, 1993, 1997). This work provides an attempt to explain why men are more criminal and, in particular, more violent than women, whether it be at the interpersonal or collective level; and why some men are more criminal and more violent than others (Bowker, 1998). In what follows, some of the main issues raised by this and earlier work are summarized under the themes of gender learning processes, power and control models, masculinities, and masculine identities, although it is recognized that there is much overlap.

Gender learning processes

Discussions of male criminality cannot be divorced from the social construction of gender and gendered subjectivities. Here, male offending is often explained in terms of the socialization processes where, on the one hand, boys experience a relative lack of informal control and, on the other hand, they learn that 'female' attributes are something to be avoided and that to be a 'man' involves being tough, fearless, and non-emotional (Walklate, 2001). Male crime is thus linked to cultural notions of 'manhood' and to the prescribed and gendered social roles that are learned and legitimated in various arenas.

- *The family*: where male offending can be correlated with prevailing social stereotypes about male behaviour, on the one hand, and with parental models, on the other hand (Oakley, 1972). According to this argument, boys learn what 'men do' and, in the pursuit of 'authentic manhood' and its approved forms of expression, boys are more likely to engage in anti-social behaviour than girls. In terms of parenting models, various risk factors for male offending have also been highlighted, including parental deprivation of love and childhood experiences of witnessing and/or suffering violence (Farrington and Painter, 2004).

- *The media*: where society's approved definition of male and female sex roles are reflected, reinforced, and exploited (Surrette, 1998).

- *Sport and leisure*: where being seen to be 'tough' is celebrated and where male violence (usually directed towards other men) comes with its own rewards (Jefferson, 1998; Williams and Taylor, 1994).

- *Social policies*: where models of 'fatherhood' and 'breadwinning' determine and constrain the choices open to men (Hobson, 2002).

- *The law*: where certain male behaviours have been condoned historically (for example, domestic violence and rape) whilst those behaviours that deviate from the sex-typed model (for example, homosexuality) have been subject to sanction (Weitz, 1998).

Sex role analyses point to the processes, extending through childhood and into adult life, through which individuals become not only conscious of their gender roles but also, through years of learning, internalize them and make them part of their own personalities. While this approach constitutes an important first step towards an understanding of gender relations and the gendered nature of criminality, it has been criticized for an under-emphasis on the inequalities between males and females and, in particular, the forms of power that men exercise over women (Stoltenberg, 2000; Walklate, 2001).

Power and control models

Stoltenberg (2000) argues that male and female roles are not equal. He highlights the social construction of masculinity as the main source of societal injustice and discrimination. Here, it is suggested that an understanding of male criminality depends upon an understanding of gendered power and power relationships and, in particular, men's use and abuse of women and women's bodies.

Power and control models of male crime owe much to radical feminists' analyses of patriarchal systems of exploitation and oppression and of the techniques for 'doing gender'. That is, the ways in which male domination is made real through acts of force and 'sexual terrorism' (Stoltenberg, 2000: 27). According to this argument, male superiority is constituted through power and control tactics such as rape, violence, prostitution, and pornography, but also through the exploitation of women's labour (at home and in the workplace) and through sexist language and harassment—acts in which women are subordinated whilst men are affirmed in their 'manhood' (Messerschmidt, 1993). Male superiority is thus not seen as 'natural'. Rather, men learn to experience their lives and, in particular, their sexuality, in terms of conquest and power (Biddulph, 1994; Seidler, 1989). So, masculine 'excellence' in this sense is based on force and anger, the one expression of emotion associated with the notion of masculinity. Moreover, it has been bolstered and legitimated by a whole range of laws and cultural norms (Weiz, 1998).

Of course, not all men are the same and not all men commit crime or are violent or sexual predators and, indeed, the victims are not all female. Violence and sexual violence are not uniquely masculine behaviours, for women can also use power in this way, albeit to a much lesser extent. Power and control models that posit two opposing categories—men and women—overlook the complex nature of power and the power relations among men and among women. For example, they cannot fully explain female violence or the changing position of women in patriarchal discourses. Nor can they fully account for the contradictory experiences of male power (for example, in the home) and powerlessness (for example, in the workplace) or the impact of power imbalances on subjective feelings and identities (Walklate, 2001). To this end, such approaches to understanding male crime and violence have been much criticized. However, they provide a useful context for the emerging focus on power relations between men and masculinities (Hearn, 2003).

Masculinities and masculine identities

There has been an increasing recognition in the field of 'masculinities studies' of the plurality of masculinities, masculine identities, and, indeed, patriarchies. Here, it is argued that there is no universal male experience. Rather, there is diversity among men and, similarly, there are many different types of masculinity and forms of patriarchal organization. Connell's (1987, 1995) work, in particular, has made a significant contribution to an understanding of the relationships between different types of masculinity and masculine identity. That is, how males see themselves as 'men'. Connell (1995) identified a range of masculinities and highlighted the cultural and historical variations. However, he argued that, in any given era, a broad delineation can be made between hegemonic, or dominant, masculinity (white, heterosexual, and middle class in contemporary Western societies) and other types of subordinated masculinities.

Hegemonic masculinity, according to Connell (1995), represents the culturally dominant ideal of 'manhood', which serves to provide individual men with a sense of self while downgrading other types of masculinity and femininity(ies). 'Successful' male identity requires a distancing from that which is perceived to be 'non-male' (Stoltenberg, 2000). Thus, 'real men' dispense with inferior feminine emotions such as compassion, fear, or distress (Mosher and Thomkins, 1988). Stoltenberg (2000) argues that there is, however, no such thing as a 'real man'. There is only the idea of it and the consequences of trying to make it seem real: the subordination of women and others identified as 'non-male'. Consider, for example, the way in which being 'a girl' is viewed in pejorative terms and the rich linguistic taunts used to define and demean so-called 'effeminate' men. While the sanctions applied to those who deviate from the hegemonic ideal may take the form of social ridicule, they may also be forced institutionally, economically, and through law. For instance, heterosexual masculinity has traditionally kept homosexual masculinity subordinate through social stigma and legal sanctions.

Connell's (1995) work suggests that, at any given time, the social structure produces numerous masculinities and femininities and different ways of being, and of seeing oneself as, male or female. It also produces sets of relationships between masculinities and femininities based on degrees of domination and subordination and stratified by age, social class, racial difference, and sexuality. Together, these practices create a gender order characteristic of the society at that particular stage. However, the gender order can be challenged, can change, and can sometimes undergo periods of 'crisis' (Connell, 1995).

In criminology, the work of Connell has been drawn upon in an increasing body of work examining the relationship between masculinities and crime (but see, in particular, Messerschmidt, 1993, 1997, 1998, 2000). This work points to the importance of understanding male crime and victimization and, indeed, male involvement in crime control, in terms of the idea of hegemonic masculinity; the social context (where different constructions of masculinity are produced); and the power relations between different groups of men.

While hegemonic masculinity's power over subordinate masculinities and femininity(ies) may negatively affect the lives of those perceived to be 'non-male', the non-identification with that which is perceived to be feminine (such as powerlessness) also has consequences for those men who are violently and/or sexually victimized. Here, gendered assumptions regarding the 'typical victim' may lead to problems for men not only in understanding themselves as 'men' but also in terms of their experiences in the criminal justice and victim support systems (see Stanko and Hobdell, 1993; Goodey, 1997; McMullan, 1990; Gadd *et al.*, 2002).

Messerschmidt (1993, 1994, 1998) argues that men construct and maintain their own masculine identities in the context of their position in society and, in particular, their access to power and resources. Here, he identifies the importance of understanding male social positioning in relation to other key variables such as age, socio-economic status, and racial difference. For example, he points to the complex way in which 'race' and class interact in the social construction of youthful masculinities and crime (Messerschmidt, 1994). He also identifies the social conditions and practices that have not only led to the construction of 'racial masculinities', but have also sought to keep black masculinities subordinate, whilst affirming white-supremacist masculinity (Messerschmidt, 1998). In his work, we can see the ways in which socially organized power differences between men produce different constructions of masculinity.

In a similar vein, various studies have shown how men who lack societal power may create a sense of themselves as men through 'compensatory' measures including crime, violence, drugs, and other forms of 'risk' behaviour (see Katz, 1995; Hobbs *et al.*, 2003; Winlow, 2004). Katz (1995), for example, points to the socio-cultural challenges to male hegemony in post-industrial capitalist societies and, in particular, the increasing economic instability and dislocation of working-class, white males. He suggests that, in response to these pressures, we have seen the development of different and exaggerated forms of masculine expression involving the physical body as a mode of aesthetic and actual power (also see Bloor *et al.*, 1998). Other writers have also suggested that socio-economic changes have led to a white, working-class culture of 'hyper-masculinity', expressed through forms of violent and abusive behaviour (see Surette, 1998; Winlow, 2004). Winlow (2004), for instance, argues that the involvement of predominantly young men in crime and violence needs to be seen as a product of their economic positioning and their need for validation of their masculinity.

Such analyses of 'underclass masculinities' (Winlow, 2004: 19) provide an important contribution to an understanding of male criminality. However, while the nature of the economy may explain why some men resort to crime, it cannot be applied to all male offending. As Katz (1988) suggests, crime can be attractive for males and it can be exciting. Campbell (1993), similarly, highlights the fun and risk elements of male involvement in crime. Here, it is important to consider the gratifications and pleasures derived from crime, which may themselves be linked to aspects of masculinity and masculine expression. Moreover, as Walklate (2001) suggests, the focus on working class masculinities may well serve, on the one hand, to legitimate the targeting of the crimes of the socially powerless and, on the other hand, to deflect attention away from the structural and political context in which offending behaviour is expressed and without which 'manhood' has no social or subjective meaning. Here, it is important to consider the processes through which certain forms of masculinity-validating power are condoned while others are condemned and criminalized.

REVIEW QUESTIONS

1 Why do you think there has been a 'masculinity turn' in criminology?

2 Can masculinity be used to explain all crimes?

3 What are some of the difficulties associated with using the concept of masculinity to explain criminal behaviour?

Gender and the criminal justice process

It has been suggested that the organizational structures of criminal justice are highly 'gendered'. That is, practices and procedures are patterned by distinguishing between males and females. Here, concerns about the neutrality of the system are bolstered by its overwhelming 'maleness': official agents at every level of the system are predominantly male. What is less clear, however, is whether this has a discriminatory impact on decision-making and, if so, in whose favour?

A common assumption—the 'chivalry hypothesis'—is that women are treated more leniently than men simply because they are women. Here, it is suggested that paternalistic decision makers extend chivalrous treatment to women and that males are discriminated against (Farnworth and Teske, 1995). To a certain extent, this view is supported by official statistics—males are more likely than females to be arrested, convicted, and, if convicted, given a custodial sentence. However, when the defendant's previous record and the nature of the offence are taken into account, the evidence for chivalry is less clear-cut, and studies which have controlled for legal variables have found that males and females are treated similarly—the 'equal treatment hypothesis' (Farrington and Morris, 1983).

Both of these hypotheses have been challenged by feminist writers, who describe the process in a very different way, viewing the system as sexist and discriminatory against women. They argue that females are treated more harshly than males for similar offences and are punished for breaching the criminal law and sex role expectations—the 'double deviance hypothesis' (see Howe, 1994 for an overview). Other writers still argue that there is no monolithic male or female experience and some men and some women are dealt with in a discriminatory manner—the 'selectivity hypothesis'. This view considers the interaction of gender with other aspects of social experience and points to the ways in which constructions of age, ethnicity, class, and sexuality affect how males and females are treated.

It is questionable whether any of the above hypotheses can ever be proved empirically (Gelsthorpe, 2001). However, a large body of research has been conducted at many different stages of decision-making process to establish whether discrimination exists in criminal justice. In what follows, some of the major issues are examined in relation to policing, punishment, and sentencing.

The culture of policing

The police occupy a crucial role in determining who enters the criminal justice process and, while there are statutory anti-discrimination requirements, it is suggested that 'extra-legal' factors frequently affect police decision-making. For example, it seems that males and females are treated differently: women are more likely than men to be cautioned rather than prosecuted and are less likely to be stopped and searched (Hough, 1995). This would seem to support the 'chivalry hypothesis'. However, the greater proportion of women cautioned by the police does not necessarily demonstrate preferential treatment. Rather, it may be that women commit less serious offences than men. Indeed, studies that take the nature of the offence into account find little evidence of leniency and instead point to equal treatment (Laycock and Tarling, 1985).

In contrast, it is suggested that, in some circumstances, females are treated more harshly than males and are more likely to be prosecuted. Gelsthorpe (1989), for example, argues that female promiscuity has, historically and contemporarily, been treated more harshly than similar behaviour by males. Hudson (1989), likewise, suggests that girls are judged by the police in terms of their 'femininity' and are treated differently to boys for identical behaviours (such as running away, sexual activity, alcohol consumption). Such research dispels the notion that females are treated chivalrously and, instead, provides evidence in support of the 'double deviance' hypothesis.

It has been well documented that socialization into a police 'culture' influences the way in which officers go about their work and relate to those with whom they come into contact (Smith and Gray, 1985; Jefferson, 1990; Reiner, 2000; Fielding, 1994). Here, it has been suggested that a pivotal feature of police culture is 'hegemonic masculinity'. Policing, like offending, is numerically dominated by men and can been seen as a form of masculine expression (Hunt, 1984). Hunt (1984) suggests that police officers routinely employ stereotypes to make sense of the world they police and tend to associate women with 'morality' and with the domestic domain. As a consequence, those few women who are processed as offenders are not considered 'real women'. This distinction between female offenders and 'real' women has been seen most clearly in relation to female prostitutes, the group of women in most regular contact with the police (see Edwards, 1987; Heidensohn, 1996).

Horn (1995) suggests that police treatment of women is more complex than simple support for the 'equal treatment', 'chivalry', or, indeed, 'double deviance' hypotheses. She argues that police officers tend to categorize women offenders in terms of their personal characteristics and the nature of the offence. So, while all women offenders may be perceived more negatively than women who do not offend, not all women offenders are treated the same, and chivalrous treatment may be reserved for those women who act in ways consistent with hegemonic assumptions of femininity. Horn (1995) proposes that essentially 'decent' women are thought to be those who have temporarily offended due to circumstances. In contrast, women who are physically violent and/or involved in drug offences or who show antagonism to the police, are thought to be 'non-women' and actually 'worse' than male offenders.

In a similar vein, there is evidence that police discretion works against young, poor, minority ethnic males. As Fielding (1994) suggests, 'cop culture' is also a white, heterosexual culture and any evaluation of policing must recognize that there are different life experiences among men and among women, depending on such factors as ethnicity, class, age, and sexuality. Moreover, opportunities for the operation of selectivity based upon assumptions, value judgements, stereotypes, and prejudices are not just confined to policing but run throughout the criminal justice process.

Punishment and sentencing

As with policing, there is a general assumption that women are sentenced and punished more leniently than men. This is often attributed to a 'courteous' attitude on the part of sentencers who may explain female offending in very different terms to male offending and who may be reluctant to send women to prison, especially if they have children (Morris, 1987). The idea of chivalrous treatment as an example of 'reverse discrimination' has been evidenced in sentencing statistics that reveal that women are far less likely than men to receive a custodial sentence, are more likely than men to receive probation or discharges, and, if given a custodial sentence, are generally given shorter sentences (see Hedderman and Hough, 1994; Gelsthorpe, 2001). However, chivalrous treatment, if it exists, is likely to be far more complex than the simple lenient treatment of all women. Belknap (2001: 132) argues that chivalrous treatment is part of a 'bartering system' or exchange relationship in which lenient treatment is extended only to certain kinds of females, according to the nature of the offence, but also according to adherence to 'proper' gender roles. The theme of punishment for breaching sex role expectations has been identified in much of the literature on women and crime, and it has been argued that the sentencing of women reflects notions of the 'ideal' woman, related to family and domestic considerations, leading to differentiation between women. Thus, being married, having dependent children, and being a 'good' home-maker may all afford women lenient treatment.

Studies of sentencing, therefore, suggest that while chivalry might well be extended to some women whose behaviour conforms to approved stereotypes, leniency will not be shown to those women who 'deviate' from notions of appropriate sex-role behaviour, who may be dealt with more harshly than other women and, indeed, men. Research on women and punishment also suggests a differential impact of sentences on men and women (see, for example, Carlen, 2002). It has, for instance, been suggested that many aspects of imprisonment which, in principle, apply equally, may have different implications for men and women. On the one hand, this may be due to the relative invisibility of female prisoners in penal policy and practice—women remain a minority of the prison population and, in a system where women emerge as 'deviations', their needs and experiences have been often misunderstood (Home Office, 2007; Morris *et al.*, 1995). On the other hand, it has been suggested that women find prison life harder than their male counterparts because regimes for women have been based on stereotypical assumptions about women's role in society and about the needs of women prisoners. This view suggests that regimes for women prisoners have been dominated by oppressive forms of 'patriarchal control' (see, for example, Eaton, 1993; Edwards, 1994; Sim, 1990). Thus, women prisoners experience a harsher disciplinary regime than men and the impact of, and responses to, imprisonment may be more severe (Smith, 2002).

In summary, there is evidence that some women are dealt with in a discriminatory manner in sentencing and punishment procedures. As Gelsthorpe (1996) concludes, those women who conform to stereotypical conceptions of 'ladies' seem to receive different sentences to those who breach these expectations. Moreover, there is no monolithic female experience that can be defined independently of other factors such as ethnicity, class, and sexuality. In this respect, distinctions are similarly drawn between different men and it would be wrong to suggest that men are treated in non-discriminatory ways. For example, poor, black, young men are over-represented in prisons and there is evidence of discriminatory treatment of some men in some situations, even when controlling for legal variables (Hood, 1992). This leads to the suggestion that the criminal justice system is based upon deeply embedded discourses around hegemonic femininity and masculinity and other variables interact with sex to provide a different pattern of criminal justice for male and female offenders.

REVIEW QUESTIONS

1 Which hypothesis do you find the most convincing?

2 Identify as many factors as possible other than gender which influence the way in which offenders are treated?

3 What groups of female offenders are likely to be viewed as deviating from so-called 'normal' sex-role behaviour?

CONCLUSION

This chapter has outlined some of the key issues in relation to sex, gender, and crime. Despite the many contributions of feminists working within criminology and, more recently, the developing criminological thinking about masculinities, many questions about the relationship between gender and crime remain unanswered. For example, the 'real' extent of male and female offending is probably unknowable but there is a need to develop more adequate gender statistics on crime and justice, not least where statistics are used to measure the impact of policy on both women and men. In addition, some areas remain relatively unexplored, such as the concept of violence as a form of feminine expression, and there is scope to develop further work on femininities and crime.

What seems clear, however, is that a consideration of gender has had an influence on academic criminology, although the precise nature of that influence is debatable. Heidensohn (2003) and Naffine (2003), for example, both suggest that questions of gender remain peripheral to mainstream criminology and criminological theory. Hearn (2003), similarly, points to the resilience of patriarchy in the discipline. It remains, after all, a discipline dominated by men studying men. Here, there is a real need to address the fundamental gender flaws in much criminological theorizing and empirical work as well as the academic gendering of the discipline itself (see also Scraton, 1990).

Finally, politicians and policy makers, like criminologists, have been slow in considering crime as 'gendered work'. There has been an increased recognition of the need to adopt anti-discriminatory procedures in recent years, given additional impetus by the recommendations of the Corston Report (Home Office, 2007) that each criminal justice agency must prioritize and accelerate preparations to implement their gender equality duty enshrined in the Equality Act 2007. Additionally, there have been developments in risk-focused prevention and interventions in relation to violent, sexist masculinities. However, the social structures which frame how individuals experience themselves as men or women and in which offending behaviour is expressed remain largely intact.

QUESTIONS FOR DISCUSSION

1 What impact has feminism had on criminology?

2 How far is the problem of crime a problem of men and masculinity?

3 To what extent is the criminal justice system composed of gendered institutions?

4 How adequately has criminology explained gendered patterns of offending?

5 Compare and contrast the different ways in which male and female offenders have been represented in: (a) criminological theories; (b) media representations; and (c) criminal justice processes.

GUIDE TO FURTHER READING

Evans, K. and Jamieson. J. (2008) (eds) *Gender and Crime*: A Reader. Buckingham: Open University Press.

A collection of both classic and groundbreaking readings which illustrate how gender informs criminology. The final chapter by the editors sets out the challenges that the gender and crime question has posed for criminology and its impact on the discipline.

Heidensohn, F. (2006) *Gender and Justice: New Concepts and Approaches*. Cullompton: Willan Publishing. Basingstoke: Macmillan.

This edited collection brings together a range of established and new writers with a shared concern for exploring the relationship between gender and justice. Its coverage is broad, examining both offending behaviour and official responses to it.

Newburn, T. and Stanko, E. (eds) (1994) J*ust Boys Doing Business: Men, Masculinities and Crime*. London: Routledge.

This edited collection explores the relationship between masculinity and crime. The chapters describe the ways in which masculinity is essential to understanding men's involvement in crime, their experiences of victimization, and the dynamics of criminal justice agencies.

Silvestri, M. and Crowther-Dowey, C. (2008) *Gender and Crime*. London: Sage.

This new textbook provides a comprehensive and critical introduction to the relationship between gender and crime and brings a human rights perspective to the debates.

Winlow, S. (2001) *Badfellas: Crime, Tradition and New Masculinities*. Oxford: Berg.

This research monograph brings complex debates around masculinity and crime to life. It draws upon covert research with professional criminals and violent men and explores the ways in which male identity is expressed each day though a range of activities including criminal ones.

WEB LINKS

http://www.asc41.com/dir4/

The American Society of Criminology has a Division on Women and Crime. It developed out of the growing interest in the study of gender and women as offenders, victims, and criminal justice professionals. The website provides links to a wide range of relevant websites.

http://www.crimeinfo.org.uk

Developed by the Centre for Crime and Justice Studies, this website contains an abundance of material about crime and responses to it. It includes factsheets on women (including young women) and crime and domestic violence plus autobiographical accounts by male and female offenders.

http://www.fawcettsociety.org.uk

The Fawcett Society is a leading organization campaigning for equality between women and men. The website details its work on women and justice and its efforts to obtain better treatment for women as victims, offenders, and criminal justice professionals.

http://www.womeninprison.org.uk

Women in Prison was set up in 1983 by an ex-prisoner as a campaign group. The website outlines the work it does providing welfare and education advice to women in prison and post-release and its work educating the public and policy makers about women in the criminal justice system and promoting alternatives to custody.

http://www.justice.gov.uk/publications/womencriminaljusticesystem.htm

The Ministry of Justice website includes an annual report which brings together data produced by a range of criminal justice agencies relating to the experiences of women within the criminal justice system.

REFERENCES

Adler, F. (1975) *Sisters in Crime: The Rise of the New Female Criminal*. New York: McGraw-Hill.

Batchelor, S. (2002) 'The myth of girl gangs', in Y. Jewkes and G. Letherby (eds) *Criminology: A Reader*. London: Sage.

Belknap, J. (2001) *The Invisible Woman; Gender, Crime and Justice* (2nd edn). Belmont, Ca: Wadsworth/Thomson Learning.

Benjamin, S., Mauthner, M., and Ali, S. (eds) (2003) *The Politics of Gender and Education: Critical Perspectives*. Basingstoke: Palgrave Macmillan.

Biddulph, S. (1994) *Manhood*. Sydney: Finch.

Bloor, M., Monaghan, L., Dobash, R., and Dobash, R. (1998) 'The body as a chemistry experiment: steroid use among South Wales bodybuilders' in S. Nettleton and J. Watson (eds) *The Body in Everyday Life*. London: Routledge.

Bowker, L. (ed) (1998) *Masculinities and Crime*. London: Sage.

Box, S. and Hale, C. (1983) 'Liberation and Female Criminality in England and Wales', *British Journal of Criminology*, 23 (1), 35–49.

Box, S. and Hale, C. (1984) 'Liberation/Emancipation, Economic Marginalisation, or Less Chivalry: The Relevance of Three Arguments to Female Crime Patterns in England and Wales, 1951–1980', *Criminology*, 22 (4), 473–98.

Budd, T., Sharp, C., and Mayhew, P. (2005) *Offending in England and Wales: First Results from the 2002 Crime and Justice Survey*, Home Office Research Study 275. London: Home Office.

Burman, M. (2003) 'Girls Behaving Violently', *Criminal Justice Matters*, 53, 20–21.

Campbell, B. (1993) *Goliath: Britain's Dangerous Places*. London: Virago.

Carlen, P. (1983) *Women's Imprisonment*. London: Routledge and Kegan Paul.

Carlen, P. (1985) 'Law, Psychiatry and Women's Imprisonment: A Sociological View', *British Journal of Psychiatry*, 146, 618–21.

Carlen, P. (1988) *Women, Crime and Poverty*. Milton Keynes: Open University Press.

Carlen, P. (2002) *Women and Punishment. The Struggle for Justice*. Cullompton: Willan Publishing.

Connell, R. (1987) *Gender and Power*. Oxford: Polity Press.

Connell, R. (1995) *Masculinities*. Oxford: Polity Press.

Danner, M. (1989) 'Socialist feminism: a brief introduction' in B. MacLean and D. Milovanovic (eds) *New Directions in Critical Criminology*. Vancouver: The Collective Press.

Dines, G. and Humez, J. (eds) (1995) *Gender, Race and Class in Media*. London: Sage.

Eaton, M. (1993) *Women After Prison*. Milton Keynes: Open University Press.

Edwards, S. (1987) 'Prostitutes: Victims of Law, Social Policy and Organized Crime' in P. Carlen and A. Worrall, (eds) *Gender, Crime and Justice*. Milton Keynes: Open University Press.

Edwards, S. (1994) 'The Social Control of Women in Prison', *Criminal Justice*, 12, 9–10.

Farnworth, M. and Teske, R. (1995) 'Gender Differences in Felony Court Processing', *Women and Criminal Justice*, 6 (2), 23–44.

Farrington, D. and Morris, A. (1983) 'Sex, Sentencing and Reconviction', *British Journal of Criminology*, 23 (3), 229–48.

Farrington, D. and Painter, K. (2004) *Gender Differences in Risk Factors for Offending*. Home Office Findings 196. London: Home Office.

Fielding, N. (1994) 'Cop canteen culture' in T. Newburn and E. Stanko (eds) *Just Boys Doing Business? Men, Masculinities and Crime*. London: Routledge.

Gadd, D., Farrall, S., Lombard, N., and Dallimore, D. (2002) *Domestic Abuse against Men in Scotland*. Edinburgh: Scottish Executive.

Gelsthorpe, L. (1989) *Sexism and the Female Offender*. Aldershot: Gower.

Gelsthorpe, L. (2001) 'Critical Decisions and Processes in the Criminal Courts' in E. McLaughlin and J. Muncie (eds) *Controlling Crime* (2nd edn). London: Sage.

Goodey, J. (1997) 'Boys don't cry: Masculinities, fear of crime, and fearlessness', *British Journal of Criminology*, 37 (3), 401–18.

Hearn, J. (2003) '"Just Men Doing Crime" (and Criminology)', *Criminal Justice Matters*, 53, 12–13.

Hedderman, C. and Hough, M. (1994) *Does the Criminal Justice System Treat Men and Women Differently?* Home Office Research and Statistics Department, 10. London: Home Office.

Heidensohn, F. (1968) 'The Deviance of Women: A Critique and an Enquiry', *British Journal of Sociology*, 19 (2): 160–75.

Heidensohn, F. (1996) *Women and Crime* (2nd edn). Basingstoke: Macmillan.

Heidensohn, F. (2002) 'Gender and crime' in M. Maguire, R. Morgan, and R. Reiner (eds) *The Oxford Handbook of Criminology* (3rd edn). Oxford: Oxford University Press.

Heidensohn, F. (2003) 'Changing the Core of Criminology', *Criminal Justice Matters*, 53, 4–5.

Hobbs, D., Hadfield, P., Lister, S., and Winlow, S. (2003) *Bouncers: Violence and Governance in the Night-time Economy*. Oxford: Oxford University Press.

Hobson, B. (ed) (2002) *Making Men into Fathers: Men, Masculinities and the Social Politics of Fatherhood*. Cambridge: Cambridge University Press.

Home Office (2007) *The Corston Report: A Review of Women with Particular Vulnerabilities in the Criminal Justice System*. London: Home Office.

Hood, R. (1992) *Race and Sentencing*. Oxford: Oxford University Press.

Horn, R. (1995) 'Not Real Criminals: Police Perceptions of Women Offenders', *Criminal Justice Matters*, 19, 15–16.

Hough, M. (1995) 'Scotching a Fallacy', *Criminal Justice Matters*, 19, 17–18.

Howard League for Penal Reform (2006) *Prison Information Bulletin 2: Women and Girls in the Penal System*. London: Howard League for Penal Reform.

Howe, A. (1994) *Punish and Critique*. London: Routledge.

Hudson, B. (1989) 'Justice or welfare? A comparison of recent developments in the English and French Juvenile Justice System' in M. Cain (ed) *Growing up Good: Policing the Behaviour of Girls in Europe*. London: Sage.

Hunt, J. (1984) 'The development of rapport through the negotiation of gender in fieldwork among the police', *Human Organisation*, 43 (4): 283–96.

Jefferson, T. (1990) *The Case Against Paramilitary Policing*. Milton Keynes: Open University Press.

Jefferson, T. (1998) 'Muscle, "Hard Men" and "Iron" Mike Tyson: Reflections on Desire, Anxiety and the Embodiment of Masculinity', *Body and Society*, 4 (1), 77–98.

Katz, J. (1988) *The Seductions of Crime*. New York: Basic Books.

Katz, J. (1995) 'Advertising and the construction of violent, white masculinity' in G. Dines and J. Humez (eds) *Gender, Race and Class in Media*. London: Sage.

Kershaw, C., Nicholas, S., and Walker, A. (eds) (2008) *Crime in England and Wales 2007/8: Findings from the British Crime Survey and Police Recorded Crime*, Home Office Statistical Bulletin 07/08. London: Home Office.

Laycock, G. and Tarling, R. (1985) 'Police Force Cautioning: Policy and Practice', *Howard Journal*, 24 (2), 81–92.

Lombroso, C. and Ferrero, W. (1895) *The Female Offender*. London: Unwin.

McIntosh, M. (1978) 'The State and the Oppression of Women' in A. Kuhn and A. Wolpe (eds) *Feminism and Materialism*. London: Routledge and Kegan Paul.

McMullen, R. (1990) *Male Rape: Breaking the Silence on the Last Taboo*. London: Gay Men's Press.

Messerschmidt, J. (1993) *Masculinities and Crime: Critique and Reconceptualization of Theory*. Totowa, NJ: Rowman and Littlefield.

Messerschmidt, J. (1994) 'Schooling masculinities and youth crime by white boys' in T. Newburn and E. Stanko (eds) *Just Boys Doing Business? Men, Masculinities and Crime*. Totowa, NJ: Rowman and Littlefield.

Messerschmidt, J. (1997) *Crime as Structured Action*. London: Sage.

Messerschmidt, J. (1998) 'Men Victimizing Men: The Case of Lynching, 1865–1900' in L. Bowker (ed) *Masculinities and Violence*. London: Sage.

Messerschmidt, J. (2000) *Nine Lives*. Boulder, Col.: Westview.

Miller, J. (1998) 'Up it Up: Gender and the Accomplishment of Street Robbery', *Criminology*, 36 (1), 37–66.

Miller, J. (2001) *One of the Guys: Girls, Gangs and Gender*. Oxford: Oxford University Press.

Ministry of Justice (2007a) *Criminal Statistics, England and Wales 2006*, London: National Statistics.

Ministry of Justice (2007b) *Sentencing Statistics, England and Wales 2006*, London: National Statistics.

Morgan, D. (1992) *Discovering Men*. London: Routledge.

Morris, A. (1987) *Women, Crime and Criminal Justice*. Oxford: Basil Blackwell.

Morris, A., Wilkinson, C., Tisi, A., Woodrwo, J., and Rockley, A. (1995) *Managing the Needs of Female Prisoners*. London: Home Office.

Mosher, D. and Tompkins, S. (1988) 'Scripting the macho man: Hypermasculine socialization and enculturation', *Journal of Sex Research*, 25 (1), 60–84.

Muncie, J. (2004) *Youth and Crime* (2nd edn). London: Sage,

Murgatroyd, L. (2000) 'Developing gender statistics in the UK', *Radical Statistics*, Issue 74.

National Offender Management Service (2008) *Prison Population and Accommodation Briefing for 8th Aug 2008*. London: National Offender Management Service.

Naffine, N. (1997) *Feminism and Criminology*. Oxford: Polity Press.

Naffine, N. (2003) 'The "Man Question" of Crime, Criminology and Criminal Law', *Criminal Justice Matters*, 53, 10–11.

Newburn, T. and Stanko, E. (eds) (1994) *Just Boys Doing Business? Men, Masculinities and Crime*. London: Routledge.

Oakley, A. (1972) *Sex, Gender and Society*. Aldershot: Gower.

Oakley, A. (1981) *Subject Women*. Oxford: Martin Robertson.

Pollak, O. (1961) *The Criminality of Women*. New York: A.S. Barnes.

Reiner, R. (2000) *The Politics of the Police* (3rd edn). Hemel Hempstead: Harvester Wheatsheaf.

Reissman, C. (1998) 'Women and medicalization: a new perspective' in R. Weitz (ed) *The Politics of Women's Bodies*. Oxford: Oxford University Press.

Scraton, P. (1990) 'Scientific knowledge or masculine discourses? Challenging patriarchy in criminology' in L. Gelsthorpe and A. Morris (eds) *Feminist Perspectives in Criminology*. Buckingham: Open University Press.

Seidler, V. (1989) *Rediscovering Masculinity: Reason, Language and Sexuality*. London: Routledge.

Showalter, E. (1987) *The Female Malady*. London: Virago.

Sim, J. (1990) *Medical Power in Prisons*. Milton Keynes: Open University Press.

Sim, J. (1994) 'Tougher than the rest? Men in prison', in T. Newburn and E. Stanko (eds) *Just Boys Doing Business? Men, Masculinities and Crime*. London: Routledge.

Simon, R. (1975) *Women and Crime*. London: Lexington.

Smart, C. (1976) *Women, Crime and Criminology*. London: Routledge and Kegan Paul.

Smart, C. (1982) 'The new female offender: reality or myth?' in B. Price and N. Sokoloff (eds) *The Criminal Justice System and Women*. New York: Clark Boardman.

Smith, C. (2002) 'Punishment and Pleasure: Women, Food and the Imprisoned Body', *Sociological Review*, 50 (2), 198–214.

Smith, D. and Gray, J. (1985) *Police and People in London*. Aldershot: Gower.

Sommers, I. and Baskin, D. (1993) 'The Situational Context of Violent Female Offending', *Journal of Research in Crime and Delinquency*, 30(2), 136–62.

Stanko, E. (1990) *Everyday Violence: How Women and Men Experience Sexual and Physical Danger*. London: Pandora.

Stanko, E. and Hobdell, K. (1993) 'Assaults on Men: Masculinity and Male Violence', *British Journal of Criminology*, 33 (3), 400–15.

Stoltenberg, J. (2000) *Refusing to be a Man. Essays on Sex and Justice* (rev. edn). London: UCL Press.

Surette, R. (1998) *Media, Crime and Criminal Justice* (2nd edn). London: Wadsworth.

Thomas, W. (1923) *The Unadjusted Girl*. Boston: Little Brown.

Walklate, S. (2001) *Gender, Crime and Criminal Justice*. Uffculme: Willan Publishing.

Walkowitz, J. (1980) *Prostitution and Victorian Society*. Cambridge: Cambridge University Press.

Weitz, R. (1998) 'A History of Women's Bodies' in R. Weitz (ed) *The Politics of Women's Bodies*. Oxford: Oxford University Press.

Williams, J. and Taylor, R. (1994) 'Boys keep swinging: masculinity and football culture in England' in T. Newburn and E. Stanko (eds) *Just Boys Doing Business? Men, Masculinities and Crime*. London: Routledge.

Winlow, S. (2004) 'Masculinities and Crime', *Criminal Justice Matters*, 55, 18–19.

18 'Race', ethnicity, and crime

Marian FitzGerald

INTRODUCTION

When the media and politicians talk about 'race relations' or focus on 'ethnic minorities' in relation to crime, there is an assumption that the public will know exactly what they mean, including which particular groups they are talking about. Yet the terms 'race' and 'ethnicity' can mean different things to different people in different contexts. Britain's post-war history largely determined which groups came to be defined as 'ethnic minorities' for official purposes, including the collection of statistics. Once 'ethnic' statistics became available in a criminal justice context, they highlighted the over-representation of some of these minorities among people suspected or convicted of crime. Although the *reasons* for this over-representation were not self-evident and likely to be complex, the New Labour Government elected in 1997 increasingly emphasized explanations to do with 'racism', particularly in the police service. Despite considerable investment in measures to tackle the problem in these terms, however, the figures have progressively got worse. This chapter takes a critical look at how we conceive of 'ethnicity' in a British context, at the reasons for the over-representation of certain groups in the criminal justice statistics, and at some of the challenges this poses criminologists.

BACKGROUND

The terms 'race' and ethnicity are often used very loosely and even interchangeably; but their precise meaning is also contested. Academics have coined different (and sometimes competing) definitions of each for many decades.

For present purposes the notion of 'race' rests on assumptions that human beings can be divided into broad groups which are in some way distinguished on the basis of inherently different biological characteristics.

It is true that certain groups of people with common ancestry and/or geographic origins may share some genetic characteristics which, for example, make them more susceptible to some types of disease. However, it is now well established that each individual has their own unique biological makeup within an overarching biological framework which is common to *all* human beings. So the term 'race' is highly contested in a scientific sense; but it is still commonly used as a way of categorizing people whose shared genetic characteristics mean they *look* broadly similar to each other and seem different to members of other groups. These distinctions are usually very crude—and they are often in the eye of the beholder.

The reason why 'race' is such a contested term (and therefore written in inverted commas) is because it has sometimes been used *as if* these crude distinctions were scientifically based and, in particular, because this pseudo-scientific usage has given spurious legitimacy to negative stereotypes of some groups. Thus, in previous centuries notions of 'racial' difference were used to divide human beings into separate species and rank them 'according to inborn worth' (Gould, 1981), thereby providing the underpinning for genocidal ideologies such as Nazism which was based on the notion of a 'Master Race'.

In situations where it is convenient to describe people according to some group characteristics (for example whether they are male or female, young or old), some academics try to avoid the term 'race' completely. Where it *is* used, though, the term is recognized as a social rather than a scientific construct,[1] thus:

…the term race is applied more often to phenotype—the physical characteristics such as colour, more frequently found in particular ethnic groups—than genotype—those distinctions which have some biological underpinning. Socially race has a significance dependent not on science but upon belief. (McEwen, 1991)

The concept of ethnicity arguably provides a more meaningful basis for distinguishing between social groups. It recognizes that some groups may have shared a particular range of experiences over centuries and developed some degree of shared culture related to this which now provides the basis for a common sense of identity.

Milton Yinger sums up many of the commonly agreed elements of ethnicity when he suggests that an ethnic group

…exists *in the full sense* when three conditions are present: a segment of a larger society is seen by others to be different in some combination of the following characteristics—language, religion, race and ancestral homeland with its related culture; the members also perceive themselves in that way; and they participate in shared activities built around their (real or mythical) common origin or culture. (Yinger, 1986, emphasis added)

However, where ethnic distinctions have been made for policy purposes (as discussed later in this chapter) these have often been criticized—whether on the grounds that the distinctions are crude and arbitrary, that they are divisive *per se*, or that they are a diversion from tackling racism or class divisions (Sivanandan, 1985). For in practice this type of categorization rests on an assumption that individuals who share these characteristics identify with each other and that they can be classified accordingly—regardless of whether they would choose to describe themselves in this way.

In Britain, the term 'ethnic minority' is now commonly used to describe groups associated with particular waves of immigration since the Second World War. It is usually associated with people who are not white and, in particular, those with origins in the Caribbean and in the Indian subcontinent since these were the predominant visible minority groups when the collection of 'ethnic' statistics for administrative purposes first began in the late 1970s and 1980s.

REVIEW QUESTIONS

1 What is the difference between 'race' and ethnicity?

2 Why are the terms controversial?

3 How would you describe your own ethnicity?

Britain's ethnic minorities

Successive British governments had tried to control immigration from at least the early part of the twentieth century; but the population of countries which were part of the

British Empire were *not* thought of as foreigners—they were British subjects. And as these countries began to gain independence in the period following the Second World War, special measures were taken to hold on to their allegiance, including by giving their citizens full rights of entry into the United Kingdom

At first many were actively recruited from the ex-colonies in the Caribbean to fill labour shortages in Britain in the late 1950s and early 1960s. This 'Caribbean' immigration was followed by a second major wave of 'Asian' immigration from the Indian subcontinent (India, Pakistan, and Bangladesh) in the 1960s and 1970s, with further additions of Asians who had settled in countries of East Africa but were now being expelled on a discriminatory basis by the governments of those States. By now, though, popular demands for immigration control as well as changes in the economic and international context resulted in progressively tighter legislation to keep out new immigrants from the 'New Commonwealth',[2] the main exceptions being spouses and children coming to join those who had already been admitted.

Previous immigrants to Britain had often suffered prejudice and discrimination; but, because they were white, they and their children had more options for blending in to the 'host' society, even if this meant sacrificing some of their ethnic identity. The post-War immigrants from the Caribbean and the Indian subcontinent, however, were *visibly* different both from the host population and from each other. That is, in terms of 'phenotype' they were readily thought of as being racially different, even though there were significant ethnic divisions between and within both groups.

Not only did they suffer overt discrimination—facing notices when seeking work or accommodation which proclaimed 'no coloureds'—they suffered physical harassment. Tensions between Caribbean immigrants and the indigenous white population erupted in violence on the streets in Nottingham and London in the late 1950s, (for overviews see Katznelson ,1973; Walvin, 1984) and this seems to have triggered a dual response from the Government which was to set the pattern for the future (Layton-Henry, 1992). On the one hand, the 1960s saw the introduction of the selective immigration controls referred to above but on the other hand the first legislation to outlaw discrimination which was also progressively strengthened over time and culminated in the 1976 Race Relations Act.

Meanwhile the Caribbean and Asian immigrants who had settled here before controls were introduced continued to be joined by other family members including children they had initially left at home. Over time, they also began to have children born in Britain—some of whom were of 'mixed' ethnic heritage as a result of relations between the Caribbean group in particular and the indigenous white population. The poorest of these groups faced ongoing disadvantages beyond the immigrant generation; and governments increasingly became aware[3] that, although discrimination still played a part in this, other factors at work were more deeply entrenched. It was apparent that special *proactive* measures would be needed to prevent this disadvantage being perpetuated from one generation to the next, affecting not only immigrants but their descendants born in Britain.

The 1976 Race Relations Act was the cornerstone of government policies for tackling both discrimination *and* disadvantage. However, to ensure that these policies were working, it would need facts about:

(a) the position of different ethnic groups compared to the average for the population at large on key indicators such as employment, housing and education; and

(b) whether their position was changing over time.

The most obvious way to capture this information was through the national Census which takes place every ten years. This already included a question on where people were born; but, for purposes of tracking what had come to be called racial disadvantage, this information was becoming increasingly unreliable, since increasing numbers of those affected were now being born in Britain. So in the 1980s local authorities and major surveys started collecting information on people's ethnicity as such; and an ethnic question was finally introduced into the Census itself in 1991. The Census question was changed and expanded in 2001 and a further question was introduced about people's religion.

Table 18.1 gives the breakdown of the population using the 16 categories which were chosen as the basis of the ethnic question in the 2001 Census, along with the five major groupings to which the results are often aggregated. Despite the preoccupation with visible minorities, by 2001 the largest single ethnic minority was actually the 'White Other' group (at 2.6 per cent) whereas all of the *visible* minorities together accounted for just over 8 per cent of the total.

In a criminological context it is commonly accepted that certain socio-economic and demographic factors are closely correlated with the risk of individuals becoming involved in the sort of crimes which may bring them to the attention of the police. These risks are greater where a higher proportion of the group is young, where young men lack educational qualifications and/or are unemployed. They can also be intensified by factors associated with household composition, as well as the extent to which people live in high crime urban areas. And the more of these factors are present, the more they may reinforce each other. Importantly for the purposes of this chapter, the Census provides information on some of these factors broken down by ethnicity. Table 18.2 provides a sample of relevant Census statistics comparing the main visible minorities[4] with the figure for the white British population.

REVIEW QUESTIONS

1 What do you think is the reason why these particular 16 categories formed the basis for a question on ethnicity in the 2001 Census?

2 What alternative or additional categories might have been included?

3 On the basis of Table 18.2, which groups appear, on average, to be most at risk of offending?

Table 18.1 2001 Census: Population of England and Wales by ethnic category

White: British	87.5	White 91.3
White: Irish	1.2	
White: Other White	2.6	
Mixed: White and Black Caribbean	0.5	Mixed 1.3
Mixed: White and Black African	0.2	
Mixed: White and Asian	0.4	
Mixed: Other Mixed	0.3	
Asian or Asian British: Indian	2.0	Asian 4.4
Asian or Asian British: Pakistani	1.4	
Asian or Asian British: Bangladeshi	0.5	
Asian or Asian British: Other Asian	0.5	
Black or Black British: Black Caribbean	1.1	Black 2.2
Black or Black British: Black African	0.9	
Black or Black British: Other Black	0.2	
Chinese or Other Ethnic Group: Chinese	0.4	Other 0.9
Chinese or Other Ethnic Group: Other Ethnic Group	0.4	

Source: Census 2001.

Table 18.2 Socio-economic and demographic characteristics Selected ethnic groups

	% Living in Inner London	% Aged 10 to 15	% of males aged 16 to 24 unemployed[5]	% aged 16 to 20 with no educational qualifications[6]	% of dependent children living in single parent households
White British	5.3	19.6	7.2	16	22.1
Mixed White and Black Caribbean	15.1	57.5	14.5	24.6	54.5
Black Caribbean	33.7	20.4	15.8	16.3	59.1
Black African	47.7	30.2	6.9	12.6	44.3
Indian	8.2	22.9	5.2	10.6	10.9
Pakistani	6.1	35.0	10.1	22.6	16.3
Bangladeshi	45.7	38.4	9.2	21.6	15.1

Source: Census 2001.

Minorities, crime, and the criminal justice system

1950s to 1970s

Caribbean immigration in particular took place in the context of a tradition of policing which is nostalgically recalled in terms of the friendly neighbourhood police officer who often kept order just by 'having a quiet word'. However, the other side of the coin was a lack of scrutiny over the way the police exercised their powers which facilitated instances of oppressive behaviour, the arbitrary application of the law, and various forms of corruption. Even if this type of malpractice was not endemic, in the climate of prejudice at that time and in the absence of any safeguards against discrimination, the new immigrants found themselves disproportionately on the receiving end of heavy-handed policing and malpractice.

By the late 1960s and early 1970s concerns were already being raised about the police treatment of Caribbean immigrants (Rose *et al.*, 1969; Hunte, 1966; Humphrey, 1972). This was despite the fact that a parliamentary inquiry into 'Police-Immigrant Relations' in 1972 concluded that crime among Asians was lower than average and, among 'West Indians' it was no higher than for whites (House of Commons Select Committee on Race Relations and Immigration, 1972).

However, the original West Indian immigrants had now begun to bring over children they had left behind in the Caribbean and this, coupled with the fact that the first generation of children born in this country was also starting to reach adolescence meant that unprecedented numbers of young black people were entering the peak age range for offending by the mid-1970s. When the same Committee held a further inquiry specifically into 'The West Indian Community' five years later, witnesses from the Metropolitan Police Service (MPS) had decided that criminality among this group *was* now higher than average (House of Commons Select Committee on Race Relations and Immigration, 1977). This coincided with a 'moral panic' about the involvement of young black men in street crime (Hall., 1978); and in London in particular this group was targeted by the police using laws which dated back to 1824 and allowed officers to arrest anyone *on suspicion* that they were *about to* commit an offence (Demuth, 1979).

1980s

The emerging stereotype of black people as offenders was then further reinforced when young black people were involved in the first civil disturbances in deprived areas of mainland Britain for over half a century, firstly in the St Paul's area of Bristol in 1980 and then in parts of London (most notably Brixton) as well as other inner city neighbourhoods including Toxteth (Liverpool) in 1981. There was a further recurrence in 1985 centring largely on Tottenham (London) and Handsworth (Birmingham). All of these disturbances were triggered by incidents involving the police; but when Lord Scarman was asked to report on the causes of the 1981 riots he insisted on widening his brief beyond the immediate police-related issues. At their core, he found, were issues of structural disadvantage as well as discrimination; and, although his report included extensive criticism of the police, he repudiated any notion of systematic discrimination (Scarman, 1981).

The riots of the early 1980s triggered major reforms not only of police training but also the regulation and scrutiny of police conduct, as embodied in the 1984 Police and Criminal Evidence Act (PACE). Among other things, this took responsibility for prosecution away from the police by setting up the Crown Prosecution Service, and it also set up new structures for local police accountability. Section 1 of PACE also gave police officers the power to stop and, as necessary, search any individual on the basis of 'reasonable suspicion' that they were carrying illegal, stolen, or prohibited goods; but they had to make a record of any such searches.

Meanwhile, Asian immigration had continued but family reunion was often long delayed, especially in the case of the poorer (Pakistani and Bangladeshi) groups. So the equivalent cohort of young people in these groups would only start to reach the peak age for offending by the mid 1990s. At the end of the 1970s, therefore, these groups continued to be seen as unproblematic in terms of criminal activity; but they too were the targets of racial attacks, just like the West Indians before them. This meant that the Government began (belatedly) to recognize the problem of racial harassment in the early 1980s in a context which lent itself to a dual form of stereotyping where 'Asians' were indiscriminately cast as victims and black people as offenders.

1990s to the present

There was no repetition of black-led disturbances after 1985. There *were* 'rural riots', though, at the end of the 1980s (Tuck, 1989) followed by further serious outbreaks of civil disorder on poor estates[7] during the 1990s; and all of these involved mainly young white people.

Despite the major changes within the police following the Scarman report and the introduction of PACE, the legacy of mistrust between the service and black people of West Indian origin persisted. In 1997 a new Labour Government was elected with a far more explicit commitment than its predecessor to tackling racism, and one of its earliest initiatives in this context was to set up a public inquiry into the MPS investigation of the racist murder of a young black man, Steven Lawrence, in 1993. The inquiry's remit was to look at why the MPS had consistently failed to ensure the prosecution of his killers; but, under the chairmanship of Lord Justice Macpherson (Macpherson, 1999), it broadened its terms of reference to look also at 'the central problem...of the lack of trust which exists between the police and the minority ethnic communities'.

Macpherson's report concluded that both the failure of the investigations into Stephen Lawrence's murder[8] and the wider 'problem' it considered were due to 'institutional racism'. As evidence, it cited in particular 'disproportionality' in searches under s. 1 of PACE (see above)—that is, the over-representation of ethnic minorities in the search figures compared with their presence in the population as shown in the Census. 'Institutional racism', it said, characterized not only the police service at large but the criminal justice system more generally, as well as other institutions. It could be defined as:

the collective failure of an organisation to provide an appropriate and professional service to people because of their colour, culture or ethnic origin. It can be seen or detected in processes, attitudes and behaviour which amount to discrimination through unwitting prejudice, ignorance, thoughtlessness, and racist stereotyping which disadvantage minority ethnic people. (Macpherson, 1999)

The Government accepted all Macpherson's recommendations and set up a steering group[9] to oversee their implementation, premised on the notion that this and other measures would reduce 'disproportionality'. It was already funding a major programme of police race relations training; and was soon to update the 1976 legislation in the form of the 2000 Race Relations Amendment Act which, among other things, removed some previous exemptions for the police.

However, two years after the publication of the Macpherson report there was a recurrence of rioting; but the disturbances this time were in deprived areas of Northern towns (notably Bradford,[10] Burnley, and Oldham) and they largely involved Asians. More specifically, they involved young people of Pakistani origin; and they also differed from the riots of the early 1980s in that they were not commonly triggered by conflict with the police, but in some instances by confrontations with groups of young whites. Just as the dust was settling on these, and the relevant inquiries had reported on their causes and likely policy implications (Ouseley, 2001; Cantle, 2002) further confusion was created by disturbances in Birmingham as a result of conflict between young Asian and Black people. Importantly, these took place not long after the London bombings of 2005; so not only did they further call into question the benign stereotype of the law-abiding 'Asian', a new and far more sinister stereotype was already attaching itself to particular sub-groups of Asians. In the context of concerns about 'Islamic' terrorism in general and the shock of discovering that those responsible for the London bombings had been born and raised in Britain, the religion question in the 2001 Census made it easy to identify the ethnic groups most 'at risk' of becoming involved in 'Islamic' terrorism as those of Pakistani and Bangladeshi origin.[11]

By 2007, new concerns began to reach the national media about crime among the growing numbers of new immigrants from Eastern Europe;[12] but these were overshadowed by a growing preoccupation with questions about whether Britain was witnessing the emergence of youth 'gangs' and the extent to which these were predominantly black (Young *et al.*, 2007).

Ethnic statistics in a criminal justice context

The development of ethnic statistics

Some of the earliest studies to highlight problems between minorities and the police had called for statistics to be kept which would provide evidence of police bias (Rose, *et al.*, 1969). The MPS itself had begun to keep its own ethnic data from at least the 1970s; and these were used to justify its conclusions that, by 1977, West Indians had become more involved in crime (see above). They also provided material for occasional statistical bulletins by the Home Office during the 1980s, as well as valuable information for a number of research studies (Demuth, 1979; Stevens and Willis, 1979; Willis, 1983). Nonetheless the Scarman report into the 1981 riots had commented critically on the absence of hard factual information about black people, crime, and policing.

National ethnic monitoring *was* introduced by the Government after the riots, but only for the prison population. However, as we have seen, by the early 1990s, the practice of recording ethnicity had become well established to the extent of including an ethnic question in the Census. This made demands for ethnic monitoring at the point of entry to the criminal justice system less controversial; and an amendment to the Criminal Justice Act in 1991 was interpreted[13] in these terms. Starting in 1996, all 43 police forces in England and Wales had to record the ethnicity of anyone they:

- searched,
- arrested, or
- cautioned.

There was, however, no requirement for the police to collect information about *victims* of crime with the exception of victims of homicides. Also, the police were only required to use four ethnic categories: 'White, Black, Asian and Other'.

The topics were chosen in part because forces were already required to provide returns to the Home Office on these items; and the crudeness of the ethnic categories was largely because the police were to classify people on the basis of what they *looked* like to the officer involved. (This was because at the time the police had successfully argued that asking people to classify *themselves* using a list of Census categories might be difficult in the course of street searches—and would, in any case, be impossible in the case of homicides).

Since then, ethnic monitoring in a criminal justice context has continued to proliferate among agencies other than the police and the prison service, though it remains patchy. (For example, at the time of writing there was no systematic data with regard to decisions to prosecute or court decisions.) Where this happens, the agencies require self-classification based on the Census codes; and the police—in addition to continuing to use their own visual classification system—were also formally required from 2003 to use self-classification.[14]

Trends, patterns, and politics

The first year's monitoring figures from the police were available to the Macpherson Inquiry (see above); so they provided quantitative support for its finding that police searches reflected 'institutional racism'. Less attention was paid to the statistics on other items and none at all to the homicide figures—even though all of these were available and they too were 'disproportionate' to some degree, at least in the case of black people (see Figure 18.1a).

Subsequently, despite the Government's commitment to tackling 'disproportionality' and the implementation of the recommendations of the Macpherson Inquiry, the over-representation of black people increased on all of these key indicators; and Asians also now started to be over-represented—albeit 'disproportionality' reduces significantly if age is controlled for (Figure 18.1b).

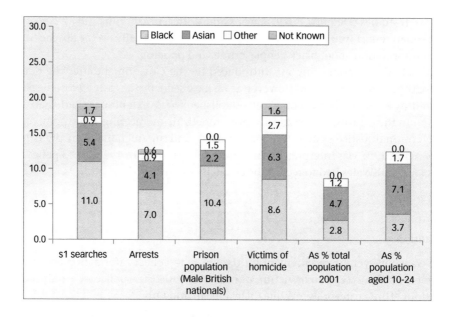

Figure 18.1a Minorities as a proportion of police searches,[15] arrests, prisoners,[16] and homicide victims 1997–98 (compared to their presence in the Census 2001)

Source: Home Office, 1998

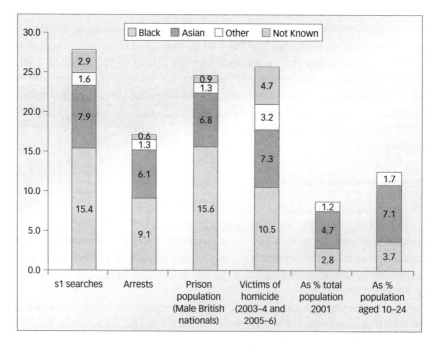

Figure 18.1b Minorities as a proportion of police searches, arrests, prisoners and homicide victims[19] 2005–06 (compared to their presence in the Census 2001)

Source: Ministry of Justice, 2007

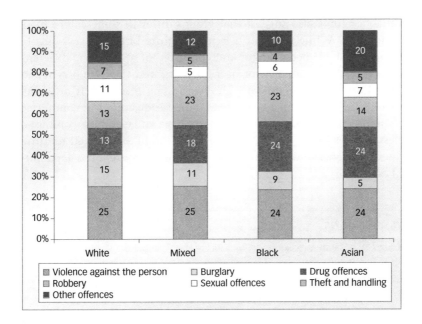

Figure 18.2a Prison population at June 2005: Sentenced British national prisoners by offence type within ethnic group

Source: National Offender Management Service, 2006

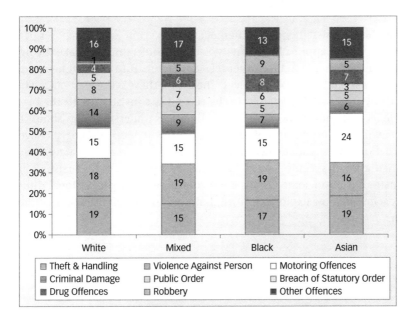

Figure 18.2b Young people aged 10 to 17 subject to disposal 2005–06 by main offence type within ethnic group

Source: Youth Justice Board, 2007.

The available figures also suggest that groups differ to some extent in their patterns of offending. While the prison figures capture only the very small number of any group who have been caught and convicted of an offence, differences have been apparent in these statistics for over 20 years; and they are now reflected also in the Youth Justice Board (YJB) data. The two systems use slightly different offence categories and the prison statistics relate to more serious offences committed largely by adults whereas the YJB data cover the 10 to 17 age range and many minor offences. Nonetheless, Figures 18.2a and 18.2b illustrate the extent to which ethnic differences[17] in the types of offences[18] which bring people into the system are apparent in both sources of data.

REVIEW QUESTIONS

1 What were the various reasons for introducing ethnic monitoring into the criminal justice system?

2 How do the ethnic categories in the published criminal justice figures relate to the 16 categories in the Census – and do you think aggregating the figures in this way could pose any problems?

3 What appear to be the main differences between groups in the offences they are caught for?

Interpreting ethnic differences in crime statistics

Interpreting these persistent ethnic differences in the crime statistics poses particular challenges. Two broad approaches to analysis are possible: one is to take the figures at face value; and the other is to take other relevant factors into account before drawing any conclusions about 'ethnic' differences. The first of these is the least satisfactory and involves largely unrecognized dangers. The second is consistent with the best traditions of intellectual enquiry because it accommodates understandings about the risks of getting involved in crime (and of getting caught) which criminologists have developed internationally over many decades. However, it fails to appreciate the impact of factors which are not specific to any particular group but whose persistent and disproportionate impact on some groups has a collective, inter-generational dimension. Both approaches are now explored in turn, followed by a brief discussion of the group dimension.

Taking the figures at face value

The over-representation of any group in the statistics, if taken at face value, could mean:

(a) that the group is discriminated against at the point of entry into the criminal justice system and then all the way through it to the point of imprisonment; and/or

(b) that the group is more involved in crime than others for reasons which are somehow particular to that group.

The Macpherson report tended to take the first of these positions in the case of police searches where it insisted that the figures must *only* be taken at face value:

> Nobody in the minority ethnic communities believes that the complex arguments which are sometimes used to explain the figures as to stop and search are valid... [and] Attempts to justify the disparities through the identification of other factors... simply exacerbates the climate of distrust. (Macpherson, 1999)

However, the persistence of 'disproportionality' in the available figures, the fact that it is apparent also in the homicide statistics, and the consistent picture of ethnic differences in patterns of crime mean this position now seems untenable.

In this context, to insist that the ethnic differences in the figures must be taken at face value leaves them open to be used as evidence of a higher level of involvement in crime which is racially or ethnically specific. Thus a former Prime Minister, Tony Blair, in the face of growing concerns about knife and gun crime tried to insist that this was not a general problem but an issue for 'the black community' to resolve (Blair, 2007).[20]

Taking other factors into account

We have already seen from the Census data in Table 18.2 that different groups vary in terms of some of the known risk factors for involvement in crime; but the statistics are also an important reminder that the very crude categories used in the criminal justice statistics mask many of these differences. Black Africans, for example, have much lower rates of youth unemployment than the Black Caribbean group, and the 'mixed' group shares many of the disadvantages of the Black Caribbean group, but its geographic distribution is very different and it is also very much younger. Among the 'Asians' the Indian group is, on average, a very high achieving group in stark contrast to the Pakistanis and Bangladeshis; yet the difference in their age structure means that these two poorer groups by now outnumber the Indians in the youth population.

Other available statistics further refine the picture which emerges from the Census and frequently highlight the particular risks for the 'mixed' and black groups. These two groups, for example, are over-represented among young people in care (Figure 18.3); and young people in care are widely recognized to be especially vulnerable to becoming caught up in the criminal justice system. The situation is reversed, though, in the case of the various Asian groups, even among the poorer Pakistani and Bangladeshi communities.

Two further sets of factors which have been relatively neglected to date but which the research evidence increasingly confirms may be relevant in this context are neighbourhood influences and the chances of offenders of different ethnic origins getting caught.

The American literature has a long tradition of setting crime and criminality in their specific local context which is most closely identified with the Chicago School of the 1920s (see for example Park and Burgess, 1925). Ethnographic studies such as Mercer Sullivan's 'Getting Paid' (Sullivan, 1989) show how these local influences may differentially influence patterns of crime among similar groups of different ethnic origins. While Britain does not have anything like the same levels of residential segregation between ethnic groups as the USA, research studies here are also beginning to highlight the extent to which the higher concentration of some groups in particular high crime areas may affect their involvement in crime.

Thus John Pitts' study of issues around youth gangs in Britain explores the specific local factors which underlie their emergence in certain areas (Pitts, 2008). In a study published in 2003 in the context of yet another moral panic about street crime, statistical modelling by Chris Hale also threw important new light on the role of neighbourhood factors in explaining the much higher involvement of black young people in this type of crime. Variations in the level of street crime between different London boroughs, Hale found, were explained entirely in terms of socio-economic and demographic factors which had nothing to do with ethnicity. The problem was greatest (and had increased fastest) in areas characterized by population change where a high proportion of children were living in poverty but also where young people from very deprived backgrounds were likely to come across more affluent sections of society. The fact that black young people disproportionately lived in these types of area *and* were disproportionately affected by factors such as child poverty (which is higher in single parent households) entirely explained their over-representation in the robbery figures (FitzGerald, Stockdale, and Hale, 2003).

Far less consideration has been given to the possibility that 'disproportionality' might also reflect the differential chance of offenders of different ethnic origins coming to the attention of the criminal justice system in the first place—even though a commonplace in discussing the limitations of police and other criminal justice statistics is that only a minority of the crimes committed may ever come to the attention of the system in the first place. However, the Home Office's Offending Crime and Justice Survey (OCJS) asks respondents whether they have ever committed a crime and also whether they have ever come into contact with the criminal justice system. The 2003 survey found *no* significant ethnic differences in the extent to which respondents who were 'non-offenders' had ever been arrested;[21] but, by contrast, black respondents who *admitted* to having 'ever'

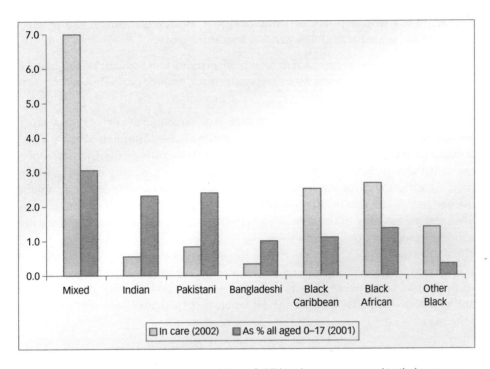

Figure 18.3 Selected minorities as a proportion of children in care compared to their presence in the population aged 0–17

Sources: Department of Health (2007) and 2001 Census.

offended were significantly more likely to have been arrested and to have been to court than their white counterparts[22] (Sharp and Budd, 2005).

Importantly, the OCJS sheds some light on the possible reasons why Black people (and also those of 'Mixed' origins) are more likely to be arrested if they offend. It identifies a number of factors which are highly correlated with the likelihood of being arrested. These include the *type* of offence people have committed—where contact crimes such as robbery are more likely to be detected because victims and witnesses can provide descriptions of the offender—and factors such as school exclusion, living in rented accommodation, and associating with people already known to the police. Again, none of these factors is ethnic-specific but they disproportionately affect the Black sample in particular and to a lesser extent also the 'Mixed' group (for a fuller discussion, see FitzGerald, 2007).

The group dimension

An approach which takes other relevant factors into account has far more intellectual legitimacy than basing politically driven conclusions on headline differences between what are, in any case, very crude ethnic categories. However, it runs into a problem which Jefferson hinted at in 1991 when he complained that:

> ...the currently dominant approach to investigating ethnicity and criminalization...is a bit like sieving flour with ever finer meshes; eventually there is too little getting through to...construct a very meaningful account.

That is, dissecting the ethnic differences in the figures according to a list of factors which have nothing to do with ethnicity *except* inasmuch as they disproportionately affect particular ethnic groups risks obscuring the fact that the resulting experiences may over time contribute to these groups' ongoing sense of a shared identity (as described by Yinger). It denies the particular configurations in which these factors may cluster around different groups and ignores the possibility that the ways in which they interact may have a specific meaning in the light of any group's shared history, especially where this includes memories of conflict with the police.

This collective impact, though, is not simply psychological. For any group, the significant over-representation of its young men in the criminal justice system will inevitably have consequences for its economic prospects and, thereby, on gender and family relations—especially where this situation is perpetuated from one generation to the next.

REVIEW QUESTIONS

1 If you were given a set of figures which showed Black people were significantly over-represented in arrests in that force compared to their presence in the local population, what information would you want to take into account before deciding whether this was due to discrimination?

2 What criminological theories do you know of which might be relevant to understanding the under- or over-representation of different groups in the criminal justice system?

CONCLUSION

So far this chapter has had nothing to say about the role of discrimination. The findings of the Offending Crime and Justice Survey are the first to suggest that minorities who have never offended are no more likely to be picked on by the police than other similar members of the public. In addition, one of the most important studies of ethnic minorities within the criminal justice system was a study of Crown Court sentencing in the West Midlands (Hood, 1992) which took a wide range of relevant factors into account in analysing the reasons for very large differences in the proportion of defendants from ethnic minorities who received custodial sentences. Once these were controlled for, most of the differences disappeared and those which remained were not evenly spread. They mainly affected adult males rather than juveniles or women; and the Crown Court centre from which the majority of the cases were drawn appeared to be completely equitable in its sentencing. That is, if discrimination *was* occurring, it was confined to a minority of cases in particular areas.

Certainly the ethnic monitoring statistics reported in this chapter are far too crude to be of much use (if any) in proving the extent of any discrimination and still less where and how this occurs. For example, the average number of s. 1 searches per constable in a given year is probably less than two per month.[23] Since nearly three-quarters of these are searches of white people and it is inconceivable that every single search of a minority is unjustified, it would be very difficult—if not impossible—to discover where any instances of discrimination were occurring simply by analysing the statistics.

This is not to say there is room for complacency about discrimination, and safeguards will always be needed. However, it is also worth bearing in mind that officials who are ready to abuse their powers on the basis of prejudice are unlikely to do so *only* in relation to ethnic minorities. In areas where they deal almost exclusively with white people, they might still discriminate, for example, against gypsies, homosexuals, or young people whose appearance offends them. So robust *systems* are needed to pick up abuse of *any* sort; but whether these systems are effective is likely to depend on supervisors routinely monitoring them by checking on the performance of the individuals for whom they have line management responsibilities rather than waiting for raw statistics to alert them to the possibility that they have been overlooking bad behaviour.

Here again, therefore, we are thrown back on the need to set the experience of ethnic minorities in a wider context. As the previous section argued, it is important to appreciate the particularity of their experience and its implications for the group as a whole; but it is essential here to distinguish between cause and effect. Well established criminological understandings about the risk factors for involvement in the criminal justice process should be the starting point for appreciating the *reasons* for the over-representation of different groups in the criminal justice system; and these, in turn, may readily be framed in terms of criminological theory.

Criminologists may differ over which theories are most relevant for this purpose; but it cannot seriously be suggested that new theories are needed to understand the particular situation of specific minorities in a peculiarly British context at this precise moment in history. The groups who have most recently been of concern in this context are themselves undergoing constant internal change; and, as we have seen, it is likely that the 'Mixed' group and the poorer Asian groups may displace the Black group as the folk devils of the future. It is arguable that these particular groups have been more vulnerable insofar as they are visibly different so a higher proportion may *de facto* be the victims of negative stereotyping and discrimination and this may endure far beyond the immigrant generation. Yet already the spotlight has started to turn on the criminal involvement of newer groups of immigrants, some of whom are white (see above).

Finally, a failure to contextualize the experiences of those minorities on whom we currently keep statistics in these ways increasingly threatens the interests of the minorities themselves. For we are now witnessing the publication of figures which year after year continue to show the same groups as over-represented among tried and convicted offenders—apparently impervious to all attempts to change this picture; and there is a real danger that this will fuel 'statistical racism'. That is, just as the scientific knowledge of past eras was used to justify racist beliefs in ways which may now appear to us as ludicrous (see Introduction), so the current reliance on ranking groups according to statistical averages could itself—as the former Prime Minister has already demonstrated—lend a cloak of respectability to generalized statements about whole groups.

QUESTIONS FOR DISCUSSION

1 How often are ethnic minorities referred to in other chapters in this volume? Would more or fewer such references be appropriate? What guidelines would you suggest to ensure consistency in the way the term is used in an edited volume such as this, bearing in mind the need to avoid over-simplification?

2 Monitor the domestic news in a range of broadsheet and tabloid newspapers and broadcast media for a week. Count the number of times each refers to the ethnic origin of individuals it reports on. Which ethnic groups are mentioned most frequently, in which media; and what proportion of these references are in a criminal justice context?

3 How would you set up a study to try to tease out the factors which underlie the apparent over-representation of certain ethnic groups in the annual statistics for your local Youth Offending Team; and how would you seek to understand the reasons for the ethnic differences they appear to show in patterns of offending?

GUIDE TO FURTHER READING

Webster, C (2008) *Understanding Race and Crime*. Maidenhead. Open University Press.

Bowling, B. and Phillips, C. (2002) *Racism, Crime and Justice*. Harlow. Longman.
For books covering these issues particularly from a British perspective (but taking rather different standpoints).

Tonry, M. (ed) (1997) *Ethnicity, Crime and Immigration: Comparative and Cross-national Perspectives*. Chicago. University of Chicago Press.

Marshall, I.H. (ed) (1997) *Minorities, Migrants and Crime: Diversity and Similarity across Europe and the United States*. London. Sage.
To get a better international comparative perspective on the issues—including insights into national differences in the groups conceived of as 'ethnic minorities', the policies pursued in relation to them, and the type of statistical information available—read these two edited volumes.

WEB LINKS

http://www.tandf.co.uk/journals/routledge/01419870.html
Currently the main British journal covering issues of ethnicity is Ethnic and Racial Studies which can be accessed via this web link or through subscribing university libraries.

http://www.nacro.org.uk/publications/racecriminal.htm
The National Association for the Care and Resettlement of Offenders has a specialist team working on issues concerning ethnic minorities. This site gives online access to their briefing papers.

http://www.justice.gov.uk/
When the Ministry of Justice was formed from the split in the Home Office in 2007 it took over responsibility for the s. 95 publications which can be accessed online through this web link. The National Offender Management Service falls within the Ministry of Justice so it is also worth searching this site for any relevant NOMS publications.

http://www.homeoffice.gov.uk/rds/

The Home Office unit responsible for Research, Development and Statistics produced the s. 95 publications from 1992 until the Home Office was split; so this site contains s. 95 material up to that point. The department has also long been responsible for a wide range of relevant research and statistical publications, some of which are cited in the references in this chapter and many of which can be accessed online.

http://english.justitie.nl

The Dutch Ministry of Justice website is accessible in English and contains a lot of research publications and statistics related to ethnic minorities in *their* criminal justice system. It may be of interest to compare these with the material produced by the Home Office and Ministry of Justice and also with the American research and statistics which are available online from two main sources, as follows.

http://www.vera.org/

The Vera Institute of Justice is a major independent American research organization which describes itself as 'an independent center for policy and practice, making justice systems fairer and more effective through research and innovation'.

http://www.ojp.gov/bjs/crimoff.htm

This link goes direct to offender statistics within the US Department of Justice's Bureau of Justice Statistics and is a good place to start. Searches can then be widened to publications from other parts of the Department of Justice and to relevant external sites.

REFERENCES

Blair, T. (2007) *Callaghan Memorial Speech. 11 April* <http://www.number-10.gov.uk/output/Page11472.asp>.

Brown, C. (1984) *Black and White Britain*. London: PSI.

Cantle, T. (2002) *Community Cohesion: a Report of the Independent Review Team*. London: Home Office.

Clegg, M. and Kirwan, S. (2006) *Police Service Strength England and Wales*. Home Office Statistical Bulletin 13/06. London: Home Office.

Daily Telegraph (2007) 'Foreigners "commit fifth of crime in London"'. 24 September.

DCSF (2008) *National Curriculum Assessment, GCSE and Equivalent Attainment and Post-16 Attainment by Pupil Characteristics, in England 2006/07* <http://www.dfes.gov.uk/rsgateway/DB/SFR/s000759/CrosstabsforSFR.xls>.

Demuth C. (1979) *'Sus': a Report on the Vagrancy Act 1824*. Runnymede Trust.

Department of Health (2007) *Children looked after by local authorities year ending 31 March 2002*. England (detailed statistics) <http://www.dh.gov.uk/en/Publicationsandstatistics/Statistics/StatisticalWorkAreas/Statisticalsocialcare/DH_4015858>.

FitzGerald, M. (2007) *Supplementary memorandum submitted by Dr Marian FitzGerald, Specialist Adviser to the Committee* in Young Black People and the Criminal Justice System Second Report of Session 2006–07: Volume II Oral and written evidence. HC 181-II. London. The Stationery Office Limited.

FitzGerald, M., Stockdale, J., and Hale, C. (2003) *Young People and Street Crime*. London: Youth Justice Board.

Gould, S.J. (1981) *The Mismeasure of Man*. London: W.W. Norton and Company.

Guardian (2008) 'Polish federation accuses Daily Mail of defamation' 15 March.

Hall, S., Crichter, C., Jefferson, T., Clarke, J., and Roberts, B. (1978) *Policing the Crisis*. London: Macmillan.

Home Office (1998) Statistics on Race and the Criminal Justice System: A Home Office publication under section 95 of the Criminal Justice Act 1991.

Hood, R. (1992) *Race and Sentencing*. Oxford: Oxford University Press.

House of Commons Select Committee on Race Relations and Immigration (1972) *Police Immigrant Relations*. London: HMSO.

House of Commons Select Committee on Race Relations and Immigration (1977) *The West Indian Community*. London: HMSO.

House of Commons Select Committee on Race Relations and Immigration (1981) *Racial Disadvantage*. London: HMSO.

Humphrey, D. (1972) *Police Power and Black People*. London: Panther Books.

Hunte, J. (1966) *Nigger Hunting in England*. London: West Indian Standing Conference.

Jansson, K. (2006) *Black and Minority Ethnic groups' experiences and perceptions of crime, racially motivated crime and the police: findings from the 2004/05 British Crime Survey*. Home Office Online Report 25/06.

Jefferson, T. (1991) 'Discrimination, Disadvantage and Police Work' in E. Cashmore and E. McLaughlin (eds) *Out of Order? Policing and Black People*. London: Routledge.

Jones, A. (1996) *Making Monitoring Work: A Handbook for Racial Equality*. Centre for Research in Ethnic Relations, University of Warwick.

Katznelson, I. (1973) *Black Men, White Cities*. London: Institute of Race Relations/Oxford University Press.

Layton-Henry, Z. (1992) *The Politics of Immigration*. Oxford: Blackwell.

Macpherson, W. (1999) *The Stephen Lawrence Inquiry*. London: The Stationery Office.

McEwen, M. (1991) *Housing, Race and Law; the British Experience*. London: Routledge.

Ministry of Justice (2007) Statistics on Race and the Criminal Justice System—2006: A Ministry of Justice publication under section 95 of the Criminal Justice Act 1991.

Modood, T., Berthoud, R., Lakey, J., Nazroo, J., Smith, P., Virdee, S., and Beishon, S. (1997) *Ethnic Minorities in Britain: Diversity and Disadvantage; The Fourth National Survey of Ethnic Minorities*. London: Policy Studies Institute.

National Offender Management Service (2006) *Offender Management Caseload Practitioners. Statistics 2005*. Statistical Bulletin 18/06. London: Home Office.

Ouseley, H. (2001) *Community Pride Not Prejudice: Making Diversity Work in Bradford*. Bradford: Bradford Vision.

Park, R. and Burgess, E. (eds) (1925) *The City*. Chicago: Chicago University Press.

Pitts, J. (2008) *Reluctant Gangsters*. Cullompton: Willan Publishing.

Rose, E.J.B., Deakin, N., Abrams, M., Jackson, V., Peston, M., Vanags, A.H., Cohen, B., Gaitskell, J., and Ward, P. (1969) *Colour and Citizenship*. Oxford: Institute of Race Relations/Oxford University Press.

Scarman (1981) *The Brixton Disorders: Report on an Inquiry by the Rt. Hon. Lord Justice Scarman OBE*. London: Her Majesty's Stationery Office.

Sharp, C. and Budd, T. (2005) *Minority ethnic groups and crime: findings from the Offending, Crime and Justice Survey 2003*. Home Office Online Report 33/05.

Shaw, C. (1988) *Latest Estimates of the Ethnic Minority Populations*. Population Trends No. 51. Spring 1988. Office of Population Censuses and Surveys.

Sivanandan, A. (1985) 'RAT and the degradation of the black struggle' *Race and Class* XXVI:4.

Smith, D. (1974) *The Facts of Racial Disadvantage*. London: Policy Studies Institute.

Stevens, P. and Willis, C. (1979) *Race Crime and Arrests*. Home Office Research Study 58. London: Home Office.

Sullivan, M. (1989) *'Getting Paid': Youth Crime and Work in the Inner City*. Ithaca, NY: Cornell University Press.

Tuck, M. (1989) *Drinking and Disorder: a study of non-Metropolitan Violence*. Home Office Research Study 108. London: Home Office.

Walvin J. (1984) *Passage to Britain*. London: Penguin.

Willis, C. (1983) *The Use, Effectiveness and Impact of Police Stop and Search Powers*. RPUP 15. London: Home Office.

Yinger, M. (1986) 'Intersecting Strands' in J. Rex and D. Mason (eds) *Theories of Race and Ethnic Relations*. Cambridge. Cambridge University Press.

Young, K. and Connelly, N. (1981) *Policy and Practice in the Multi-Racial City*. London: Policy Studies Institute.

Young T., FitzGerald M., Hallsworth S., and Joseph I. (2007) *Groups, Gangs and Weapons*. London. Youth Justice Board.

Youth Justice Board (2007) *Offences Resulting in a Disposal 2005–6* <http://www.yjb.gov.uk/NR/rdonlyres/FE75681B-BD24–4D6F-864D-D483CC2A97B8/0/AnnualStatistics200506RegionalOffencesresultinginadisposal.xls>.

NOTES

1. Use of the term becomes unavoidable when discussing 'racism'—that is prejudice against particular groups based on the 'beliefs' referred to by McEwen.

2. The 'New' Commonwealth comprised countries where the majority of citizens were non-white, as opposed to 'Old' Commonwealth countries such as Canada, Australia, and New Zealand, many of whose citizens were descended from people who had emigrated from Britain in the first place.

3. A major study in the mid-1970s was particularly influential in this regard (Smith, 1974) and the issues were again taken up by the House of Commons Home Affairs Committee in its report on 'Racial Disadvantage' in 1981.

4. That is, the groups which accounted for 0.5 per cent or more of the population—with the exception of the 'Other Asian' group which is omitted for the sake of simplicity since its composition is very uncertain.

5. This figure shows the percentage of 16–24 year olds who said they were economically active at the time of the Census. People who are 'economically active' include students as well as those in work and seeking work.

6. The published Census table does not give any further breakdown by gender. Figures published by the Department for Children Families and Schools consistently show that boys lag behind girls in attainment at this age and that the gulf is much higher than average in some groups. In 2007, for example, only 41.5 per cent of Black Caribbean boys achieved five GCSEs at grades A-C, compared with 55.2 per cent of White British boys and 56.2 per cent of Black Caribbean girls. The results for Pakistani pupils showed similarly stark gender differences (DFES 2007).

7. Most notably Meadowell (Tyneside) and Blackbird Leys (Oxford) in 1991.

8. The second police investigation had, in fact, identified the suspects but the Crown Prosecution Service decided not to charge them.

9. This included one of the members of the inquiry team and the mother of the murdered boy.

10. Bradford had already experienced rioting in 1995, although these events were depicted in classic terms of conflict with the police.

11. According to the 2001 Census, over 90 per cent of Pakistanis and Bangladeshis are Muslims; and they accounted for nearly 70 per cent of the Muslim population of England and Wales. However, it is worth noting that, of the four bombers, one was of black Caribbean heritage and a convert to Islam.

12. Thus in 2007 a number of chief constables began to raise concerns about the impact on their crime figures of new immigrants and the issues raised by this (see, for example, *Daily Telegraph*, 24 September 2007). Those from Eastern Europe in particular could not readily be identified in their ethnic monitoring returns since they would be classified as white; and comparisons with population statistics from the Census would be distorted since many of these individuals would not have been counted in 2001. Meanwhile, though, sections of the media had begun persistently to run stories about Polish criminals (see *Guardian*, 15 March 2008).

13. Home Office circular 70/92 to all police forces one year later entitled 'Implementing s 95 of the Criminal Justice Act 1991 and Ethnic Classifications' heralded the introduction of ethnic monitoring. This was followed two years later by circular 34/94, giving more precise details of the information to be collected from April 1996.

14. However, the fact that these figures had not yet been published five years later suggests that these remained incomplete or unreliable or both—possibly vindicating the police's original arguments for visual classification referred to earlier.

15. The police have several different powers under which they can search members of the public; but by far the most common are searches under s. 1 of PACE which requires an officer to have 'reasonable grounds for suspicion' that anyone they search is carrying illegal, prohibited, or stolen goods (and, as of 2003, items for committing criminal damage).

16. Figures are given for male prisoners with British nationality only since women form only a very small proportion of all prisoners and they tend to be sentenced for different types of offence from men. Also, the very high proportion of foreign female prisoners in the black group can seriously distort inter-ethnic comparisons.

17. Both systems by 2005 were based on self-classification using the 16 Census categories and the figures are aggregated to five categories (that is, including a 'mixed' category of individuals who might previously have been classified under any of the 'White', 'Black', 'Asian', or 'Other' headings).

18. In both cases, a number of offence categories which individually accounted for less than 5 per cent in any ethnic group have been subsumed into a single 'other' category for the sake of simplicity.

19. Figures given here exclude the 20 Chinese cockle pickers drowned in Morecambe Bay which significantly inflated the 'Other' category for that one year.

20. The homicide figures for 2003–04 and 2004–05 combined do, indeed, show that black victims of homicide were more likely than others to have died from a sharp instrument or by shooting (Ministry of Justice, 2007). However, Blair made his argument on the basis of disproportionality alone, ignoring the fact that black people still accounted for only a *minority* of all victims in these categories (at 13 per cent and 35 per cent respectively).

21. These were people who hadn't committed any of the offences the survey asked about, although they might still (legitimately) have been arrested for other reasons.

22. Although the proportion is also higher for the 'Mixed' group, the difference is not statistically significant (possibly due to small numbers) whereas it is noticeable that 'Asians' who say they have offended are significantly *less* likely to have come to the attention of the system.

23. In 2006 there were 109,228 police constables (Clegg and Kirwan, 2006) and 878,153 recorded s. 1 searches (Ministry of Justice, 2007). Even if only half of those constables were on active duty they would average 16 searches per year.

19 Young people and crime

Derek Kirton

INTRODUCTION

There are many reasons for examining the relationship between young people and crime. One of the more obvious is that levels of involvement in criminal activity, whether judged by official statistics or self-report studies, are at their highest in the teenage years. Crime statistics for England and Wales show peak ages for offending as 17 for males and 15 for females (Ministry of Justice, 2007). These statistics relate to committing the most serious (i.e. indictable) offences. A similar pattern emerges from self-studies which consider a wider range of offences. The 2006 Offending, Crime and Justice Survey found that the peak ages for offending were between 14 and 17 for males and between 12 and 17 for females (Roe and Ashe, 2008). A second reason is that childhood and youth are commonly seen as times when patterns for later life are being set. Effective intervention, or the lack of it, may decide whether young offenders become 'hardened criminals'. Moral panics regarding the 'youth of today' have recurred throughout history (Pearson, 1983).

This chapter focuses on analysing both youth crime and responses to it. The latter are concentrated largely on the youth justice system, but may also involve initiatives relating to parenting, schooling, problem drug or alcohol use, or social inclusion. In the main body of the chapter, we will discuss the key principles around which youth justice has evolved and how the balance between them has changed over time. This will be followed by examination of some of the main theories and models that have been put forward to explain youth crime, including patterns linked to social divisions such as those based on class, ethnicity, and gender. Finally, a review of recent developments and future directions in youth justice is provided. First, however, the context will be set with an overview of some key concepts and debates relating to young people and crime.

BACKGROUND

Before looking at what is distinctive about young people and crime, it is important to acknowledge that there are many similarities with the treatment of adult offenders. For example, in both instances there are debates regarding the appropriate balance between punishment, rehabilitation, and deterrence, and the rights and responsibilities (including to victims) of offenders. Similarly, there is a broad range of sentencing options from fines and discharges to custody. Within the field of criminology, the tensions between crime as an act of free will or as a product of psychological, sociological, or biological factors apply to young and adult offenders alike. It should be noted here that 'young' has different meanings depending on context. Within the criminal justice system in England and Wales, those aged between 10 and 17 are dealt with through a distinctive youth justice system with its own courts, custodial institutions, professional personnel, and, in many cases, sentences. Young adulthood is also marked through separate custodial facilities, with Young Offender Institutions catering for those between the ages of 15 and 21. In research, young has sometimes been taken up to the age of 25 or even 30, largely in order to explore further the process of 'growing out of crime'.

Despite the similarities, however, there are also important differences between the domains of 'young' and 'adult' offenders, differences that, in broad terms, are reflective of perspectives on childhood and youth as life stages. Crucially, they are seen as periods of evolving understanding and morality, rendering children and young people less responsible than adults for their actions. This is generally embodied within criminal justice systems in four main ways. First, there is a minimum age of criminal responsibility (currently ten in England and Wales and Northern Ireland and eight in Scotland), below which the child cannot legally commit a crime. The rationale for this is that they lack the *mens rea* (or 'guilty mind') required. Second, even above the age of criminal responsibility, children and young people tend to be treated differently from adult offenders in various ways. Typically, these will include separate courts (or alternatives to courts) and certain sentencing options that are specific to young offenders. A third feature is that of parental responsibility, either directly for their children's behaviour or through failure to control their offspring. Finally, the State is usually regarded as having responsibilities not only to address the behaviour of young people but also to protect their rights and ensure their 'welfare'. However, these seemingly straightforward features of youth justice systems hide great complexity and often fierce controversy. One example of this is that the age of criminal responsibility has varied significantly over time and between countries—currently ranging in Europe from seven to 18 (see Muncie and Goldson, 2006a).

As will be seen below, understandings of, and responses to, youth crime were transformed during the nineteenth century and much of the twentieth. A growing sense of childhood 'innocence' was reflected in separation from adult offenders and other corrupting influences. Links were increasingly drawn between childhood deprivation and later involvement in crime. This gave rise to what is generally referred to as a welfare model for dealing with youth crime, in which offending is taken to be a symptom of psychological or social deprivation. The response rests with providing expert-led treatment in order to meet the child's needs and so reduce offending. The high point of the welfare model occurred in the late 1960s, but thereafter, its core assumptions were largely rejected and replaced by what became known as the justice model. Rather than focusing on deprivation and needs, the justice model places the offence at the centre, regarding it as an act of free will, with the offender to be punished in line with the seriousness of the crime.

The shift from welfare to justice highlighted a crucial aspect of responses to youth crime, namely that intervention can sometimes be seen as counter-productive. This may occur through the effects of labelling young people as criminals (see Chapter 4) but also because any reoffending tends to provoke more severe ('high tariff') sentences. This may accelerate young offenders' paths towards custody and deepen their involvement in offending. Interventions for young people who have committed minor offences or even those judged to be at 'risk' of offending are often characterized as net-widening, to describe the way they draw young people into the youth justice system, perhaps unnecessarily and with negative consequences. In the case of young offenders, attempts to avoid the effects of net-widening are underpinned by the notion that young people generally 'grow out of crime' and that diversion from the youth justice system is more effective. The strategy of diversion describes efforts to minimize young offenders' involvement with the formal youth justice system, steering them away from the more punitive sentences such as custody, and where possible keeping them out of the system entirely.

While debates on welfare, justice, diversion, and net-widening focus on the perceived effectiveness of particular interventions, some analysts have argued that the youth justice system is driven by other considerations, notably concern with management of the system and its 'value for money'. The concept of corporatism was developed by Pratt (1989). Its main elements are those of centralization, government intervention, and cooperation of agencies and professionals working towards common goals. Typically, it has also been associated with the use of targets, and prescribed ways of working.

The development of youth justice in England and Wales

A specific focus on young offenders is generally traced to the early years of the nineteenth century when organizations emerged to highlight the issue and campaign for reform (Muncie, 2004). At the heart of their work was a plea for a move away from harsh, generally physical punishment towards more subtle means. A growing sense that children and young people could be moulded heightened awareness of the potential for both rehabilitation and corruption.

The rise of the welfare model

During the nineteenth century, there was increasing separation from adult offenders through the establishment of juvenile prisons and the Reformatory and Industrial Schools of the 1850s (subsequently named approved schools), which emphasized strict discipline and training for modest but respectable trades, but also sought to offer children a more caring environment. Such developments can, in turn, be seen as part of a wider movement to regulate childhood through protective legislation, removal from the streets, compulsory schooling, and organized leisure (Hendrick, 1994).

In line with ideas of childhood as a period of 'natural innocence', stronger links were drawn between deprivation and involvement or risk of offending. Establishment of juvenile courts and separate custodial institutions (known as 'Borstals') under the Children Act 1908 marked a clearer separation from adult criminal justice, while the Children and Young Persons (CYP) Act 1933 highlighted the need to protect children from bad company, moral danger, and neglect, and strengthened the legal powers to remove children from their families. Young offenders were now more likely to be seen as victims of circumstance, and in principle to be treated more sympathetically. However, the changes also brought closer surveillance of families and intervention aimed at preventing future offending (Donzelot, 1980).

These trends continued after World War II, as offending came to be explained more in psychological and sociological terms, and social workers were increasingly deployed to work with 'problem families' as a means to reducing youth crime. This welfare-based strategy was buoyed by the failure of approved schools and custody to reduce reoffending (Minty, 1987). The new orthodoxy that youthful offending had to be understood and addressed in the context of child welfare was enshrined in the CYP Acts of 1963 and 1969 which among other measures raised the age of criminal responsibility from 8 to 10 and then to 14 respectively. Decriminalization was also reflected in a significant transfer of responsibility for young offenders from the criminal justice system to local authorities, with offending one of the grounds for making a care order, under which authorities acquired parental rights.

The return to justice

In hindsight, the CYP Act 1969 can be seen as the high point of the welfare model, as it quickly came under attack from various quarters. The emerging 'new right' blamed 'permissiveness' for a rising crime rate (Hall *et al.*, 1978) and portrayed the welfare model as 'soft on crime'. The incoming Conservative Government declined to implement the new age of criminal responsibility, leaving it at 10. There was also opposition from police and magistrates, and a sharp rise in custodial sentences seemed to reflect the latter's desire to ensure punishment and retain greater control over the treatment of young offenders.

While criticism from the political right was predictable, the welfare model also came under fire from the left, arguing that whatever the intentions behind the model, its effects were often harsh (Thorpe *et al.*, 1980). For example, care orders could last many years (until age eighteen), effectively creating indeterminate sentences. Net-widening occurred as those committing relatively minor offences or even adjudged 'at risk' of offending could be drawn into supervised activities and treatment regimes. In addition to raising civil liberties questions, this could lead to harsher sentences if a young person (re)offended while taking part, a phenomenon known as 'raising the tariff'. The dangers of net-widening were greater because, as Thorpe *et al.* (1980) suggest, the welfare model had effectively been grafted onto the existing system, rather than replacing it. These pressures led to the development of what became known as the justice model (see above) (Morris *et al.*, 1980). For those who worked with young offenders, the model was to shift the focus on to the behaviour and away from the background of the offender.

Diversion in the 1980s: a quiet revolution

The 1980s present something of a paradox in relation to youth justice. The Conservative Government elected in 1979 was strongly committed to taking a tough stance on crime. Yet during the following decade there was a very sharp fall, from 7,700 in 1981 to 1,400 in 1991, in the number of young offenders sentenced to custody (Smith, 2007). As Pitts (2001) argues, the scale of this change is not explicable in terms of falling youth crime, but rather from the way in which the Conservative Government sought to reconcile its commitment to tough 'law and order' policies with a desire to contain public expenditure. In broad terms, the answer was to be found under the slogan 'punishment in the community', with sentences that could be presented as alternatives to custody (Bottoms *et al.*, 1990). Within the new community programmes, youth justice workers were able to develop a strategy of 'diversion'.

At its heart, diversion meant pursuing the 'least restrictive alternative' for offenders, avoiding custody at the higher end of the tariff and using cautions and warnings at the lower end. The underpinning rationale for diversion was that most young offenders 'grow out of crime' and that strong intervention from the criminal justice system tends to be counter-productive. To effect this strategy, youth justice workers developed programmes that proved acceptable to the courts, largely by emphasizing responsibility on the part of offenders, including making reparation to victims or to the wider community.

Despite high youth unemployment, withdrawal of welfare benefits, and numerous inner city disturbances in the 1980s, offending by young people generated few moral panics. It was thus that the 'quiet consensus' (Haines and Drakeford, 1998: 32) developed in support of the diversionary strategy and its principles were enshrined in the Criminal Justice Act 1991. This stressed custody as a last resort and introduced measures to reduce its use, while community sentences were promoted as 'tough alternatives' and the responsibilities of parents for their children were strengthened. Despite its 'success', however, some critics argue that the diversionary model and its fit with a 'just deserts' model meant that there was often little engagement with the personal difficulties experienced by offenders or wider issues of inequality and social justice (Pitts, 2001; Brown, 2005).

The punitive turn

Repeating in many respects the earlier fate of welfarism in the 1970s, the diversionary philosophy of the Criminal Justice Act 1991 was soon undermined due to mounting opposition and a series of moral panics. Pitts (2001: 11) suggests that there was a growing realization both that many young people were not 'growing out of crime' and that some youth crime was 'serious'. Combined with increased awareness of victimization, especially in economically deprived areas, this called into question the relatively 'hands off' approach embodied in the Act. Equally influential, however, was a string of moral panics. Debate on an emerging 'underclass' in Britain (Murray, 1990; Dennis and Erdos, 1992) was augmented by a series of folk devils, both individual ('rat boy' and 'safari boy') and collective (the 'joyrider', 'bail bandit', and 'persistent young offender') (Hagell and Newburn, 1994). The common thread, however, was that of growing lawlessness and dangerous young criminals who had become 'untouchable'. Into this volatile situation came the tragic murder of toddler James Bulger by two boys barely above the age of criminal responsibility, an event which seemed to signify the demise of 'childhood innocence' (Jenks, 1996).

Responding to John Major's call to 'condemn a little more and understand a little less' (*The Mail on Sunday* 21 February 1993), the Government introduced a wide-ranging set of 'get tough' measures. The use of cautions was restricted and bail conditions tightened. The anti-custodial emphasis of the 1991 Act was overturned by changes that allowed longer custodial sentences and for these to apply to younger offenders. Secure Training Centres (widely characterized as 'junior prisons') were introduced for persistent young offenders aged 12 to 14. The changes prompted a 40 per cent rise in custody for young offenders between 1992 and 1997 (Audit Commission, 2004). To further emphasize toughness, custodial regimes were to be modelled on US style 'boot camps' and use of the army's 'glass house' was proposed. This punitive turn went hand in hand with what Pitts (2001) has referred to as 'dejuvenilization'; that is, eroding the principle of treating children and young people separately from adults. Electronic tagging was extended to those under 16, and the Crime (Sentences) Act 1997 allowed young offenders to be named publicly. Dejuvenilization brought the UK into increasing conflict with those who monitor the United Nations Convention on the Rights of the Child (UNCRC), ironically signed by the UK Government very shortly before the punitive turn took place. This conflict will be discussed further later in the chapter.

New Labour—'tough on crime and tough on the causes of crime'?

Tony Blair's famous soundbite indicated that New Labour would attempt to match the Conservatives in terms of 'toughness' but also outflank them with a wider approach to preventing crime. Once in government, New Labour launched an ambitious new programme, with the provisions contained in the Crime and Disorder Act 1998 and subsequent legislation. The main measures in relation to youth justice can be summarized as follows:

- removal of *doli incapax*;
- custody and tough community sentences;
- strengthening warning systems;
- reparation and restorative justice;
- anti-social behaviour orders;
- curfews;
- child safety orders;
- parental involvement;
- establishing a national Youth Justice Board to oversee the youth justice system and multi-agency Youth Offending Teams based in all local authority areas.

The ancient presumption of *doli incapax* (literally 'incapable of evil') meant that for offenders under 14, courts had to establish clearly that they understood the consequences of their actions. Its removal was intended to symbolize the Government's rejection of 'excuses' but was controversial in its implication that children of this age held an 'adult' understanding of their behaviour. The aims of punishment and reintegration were enshrined in a new Detention and Training Order (DTO), allowing sentences to be split between custody and the community, the latter operating close monitoring alongside supervised activities. In 2001, the 'Intensive Supervision and Surveillance Programme' (ISSP) was introduced to provide a tough community-based intervention for persistent or serious offenders. ISSP comprised a minimum of 25 hours per week supervised activity aimed at reducing offending behaviour, while the surveillance component included measures such as tracking, tagging, voice recognition, and police intelligence (for research on ISSP, see Gray *et al.*, 2005).

The Labour Government was also keen to promote the use of restoration within youth justice, with the offender through word, deed, or by other means making direct restoration to the victim (or community) for the offence. Restorative youth justice was enshrined in measures such as the reparation order and subsequently the referral order (made under the Youth Justice and Criminal Evidence Act 1999). The latter entailed first-time offenders being referred to a Youth Offender Panel whose main focus would be to consider how restoration could be made. Membership of Panels comprises two volunteers from the local community and one representative from a Youth Offending Team.

While measures to combat poverty and social exclusion and initiatives such as Sure Start were seen as contributing to crime reduction, being 'tough on the causes of crime' focused above all on preventing it through early intervention. Such intervention, however, entailed controversial extension of legal powers. Drawing on principles of 'zero tolerance', young people could be made the subject of anti-social behaviour orders (ASBOs) or subject to curfews. Meanwhile the child safety order was introduced to allow intervention for 'offenders' under the age of 10, for critics effectively lowering the age of criminal responsibility by the back door. Another key element in the strategy of early intervention lay in addressing perceived deficiencies of parenting, including the introduction of the parenting order, obliging parents of young offenders to attend classes to improve their skills (Drakeford and McCarthy, 2000).

Corporatism and managerialism: an alternative explanation?

Thus far, this historical review has been couched largely in term of competing principles or philosophies relating to youth crime—welfare and justice, diversion and intervention. However, some writers argue that better explanations can be found by examining the ways in which youth justice services have been organized and managed. 'Corporatism' (described earlier), with its emphases on management, performance, and cost-effectiveness, became more prominent during the 1980s. In the 1990s, these concerns were reflected in the growing influence of the Audit Commission, which produced a series of reports on the operation of youth justice services (1996; 1998). These reports highlighted organizational inefficiencies such as delays in taking offenders to court, but also promoted the idea of early 'preventive' interventions as a means of saving public money in the longer term. For its critics (Smith, 2007), corporatism is seen as a repressive force, using state power to increase surveillance and control over those who deliver and receive services. For supporters, however, it offers potential for 'joined up' responses, with agencies working together towards the common goal of reducing offending. This view was readily apparent in the Labour Government's establishment of a Youth Justice Board and local Youth Offending Teams, with representation from police, probation, social services, health, drug and alcohol services, housing, and education.

REVIEW QUESTIONS

1 How would you explain the rise and fall of the welfare model in youth justice?

2 Can the diversionary strategies pursued during the 1980s be regarded as successful?

3 Is Pitts right to say that recent decades have seen a process of dejuvenilization in youth justice?

Understanding youth crime

As noted earlier, explanations advanced for youth crime are similar in many ways to those within criminology more generally (see Chapter 4), but are also significantly influenced by perspectives on childhood and youth as life stages, including questions as to whether and how young people may 'grow out of crime'. These issues, along with consideration of parenting and schooling, are rarely applied to older offenders! It is not our intention here to offer a review of theoretical explanations, including those addressing the ways in which youth crime has been defined and 'constructed' as a social problem (for a discussion see, for example, Muncie, 2004). Rather, our focus rests with the relationship between explanations and policy and practice in youth justice. Earlier, it was seen how ideas about deprivation influenced the rise of the welfare model and how interactionist accounts of 'labelling' effects and stigma (Becker, 1963; Lemert, 1967) helped to underpin diversion strategies. Similarly, the influences of realist perspectives can be seen from the 1980s onwards. For 'right realism' this meant emphasizing personal responsibility and moral culpability while for 'left realism', a focus on social causation had to be tempered by 'taking crime seriously'. In both instances, a stronger focus on victims supported the growing interest in restorative justice.

Risk factors: the new orthodoxy

For most of the past decade, the dominant paradigm for understanding and addressing youth crime has been provided by the concept of risk factors, particularly associated with work from the Cambridge Institute of Criminology (West, 1973; Farrington, 1996). During a period of some pessimism regarding youth crime, the risk factor approach appeared to point a way forward, identifying a range of factors associated with youth crime, which might then be targeted for intervention, singly or in combination. Farrington and West's research was based on a longitudinal study, following a group of 411 working class boys from the age of eight in 1961 through to 32. Its obvious strength was the potential to track offending careers over many years and to identify factors associated with their progression. Farrington (1996) highlights the following major risk factors:

- low income and poor housing;
- living in 'deteriorated' inner city areas;
- high degree of impulsiveness and hyperactivity;
- low intelligence and low school attainment;
- poor parental supervision and harsh and erratic discipline;
- parental conflict and broken families;

to which might be added:

- the influence of delinquent friends/gang membership;
- use of drugs or alcohol.

(Smith and McVie, 2003)

The risk factors approach has been taken up by the Youth Justice Board (2001) and is reflected in risk assessment tools such as ASSET which score a list of factors to gauge the likelihood of reoffending. For New Labour, while the above risk factors could readily be linked to wider initiatives in respect of social exclusion and education, arguably the most influential to be taken up was the notion of parenting deficit. Not only were family stability and parental supervision directly important in lowering the risk of offending, but they could also be seen as relevant to reducing those risks that stemmed from material deprivation or educational failure (Utting *et al.*, 1993). This research seemed to point towards the value of early intervention and was supported by other studies suggesting that potential persistent offenders could readily be identified from their early behaviour (Chief Secretary to the Treasury, 2003).

The risk factors approach and supporting research have been criticized, however, especially for their lack of social and political context (Haines and Drakeford, 1998; Smith, 2007). For example, risk factors identifiable from the 1960s and 1970s may be less applicable to today's society, with its different ethnic make-up, family structures, and lifestyles. Moreover, risk factors cannot be assumed to work in a similar fashion irrespective of social context. Pitts (2000: 11) cites US research by Wikstrom and Loeber showing that individual risk factors can be significantly outweighed by neighbourhood factors. It may also be argued that in practice, the risk factors approach allows the locus of 'responsibility' to rest firmly with young people and their families. Offending behaviour has been explained in terms of the way young people 'think' and their lack of self-control rather than as a product of the situations in which they find themselves. Similarly, Smith (2007) suggests that poor parents are treated as 'shock absorbers', charged with instilling self-control in their children regardless of the effects of unemployment, poverty, or homelessness. A further difficulty with the risk factors approach is that it may be stigmatizing, labelling those who fall into the risk categories as 'potential offenders' and often targeting them for intervention. Work emanating from the longitudinal Edinburgh Study of Youth Transitions and Crime (<http://www.law.ed.ac.uk.cls/esytc/>), some of which is reported below, attempts to explore further the links between individual and wider social risk factors, including those such as friendship groups and gang membership. However, it must be remembered that the risk factors approach is focused on prediction based on statistical correlation rather than 'causal' explanation of offending. In this context, qualitative research can be useful for exploring contingencies and the part played by 'life events' in offending careers (Webster *et al.*, 2006).

Profiling youth crime: lessons from self-report surveys

In recent years, knowledge of youth crime has been boosted by a series of self-report studies, typically sampling around 5,000 young people of varying ages between 10 and 25 or even 30 (see for example, Graham and Bowling, 1995; Flood-Page *et al.*, 2000; Roe and Ashe, 2008). Collectively, these self-report studies provide a useful complement and counterweight to official statistics, bearing in mind that most 'crime' goes undetected. These studies show a fairly consistent pattern over time and tend to confirm a number of key aspects of youth offending. One of these is that it is by no means uncommon. The 2006 Offending, Crime and Justice Survey found that 22 per cent of respondents aged between 10 and 25 had committed at least one offence in the previous year (Roe and Ashe, 2008). A second is that a relatively small number of young people account for a significant proportion of crime, with the 2005 version of the same survey finding that 7 per cent of their sample reported responsibility for 83 per cent of offences. Surveys also show that only a minority of offenders are 'caught', with only around 10 per cent of self-confessed offenders reporting being arrested during the past year and only 5 per cent being taken to court (Wilson *et al.*, 2006). Another key finding, as noted earlier, is that the vast majority of those involved in youth offending do indeed 'grow out of crime'. Interestingly, although some offenders stopped after being caught by the police, on balance this appeared to delay the process of desistance, adding support to 'labelling' perspectives (Smith, 2006). The surveys confirm the importance of the risk factors cited above, grouping them into domains such as family, schooling, community, and individual/personal, but often giving them different weight. This highlights the fact that statistical association does not demonstrate that risk factors 'cause' crime, and complex questions remain about how they interact. It should also be noted that self-report studies raise important methodological issues, including sampling, response rates, and perhaps above all, reliability, and data from them must be interpreted with caution (Coleman and Moynihan, 1996).

Young people as victims: a neglected story?

When young people and crime hit the headlines it is most frequently when 'they' (young people) are perceived as a threat to 'us' (respectable, 'adult' society). Young people have not been included in the British Crime Survey (although there are plans to include them in future) and until some studies carried out in the 1990s, there was little focus on them as victims of crime, whether perpetrated by adults or by other young people (Anderson *et al.*, 1994; Hartless *et al.*, 1995). One of the most striking findings from these studies was that young people suffered higher levels of victimization than adults, including from 'normal crimes', such as theft, violence, or harassment as well as abuse within the family. Surveys have also shown how widespread 'fear of crime' is by no means restricted to adults (MORI, 2003).

Another important finding to emerge is that levels of victimization are higher among those who are involved in offending or excluded from school (Smith and McVie, 2003). The reasons for these links are complex and may include participation in risky activities, and the higher incidences of crime and victimization found in particular areas, or among peer groups (Smith, 2004; Smith and Ecob, 2007). While offending can lead to victimization both directly (for example, if a victim retaliates) or indirectly (for example, through becoming a victim whilst placed in custody), it is also the case that many offenders have themselves previously been victims. Boswell (1995), for example, found that 72 per cent of young offenders committing the most serious crimes had been the victims of abuse. Child welfare campaigners might broaden this argument, claiming that young offenders are almost invariably victims, if only in the sense of having been failed by (adult) society.

REVIEW QUESTIONS

1 What are the key strengths and weaknesses of the 'risk factors' approach to youth crime?

2 How useful are self-report studies in understanding youth crime?

3 What can be learnt from the study of young people as victims of crime?

Young people, crime, and social divisions

In discussing youth crime, it is important to remember that the term 'youth' brings together those with widely differing backgrounds and circumstances, not least arising from major social divisions, such as those of class, ethnicity, and gender.

Class

There is a long-established pattern of over-representation in official crime statistics of those from working class backgrounds. Debate, however, has often raged as to whether this reflects levels of participation in crime or is generated by discriminatory policing and processes within the criminal justice system (Muncie, 2004).

Findings from self-report studies suggest that both factors are present to a degree. The importance of socio-economic deprivation as a risk factor has already been noted, and self-reported offending rates in Social Class V have been found to be roughly twice those in Class I (Flood-Page *et al.*, 2000: 22; Smith and McVie, 2003: 185). Explaining 'over-representation' is arguably as difficult and controversial as gauging its extent. Conceptualizations of class are varied and have their own complex relationships with factors related to education, unemployment, drug use, and neighbourhood. Additionally, they are open to cultural/behavioural and structural interpretations which provide very different explanations for involvement in crime. White and Cunneen (2006) argue that class continues to be important in understanding youth crime, whether in terms of the impact of marginalization in a globalized economy or the contribution of street culture to identities when those rooted in work and consumption are denied.

'Race' and Ethnicity

Debate on minority ethnic over-representation has focused particularly on young black people and those of mixed parentage, whose presence in the youth justice system is roughly twice that in the population (House of Commons Home Affairs Committee, 2007). Findings from self-report studies have to date cast little light on how far this reflects their greater involvement in crime. For while some have found higher levels of offending than among their white peers, in others the levels have been similar or lower (Flood-Page *et al.*, 2000; MORI, 2003; Armstrong *et al.*, 2005). There is evidence from these surveys that young black people committing offences are more likely to be arrested, whether because of the types of crime involved, use of public space, greater surveillance, or discriminatory policing (House of Commons Home Affairs Committee, 2007).

Over-representation has also given rise to claims of discrimination within the various stages of the criminal justice system. In a recent and very detailed examination, Feilzer and Hood (2004) concluded that while there was no pervasive discrimination in the youth justice system, there were aspects and processes that had discriminatory effects. For young black people and especially those of mixed parentage, there was less likelihood of pre-court disposals and unconditional bail, and greater likelihood of referral to Crown Court, more restrictive community penalties, and longer custodial sentences.

From its deliberations, the Home Affairs Committee concluded that over-representation of young black people reflected the interaction of social exclusion, community factors such as family breakdown and lack of positive role models, and the workings of the criminal justice system. However, it can be argued that this analysis fails to engage with complex and dynamic nature of ethnicity and processes of racialization, including their localized 'community contexts' (Webster, 2006).

Gender

Gender inequalities raise a qualitatively different set of issues from those associated with class or ethnicity. Young women are far less likely than young men to appear in criminal statistics, although self-report studies suggest that they under-estimate female involvement in youth crime. Nonetheless, the studies show that young male offenders outnumber females by ratios in the range of two or three to one and even higher for persistent or serious offenders (MORI, 2003; Smith and McVie, 2003). Smith and McAra (2004) suggest that crimes such as carrying a weapon, housebreaking, robbery, theft from cars, and cruelty to animals are overwhelmingly committed by young men. There are many competing explanations for such differences (see Chapter 17 for fuller discussion) but part of the answer clearly lies with different patterns of socialization, where conformity is highly valued for girls and young women and their behaviour more tightly monitored and controlled. Feminist writers highlight that girls are already 'policed' heavily, historically in terms of sexuality and more recently in terms of alcohol use, prior to any contact with the criminal justice system (Gelsthorpe and Sharpe, 2006). Gender stereotypes tend to portray offending as relatively 'normal' for young men, while running counter to the 'nature' of women. Yet, as Brown (2005) argues, these norms may be so taken for granted that the relationship between masculinity and crime is rarely scrutinized.

Stereotyping appears to produce mixed results for young female offenders. On the one hand, beliefs that they are less likely to become persistent or serious offenders may lead to more lenient treatment and sentencing patterns lend some support to this (see Table 19.1).

Table 19.1 Type of disposals for offenders (aged 10 to 17) by gender

	Male (%)	Female (%)
Pre-court	40	60
first tier (*)	37	27
community disposals	19	12
custody	4	1

Source: adapted from Youth Justice Board (2006:17)
(*) most commonly referral orders (39%), compensation orders (21%), fine (18%)
conditional discharge (12%)

However, young women may also suffer more from the negative aspects of welfarism and when they commit violent crimes, may be 'doubly damned', having transgressed the bounds of femininity as well as the criminal law (Brown, 2005). Custodial sentences for young women have risen rapidly in recent years, a rise attributed by some to backlash against women's liberation (Worrall, 2001) and moral panic regarding women becoming more violent, even though there is little evidence to support this (Bachelor *et al.*, 2001).

REVIEW QUESTIONS

1 What are the most likely explanations for the over-representation of working class and minority ethnic young people in the official crime statistics?

2 How do gender stereotypes affect responses to youth crime?

Contemporary youth justice and future directions

In this section, we will seek to review the main characteristics of current youth justice policy in England and Wales and consider the principal debates surrounding its future direction. Since its election in 1997, the Labour Government has continued to emphasize 'toughness' in sentencing, promotion of responsibility on the part of young offenders and their parents, and a wide range of early intervention measures. A major concern has been to 'take crime seriously' in order to limit political vulnerability when public and media opinions are generally seen as punitive. This stance has, however, set the Government at odds with penal reform groups, major children's charities, children's rights bodies, and many youth justice professionals who claim that it treats young people as 'offenders first, children second'. In seeking to reverse this priority, the pressure groups are in many ways drawing upon ideas associated with the welfare model, suggesting that rumours of its death have been exaggerated. We will return to these arguments below, but first consider how the current Government's youth justice policy has evolved.

A key element in 'taking crime seriously' has been to ensure that 'something happens' as a consequence of crime. This has been reflected in a significant fall in low tariff sentences, such as cautions, fines, and discharges, and a rise in those (especially restorative measures and community sentences) perceived as having greater consequences for young offenders. The modest increases in custody hide significant rises among those groups, notably female offenders and younger (aged 10 to 14) male offenders, for whom custody was rarely used in the past.

Whatever the debates about the appropriateness of custody and whether it 'works', concerns for cost-effectiveness tend to militate against its use, instead favouring community sentences (Audit Commission, 2004). The high cost of custody is also relevant to a broader preventive strategy where it is argued that modest early expenditure may produce savings on individual offenders of £70,000 or even £140,000 in the longer term (Scott *et al.*, 2001; Audit Commission, 2004: 93). Despite its persuasive logic, however, this argument makes bold assumptions regarding the ability to identify future offenders and divert them from criminal careers. Equally, it appears to gloss over the negative consequences that may arise from intervention. Nonetheless, prevention and early intervention continue to play important parts in youth justice policy. This includes activity-based programmes such as SPLASH, Positive Activities for Young People, and the Youth Inclusion Programme introduced in 2000 and now targeting 'at risk' 8- to 17-year-olds in high crime areas. Younger children and their families have also been targeted, initially through the On Track programme for 4- to 12-year-olds, and more recently Youth Inclusion and Support Panels for those aged 8 to 13. In line with a 'joined up' approach to crime reduction, panels may refer children and parents to a range of activities, advice, mentoring, or counselling services. (For a review of On Track see Hine and Harrington (2004) and for details of other initiatives <http://www.yjb.gov.uk/en-gb/yjs/Prevention/>.) Restorative justice has established a prominent place in youth courts, with referral orders now accounting for around 30 and 40 per cent of sentences for young male and female offenders respectively in 2006 (Ministry of Justice, 2007). However, it has proved difficult to engage victims directly in the process. Newburn *et al.* (2002) found victims attending Youth Offender Panels in only 6 per cent of cases.

Children first?

The proposition that young offenders should be treated as 'children first' draws significantly upon discourses of children's rights as set out in the United Nations Convention on the Rights of the Child 1989 (UNCRC) and domestically in the Children Act 1989. Monaghan *et al.* (2003) set out six key requirements for a child-centred youth justice, which should:

(a) be in line with the principles of the UNCRC;

(b) be distinct and separate from the adult criminal justice system;

(c) have children's 'best interests' as its guiding principle;

(d) raise the age of criminal responsibility;

(e) treat offenders as children first, that is, in line with children's legislation; and

(f) use secure accommodation only as a last resort and ensure it provides a safe and caring environment.

In policy terms, the two most important elements are support for decriminalization and opposition to custody. Decriminalization is partly a matter of raising the age of criminal responsibility (14 is typically the preferred age) but also entails moving away from the 'adversarial' court towards more welfare-focused settings, such as the Scottish hearings system. 'Children first' opposition to custody focuses strongly on the failure of custodial regimes to protect and meet the needs of vulnerable young people. As noted earlier, young offenders have often experienced troubled and abusive childhoods and studies show that up to a third of male and half of female prisoners have been in public care (Worsley, 2007). Mental health problems are estimated to affect between 46 and 81 per cent of those in custody (Hagell, 2002), with significant incidence of (attempted) suicide (Downey, 2002). Penal reform groups, most notably the Howard League for Penal Reform, have waged a long, and at least partially successful, campaign to prevent young offenders being remanded to adult prisons and to establish that the protections of the

Children Act 1989 apply to Young Offender Institutions (YOIs). They have also sought to promote the use of local authority secure accommodation over YOIs, the former being generally regarded as providing better care and education, albeit at greater expense (Audit Commission, 2004).

Some supporters of a 'children first' position also oppose restorative justice measures when they take place within a framework of threats and sanctions and are grafted onto a system based on very different principles (Pitts, 2001). Haines and O'Mahony (2006) argue that pressuring young offenders to apologize and make reparation can be very one-sided in situations where they may be more sinned against than sinners. From this perspective, the pendulum has swung too far towards emphasizing young people's responsibilities at the expense of their rights and the responsibilities of others to them (Haines and Drakeford, 1998).

REVIEW QUESTIONS

1 Has New Labour's approach to youth crime been successful?

2 Assess the arguments for and against treating young offenders as 'children first'.

CONCLUSION

In this chapter we have reviewed key aspects of the relationship between young people and crime, whether as offenders, victims, or recipients of youth justice. We have seen how, through the many changes taking place over the past two centuries, certain enduring questions can be identified. These relate to whether young offenders should be treated differently from adults, and if so, in what ways? Responses have been shaped by the need to address (youth) crime effectively while also dealing appropriately with offenders as children and young people. It is important here to remember that 'childhood' and 'youth' are socially constructed terms and can vary according to time and place. Different constructions may point to different approaches, such as those based on welfare and justice principles respectively. Competing perspectives on whether young people 'grow out of crime' may support diversion or early intervention strategies. Following a long period of growing separation between the respective treatment of young and adult offenders, recent decades have witnessed a reversal of this trend. It is clear that successive governments have felt obliged to take a 'tough' stance on youth crime to meet media and public demands, but by doing so they have tended to amplify moral panics surrounding youth crime, while reinforcing the image of youth justice as 'too lenient'. This amplification process has seen relentless expansion and tightening of the youth justice net, during a period when youth crime has by most measures declined or been static (Fionda, 2005).

While successive UK governments have looked to the US for inspiration, 'children first' advocates favour European models as the way forward. These remain more rooted in welfarist ideas, with much lower rates of custody, higher ages of criminal responsibility (the European average being between 14 and 16), investigative enquiry into the offender's circumstances, and emphasis on promoting social inclusion (Pitts, 2001). Although transplanting ideas from one culture to another is a difficult process, it seems strange that policy makers look towards the US with its high crime rate and vast prison population rather than to Europe where both are generally much lower. As Muncie and Goldson (2006b) observe, while there has been an overall international trend away from welfarism, this is by no means universal, with some countries pursuing decarceration and/or eschewing more punitive policies.

If currently the main political parties in the UK appear only to offer variations on a theme of 'toughness', there remains a significant liberal opposition advocating a response to youth crime based on children's rights and welfare (see for example, Solomon and Garside (2008)). While marginalized in many respects, this opposition draws strength from the wider framework of children's rights and the persistence of welfare concerns in the lives of young offenders. A youth justice system in England and Wales based on 'children first' appears very unlikely at present, but it would be unwise to assume that this cannot change in the future.

QUESTIONS FOR DISCUSSION

1 Should the age of criminal responsibility be raised to 14?

2 Do young offenders have too many rights and too few responsibilities?

3 Based on this chapter and Chapter 8, to what extent do you consider that the moral panics surrounding youth crime can be blamed on media coverage?

4 Is legislation on anti-social behaviour likely to help reduce offending by young people?

5 'Reducing social inequalities such as those based on class and ethnicity is a vital part of the fight against youth crime.' Discuss.

GUIDE TO FURTHER READING

Goldson, B. (2008) *A Dictionary of Youth Justice*. Cullompton: Willan Publishing.

This recent work provides broad coverage in dictionary format of a range of issues—historical, legal, theoretical, policy, practice, and research—relating to youth justice in the UK.

Goldson B. and Muncie, J. (eds) (2006) *Youth Crime and Justice: Critical Issues*. London: Sage.

This edited collection covers a very wide range of topics relating to youth justice, including its relationship to social divisions, and wider policy contexts as well as practice issues.

Muncie, J. (2004) *Youth and Crime: a Critical Introduction* (2nd edn). London: Sage.

This book is probably the most useful of the overview texts in the field of youth crime and youth justice. It provides a good historical account of youth crime and locates discussion in a wider context of theorizing about youth and youth culture(s).

Muncie, J. and Goldson B. (eds) (2006) *Comparative Youth Justice: Critical Issues*. London: Sage.

This collection comprises analyses and commentary on youth justice in 12 countries and a useful concluding chapter discussing broad trends and variations between and within countries.

Smith, R. (2007) *Youth Justice: Ideas, Policy, Practice* (2nd edn). Cullompton: Willan Publishing.

The main strength of this book is its very detailed analysis of the workings of youth justice, making it complementary to Muncie's book in many respects.

WEB LINKS

http://www.barnados.org.uk

Like other major children's charities, Barnardo's takes a keen interest in youth justice, crime, and victimization. The website provides details of the project work undertaken and of relevant research.

http://www.yjb.gov.uk/en-gb

The website for the Youth Justice Board provides an excellent guide to the workings of the youth justice system, including information on sentences, courts, and custody. It also highlights the YJB's publications and research and provides links to relevant legislation and reports.

http://www.nayj.org.uk

The National Association for Youth Justice broadly advocates an approach to youth justice based on the rights of children and young people. It publishes a newsletter and the journal *Youth Justice* which includes many topical articles on the workings of the youth justice system.

http://society.guardian.co.uk/youthjustice/

This section within the *Guardian's* Society website provides useful links to other relevant sites and details of recent articles dealing with youth crime and youth justice.

http://www.howardleague.org

Along with other penal reform groups such as Nacro, the Howard League runs various projects and campaigns linked to youth justice in addition to producing publications and reports.

REFERENCES

Anderson, S., Kinsey, R., Loader, I., and Smith, C. (1994) *Cautionary Tales: Young People, Crime and Policing in Edinburgh*. Aldershot: Avebury.

Armstrong, D., Hine, J., Hacking, S., Armaos, R., Jones, R., Klessinger, N., and France, A. (2005) *Children, Risk and Crime: the On Track Youth Lifestyles Surveys*. Home Office Research Study 278. London: Home Office.

Audit Commission (1996) *Misspent Youth: Young People and Crime*. London: Audit Commission.

Audit Commission (1998) *Misspent Youth '98: the Challenge for Youth Justice*. London: Audit Commission.

Audit Commission (2004) *Youth Justice 2004: A Review of the Reformed Youth Justice System*. London: Audit Commission.

Bachelor, S., Burman, M., and Brown, J. (2001) 'Discussing Violence: Let's Hear it from The Girls', *Probation Journal*, 48 (2): 125–34.

Becker, H. (1963) *Outsiders: Studies in the Sociology of Deviance*. New York: Free Press.

Boswell, G. (1995) *Violent Victims*. London: Princes Trust.

Bottoms, A., Brown, P., McWilliams, B., McWilliams, W., and Nellis, M. (1990) *Intermediate Treatment and Juvenile Justice: Key Findings and Implication from a National Survey of Intermediate Treatment Policy and Practice*. London: HMSO.

Brown, S. (2005) *Understanding Youth and Crime: Listening to Youth?* (2nd edn). Buckingham: Open University Press.

Chief Secretary to the Treasury (2003) *Every Child Matters* (Green Paper), Cm 5860. London: Stationery Office.

Coleman, C. and Moynihan, J. (1996) *Understanding Crime Data*. Buckingham: Open University Press.

Dennis, N. and Erdos, G. (1992) *Families Without Fatherhood*. London: Institute of Economic Affairs.

Donzelot, J. (1980) *The Policing of Families*. London: Hutchinson.

Downey, R. (2002) 'Youth Crimes and Punishment', *Community Care* (14–20 February): 30–2.

Drakeford, M. and McCarthy, K. (2000) 'Parents, responsibility and the new youth justice' in B. Goldson (ed), *The New Youth Justice*. Lyme Regis: Russell House Publishing.

Farrington, D. (1996) *Understanding and Preventing Youth Crime*. York: York Publishing Services.

Feilzer, M. and Hood, R. (2004) *Differences or Discrimination?: Minority Ethnic Young People In The Youth Justice System*. London: Youth Justice Board.

Fionda, J. (2005) *Devils and Angels: Youth Policy and Crime*. Oxford: Hart Publishing.

Flood-Page, C., Campbell, S., Harrington, V., and Miller, J. (2000) *Youth Crime: Findings from the 1998/99 Youth Lifestyles Survey*. London: Home Office.

Gelsthorpe, L. and Sharpe, G. (2006) 'Gender, youth crime and justice', in B. Goldson and J. Muncie (eds) *Youth Crime and Justice: Critical Issues*. London: Sage.

Graham, J. and Bowling, B. (1995) *Young People and Crime*. Home Office Research Study no. 145. London: HMSO.

Gray, E., Taylor, E., Roberts, C., Merrington, S., Fernandez, R., and Moore, R. (2005) *Intensive Supervision and Surveillance Programme: The Final Report*. London: Youth Justice Board.

Hagell, A. (2002) *The Mental Health Needs of Young Offenders*. London: Mental Health Foundation.

Hagell, A. and Newburn, T. (1994) *Persistent Young Offenders*. London: Policy Studies Institute.

Haines, K. and Drakeford, M. (1998) *Young People and Youth Justice*. Basingstoke: Macmillan.

Haines, K. and O'Mahony, D. (2006) 'Restorative approaches, young people and youth justice', in B. Goldson and J. Muncie (eds) *Youth Crime and Justice: Critical Issues*. London: Sage.

Hall, S., Critcher, C., Jefferson, T., Clarke, J., and Roberts, B. (1978) *Policing the Crisis: Mugging, the State and Law and Order*. London: Macmillan.

Hartless, J, Ditton, J, Nair, G., and Phillips, S. (1995) 'More Sinned Against Than Sinning: a Study of Young Teenagers' Experiences of Crime', *British Journal of Criminology,* 35 (1): 114–33.

Hendrick, H. (1994) *Child Welfare, England 1872–1989*. London: Routledge.

Hine, J. and Harrington, V. (2004) *Delivering On Track*. Development and Practice Research Report 12. London: Home Office.

House of Commons Home Affairs Committee (2007) *Young Black People and the Criminal Justice System Second Report of Session 2006–07 Volume I*. HC 181-I

Jenks, C. (1996) *Childhood*. London: Routledge.

Lemert, E. (1967) *Human Deviance, Social Problems and Social Control*. Englewood Cliffs: Prentice-Hall.

Ministry of Justice (2007) *Criminal Statistics England and Wales 2006*. London: Stationery Office.

Minty, B. (1987) *Child Care and Adult Crime*. Manchester: Manchester University Press.

Monaghan, G. Hibbert, P., and Moore, S. (2003) *Children in Trouble: Time for Change*. Ilford: Barnardo's.

MORI (2003) *Youth Survey 2003*. London: MORI.

Morris, A., Giller, H., Geach, H., and Szwed, E. (1980) *Justice for Children*. London: Macmillan.

Muncie, J. (2004) *Youth and Crime: A Critical Introduction* (2nd edn). London: Sage.

Muncie, J. and Goldson, B. (eds) (2006a) *Comparative Youth Justice*. London: Sage.

Muncie, J. and Goldson, B. (2006b) 'States of transition: convergence and diversity in international youth justice' in B. Goldson and J. Muncie (eds) *Comparative Youth Justice*. London: Sage.

Murray, C. (1990) *The Emerging British Underclass*. London: Institute of Economic Affairs.

Newburn, T., Crawford, A., Earle, R., Goldie, S., Hale, C., Hallam, A., Masters, G., Netten, A., Saunders, R., Sharpe, K., and Uglow, S. (2002) *The Introduction of Referral Orders into the Youth Justice System: second interim report*. London: Home Office.

Pearson, G. (1983) *Hooligan: a History of Respectable Fears*. London: Macmillan.

Pitts, J. (2000) 'The New Youth Justice and the Politics of Electoral Anxiety', in B. Goldson (ed), *The New Youth Justice*. Lyme Regis: Russell House Publishing.

Pitts, J. (2001) *The New Politics of Youth Crime: Discipline or Solidarity*. Basingstoke: Palgrave.

Pratt, J. (1989) 'Corporatism: the Third Model of Juvenile Justice', *British Journal of Criminology,* 29 (3): 236–54.

Roe, S. and Ashe, J. (2008) *Young People and Crime: Findings from the 2006 Offending, Crime and Justice Survey,* Home Office Statistical Bulletin 09/08. London: Home Office.

Scott, S., Knapp, M., Henderson, J., and Maughan, B. (2001) 'Financial Costs of Social Exclusion: Follow up Study of Antisocial Children into Adulthood', *British Medical Journal,* 323: 191–94.

Smith, D. (2004) *The Links Between Victimization and Offending*. Edinburgh Study of Youth Transitions and Crime, Research Digest, No. 4.

Smith, D. (2006) *Social Inclusion and Early Desistance from Crime*. Edinburgh Study of Youth Transitions and Crime, Research Digest, No. 12.

Smith, D. and Ecob, R. (2007) 'An Investigation into Casual Links between Victimization and Offending', *British Journal of Sociology*, 58 (4); 633–59.

Smith, D. and McAra, L. (2004) *Gender and Youth Offending.*, Edinburgh Study of Youth Transitions and Crime, Research Digest, No. 2.

Smith, D. and McVie, S. (2003) 'Theory and Method in the Edinburgh Study of Youth Transitions and Crime', *British Journal of Criminology*, 43 (1): 169–95.

Smith, R. (2007) *Youth Justice: Ideas, Policy, Practice* (2nd edn). Cullompton: Willan.

Solomon, E. and Garside, R. (2008) *Ten Years of Labour's Youth Justice Reforms: An Independent Audit,* London: Centre for Crime and Justice Studies.

Thorpe, D., Smith, D., Green, C., and Paley, J. (1980) *Out of Care: the Community Support of Juvenile Offenders*. London: Allen & Unwin.

Utting, D., Bright, J., and Henricson, C. (1993) *Crime and the Family: Improving Childrearing and Preventing Delinquency*. London: Family Studies Policy Centre.

West, D. (1973) *Who Becomes Delinquent*. London: Heinemann.

Webster, C. (2006) ' "Race", Youth Crime and Justice', in B. Goldson and J. Muncie (eds) *Youth Crime and Justice: Critical Issues*. London: Sage.

Webster, C., MacDonald, R., and Simpson, M. (2006) 'Predicting Criminality? Risk Factors, Neighbourhood Influence and Desistance', *Youth Justice*, 6 (1): 7–22.

White, R. and Cunneen, C. (2006) 'Social class, youth crime and justice', in B. Goldson and J. Muncie (eds) *Youth Crime and Justice: Critical Issues*. London: Sage.

Wilson, D., Sharp, C., and Patterson, A. (2006) *Young People and Crime: Findings from the 2005 Offending, Crime and Justice Survey*, Home Office Statistical Bulletin 17/06. London: Home Office.

Worrall, A. (2001) 'Girls At Risk?: Reflections on Changing Attitudes To Young Women's Offending', *Probation Journal*, 48 (2): 86–92.

Worsley, R. (2007) *Young People in Custody 2004– 2006: An Analysis of Children's Experiences of Prison*. London: HM Inspectorate of Prisons/Youth Justice Board.

Youth Justice Board (2001) *Risk and Protective Factors associated with Youth Crime and effective interventions to prevent it*. London: Youth Justice Board

Youth Justice Board (2006) *Youth Justice Annual Statistics 2005/06*. London: Youth Justice Board.

20 'Ageing' in prison: crime and the criminal justice system

Azrini Wahidin

INTRODUCTION

This chapter will review what is known about older people and crime. We will start by defining the term 'older offender', and then critically explore why older people in the criminal justice system have been constructed as victims rather than perpetrators and why crimes committed by elders are absent from the criminological agenda. Work in this area has been led by American researchers and it is only in the last ten years that researchers in the UK (see Phillips, 1996; Manthorpe, 1983; Wahidin, 2004; Wahidin and Cain, 2006) have examined the relationship between ageing and crime. I will identify the key issues and current debates in criminology surrounding older people and crime and will focus on the specific issues an ageing population poses to the criminal justice system (with reference to the prison system in England and Wales). The first section offers an exploration of why, when we think about elders and the criminal justice system, we equate the stereotypical image of a vulnerable frail person as being the victim rather than the offender.

The chapter will provide an introduction to the area, contextualize the age demographics of the prison population, discuss age-specific theories of crime, raising epistemological questions about the nature of imprisonment, and, finally, examine the role that age-specific programmes can play in reducing the pains of imprisonment. I will argue that it is only by systematically addressing the needs of elders in prison, rather than reacting to them, that we can begin 'to look after them with humanity and help them lead law-abiding and useful lives in custody and after release'. (This statement may be seen displayed at the entrance of every prison. Go to <http://www.hmprisonservice.gov.uk/> to enter HM Prison Service website.)

We are unaccustomed to thinking about people in later life as criminal offenders. Usually, when the elderly receive publicity, they are represented as the victims of crime, not its perpetrators. Some women and men in later life, nevertheless, do commit crimes, some are arrested, some are convicted, some are sent to prison, and some grow old in prison. A decade ago we would never imagine it possible that people were committing crimes in later life, growing old behind bars, and that prison nursing homes would be a feature of the prison landscape. This section will address the relationship that criminology has to the study of age and crime.

BACKGROUND

It is difficult to draw precise conclusions about the extent of crimes committed by persons in later life. The initial problem arises with the definition of the 'elder', which can produce information that at first appears contradictory. Social scientists who have researched older persons and their criminal behaviour have failed to come to a uniform agreement on what age constitutes 'old'. Although there is no definitive, nationwide, or international standard for what constitutes an 'older offender'; most researchers identify 50 as the threshold age. The inability to agree on what constitutes an older offender is one of the most troubling issues involved in comparing research outcomes on both sides of the Atlantic. For the purpose of this chapter, the term 'older' or offender in later life will be used to denote a person aged 50 or over.

Age and crime: the usual suspects?

Criminal behaviour and criminological studies have focused predominantly on young people's activities. While young people have for long been associated with crime, it appears that, as is the case with social class, different age groups commit different types of crime. Yet many theories deal almost exclusively with juvenile delinquency. It has been stated that '[o]ne of the few facts agreed on in criminology is the age distribution of crime' (Hirschi and Gottfredson, 1983: 552). A series of moral panics have 'demonized young people, from the teddy boys, mods and rockers of the 1960s, through to punks, skinheads, muggers, joyriders, "rat" boys' (Curtis, 1999: 28), girl gangs, and mobile phone snatchers of 2000 (see for example, Cohen, 1973; Pearson, 1983). However, the assumption that crime is overwhelmingly a young person's activity must be called into question (see Chapter 19).

Victimology and old age

In popular and political discourses the 'problem of crime' is associated with 'youth crime' as if they were synonymous. As a result, all manner of myths and stereotypes about 'troublesome' people and spaces have come into play. The vast majority of research on youth and crime in the UK has focused on young people as offenders rather than as victims of crime (Williams, 1998; Wahidin and Powell, 2005). They have long been positioned outside the boundaries of the 'ideal victim'; they are, as Presdee (1994) argues, 'invaders of space' (see Chapter 19). 'Youth' and 'old age', and much that we can connect with these categories can be viewed as cultural and historic constructs; the meaning they carry varies over time and space. Conditions often associated with older people are more a result of how society constructs them rather than as a product of the biological ageing process.

The elderly population should be a source of concern if only because it is a growing population. The United Nations estimates that by the year 2025, the global population of those aged 60 years and over will have doubled from 542 million in 1995 to around 1.2 billion people (Krug, 2002: 125). In 2002 there were 19.8 million people aged 50 and over in the UK. The number is projected to increase by a further 41 per cent by 2031, when there will be close to 28 million people aged 50 and over (National Statistics Online, November 2007: <http://www.statistics.gov.uk/>).

Fear of crime

Victims and offenders are constructed in opposition to each other: good and evil, innocent and guilty, predators and prey, and so on. This is important when we come to think about older people as victims of crime. However, this is not just an oversimplification of a complex phenomenon but a deliberate attempt to ignore or at least to overlook the striking similarities, affinities, and overlap between these two populations (see Chapter 24). Within the literature on the fear of crime, older people are usually discussed as experiencing a high level of fear. However, the high-fear/low-risk equation has been questioned in a number of studies that suggest that elders are not in fact any more fearful of crime than younger people (Ferraro, 1995: Crawford *et al.*, 1990; Pain, 1995; Holloway and Jefferson, 2000). Studies from the British Crime Survey have shown that the elderly are less at risk from both violent crime and burglary, and that young men are the group most at risk from assault.

If older people are characterized by an overall low degree of victimization, then why have they been singled out as a specific group in research into the impact of crime? Although the aged are among the least victimized with regard to many serious crimes, there is evidence to suggest that this is not true for certain specific crimes. Second, why do elderly victims of crime provoke such a public outcry? Two possible answers can be found in the portrayal and construction of old people. The image of the older victim as vulnerable wins votes and sells newspapers; neither criminal activity nor the inhumane denial of the special needs of elders in prison are easily squared with this attitude of paternalistic concern. Moreover, the literature suggests that, irrespective of age, those more concerned with the problem of crime and expressing most fear of crime are not necessarily the most likely to have experiences of victimization. In terms of actual rates of victimization, older people are at relatively low risk from crime (although elder abuse, which is not considered here due to the lack of space and nature of discussion, is certainly under-reported (Mawby and Walklate, 1994). As with other characteristics which make people vulnerable to victimization, it is difficult to disentangle the age factor from others, which means that older people figure prominently among those for whom victimization has a high impact. However, while the aged may be relatively unlikely to become victims of crime, their fears are understandable: if they are poor, in poor health, live in bad neighbourhoods, isolated, house-bound, and if they feel vulnerable, the risk of victimization substantially increases (Zedner, 1997). Moreover, one must stress that the experience of *fear* is very real to the individual and thus makes measuring degrees of fear an impossibility. Sparks (1992) rhetorically asks, 'What is a rational level of fear?' In other words, if *fear* is *experienced*, then ultimately, it is real.

A hidden minority

When thinking about elders as perpetrators of crime we associate them with relatively minor offences such as: breach of the peace, shoplifting, or driving under the influence of alcohol. We are unlikely to associate this group with crime serious enough to result in prison sentences continuing into old age. However, there have been recent exceptions with high profile cases such as Harold Shipman, Rosemary West, and the general rise in the number of men who have been convicted in later life for sex-related offences, including those charged with 'historical offences' (offences committed two/three decades ago). The majority of men in prison aged 60 and over (56 per cent) have committed sexual offences and 52 per cent of 60- to 69-year-old prisoners are sexual offenders and among the over 70s it is 73 per cent (Prison Reform Trust, 2007).

Ageing, in criminological literature, is not seen to be an issue, which in itself reflects how the age and crime relationship has been constructed. Contrary to popular belief, the most common offences for the older female age group are not perpetrated by the menopausal shoplifter; they are not theft and handling or fraud and forgery, but

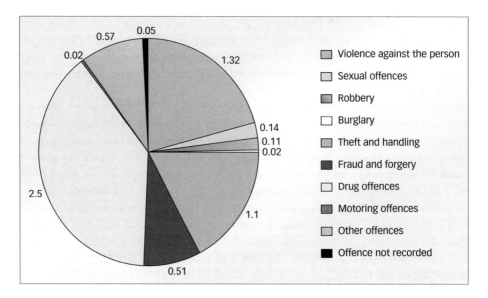

Figure 20.1 Percentage of all offences across all sentence lengths for females aged 50 and over (30 June 2007)

Source: Data adapted from the Prison Reform Trust, 2008. The data was obtained from the prison IT system. Some data items total less than 50. Due to their relative size, their accuracy at this level of detail cannot be guaranteed.

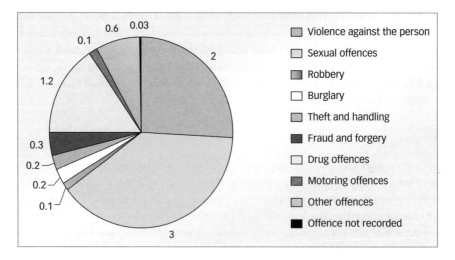

Figure 20.2 Percentage of all offences across all sentence lengths for men aged 50 and over (30 June 2007)

Source: Data adapted from the Prison Reform Trust, 2008. The data was obtained from the prison IT system. Some data items total less than 50. Due to their relative size, their accuracy at this level of detail cannot be guaranteed.

Table 20.1 Cross tabulation of age against sentence length for all prisoners aged 50 and over (June 2007)

Sentence	0< 6 months	6<12 months	12<4 yrs	4<Life	Life	Total
No. of prisoners	164	102	1,116	3,129	1,557	6,069

Source: Data adapted from the PRT 2008. The data was obtained from the prison IT system. Some data items total less than 50. Due to their relative size, their accuracy at this level of detail cannot be guaranteed.

violence against the person and drug offences. By comparison, the most common offences for men in this group are sexual offences, violence against a person, and drug offences.

The 'greying' of the prison population: too few to count?

Women in prison of all ages form only a very small proportion of the total prison population although the number women in prison has more than doubled over the past decade. On 30 June 2007 the total prison population for England and Wales was 81,040. The women's prison population in England and Wales stood at 4,390; women over 50 represent only 6 per cent of the total female prison estate and in terms of actual figures there were 247 women over the age of 50 on 30 June 2007.

Men in prison constitute 94 per cent of the total prison population and on 30 June 2007 the total male prison population was 76,299. For the same period men over 50 represent 8 per cent of the male estate and in terms of actual numbers, there were 5,946. Ethnicity research conducted by Wahidin (see 2005) notes that a significant difference between male and female older prisoners is in the proportion of black and white offenders. More than one in ten male older prisoners who are over 60 belong to a minority ethnic group, which is far higher than the proportion of the general population (Prison Reform Trust, 2007).

The Ministry of Justice of England and Wales has no overall policy or strategy for dealing with older females or older males in prison, although they do have a policy document for every prison entitled the 'Statement on Decency'; however this document fails to incorporate older offenders. Although the Prison Service has elderly units for men, such as HMP Norwich, HMP Frankland, and HMP Wymott, to date, there has been no discussion or plans for similar arrangements to be made for women.

REVIEW QUESTIONS

1 How and why are elders portrayed as victims of crime rather than perpetrators of crime?

2 Discuss the idea that a decade ago we would never have thought it possible that prison nursing homes would become a necessity.

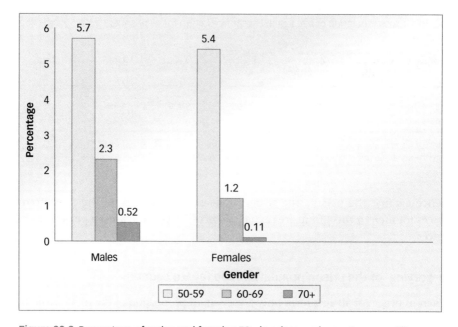

Figure 20.3 Percentage of males and females 50+ in prison under sentence on 30 June 2007

Source: Data adapted from the PRT 2008. The data was obtained from the prison IT system. Some data items total less than 50. Due to their relative size, their accuracy at this level of detail cannot be guaranteed.

Lost offenders in forgotten places

The elderly prison population is likely to increase because our population is ageing (Newman, Newman, and Gerwitz 1984: xvii), more and more people are being incarcerated, and the times served by people subject to mandatory sentences (the mandatory life sentence is the only sentence available to the courts for persons over the age of 21 found guilty of murder), are getting longer (Flynn, 1992; James, 1992; Steffensmeier and Moti 2000). In 1984, the mean time served by females serving a mandatory life sentence was three years and, by 1994, the time served went up to 13 years (see Home Office, 2001, 2001a; NACRO, 1992a). If more and more people are receiving longer mandatory sentences, this will mean that some will remain imprisoned until they are old. This phenomenon is known as the 'stacking effect' (Aday, 2003). A related fact is that those serving life sentences in general are older than the average age of the prison population as a whole. From 1996 to 2000, the over-50 lifer female population rose by 45 per cent and by comparison the lifer male population rose by 66 per cent.

Age breakdown of prison population

The population of women prisoners in England and Wales has features that distinguish it from that of men (Home Office, 1999, 2002; Ministry of Justice, 2007; HMCIP 2001,

2002a; HMIPP, 2001). Between 1993 and 2001, the female prison population rose 140 per cent as against 46 per cent for men, reflecting sentencing changes (Ministry of Justice, 2008: 4; see also Home Office, 2001b). In 1999, the female prison population (only those convicted and sentenced to custody) stood at 2,443 and by 30 June 2007 the population stood at 4,390 which is an increase of 80 per cent. The long-term trend is for the population to continue to rise even though many of the women's prisons have re-rolled into men's prisons, reducing the number of women's prisons from 18 to 14) (personal communication with women in prison, 12 January 2008).

The largest concentrations of male prisoners aged 50-plus are at HMP Whatton, a Category C prison, and HMP Wakefield, which is designed to hold Category A and B prisoners. The highest percentage of women in the 50-plus category are held at HMP Downview, which is a closed prison, and HMP Morton Hall, a semi-open prison which is also the only female foreign detention centre in England and Wales As numbers are predicted to increase (as a result of bifurcation in sentencing), this will surely pose particular problems in terms of the physical environment, healthcare facilities, and resettlement programmes required to fulfil the statement of purpose, the Discrimination Acts 1995, 2005, and the Human Rights Act 1998 (implemented in October 2000). This was heralded by Jack Straw as the 'the most significant statement of human rights in domestic law since the 1968 Bill of Rights' (cited in Sim, 2000: 186).

Old age and crime

Old criminals offer an ugly picture and it seems as if even scientists do not like to look at it for any considerable amount of time...On the other hand, if the thesis of the interrelationship between age and crime is to hold, an investigation of all its implications has to yield results, and with the tendency of our population to increase in the higher age brackets, a special study of criminality of the aged seems to meet a scientific as well as a practical need. (Pollak, 1941: 212)

The absence of elders in the criminological imagination mirrors where the study of female offenders in criminology was 30 years ago. The lack of research in this area is an implicit form of ageism that implies that the problems of this group can be disregarded, or that ageing criminals are simply not worth discussing. The explanation frequently given for the lack of statistical information on this topic is that at present the numbers involved are too small to yield significant information, with the implication that this justifies excluding and ignoring the rights of elders in prison. Yet there has been no assessment of the implications of this, or recognition that England and Wales, like the US, are facing an ageing prison population. This phenomenon has become known as the 'geriatrification' of the prison population.

If Pollak's view was accurate in 1941, it is even more so today, over 60 years later. With the elder prison population representing the fastest growing age group in our prison system, we have reached an important juncture in the disciplines of gerontology and criminology.

A historical view of older offenders

The literature available on older offenders is restricted to predominantly American-based research (Newman, 1984). It was in the 1980s in America that there was renewed interest in ageing offenders (Ham, 1976; Rubernstein, 1984). However, research interest in criminal behaviour among the elderly dates back to the end of the nineteenth century—the phenomenon was first discussed at a criminology conference in Budapest in 1899 (Pollak, 1941: 213 cited in Gewerth, 1988: 15). The work of Aday (1994, 1994a, 2003) has been instrumental in raising the profile of older offenders in the US and he identifies a void in the literature regarding the ageing prison population in general. In contrast to Aday's work, there has been only one study in the UK that addresses the needs of the older male and female prison population (Wahidin, 2004; Wahidin and Cain, 2006).

Types of offenders

We know that there are different types of offenders, ranging from the:

- older first time offender currently serving a term of imprisonment;
- the older offender who has had previous convictions but not served a prison sentence before;
- the recidivist who may have spent a significant amount of her or his life in and out of prison;
- prisoners fulfilling a life sentence and who have grown old in prison;
- long-term inmates.

Typically, the crimes committed by the above mirror those of young offenders. However, in all five groups, the ageing prison population is a special one in terms of health and social care needs, individual adjustment to institutional life, maintaining kinship networks, and end of life issues (Gallagher, 1990). This group challenges the structure of the prison system regarding purposeful activity, rehabilitation, and resettlement needs of offenders in later life.

Theories of crime

The search for causes of crime at any age has been the principal concern of criminologists from Cesare Lombroso and Guglielmo Ferrero in 1895 to Richard Herrnstein and Charles Murray in 1994 (see Chapter 6). The literature on crime in later life has largely been descriptive, with little attempt to provide a theoretical perspective to account for growing numbers of older offenders encountering the criminal justice system.

What this chapter attests to is that women and men across the life course engage in crime for very different reasons. We know that women's experiences of incarceration are qualitatively different to the experiences of men (Carlen, 2002). In the same way, one can argue that older offenders may engage in criminal activities for different reasons to young offenders. Moreover, their experience of incarceration is qualitatively different to the younger able-bodied prison population. The non-age-specific theories of crime emphasize either of two primary influences in illegal behaviour. These are the 'gains' derived from legitimate versus illegitimate activities and the extent to which an individual undergoes social integration and internalization of conventional norms (Hirschi, 1969).

Although non-age-specific theories may differ with respect to the emphasis placed on a particular independent variable, a summary of the crucial predictors would probably include at least some of the following factors:

(a) age;

(b) ethnicity;

(c) gender;

(d) marital/partnership status;

(e) socio-economic status (occupation, education);

(f) criminal associations.

Those few theories that focus on older persons identify the same causes and correlations as more general theories of lawbreaking. Indeed, in most cases, the explanations offered for elders engaging in illegal behaviour might better qualify as 'speculation' than 'theories'. What one can ascertain from the literature is that there are causes and correlates of illegal behaviour that influence:

(a) all age groups equally;

(b) elders and non-elders differentially; and/or

(c) elders uniquely.

Elders in prison

The increase in the proportion of elders is having far reaching effects on all components in the criminal justice system. This section will examine how prisons can begin to address the needs of the older prison population. Once in prison, the vulnerabilities of age are exacerbated by the lack of adequate facilities to enable elders to lead 'law abiding and useful lives in custody and after release' (this statement can be found at every prison in England and Wales). The lack of facilities catering for individual needs increases the pain of imprisonment where the prisons focus resources and facilities, such as training and educational programmes, on the young and able-bodied. This is a good example of how the discourse of ageism and the idea of less eligibility operate when faced with limited resources. Prison officers/prison personnel fail to place elders on educational or training programmes, assuming that, due to their age, they are less likely to find employment.

The lack of help and rehabilitation renders elders a 'hidden minority'. Once prisoners are released, the effect of the discontinuity of pension contributions will leave them with insufficient contributions and consequently they will be in receipt of either a partial pension or none at all. The current wave of anti-social legislation,[1] such as the Housing Act of 1988, (reducing the housing available for ex-prisoners), the Criminal Justice and Public Order Act of 1994, and the Crime and Disorder Act of 1998, the diminishing value of the basic retirement pension, and the complexity of the forms that need to be completed, have in turn led to low take-up rates of benefits by elders in the wider society (Phillipson and Walker, 1986).

A useful initiative would be to introduce independent advice centres in prisons, ensuring that the prisoners had information about available benefits and access to legal resources. A network of employment schemes, linking offenders across the life-course to jobs, would provide occupational skill, an employment record, and promote self-esteem. The continuation of National Insurance contributions whilst in prison is an obvious necessity for offenders across the life-course. Furthermore, a network of halfway houses needs to be established, and facilities/schemes comparable to those at Grendon Underwood[2] and Latchmere House.[3] Such schemes have already been successfully introduced, but far more is needed to ensure that all eligible prisoners are able to access this kind of support.

Women and men in later life need improved health services, better pensions, different types of housing, age-sensitive regimes, and a variety of aids when they become disabled. We have to recognize that the elderly inmate, due to the effects of ageing, has far different needs and places far different demands on a system that is designed for the younger inmate. But they also need a reason for using these things. 'In our society the purpose of life in old age is often unclear...Old age is seen as a "problem" with the elderly viewed as dependants; worse still, they are often described as a non-productive burden upon the economy' (Phillipson, 1982: 166). It is not surprising then that elders experience isolation and alienation when they are denied access to the sources of meaning valued by the society in which they live (Phillipson and Walker, 1986; Turner, 1988).

Although little research has been undertaken in England and Wales into the health of older female and male prisoners, Wahidin (2006) found that women prisoners compared to men over 50 considered themselves disadvantaged in preventative health and wellness schemes (55–6). Similarly, in the USA Kratcoski and Babb (1990), (cited in Kerbs, 2000: 219), found that older female prisoners were less likely than men to participate in recreational programmes, and reported significantly higher levels of poor or terrible health (46 per cent versus 25 per cent), with depression and generalized 'worry' being the two most persistent health problems they experienced. McDonald's (1995) study identified several conditions that have forced prison health care costs in the US to rise. A similar pattern is emerging in the prison system in England and Wales. The factors influencing the increase in expenditure are the following:

(a) the rising cost of health care in society at large;

(b) the increasing number of prisoners in the prison system;

(c) the general ageing of the prison population;

(d) the higher prevalence of infectious diseases among prison populations.

As long as these trends continue, prison health-care costs will continue to increase. Like prisoners in general, ageing prisoners have not had proper access to health care on the outside. They often come into the prison system with numerous chronic illnesses and consume multiple medications. Jonathan Turley, Director of the Project for Older Prisoners (POPS), noted that: 'the greatest single contributor to the high costs of older prisoners is medical expenditures' (Turley, 1990: 26). On average, prisoners over the age of 50 suffer at least three chronic health problems, such as hypertension, diabetes, and emphysema (Acoca, 1998; Turley, 1990). Prisoners, as a population, traditionally have medical and social histories that put them more at risk for illness and disease than their non-inmate peers (Marquart *et al.*, 1997, 2000). As the number of older prisoners increases, the prison system will be even more challenged to provide adequate health and social care provision.

The health needs profile of the ageing offender is hard to map in the absence of statistical information relating to health care costs in prisons in England and Wales. We know that in the US, daily medical care for the general prison population costs $5.75 per offender. On average, for an offender over 50 years of age, the cost of incarceration is approximately three times as much as a prisoner aged under 50 (Neeley, Addison, and Moreland-Craig, 1997; Fazel *et al.*, 2001). Statistics for 2001 provided by the Florida Corrections Commission, support the above findings and demonstrate that prisoners over 50, despite making up only 9 per cent of the total prison population, were responsible for 19 per cent of the costs paid for ambulatory surgery episodes, 17 per cent of costs for non-emergency room episodes, 31 per cent of costs for ancillary care episodes, 20 per cent of costs for specialty care episodes, and 29 per cent of costs for inpatient care episodes.

With a predicted rise in the number of offenders who are older, sicker, and serving longer sentences, coupled with institutions' stretched resources, it is reasonable to argue that if we fail to address the needs of elders in prison, we will be facing an inevitable crisis (Prison Reform Trust, 2003). As more cohorts enter the latter stages of life, the age revolution will significantly affect all facets of the criminal justice system.

REVIEW QUESTIONS

1 How might we define ageism? Give three examples of ageist behaviour or language.

2 What are the effects of growing medical costs on the prison system and what strategies can be employed to improve healthcare in the prison system?

3 Is there much point in providing a rehabilitation programme for a 50-, 60-, 70-year-old offender serving a five to ten year sentence? Please give reasons for your answers.

Policy recommendations

To alleviate some of the pains of imprisonment, the prison authorities should be turning their attention to literature relating to residential homes (Atherton, 1989; Coleman, 1993; Hockey, 1989). There are many simple measures and this is not an exhaustive list, that could be taken which would allow elders control over their immediate physical environment, for example, installing doors and windows which they could open easily, and radiators which they could adjust themselves, replacing the harshness of the prison corridors with appropriate carpet tiles, use of electricity sockets which would allow all elders the opportunity to listen to the radio, and replacing the glare of the strip light with something less harsh. Such measures would at once make prison a less hostile and more accessible place. In addition, due to the impairment of sight, hearing, memory, and reflexes, and also the general slowing of movement and mental responsiveness, elders need to be cared for by staff members who are specifically trained in the needs of elders in prison.

Segregation versus integration

The American criminal justice system has been at the forefront of delivering special programmes for older offenders (Krajick, 1979; Aday and Rosefield, 1992). 'Special programmes', here constitute the distinctive treatment of the elderly prisoner housed in an age-segregated or in an age-sensitive environment. Segregation provides a concentration of specialized staff and resources for the elderly, thereby reducing costs (Florida Corrections Commission, 1999).

Previous research supports the notion that participation in a specific group increases self-respect and increases capability to resume community life once released. A choice of age segregation or age integration provides older prisoners with the opportunity for forming peer networks, while at the same time reducing vulnerability and violence they may encounter in the mainstream of prison life. Fattah and Sacco state:

> Concern for their safety and the need to protect them against victimisation, exploitation and harassment outweigh any stabilizing effect their integration may have. (1989: 101)

It is imperative that the prison system provides not only comprehensive opportunities whilst in prison and appropriate resettlement programmes, but also alternatives to the traditional custodial framework in which elders find themselves growing old. What is needed is the flexibility of having accommodation and provision reserved for elders, without creating a separate prison or excluding elders from the main prison environment. Aday succinctly states: 'Like the elderly in the free world, they are familiar with life in the general population and perceive that it has a mark of independence' (2003: 146). The criminal justice system in England and Wales, unlike the American criminal justice system, is still operating without a comprehensive plan to respond adequately to a pending crisis. The needs of elders in prisons are substantial, and can include physical, mental, and preventative health care; custody allocation to special housing, educational, vocational, or recreational programmes, physical exercise, and rehabilitation programming; dietary considerations; and long-term geriatric and nursing care.

An overriding theme within the integration versus segregation debate is that the way forward is to provide flexible accommodation, not through segregation, but through integration, within a framework of tolerance, understanding, and adaptability. The ageing prison population poses a true dilemma, and deserves recognition both among those interested in the wellbeing of those in later life and those executing prison policy. Age, in time, will be considered as one of the biggest issues that will continue to affect the criminal justice system and prison health care in the future. With the continued increase in criminal activity among the elderly population as a whole, learning more about crime and ageing, and about institutional adjustment, recidivism, and release, seems imperative.

Today, we have family courts, juvenile courts, and a large variety of special courts to handle specific problems (Wahidin and Cain, 2006). Along with the medley of juridical experts, from child psychiatrists to social workers, in the future will we see court reports and parole boards informed by gerontologists? Could we be accused of infantilizing the older offender if we were to advocate a court that deals specifically with the older offender? The literature suggests the following initiatives. This is not by any means an exhaustive list, but it does raise various policy questions:

- Should we change our sentencing structure to reflect probable years remaining in the offender's life?[4]
- Should older prisoners be segregated from the general prison population or should they be integrated into the mainstream of prison life?
- What are the alternatives to imprisonment for this cohort (dependent on risk, nature of offence, and time served)?

The limited knowledge concerning elders and crime and the absence of relevant policies and planning in this area, lead one to suggest that the criminal justice system should be turning its attention to:

- an examination of existing formal and informal practices regarding elders, as the first step in developing an explicit and integrated set of policies and programmes to address the special needs of this group;
- developing a comprehensive and gender-sensitive programme for elders, which fosters personal growth and accountability and value-based actions that lead to successful reintegration into society;
- preparing all personnel of the criminal justice system to understand and appropriately address elder-specific topics and issues.

In terms of being able to address the needs of elders in the criminal justice system, the Prison Policy Unit for England and Wales should be able to institute the following:

- adopting the age of 50 as the definition of an older offender;
- compiling comprehensive data on the over 50s in the criminal justice system from arrest to custody, through to re-entry to wider society;
- introduction of specific programmes geared towards the needs of the elderly;

Age	Percentage
16–18	>70
45–49	27
50–64	22
65 and older	7

Table 20.2 The correlation between age and reoffending

Source: Annual report of the CMA incarcerating elderly and aging inmates: medical and mental health implications: <http://www.doh.state.fl.us/cma/reports/agingreport.pdf> cited in Wahidin (2004).

- identification of the costs of long-term incarceration of infirm prisoners and the potential risks of early release or extended medical leave for this population;
- adoption of the National Service Framework for Older People;
- introduction of a national strategy that addresses the health and social care needs of older prisoners from imprisonment to release;
- addressing 'end of life' issues and providing palliative care. We should also open a debate to discuss the role of prison 'care' homes that can provide hospice care facilities.

Elders in prison are less likely to be a risk to society, and less likely to reoffend, and this allows for the possibility of designing future prisons/alternatives to prisons with the older person in mind (see Table 20.2). In a report produced by the Florida Corrections Commission (1999), it was found that elderly prisoners have the lowest recidivism rate of any group examined (see Table 20.2).

In England and Wales, the only figures that compare release by age are in relation to the Home Detention Curfew (HDC was introduced across England and Wales in 1999). It allows short-term prisoners to spend up to the last two months of their custodial sentence subject to an electronically-monitored curfew for at least nine hours per day). Figures suggest that the release rate on HDC tends to increase with age and it is more likely to be used for the 50-plus groups. The association here is that there is a higher risk of reconviction for younger offenders (Home Office, 2001c; Johnson and Alozie, 2001; Long, 1992).

Whilst further research is needed to ascertain how these figures break down for the female and male prison population, one could certainly imagine a future in which imprisonment of elder females and males is a rarity, reserved for those who are convicted of truly heinous crimes of a nature indicating a continuing risk to society. Male and female prisoners are not comparable; they have different criminal profiles, in terms of types of offences committed, previous offending history, and reconviction rates. It has been suggested that a gender-specific policy based on substantive equality will improve the plight of women in prison across the life-course (Carlen, 2002; NACRO, 1993, 1994). It can be argued that women in later life compared to older men who are in prison are a low-risk group in terms of repeat offending and nature of offence. Thus, it can be argued that a pilot group from this age cohort, who are assessed as low risk, could be used to explore alternatives to imprisonment. This could lead to savings being made on both a humanitarian and fiscal level.

A good example of diverting or reducing custodial sentences for elders is an early release scheme orchestrated by the Project for Older Prisoners in the US. Candidates must be over 50 years of age, have already served the average time for their offences, and have been assessed as low risk and thus unlikely to commit further crimes. Another unique requirement of this programme is that the victim, or the victim's family, must agree to early release. As a result of these strict standards, no prisoner released under the Project for Older Prisoners has ever been returned to prison for committing another crime (Turley, 1992). The programme helps them find employment and housing, and ensures that they receive their full entitlement to benefits. Such a scheme could beneficially be extended to England and Wales, to include a large number of older prisoners, and, if successful, could foster a willingness within the penal system to consider shorter or non-custodial sentences for this low-risk group.

REVIEW QUESTIONS

1 Explain why prison nursing homes have become a necessity.

2 Can we use old age as a bona fide legal defence as a mitigating factor in the court of law?

3 What are the advantages and disadvantages of holding elderly offenders?

CONCLUSION

Traditionally, questions concerning discrimination in criminal processing have focused on the effects of factors such as gender, ethnicity, disability, sexuality, socio-economic status, and age (for those between 10 and 18), but have neglected later-life issues. It has been argued throughout this chapter that crimes committed by elders are of sufficient importance to warrant increased research, better reporting of the age of offenders once released, and research into where they go after serving their sentence. Research is required to investigate their domestic responsibilities prior to imprisonment and the possibility of designing future prisons with elders in mind. Their experiences have remained marginalized in the debates around policy, and how the criminal justice system responds to these changes remains yet to be seen.

In light of this growing population, we have to begin to re-evaluate fundamental theories of punishment, deterrence, retribution, and rehabilitation for this particular group. One also has to consider the types of offence, risk, and need in relation to the above. This hidden minority will pose challenges to the jurisprudence and due process system. It is because of the failure to provide adequate facilities in prison that elders are unable to have a reasonable quality of life behind and beyond the walls.

Professionals in the field of criminology and gerontology can provide a greater awareness and under-standing of the problems facing persons who encounter the criminal justice system in later life. For it is only in the context of heightened understanding of ageing in general that the problems of offending, prison adjustment, and successful re-entry to society of the aged can be fully addressed. Policymakers will have to address the special needs of prisoners who will spend the remainder of their lives in prison as well as those who will be released in late old age.

For many years, both gerontologists and criminologists have concentrated their attention exclusively in their respective fields (Malinchak, 1980). In this chapter, I have tried to make the case for a combined criminological and gerontological approach to the area. Both disciplines bring a richness to understand-ing the experiences of older men and women who find themselves lost in the criminal justice system that treats adults the same, be they 25 or 74. It is only by having an integrated approach that we can begin to fully understand the complexity of ageing in the criminal justice system and, in turn, put the needs of elders firmly on the research and penal policy agenda.

If society has little place for elders in general, it has even less place for the elderly prisoner or ex-convict. Some have served an extremely long sentence in prison and find that they have no family or social networks on the outside and it is on this basis release can be denied. So what happens to the elderly offender who has nowhere to go? Prison does not stop at the prison gates (see Social Exclusion Unit, 2002; Halliday Report, 2001, HMIP 2002a). Women and men who leave prison bring with them the effects of a custodial sentence and, on release, they encounter suspicion, rejection, and hostility as they make this transition from prison to a society which discriminates against the elderly.

Figure 20.4 State Prison #4017.

Source: Sandy Campbell, Tennessean, 10 April 1994, © *The Tennessean*

QUESTIONS FOR DISCUSSION

1 What are the advantages and disadvantages of having separate prisons for older offenders?

2 What are the advantages and disadvantages of having an integrated elderly unit for older offenders?

3 What would be the advantage of setting up a similar early release scheme such as the Project for Older Prisoners in the UK?

4 Give three examples of the future challenges an older prison population will pose for the criminal justice system.

GUIDE TO FURTHER READING

Aday, R.H. (2003) *Aging Prisoners: Crisis in American Corrections*. Westport CT: Praeger.

This is an excellent introduction to the profile of older offenders in US prisons. It provides a comprehensive view of the needs of offenders in later life, and recommends policy initiatives to address this growing population.

Biggs, S. (1993) *Understanding Ageing—Images, Attitudes and Professional Practice*. Buckingham: Open University Press.

Simon Biggs examines theoretical approaches to understanding old age. His book provides new insights into how older age is imagined, defined, and experienced. By studying self-perception, communication, and power relations, and applying his conclusions to the helping professions, institutions, and community care, Biggs offers a new framework for constructive social gerontology and reflexive praxis.

Bond, J., Coleman, P., and Peace, S. (eds) (1993) *Ageing in Society—An Introduction to Social Gerontology*. London: Sage.

This book provides a comprehensive coverage of gerontological issues while capturing the complexity inherent in the processes of ageing. The book emphasizes diversity in the experience of ageing as a function of cultural, social, racial/ethnic, and individual variability.

Rothman, M.B., Dunlop, B.D., and Entzel, P. (2000) Elders, *Crime and the Criminal Justice System*. New York: Springer.

The Rothman *et al.* collection is the only book that provides an international perspective on ageing offenders. This edited book examines the relationship between old age and crime and the criminal justice system.

Wahidin, A. (2004) *Older Women in the Criminal Justice System: Running out of Time*. London: Jessica Kingsley.

This book introduces the reader to key debates and issues surrounding the needs of the older prison population in England and Wales. In particular, this book is based on a national study of older women and their experiences of imprisonment. The author uses her recent work on older men in prisons and the management of the older prison population in the US and the UK to highlight implications for older offenders.

Wahidin, A. and Cain M. (eds) (2006) *Age, Crime and Society*. Cullompton: Willan Press.

The starting point of this book is that 'age' is under-theorized and viewed as unproblematic in criminology. There is very little material on 'elder' or later life crime, little on the victimization of elders except in relation to the presumptively irrational nature of their fears. The book examines some of the issues and concerns in the field of elder abuse and neglect and argues the case that criminology as a discipline must address issues of ageing and its complex relationship with crime. This book is the first comprehensive text to tackle these issues.

WEB LINKS

http://www.gwu.edu/~ccommit/law.htm

This website details the largest volunteer prison assistance project for older offenders.

http://www.elderabuse.org.uk

Action on Elder Abuse is a site giving information about conferences and news as well having a special link page for students who are researching the topic of elder abuse.

http://www.howardleague.org

The Howard League is the oldest penal reform charity in the UK. The site gives access to publications, conferences, and information pertaining to the criminal justice system in the UK.

http://www.hmprisonservice.gov.uk/

An extremely useful site, this includes a range of link pages to government departments, statistical information and is the official site of HM Prison Service.

REFERENCES

Acoca, L. (1998) 'Defusing the Time Bomb: Understanding and Meeting the Growing Healthcare Needs of Incarcerated Women in America', *Crime and Delinquency*, 44, 49–70.

Aday, R.H. (1994) 'Aging in Prison: A Case Study of New Elderly Offender', *International Journal of Offender Therapy and Comparative Criminology*, Vol. 1, Part 38: 79–91.

Aday, R.H. (1994a) 'Golden Years Behind Bars: Special Programs and Facilities for Elderly Inmates', in *Federal Probation* 58: 2: 47–54.

Aday, R.H. (2003) *Aging Prisoners: Crisis in American Corrections*. Westport USA: Praeger.

Aday, R.H., and Rosefield, H.A. (1992), 'Providing for the Geriatric Inmate: Implications for Training', *Journal of Correctional Training*, 12, 14–16, 20 Winter.

Atherton, J.S. (1989) *Interpreting Residential Life—Values to Practice*. London, Tavistock: Routledge.

Biggs, S. (1993) *Understanding Ageing—Images, Attitudes and Professional Practice*. Buckingham: Open University Press.

Bond, J., Coleman, P., and Peace, S. (eds) (1993) *Ageing in Society—An Introduction to Social Gerontology*. London: Sage.

Bowling, B., and Phillips, C. (2002) *Racism, Crime and Justice*. London: Longman.

Bytheway, W.R., and Johnson. J. (1990) 'On Defining Ageism', *Critical Social Policy*, Vol. 27.

Carlen, P. (2002) *Women and Punishment: The Struggles for Justice*. Cullompton: Willan.

Cohen, S. (1973) *Folk Devils and Moral Panics*. Oxford: Martin Robertson.

Coleman, P. (1993) 'Adjustment in later life' in J. Bond, P. Coleman, and S. Peace (eds) (1993) *Ageing in Society—An Introduction to Social Gerontology*. London: Sage.

Crawford, A., Jones, T., Woodhouse, T., and Young, J. (1990) *Second Islington Crime Survey*. Middlesex: Middlesex Polytechnic.

Curtis, S. (1999) *Children Who Break the Law*. London: Waterside Press.

Devlin, A. (1998) *Invisible Women*. Winchester: Waterside Press.

Fattah, E.A. and Sacco V.F. (1989) *Crime and Victimisation of the Elderly*. New York: Springer-Verlag.

Fazel, S., Hope, T., O'Donnell, I., Piper, M., and Jacoby, R. (2001) 'Health of Elderly Male Prisoners: Worse than the General Population, Worse than Younger Prisoners', *Age and Ageing* 30: 403–407.

Featherstone, M. and Hepworth, M. (1993) 'Images of ageing', in J. Bond, P. Coleman, and S. Peace (eds) (1993) *Ageing in Society—An Introduction to Social Gerontology*. London: Sage.

Ferraro, K. (1995) *Fear of Crime: Interpreting Victimisation Risk*. New York: State University of New York Press.

Florida Corrections Commission (1999) Annual Report Section 4: Status Report on Elderly Offenders. Florida Corrections Department.

Flynn, E. (1992) 'The greying of America's prison population', in the Prison Journal, Vol. 72 Nos. 1 and 2, 77–98.

Gallagher, E. (1990) 'Emotional, Social, and Physical Health Characteristics of Older Men in Prison' *International Journal of Aging and Human Development*, Vol. 31 (4): 251–65.

Genders, E. and Players, E. (1995) *A Study of a Therapeutic Prison*. Oxford: Oxford University Press.

Gewerth, K. (1988) 'Elderly Offenders: A Review of Previous Research', in B. McCarthy, *Older Offenders*. New York: Praeger.

Government Actuary's Department <http://www.gad.gov.uk/Demography_Data/Population_projections_background.asp>.

Halliday, J. (2001) *Making Punishments Work: Report of a Review of the Sentencing Framework for England and Wales*. London: Home Office.

Ham, J. (1976) *The Forgotten Minority an Exploration of Long-Term Institutionalized Aged and Aging Prison Inmates*, PhD. Diss., University of Michigan.

Her Majesty's Chief Inspector of Prisons (HMCIP) (1997) *Women in Prison: A Thematic Review*. London: The Home Office.

Her Majesty's Chief Inspector of Prisons (HMCIP) (2001) Annual Report 1999–00, Inspector's Report via <http://inspectorates.homeoffice.gov.uk/hmiprisons/inspect_reports/hmp-yoi-inspections.html/550815/kingston011.pdf?view=Binary>.

Her Majesty's Chief Inspector of Prisons (HMCIP) (2001a) *Report on a Full Announced Inspection of HMP Kingston: 12–16 February 2001*. Inspection Reports via <http://inspectorates.homeoffice.gov.uk/hmiprisons/inspect_reports/hmp-yoi-inspections.html/550815/kingston011.pdf?view=Binary>.

Her Majesty's Inspectorate of Prisons for England and Wales (2002a) *Report of HM Inspectorates of Prison and Probation Conference: Through the Prison Gates*. London: The Stationary Office.

Her Majesty's Inspectorates of Prisons and Probation (HMIPP) (2001) *Through the Prison Gate: A Joint Thematic Review*. London: HMIP.

Herrnstein, R., and Murray, C. (1994) *The Bell Curve—Intelligence and Class Structure in American Life*. London: The Free Press.

Hirschi, T. (1969) *Causes of Delinquency*. Berkeley: University of California Press.

Hirschi, T. and Gottfredson, M. (1983) 'Age and the Explanation of Crime', *American Journal of Sociology*, 89: 552–84.

Hockey, J. (1989) 'Residential Care and the Maintenance of Social Identity: Negotiating the Transition to Institutional Life', in M. Jefferys *Growing Old in The Twentieth Century*. London: Routledge, 201–218.

Holloway, W. and Jefferson T. (2000) 'The Role of Anxiety in Fear and Crime', in T. Hope and R. Sparks (eds) *Crime, Risk and Society*. London: Routledge.

Home Office (1994) *Does the Criminal Justice System Treat Men and Women Differently?* Research Findings No. 10. London: HMSO.

Home Office (1999) *Statistics on Women and the Criminal Justice System—A Home Office Publication Under Section 95 of The Criminal Justice Act 1991*. London: HMSO.

Home Office (2001) *The Halliday Report: Making Punishment Work: review of Sentencing Framework for England and Wales*. London: HMSO.

Home Office (2001a) *The Government's Strategy for Women Offenders: Consultation Report*. London: HMSO.

Home Office (2001b) *Home Office Prison Population Brief*. London: HMSO.

Home Office (2001c) *Prison Statistics of England and Wales*. National Statistics Cm. 5743.

Home Office (2002) *Statistics on Women and the Criminal Justice System: A Home Office Publication Under Section 95 of the Criminal Justice Act*. London: HMSO.

James, M. (1992) 'Sentencing of Elderly Criminals', *American Criminal Law Review* Vol. 29: 1025–44.

Johnson, W. (1989) 'If only, the Experience of Elderly Ex-Convicts', *Journal of Gerontological Social Work*, 1989 Vol. 14: 191–208.

Johnson, W., and Alozie, B.O. (2001) 'The Effect of Age on the Criminal Processing: Is there an Advantage in Being "Older"'? *Journal of Gerontological Social Work*, 35, 47–62.

Jones, G.M. (1987) 'Elderly People and Domestic Crime', *British Journal of Criminology*, Vol. 27, 191–201.

Kerbs, J. (2000) 'The older prisoner: social, psychological and medical considerations' in M. Rothman, B. Dunlop, and P. Entzel (2000) *Elders, Crime and The Criminal Justice System—Myth, Perceptions, and Reality in the 21st Century*. New York: Springer Publishing Company.

Krajick, K. (1979) 'Growing Old in Prison'. *Corrections Magazine*, 5(1), 32–46.

Krug, E.G. (2002) *World Report on Violence and Health*. Geneva: World Health Organisation.

Lombroso, C. and Ferrero, G. (1895) *Female Offender*. London: Appleton.

Long, L.M. (1992) 'A Study of Arrests of Older Offenders: Trends and Patterns' *Journal of Crime and Justice*, 15, 157–75.

Malinchak, A.A. (1980) *Crime and Gerontology*. Englewood Cliffs, NJ: Prentice Hall.

Manthorpe, J. (1983) 'With Intent to Steal in the New Age', *Journal of Offending Counselling Services and Rehabilitation*, 13 (Spring) 25–28.

Marquart, J.W., Merianos, D.E., Herbert, J.L., and Carroll, L. (1997) 'Health Condition and Prisoners. A Review of Research and Emerging Areas of Inquiry' *Prison Journal* 77, 184–208.

Marquart, J.W., Merianos, D.E., and Doucet, G. (2000) 'The Health Related Concerns of Older Prisoners: Implications for Policy', *Aging and Society* 20, 79–96.

Mawby, R. and Gill, M. (1987) *Crime Victims: Needs, Services and the Voluntary Sector*. London: Tavistock.

Mawby R. and Walklate S. (1994) *Critical Victimology: The Victim in International Perspectives*. London: Sage.

Mcdonald, D.C. (1995) *Managing Prison Health Care and Costs*. Washington, DC: National Institute of Justice, US Department of Justice.

Ministry of Justice (2007) *Sentencing Statistics 2006, England and Wales*. London: RDS.

Ministry of Justice (2008) *Statistics on Women in the Criminal Justice System 2005/6*. London: MOJ.

NACRO (1992a) *Women and Criminal Justice: Some Facts and Figures*. NACRO Briefing No. 91 (August). London: NACRO.

NACRO (1993) *Women Leaving Prison*. London: NACRO.

NACRO (1994) *Prison Overcrowding—Recent Developments*. NACRO Briefing No. 28 (July). London: NACRO.

Neeley, L.C., Addison, L., and Moreland-Craig, D. (1997) 'Addressing the Needs of Elderly Offenders', *Corrections Today*, August, 59, 120–24.

Newman, E. (1984) 'Elderly Offenders and American Crime' in E. Newman, D. Newman, M. Gewirtz (eds) *Elderly Criminals*. Oelgeschlager, Massachusetts: Gunn and Hain Publishers Inc., Cambridge.

Newman, E., Newman, D., and Gewirtz, M. (eds) (1984) *Elderly Criminals*. Oelgeschlager, Massachusetts: Gunn and Hain Publishers Inc. Cambridge.

Pain, H.R. (1995) 'Elderly Women and Fear of Violent Crime: the least likely Victims', *British Journal of Criminology*, 38 (4), 584–98.

Pearson, G. (1983) *Hooligan: A History of Respectable Fears*. London: MacMillan.

Pertierra, J.C. (1995) 'Do the Crime: Do the Time: Should Elderly Criminals Receive Proportionate Sentences?' *Nova Law Review*, Winter: 1–25.

Penal Affairs Consortium (1996) *The Imprisonment of Women: Some Facts and Figures*. London: (March).

Phillips, J. (1996) 'Crime and Older Offenders', *Practice*, Vol. 8, 1, 43–55.

Phillipson, C. (1982) *Capitalism and the Construction of Old Age*. London: Macmillan.

Phillipson, C., and Walker, A. (eds) (1986) *Ageing and Social Policy, A Critical Assessment*. Aldershot: Gower.

Pitts, J. (1988) *The Politics of Juvenile Crime*. London: Sage.

Pollak, O. (1941) 'The Criminality of Old Age', *Journal of Criminal Psychotherapy*, 3, 213–35.

Presdee, M. (1994) 'Young people, culture and the construction of crime: doing wrong versus doing crime' in G. Barak (ed) *Varieties of Criminology*. Westport CT: Praeger.

Prison Reform Trust (2003) *Growing Old in Prison: A Scoping Study on Older Prisoners*. London.

Prison Reform Trust (2008) *Bromley Briefings Prison Factfile*. December. London

Rothman, M.B., Dunlop, B.D., and Entzel, P. (2000) *Elders, Crime and the Criminal Justice System*. New York: Springer.

Rubernstein, D. (1984) 'The Elderly in Prison: A Review of the Literature' in E. Newman, D. Newman, M. Gewirtz *et al.* (1984) *Elderly Criminals*. Oelgeschlager, Cambridge, Massachusetts: Gunn and Hain Publishers Inc., 153–68.

Sim, J. (2000) 'One Thousand Days of Degradation: New Labour and Old Compromises at the Turn of the Century', *Social Justice* Vol. 27 (2), 168–92.

Social Exclusion Unit (2002) *Reducing Re-offending by Ex-prisoners*. London: Office of Department of Prime Ministers.

Sparks, R. (1992) 'Television and the Drama of Crime—Moral Tales and the Place of Crime' *Public Life*. Buckingham: Open University.

Steffensmeier, D., and Moti, M. (2000) 'Older Women and Men in the Arms of Criminal Law; Offending Patterns' *The Journal of Gerontology*, 5141–51.

Turley, J. (1990) 'Long-Term Confinement and the Aging Inmate Population', US Department of Justice, Federal Bureau of Prisons, Form on Issues in Corrections, 'Alternative Solutions'. Washington DC: US Government. Printing Office.

Turley, J. (1992) 'A Solution to Prison Overcrowding' USA Today Magazine, November 12, 80–81.

Turner, B. (1988) 'Ageing, Status Politics and Sociological Theory' *British Journal of Sociology*, Vol. 40, No. 4: 589–605.

Wahidin, A. (2000) 'Life Behind the Shadows: Women's Experiences of Prison in Later Life' R. Horn and S. Warner (eds) *Issues in Forensic Psychology, Positive Directions for Women in Secure Environments*. London: The British Psychological Society.

Wahidin, A. (2004) *Older Women in the Criminal Justice System: Running Out of Time*. London: Jessica Kingsley.

Wahidin, A. (2005a) 'Managing the Needs of Older Male and Female Offenders, "Re-Awakening the Criminological Imagination"', British Society of Criminology Conference, Leeds University. Unpublished paper.

Wahidin, A. (2006) 'No problems: old and quiet: imprisonment in later life' in A. Wahidin and M. Cain (eds), *Ageing, Crime and Society*. Cullompton: Willan Press.

Wahidin, A. and Powell, L.J. (2005) 'Age, victimisation and crime' in P. Davis, P. Francis, and C. Greer (ed), *Crime, Violence and Victimisation*. London: Sage.

Wahidin, A. and Cain, M. (eds) (2006), *Age, Crime and Society*. Cullompton: Willan Press.

White, P., Woodbridge, J., and Flack, K. (1999) *Projections of Long Term Trends in the Prison Population to 2006:* Home Office Statistical Bulletin Issue1/99: 20th January 1999.

Williams, B. (1998) *Victims and the Criminal Justice System*. London: Longman.

Zedner, L. (1997) 'Victims' in M. Maguire, R. Morgan and R. Reiner (eds.) *The Oxford Handbook of Criminology*. Oxford: Oxford University Press.

NOTES

1. The Housing Benefit, Council Tax Benefit and Income Support (Amendments) Regulations 1995 ended the previous practice of using housing benefit to meet rent payments of convicted prisoners serving up to a year in custody. Assistance is now confined to prisoners serving sentences of up to six months who receive conditional discharge subject to good behaviour after 13 weeks in custody. These changes have increased homelessness among released prisoners by causing a substantial number of prisoners to lose their homes during periods in prison, from between 13 and 52 weeks. A report, *Housing Benefit and Prisoners* (Penal Affairs Consortium, November 1996) estimates that 5,000 additional prisoners could be released as homeless each year as a result of this change (Devlin, 1998: 42).

2. Grendon prison was opened in 1962, as a unique experiment in the psychological treatment of offenders whose mental disorder did not qualify them for transfer to a hospital under s. 72 of the Mental Health Act 1959. Grendon is a category B training prison and may be described as a multifunctional establishment, accommodating three adult therapy wings which operate as therapeutic communities, an assessment and induction unit, and a treatment wing designed specifically for sex offenders (see Genders and Players, 1995).

3. HMP Latchmere House is a resettlement prison, which holds male adult prisoners serving a sentence of four years or more, including up to 20 life-sentenced prisoners, and assists them to prepare for release.

4. Cristina Pertierra (1995) presents a series of cases brought to the American Court of Appeal in which elderly offenders, under the 18th Amendment, have claimed that, given their ages and life expectancies, the sentences imposed amount to life imprisonment, and are thus disapropriate to the crimes committed. For further details, see *United States* v *Angiulo*, 85 2F. Supp. 54, 60 (D. Mass. 1994); see also *Alspaugh v State*, 133, So. 2d 597, 588 (Fla. 2d dist. Ct App.1961).

Part Four
RESPONSES TO CRIME

21

The politics of law and order

Chris Hale and Marian FitzGerald

INTRODUCTION

One function of the modern State is to guarantee the safety and wellbeing of its citizens. Governments are expected to protect them from both external threats (such as invasion and, more recently, acts of terrorism) and internal threats, including the risk of becoming a victim of crime. More specifically, they are expected to minimize the risk of crime and to deal effectively with those who commit it through the operation of the Criminal Justice System (CJS), the chief agencies of which are: the Police, the Crown (soon to be Public) Prosecution Service, the Courts, and the Probation and Prison services (see Uglow, Chapter 22 below). How effectively the system serves the Government in meeting these two aims, though—and whether citizens are confident that it is doing so—has increasingly been the subject of political debate.

BACKGROUND

In the UK it has now become commonplace to hear representatives of the main political parties making public statements which are designed to make them appear tough on crime. Fear of the political consequences of seeming to be soft on criminals has resulted in record numbers in jail. The Government's claims about the actual level of crime are hotly contested by the opposition and are greeted with scepticism by the electorate. In turn, voters' concerns about crime may have been heightened by the fact that politicians themselves have chosen to make it a high-profile party political issue; but they also reflect the fact that over the long term crime (including serious violent crime) *has* steadily been rising and, for all their rhetoric, politicians seem unable to stem this tide. In addition changes in the national and international context add to the underlying insecurities which fuel what is often referred to as 'fear of crime'.

Yet there was a time following the end of World War II when crime and criminal policy had a relatively low profile and were dealt with on the basis of consensus.

In the space of this chapter we can only outline the main developments which have increasingly politicized the debate about crime and criminal justice policy in Britain; but it is important to start with a reminder that the acts which are treated as 'crimes' are always in some sense political. They may change over time, across cultures and political ideologies (see Morrison, Chapter 1 above); and the criminal justice system is weighted towards some rather than others for reasons which are also political to some extent. Thus, Parliament passes the laws which define which acts are criminal; and politicians decide what resources will be allocated to the CJS. Since these resources are finite, choices have to be made about which crimes to prioritize; and these priorities tend to reflect the interrelated preoccupations of the public, the media, and politicians. So crimes committed by businesses receive less attention than the types of crimes committed by relatively disadvantaged individuals—even though the former may inflict more damage on society (see Tombs, Chapter 13 above). Additionally, governments may influence priorities more directly by allocating funding to tackling particular types of crime or by setting targets in relation to some offences but not others (see Jones, Chapter 25). They can also determine how particular types of crime should be dealt with and they can even try to influence public *perceptions* of crime by determining how it gets measured.

Arguably this direct political influence has grown significantly in recent years to the point of calling into question the long-standing belief that the British[1] CJS is relatively free from political interference. This belief reflects the fact that key decision makers *within* the system are not elected by voters and they are expected to remain above party politics in their public pronouncements. It also rests on a tradition which, until recently, held that, while Parliament made the laws, it should not interfere in how they were applied. Judges and magistrates in particular might be encouraged, exhorted, informed, and reasoned with, but they could never be instructed by politicians. As a former Home Secretary put it:

> It is not for the Home Secretary, Government or the House to lay down to the courts how many people they send to prison. It is our job to provide places for them. (*Hansard*, 5 November 1987, column 1055)

Even before this belief began to erode, though, the political salience of crime had begun to increase in the context of broader debates over the last 30 years or so. Hall *et al.* (1978) suggest that crime is often an indicator, a metaphor for more general feelings of social anxiety and apprehension, a theme pursued historically by Pearson, who sees the respectable preoccupation with disorder as serving:

> ...an ideological function within British public life, as a convenient metaphor for wider social tensions which attend the advance of democratization. (Pearson 1983: 230)

That is, political debates about crime may be seen as a way of raising broader questions about what type of society we are—or wish to be.

REVIEW QUESTIONS

1 In what senses is crime political?
2 How can crime serve as a metaphor?

The politics of law and order in the UK since 1945

Trends in crime

No discussion of the politics of law and order can ignore the large growth in recorded crime since 1945.

Figure 21.1 shows how crime in England and Wales changed from an exceptional experience to one that has become relatively normal. From a low of around 430,000 in 1954, recorded offences increased nearly 13-fold to peak at over 5.5 million in 1992, with a further new peak of over 6 million in 2003–04. Criminal victimization moved from the margins to '...become a routine part of modern consciousness a standing possibility that is constantly to be "kept in mind"' Garland (2001). Some idea of the magnitude of the

Figure 21.1 Recorded crime in England and Wales 1945 to 2006/07 (changes to counting rules indicated by *)

Source: Home Office Criminal Statistics

shift may be taken from the fact that the *increases* in recorded crime from both 1989 to 1990 and 1990 to 1991 were larger than the total level of crime in any year until 1959.

This overall rising trend has not been uniform; rather, building on Hale (1999) and McClintock and Avison (1968) it is possible to identify four distinct periods:

(a) Crime period 1: 1945–54—recorded crime fluctuates around low level;

(b) Crime period 2: 1955–72—recorded crime begins to grow steadily;

(c) Crime period 3: 1973–92—recorded crime growth accelerates;

(d) Crime period 4: 1992 to the present: levels of recorded crime become more volatile—falling, then appearing to rise, then to fall again.[2]

The overall upward trend, followed by a downturn in the early 1990s, is not peculiar to Britain. It has been observed in other similar economies over the same period; and the main factors at work have been identified as a combination of long-run economic and social trends with short-term economic fluctuations affecting the balance between violent crime and property crime within this (Field, 1990). The main long-term changes have been summarized by Loader and Sparks (2007) as structural changes at the level of economic, social, and cultural relations.[3] Some of these will be discussed below while others, particularly economic changes, are considered in more detail in Chapter 16. The four that Loader and Sparks list may be summarized as:

(a) the shift from economies predominantly based on manufacturing industry to ones based on the service sector and the rise of consumerism;

(b) changes in family structures and living arrangements (including the suburbaniza-
tion of cities);

(c) the proliferation of electronic mass media; and

(d) a 'democratization' of everyday life ', including altered relations between men and
women, parents and children, and, more generally, a marked decline in unthink-
ing adherence towards authority.

Trends in the politics of crime

Faced with these trends in recorded crime—and in view of the public's expectations
that governments have a responsibility to protect them from crime—political interest
in crime control might have been expected to increase over the same period. However,
many other factors have influenced the form this interest has taken, including developments within the political parties themselves, as well as wider, unexpected developments which challenged the governments of the day and were therefore often politically
exploited by the opposition.[4] It is important to remember here that of the 17 elections
since 1945 (see Table 21.1), the Conservative Party won a clear majority in eight and the
Labour Party in eight, the 17th being February 1974 when Labour was only able to form
a minority Government with Liberal Party support.

Table 21.1 Post-1945 general elections in the United Kingdom

Date	Result
1945	Labour victory
1950	Labour victory
1951	Conservative victory
1955	Conservative victory
1959	Conservative victory
1964	Labour victory
1966	Labour victory
1970	Conservative victory
1974 (Feb)	Labour Government but only with Liberal support
1974 (Oct)	Labour victory
1979	Conservative victory
1983	Conservative victory
1987	Conservative victory
1992	Conservative victory
1997	Labour victory
2001	Labour victory
2005	Labour victory

Until the 1997 election, the Conservative Party had dominated the post-war political scene with two lengthy periods in power—the first, for 13 years, from 1951 until 1964 and the second, for 18 years from 1979 until 1997. While both main parties have kept the same names, there have been significant changes in their political ideologies in this period,[5] and changes in the terms of the political debates around law and order reflect these party political developments at least as much as any objective change in the level and nature of crime; so they do *not* correspond to the four distinct crime periods identified above. According to Downes and Morgan (2002) they fall into three phases:

(a) Politics phase 1: 1945–70—political census around support for penal-welfare approach.

(b) Politics phase 2: 1970–92—political division and sharp disagreements between the main political parties.

(c) Politics phase 3: 1992–present—a new consensus based around 'populist punitiveness'.

Each is now examined in turn.

REVIEW QUESTIONS

1 Describe the major trends in recorded crime in England and Wales since 1945.

2 What are the main explanations for these trends?

3 What were the key political phases in the UK since the end of World War II?

Politics phase 1: 1945–70

Prior to the UK general elections of 1974 and 1979, the approach to crime and offending by the Conservative and the Labour Parties was essentially bi-partisan. They shared an understanding of the problems and a belief that solutions lay in policies combining elements of both punishment and welfare. The administration of this 'penal-welfare state' (Garland, 2001) was largely to be left to the institutions of the CJS (see above) by contrast with political divisions over other policy areas such as economic management, foreign affairs, health, or education.

Loader and Sparks (2007: 79) see the penal-welfare state as being organized around three 'mutually reinforcing axioms':

- 'crime' as conceptually unproblematic and geographically and socially delimited;

- a causal theory that understood crime as a presenting symptom of more deep-seated social problems;

- an attachment to the idea of crime control policy as the province of 'experts' and expert knowledge.

The first of these axioms (a shared belief in what crime was, where it happened, and who did it) meant that, prior to the 1970s, the emphasis was on identifying and reforming the individual 'delinquent'. This 'rehabilitative ideal' was part of a broader modernist agenda which aspired to apply scientific knowledge to reforming individuals and improving social conditions. The second was reflected in policies which aimed at improving housing and education, alongside increasing social welfare and family support, coupled with '… "correctionalist" treatment programmes oriented at returning individual offenders to the fold of social democratic citizenship' (Loader and Sparks, 2007: 84). The third meant that the direction of crime policy could (and properly *should*) be left to a small group of civil servants and senior CJS practitioners free of influence from politicians or public opinion.

The period from 1930 to 1948 had seen deepening economic crisis and political unrest, with crime growing at around 7 per cent per annum. However, the major economic crises of the 1920s and 1930s had led to greater economic intervention by governments, a trend reinforced by experiences of the economic planning during the war. Meanwhile the Beveridge Report (Beveridge, 1942) had laid the foundations for the wide-ranging system of social security that became the Welfare State whereby government would actively promote social progress by improving health, housing, and diet. The interventionist 'welfarist' approach adopted by the Labour Government of 1945 to 1951 continued under the Conservative Governments of the 1950s and became part of the consensus of British political life. As McClintock and Avison (1968: 19) note, the expectation at this time was that crime had stabilized and indeed would begin to fall. At this time unemployment was low but the rationing introduced in the war continued, so levels of consumption grew only slowly; and crime levels per head were actually about 18 per cent lower by 1954 than in 1948.

The expectation that crime would continue to fall, though, was dashed when the level started to rise again from 1955, with the figures showing a steady, and seemingly inexorable, growth of around 10 per cent each year. This coincided with the beginning of the consumer boom after years of post-war austerity, at a time when, according to then Prime Minister, Harold Macmillan, Britons had '…never had it so good'. Yet the UK's global economic position was already in relative decline and, as the post-war expansion began to falter in the early 1960s, the Labour Government effectively abandoned its commitment to full employment, pursuing policies which in 1967 led to a major rise in industrial unrest. The 1960s was also a time when the post-war baby boom generation reached their teenage years; and political upheavals around the globe, particularly in 1968, further fuelled moral panics around the behaviour of increasingly rebellious youth.

Debates over crime and punishment during the years from 1945 to 1970, however, reflected what historians see as a period of relative consensus between the Conservative and Labour Parties. Downes and Morgan (1994, 1997, 2002, 2007) note that when the Conservatives promised to review the Criminal Justice System in 1959 this was the first time any of the party manifestos for general elections had referred to these issues at all. By 1964, adopting themes still familiar today, they were promising to strengthen the police, to introduce tougher measures against hooliganism, and to counter delinquency by supporting family ties. Yet despite the rise in crime under Conservative Governments since

1951, the Labour Party remained silent on the topic. This changed in 1966 when, for the first time, after two years in power, Labour devoted as much space as the Conservatives to crime issues. As yet, though '...no party manifesto suggested that the level or form of crime was itself attributable to the politics of the party in government' (Downes and Morgan, 1994: 187).

REVIEW QUESTIONS

1 What were the main aims of the Welfare State?

2 What happened to the relative global economic position of the UK between 1945 and 1970?

3 What were the main points of the political debates around law and order?

Politics phase 2: 1970–92

In the period 1970 to 1992, not only were increases in the numbers of recorded offences very large by historical standards, they coincided with recurrent outbreaks of mass disorder in a variety of different contexts. Against this backdrop, the problem of rising crime could no longer be ignored: crime had now become symbolic of wider and more deepseated problems—a symptom of the threat to the rule of law and order in society. The temperature of the political debate rose accordingly, and by the 1970 election campaign the post-war consensus had broken down. All parties were devoting more words than ever before to the issue; and, for the first time, the Conservatives made links between the worsening crime problem and the Labour Government. They also began to identify crime with mass forms of unrest, including political protest and industrial disputes and picketing, even though, at this time, these were rarely associated with violence. The law needed modernizing the Conservatives claimed '...for dealing with public order—peculiar to the age of demonstration and disruption' (Conservative Party, 1970). Labour's response was to deplore the 'cynical...attempts of our opponents to exploit for Party political ends the issue of crime and law enforcement'. They reassured voters that the streets of British cities were as safe as any in the world; but this did not prevent them losing the election.

The Conservatives won in 1970 promising radical economic reform and a commitment to allowing market forces to operate, with wages allowed to find their own level and traditional manufacturing industries struggling to survive in the global economy without government help. However trade union resistance forced the Government to discard its non-interventionist policies and turn once more to income policies and Keynesian demand management.

Crime rates were fairly constant between 1970 and 1973, and, in the first of the two general elections of 1974 (see Table 21.1) the Conservatives claimed they had been successful as a government in fighting crime. They attributed this to the growth in police numbers, tougher penalties for offences involving firearms, and the ability of the courts to impose compensation orders (Downes and Morgan, 1994: 91). The Labour Party returned to its strategy of silence on both the Conservative's record and their own plans. By the second

1974 election, with Labour now precariously in power, the Conservatives returned to the attack, explicitly criticizing Labour's record on crime and, for the first time, questioning their integrity on the issue, accusing Labour of failing to support the 'rule of law' because some Labour MPs and shadow cabinet members had supported the use of mass picketing in the 1973 miners' strike.

Labour nonetheless secured the majority it needed, but by 1975 was itself arguing that high unemployment was part of the price to be paid for combating high inflation. The Government's efforts to restrict money supply and cut public expenditure intensified after a series of currency crises and visits from the International Monetary Fund (IMF) in 1976, and by the late 1970s there were widening divisions between those in relatively secure full-time work and those with unskilled, often part-time, but certainly insecure, jobs. The Government presented its abandonment of welfarism and adoption of monetarism as externally imposed by the IMF because of circumstances which required everyone to make sacrifices; but its imposition of blanket pay rises for public sector workers, including the lowest paid, resulted in widespread strikes in the winter of 1978–79. These badly affected the public at large since the strikers tended to be involved in menial but essential jobs such as refuse disposal and digging graves. So in the run up to the 1979 general election, the Conservative Party embraced monetary discipline and reductions in government borrowing and spending, but they won it using law and order as a central unifying theme in the wake of 'The Winter of Discontent'. Their approach was to align industrial militancy and public protest with a general decline in morality and breakdown of respect for authority which, in turn, they blamed on the dependency culture fostered by the Welfare State. The crimes of individuals were now seen as a symptom of the moral and economic decline of the nation:

> In their muddled but different ways, the vandals on the picket lines and the muggers in our streets have got the same confused message—'we want our demands met or else' and 'get out of the way give us your handbag'. (Margaret Thatcher, 1979)

For the new Conservative Government of 1979, law and order meant new forms of social discipline, based on a form of morality which emphasized individual effort and endeavour as essential to self-discipline. This informed their approach to crime which insisted that social conditions were irrelevant to criminality: it was the individual who was basically bad. Punishment and retribution were central to their policy, reinforced by the view that with offenders 'nothing works'[6]—that is, that programmes aimed at rehabilitation and reform of individuals were having no impact (see Worrall, Chapter 26 below). The focus therefore shifted to crime *prevention*, with a strong emphasis on the need for individual citizens to take responsibility through greater vigilance and awareness coupled with an increase in police numbers.

Between 1979 and 1988 the number of police officers increased by 11 per cent, there was a 12 per cent increase in civilians employed, and a 64 per cent increase in real terms in total police expenditure. At the same time the Conservative Government implemented a major prison-building programme, while the numbers imprisoned increased from an average 42,220 in 1979 to 47,200 in 1986–87, a figure 13 per cent above the capacity of the prison system (Brake and Hale, 1992). This punitive approach linked to enhanced investment was reflected in their success in marshalling the police and the courts to break organized working-class resistance to their economic and social programme (for example, the 1984 miners' strike). Yet the Conservatives' claims with regard to law and order more generally were challenged in other, unexpected ways. Within a year of them taking office they faced the first major, sustained outbreak of public disorder on the British mainland since before the Second World War. The civil disturbances of 1980 were triggered by conflict between black people and the police, and were followed on a larger scale by similar outbreaks in 1981. With the crime rate rising at the same time, the Government tried initially to find ways to prove to the electorate that it could control these developments. However, it gradually became apparent that strong policing and tough sentencing were having little impact on crime levels.[7] Rather than taking the tough response to the disturbances of the early 1980s which might have been expected, the Government pursued a strategy based on urban regeneration and police reform (which culminated in the 1984 Police and Criminal Evidence Act).

By the 1983 election, Conservative rhetoric on law and order was again changing with a further perceptible shift to the 'responsibilization' of the individual. It was no longer just a matter of extolling the virtues of strong police powers and tougher sentencing to curb crime. Now:

> Dealing with crimes, civil disobedience, violent demonstrations and pornography are not matters for the police alone. It is teachers and parents—and television producers too—who influence the moral standards of the next generation. There must be close co-operation and understanding between the police and the community they serve. (Conservative Party, 1983)

Between 1983 and 1987 recorded offences increased by just under 20 per cent, and 1985 saw a further recurrence of inner city rioting similar to that of the early 1980s, this time involving loss of life. From being an electoral asset, law and order by now risked becoming the Conservatives' biggest failure. Pragmatically the Government's rhetoric now shifted again in ways calculated further to distance it from any responsibility for these developments. The risk the Conservatives had taken in their response to the earlier disturbances had not paid off and their current Home Secretary signalled a change in mood when he claimed these riots were 'not a cry for help but a cry for loot', while several of his parliamentary colleagues were quick to make associations with the race equality policies pursued by the Looney Left Labour authorities in the areas where they occurred (FitzGerald, 1987, 1989). The role of the police in ensuring order was itself also now played down in favour of increasing stress on the importance of 'community' and the 'active citizen'.

Importantly, the Conservatives were not alone in this. Thanks in part to the work of the New Left Realists (see, for example, Lea and Young, 1984) the Labour Party had itself begun to recognize that there were votes to be lost if it continued to neglect the impact of crime on its traditional supporters. Crime prevention was endorsed by all the major parties in the 1987 election. But while for the Labour Party the approach was to be a collective one through the local authorities, the Conservatives placed responsibility on individual householders and voluntary local schemes.

While the 'active citizen' now became the cornerstone of the Conservative approach to prevention (through their involvement, for example, in Neighbourhood Watch schemes), the numbers in prison were becoming an increasing cause for concern to a cost-conscious government. This led to a schizophrenic approach in the 1980s, with Home Office Ministers arguing consistently that prison was only to be used for violent and serious offenders, but also (see earlier) that the Government's role was to provide prison places without interfering with the judicial process. Despite various measures to reduce the numbers imprisoned, the Conservatives sustained their punitive rhetoric in public, and expenditure on the prison service rose considerably—by 36 per cent in real terms between 1979 and 1989. This led to the growing awareness that prison was an expensive way of making bad people worse[8] and to a further attempt to persuade courts and the public that non-custodial community sentences (see Worrall, Chapter 26) were not soft options but were tough measures, if properly applied. This culminated in the 1991 Criminal Justice Act (CJA) which had at its core the principle that the sentencing decision should focus on the seriousness of the offence and that normally the offender's previous convictions were not to be taken into account. It embodied the 'just deserts' theory of punishment by outlining a clear hierarchy of sentences of increasing severity from discharge through fines to community-based sentences to custodial sentences which should be related to the seriousness of the offence, such that custody should be imposed only for the most serious offences, or in the case of violent or sexual offences if it was necessary to protect the public.

By the end of the decade, further disturbances—this time in all-white, rural areas—had taken the Government by surprise (see FitzGerald, Chapter 18). They were followed in 1990 by rioting associated with its introduction of the poll tax and again in 1991 by riots by young whites on outer estates in several British cities triggering media-fuelled anxiety over joyriding and ram raiders. Meanwhile, ongoing concerns over football hooliganism which had first become an issue in the 1960s risked seriously tarnishing Britain's image abroad, particularly after it resulted in fatalities at the European Cup Final in Belgium in 1985. Coinciding with the severe economic recession of 1989–92, recorded crime in 1992 was 50 per cent more than in 1988. Yet despite this, Labour was unable to seize power in the 1992 general election.

REVIEW QUESTIONS

1 What links did the Conservative Government elected in 1979 make between crime and industrial unrest?

2 What did the Conservative Government of the 1980s believe had been the effect of the Welfare State?

3 What happened to crime between 1979 and 1992?

4 What factors caused Conservative policies on crime to change?

5 What changes occurred in Conservative policies on law and order?

Politics phase 3: post-1992

The third, most recent phase in the politics of law and order is distinguished primarily by the development of competition between the two main political parties over which could persuade the electorate it was tougher on crime. We have seen how in the previous crime phase miscellaneous, recurrent outbreaks of violent group disorder fuelled the social anxiety and apprehension referred to by Hall, above, such that the issue of crime was now inexorably framed within more fundamental concerns about law and order. The third phase effectively divides into two. It opens with (New) Labour in opposition actively tapping in to this social anxiety and apprehension by widening the scope of criminal justice policy to include minor, everyday 'incivilities' which were already known to be closely associated with what had come to be known as 'fear of crime'. After the watershed of the 1997 general election with New Labour now in government, it too faced outbreaks of disorder from unexpected quarters; but these did not have the same political salience as they had done for the new Conservative Government of 1979. Rather, the agenda the New Labour Government had created around law and order was further widened by the need to accommodate the threat of terrorist attacks. By contrast with its predecessors' strategies for distancing themselves from events which they could not control, one of the hallmarks of the New Labour administration was its efforts to micro-manage the running of public services and their implementation of government policies while subjecting them to major reform in the name of 'modernization'. So politics phase 3 may come to be associated with a greater degree of political intervention in the criminal justice system than ever before—and one which seriously challenged its long-held tradition of independence.

1992–1997

If the recession of 1988–92 dented the Conservatives' reputation for sound economic management, a further blow fell in September 1992 when currency speculation forced Sterling out of the European Exchange Rate Mechanism (ERM).[9] As Faulkner (2001: 122) notes, a fundamental and dramatic change in the Conservative Government's political style occurred during 1993. He traces this in part to rising crime figures and difficulties within the Conservative Party following the ERM withdrawal and the accession to the Maastricht Treaty.

> These events created an urgent need for the Government to re-unite the Party around a suitable populist issue, and crime and law and order were a natural choice. (Faulkner, 2001: 122)

Faulkner also points out that the change was not challenged by the other parties since none could easily oppose such a populist based campaign once it had gathered impetus. On 12 February 1993, the toddler James Bulger was abducted and brutally murdered by two ten-year-old boys and the case had a major impact on public perceptions of youth crime:

> The Bulger case has become a powerful symbol of our collective helplessness, of a malaise that goes beyond a single case, beyond even crime figures. (*Independent on Sunday*, 28 February 1993)

By now, the 1991 CJA (see above) had come into operation following a lengthy training programme to ensure its smooth introduction, and its diversionary impact was already becoming clear. The monthly prison population figures peaked at 47,605 in April 2002 and had thereafter showed a continuous downward drift to 40,722 by the end of December. The *Independent on Sunday* (IOS) referred to this reduction as the '…largest and swiftest decline in living memory'. However, their new populist strategy saw the Conservatives rapidly and dramatically abandoning the liberal thinking behind the Act. Recognizing that they had been lucky to win the 1992 election so they might be living on borrowed time, they embarked on a strategy which seemed to be designed to damage their Labour opponents by flushing them out as weak on law and order issues. In a speech to the 1993 Conservative Party Conference, its new Home Secretary Michael Howard jettisoned the view that prison was an expensive way of making bad people worse; and his bald assertion that 'prison works' was followed (unsurprisingly) by a further increase in the prison population. More broadly the Conservatives made a high profile return to the punitive authoritarian approach of the 1970s with a call to go 'back to basics'.[10]

Meanwhile, Labour had begun a major overhaul of its own criminal justice policies, partly in order to challenge the belief that the Conservatives were *the* party of law and order. Although between 1993 and 1996 the party was to produce several policy papers that linked crime with social problems; publicly it focused on criticizing the operation of the criminal justice system under the Conservatives (Downes and Morgan, 1997).

That is, far from falling into the Conservative's trap to flush them out as soft on crime, the Labour front bench's response was to refuse to allow any clear blue water to open between the two parties. The more punitive the Government became, the more determinedly the Opposition seemed to swim after them. Labour's attack on the 1991 CJA and Conservative policy generally was in terms of criticisms of the Act's 'just deserts' approach and the inadequacies of the CJS under the Conservatives, as exemplified by falling conviction rates and delays in dealing with juvenile offenders. They made no attempt to imply that the rise in crime was related to the economic and social consequences of the Conservative policies, despite the apparent connection made between the two by Tony Blair when, as Shadow Home Secretary, he announced that New Labour would be 'tough on crime and tough on the causes of crime' (Blair, 1993). Indeed the main aim of this sound-bite seems to have been to resonate with the public's fear of, and anger about, rising crime and to convince them that the party would now be 'tough on crime' *whatever* its causes (Downes and Morgan, 2002: 296).

Michael Howard continued to raise the stakes—for example, by doubling the maximum custodial sentence for 15- to 17-year-olds, and introducing new custodial sentences for 12- to 14-year-olds. However, far from withdrawing from this bidding war on toughness, Blair and his successor as shadow Home Secretary often appeared to take the lead. Jack Straw's enthusiasm for the New York-style policing (see Jones, Chapter 25 below) with its 'zero tolerance' of low-level nuisance was reflected in his attacks on beggars and car washers at traffic lights (Guardian, 5 September 2005) and was also successful in generating headlines for the party. We were treated, in Newburn's words, to the '…unedifying spectacle of the Home Secretary and his Labour Shadow fighting to out-tough each other' (Newburn, 2003).

New Labour did not ignore the wider social issues related to crime and in papers such as *Tackling the Causes of Crime* (Labour Party, 1996a) linked crime with a range of social problems including: parenting; schools and truancy; drugs and alcohol abuse; unemployment and recession; care in the community; homelessness; and the inadequacies of the youth service. These, in turn, all related to the development of a key New Labour agenda around tackling social exclusion (see Young and Matthews, 2003; Hale and FitzGerald, 2007; Hale, Chapter 16 above). Yet in the run up to the 1997 election, the Party's public pronouncements on crime emphasized the need for more secure places for juveniles, proposals for lengthy periods of imprisonment for breaches of community safety orders, and support for new approaches to clamp down on forms of low level crime and 'incivilities' which were referred to under the generic label of 'anti-social' behaviour—for example by introducing Anti-Social Behaviour Orders (ASBOs) as a way of tackling 'neighbours from hell'.

1997 to the present

The electoral competition to look tough on crime, coupled with New Labour's discovery of the anti-social behaviour agenda, has so successfully dominated the headlines since 1992 that the public might have been forgiven if it failed to notice that recorded crime had actually been falling year on year until the change of government in 1997. This trend continued in New Labour's first year in office as it started to set out its priorities for all public services along with arrangements for monitoring (not to say to managing) their efforts to meet these. All 43 police forces were set specific targets for reducing domestic burglary and motor vehicle crime by 25 per cent by 2004–05, while five were additionally set targets for reducing robbery. The Government backed this with a £400 million Crime Reduction Strategy which was to be spent on specified crime reduction initiatives and their evaluation.

Meanwhile, Jack Straw, as New Labour's first Home Secretary, introduced its blueprint for tackling crime in the form of the 1998 Crime and Disorder Act (CDA) which, as Newburn (2003: 121) points out, is an amalgam of preventative, ameliorative, and punitive elements. Key elements were:

- an emphasis on working with partners outside the criminal justice system (in particular through the newly created local Crime and Disorder Reduction Partnerships);

- a new approach to tackling youth crime by setting up a new Youth Justice System along with tougher measures including juvenile curfews and doing away with *doli incapax*;[11]

- a tougher approach to the sentencing of offenders in general (including the introduction of US-style '3 strikes' policies whereby repeat offenders were subject to minimum mandatory sentences for certain offences);

- new provisions for tackling anti-social behaviour including the introduction of Anti-Social Behaviour Orders (ASBOs) and parenting orders.

In the same year the Government also introduced the first of two important changes to the police recording of crime (see Figure 21.1; Hope, Chapter 3; and also below) which, in this instance, increased the total by including 'common assaults' which until now had not been counted in the official figures.

Taken together these early initiatives were to set the pattern for New Labour's approach to law and order up to the time of writing. Amid a profusion of new legislation it relentlessly reorganized and reformed existing institutions while creating new ones; it constrained the use of some powers but extended others and added to them. The overall thrust of many of these initiatives was to prioritize tackling anti-social behaviour and youth crime; but the Government's heavily managerialist style was apparent in a narrow focus on selected offences and an emphasis on measuring success, often in ways which obfuscated trends.

By the time it had been in power for 11 years the New Labour Government was estimated to have enacted between 50 and 70 criminal-justice related statutes and created 3,000 to 4,000 new offences (Morgan, 2008). No single institution of the criminal justice system had been unaffected by its zeal for reform, with major structural changes at national level and also locally, with all agencies required to work together within Local Criminal Justice Boards from 2003. The Government's rhetoric around toughness persisted, but there were shifts in emphasis during its second term—in particular from its original targets for crime reduction to improving detection rates (otherwise referred to as increasing the number of 'offences brought to justice') and with repeated references by ministers to the need to 'rebalance the criminal justice system in favour of the victim'.

Threats to merge police forces and for the Home Secretary to take measures of direct control over them were abandoned; but a Policing Standards Unit was set up in the Home Office to oversee improvements in performance followed by the creation in the Government's third term of a National Police Improvement Agency. A merger of two existing bodies and parts of another created the Serious Organised Crime Agency in 2006. Responsibility for charging offenders moved from the police to the Crown Prosecution Service; but officers on the ground were given increasing new powers for tackling anti-social behaviour (such as dispersal orders and the power to issue fixed penalty notices) which they could exercise summarily—that is, without recourse to the courts. While there were only modest increases in the basic grant to police authorities to support local policing, extra money was made available specifically to recruit new police officers and to supplement these with a new type of much cheaper officer (the Police Community Support Officer or PCSO) who would have less training and limited powers. Together they were to provide the Neighbourhood Policing Teams promised by the Government as it approached its third term facing a bidding war with other parties over which would put more 'bobbies on the beat'.

Agencies outside the CJS (such as schools and providers of social housing) were also increasingly given powers related to the anti-social behaviour agenda—for example with the right to apply for parenting orders and ASBOs. And both they and the police were under pressure fully to avail themselves of these powers from an Anti-Social Behaviour Unit set up within the Home Office in 2003 which was later elevated to the status of a cross-departmental 'Respect Task Force' following the 2005 general election (although it was subsequently disbanded after Gordon Brown took over as Prime Minister in 2007).

If magistrates' courts appear to have been undermined by the expansion of summary justice, this compounded the removal of their responsibility for many first time young offenders with the introduction of Referral Orders administered by new panels which included 'community' representation (Crawford and Newburn, 2003). However, magistrates had also been offered a sometimes bewildering array of new sentencing options by the Powers of Criminal Courts (Sentencing) Act 2000, while the Criminal Justice Act of 2003 enhanced their powers (including the scope for imposing longer custodial sentences) 'so that fewer cases have to go to the Crown Court' (TSO, 2003). In the Crown Court, judges found their discretion in individual cases increasingly constrained, not least with the introduction under the 2003 Act of mandatory 'indeterminate' sentences for those found guilty of particular serious crimes—meaning that instead of serving a fixed term they could be held in prison for as long as they were deemed to pose a risk to the public. Both courts were to be subject to a new Sentencing Guidelines Council and their overall administration was moved in 2003 also from the Lord Chancellor's Department to a new Department of Constitutional Affairs (DCA).

These changes to sentencing in the context of the Government's 'rebalancing' rhetoric were to have major implications for the prison population which, at the start of its third term had risen by nearly a quarter, standing at just over 76,000 in June 2005. By this time the Prison Service itself had been brought together with a serially reformed Probation Service under a new National Offender Management Service (NOMS) in 2004; and responsibility for this in turn shifted when the Government's appetite for reorganization reached new heights in 2007 and the Home Office itself was split in two, with NOMS moving to the new Ministry of Justice which now absorbed the four-year-old DCA.

In its early days, the new Government effectively had a walkover in the field of criminal justice. Its strong emphasis on anti-social behaviour clearly struck a popular chord which the Conservatives appeared to have neglected while they were in power; but, in any case, the latter were in disarray for some time in the wake of their 1997 defeat. By the general election of 2005, though, they were beginning to rally around their third new leader, the ex-Home Secretary Michael Howard, at a time when the Government had now been in power for eight years and could no longer blame everything on its predecessors. It, too, had by now also started to be overtaken by unexpected events. It had weathered unexpected outbreaks of civil disorder (see FitzGerald, Chapter 18) by treating them as issues of social cohesion and creating another special unit in the Home Office to manage them. However, the large numbers of young people who began to acquire mobile phones after the turn of the century had rapidly pushed the figures for recorded robberies way off the Government's target, and in 2002 the Prime Minister, Tony Blair, had chosen personally to oversee a well-funded initiative to reverse the trend within six months, as necessary at the expense of other policing priorities. The impact of government policies on the prison population was compounded by the increase in foreign prisoners which, in turn, reflected growing political concerns about the scale of immigration (to which Tony Blair had also personally responded in 2004 by setting yet another target for the removal of illegal immigrants). And all of these developments had occurred in the context of a new, major, international threat to law and order which dramatically impacted on public consciousness with the terrorist attacks in New York of September 2001.

With regard to crime as such, the Government had changed the rules for police record-ing yet again in 2002–03 (see Figure 21.1 above and Hope, Chapter 3), thereby further inflating the total, although subsequent dispensations to the police over how the rules were to be applied soon helped to bring the figures down. The Home Office was now insisting that its own British Crime Survey (BCS) was the only reliable indicator of trends—even though Tony Blair had launched his Street Crime Initiative at a time when the BCS was showing no rise in robbery. The Government also claimed that detection rates were up, although the rise did not represent an increase in the numbers of people charged with an offence: it was entirely due to a growth in the use of cautions and the rise in fixed penalty notices imposed summarily by police officers and PCSOs.

So New Labour went into their third general election with a manifesto which for the first time bracketed immigration issues with crime under the title 'Crime and security: Safe communities, secure borders', and which claimed that:

> Today, there is less chance of being a victim of crime than for more than 20 years. Labour Party (2005)

The Conservatives predictably chose to cite the police figures rather than the BCS, and highlighted in particular the rise in violent crime which (with the partial exception of robbery) had not featured in the Government's crime reduction strategy.

> Crime today is out of control. There is a gun crime every hour. A million violent crimes are committed each year. Conservative Party (2005)

They also mocked the Government's claims about improved detection rates, asserting that:

> Fewer than one in four crimes are now cleared up. Criminals have a better chance of getting away with breaking the law today than at any time in the last 25 years.

Somewhat cheekily, given their own record in office, the Conservatives also attacked the Government on its failure to deal with 'Anti-social behaviour [which]...is a growing concern in all our communities' and they promised to trump New Labour by recruiting 5,000 new police officers 'each year'.

Neither of the main parties saw fit to make terrorism a political issue. Yet the Labour Party was known to be split over the leadership's commitment to introducing identity cards and civil libertarians were already expressing concerns about many other measures taken (or known to be under consideration) by the Government in the name of 'secur-ity'. These included the introduction shortly before the election of 'control' orders which allowed restrictions to be imposed for at least a year on individuals *suspected* of involve-ment in activities related to terrorism. It fell to the Liberal Democrats to challenge them on these issues in their own manifesto which claimed:

> This Government just keeps trying to take away citizens' basic freedoms...They plan to charge every citizen nearly £100 each to hold a compulsory identity card, despite the fact that other countries have found that they don't work. It's all done in the name of cutting crime and tack-ling terrorism; but it is the terrorists who want to take away freedom and democracy—our government should defend our liberties. Liberal Democrats (2005)

Shortly after the election, the fears of politicians and the public alike were realized when bombs fatally exploded at several locations on the London transport system on 7 July 2005, followed by a further failed attempt two weeks later. Later foiled plots occasionally became matters of public knowledge; but so too did apparently bungled counter-terrorism initiatives, most notably the killing of an innocent man who was mistaken for a terrorist suspect in the weeks following the 2005 bombings. However, it was the failure to deport foreign prisoners following their release which forced the resignation in 2006 of Charles Clarke as Home Secretary.

By the time his successor split the Home Office a year later (see Uglow, Chapter 22) the numbers of police constables was steadily falling from its election year peak although there had been a 13-fold rise in PCSOs since 2004 (Bullock and Gunning, 2007). Detection rates continued to improve, but only because the numbers of cautions and fixed penalty notices continued to escalate and were further boosted by a dispensation also to count formal warnings given to people found in possession of cannabis. The new Justice Minister (Jack Straw) was soon asking the Treasury to fund the building of three new 'Titan' prisons to hold 2,500 inmates each (Ministry of Justice, 2007) while appearing to try to row back from the drive to imprisonment which had begun when he was first Home Secretary, urging magistrates in particular to consider community sentences in preference to custody (Ministry of Justice, 2008).

The Government was by now experiencing cumulative setbacks to its criminal justice policies and challenges to the claims it had been making about their success. Far from reassuring the public that they were safer as a result of the Government's tough, hyper-active law and order programme, the BCS of 2006–07 showed that 65 per cent of respondents now believed crime had increased over the previous two years (Nicholas, Kershaw, and Walker 2007) compared to 59 per cent when it first came to power (Mirrlees-Black and Allen, 1998). As the legacy of additional resources from the Street Crime Initiative dried up, robberies had again started to rise. The head of the Youth Justice Board resigned after repeatedly adding his voice to those who claimed that Government rhetoric was damaging the image of young people and its policies were criminalizing many unnecessarily. And it became impossible to play down a long-run rise in serious violence when murders of young people by other young people in different parts of the country began relentlessly to hit the headlines. By February of 2008 the National Audit Office had highlighted the absence of any coherent government strategy for tackling the problem; and its report coincided with the launch of a new government 'Action Plan for Tackling Violence', setting a further round of targets to be met by 2011. Shortly afterwards figures appeared showing that ASBOs—for so long the flagship of its anti-social behaviour agenda—were not only falling in number but, in any case, nearly two thirds of those imposed on teenagers were breached (Home Office, 2008). The law lords had ruled in 2007 that aspects of the control orders for terrorist suspects created by the Prevention of Terrorism Act 2005 breached the human right to liberty; and by June 2008 the Government was having serious difficulty trying to persuade MPs to back legislation to allow terrorist suspects to be detained without charge for up to 42 days.

Importantly, these setbacks were occurring in a context of increasing economic polarization since, despite the Government's efforts to tackle social exclusion and the policies to reduce child poverty pursued by its new Prime Minister, Gordon Brown, when he was Chancellor of the Exchequer, the gap between the rich and poor had steadily grown. Meanwhile, the Conservatives, under another leader and a new frontbench team had begun to take a different line on issues of law and order and to exploit New Labour's internal divisions on issues of security. They now indicted the Government for its short-termism and its failure to heal the 'broken society' which had given rise to the current spate of teenage killings (Daily Telegraph, 25 August 2007). While promising nonetheless to build *more* new prison places than the Government, the new Conservatives combined this with research-based proposals for reducing re-offending by the introduction of a range of therapeutic and rehabilitation programmes (Conservative Party, 2008). They promised to scrap the Government's identity card scheme and they positioned themselves as champions of Britain's civil liberties in opposing the Government's introduction of 42-day detention for terrorist suspects.

REVIEW QUESTIONS

1 Why did the Conservative Government return to a punitive penal policy in 1992?

2 What happened to recorded crime after 1992?

3 Why did the Labour Party seek to be tough on both crime and the causes of crime?

4 How do the New Labour policies on law and order fit with those on social exclusion?

CONCLUSION

This chapter began by arguing that crime is in some measure politically defined; and the New Labour Government from 1997 has illustrated this in the extent to which it has, on the one hand, created new offences, and, on the other, redefined what officially counts as crime. The chapter has also shown how crime as such has assumed increasing political salience in the context of more general insecurity among the electorate about threats to law and order which, in turn, have challenged the ability of the Government of the day to provide the protection expected by the public. In the third of our political phases in particular these threats have had an increasingly international dimension which makes it ever more difficult for the Government to claim that it can control them. Yet, at the same time, the competition for electoral advantage makes it irresistible for opposition parties to exploit any apparent weakness on the part of Government, as necessary, by playing on the fears of the public. Thus New Labour in opposition discovered the largely untapped political potential of anti-social behaviour, though it may thereby have let the genie out of the bottle. For, on the one hand, the public's generalized fears and insecurities are to some extent *projected onto* acts of anti-social behaviour rather than simply *caused by* them (see Hale, 1996 for discussion[12]); and, on the other, its rivals will not give the Government credit for recognizing the problem but will inevitably try to score political points over its 'failure' to tackle it effectively.

That is, crime as a metaphor for wider political concerns is providing an increasingly important site for political competition. Moreover, these developments are not peculiar to Britain but are being observed internationally. Jonathan Simon has suggested that what we see now is 'governing through crime'

(Simon, 2007)—that governments are setting their agenda by legislating about crime and looking to control certain types of behaviour by making them illegal. Although Simon's discussion focuses on the particularities of the US federal system, Gilling (2007) identifies a similar phenomenon in the UK which he refers to as 'governing through disorder' and which, in turn, implies proactive efforts by politicians to heighten public fears, such that:

> …public feelings of insecurity seem to have been actually produced or at least amplified by political elites in search of moral panics and public enemies. (De Giorgi, 2008)

At first sight this seems a high-risk strategy since any short-term gains may be more than offset if politicians then fail to allay the feelings of insecurity they have inflamed—especially since, as we have seen, they may be overtaken by developments beyond their control which significantly increase these feelings. However, such tactics need to be understood in the context of globalization—and in particular the role of international capital, as well as factors such as increased international mobility and communication—which have increasingly resulted in a loss of control by the nation state over the factors which affect the lives of its citizens. National politicians nonetheless continue to compete for 'power' on the basis of whatever issues are likely to have an impact on an increasingly disinterested and fickle electorate. These issues merit much fuller discussion than is possible here; but it is worth concluding with the following succinct overview by the Norwegian criminologist Nils Christie:

> There are so few other arenas left, arenas for the national exposure of the politicians as political figures, and for the party line. Where the dominant goal of life is money and the dominating idea is that an unregulated market economy is the road to this goal, in such a system crime becomes the major arena for what is left of politics. Here it is possible to present oneself as a person deserving votes, with values common to a population of affluent consumers. (Christie, 2004: 37)

QUESTIONS FOR DISCUSSION

1 In what senses are crime and responses to it always political?

2 When and why did crime become a party political issue?

3 What were the main characteristics of the bi-partisan approach to law and order?

4 Compare and contrast 'penal welfare' and 'punitive populist' approaches to crime and punishment.

5 Why has globalization contributed to the increased prominence of law and order as a political issue?

GUIDE TO FURTHER READING

Brake, M. and Hale, C. (1992) *Public Order and Private Lives: The Politics of Law and Order*. London: Routledge.
Covers the impact of Conservative policies through the 1970s and 1980s.

Downes, D. and Morgan, R. (1992, 1997, 2002, and 2007) in M. Maguire, M. Morgan and R. Reiner (eds) *The Oxford Handbook of Criminology*. Oxford: Clarendon Press.

Downes and Morgan provide the most comprehensive reviews of the politics of law and order in the period since 1945.

Garland, D. (2001) *The Culture of Control: Crime and Social Order in Contemporary Society*. Oxford: Oxford University Press.

Provides a broad review of all of these issues.

Young, J. and Matthews, R. (2003) 'New Labour Crime Control and Social Exclusion' in J. Young and R. Matthews (eds) *The New Politics of Crime and Punishment*. Cullompton: Willan Publishing

Includes chapters covering various aspects of New Labour's law and order policies.

WEB LINKS

There are no websites dedicated to the politics of law and order. You should check out the websites of the main parties to see how their views and policies are developing.

http://www.conservatives.com/
The website of the Conservative Party.

http://www.labour.org.uk/
The website of the Labour Party.

http://www.libdems.org.uk
The website of the Liberal-Democrat Party.

For helpful information and critiques of current policies the websites of the campaigning groups are useful as follows:

http://www.nacro.org.uk/
The website of NACRO.

http://www.prisonreformtrust.org.uk/
The website of the Prison Reform Trust.

http://www.howardleague.org/
The website of the Howard League for Penal Reform.

REFERENCES

Beveridge, W. (1942) *Social Insurance and Allied Services*. London: HMSO.

Blair, T. (1993) 'Why Crime is a Socialist Issue', *New Statesman*, 29(12), 27–8.

Bottoms, A.E. (1995) 'The philosophy and politics of punishment and sentencing' in C. Clark and R. Morgan (eds) *The Politics of Sentencing Reform*. Oxford: Clarendon Press.

Brake, M. and Hale, C. (1992) *Public Order and Private Lives: The Politics of Law and Order*. London: Routledge.

Bullock, S. and Gunning, N. (2007) *Police Service Strength England and Wales 31 March 2007*. Home Office Research Development and Statistics Directorate Statistical Bulletin 13/07.

Carter, P. (2003) *Managing Offenders, Reducing Crime: A new approach*. London: Prime Minister's Strategy Unit.

Christie, N. (2004) *A Suitable Amount of Crime*. London: Routledge.

Conservative Party (1970) *A Better Tomorrow*. London: Conservative Party.

Conservative Party (2005) *Are you thinking what we're thinking? It's Time for Action: Conservative Election Manifesto 2005*. <http://www.conservatives.com>.

Conservative Party (1979) *Conservative Party Manifesto*. London: Conservative Party Central Office.

Conservative Party (1983) *Conservative Party Manifesto*. London: Conservative Party Central Office.

Conservative Party (2008) 'Prison with a Purpose.' Security Agenda. Policy Paper No. 4. London: Conservative Party Central Office.

Crawford, A. (1998) *Crime Prevention and Community safety: Politics, Policies and Practices*. Harlow: Longman.

Crawford, A. and Newburn, T. (2003) *Youth Offending and Restorative Justice: Implementing Reform in Youth Justice*. Cullompton: Willan Publishing.

De Georgi, A. (2008) 'Book review. Ruth Gilmore, Golden Gulag. Prisons, Surplus, Crisis, and Opposition in Globalizing California', *Critical Criminology*, 16 (2), 157–163.

Downes, D. and Morgan, R. (1994) '"Hostages to Fortune"? The Politics of Law and Order in Post War Britain' in M. Maguire, M. Morgan, and R. Reiner (eds), *The Oxford Handbook of Criminology* (1st edn). Oxford: Clarendon Press.

Downes, D. and Morgan, R. (1997) 'Dumping the "hostages to fortune"? The politics of law and order in post war Britain' in M. Maguire, M. Morgan, and R. Reiner (eds) *The Oxford Handbook of Criminology* (2nd edn). Oxford: Clarendon Press.

Downes, D. and Morgan, R. (2002) 'The skeletons in the cupboard: The politics of law and order at the turn of the Millennium' in M. Maguire, M. Morgan, and R. Reiner (eds) *The Oxford Handbook of Criminology* (3rd edn). Oxford: Clarendon Press.

Downes, D. and Morgan, R. (2007) 'No turning back: The politics of law and order into the Millennium' in M. Maguire, M. Morgan, and R. Reiner (eds) *The Oxford Handbook of Criminology* (4th edn). Oxford: Clarendon Press.

Faulkner, D. (2001) *Crime, State and Citizen: A Field Full of Folk*. Winchester: Waterside Press.

Field, S. (1990) *Trends in Crime and their Interpretation: a Study of Recorded Crime in Post-war England and Wales*. Home Office Research Study No. 119. London: Home Office

FitzGerald, M. (1987) *Black People and Party Politics in Britain*. London: The Runnymede Trust.

FitzGerald, M. (1989) 'Race in the 1987 Election Campaign' in M. Crewe and M. Harrop, *Political Communications: the General Election Campaign if 1987*. Cambridge: Cambridge University Press.

Garland, D. (2001) *The Culture of Control: Crime and Social Order in Contemporary Society*. Oxford: Oxford University Press.

Gilling, D. (2007) *Crime Reduction and Community Safety: Labour and the Politics of Local Crime Control*. Cullompton: Willan Publishing.

Hale, C. (1996) 'Fear of Crime', *International Review of Victimology*, 4, 79–150.

Hale, C. (1999) 'The labour market and post-war crime trends in England and Wales' in P. Carlen and R. Morgan (eds) *Crime Unlimited? Questions for the 21st Century*. Basingstoke: Macmillan.

Hale, C. and FitzGerald, M. (2007) 'Social Exclusion and Crime' in D. Abrams, J. Christian, and D. Gordon (eds) *The Multidisciplinary Handbook of Social Exclusion Research*. Chichester: John Wiley and Sons.

Hall, S., Critcher, C., Jefferson, T., Clarke, J., and Roberts, B. (1978) *Policing the Crisis: Mugging, the State and Law and Order*. London: Macmillan.

Home Office (2008) ASBOS issued at all courts by area, April 1999 to December 2006 <http://www.crimereduction.homeoffice.gov.uk/asbos/asbos02a.xls>.

Hope, T. and Shaw, M. (1988) 'Community approaches to reducing crime' in T. Hope and M. Shaw (eds) *Communities and Crime Reduction*. London: HMSO.

Kershaw, C., Budd, T., Kinshott, G., Mattinson, J., Mayhew, P., and Myhill, A. (2000) The 2000 British Crime Survey, England and Wales. Home Office Statistical Bulletin 18/01. London: Home Office.

Labour Party (2005) *Britain Forward not Back: Labour Party Manifesto 2005*. <http://www.labour.org.uk>.

Labour Party (1996a) *Tackling the Causes of Crime*. London: Labour Party.

Labour Party (1996b) *Tackling Youth Crime, Reforming Youth Justice*. London: Labour Party.

Lea, J. and Young, J.(1984) *What is to be Done about Law and Order?* Harmondsworth: Penguin.

Liberal Democrats (2005) *The Real Alternative*. London: Liberal Democrats.

Loader, I. and Sparks, R. (2007) 'Contemporary Landscapes of Crime, Order and Control: Governance, Risk and Globalization' in M. Maguire, M. Morgan, and R. Reiner (eds) *The Oxford Handbook of Criminology* (4th edn). Oxford: Clarendon Press.

McClintock, F.H. and Avison, N.H. (1968) *Crime in England and Wales*. London: Heinemann.

Martinson, R. (1974) 'What Works? Questions and Answers about Prison Reform', *The Public Interest*, 35, 22–54.

Ministry of Justice (2007) <http://www.justice.gov.uk/news/newsrelease051207a.htm>.

Ministry of Justice (2008) <http://www.justice.gov.uk/news/newsrelease280208a.htm>.

Mirrless-Black, C. and Allen, J. (1998) Concern about Crime: Findings from the 1998 British Crime Survey. Home Office Research Development and Statistics Directorate. Research Findings 83. London: Home Office.

Morgan, R. (2008) *Engaging with Honest Politicians*. Criminal Justice Matters. Issue 72. June 2008. Colchester: Routledge Taylor and Francis Group.

Newburn, T. (2003) *Crime and Criminal Justice Policy* (2nd edn). London: Pearson Longman.

Nicholas, S., Kershaw, C., and Walker, A. (eds) (2007) Crime in England and Wales 2006/07. Home Office Research Development and Statistics Directorate Statistical Bulletin 11/07 London: Home Office.

Pearson, G. (1983) *Hooligan: The History of Respectable Fears*. London: Macmillan.

Pitts, J. (2003) 'Youth Justice in England and Wales' in J. Young and R. Matthews (eds) *The New Politics of Crime and Punishment*. Cullompton: Willan.

Prison Reform Trust (2003) *Briefing from Prison Reform Trust February 2004*. London: Prison Reform Trust.

Simon, J. (2007) *Governing through Crime: How the War on Crime Transformed American democracy and Created a Culture of Fear*. Oxford: Oxford University Press.

Social Exclusion Unit (2002) *Reducing Re-offending by Ex-prisoners*. London: Office of the Deputy Prime Minister.

Thatcher, M. (1979) Speech in Birmingham, 19 April.

TSO (2003) Explanatory Notes to The Criminal Justice Act 2003, The Stationery Office Limited. ISBN 010 564 403 X. Available at <http://www.opsi.gov.uk/acts/acts2003/en/ukpgaen_20030044_en_1>.

Walmsley, R. (2003) *World Prison Population List* (5th edn). Home Office Research Development and Statistics Directorate Findings 234. London: Home Office.

Young, J. (2003) 'Winning the fight against crime? New Labour, populism and lost opportunities' in J. Young and R. Matthews (eds) *The New Politics of Crime and Punishment*. Cullompton: Willan.

Young, J. and Matthews, R. (2003) 'New Labour crime control and social exclusion' in J. Young and R. Matthews (eds) *The New Politics of Crime and Punishment*. Cullompton: Willan.

NOTES

1. Strictly speaking, the system comprises three separate systems (England and Wales, Scotland, and Northern Ireland), each of which differs in some respects from the others.

2. This volatility in large measure reflects two major changes to the way crime had previously been recorded, the first in 1988–99 and the second in 2002–03 (see Hope, Chapter 3 above).

3. It is worth emphasizing that quite dramatic changes have taken place leading many to talk about a new era of 'late' or 'post' modernity distinguishable from the era of modernity.

4. Any attempt to summarize political beliefs in a short endnote is bound to distort and miss important nuances. Broadly speaking, the Conservative Party emphasizes individual freedoms and responsibilities, and with its belief in the benefits of allowing market forces free rein is often seen as the party that represents the interests of business and landowners. The Labour Party, while moving some way recently from its roots in the Trade Union movement, is still more willing to acknowledge structural factors as causing social problems even if in practice they do not always seek their solution in collective rather than individual responses. The Liberal Democrats are closer to New Labour than the Conservatives and in many respects offer a more radical perspective on many issues than either of the main parties.

5. Perhaps dominant political ideologies would be more accurate since both parties are made up of competing factions who have held internal sway at different times. For example, the pro- and anti-Europeans in the Conservative Party, and the modernizers and old guard within New Labour.

6. See Martinson (1974) for a clear statement of this view. Although by 1979 Martinson was to recant his pessimistic view, the 'nothing works' slogan was to become very powerful and contribute to the crisis of confidence in treatment programmes for offenders.

7. Especially, cynics might observe, when set alongside economic policies that had led to increased unemployment and tightening welfare support.

8. For example, in 1989 NACRO (the National Association for the Care and Resettlement of Offenders) published figures showing the annual cost in 1986–87 of keeping an offender in prison was £14,976 compared to £900 for Probation Orders and £520 for Community Service Orders. See Chapter 26 for further discussion of the use of non-custodial sentences.

9. This devaluation led to a period of sustained and steady economic growth that still continued in 2004. Ironically this improving economic situation has arguably had at least as much to do with declining crime over this same period as punitive approaches to dealing with offenders or crime prevention initiatives.

10. This was, however, somewhat undermined by revelations of extra-marital affairs involving several senior Conservatives and allegations of sleaze.

11. The presumption that a child between the age of ten and thirteen is incapable of committing a criminal offence.

12. In the fear of crime literature, anti-social behaviours are commonly referred to as 'incivilities'.

22 The criminal justice system

Steve Uglow

Within civil society, it is criminal justice that most highlights the coercive nature of the State—detaining people against their will and punishing them brings into sharp relief the beliefs and principles about how we live with one another. To interfere with such fundamental rights requires clear principles about why we should make certain sorts of conduct criminal but not others, about those whose behaviour requires investigation, about the limits of State investigation of private life, and about the objectives of any punishment. Any examination of criminal justice requires consideration of the extent of individual freedom, the nature of common interests, and the problems of fair treatment. There are no simple answers and criminal justice is a complex process with many dimensions, ethical, political, constitutional, and economic, all of which affect criminal justice policy making (see Hale, Chapter 21).

This chapter examines the adult[1] criminal justice system in England and Wales.[2] We devote significant public resources to the criminal justice system—an independent audit (Solomon et al., 2007) concluded that, in 2007–2008, we would spend £22.7 billion on police forces, prosecution and defence lawyers, courts, probation, and prisons. Despite this investment, the criminal justice system comes under significant criticism. Perhaps one problem is that 'system' is perhaps the wrong, albeit convenient, word. A system implies clear and consistent objectives, transparent demarcation of responsibilities and lines of management, understood procedures and good communication between the different elements. Some public services, such as education or health, are characterized by such unifying purposes and principles, clear organizational structures, identifiable lines of management, and recognized and effective means of accountability, normally ending with ministerial responsibility to Parliament. Such a description may be seen as a rose-tinted view of our education or health systems, but it is basically accurate. It is difficult to identify any of these characteristics within the English and Welsh criminal process.

The reason for this is that criminal justice is a collection of autonomous and semi-autonomous agencies, such as the police, the Crown Prosecution Service (CPS), the Crown and magistrates' courts, and the correctional services. Each has its own objectives, principles, and core responsibilities—prosecuting and punishing offenders, reducing crime, maintaining community safety, caring for victims, as well as protecting the rights and interests of the accused. The perspective of the probation officer may be poles apart from that of the prison officer; the police investigator sees the defence solicitor as an opponent; the volunteer supporting the victim seeks to protect the witness; while the barrister[3] sees her as simply a means to an end. It is as if the whole system is contaminated by the competitive, adversarial nature of the criminal trial itself.

The extraordinary fact is that there is no overarching ministry with parliamentary responsibility for the whole structure. There have been two, relatively recent, Royal Commissions in this area—in 1981 the Royal Commission on Criminal Procedure (RCCP) and in 1993 the Royal Commission on Criminal Justice (RCCJ). Neither considered the manner in which we manage criminal justice: yet the critical flaw is the lack of overall structure. Indeed the most recent reform was the creation of the Ministry of Justice in 2007 which was undertaken without any public review or debate. As a result, different ministries assume responsibilities for different parts of the system—from May 2007, the Ministry of Justice took over the responsibilities of the Department for Constitutional Affairs, itself the successor of the Lord Chancellor's Department. These responsibilities include constitutional affairs, criminal law, criminal justice and sentencing policy, the courts' service, legal aid, probation, prisons, youth justice, and parole; the Home Office remains responsible for the police, security, counter-terrorism, and immigration and border controls; the Attorney General is responsible for the Crown Prosecution Service (CPS) and the Director of Public Prosecutions as well as the Serious Fraud Office and HM Revenue and Customs (HMRC) Prosecution Office. But even this ministerial responsibility is limited—for example, government ministers are not answerable in Parliament for day-to-day operational matters relating to the police and the courts. Such a structure, allied to the autonomy of the agencies, invariably affects the extent of mutual cooperation and shared coherence of policy objectives.

After a short overview of the system as a whole, there follow individual sections on the main components of the system—police, prosecution, legal representation, and the courts.

BACKGROUND

This chapter aims to describe and analyse the key elements of the criminal justice system—from arrest to trial and appeal. The following is an outline of the building bricks of criminal justice:

- *Substantive criminal laws*—the police and the courts require legal authority to exercise their powers of investigation and trial. These are all based upon the existence of criminal offences—laws that forbid particular conduct and lay down punishments. Such offences must be created in a constitutionally proper fashion; all offences are nowadays created through legislation passed by Parliament. These statutory offences can be contrasted with 'common law' offences which are based on the decisions of courts. Originally the courts themselves were able to create criminal offences and some crimes, such as murder and manslaughter, are still based on common law. Nowadays the courts no longer have the capacity to create new crimes, although their decisions inevitably shape the boundaries of statutory offences.

- *Procedural criminal law*—procedural laws empower and constrain law enforcement agencies in their investigation of crime, providing them with the legal powers for arrest, detention, and trial of suspects, but also ensuring that suspects are treated with due respect. Pre-trial procedures affect the investigation and prosecution of crime—the work of the police and the CPS. Their powers and procedures are primarily governed by such statutes as the Police and Criminal Evidence Act 1984, the Criminal Procedure and Investigations Act 1996 or the Regulation of Investigatory Powers Act 2000. The trial procedures themselves deal with the manner in which the accusations are put to the defendant, the selection and function of the jury, the functions of the judge, the roles of the prosecuting or defending lawyers, the presentation of evidence, the questioning of witnesses, or the taking of verdicts. The trial itself is not an inquiry into truth where the judge calls and questions witnesses with the aid of lawyers, but an adversarial process where the prosecution and defence present conflicting accounts, call their own witnesses, and critically examine the other party's evidence and witnesses. Procedure is a highly technical area but the rules reflect key ethical principles and are underpinned by the key concept of a 'fair' trial, a right reinforced by Article 6 of the European Convention on Human Rights.

- *Law enforcement agencies*—the police service (see Jones, Chapter 25) is the key agency responsible for the investigation of criminal offences, but other agencies are also involved in law enforcement such as HMRC. The role of the police is not narrowly circumscribed. While they have specific responsibilities for investigating crime, gathering of evidence, interviewing witnesses and suspects, and preparing the case for the prosecuting authorities, their functions also include such matters as the maintenance of public order, the prevention of crime, and the regulation of traffic. Recently, the police and local authorities were given joint responsibility for community safety in local crime and disorder partnerships under the Crime and Disorder Act 1998.

- *Prosecution of offenders*—the preparation of a case for trial and the presentation of that case at magistrates' and Crown Courts is predominantly undertaken by the CPS, although agencies such as HMRC may take responsibility for mounting their own prosecutions.

- *Legal representation of offenders*—the criminal justice system also provides for defendants to be assisted by lawyers, paid out of public funds. From April 2000, the Legal Services Commission has been responsible for the public funding of defence work. The Commission established the Criminal Defence Service—this is introducing a mixed system by which criminal defence will be organized through, on one hand, contracted private practitioners and on the other, public salaried employees.

- *Trial and sentencing of the accused*—magistrates' and Crown Courts are responsible for making the initial decision of guilty or not guilty as well as for imposing penalties. These range from the financial to community-based sanctions to imprisonment (see Worrall, Chapter 26 and Matthews, Chapter 27). These decisions are subject to appeal, either on the question of the conviction itself or the appropriateness of the sentence. The initial appeal is normally to the Court of Appeal with the possibility of a further appeal to the House of Lords. These courts are responsible for examining whether the law has been properly applied and that the sentence guidelines have been followed.

- *A correctional system*—there are three different sorts of sentence laid down by a court: fines are administered by the magistrates' court; community sentences are the responsibility of the National Probation Service; and custodial sentences are in the hands of the Prison Service Agency. The enforcement of sentences passed by the Youth Court is locally in the hands of Youth Offending Teams, overseen nationally by the Youth Justice Board (see Kirton, Chapter 19).

- *Policy formulation*—this is undertaken by a range of government departments responsible for differing parts of the criminal justice system. The Home Office (police and security), the Ministry of Justice (the court service and prisons), the Attorney General (the prosecution system) all play a role, as do executive agencies such as the Youth Justice Board and the Audit Commission. In recent years, local authorities have played an important role in local community safety policies. A National Criminal Justice Board has been created and local policy is also influenced by local criminal justice boards that have been set up in all 42 criminal justice areas.

A criminal justice system is concerned first and foremost with 'crime'. This immediately raises difficult issues about what is or should be designated as criminal within a society (see Morrison, Chapter 1). Similar questions arise about when criminal laws are enforced and against whom (see Tombs, Chapter 13). This chapter avoids these debates and takes 'crime' for granted as acts which are forbidden by law—we have all seen crimes being committed and we have all committed them. But even here, mapping the extent of crime throws up problems (see Hope, Chapter 3). Before any incident is

Table 22.1 Recorded crime 1950–2007

Year	Number of offences	Offences per 100,000
1950	479,400	n/a
1980	2,520,600	5,119
1990	4,363,600	8,630
1992	5,383,500	10,535
2002/2003	5,899,450	11,327
2006/2007	5,428,300	n/a

Source: Home Office 2006.

Table 22.2 BCS estimates of crime for selected years

Year	Number of offences
1981	11.045m
1991	15.075m
1993	18.561m
1995	19.152m
1997	16.486m
2002/03	12.308m
2006/07	11.287m

Source: Home Office 2007.

recorded as a crime, the criminal justice system needs to be mobilized and this is usually done by a member of the public, who is a victim or a witness, who defines the event as a crime and who reports it to the police. The police must agree that an offence has taken place and may choose to record the incident as a crime. From these records, the Home Office publish the official criminal statistics annually (Home Office, 2006).[4]

Table 22.1 shows that recorded crime increased dramatically since the 1950s but particularly in the 1980s, peaking in 1992. It has declined by over 40 per cent since that time. This decline is not apparent in the figures, but this has been due to changes in recording practice (Simmons *et al.*, 2003).

The police record of crime is not complete—they recorded over five million incidents as crimes in 2006/07. This does not represent the totality of crime as the public may not report incidents, or the police may choose not to record the incident as an offence. The generally accepted measure in recent years has been the British Crime Survey (BCS).[5] The survey shows crime peaking in the mid-1990s, but significantly declining from that time. The survey's estimate of criminal offences in 2007 is 11.287 million, over twice that of the official figures gathered by the Home Office (Home Office, 2007), but over 30 per cent less than the figure in 1995 (see Table 22.2 and Hope, Chapter 3).

Once an offence has been recorded by the police, the legal process that operates is set out in straight-forward terms in Figure 22.1:

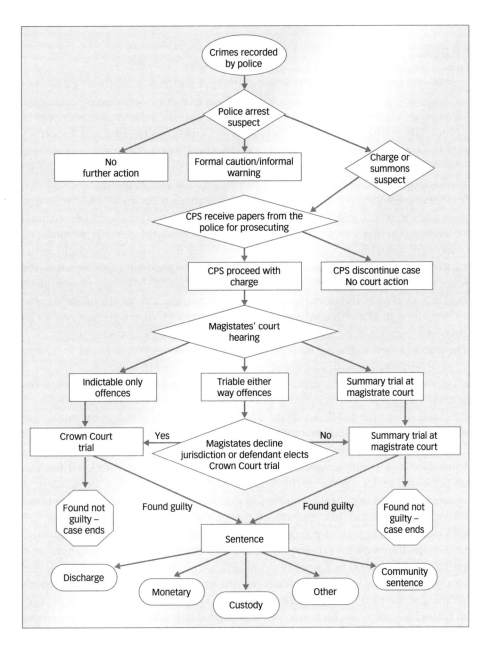

Figure 22.1 The prosecution process

Source: CJS Online 2004; © Crown Copyright.

The police

The police are the pivot of criminal justice—first they are the most visible of all the agencies. Routinely we see patrolling police officers, on foot or in cars. The media captures their presence at any major incident or crime and a police spokesperson will brief the press not only on the progress of the investigation but also on the trial and its outcome. The police are positioned at the heart of the action because they are under a legal obligation to investigate crime and have the requisite powers to search, seize material, mount surveillance, detain, and interview to achieve this (see Jones, Chapter 23).

It is these powers that enable the police to play such a significant role in criminal justice—while they may decide to investigate, they possess discretion as to which offences to investigate and to what extent. For example, finite resources have increasingly meant that an investigation may be limited to the telephone where the nature and circumstances of the incident warrants it. This in turn means that the police do not merely exercise legal powers; they are the key decision makers at this pre-trial stage. Such decisions are frequently about individual cases, but collectively senior police management are the major players in the formulation of local criminal justice policy and, through their organizations such as the Association of Chief Police Officers (ACPO), strongly influence national policy.

The police possess extensive legal powers; they are autonomous decision makers and are heavily involved in policy formulation. It is unsurprising that the police are seen as the authoritative agency for all matters connected with criminal justice, more so than magistrates or judges, prosecutors or prison officers. This might be compared to the Netherlands where the public prosecutors are perceived in this light, or to France where the judiciary dominate all matters of criminal justice. These cultural perceptions are in part the result of the way in which the police are organized.

Unusually for a public service today, the police are not a single national force directly organized under a government department. From the origins of the police in the mid-nineteenth century, local authorities have been under an obligation to maintain an efficient police force and this emphasis on the local nature of policing means that there are 43 local forces, organized geographically either on the basis of urban conurbations (the Metropolitan force for London or the West Midlands force for Birmingham) or on counties (such as Sussex) or groups of counties (such as the Thames Valley force). These forces are financed by local and national government, but are autonomous legal entities which determine their own operational strategies and are independent of political control. Forces have their own identities, often associated with a particular policing strategy such as community or geographic policing, problem-oriented policing, or intelligence-led policing (Tilley, 2003).

Although there is no political control, there is considerable political influence. Conventionally, the management of the police service is seen as having a tripartite structure:

- The Chief Constable of each force—this officer has the legal power to direct and control the force. This is the power of day-to-day operational management.

- Local government—this is exercised through a separate police authority, independent of the local council, that has the duty to maintain an efficient and effective force. This involves appointing senior officers, supervising finances, and keeping a watching brief over the quality of local policing as well as carrying out 'best value' assessments.[6] They have no power to influence police operational decisions.

- National government through the Home Office. The Home Secretary has no operational control but has the statutory duty to promote efficiency and effectiveness. This is done through setting national objectives and performance targets as well as publishing a national policing plan. Furthermore, the Home Office influences forces by a system of circulars which advise chief officers on all aspects of running a force, be that financial management, best practice on operational matters, or criminal justice strategy. Because government provides 75 per cent of police funding, the Home Secretary is in a position to make such interventions count. A minister can now require police authorities to take specific remedial action and exerts considerable influence over all aspects of policing—while remaining unaccountable to Parliament for any operational matters. The Home Office monitors the quality of policing through the Inspectorate of Constabulary and the Police Standards Unit.

In the criminal justice process, the police have the responsibility to investigate crime, to gather the evidence, and to initiate action against the suspect. It is usually a member of the public who will report matters to the police. The police have a certain discretion whether to record the incident as a crime and whether to invest resources into an investigation. This may involve forensic examination of the scene, house-to-house inquiries, tracking down and questioning witnesses, the use of informants, covert surveillance, and the interviewing of suspects. However, most crimes are not resolved—the detection rate was 27 per cent in 2005 (Home Office, 2006: Table 1.1; see Hope, Chapter 3). Those that are resolved frequently resolve themselves—the suspect is still at the scene or is clearly identified by a witness; a suspect arrested for one offence admits to committing other crimes.

When the police are satisfied that a suspect has committed the offence and that they have gathered sufficient evidence, they have various options. They may decide:

- to take no further action;

- to issue a formal caution on occasion, with conditions so that breach of those conditions or a further offence will result in a prosecution;[7]

- to charge the individual with a view to a prosecution in the magistrates' court or Crown Court.

The police will now hand the prosecution of the case to the CPS.

Prosecution

For much of the twentieth century, the police acted not only as investigators but also as prosecutors. Police forces developed prosecuting solicitors' departments which employed barristers to appear in the Crown Court. In magistrates' courts it was often a uniformed police inspector who was the prosecutor. The system was inefficient, especially in the preparation of cases; unfair because, in principle, investigation and prosecution should be separate processes; and lacked any executive or democratic accountability (Royal Commission on Criminal Procedure, 1981). In 1985, an independent prosecuting body, the CPS, was set up, organized on a regional basis—there are 42 CPS areas so that each is co-terminous with the police. Each has a Chief Crown Prosecutor who is answerable to the national executive director, the Director of Public Prosecutions (DPP), who in turn answers to the Attorney General who is responsible to Parliament.

Has the new system addressed the problems? There is now a clear distinction between the processes of investigation and prosecution as well as proper systems of accountability. But the Government still regards the criminal justice system as inefficient—the British Crime Survey estimates that there were 11.287 million criminal offences in 2007. In that year the National Criminal Justice Board concludes that merely 1.445 million were 'brought to justice'. The attrition rate is the product of many factors but the prosecution process is one of them. One aspect of this is that the relationship between the police and CPS remains ill-defined, particularly in relation to charging and the gathering of further evidence. CPS lawyers increasingly play a role at the investigative stage. Under the Criminal Justice Act 2003, the CPS have been given more responsibility for determining the charge in cases other than for routine offences or where the police need to make a holding charge. By involving the prosecutor at an earlier stage, after a suspect has been identified, but before a charge is preferred, investigators are in a better position to ensure that relevant and sufficient evidence is obtained and that the suspect is charged with the appropriate offence. Nowadays CPS Direct provides out-of-hours charging advice to the police. Even with such collaboration, at court the CPS often choose to offer no evidence so that the accused is immediately discharged by the judge or magistrates, or otherwise the CPS present such a weak case that the magistrates throw out the case or the judge directs the jury to acquit. There are many factors that can lead to such 'cracked' cases but one of these is the adequacy of the preparation of contested cases.

In other jurisdictions, such as the Netherlands or the USA, the prosecutor is the lynchpin of the criminal justice system. In the UK, the two symbolic reference points are instead the police officer and the judge. The CPS is a relatively anonymous office, reflected by public ignorance of their function. What, after all, do prosecutors do? The functions of the CPS are to:

- advise the police at the investigatory stage and in some cases be responsible for framing the charge;

- review prosecutions started by the police to ensure the right defendants are prosecuted on the right charges before the appropriate court;

- prepare cases for court and prosecute people in England and Wales who have been charged by the police with a criminal offence. The CPS lawyer will always present the case in magistrates' courts and more occasionally will act as advocate in Crown Court;

- work with other agencies such as the police and the courts to improve the effectiveness and efficiency of the criminal justice system through local and national criminal justice boards.

The decision to prosecute

The files of individual cases will be assigned to a prosecutor for review. They will ask questions such as:

- Is the nature and level of charge appropriate given the evidence?

- What mode of trial (magistrates' court or Crown Court) would be suitable?

- What is the quality of the evidence—is it relevant, credible, and substantial?

- Is there a realistic prospect of conviction?

- Is there any reason in the public interest why this prosecution should not proceed?

We have seen that the police act as a preliminary filter, removing cases from the conveyor belt of justice, by decisions either to take no further action or to caution. The CPS acts as a second filter using their power to discontinue prosecutions. The criteria they use are to be found in the Code for Crown Prosecutors (CPS, 2004). There are two basic issues:

(a) Whether there is sufficient evidence—namely if there is a realistic prospect of conviction. This is an objective test, namely whether a court would be more likely than not to convict the defendant of the charge alleged. The prosecutor must consider whether there is admissible, substantial, and reliable evidence to support the accusation.

(b) Whether a prosecution is in the public interest—the prosecutor should then consider whether the public interest requires a prosecution. Not every suspected crime should automatically be prosecuted, but reading the Code suggests that there is a presumption in favour of prosecution. The Code's constant refrain is the 'seriousness' of the offence and the prosecutor is enjoined that, broadly speaking, the graver the offence, the more likelihood that the public interest requires prosecution. Factors against prosecution include the trivial nature of the incident and the likelihood of a nominal penalty, any delay in bringing proceedings, and the health and age of the accused.

There is also the possibility of negotiation—discontinuance of all charges is not the only option since the defendant may well wish to plead guilty to a lesser charge while maintaining a plea of not guilty to more serious charges. There are often hidden negotiations known as 'plea bargaining'. The CPS can accept such 'deals', but the Code's strictures are that the overriding consideration in considering acceptance of guilty pleas is that the court must not be left in the position where it is unable to pass a sentence consistent with the gravity of the actions. The danger in such practices is that administrative convenience is taking precedence over interests of justice.

Legal representation for the defendant

Defendants were not permitted professional assistance to examine witnesses or to speak on their behalf until 1836, but it is now taken for granted that the right to a fair trial includes legal representation, not only in court but also in the police station and for other pre-trial procedures. For most defendants, the cost of legal advice and representation would be prohibitive. The legal aid scheme allows for the costs of conducting the defence to be borne by the State and not by the defendant. The scheme includes the right of a suspect in police custody to the advice of a lawyer, usually one provided under a 'duty solicitor' scheme organized by local solicitors.[8] At court, the scheme provides for legal representation in most criminal proceedings.

The management of this has been recently reformed—the Legal Services Commission took over the public funding of defence work from the Legal Aid Board in April 2000.[9] The Commission established the Criminal Defence Service (CDS) which is introducing a mixed system by which criminal defence will be organized through, on one hand, public salaried employees and, on the other, contracted practitioners—private solicitors who are accredited and publicly funded.

The radical departure is the introduction of salaried public defenders. The scheme in England and Wales is currently being piloted (Bridges, 2007). Such schemes are common in North America and Australia and a review of research (Scottish Office, 1998) found that the average case costs of staff lawyers are cheaper than private lawyers and that, despite the lower average costs, staff lawyers were found to achieve broadly similar or slightly better outcomes for their clients than private lawyers.

It is only in magistrates' courts that defendants will be unrepresented. Recent reforms (Home Office, 1997) have provided for an enhanced court duty solicitor scheme and defendants who might formerly have been unrepresented are now getting advice. For those who remain unrepresented, magistrates' courts are much less adversarial than higher courts and both the bench and the clerk often question the defendant to obtain the information that they need, whether for the purpose of the plea itself, mitigating circumstances before sentence, or working out a suitable payment plan for the fine. In provincial courts, this may come over as benevolent paternalism (McBarnet, 1981).

The courts

There are currently two systems of courts that hear and decide criminal cases: the magistrates' courts for minor, summary, cases and the Crown Courts for more serious cases heard on indictment. Decisions in these courts can be challenged through a number of channels. These structures can be seen in Figures 22.2 and 22.3.

Quantitatively 95 per cent of all criminal cases will be dealt with in the magistrates' courts. Some 1.895 million defendants were dealt with in magistrates' courts in 2005

Figure 22.2 Trial on indictment

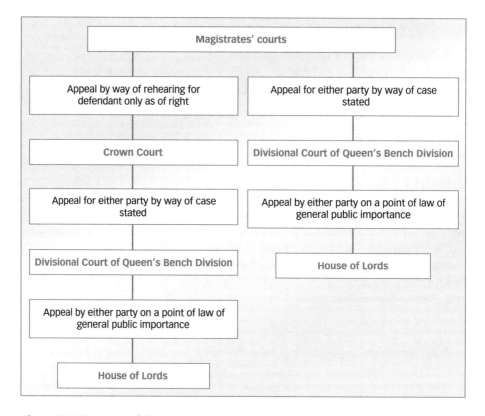

Figure 22.3 Summary trial

whereas approximately 76,000 were tried at the Crown Court (Home Office, 2006: Table 1.1).

In magistrates' courts, the justices of the peace who hear cases are local people with no legal background, taking time from their jobs to serve as unpaid judges. There are paid and legally qualified magistrates in major conurbations. In contrast the Crown Court has a judge who will have been a lawyer of some experience before being appointed to the judiciary. The trial takes place in front of a jury, a body of 12 people randomly selected from the local community.

Magistrates' and Crown courts deal with different levels of offence. There are three categories:

(a) *Summary offences:* these are the most minor crimes and are only triable 'summarily' in the magistrates' court. 'Summary' does not refer to the speed or the lack of quality of justice in magistrates' courts (although often dozens of cases may be dealt with in a morning), but to the process of ordering the defendant to attend the court by summons, a written order usually delivered by post.

(b) *Triable either way:* these are triable either in magistrates' court or in Crown Court. The most common examples are theft and burglary, but the category also includes indecent assault, arson, and criminal damage. There is no clear conceptual boundary here: theft is triable either way whereas social security fraud is a summary offence.

(c) *Indictable offences:* these are the most serious crimes, triable only on indictment (discussed below) in a Crown Court in front of a judge and jury. This category includes homicide, serious assault, rape, kidnapping, robbery, conspiracy, and Official Secrets Acts offences.

Where an offence is triable either way, summary trial is only possible if both the accused and the magistrates assent to it. The defendant has the right to insist on jury trial and if the magistrates consider summary trial inappropriate, they too can elect for trial on indictment. Most defendants opt for summary trial, not least because of the speed of the proceedings and the ceiling placed on the punishments that magistrates' courts can impose. If the offence can only be heard on indictment, the magistrates' involvement is limited—there may be a decision on whether to grant bail but the case is then to be passed to the Crown Court.

Magistrates and clerks

The unqualified, unpaid magistrates' justice of the peace (JP) may be seen, alongside the jury, as an exemplar of the 'active community' with the ordinary citizen's input into the processes of justice. In 2006, there were approximately 30,000 magistrates and 140 district judges in England and Wales (Ministry of Justice, 2007, chapter 7).

Magistrates are appointed by the Lord Chancellor acting on the advice of local advisory committees. There are over 100 of these and each is left to devise its own methods of generating applications. Individuals and organizations can put forward candidates for consideration. Local political parties often nominate candidates. The Constitutional Reform Act 2005 now provides for the Judicial Appointments Commission to appoint magistrates but the timetable for this transition has not yet been put in place. The magistrates' bench should 'reflect the community it serves', but the problem that occurs is one of balance, less in terms of gender than of age, race, and class. It has proved very difficult to appoint sufficient working class or ethnic minority magistrates. Magistrates are unpaid, receiving only a modest allowance for financial loss and subsistence. They are also not qualified, although there is compulsory training before they are allowed to adjudicate as well as continuing refresher courses—JPs will spend about a week a year on training activities. Typically, they serve for between 10 and 20 years. They are required to sit for a minimum of 26 half-day court sittings each year, but on average sit 40 or more times a year.

Sitting part time and normally in benches of three, magistrates deal mainly with criminal matters, but also with some civil cases, in the main family matters. In many conurbations, a legally qualified and paid magistrate often takes the place of the lay magistrates. Once called stipendiary magistrates, they are now known as district judges. They are drawn from the ranks of practising lawyers and normally sit alone.

There is also the youth court dealing with criminal offences by defendants aged 17 or under. The magistrates who sit in the youth court are specially selected and the rules and procedures are different from the adult court, as is its philosophy, based as it is on the welfare of the child (see Kirton, Chapter 19).

The 'clerk to the court' assists the magistrates. The clerk, a fully trained and paid lawyer, is the focal point of the court. They are responsible for legal advice tendered to the justices and for the administration of the courthouse: listing cases for hearing; summoning witnesses; handling adjournments; collecting the fines; as well as managing the personnel of the court. In court, the legal adviser has the duty to provide justices with any advice they require to properly perform their functions, but must not play any part in making findings of fact, although they may ask questions of witnesses and the parties. The overall duty is to ensure that every case is conducted fairly. Problems can arise when clerks are seen to be too involved in the decision making.

Unlike trial in the Crown Court, an accused does not have to be present for summary trial. Cases can take place in the absence of the accused who may have pleaded guilty by post or simply have failed to turn up. The CPS will normally conduct the prosecution. The accused may be legally represented, either by a barrister or solicitor, although one may choose to represent oneself. The clerk should assist an unrepresented defendant in explaining the procedure and perhaps suggesting the sort of questions that may be asked in cross-examination.

Where there is a 'not guilty' plea, the prosecution and defence will call and examine their witnesses, who will be subject to cross-examination by the other party's lawyer. Both sides have the opportunity to address the court although the defence does have the right to the last word. The magistrates listen to the evidence, but will play no part in calling or examining witnesses. At the conclusion of a contested case, they will reach a verdict. If they find the accused 'guilty' (or where the defendant has pleaded 'guilty'), they proceed to sentence. There is a range of penalties from discharges to fines to community penalties to imprisonment. The maximum penalty will be specified in the statute creating the offence, but a magistrates' court cannot imprison anyone for more than six months for any single offence or for more than one year where they are dealing with more than a single offence. Where the magistrates have tried a case summarily but have decided that their sentencing powers are insufficient, they can commit the defendant to the Crown Court for sentence. Crown Courts also hear appeals against conviction or sentence from the magistrates' courts.

The Crown Court

When an offence is too serious for the magistrates' court, an indictment is drawn up for trial in Crown Court. The Crown Court is more formal and traditional than magistrates' courts—at the front of the court will be the raised bench where the judge sits beneath the Royal coat-of-arms. A private door will lead to the judge's room. Below the judge sits the clerk to the court, a less qualified and influential figure than the justices' clerk. Facing the judge will be the dock where the accused stands and in front of the dock will be the benches for the lawyers. At one side is the jury box with two rows of six seats and on the other is the witness box where witnesses enter to testify. There will be a public gallery at the back. There may be an area for probation officers or police officers.

A trial in Crown Court is based on an indictment, a formal document containing the alleged offences. This document supersedes all other accusations (the police charge or the information laid before the magistrates) and it is to the indictment that the accused pleads guilty or not guilty. It is the indictment that should provide the starting point for the judge and the jury. Presiding in the Crown Court is a single 'professional' judge who will be a lawyer of at least ten years' experience, recommended by the Judicial Appointments Commission. He or she sits with a randomly selected jury. There are different categories of judge—the most senior are High Court judges, normally attached to the Queen's Bench Division in London; the routine work will be handled by a circuit judge or recorder—the latter are equivalent to circuit judges but their appointment is only part time. Circuit judges and recorders handle 95 per cent of the work of the Crown Court.

The jurisdiction of the Crown Court is less varied than the magistrates'—the major work is hearing criminal trials on indictment, both for offences that are indictable only and for those that are triable 'either way'. The court has exclusive jurisdiction over such trials. There is a wide diversity in the complexity and seriousness of cases and this is reflected in the division of work between High Court judges and circuit judges.

Guilty pleas are less common in the Crown Court than in the magistrates' courts—approximately 66 per cent of those tried in 2005 pleaded guilty at Crown Court. (Home Office, 2006: Tables 2.9–2.11) The course of a contested trial is very similar to that in a magistrates' court with both the prosecution and defendant examining their own witnesses and cross-examining those of the other side. However, after the closing speeches, the judge will address the jury, explaining the legal issues that have to be decided, summarizing the evidence, and explaining the burden of proof. After the judge's summing up, the jury retire to consider their verdict.

REVIEW QUESTIONS

1 What is the structure of the criminal courts?

2 Describe the work of the magistrates' courts and the Crown Court.

3 Who are the magistrates and how do you become one?

4 What is the job of the clerk to the magistrates' court?

Sentencing and the correctional system

If the magistrates or jury acquits an accused, they are free to leave the court. If they are convicted, the court proceeds to the sentencing stage. For the Crown Court judge, the maximum penalty will be specified in the statute creating the offence but, as mentioned above, a magistrates' court has a maximum of one year's imprisonment.

Courts have a certain freedom in what punishment to impose—the only mandatory sentence is a life sentence for those convicted of murder.[10] In general, a statute that creates an offence will specify a maximum rather than minimum penalty. A court can choose from the range of penalties from the minimum (an absolute discharge) to the maximum specified for the particular offence (Dickson, 2002). The possible punishments include:

- absolute and conditional discharges;
- fines;
- community punishments including community rehabilitation orders and community punishment orders (see Worrall, Chapter 26);
- prison (see Matthews, Chapter 27).

But a court cannot exercise an unfettered discretion in imposing a sentence—there is a statutory sentencing framework, originally introduced in 1991 but now contained within the Criminal Justice Act 2003. This conceives of sentencing as a two-stage process:

(a) The primary decision is the type of penalty, namely fine, community penalty, or custody. The fine is the presumptive penalty and the court must be satisfied, if it wishes to move from a fine to a community penalty or from there to custody, that the offence is sufficiently serious to warrant this.

(b) The secondary decision is that of the tariff. Having decided on the type of penalty, the court must decide on the size of the fine, the content of the community sentence, or the length of the prison sentence.

The sentencing court's discretion is also subject to other controls and influences. Defendants have the right to appeal against sentence (discussed below) and this means that the Court of Appeal exercises a significant oversight and regularly issued guideline judgements as to the appropriate level of sentencing for particular offences. For example, in *Billam*[11] the court provided sentencing guidelines for offences of rape, including aggravating and mitigating factors. This role has been taken over by the Sentencing Guidelines Panel, which works with the Sentencing Advisory Panel. The latter produces research reports on which to base guidelines. Its most recent report in 2008 was on sentencing in offences involving death by driving (Hough *et al.*, 2008).

The enforcement of the sentence will rest with different agencies—fines are administered by the magistrates' court;[12] community sentences are in general the responsibility of the National Probation Service; and custodial sentences are in the hands of the Prison Service Agency. For those prisoners serving more than four years, the decision to release is in the hands of the Parole Board whose function is to make decisions on the release and recall of prisoners on the basis of risk assessments.

The organization of the probation and prison services is in the process of change. As a result of the Carter Report (Carter, 2003) and the subsequent White Paper (Home Office, 2004), the latter two agencies were to amalgamate into a single organization, the National Offender Management Service (NOMS). The expectation was that integrating the management of offenders whilst in custody or under supervision in the community is the most effective and efficient way forward. However this objective has not been realised. NOMS is currently an executive agency that brings together the headquarters of the two services but probation and the prison service remain distinct entities whose job is to ensure that the sentence of the court is carried out. NOMS is a policy agency, organized at regional level where '... effective links can be forged and joint strategies developed with complementary services, including health, education, and employment' (Home Office, 2004: 10). In April 2008, NOMS remains responsible for commissioning and delivering adult offender management services, overseeing the contracts of privately run prisons, managing probation performance, and creating probation trusts.

REVIEW QUESTIONS

1 Describe the range of sentences available to a court.

2 What is the sentencing framework?

3 What limits are put on the sentencing powers of a magistrates' court?

4 What controls exist over the court's discretion in passing sentencing?

The Youth Justice System

The New Labour administration significantly reformed the youth justice system. Following the White Paper, *No More Excuses* (Home Office, 1997), the Crime and Disorder Act 1998 established the Youth Justice Board with the national remit to set standards, monitor performance, and develop policy. On a local level, Youth Offending Teams (YOTs) were set up as multi-agency partnerships with input from police, probation, health, social services, and education.

Both at national and local level, there is support for early, non-court, intervention such as youth inclusion programmes, parenting interventions, or the Safer Schools Partnerships. But the system remains punitive—the Government has maintained the age of criminal responsibility at 10. This can be compared with Scandinavian countries where the age of responsibility is 15. Rates of custody of young people are higher than other European countries—there are secure training centres for children as young as 12. In February 2008, there were 2,348 children aged between 15 and 17 either on remand or under sentence in England and Wales. At that time, there were approximately 9,546 young adults (18–21) in custody (Ministry of Justice, 2008).

When a young person has been arrested and taken to a police station, there are special provisions under the Police and Criminal Evidence Act 1984 Code of Practice—as well as the right to legal advice, there must be an appropriate adult present who is expected to advise the youngster and ensure that the interview is being conducted fairly.

The police can choose to divert the child from court through formal warnings. Where the youngster admits responsibility, the Crime and Disorder Act sets up a cautioning system. First there can be a reprimand which is a verbal warning given by a police officer on first offence. This can lead to a referral to the YOT. Secondly there can be a final warning—a verbal warning given by a police officer on first or second offence where the youngster is referred to a YOT to be assessed to determine the causes of their offending behaviour and for a programme of activities created to address those causes.

There can also be diversion by other pre-court interventions such as acceptable behaviour contracts where the local authority and YOT identify the youngster who is behaving anti-socially, albeit at a low level. A contract is drawn up so that the youngster agrees to stop this behaviour and undertake activities to address any problems. A breach of the ABC can lead to an Anti-Social Behaviour Order which is available for anyone aged 10 or over, causing harassment, alarm, or distress.

Where diversion has failed, youngsters can be taken to the Youth Court. This is within the magistrates' court system but there is special selection of magistrates, the proceedings are separate from adult courts, and there are restrictions on the press and public. Very serious cases still go to Crown Court under ss. 90 and 91 of the Powers of Criminal Courts Act 2000, although this practice was criticized by the European Court of Human Rights in *Venables v UK*.[13]

Where not sentenced at first hearing, the youngster may be allowed release on bail, and YOTs have bail support and supervision programmes. But in February 2008, 513 15- to 17-year-olds were held on secure remand, of whom 348 were untried and 165 were unsentenced (Ministry of Justice 2008).

The youth court has a wide range of sentencing powers. But importantly, where a young person is before court for the first time AND pleads guilty, the court must normally make a referral order which involves a referral to a Youth Offender Panel consisting of two community members working with a YOT member. This has elements of restorative justice as the Panel works out a contract with the youngster. However, so far there is only a limited role for victims. The successful completion means that the conviction is spent and need not be disclosed.

Other non-custodial sentences involve discharges, fines, curfew orders, reparation orders, action plan orders, attendance centre orders, supervision orders, care orders, community rehabilitation orders, or community punishment orders. There are also a range of interventions which exist alongside sentences, such as child safety orders, parenting orders, or drug treatment and testing orders.

The basic custodial sentence for 12- to 17-year-olds is a detention and training order which is a two-part sentence that combines a period of custody and a period of supervision in the community. This can last from 4 to 24 months. Longer sentences for serious offences are available under ss. 90 and 91 of the Powers of Criminal Courts Act 2000.

The Youth Justice Board is responsible for placing young people under 18 years of age in secure accommodation. There are three types of secure accommodation. First, there are secure training centres which are purpose-built centres for young offenders up to the age of 17 with a high staff-offender ratio and a high level of education and training. Secondly, there are secure children's homes which are generally small facilities, run by local authority social services departments, again with a high ratio of staff to young people. Finally there are young offender institutions which can accommodate young people from 15 to 21. These have lower staff-offender ratios and tend to be less able to address individual needs.

REVIEW QUESTIONS

1 What mechanisms are available to divert youngsters from the criminal justice system?

2 What sentences are available to a youth court?

3 Should young people be held in custody?

Appeals

The right of appeal is an essential element of any criminal justice system. The review of decisions allows justice to be done to individual defendants, to bring finality to the process, and to enhance public confidence. But the appellate system in England and Wales is far from straightforward and has mixed and overlapping routes. The process of appeal from a magistrates' court demonstrates this. A defendant can appeal in two ways from the decision of a bench of justices:

(a) *To Crown Court*—the defendant can appeal as of right against conviction or sentence. The appeal takes the form of a complete re-hearing of the entire case, calling the original witnesses and hearing the legal arguments again. The circuit judge is assisted normally by two JPs and they can uphold or quash the conviction or vary the sentence.

(b) *To Divisional Court of Queen's Bench*—either the prosecution or the defence can appeal by way of 'case stated' to the Divisional Court of the Queen's Bench Division. This is an ancient jurisdiction by which the Queen's Bench controls the decisions of inferior judicial bodies. But this is an appeal on the law—there is no rehearsing of the evidence and the hearing will consist of legal argument that the magistrates applied the law wrongly.

If convicted in the Crown Court, a defendant may appeal against conviction or sentence to the Criminal Division of the Court of Appeal. Appeal against conviction is governed by s. 2 of the Criminal Appeals Act 1995. The appellant must establish that the conviction should be quashed according to the sole criterion that it was 'unsafe'. The 'safety' of a conviction is a difficult concept. The court's practice is not to review the evidence in order to substitute their judgment for that of the jury. Nor is it a re-hearing of the case, although the court can receive fresh evidence and is free to assess the evidence as it sees fit. An 'unsafe conviction' exists where the judge has made an error in explaining the law to the jury, in allowing the introduction of inadmissible evidence, or in some other significant procedural fashion. Where the appeal is successful, the court can quash the conviction, vary the sentence, or order a re-trial.

The final court of appeal in criminal matters in this country is the Judicial Committee of the House of Lords. A panel will consist of five senior judges. Appeals must involve a point of law of general public importance. It deals with little criminal work—in 2006, it dealt with 19 criminal matters, of which 5 were successful (Ministry of Justice, 2007). This will be replaced by the Supreme Court in October 2009.

The Criminal Cases Review Commission

Wrongful convictions can stem from police malpractice, from the prosecution withholding evidence, from trial judge bias, from faulty forensic evidence. It is the job of the Court of Appeal to ensure that such errors are rectified. They have frequently been proved inadequate for this task. In the 1980s there was growing anxiety about the performance of the Court of Appeal. Again and again cases have had to be referred back to the court by the Home Secretary. The Birmingham Six were men of Irish origin who were convicted of the Birmingham pub bombings that occurred in 1974. They appealed against conviction originally in 1976 (Mullin, 1986). This appeal was rejected, but the Home Secretary referred the case back to the Court of Appeal in 1987 and the appeals were dismissed again. Referred again in 1990, the DPP decided not to resist the appeal, thus pre-empting the court. However, the court went ahead with the hearing and quashed the convictions in 1991. The 'fresh' evidence was that the confessions had been obtained by coercion and that there were flaws in the expert forensic testimony which stated that they had been handling explosives. In its essentials that evidence had been heard by the court in 1987, but at that time the convictions were still upheld. It is hard to understand why the Lord Chief Justice, Lord Lane, and his colleagues were unable to discover a 'lurking doubt' that had been patently obvious to most observers.

It was clear that the Court of Appeal were unlikely to ensure that wrongful convictions would always be rectified. What was often required was an organization to instigate and supervise further investigation, a function which is ill-suited to a court. For many years, it was a department in the Home Office that undertook this function and occasionally referred cases to the Court. In 1995 an independent Criminal Cases Review Commission was set up to take over this work and be responsible for referring cases back to the Court of Appeal. It deals with approximately 1,000 applications a year, and refers them to the court where it considers that there is a 'real possibility' that a conviction would not be upheld. It is an investigative body and reports to the Court of Appeal on any matter in an appeal referred to it by the Court.

Prosecution appeals

The English common law never allowed the prosecution any right to appeal against acquittal or sentence. This was the rule against 'double jeopardy'—once the jury had acquitted, that was the end of the matter as far as the State was concerned. But there are now a series of mechanisms that give the prosecution a limited right of appeal. The case stated procedure discussed earlier allows the prosecution to appeal on a point of law to the Divisional Court of Queen's Bench. This can be from the magistrates' court. Recent statutes gave a right of appeal regarding 'tainted acquittals' where a person has been convicted of intimidating or interfering with a juror or witness that has led to an acquittal. The Attorney-General's Reference system, introduced in 1972 by the Criminal Justice Act, permits the Attorney-General to refer to the Court of Appeal any point of law even though the defendant was acquitted—this does not affect the status of the original verdict. Finally there can be an appeal against sentence where a defendant has been convicted, but in the eyes of the prosecution has been given an 'unduly lenient' sentence.

The Criminal Justice Act 2003, in allowing retrial for a number of serious offences where new evidence has come to light, has undermined the rule against double jeopardy itself. Further this legislation allows the prosecution to appeal rulings before trial, during the hearing of the prosecution case and of 'no case to answer' as well as other 'terminating rulings'.

The European Court of Human Rights

A final port of call for those who feel that they have been mistreated by the UK criminal justice system is the European Court of Human Rights. The basis of any individual application to the Court is that a State has acted in breach of its obligations under the European Convention on Human Rights, such as by denying a person a fair trial (under Article 6) or by infringing a person's right to liberty, privacy, or freedom of expression. A judgement upholding such an application is an embarrassment for the Government, but does not overturn a domestic judgment or invalidate government action. There is a moral pressure for the Government to amend the domestic law so that it is compatible with the European Convention on Human Rights. Mostly, the Government does pass amending legislation.

To an extent, applications to Strasbourg will become less significant with the passage of the Human Rights Act 1998. Although this does not make the European Convention part of English law, it obliges public authorities, including the courts, to act in a manner which is compatible with Convention rights. It requires courts to interpret all legislation in a way that is compatible with Convention rights, if this is possible. Courts must take account, not merely of the Convention itself, but of the body of jurisprudence that has been built up through the decisions of the European Court of Human Rights. If it is not possible to interpret the law in this way, a superior court may make a 'declaration of incompatibility'. But it is still a matter for the Government to amend the law—or not! The impact of this for the criminal justice system is considerable—these guarantees have already compelled the Government to make amendments to laws which allowed inferences to be drawn from silence or the use as evidence of answers obtained under compulsion.

REVIEW QUESTIONS

1 Describe the process of appeal from conviction in magistrates' court.

2 To whom do you appeal from conviction in Crown Court and on what grounds?

3 When can the prosecution appeal?

4 By what means do we aim to prevent miscarriages of justice?

CONCLUSION

As we have seen, the criminal justice system in this country is a complex amalgam of different agencies, pursuing their own aims. The key unifying principle to which all should subscribe is that the accused has the right to a fair and just process, from investigation to arrest, to trial and sentencing, through to release from prison. In most areas, the criminal justice system in this country measures up to this yardstick. In many ways, this is a creation of history, notably through the decisions of courts and judges and Parliament. Out of these decisions came a number of checks and balances on the power of the State which, when put together, can be seen as ensuring that an accused person has the right to a fair trial: the presumption of innocence, the burden of proof resting on the State, the strict rules governing the admissibility of evidence, the principle that penal legislation should be narrowly interpreted, among many others. Such safeguards have been reinforced by the passage of the Human Rights Act 1998.

But judges and juries, as well as parliaments, have assaulted individual rights as often as they have protected them. In 1791, Thomas Paine wrote *The Rights of Man* arguing for equal political rights. It was a jury that convicted him of seditious libel, although Paine had already fled to France. The institutions of criminal justice provide the State with the most coercive powers in civil peacetime society: people under arrest lose their freedom of movement until it is restored by the police or by a court; they are under an obligation to account for their actions and behaviour either to police officers or to a court; on conviction they are liable to lose their property through fines, their leisure through community punishments, or their liberty through imprisonment. States frequently seek to expand these powers, seeking greater control over the population. Recently, Parliament has passed legislation that has permitted extensions to detention without trial (Terrorism Act 2001), abandoned the double jeopardy rule (Criminal Justice Act 2003), and considered the possibility of reducing the standard of proof to be applied in criminal trials from 'beyond reasonable doubt' to 'on the balance of probabilities'. For those who believe in the rule of law, it is the State that increasingly appears as the 'last enemy'. The real debate should always be about the constraints on State power, with the burden always on the State to demonstrate the absolute necessity for the increased coercive powers rather than on individuals to justify their freedom of movement and action.

QUESTIONS FOR DISCUSSION

1   What should be the principal objectives of a criminal justice system?
2   What would be the advantages and disadvantages of a 'Minister for Justice' responsible for all aspects of criminal justice?
3   To what extent should the police be subject to local or national political control?
4   Should investigation and prosecution be dealt with separately?
5   What elements (procedures, personnel, rights, and so on) are necessary for a 'fair trial'?
6   What factors should a court consider in sentencing an offender?
7   Should the prosecution have a right to appeal against conviction and/or sentence?
8   Is the system of appeal too complex? How could it be simplified?

GUIDE TO FURTHER READING

Ashworth, A. and Redmayne, M. (2005) *The Criminal Process* (3rd edn). Oxford: Oxford University Press.

Davies, M., Croall, H., and Tyrer, J. (2005) *An Introduction to the Criminal Justice System* (3rd edn). London: Longmans.

Home Office *Justice for All* (Cm 5563) (2002). London: Home Office.

McConville, M. and Wilson, G. (2002) *The Handbook of the Criminal Justice Process*. Oxford: Oxford University Press.

Padfield, N. (2004) *Text and Materials on the Criminal Justice Process* (3rd edn). London: Butterworths.

Sanders, A. and Young, R. (2006) *Criminal Justice* (3rd edn). London: Butterworths.

Uglow, S. (2002) *Criminal Justice* (2nd edn). London: Sweet & Maxwell.

WEB LINKS

The following websites contain links to most official criminal justice system webpages:

http://www.homeoffice.gov.uk
Home Office.

http://www.justice.gov.uk/
Ministry of Justice.

http://www.cjsonline.org
Criminal Justice Online.
More specialist webpages include:

http://www.acpo.police.uk/
Association of Chief Police Offices.

http://www.courtservice.gov.uk
The Court Service.

http://www.ccrc.gov.uk
Criminal Cases Review Commission.

http://www.criminal-courts-review.org.uk/
Criminal Courts Review (the Auld Report).

http://www.legalservices.gov.uk/criminal.asp
Criminal Defence Service.

http://www.cps.gov.uk
Crown Prosecution Service.

http://www.cps.gov.uk/direct/
CPS Direct.

http://www.judicialappointments.gov.uk/
Judicial Appointments Commission.

http://www.law.leeds.ac.uk/cjlinks
Leeds Centre for Criminal Justice weblinks.

http://www.magistrates-association.org.uk
Magistrates' Association.

http://www.noms.justice.gov.uk/
National Offender Management Service (archived August 2008).

http://www.lcjb.cjsonline.gov.uk/ncjb/
National Criminal Justice Board.

http://www.paroleboard.gov.uk/
Parole Board.

http://www.homeoffice.gov.uk/police/
Police Service.

http://www.hmprisonservice.gov.uk/
Prison Service.

http://www.probation.homeoffice.gov.uk
Probation Service.

http://www.sentencing-guidelines.gov.uk/
Sentencing Advisory Panel and Sentencing Guidelines Panel.

http://www.victimsupport.com
Victim Support.

http://www.youth-justice-board.gov.uk
Youth Justice Board.

REFERENCES

Bridges, L., Cape, E., Fenn, P., Mitchell, A., Moorhead, R., and Sherr, A. (2007) *Evaluation of the Public Defender Service*. London: Legal Services Commission.

Carter, P. (2003) *Managing Offenders, Reducing Crime*. London: Home Office.

CPS (2004) *Code for Crown Prosecutors* (with addendum 2004; available at <http://www.cps.gov.uk/publications/code_for_crown_prosecutors/index.html/>) (accessed April 2008).

Dickson, L. (2002) 'Issues in sentencing' in S. Uglow, *Criminal Justice* (2nd edn). London: Sweet & Maxwell.

Duff, P. and Hutton, N. (1999) (eds) *Criminal Justice in Scotland*. Aldershot: Dartmouth.

Home Office (1997) *Review of Delay in the Criminal Justice System*. London: Home Office.

Home Office (1997) *No More Excuses*. London: Home Office Cm 3809.

Home Office (2002) *Narrowing the Justice Gap—A Framework Document*. London: Home Office.

Home Office (2004) *Reducing Crime—Changing Lives*. London: Home Office.

Home Office (2006) *Criminal Statistics 2005* (Home Office Statistical Bulletin 19/06). London: Home Office

Home Office (2007) *Crime in England and Wales 2006/2007* (Home Office Statistical Bulletin 11/07). London: Home Office.

Hough, M., Roberts, J., Jacobson, J., Bredee, A., and Moon, N. (2008) *Attitudes to the sentencing of offences involving death by driving*. London: Sentencing Advisory Panel: Research Report 5.

McBarnet, D. (1981) *Conviction*. London: Macmillan.

Ministry of Justice (2007) *Judicial and Court Statistics 2006* Cm 7273. London: HMSO.

Ministry of Justice (2008) *Population in Custody February 2008* London: HMSO.

Mullin, C. (1986) *Error of Judgement*. London: Chatto and Windus.

Royal Commission on Criminal Procedure (1981) *Report* Cmnd 8092. London: HMSO.

Royal Commission on Criminal Justice (1993) *Report* Cm 2263. London: HMSO.

Scottish Office (1998) *A Literature Review of Public Defender or Staff Lawyer Schemes*. Legal Studies Research Findings 19. Edinburgh: Scottish Office.

Simmons, J., Legg, C., and Hosking, R. (2003) *National Crime Recording Standard: an analysis of the impact on recorded crime*. Home Office Online Report 31/03. <http://www.homeoffice.gov.uk/rds/pdfs2/rdsolr3103.pdf>.

Solomon, E., Eades, C., Garside, R., and Rutherford, M. (2007) *Ten Years of Criminal Justice Under Labour: An Independent Audit*. London: Centre for Crime and Justice Studies.

Tilley, N. (2003) 'Community policing, problem-oriented policing and intelligence-led policing' in T. Newburn (ed) *Handbook of Policing*. Cullompton: Willan.

NOTES

1. The youth justice system deals with offenders who are 17 or under. A description of the system can be seen at the Youth Justice Board website at <http://www.yjb.gov.uk> (see Kirton, Chapter 19).

2. An account of the Scottish system can be found in Duff (1999) or on the Scottish Executive website at <http://www.scotland.gov.uk>. Information on the system in Northern Ireland can be found at <http://www.cjsni.gov.uk>.

3. There are two categories of lawyer in England and Wales: the solicitor is the general practitioner, available to the public for legal advice and limited representation; the barrister is the consultant and advocate (only available through a solicitor) who will provide specialist advice and represent clients in court.

4. The 2005 criminal statistics can be accessed at <http://www.homeoffice.gov.uk/rds/pdfs06/hosb1906.pdf>.

5. The BCS is best accessed through <http://www.homeoffice.gov.uk/rds/bcs1.html>.

6. Best value reviews of performance arise from the duty of continuous improvement for local authorities as set by the Local Government Act 1999.

7. There is a separate statutory scheme involving reprimands and final warnings for young persons under the Crime and Disorder Act 1998.

8. This is provided for by ss. 58 and 60 of the Police and Criminal Evidence Act 1984.

9. Access to Justice Act 1999; <http://www.legalservices.gov.uk/>.

10. There are other mandatory sentences under the Crime (Sentences) Act 1997 although these are rarely applied.

11. [1986] 8 Crim App Rep (S) 48.

12. There are other financial penalties such as compensation orders. Confiscation of assets is also possible under the provisions of the Proceeds of Crime Act 2002.

13. [1999 (2000) 30 EHRR 121; [2000] 2 All ER 102.]

23 Surveillance

Richard Jones

INTRODUCTION

In this chapter I will discuss the topic of surveillance. The aims of this chapter are: to introduce and discuss what is meant by surveillance within criminology; to introduce key theories relating to the concept of surveillance; to summarize some criminological research on surveillance; and to identify some new surveillance technologies and discuss their implications. The topic is now fairly broad and extensively researched within criminology, so by necessity any introduction has to be selective.

BACKGROUND

The Oxford English Dictionary (OED) 2nd edition (1989) defines 'surveillance' as, 'a. Watch or guard kept over a person, etc., [especially] over a suspected person, a prisoner, or the like; often, spying, supervision; less commonly, supervision for the purpose of direction or control, superintendence. … b. [an attribute, especially] of devices, vessels, etc., used in military or police surveillance.' The term 'surveillance' seems to imply practices of watching or listening not merely briefly, but rather over an extended period of time.

Within criminology, forms of surveillance can be understood to include: audio or visual surveillance; surveillance of written communications; positional surveillance of people or things; Neighbourhood Watch schemes; CCTV systems, including in city centres, banks, shops, hotels and restaurants, at airports, and on public roads; in prisons; in relation to Internet usage; and the electronic monitoring of offenders ('tagging'). An important distinction can be drawn between surveillance of specific individuals and surveillance of the public in general. Applications of surveillance falling outside usual criminological boundaries but nevertheless conceptually related to it include military surveillance; workplace surveillance; surveillance (of various types) carried out by intelligence agencies; satellite surveillance, both military and civilian (of weather patterns, crop status, and so on); and medical surveillance of individuals and populations (epidemiological monitoring of the spread of viruses, for example).

Academic and political attention to the topic of surveillance came to the fore in the UK in the 1980s, following a combination of interest in (and concern regarding) urban policing tactics, the policing of various workers' strikes and political marches and demonstrations; the 'Zircon' spy satellite saga; the emergence of the 'personal microcomputer'; the presence of CCTV cameras in some central London streets; the suspected wiretapping and 'bugging' by the security services of certain politicians and activists; and renewed public interest in George Orwell's novel *1984*. Public and political concern regarding surveillance centred on the powers of the new technologies, their potential political uses, and on the consequent possible threat to civil liberties, a perspective that is still strong today. Criminological interest in surveillance theory was stimulated partly by Marxist criminology and sociology, but also by the publication in the UK of Michel Foucault's (1979) *Discipline and Punish* (see below). The study of surveillance thus has many aspects, and has links with many other topics, including policing, the politics of law and order, punishment in the community, prisons, terrorism, crimes of the state, and media images of crime. In the following section, key theoretical perspectives on surveillance will be introduced and discussed.

Theories of surveillance

Marxism, social control, and surveillance

Following Karl Marx (1818–83), Marxists emphasize social control's class basis, and hence what they regard as the socially unjust nature of social control. It is convenient to distinguish between two types of social control, namely formal social control and informal social control. Formal social control refers to the criminal law, the police, and the criminal justice system. Informal social control, on the other hand, refers to compliance with social norms (such as that people should obey the law) demanded by an individual's own family, friends, teachers, neighbours, workmates, or fellow citizens. The concepts of formal and informal social control are used by Marxists and non-Marxists alike. Marxists offer a particular interpretation of these two forms of social control, seeing them as key means by which the ruling class maintain their dominance over the working class.

Both informal and formal social control may involve forms of surveillance. In the case of informal social control, the form of surveillance involved would seem to be primarily of an interpersonal kind. In the case of formal social control, though, it may be that along with surveillance at the local, human level (by police officers out walking the beat, for example), specific surveillance technologies are also employed in order to gain additional or alternative quality surveillance information (for example, via CCTV). In all cases, Marxists would interpret the surveillance employed in terms of its social control 'role' or even 'function' within society. Various studies on social control were published during the 1980s which, while not necessarily Marxist, shared Marxists' vision of social control as one that was essentially controlling or repressive, whether intentionally or unintentionally so (see for example, Cohen, 1985; and Cohen and Scull, 1983). Marxist analyses can be complex, sophisticated, and subtle, and can offer interpretations of a variety of surveillance practices including State-sanctioned surveillance, by intelligence agencies (they are protecting the State, which is said principally to serve ruling class interests); CCTV schemes (they might be said, for example, to be directed primarily at protecting retailers' profits, or against working class public order disruption); and informal, peer surveillance (which may be a key mechanism by which bourgeois norms are upheld).

Foucault, 'discipline', and surveillance

Many contemporary accounts of surveillance remain strongly influenced by Michel Foucault (1926–84) and his work on discipline, set out in closest detail in his book *Discipline and Punish*. The original title of the book on its publication in France in 1975 was *Surveiller et Punir*. On its translation into English, the publishers discussed with Foucault what English title to give the book; he thought 'discipline' a better word to use than 'surveillance', perhaps because the latter usually has a more detached meaning in English, usually implying only the watching rather than the correcting of behaviour, and thus fails to capture the interactive quality of 'corrections' that Foucault's book sets out to describe. Nevertheless, surveillance, optics, observation, and knowledge, are all central themes of Foucault's book, and the book has made a distinctive contribution to a certain type of critical sociological criminology, particularly in the areas of the sociology of punishment and the study of social control.

At the same time, it is important to realize that Foucault was not a criminologist, that his book is not intended as a criminological text as such, and that his interest ultimately is in the study of the Western 'subject' (perceiving person) in modern societies. It makes a certain sense to think, at least in the first instance, of the criminological topic of *Discipline and Punish* as one Foucault happened by chance to use as the case study for his book; he could have written the same book, he once noted, instead about the school, factory, hospital, or army barracks.

Discipline and Punish (Foucault, 1979) famously opens with brief descriptions of two, very different, forms of punishment from French history: the brutal execution of Damiens the regicide in 1757, and a prison timetable from about 1838. The public execution is gory and brutal, taking place in public before a large crowd, and today seems quite barbaric to us. The prison timetable, in contrast, appears infinitely more civilized and modern and, in its specifications of when and where prisoners should be doing things at different times of the day, in its form strikes us as familiar today, even if its content is now somewhat old-fashioned. Foucault notes that these two very different types of punishment are separated by a period of only about 80 years. How, he asks, did the change from one to the other come about? His answer rejects the obvious liberal explanation that the change is attributable to French society becoming more civilized and humane. Instead, and controversially, he suggests that modern prisons evolved not because they are *kinder* ways of punishing but because they are more *efficient* ways of punishing; to use Foucault's terminology, modern prisons are based on a more efficient 'technology of power'.

A technology of power, Foucault writes, is a particular, historically specific way by which humans exercise power over one another. A technology of power is comprised both of *knowledges* and of *practices*. Different technologies of power are dominant during different phases of history. Foucault's model of history is reminiscent of Rusche and Kirchheimer's (1968), in that it characterizes history as being composed of a succession of phases (each phase lasting for decades or centuries). During each phase, social organization follows certain patterns. But social life changes dramatically at certain points, as one phase gives way to another. (As such, Foucault rejects the conventional liberal understanding of history as a process of continual and gradual change.)

According to Foucault, technologies of power are to be found within all areas of social life, including health and medicine, education, the military, and factories. *Discipline and Punish* is concerned specifically with the role that three, historically successive, technologies of power play within the spheres of punishment and of social control: monarchical power, juridical power, and disciplinary power. Monarchical punishment is the spectacular, brutal, public form of punishment being carried out in the execution of Damiens. It is a display of the monarch's absolute power, and typically involves some sort of visible marking or disfiguring of the offender's body; but it is also, says Foucault, an unstable, hard-to-control, form of punishment; its use of brute force and heady emotions can backfire, and the impassioned crowd might even turn on the executioner and the State. Juridical punishment is the punishment of classical criminology ('let the punishment fit the crime') from the late eighteenth century. Punishment is to be proportionate, with length of time spent in prison intended to reflect the gravity of the offence committed. It is not particularly concerned with the offender as such, readmitted as a full citizen once the prison sentence has been served.

According to Foucault, disciplinary punishment began towards the beginning of the nineteenth century, after 'discipline' (an older set of techniques that had been used in places such as monasteries for several centuries) took root in the newly formed modern prisons, and began guiding penal practices and knowledges. Discipline is based on supervision, training, correction of unwanted behaviour, and the continual examination and testing of each individual person. (The illustrations in the middle of the book *Discipline and Punish* are helpful in quickly grasping what Foucault had in mind.) Rather than seek to crush an offender (an aim of monarchical punishment), or merely incarcerate them for a time but do little more (as juridical punishment had done), disciplinary punishment seeks to rehabilitate. Discipline utilizes measures of time and space to bring order to the social world. Groups of soldiers can be taught to march in step in orderly rows and columns, the sick can each be assigned one hospital bed, schoolchildren a desk each, and prisoners their own cell. By individualizing each person in this way, 'abnormal' or 'incorrect' behaviour becomes easier for a supervisor to identify, study, and address. Foucault argues that this is what surveillance is; a system by which a small number of supervisors can efficiently exercise dominance and control over individuals and groups by constituting them in a certain way. The aim is to 'normalize' each person, by identifying and dealing with any abnormal behaviour, however small. Once this has been done, the individual can successfully and safely be handed over to a different, less intensive part of the surveillance apparatus. But remember that it is a very specific form of dominance, in that its aim is not violent repression, but rather the detailed study of each individual's behaviour, record, and history, with a view to reforming and rehabilitating them, at least in part. Foucault notes that 'experts' have an important role to play here (particularly in the more problematic cases) because of their role in generating and applying specific knowledge within each field, but that equally important are the specific practices facilitated by each institution's architecture. Foucault sees Jeremy Bentham's 'Panopticon' prison design as an illustration of the relationship between knowledge and architecture within institutions, as well as epitomizing disciplinary surveillance in particular. The circular prison design, featuring a central guard's tower from which a guard can see into every single prison cell while themselves remaining hidden, separates the prisoners (one to each cell), thus helping control order in the prison, but also generates knowledge and practices relating to the prisoners through facilitating study of them as individuals.

Foucault claims that the social scientific study of people, and in particular academic disciplines such as psychology and criminology ('the disciplines') emerged at this time, alongside the birth of the modern prison. But the maximum security prison is not the only place within the criminal justice and crime control system in which discipline and surveillance (in Foucault's sense) are to be found. Disciplinary punishment, Foucault claims in his 'dispersal of discipline' thesis, underpins not only all other, less secure prisons, but also probation work, diversion schemes, half-way houses, and outreach work—a network that he terms the 'carceral archipelago'. Moreover, disciplinary surveillance penetrates deep into the social body, with various professions exercising implicit watching-and-judging powers through their specialized forms of surveillance: the teacher-judge, the lawyer-judge, the police officer-judge. Further still, this judging (surveillance and normalization) is exercised to some extent by us all. In this way, disciplinary punishment and disciplinary social control are 'genetically' related to one another, as it were, with discipline (active surveillance) being their shared characteristic.

As David Garland (1990) has noted, Foucault's account of discipline and surveillance practices constitutes an original and thought-provoking reinterpretation not only of punishment in modern society but also of the connections between punishment and social control. As Garland has also noted, there are various problems with Foucault's account. Garland (1985) has shown that in England, at least, disciplinary punishment actually appears to have begun almost a century later than Foucault claims. Moreover, Foucault's 'power perspective' (his insistence that social relations and historical change must be understood exclusively in terms of power and domination), and his related 'anti-humanist' approach, are highly questionable as analytic frameworks. They also beg certain questions: Is power really as one-sided as Foucault portrays? Is resistance to power possible? Are people really primarily motivated by (and is history really explicable in terms of) power alone? To some extent, Foucault addresses these and other criticisms in interviews and essays after *Discipline and Punish* was first published (see for example, Gordon, 1980), though in other respects they remain fundamental objections to his whole approach during the early to mid-1970s.

There is a certain limited connection between Marxist accounts of social control (both types) and Michel Foucault's account of disciplinary surveillance—and indeed some Marxist accounts have been influenced by Foucault's work—but there are also differences. (See Sumner, 1990 for an approach that draws both from Marxism and Foucault.) What is important to us here, however, is to recognize that although Foucault (1979) was clearly very interested in the topic of surveillance, and indeed built this whole book around a particular, unique interpretation of this term, he was only partly concerned with alerting his readership to the 'Big Brother' nature of the State, and instead more concerned with trying to say something about the individualizing practices of surveillance—about the *formation* of the modern disciplined individual, rather than the *repression* of the individual as Marxists would have it. Foucault was interested in this greater issue, namely of the history of Western subject, about how this particular subject formation came about, about knowledge-production, and relations between knowledge formations and power formations (note however that Foucault does not say 'knowledge is power') (see Dreyfus and Rabinow, 1982). Nevertheless, Foucault's work continues to be influential within the study of surveillance today, perhaps because of his account of the insidious, social-controlling functions of surveillance, and perhaps because of the apparent applicability of his discussion of the Panopticon to electronic surveillance technologies: 'the electronic Panopticon' (see Lyon, 1993; 1994).

'Post-disciplinary' theories of surveillance

In the early 1990s, Feeley and Simon (1992) claimed that a new guiding logic was emerging within punishment, which they termed 'The New Penology'. They suggested that this new logic was a historical successor to disciplinary punishment, or at least that it stood in sharp contrast to it. The characteristics of the new penology were said to involve an interest in aggregates rather than individuals; use of actuarial analysis; and incapacitation rather than rehabilitation as a sentencing rationale. In a subsequent essay, Feeley and Simon (1994) extended the new penology argument and argued that similar practices could be seen emerging across various different parts of criminal justice and crime control systems; they termed this 'actuarial justice'. The relevance of their work to the study of surveillance lies in their identification of a crime control approach that utilizes a form of surveillance seemingly rather different to the involved, individualizing approach modelled by Foucault. In a discussion of screening techniques used in airport security checks of passengers, Feeley and Simon (1994: 177) argue that such screening may now be based on identifying typical offender risk factors, and utilizing this information in risk identification systems. In the busy world of the airline industry, where it is important to maintain security without delaying the majority of passengers unduly, a risk factor system aims to flag-up certain passengers as potentially 'high risk' based on a simple calculation. By using basic information such as a passenger's age, nationality, transit origin and destination, and so on, a risk instrument can quickly derive an initial risk 'score' for each passenger. Passengers scoring above a certain predefined level can be searched, questioned, or investigated further, or discreetly put under surveillance within the airport terminal. Even the proponents of such systems do not claim that they are foolproof; rather the aim is to help allocate the scarce resources of airline security (equipment, personnel, and their time) in focusing on potentially higher risk individuals. Thus it may not be the actual immediate behaviour of certain passengers that draws the attention of the surveillance system but instead various prior factors.

Critics of such risk checklists claim that they may involve stereotypes (of race, religious faith, nationality, or gender, for example); that sometimes there is little social scientific research underpinning them; that there could be a circularity involved, in that risk factors may simply reflect outcomes of past practices and beliefs (which may be biased or partial); or that even in the absence of actual bias, the resulting decisions can still seem somehow profoundly unfair (see also Simon, 1988). It could be, though, that these problems are only present in poorly researched and implemented screening systems, and that properly researched, evidence-based screening systems that have been properly evaluated and revised as necessary are a useful additional tool. However, the key point for us here is that, to the extent that such checklists and other risk factor-based screening systems are used in various crime control and criminal justice 'surveillance' systems, it could be argued that their usage might represent a move *away* from Foucauldian surveillance practices and *towards* a new, 'post-disciplinary' form of surveillance (a historical shift which seems to have been hinted at, at least, by Feeley and Simon (1992) in the title of their original article). However, it could be that the risk-based practices Feeley and Simon identify are indeed historically fairly novel and sociologically significant, but that these newer practices overlay and complement existing (and more Foucauldian) surveillance practices rather than simply replacing them.

Another approach, similar in certain respects to Feeley and Simon's, involves a particular reading of Michel Foucault's (1991) notion of 'governmentality'. Governmentality is a neologism of Foucault's used to describe particular techniques and practices of government used to nurture the economic, social, and medical health of the population as a whole (a good introduction and discussion can be found in Garland, 1997). These 'arts of governing' were developed over the centuries, but are particularly associated with the development of the disciplines of economics and public health. On one reading, adopted by a number of UK, US, and Australian commentators (see Barry *et al.*, 1996), Foucault's work on governmentality is concerned with analysing neo-liberal politics (as emerging in the mid-1970s, around the time at which he began studying governmentality), and is taken to be suggesting that governmentality somehow comes to supplant discipline. On this reading, in respect of the specific fields of crime control and criminal justice, individualizing surveillance is said gradually to be replaced, as from about the 1980s, by aggregating, actuarial surveillance, of the kind on which Feeley and Simon focus. However, an alternate reading is that, while Foucault undoubtedly was interested in the rise of neo-liberalism, he envisaged governmentality as augmenting discipline, not replacing it. If this is correct, then his concept of governmentality relates to State-level power, augmenting his account in *Discipline and Punish* of power/knowledge within institutions, and therefore should not be regarded as *post*-disciplinary. The notion of governmentality may possibly have some utility in analysing surveillance and classification practices at the level of the State, for instance in relation to national identity cards of the sort the UK Government has been considering introducing. However, from the perspective of governmentality, such ID cards would be seen less as an historical innovation indicative of something distinctly 'new' happening, and more as merely the latest in a long series of historical measures, including letters of passage, passports, national insurance numbers, visas, driving licences, and birth certificates.

Rather different 'post-disciplinary' perspectives can be found in two separate essays by French post-structuralist writers Jean Baudrillard (1929–2007) and Gilles Deleuze (1925–95). In a short, critical book entitled *Forget Foucault*, Baudrillard (1987) claims that Foucault's work in *Discipline and Punish* gives too much credence to the concept of power, and indeed that Foucault's book was itself part of a fading era; as such, Baudrillard seems to reject Foucault's power perspective, including the concept of 'technologies of power'. Baudrillard (1983; 1993) argues instead that contemporary Western societies are societies of 'simulation' (of surface, image, appearance, digitization, and perfect replicability, an era in which the electronic or genetic 'copy' is indistinguishable from the 'original'). From this perspective, the imagery produced by CCTV cameras, for example, should not be theorized in terms of attempts to 'know' the truth about the person under surveillance, but instead as part of society's safety-inspired desire to achieve an exact yet sterile reflection of itself. Although Baudrillard considered himself as standing in stark opposition to Foucault, others see certain linkages between their work. Bogard (1996) has argued that Foucault's work on surveillance can be combined with Baudrillard's work on simulation, suggesting that electronic forms of surveillance today may involve elements both of Foucauldian surveillance and of Baudrillard's simulation in their (digital) representation of the person under surveillance. With the emergence of electronic forms of surveillance producing electronic representations of the person or thing under surveillance, we also enter an era in which those representations can be electronically recorded, analysed, and replayed. For Bogard, the possibilities that various electronic surveillance systems offer in terms of their enabling surveillance to begin to escape from the ties of the here-and-now, are tied into the wider emergence not just of an information society but of 'the conversion of persons and social relations into the universal ether of information, which is their simulation' (1996: 69).

Deleuze, too, has contributed (albeit in brief) to post-disciplinary perspectives in an essay suggesting that Foucault's third type of 'technology of power' (disciplinary power) may presently be being replaced by a fourth, which he terms 'control'. Deleuze's (1995) essay is more than a little opaque, but he seems to be suggesting that contemporary capitalism, with its electronic communications, dynamic consumer economy, geographic mobility, and fluid organizational techniques, gives rise to a cultural form in which disciplinary institutions become superseded by life-long flow control systems (see Jones, 2000; Haggerty and Ericson, 2000; see also Lyon, 2003). Haggerty and Ericson develop these themes in their notion of the 'surveillant assemblage' (2000). Deleuze might point to electronic tagging of offenders (particularly involving satellite tracking) as an example of this form of control—rather than being detained in a prison, today's society is able to punish and control even while 'setting free'. Tracking tags, like electronic access cards, can permit/disallow (cards) or warn against (tags) entry to a particular zone or place, possibly at a particular time or day. In this way, such tags 'modulate' a given offender's daily routine, rather than simply restricting it or subjecting it to traditional surveillance supervision. Moreover, tracking tags themselves appear from this perspective as just another instance of a greater system of electronic access controls, swipe cards, RFID cards (see below), PIN numbers, biometric recognition systems, login names and passwords, and so on—each with their own 'access privileges' and restrictions. In a suitably equipped apartment block, an RFID card waved at the shared entrance can grant all residents access to the foyer, but waved at a sensor in one of the lifts, allows each resident access only to the floor on which their apartment is situated. (There's a certain analogy with users logging on to a computer system and being able to access certain shared folders, but only their own private folders, on a shared network server.) As such, if there is surveillance at work here, it is less the tracking of individual users, and more simply the granting of electronic 'keys', which allows users to lead their lives just as with any other sort of keys. In some cases, such keys may be enabling or even liberating. Yet they are also likely to leave a little digital trace somewhere in a digital archive each time they are used. From the point of view of the key issuer, day-to-day surveillance of the vast majority of users probably is not necessary; the archived record is a way to reconstruct events should something go awry. But nevertheless, the potential to combine this mass of stored data and to build up a 'picture' of a person's activities, communications, interests, financial transactions, and so on, seems to bring us back towards the intensive, person-centred focus of Foucauldian surveillance.

New themes within surveillance studies

Surveillance studies have developed apace over the past few years. The field is now wide-ranging, but certain themes can be identified within the literature. David Lyon has argued that an important characteristic of surveillance today is its role in what he terms 'social sorting'—the 'drive of contemporary surveillance' to classify and record data, in order better to 'plan, predict and prevent' (2003: 13). Searchable databases play a key role in such surveillance, informing the management of populations, by sorting and classifying data about individuals. Access to social opportunity is now policed at virtual 'gates and barriers', which effectively 'sort populations and persons'. If 'dataveillance' (see Lyon, 2007: 16) is the practice of surveillance as data gathering, social sorting is the use of this data in social governance. Three related themes include a focus on globalization, in recognition of the ease with which electronic surveillance data has the potential to circulate globally (see Lyon, 2001: chapter 6; Zureik and Salter, 2005); an interest in the role of borders and gateways (see Franko Aas, 2007); and, allied to this, an awareness that biometric identification of people's bodies is becoming increasingly common, with interesting consequences (see Lyon, 2007: chapter 6; Franko Aas, 2006).

The social implications of new surveillance technologies seems set to continue to be an energizing theme within surveillance studies, not least because new technologies will continue to be invented, and will thus continue to pose challenges to existing social, political, and legal systems. Privacy is also an important theme informing contemporary surveillance studies and related academic areas. As Goold (2007: 69) notes, concepts of '[s]ecurity, surveillance, identity and privacy are intimately connected'. Surveillance studies today involves exploration of these themes across a range of contexts, from criminal justice, policing, and state security, to the military, commerce, the Internet, and the workplace (see for example the essays in Lyon, 2006). Lastly, writers in this field continue to be engaged in identification of, and involvement in, the political aspects of surveillance. Sub-themes within this area include concern over 'function creep' (the possibility that surveillance systems may be introduced on certain grounds, only to take on new (and possibly more troubling) functions once in operation); and the study of resistance to surveillance, challenging the idea that intrusive surveillance systems are inevitable, either socially or politically (see, for example, Haggerty and Ericson, 2006; Monahan, 2006; Lyon, 2003).

REVIEW QUESTIONS

1 What does Foucault mean by 'discipline' and 'surveillance'? For Foucault, what is the relationship between punishment and social control?

2 What are 'post-disciplinary' theories of surveillance, and why might there be a need for such theories today?

Surveillance technologies

Having considered some of the main theoretical *perspectives* within sociological criminology on the topic of surveillance, this section will discuss various different surveillance *technologies*.

Surveillance cameras

Perhaps one of the best-known forms of surveillance today is closed-circuit television (CCTV) camera surveillance. In the UK, CCTV camera usage expanded dramatically during the 1990s, partly as a result of Home Office backing of CCTV city street schemes. The number of CCTV cameras also increased over this same time period in shopping centres and malls, on roads and highways, within private premises (homes, offices, shops), and in institutions such as prisons. Their increase in usage over this time is probably due to the technology becoming more affordable, a belief that CCTV cameras would somehow 'deter' crime, and a wider shift toward usage of situational crime prevention measures generally on the part of individuals and organizations (see Garland, 2001).

CCTV is often thought of as being a form of situation crime prevention (SCP), following Clarke's (1995) classic classification of situational crime prevention techniques. Clarke identifies 'increasing the risk of detection' as one of the three main ways in which SCP can work. During the 1990s it was often presumed that the appearance of CCTV cameras in a place or area would 'deter' offenders from offending because of the offender's perception of the greatly increased risk of getting caught. Much of the research into CCTV during this time were evaluations of schemes (whether in a city centre, or certain shops or institutions), trying to establish whether schemes did indeed have such an effect; whether they were having no effect; whether they were instead merely 'displacing' criminal activity to other areas nearby lacking CCTV; or whether they were not only working but were also 'diffusing' benefits to other areas nearby lacking CCTV (Brown, 1995; Tilley, 1993; Ditton and Short, 1999). Research findings are mixed, but seem to suggest that in many cases CCTV schemes do not seem nearly as effective at crime reduction as their early proponents had hoped, and indeed research suggests that something as simple as improving street lighting may be more effective. It should be noted that a scheme's effectiveness may depend on various factors, and that effectiveness may vary over time. In a review of research on the effectiveness of the crime preventive effects of CCTV surveillance cameras, Welsh and Farrington found that studies 'showed that CCTV had a small but significant desirable effect on crime, has been most effective in reducing crime in car parks, has been most effective when targeted at vehicle crime ... and has been more effective in reducing crime in the U.K. than in North America'. They note too that greater public support 'for the use of CCTV cameras in public settings to prevent crime' has been found in the UK than has been found in North America (Welsh and Farrington, 2007: 204–5).

However, in addition to (or in place of) any deterrent effect achieved, a feature of CCTV surveillance is that even if it does not deter an offence, if the camera is pointing in the right direction and the video feed is being recorded then a visual record of the offence is made which could be used to apprehend the offender and/or secure conviction in a court. (Issues relating to (poor) image quality and recording quality seem likely to become less significant as technology improves; indeed, the latest systems feature digital recording.) During the commission of an offence, CCTV surveillance cameras may prove useful in coordinating police or security staff deployment, with a central operator able to radio staff on the ground as to the exact location(s) they should go, the nature of the offence(s), and the appearance of the offender(s). It may be that these applications of CCTV, involving their combination with recording and communications technologies, which lend them evidential and resource-allocation applications respectively, eventually take over as the 'justification' for CCTV. As McCahill (2002) shows, however, the cultural and organizational context is significant in shaping the ways in which CCTV systems are actually used and the ends to which the information they provide is actually put. Other researchers have pointed out that, in practice, CCTV may be used to target certain people or categories of person who are not necessarily offenders, such as the homeless or groups of young males, but who are perceived as (potentially) disorderly by CCTV operators and security staff.

Norris *et al.* (1998) raise a third possible way in which CCTV can be combined with other technologies, namely, the connecting of camera output to a computer running facial recognition software. The computer can attempt to match facial image data from CCTV live feeds with facial image data stored on a database of known individuals (known or suspected offenders, for example). The software uses techniques which in theory can match images even where an offender has sought to disguise themselves. A city-centre scheme using the technology is in use in Newham, East London. Norris *et al.* (1998) characterize such systems as 'algorithmic surveillance', and suggest that they represent an intensification of surveillance and a step toward intensified social control. It seems possible, however, that CCTV visual recognition systems will turn out to have one of two specific uses. The first is as a technical assistant to busy CCTV operators, flagging up 'known offenders' as they appear on a street. There are various possible objections to such practices, yet they may still become integrated into surveillance practices. A second role is likely to be as part of a biometric identity validation device, for entry control systems (such systems are presently being introduced at certain European airports, for restricted personnel areas, or at passenger security gates).

Two important aspects of the development of surveillance cameras seem likely to shape their usage over the next decade. The first is camera miniaturization, concealment, or ubiquity, leading to the increasing possibility of cameras recording private activities (whether such surveillance is being carried out lawfully or not). This is likely to have social ramifications as areas previously hidden from public view become more visible, with attendant social consequences (see also Goffman's (1990) distinction between 'back stage' and 'front stage' activities). Areas targeted by such 'surveillance' might include workplaces and residences, but also places such as police stations and prisons. A second (and related) aspect seems likely to be the connection of miniature video cameras to mobile communications devices, which becomes increasingly feasible as the connection speed of mobile data networks increases. Both aspects enable the surveillance of areas of social life that may already have been accessible but whose activities had previously been undocumented. Both developments have the potential to contribute to social change.

It is important to note that although in terms of CCTV applications, we are most familiar with city-centre CCTV schemes and with CCTV in and around private properties (offices, shops, homes, and so on), there are various other possible applications of CCTV in relation to crime control and criminal justice, not all of which can be described as involving 'surveillance'. Among these are the use of CCTV in prisons, on roads and motorways, in cashpoint machines as a check against bank and credit card fraud, in courts as a way of linking proceedings between remote sites, and in the custody suites in police stations. On this last topic, Newburn and Hayman (2002) conducted detailed sociological research on the effects of the introduction of CCTV in the custody suite in a police station in London, England. Their study shows how the roles the CCTV system performed were not always as had been anticipated, and that to understand CCTV's use and effects one needs to understand the social dynamics of the police custody suite itself. Such studies thus suggest that CCTV does not have some generic or intrinsic 'function', but rather that the uses to which it is put depend on various contingent local factors. Studying specific implementations of CCTV can also challenge the assumption that they have a particular 'function', or their introduction heralds the departure from established practices. Goold (2004: 212), for instance, studied policing practices in six towns in the South of England, and found that they 'did not change significantly as a result of the introduction of CCTV'. Neyland (2006) argues that the themes of 'privacy, surveillance and trust' can be used to guide exploration of emergent interactions between CCTV operator staff, police officers, and the public. Lastly, Smith (2007) shows how ethnographic study of CCTV control rooms can reveal how CCTV operators manage the emotional strains of their jobs through the creative construction of narrative to accompany the events they witness on screen.

Electronic monitoring of convicted offenders

Research into the possibility of 'electronically tagging' convicted offenders can be dated back to the early 1960s. In 1964, four Harvard University academics published an article on 'behavioural electronics', one of whom by 1970 had developed a prototype electronic system for tracking a person's movements within a city (Schwitzgebel *et al.*, 1964; Schwitzgebel, 1970). Bulky, cumbersome, and impractical, their device was essentially experimental. By 1982, however, the advent of the silicon chip permitted smaller electronic devices to be developed, and in the US a New Mexico judge is said to have pioneered the introduction of the electronic monitoring of convicted offenders as a feasible sentencing option for the courts (Nellis, 2005). The first time a person in England was electronically tagged in a criminal justice context was in 1989, when a man was granted bail on condition that he 'voluntarily agreed' to have a device attached to him (Lilly and Himan, 1993: 1). Various pieces of legislation were introduced by the then Conservative Government in the UK during the late 1980s and early 1990s. Tagging schemes were opposed on moral and ethical grounds by various groups. The Labour Government elected in 1997 has since sought to expand rather than contract such schemes, and opposition on political or ethical grounds to the electronic tagging of offenders, though still occasionally voiced, is presently much less pronounced.

In formal terms, from the 1980s through to today, courts and the law have presented the 'tagging' of offenders with electronic 'tags' not as a punishment in and of itself, but rather as a means by which compliance with a specific other penalty can be monitored. In the 1980s and 1990s, the most common application of the electronic monitoring of offenders was alongside a home detention curfew order. The 'first generation' of electronic tags do not have any capability of 'tracking' an individual tagged offender's movements as such. Rather, the limited range of the radio transmitter technology used in the tags—which is similar to that found in short-range (30 to 100 metres) domestic cordless telephones—is exploited to ensure that an individual is in fact at home in compliance with their home curfew order (which may be between 7 p.m. and 7 a.m., for example). The tag is attached to the offender after sentencing, usually in the form of a small plastic anklet in which the transmitter is encased, and a base unit is installed in the offender's home and connected to a dedicated telephone line. During the pre-arranged curfew hours, the base unit 'listens' out for an intermittent signal pulse transmitted by the anklet. As long as it hears the pulse, nothing happens. But if no pulse is detected—because the offender has moved out of the receiving range of the base unit, and hence must therefore no longer be at home—the base unit automatically dials a monitoring centre, which can then alert a member of their staff (or potentially a probation or police officer) and request they investigate the breach. Electronic monitoring using this technology has been implemented in a number of jurisdictions including England and Wales, Scotland, several US states, Canada, Sweden, New Zealand, and Australia (see Black and Smith, 2003; Scottish Executive, 2000). Courts in England and Wales seem to have been relatively reluctant to adopt electronically monitored curfew orders as an initial disposal, possibly because of uncertainty as to its severity as a punishment or its appropriateness for particular offences or offenders. In England and Wales today, many offenders being electronically monitored at any given moment are not in fact offenders whom a court has so sentenced, but are instead selected prisoners who have been granted early conditional release from their medium-term prison sentences, the conditions including that they must not re-offend and that they must abide by an electronically-monitored home detention curfew order for the remainder of the time that would have been their prison sentence duration (see Home Office, 2001). Many prisoners have now passed through this scheme.

While the electronic monitoring of offenders' compliance with a home detention curfew order is surveillance of sorts, it is also in certain respects only of a fairly limited kind. The above 'first generation' of tag does not 'know' the location of the tagged offender as such, merely whether they are or are not at home. Nor does it know what the offender is doing while they are at home, nor where they are or what they are doing during non-curfew hours. As such, and while this practice bears some relation to Foucauldian disciplinary surveillance, it also appears somewhat different in operation.

Recent years, however, have witnessed the emergence of a 'second generation' of electronic tags, which look set gradually to supersede and replace the first generation tags. These newer 'tracking' tags have been trialled in England and Wales and incorporate Global Positioning System (GPS) technology (Shute, 2007). The GPS technology enables the tag to identify its wearer's exact geographical location, and so can be used to monitor compliance not only with home curfew orders, but also with attendance or exclusion orders. Whilst the initial application of such tags is likely to be in monitoring compliance with such orders, it is not hard to see how these 'tracking tags' could in the future permit a far more continual and detailed form of surveillance. Advocates of such tags argue that a possible benefit of their implementation could be that they could provide additional geographical evidence linking the tagged offender with any subsequent offences (or indeed exonerating them of these offences), and that they might provide further reassurance to the public while contributing to a reduction in reliance on custodial sentences. Critics argue that, as with the earlier tags, tagging by itself does nothing meaningful by way of addressing an offender's offending behaviour; and that the continual, detailed geographical monitoring of a person's movements (even those of a convicted offender), is a worrying development within liberal democratic societies. However, this argument is less compelling where the alternative to such electronic monitoring of curfew/attendance/exclusion orders is a prison sentence, which would seem to be even more restrictive in terms of curtailment of freedom of movement and privacy; and quite possibly less likely to command public support when it becomes common for consumer devices such as mobile phones to feature position-locating technologies.

Internet surveillance

Internet 'surveillance' can take many forms, but arguably can be reduced to one of two main types. The first type involves gathering information about a specific user. The second type, on the other hand, involves gathering aggregate data about a large group of Internet users (for example, all visitors to a particular website) in search of patterns or time trends. Surveillance of the first kind (a specific user's Internet usage) might be carried out, for example, by an employer who suspects an employee of improper Internet usage, or of betraying commercial secrets to a rival company. Internet surveillance of an individual might also be carried out by the police (for example, investigating an individual suspected of downloading or trading in computer images of child pornography), or indeed by State intelligence agencies seeking to gather information on a specific individual's or group's communications, activities, or associates. Monitoring of groups of people's usage of the Internet, on the other hand, might be conducted by a website administrator, an Internet Service Provider interested in patterns of usage by their customers, or by a computer security chief tracking the changing methods used by the many hackers trying to hack into their organization's network.

Surveillance of individual Internet users might be carried out by a company or institution simply by examining log files routinely generated by network servers, which record which user logged on from which computer, at what time, and for how long; by examining server or router logs which may reveal which websites an individual visited; or email servers to establish what emails a user has sent, when, to whom, and what information these contained (Casey, 2004). In addition, considerable information may be obtained by examining the hard disc drive of a specific computer or, alternatively, by capturing a copy of network traffic as it passes through a network. Additional means of tracking an individual user's computing activities include keystroke monitors; spyware installed on the computer; and remote screen-view software, enabling remote viewing of an individual's computer screen in real time. Most computer activities leave an electronic 'trace' of some sort, on a hard disc or on a network server, or both, and network activity is usually traceable back to specific network addresses and ultimately back to specific computers. However, as with all forms of surveillance, the more knowledgeable the person (potentially) under surveillance is about the surveillance practices likely to be used against them, the more strategies they can employ to try to evade surveillance.

In practice, much 'surveillance' of employees' Internet usage is likely to remain at a general background level, at least until a case of improper Internet usage comes to the attention of someone in computing security, company management, or law enforce-ment. Their attention may be drawn by a complaint from someone within or outside their company; by the police; by a routine sweep of log files by a computing officer look-ing for suspect sites visited or files downloaded; or by a piece of monitoring software set to run in the background on a network, looking out for certain suspicious network activity. When one of these events alerts an organization to a potential problem, they can then proceed with a forensic investigation in search of data, which may or may not involve ongoing surveillance of particular users or computers.

Schafer (2006) has drawn attention to a potential development in Internet surveil-lance, namely that Internet surveillance could in the future theoretically be conducted not by humans but by 'autonomous agent' computer programs. In short, software pro-grams could be designed to traverse the Internet in search of wrongdoing. An interesting aspect of such programs is their potential for autonomous decision-making, following certain rules (such as the law of evidence) and/or their own acquired knowledge (in the case of artificial intelligence (AI) systems).

Surveillance of wireless communications

Wireless communications can be voice or data transmissions, and can be done over vari-ous systems, such as mobile cellular telephones, wireless Internet connections ('WiFi'), short-range wireless connection technologies such as 'Bluetooth', miniature radio tags such as RFIDs, or microwave or satellite links. In many respects, the surveillance of wireless communications is conceptually no different to the surveillance of telephone data, or other landline telecommunications. Nevertheless, there are certain differences between landline and wireless communications. The first is that wireless communica-tions involve the broadcasting of data (even if this is very low power and hence over a very short range), and as such it has a certain intrinsic 'openness' leaving it susceptible to eavesdropping. With wireless communications of all kinds likely to become ever more ubiquitous, this would seem to present various additional opportunities for communica-tions to be subjected to surveillance. The second is that wireless communications may be used to track a person's location (see above). Thirdly, because wireless communication enables mobility, surveillance of wireless communications potentially allows for surveil-lance of mobile individuals.

A form of surveillance of sorts is presently emerging in respect of the tagging of goods in retail stores using miniature identifier tags. These tags potentially can be concealed within a product's packaging or indeed within the product itself. These RFID (Radio Frequency Identification) tags transmit data which identify such things as exact details of the product (which might be anything from a carton of milk, or a pair of shoes, to a pallet of goods), its price, and the name of the retail store or warehouse in question. RFID tags have a short detection range, but the 'active' type has a range sufficient for a store to use the tags' movements in order quickly to calculate the total price of a basket of groceries at a supermarket; to track points of interest for marketers such as which goods are picked up, examined, but ultimately put back on the shelves by consumers; and as a means of combating shoplifting, the idea being that the tiny tags are hard to find and remove. Because of their tiny size, the fact that a person may not be aware they are carrying RFID tags about their person, and because RFID readers can operate without being seen, their use has potential surveillance applications, but also implications for privacy and data protection.

Other technologies used in surveillance

The above represent just some of the many different surveillance (and related) technologies in use today. A few additional types are worth mentioning. Geographic information system (GIS) technologies—essentially, computerized mapping—can be used in conjunction with geographic location technologies such as Global Positioning System (GPS) technology, or mobile phone handset positioning using signal triangulation. GIS technologies offer a convenient and powerful way of storing, manipulating, and visualizing positional data. Satellite imagery can further enhance geographic visualization. As more commercial applications for real-time positional data are found, and as more consumer devices become positionally locatable or positionally aware, it will become increasingly possible for surveillance of the locations of individuals, vehicles, and goods to be conducted for commercial or crime control purposes (see Monmonier, 2002).

Another surveillance technology worth mentioning briefly, not least because of its likely expansion over the coming years, is the biometric sensor (see Lyon, 2001: Chapter 5; Van der Ploeg, 2003; Franko Aas, 2006). Biometric sensors can be used in conjunction with a smart card in order to authenticate a person (in place of a PIN code, for example); or can be compared with data stored on a remote computer database in order to identify individuals. Such sensors work by obtaining various measurements of biological features unique to each individual, such as iris pattern, fingerprint, or handprint, and comparing this data to previously recorded data of the same type. An increasingly common application for biometric devices is as part of access control systems, such as for airport check-in, at immigration desks, office entry systems, or in order to log on to a computer. However, as with any such access control information, the information about who has passed through the access control could be used for surveillance purposes, either of a generalized kind (aggregate information) or for conducting surveillance of a specific individual. The difference between biometric access control systems and other types (such as using passwords, identity documents, or electronic cards) is that it is much harder for an individual to use a false identity. A separate type of technology that measures aspects of a person's body is the drug or alcohol test. Whereas biometrics measures bodily characteristics that remain the same over time, drug and alcohol tests can be used as a form of surveillance of a person's recent use of drugs or alcohol, or of their medical condition. Alcohol 'breathalysers' have been used for several decades in countries around the world, principally in the area of motoring, though they appear increasingly to be used in other areas of transportation, such as to ensure that airline pilots are not intoxicated prior to flight. Drug testing of arrestees at police stations is another application of such testing technology, in this case principally in order to try to gather data on patterns and trends in illegal drug use among the arrestee population.

The 'architecture' of surveillance and monitoring

In this section, I will present my own interpretation of surveillance practices and technologies, and in so doing attempt to contribute to existing theoretical models of surveillance.

Table 23.1 is an attempt at a typology of different kinds of surveillance. The aim of the typology is to distinguish between the various different types of surveillance discussed in this chapter, and to help compare and contrast between them. (Incidentally, the typology can be applied both to surveillance in the real world and on the Internet (one can imagine

Table 23.1 A typology of surveillance

By whom	Of whom or what	Overt or covert	Method	Comments
1. Intelligence agencies	Political or criminal threats to state security	Covert	Human and/or technological	
2. Law enforcement agencies	Suspected (serious) criminals	Covert	Human and/or technological	
3. Employers, private detectives, individuals	Specific individuals suspected of wrongdoing	Covert	Human and/or technological	
4. Public sector staff or private sector management	Institutionalized or employees	Overt	Mostly human, some technology	Foucauldian surveillance, 'discipline'
5. Guardians of places, people, or things	A place, person(s), or thing(s)	Overt, but may be covert	Human and/or technological	Police, neighbourhood watch, private security guards, CCTV, 'tags'
6. Anyone	Behaviour of family, friends, workers, public	Overt	Human	Informal social control

each of the types in the context of the Internet) and thus provides us with a model for studying surveillance on the Internet generally.) The typology draws attention to the range of different targets, aims, and forms of surveillance that exist, and can be useful for thinking about the differences between different types of surveillance. Despite these differences, are there particular characteristics that all forms of surveillance share?

One possible characteristic of surveillance is that it is imposed on people, since, given the choice, most people would prefer not to be under surveillance. Imposition is not unique to surveillance (it is also characteristic of penal sanctions, for example), but is nevertheless useful to consider. Indeed, it is possible that it is precisely the 'inescapability' of surveillance and the compliance with surveillance so demanded that lends surveillance its peculiar quality, and one that many people find so objectionable. There are many reasons why a person may not wish to be subjected to surveillance (for example, loss of privacy, autonomy, trust, or control) and may thus actively resist or seek to subvert it. Given this, we can see that to be effective, surveillance needs to ensure it is not easily defeated by the person(s) being targeted; it needs to be difficult to counter, otherwise it is likely to be ineffective. Two classic ways in which surveillance may attempt to do this are by acting covertly (since it is harder to counter surveillance if one is unaware that one is under surveillance); or conversely, by acting very overtly, for example by an ever-present supervisor or prison warden (and which seems to derive its power more from a form of intimidation). There may, therefore, be a linkage between surveillance studies and the study of compliance in the context of criminal justice. Bottoms (2001) has pioneered work on the topic of compliance and criminal justice sanctions, and has distinguished between various ways in which compliance can be sought, including threats of penalties for non-compliance, affective attachment, perceived legitimacy, and others. Conceptually related research includes that on situational crime prevention (Cornish and Clarke, 2003), and on the regulation of the Internet (Lessig, 2006). Although of likely relevance to the study of surveillance, there is insufficient space here to explore all the various social mechanisms at play in surveillance, so I will focus on just one, namely a compliance mode that Bottoms terms 'constraint-based compliance' and which I term 'architectural' (following Lessig, 2006). The particular aspect of interest of the architectural/constraint mode of compliance is that it refers to the 'designing in' of features or systems such that (in theory, anyhow) a person has no choice but to comply. The architectural mode typically exploits physical, real-world properties, or virtual, software properties in order to try to ensure compliance.

On reflection, we can see that the exploitation of physical properties lies at the very heart of surveillance. Human surveillance is based on proximity, lines of sight, observation, or hearing what another is saying. Foucault's disciplinary surveillance is centrally concerned with the observable, with the capacity of the human body to be trained, and with physical segregation and isolation; and in the figure of the Panopticon we find Bentham's ingenious exploitation of architecture and optics, such that the central prison official can see all the prisoners but not vice versa. More recently, we can see that biometric sensors exploit certain unique identifiers of our bodies and our inability to escape from our given body; CCTV cameras exploit optics, but are also themselves constrained by lines of sight; contemporary telephone surveillance can exploit features of digital telephone exchanges to obtain lists of numbers dialled and calls received, and can make electronic recordings of calls; websites can use information automatically received by the web server about each visitor to the website to identify the approximate geographical location of the visitor; RFID tags offer an architectural solution to the problem of keeping track of moveable goods; and lastly, the covert surveillance practices of types 1–3 in the typology rely on their hidden nature to obtain information. However, resistance to surveillance also typically exploits physical properties and the limits of the surveillance practice in question, as in the case of political activists or criminals concealing their identity from CCTV cameras by the simple device of wearing a mask, a cap, or a hood.

As Lessig (2006) notes, governments or hardware and software manufacturers sometimes try to 'design in' user restrictions or surveillance features in relation to computer, electronic, or network systems. The concept of architecture is useful here, because, as Lessig explains, what may appear merely a technical question of system design often (intentionally or unintentionally) masks political and social choices and the implementation of certain preferred social and political values. This sometimes happens without any prior public debate. (Lessig offers the example of user anonymity in online forums; anonymity may encourage freedom of speech but also facilitate anti-social behaviours (verbal attacks on other users, or hate speech), whereas denying anonymity may restrict anti-social behaviour but also inhibit freedom of expression.) An implication of this is that it is important to recognize that architecture and constraint-based compliance systems are not homogeneous, but are instead quite diverse, and that society has a choice as to what *sort* of architectures it wants for its surveillance systems. Moreover, although architectures constrain, they also always simultaneously enable certain practices. In the case of surveillance architectures, the least objectionable of them today may be those technologies that are sufficiently effective while remaining as unobtrusive, uninvasive, and speedy as possible. Where surveillance does not achieve these qualities, it seems more likely to be resented or even actively resisted (possibly also by 'architectural' means).

In summary then, the concept of 'architecture' provides a way of analysing both how surveillance works (and in particular its technological dimension, the way it utilizes physical or virtual properties) and what its limits may be. The architectural dimension is nevertheless just one aspect of surveillance and other dimensions such as social norms, law, and market forces are also important. Finally, the concept of architecture is useful because it also helps draw attention to the relationship between technical design and political values.

REVIEW QUESTIONS

1 Identify three different surveillance technologies (for example, CCTV cameras). In relations to the typology, by whom would you say could each technology be used?

2 Why and how might people resist surveillance systems? Under what circumstances, or in what forms, do you think people are likely to find surveillance more acceptable?

CONCLUSION

This chapter has covered a number of topics, including definitions of surveillance and monitoring, some key theoretical models, and some particular contemporary technologies of surveillance and monitoring. Foucault's theoretical work on disciplinary surveillance remains influential, but his critique of surveillance was originally directed not so much at the 'Big Brother' State, as at our everyday institutions and at social science itself. Critical (civil libertarian, or Marxist) approaches to surveillance technologies importantly emphasize the political abuses to which these technologies could be put. Today, we are faced with a plethora of technologies (and with new technologies emerging all the time) whose applications vary widely—from intentional, covert surveillance at one extreme, to CCTV cameras in shops, through to systems whose everyday applications may not really have been designed for surveillance purposes at all but which could possibly be put to such ends (for example, entrance swipe cards or RFID chips in retail products). Many normative issues about surveillance ultimately return to questions of security, trust, convenience, and privacy; while accounts of the actual operation of surveillance frequently return to the study of law, social norms, commerce, and technology.

QUESTIONS FOR DISCUSSION

1 What is Michel Foucault's contribution to the study of surveillance, and what are the similarities and differences between his approach and that of Marxists?

2 What are some of the different types of surveillance that could be carried out? What sort of technologies could this surveillance use and what information would these technologies help gather?

3 Compare and contrast surveillance carried out directly by people, with that conducted using technology. From the point of view of the person or organization conducting the surveillance, what are the strengths and weaknesses of the two?

4 How should society balance surveillance and privacy?

5 Why might someone try to resist surveillance, and how might they try to do this?

GUIDE TO FURTHER READING

Bogard, W. (1996) *The Simulation of Surveillance: Hypercontrol in Telematic Societies*. Cambridge: Cambridge University Press.
A suggestive postmodern exploration of contemporary and future surveillance.

Foucault, M. (1979) *Discipline and Punish: The Birth of the Prison*. London: Penguin.
While primarily concerned with punishment, and not always an easy read, this book nevertheless remains an essential part of the repertoire for anyone interested in surveillance. See especially centre illustrative plates, pp. 3–8, Parts 3.2, 3.3, and 4.3.

Lyon, D. (2007) *Surveillance Studies: An Overview*. Cambridge: Polity Press.
An excellent introduction and overview of contemporary surveillance theories, technologies, and issues.

WEB LINKS

http://www.queensu.ca/sociology/Surveillance/

The Surveillance Project. Run by David Lyon and colleagues at the sociology department of the Queen's University, Canada.

http://www.surveillance-and-society.org

Surveillance and Society. Online surveillance studies journal.

http://www.liberty-human-rights.org.uk

Liberty. Website of a leading UK civil liberties pressure group. Includes information on their privacy concerns regarding various surveillance policies and technologies.

http://www.wired.com

Wired. US-based magazine containing a wide range of news stories and features on the latest technological developments, including cultural, governmental, and privacy issues.

http://www.homeoffice.gov.uk

Home Office. Website of a UK ministry responsible for dealing with crime, policing, criminal justice, counterterrorism, and immigration.

REFERENCES

Barry, A., Osborne, T., and Rose, N. (eds) (1996) *Foucault and Political Reason: Liberalism, Neo-Liberalism and Governmentality.* London: UCL Press.

Baudrillard, J. (1983) *Simulations* [aka 'Simulacra and Simulations']. New York: Semiotext(e).

Baudrillard, J. (1987) *Forget Foucault.* New York: Semiotext(e).

Baudrillard, J. (1993) *Symbolic Exchange and Death.* London: Sage.

Black, M. and Smith, R.G. (2003) 'Electronic Monitoring in the Criminal Justice System', Trends and Issues in Crime and Criminal Justice No. 254. Canberra: Australian Institute of Criminology.

Bogard, W. (1996) *The Simulation of Surveillance: Hypercontrol in Telematic Societies.* Cambridge: Cambridge University Press.

Bottoms, A.E. (2001). 'Compliance and community penalties', in A.E. Bottoms, L. Gelsthorpe, and S. Rex (eds) *Community Penalties: Change and Challenges.* Cullompton: Willan.

Brown, B. (1995) *CCTV in Town Centres: Three case studies* (Crime Detection and Prevention Series: Paper 68). London: Home Office, Police Department.

Casey, E. (2004) *Digital Evidence and Computer Crime* (2nd edn). London: Academic Press.

Clarke, R.V. (1995). 'Situational crime prevention', in M. Tonry and D. Farrington (eds) *Building a Safer Society: Crime and Justice: A Review of Research,* Vol. 19. Chicago: University of Chicago Press.

Cohen, S. (1985) *Visions of Social Control: Crime, Punishment and Classification.* Cambridge: Polity.

Cohen, S. and Scull, A. (eds) (1983) *Social Control and the State.* Oxford: Martin Robertson.

Cornish, D. and Clarke, R.V. (2003). 'Opportunities, Precipitators and Criminal Decisions: A Reply to Wortley's Critique of Situational Crime Prevention', in M. Smith and D. Cornish (eds) *Theory for Practice in Situational Crime Prevention.* Cullompton, UK: Willan Publishing.

Deleuze, G. (1995) 'Postscript on control societies', in *Negotiations: 1972–1990.* New York: Columbia University Press.

Ditton, J. and Short, E. (1999) 'Yes, it works—no, it doesn't: Comparing the effects of open-street CCTV in two adjacent town centres', *Crime Prevention Studies,* Vol. 10: 201–23.

Dreyfus, H. and Rabinow, P. (1982) *Michel Foucault: Beyond Structuralism and Hermeneutics.* Hemel Hempstead: Harvester Wheatsheaf.

Feeley, M. and Simon, J. (1992) 'The New Penology: Notes on the Emerging Strategy of Corrections and its Implications', *Criminology,* Vol. 30 (4): 449–74.

Feeley, M. and Simon, J. (1994) 'Actuarial justice: the emerging new criminal law', in D. Nelken (ed) *The Futures of Criminology*. London: Sage.

Foucault, M. (1979) *Discipline and Punish: The Birth of the Prison*. London: Penguin.

Foucault, M. (1991) 'Governmentality' in G. Burchell, C. Gordan and P. Miller (eds) *The Foucault Effect: Studies in Governmentality*. Hemel Hempstead: Harvester Wheatsheaf.

Franko Aas, K. (2006) '"The body does not lie": Identity, risk and trust in technoculture', *Crime, Media, Culture*, Vol. 2(2): 143–158.

Franko Aas, K. (2007) 'Analysing a world in motion: Global flows meet "criminology of the other"', *Theoretical Criminology*, Vol. 11(2): 283–303.

Garland, D. (1985) *Punishment and Welfare: A History of Penal Strategies*. Aldershot: Gower.

Garland, D. (1990) *Punishment and Modern Society: A Study in Social Theory*. Oxford: Clarendon.

Garland, D. (1997) '"Governmentality" and the Problem of Crime: Foucault, Criminology, Sociology', *Theoretical Criminology*, 1(2): 173–214.

Garland, D. (2001) *The Culture of Control: Crime and Social Order in Contemporary Society*. Oxford: Oxford University Press.

Goffman, E. (1990) *The Presentation of Self in Everyday Life*. London: Penguin.

Goold, B. (2004) *CCTV and Policing*. Oxford: Oxford University Press.

Goold, B. (2007) 'Privacy, Identity and Security' in B. Goold and L. Lazarus (eds) *Security and Human Rights*. Oxford: Hart Publishing.

Gordon, C. (ed) (1980) *Power/Knowledge: Selected Interviews and Other Writings*. Hemel Hempstead: Harvester Wheatsheaf.

Haggerty, K. and Ericson, R.V. (2000) 'The surveillant assemblage', *British Journal of Sociology*, 51 (4): 605–22.

Haggerty, K. and Ericson, R.V. (eds) (2006) *The New Politics of Surveillance and Visibility*. Toronto: University of Toronto Press.

Home Office (2001) *Electronic monitoring of released prisoners: an evaluation of the Home Detention Curfew scheme: Home Office Research Studies 222*. London: Home Office.

Jones, R. (2000) 'Digital Rule: Punishment, Control and Technology', *Punishment and Society*, 2 (1): 5–22.

Lessig, L. (2006). *Code: Version 2.0*. New York, NY: Basic Books.

Lilly, J.R. and Himan, J. (eds), (1993). The Electronic Monitoring of Offenders: Symposium Papers, Second Series. Leicester: De Montfort University Law School Monographs.

Lyon, D. (1993) 'An Electronic Panopticon? A Sociological Critique of Surveillance Theory', *Sociological Review*, 41 (4): 653.

Lyon, D. (1994) *The Electronic Eye: The Rise of Surveillance Society*. Cambridge: Polity.

Lyon, D. (2001) *Surveillance Society: Monitoring Everyday Life*. Buckingham: Open University Press.

Lyon, D. (2003) *Surveillance after September 11*. Cambridge: Polity Press.

Lyon, D. (2003) 'Surveillance as social sorting: Computer codes and mobile bodies' in D. Lyon (ed) *Surveillance as Social Sorting: Privacy, Risk and Digital Discrimination*. London: Routledge.

Lyon, D. (ed) (2006) *Theorizing Surveillance: The panopticon and beyond*. Cullompton: Willan Publishing.

Lyon, D. (2007) *Surveillance Studies: An Overview*. Cambridge: Polity Press.

McCahill, M. (2002) *The Surveillance Web: The rise of visual surveillance in an English city*. Cullompton: Willan Publishing.

Monahan, T. (ed) (2006) *Surveillance and Security: Technological Politics and Power in Everyday Life*. New York: Routledge.

Monmonier, M. (2002) *Spying with Maps: Surveillance technologies and the future of privacy*. Chicago: Chicago University Press.

Nellis, M. (2005) 'Out of this World: The Advent of the Satellite Tracking of Offenders in England and Wales', *The Howard Journal*, Vol. 44(2): 125–150.

Newburn, T. and Hayman, S. (2002) *Policing, Surveillance and Social Control*. Cullompton: Willan Publishing.

Neyland, D. (2006) *Privacy, Surveillance and Public Trust*. Basingstoke: Palgrave Macmillan.

Norris, C., Moran, J., and Armstrong, G. (1998) 'Algorithmic surveillance—The future of automated visual surveillance', in C. Norris, J. Moran, and G. Armstrong (eds) *Surveillance, Closed Circuit Television and Social Control*. Aldershot: Ashgate.

Rusche, G. and Kirchheimer, O. (1968) *Punishment and Social Structure*. New York: Russell & Russell.

Schafer, B. (2006) 'The Taming of the Sleuth—Problems and Potential of Autonomous Agents in Crime Investigation and Prosecution', *International Review of Law Computers and Technology*, Vol. 20 (1&2: 63–76).

Schwitzgebel, R.K. (1970) 'Behavioral Electronics Could Empty the World's Prisons', *The Futurist*, April 1970: 59–60.

Schwitzgebel, R.K., Schwitzgebel, R., Pahnker, W., and Hord, W. (1964) 'A Program of Research in Behavioral Electronics', *Behavioral Electronics*, 9: 233–8.

Scottish Executive (2000) *Tagging Offenders: The Role Of Electronic Monitoring In The Scottish Criminal Justice System* (Consultation paper). Edinburgh: Scottish Executive.

Shute, S. (2007) *Satellite Tracking of Offenders: A Study of the Pilots in England and Wales* (Research Summary 4). London: Ministry of Justice.

Simon, J. (1988) 'The Ideological Effects of Actuarial Practice', *Law and Society Review*, 22: 772–800.

Smith, G. (2007), 'Exploring Relations between Watchers and Watched in Control (led) Systems: Strategies and Tactics', *Surveillance & Society*, Vol. 4(4): 280–313.

Sumner, C. (ed) (1990). *Censure, Politics and Criminal Justice*. Buckingham: Open University Press.

Tilley, N. (1993). *Understanding Car Parks, Crime and CCTV: Evaluation Lesson from Safer Cities* (Crime Prevention Unit: Paper 42). London: Home Office.

Van der Ploeg, I. (2003). 'Biometrics and the body as information', in D. Lyon (ed) *Surveillance as Social Sorting*. London: Routledge.

Welsh, B. and Farrington, D. (2007). 'Closed-Circuit Television Surveillance', in B. Welsh and D. Farrington (eds), *Preventing Crime: What Works for Children Offenders, Victims and Places*. New York: Springer.

Zureik, E. and Salter, M. (eds) (2005) *Global Surveillance and Policing: Borders, Security, Identity*. Cullompton: Willan Publishing.

24 'Victims'

Brian Williams[1]

INTRODUCTION

This chapter introduces the reader to the study of victims of crime and to the political and social changes which have brought victims increasingly to the centre of debates about crime. Academic research has helped to change our understanding of victimization, assisted by the insights and pressure of a growing victims' movement. The criminal justice system has itself gradually changed to reflect increased understanding of victims' needs, and they have been accorded greater entitlements and rights—at least on paper. Some of the difficulties which prevent victims from taking up these rights are considered, and the effectiveness of particular approaches to meeting victims' needs in different countries is discussed. The greater centrality of victim issues is not necessarily reflected in greater sensitivity on the part of politicians or criminal justice practitioners, and the links between policies and practice are considered.

BACKGROUND

The academic study of victims of crime is a comparatively recent phenomenon, and the importance of victimology as a discipline has increased along with the growing social and political attention to issues of criminal victimization and how the criminal justice system should respond to victims. Since the 1970s, at first in North America and then elsewhere, the emergence of a vocal victims' movement has helped to increase the momentum for change in criminal justice policies affecting victims. In turn, this has increased the demand for research and knowledge about the effects of crime upon victims and the best ways of responding to their needs.

However, the first systematic study of victims was in the late 1940s, and its approach was extremely influential. It sought to understand the victimization process by examining the relationships between victims and offenders and classifying victims according to the degree to which they could be regarded as 'prone' to victimization (von Hentig, 1948). This attempt to produce a typology of victimization was emulated by a number of subsequent studies which tried to place victims on a spectrum from the randomly chosen to those who in some way helped to precipitate the crime (Mendelsohn, 1956; Wolfgang, 1958; Amir, 1971; Gottfredson, 1984). In the process, the authors of these studies were perpetuating the idea that there are 'innocent' victims and others who—to a greater or lesser extent—contribute to their own victimization (Elias, 1993). Politicians, policy makers, and criminal justice practitioners based their beliefs about victims on an understanding that there was a spectrum of blameworthiness, with some types of victims less deserving of credence and support than others.

It was only with the increasing influence of feminist criminologists that this stereotype (or ideal type) was challenged as a form of victim-blaming (see Mawby and Walklate, 1994; Williams, 1999). The early victimological studies used questionable research methods (often not involving any direct contact with victims themselves) and in many cases it was not difficult for critical criminologists from the 1970s onwards to challenge them on an intellectual level (Temkin, 1987; Radford, 2001). The damage in terms of the social and political influence of their publications had already been done, however, and there remains work for criminologists to do in terms of challenging commonsense beliefs about victims ('if you drive a Vauxhall Astra, it's bound to get stolen'; 'this fire seems suspicious—was it an insurance job?'; 'she asked for it, going out dressed like that').

This is not to deny that commonsense beliefs may have some foundation in reality, but rather to suggest that often they may not have the explanatory power necessary to justify giving them greater credence than hard evidence. The Vauxhall Astra *is* a relatively easy car to steal, but being told this does little to help the person reporting its theft, and may make her feel that the police are blaming her for her own victimization (Curry *et al.*, 2004). Perhaps the manufacturers should do something about the car's security systems. People undoubtedly do set fire to unsuccessful businesses in order to escape their debts, but this is not the only possible explanation for a pub catching fire, and the residents who narrowly escape a fire may not take kindly to being treated as arson suspects. The concept of 'contributory negligence', based upon a belief that women can provoke men to rape them by dressing in particular ways, depends upon particular beliefs about male sexuality which are not justified by the facts (Mullender, 1996; Kennedy, 1993). It also ignores the power dynamics involved—and this is a common theme in the more recent victimological writing which questions victim-blaming approaches and links them to hate crime against, for example, black people, people with disabilities, and lesbian and gay people (Bowling, 1998; Shakespeare, 1996; Moran, 2001). For women, too, issues of power are central in relation to the criminal justice system. As senior barrister Helena Kennedy put it in the context of defence lawyers' tactics sometimes used in the case of 'domestic' murders by men (1993: 69), 'within the male stronghold of the court it is all too easy to create the feeling that a women had it coming to her'.

The academic and policy challenges posed by the women's movement (and subsequently by campaigns against other forms of discrimination) led to a number of different approaches to studying victims of crime. Rather than relying heavily upon statistics and case records compiled by criminal justice agencies, as the early victimologists did, researchers began to ask victims themselves about what had happened. This occurred both in the form of victim surveys (on local, national, and international levels), and in a change of approach towards research methods which increasingly relied upon victims' own detailed accounts. Thus, victimology began to embrace both large scale empirical work aimed at producing reliable statistics on the prevalence and distribution of victimization, and smaller scale qualitative work which tried to hear and understand victims' experiences (for examples of survey methodology see Koffman, 1996; O'Mahony *et al.*, 2000; Kershaw *et al.*, 2001; MVA Consultancy, 2000; van Dijk, 2000; for qualitative studies see for example Boswell, 1999; Bowling, 1998; Temkin, 2002; Curry *et al.*, 2004). In the process, questions began to be raised about whether some people who had suffered criminal victimization were ever officially defined as victims, and about the processes which led to the systematic exclusion of some types of victims from the statistics. Where particular offences are less likely to be reported, there is a larger 'dark figure' of victims as well as of offenders. Some offences which are not generally accepted as such are particularly unlikely to yield large numbers of victims seeking help (obvious examples being so-called domestic violence, crimes committed against residents of institutions, and crimes with victims with difficulties in expressing their views, for example people with severe learning difficulties or communication problems). Increasingly in the UK, research since the 1990s has also taken the form of evaluative studies assessing the impact of criminal justice policies and practices on victims and the effectiveness of particular forms of victim services.

In the UK, the initial move in the late 1970s towards crime surveys which took victims' perceptions seriously was largely motivated by local government concerns about fear of crime and the concentration of some types of crime in poorer areas (see Williams, 1999: 47–8; Zedner, 2002: 421–5), as well as a desire to bring 'hidden' crime such as violence within the home out into the open. Crime surveys made a major contribution to increasing awareness of the real risks of criminal victimization, and they also had an impact upon the ways in which academic research was subsequently done (as had happened earlier in the USA). More recently, an international crime victimization survey has made it much easier to make reasonably valid comparisons between countries (van Dijk, 2000). Increasingly, victim surveys include questions about victims' views on the treatment they receive at the hands of the criminal justice system as well as their victimization rates. Survey methodology is usually designed to reveal unreported crimes as well as more obvious offences, which is important in increasing understanding of the consequences of crime, given that the criminal justice system largely ignores victims who do not come forward for assistance. (The great majority of referrals to victim support agencies come via the police, who clearly cannot refer people for assistance if crimes go unreported.)

As legislation and policies make greater demands upon the criminal justice and related professions in terms of how they deal with victims of crime, research attention has increasingly turned to service delivery and victims' perceptions of the ways in which they are treated. Impassioned debates are taking place about such issues as:

- the effectiveness of Victim Impact Statements (Victim Personal Statements in England and Wales) in meeting victims' need to make their views known to sentencers (see for example Erez and Rogers, 1999; Sanders *et al.*, 2001);

- the possible dangers and benefits of restricting defendants' right to cross-examine alleged rape victims in court (see for example Temkin, 2002);

- the benefits and pitfalls of restorative justice, which involves victims and offenders in direct contact or indirect discussion of how best to resolve the problems caused by a crime (see for example Johnstone, 2002; Home Office, 2003);

- how much, if anything, victims should be told about the sentencing and subsequent treatment of 'their' offender, and how much help criminal justice agencies should provide to victims in the process of eliciting their views (see for example, Williams, 2002, 2005; Newton, 2003).

These debates and the extent to which research into victims' needs and views inform them, demonstrate the relevance and the applied nature of much recent victimological research. This chapter now turns to consider the needs of victims of crime and the extent to which the criminal justice system has responded appropriately in its increasing anxiety to be seen to meet such needs.

REVIEW QUESTIONS

1 In what ways did the early development of academic victimology impact upon attitudes to and policy about victims of crime?

2 How did the rise of the women's movement and of an organized victims' movements alter the academic approach to the study of victims in the 1970s?

3 Are some victims guilty of 'contributory negligence', bringing their victimization upon themselves by their own behaviour or status?

The reactions and needs of victims of crime

Individual victims experience crime in very different ways, and this is an important consideration when it comes to meeting their needs within the framework of criminal justice. A 'one size fits all' approach is unlikely to succeed. However, criminal justice agencies are not necessarily very good at responding flexibly to individual needs.

Some victims—particularly in serious cases—will be sufficiently traumatized by what has happened to them that they need expert help. This is a small minority of cases, but the system has found such needs hard to accommodate. In cases where a victim is in need of psychiatric treatment or counselling before the trial of the accused takes place, it has only recently been agreed in England and Wales that the victim's needs should take priority even if this puts the prosecution at risk. After sentencing, victims in more serious cases are routinely put in touch with Victim Support and (less systematically) with other agencies which may be able to help them such as Rape Crisis, the NSPCC, and Women's Aid (Newton, 2003). There is, however, a degree of selectivity on the part of the police in some parts of the country in relation to which types of victims' details are passed on to the helping agencies (Spackman, 2000: 19). This means that victims only receive services if they are aware of their existence and have the confidence to make contact with the agencies concerned. In many cases, particularly less serious ones, victims do not need specialist help of this kind, but they may still welcome the opportunity to give vent to their feelings with a neutral person: those who are closest to the victim may quickly tire of discussing an incident repeatedly, and an independent person such as a Victim Support volunteer can provide a welcome listening ear.

There is a good deal of research evidence that victims of crime benefit from being kept informed about the progress of the criminal cases in which they are involved, and that failure to provide this information can make life more difficult for them (Mawby and Walklate, 1994; Tudor, 2002). Since the early 1990s, the probation service has been responsible for giving victims of serious crime in England and Wales a choice about whether they wish to be kept informed about the outcomes of their cases, and, where an offender is sentenced to custody, about the subsequent treatment and eventual release of the person concerned. Since 2000, this has applied to all cases in which the offender is sentenced to 12 months or more in custody, and after some teething problems the requirement is now being implemented successfully in the great majority of cases (HMIP, 2003). Particularly where the shorter sentences are concerned, rates of take-up of the offer of information are lower than might be expected, however—and male victims are much less likely to make contact with the probation service than their female counterparts (Newton, 2003). Since the introduction of the Domestic Violence, Crime and Victims Act of 2004 this service has now been extended so that it is open to victims of mentally disordered offenders who were not previously eligible.

In more general terms, it is clear that victims feel better about the criminal justice system when its agencies have made serious efforts to keep them properly informed, and they are correspondingly dissatisfied when this is not done (Reeves and Mulley, 2000;

Curry *et al.*, 2004). Victims are often having their first contact with the criminal justice system, and hardened professionals who are familiar with its workings need to bear this in mind (but do not always do so).

Reactions to victimization may include seemingly irrational responses such as guilt and shame: helping agencies can often assist by providing reassurance that such reactions are not unusual. Victims may also benefit from an opportunity to express their anger, anxiety, or depression in a safe environment.

A frequently expressed, and hardly unreasonable, desire on the part of victims is to be treated with respect by the criminal justice system and its various staff. To meet this need, the agencies concerned need to provide their staff with appropriate training and resources. Police officers, in particular, tend to underestimate the impact of some types of crime upon their victims (Mawby and Walklate, 1994; Williams, 1999; Reeves and Mulley, 2000; Curry *et al.*, 2004). Some of the agencies have frequently also failed to respond sensitively to the varying needs of victims arising from their membership of different racial groups, their gender, sexuality, age, religion, or disability. The most glaring example is the failure of the Metropolitan Police to provide a professional or even non-racist service to Duwayne Brooks, who was with black murder victim Stephen Lawrence when he died (Bowling, 1998). The inquiry report on this case has had a considerable influence upon practice within a number of criminal justice agencies (Chouhan, 2002; Downes and Morgan, 2002). Other criminal justice agencies have also been criticized for their insensitivity towards victims of hate crimes (McManus, 2002), where apparently minor incidents may build up into almost intolerable patterns of harassment and discrimination (Bowling, 1998; Sanders *et al.*, 1997).

Victims often simply want practical help, which may include:

- compensation/reparation for damage;
- protection from further victimization and advice about crime prevention;
- assistance in giving evidence in court;
- making their premises safe after a break-in.

Obstacles to victim take-up of services and entitlements

As already noted, one problem for victims in obtaining services is that they are frequently unfamiliar with the workings of criminal justice and may not even know of the existence of agencies which could offer them help. Substantial efforts have been made to remedy this problem, and the level of victims' awareness of the services of Victim Support (for example) is steadily increasing (Maguire and Kinch, 2000). Initiatives such as the *Victim's Charter* (Home Office, 1996), however, have been criticized for failing to provide victims with the information they need to access a range of appropriate services. Some voluntary organizations have been supported and promoted by central government while others have not received such support to anything like the same extent (Williams, 1999). There have been recent changes in this area including some level of statutory funding for Rape Crisis and Women's Aid, and Independent Domestic Violence Advisors and Independent Sexual Advisors have been introduced to help guide victims about services they can access; however, it is too early to say how effective these new initiatives will be in easing difficulties in accessing services for victims.

The ways in which services are delivered may also create a barrier. For example, in a Scottish survey, victims of commercial crime welcomed the crime prevention advice they received from the police, but some victims of personal crime found it patronizing or alarming. In particular, advice about the likelihood of repeated offences needs to be delivered with some sensitivity (Curry *et al.*, 2004). Some victims contacted by the probation service, particularly when the implementation of the responsibility to keep victims of more serious crimes informed first began, found such approaches insensitive and unwelcome (Williams, 1999: 110–16). Low response rates by victims to contacts from the probation service may be explained in a number of ways,[2] but until recently no research has so far been undertaken to find out victims' own views (Newton, 2003). A MORI poll was conducted in 2004 which investigated victim's experiences of using the Probation Victim Contact Scheme. This found that victims tended to be very positive about the support received from their victim contact officer, though less positive about the level of information that they receive from them about the progress of their case.

There is considerable evidence that victims of sexual offences frequently find the process of reporting such crimes, attending court, and giving evidence extremely distressing, despite a number of improvements made to the system since the 1970s (Temkin, 2002; Williams, 2005). A significant proportion of such victims interviewed about their experiences refer to the criminal justice process as a re-victimization, and reporting rates for some offences are believed to be artificially low as a result.

The issue of the 'ideal victim' discussed earlier also has a bearing upon access to and take-up of services. For example, a young Albanian woman who has been abducted, raped and trafficked, and forced to work as a prostitute in this country, is likely to be treated by official agencies first as an illegal immigrant and only secondly, if at all, as a victim of crime. She is far from the stereotypical victim of crime: she has no right to be in the country in the first place, and she works in the sex trade, albeit under duress. She is, nevertheless, in need of protection and access to services—both of which are in very short supply for people in these sorts of circumstances in the UK. Power and the lack of power are important determining factors here.

The distinction between the ideal and the guilty victim also has less dramatic effects. For example, it can mean that people with criminal convictions are frequently refused criminal injuries compensation, even when they suffer the most serious assaults. The likely success of efforts to 'put victims at the heart of the criminal justice system' (Criminal Justice Online, 2002) depends to a large extent upon the breadth of the definitions of victims employed.

Advances in the treatment of victims of crime

The law and agencies' policies in England and Wales have been changed a good number of times since the 1960s with a view to improving the treatment of victims of crime, and there is insufficient space here to go into great detail (see Williams, 1999; Williams,

2002; Zedner, 2002). However, it is worth noting the broad areas in which significant changes have been made:

- criminal injuries compensation for the victims of violent crime was introduced in 1964 and the UK system is among the most generous in the world, despite its limitations;

- in legislation since the 1970s, the arrangements for court-ordered compensation of victims by offenders have been strengthened;

- women's aid refuges and rape crisis centres have been established by voluntary organizations and in recent years they have begun to receive some State financial support;

- Victim Support, established in the 1970s, soon achieved national coverage and now receives substantial financial support from the State for a volunteer-based service;

- the identity of complainants in rape cases has been increasingly protected, and they have gradually been shielded from aggressive questioning by investigating police officers and cross-examination in court (although more needs to be done);

- victim-offender mediation and other forms of restorative justice which offer choices to victims have increasingly been introduced, in youth justice in the 1990s and in relation to adult offenders more recently (see the final section of this chapter, below);

- international organizations including the United Nations and the Council of Europe have been active since the 1980s in highlighting States' responsibilities towards victims of crime, and policy and legal changes have followed (see <http://www.victim-ology.nl> for some of the relevant international agreements);

- telephone advice services such as Childline and the Victim Supportline have been introduced;

- programmes confronting offenders with their crimes' consequences for victims have become increasingly common and comprehensive;

- vulnerable witnesses have received increasing legal protection and opportunities (for example) to give evidence via video links, with major legislation in 1999 gradually coming into effect in subsequent years;

- provisions for keeping victims informed at various stages of the criminal justice process have been introduced (although this is another field where much more could still be done). Witness Care Units have been introduced to try to improve the flow of information to witnesses going through the criminal justice system by co-locating staff from the police and Crown Prosecution Service.

The Domestic Violence, Crime and Victims Act was passed in 2004 and was hailed as the biggest shake up of domestic violence laws for 30 years. This introduced Domestic Violence Homicide Review Panels and the Victims Code which came into force in 2006. Hoyle (2007) outlines some of the changes included in the Act that are aimed at tackling domestic violence, including making common assault an arrestable offence.

REVIEW QUESTIONS

1 Given that some victims need assistance from outside their own circle of family and friends, what obstacles currently prevent them from obtaining access to this help?

2 What are the main needs expressed by victims of crime, and how does the criminal justice system go about responding to these?

3 What forces have driven the increased emphasis upon victims of crime in UK policy-making?

Effectiveness and international comparisons

It can be instructive to compare the ways in which different legal systems respond to the demands of new pressure groups. In this section, a small number of specific examples of innovation in relation to the rights and needs of victims of crime will be briefly considered in a comparative perspective.

In various jurisdictions, changes have been made in response to consistent research findings about victims' desire to be kept better informed about the progress of cases. One of the key questions is which agency is in the best position to undertake such work. The police have the necessary information and they have direct contact with victims at an early stage. The prosecution service has information about every stage of the case but has no tradition of direct contact with victims. The probation service has no such experience either, but it has staff with relevant training in supporting people at difficult times. In different countries, each of these agencies has been entrusted with the responsibility for making and sustaining contact with victims who require information.

In the Netherlands, the police were given this role and it is clear that when they implement the policy which requires them to keep victims informed, this increases victims' overall satisfaction with the criminal justice system. Sadly, implementation is inconsistent and according to several research studies in the 1990s fewer than 40 per cent of those entitled to information were actually provided with it (Wemmers, 1996). Victim satisfaction with their treatment is likely to be adversely affected by offers of help which do not actually materialize, and this is clearly the case when the police offer to keep people informed and then fail to follow this through in practice (Curry *et al.*, 2004).

Given the difficulty of delivering this service by adding it to the duties of hard-pressed police officers, there is a good deal to be said for approaching the problem in a different way. In England and Wales, the problem was recognized in the *Victim's Charter* (Home Office, 1990; 1996) which added this task to the responsibilities of the probation service, initially only in respect of victims whose offenders were sentenced to lengthy terms of imprisonment. Over subsequent years, the scheme has been extended to cover most victims in cases where the offender is imprisoned (that is, the victims of more serious offences). There were considerable problems in implementing the new arrangements, not least because the probation service was initially provided with no additional resources with which to do so. Many staff also found the idea of working with victims unattractive, and this was a considerable cultural obstacle to change. Over a period of years, these difficulties were overcome (Williams, 2002), but victim take-up of the service remains relatively low: under 40 per cent overall, and a little over 50 per cent in the case of sexual offences, according to one study (Newton, 2003). It seems likely that victims' attitudes towards the probation service, which remains primarily concerned with the surveillance of offenders, are a key factor in this low response to offers of a service which victims consistently demand when asked about their expectations of the criminal justice system.

A different approach has been taken by the criminal justice system in Scotland, where in more serious cases the provision of information to victims has been entrusted to a Victim Information and Advice Service within regional offices of the Procurator Fiscal Service. This is a relatively recent development which has yet to be evaluated, but it will be interesting to see how the experience of delivering the service in this way compares to the successes and difficulties encountered elsewhere. It seems likely that the perceived independence of the people offering the service may encourage higher take-up rates.

It would appear that there is a recognition that victims do need to be provided with information, and in some countries this has been made into a firm entitlement, but implementation can be problematic. If the necessary resources are not made available, policy changes may actually make matters worse by raising victims' expectations but not meeting them in more than a minority of cases.

Another need expressed by victims is that for financial compensation. Many criminal justice systems have responded to the evidence by establishing State compensation schemes, and this is often the first legislative attempt to accommodate victims' needs, but there are considerable differences between these arrangements. In most jurisdictions, State-funded compensation is restricted to victims of violent crime.[3] The extent to which offenders can (additionally or alternatively) be required to pay compensation to their victims through the courts varies considerably from country to country. In England and Wales, such payments can now be made by the court to the victim and recovered from the offender, which is an improvement on the previous system under which offenders often made small and infrequent payments by instalments.

While the UK criminal injuries compensation arrangements are among the best-funded in the world (Brienen and Hoegen, 2000), they have been consistently criticized by victims' organizations (see for example Victim Support, 1995). The lowest levels of award (currently starting at £1,000) can be perceived as belittling victims' injuries: an award of £1,000 for what is seen by the victim as a serious offence can feel insultingly small. Restrictions on claims by victims who happen to have criminal convictions themselves, or who delayed reporting offences to the police, or who are claiming State benefits, have been seen as discriminatory (Williams, 2005). The administration of the scheme is often slow and it is certainly bureaucratic, involving the completion of complex forms and the provision of extensive evidence, especially where claims involve compensation for psychological injuries. Perhaps most importantly, many victims simply are not told that they can claim. Victims' organizations thus find themselves in the position of promoting the scheme, although they have reservations about its operation, and advising individual claimants about how to appeal against decisions. Nevertheless, the UK scheme was set up as long ago as 1964 (a year after the first such system in New Zealand). As such, it has provided a model for similar arrangements elsewhere, and perhaps some lessons have been learnt from its advantages and disadvantages. Unlike discretionary schemes in countries such as Italy, the UK compensation fund is on a statutory basis and it covers domestic violence offences (which are specifically excluded from some European countries' schemes: see Brienen and Hoegen, 2000).

Victims also want direct services, as shown by the high levels of take-up of such services where they are provided. The type and extent of service provision varies enormously between countries, as Mawby (2003) has shown. In the US, there is a strong emphasis upon providing victims with professional counselling, whereas a self-help model prevails in western Europe, where volunteers are more likely to be deployed to provide neighbourly support to victims and referral on to professional services where required. In the UK, Victim Support prioritized property offences for many years (particularly burglary, although this has since changed), while North American victim agencies concentrated upon victims of violent offences.

In the Netherlands, services to support victims were originally set up by the probation service, and there has always been a strong emphasis upon victim–offender mediation (which is viewed with suspicion in many other countries) and referral to professional counselling agencies (which is beyond the resources of other jurisdictions). The Dutch victim support arrangements have always covered victims of road traffic accidents, while in England and Wales this has not formally been the case—although extending services to such victims is now under discussion here. While victim support services in countries such as the Netherlands, England and Wales, and Scotland are provided on a national, fairly standardized basis, this is far from being the case in countries with federal systems such as the US or Belgium. In other jurisdictions, such as Germany and most eastern European countries, provision is much more patchy, depending upon locally available resources. German victim support agencies tend to concentrate upon providing legal and financial rather than emotional support. Services for victims are generally not well-developed in countries with no tradition of voluntary activity by non-governmental organizations. Engagement with the victims of more serious crimes is the exception rather than the norm internationally, and appears to be at its most sophisticated in western Europe and North America—which is to say, in the richer countries—although it is also developing in response to unmet needs in countries in violent transition such as South Africa.

As a final case study, this section concludes with a discussion of the introduction of victim impact statements in a variety of countries (VIS, known in England and Wales as Victim Personal Statements). First introduced in the USA, VIS were intended to improve victims' position in the criminal justice system by creating an opportunity for them to give information about the loss and damage suffered as a result of the offence, and express their feelings about this. Not only would this involve victims in a system which had traditionally marginalized them (and it might thus to some extent empower them), it was also intended to alter the culture of the system by allowing case-hardened practitioners to obtain a victim perspective.

In the US, the use of VIS ran into constitutional problems from a fairly early stage: emotive victim statements were being read to courts, even in capital cases, and inflaming emotions in a way which made decision-making more difficult. As a result, the higher courts ordered restrictions on the use of the statements in the most serious cases—which also happened for different reasons in the UK (Doerner and Lab, 2002; Zedner, 2002). Take-up rates were relatively low among victims in the US and, later, elsewhere, although it was initially unclear what reasons lay behind this (Doerner and Lab, 2002; Hoyle *et al.*, 1998). Possible explanations included difficulty in tracing victims, failure to inform them of their right to make a statement, and victims choosing, for a variety of reasons, not to take part. Research established that these reasons included fear of retaliation by offenders, general dissatisfaction with and distrust of the criminal justice system, and a disinclination to expose themselves to further emotional distress (Erez and Tontodonata, 1992). There was also a belief on the part of some participants that no notice would be taken of what they said, a feeling also observed when Victim Personal Statements were piloted in England (Hoyle *et al.*, 1998). There was considerable controversy among researchers and practitioners about the extent to which participating in the VIS process made victims feel any better or made judges feel better-informed (Sanders *et al.*, 2001; Erez, 1997), and low levels of participation made the argument that VIS empowered victims ring somewhat hollow. Nevertheless, as so often in criminal justice policy, the American arrangements were adapted or emulated in a number of other jurisdictions, including Australia, Canada, England and Wales, Ireland, and Scotland.

Some authors have suggested that US politicians introduced VIS primarily for political reasons—to show that 'something was being done' for victims (Garland, 2001; Ashworth, 2000). Given the ambiguity of the research evidence briefly reviewed above, it does seem difficult otherwise to explain the enthusiasm of legislators in other jurisdictions for undertaking similar experiments in their own countries. While it is true that (for example, in Ireland, England and Wales, and Scotland) some of these VIS schemes were explicitly designed to avoid some of the pitfalls observed in the US, they all derive from the same principles and they are likely to face at least some of the same problems (Walklate, 2002). New ideas spread rapidly in criminal justice, and politicians do not always take sufficient (or any) notice of research evidence. The careful, measured evaluation of the pilot VIS scheme in England and Wales by Hoyle *et al.* (1998) in which evidence for not introducing VIS in England and Wales was provided, was swiftly followed by the Home Office decision to 'roll out' Victim Personal Statements nationally, and the authors became somewhat more impassioned in their subsequent discussions of the issues (Sanders *et al.*, 2001).

CONCLUSION

A number of general issues emerge from this brief exercise in international comparisons. While more comparative research is needed (Mawby, 2003) it seems clear that the extent to which victim services exist in a particular country has less to do with levels of need than with the availability of resources and the existence or otherwise of voluntary organizations willing to take on the task.

Whereas some services are introduced in response to research evidence about victims' wishes and needs, other reforms are carried out despite what is known about victims' wishes and responses to experimental projects.

Legislation is not always effectively implemented—which is generally true in a number of fields, but seems to apply particularly to laws and policies relating to victims of crime. This being the case, a number of authors have expressed the suspicion that politicians are particularly prone to making rhetorical statements about the need to assist victims of crime and accordingly putting forward what might be called rhetorical legislation, which looks good but is not properly brought into effect (Williams, 2005; Walklate, 2002). Whether sufficient resources are allocated to ensure the success of new initiatives is one test of the seriousness of those who bring forward the legislation, and a recurrent theme in the discussion above (and in the literature generally) is the failure to make adequate resources available to allow effective implementation of reforms in this area of policy. A linked issue is that of publicity: a number of the initiatives described have been less successful than they might have been due to inadequate publicity. The cynical observer might say that one way to limit take-up of services is to ration the knowledge of the public about their availability (Williams, 1999).

Internationally, there is a growing tendency to experiment with—and in some cases even to replace traditional adversarial criminal justice approaches with—restorative methods. There is insufficient space here to debate the merits of restorative justice (see Johnstone, 2002) and there has not yet been enough research on the merits or otherwise of the experimental projects in the UK to be clear about how successful they are. However, such approaches have been remarkably successful in other jurisdictions (notably in Austria and New Zealand) and they appear to show considerable promise in terms of keeping victims of crime better informed, involving them and giving them a say in the criminal justice process if they so wish, and ensuring that the victims who do decide to take part in such approaches are treated respectfully and get something out of their involvement (see Williams, 2005).

Finally, and perhaps most importantly, many reforms in the area of services for victims have been initiated by people whose primary concern is the welfare and fair treatment of offenders, and praiseworthy as this is, it tends to make victims somewhat wary.

QUESTIONS FOR DISCUSSION

1 Whose interests, apart from those of the victims themselves, are served by legislation and policies which purport to meet the needs of victims of crime?

2 What prevents legislation and policy on victims of crime from being effectively implemented—and what reasons might help to explain this?

3 Why did services for victims of crime only begin to emerge in the 1960s, and why have policy initiatives and legislation in this area become so much more common in recent years?

4 Why are some groups of victims seen as more 'deserving' than others? Which groups does this particularly apply to? What are the practical consequences?

5 Many services for victims of crime have been initiated by groups whose primary focus is upon offenders (for example, the restorative justice movement, Victim Support, Victim Impact Statements). What possible explanations are there for this, and what consequences might it have?

GUIDE TO FURTHER READING

Doerner, W.G. and Lab, S.P. (2002) *Victimology* (3rd edn). Cincinnati: Anderson.

Although it fails to consider most of what is happening outside North America, this is a useful textbook, providing evidence about the growth of victim services and the victims' movement in North America which is based upon research.

Goodey, J. (2005) *Victims and Victimology: Research, Policy and Practice*. Harlow: Longman.

An up-to-date textbook on victims policy internationally; particularly strong on gender issues.

Johnstone, G. (2002) *Restorative Justice: Ideas, Values, Debates*. Cullompton: Willan.

A carefully argued critique of some of the central claims of restorative justice, including the issues affecting victims of crime. This book also gives examples of what restorative justice involves in practice and how it is implemented. Draws upon philosophical evidence but is clearly and accessibly written.

Mawby, R.I. and Walklate, S. (1994) *Critical Victimology: International Perspectives*. London: Sage.

Although now somewhat dated, this remains the key text on the victims' movement, the needs of victims, and provision for them across the western world. It introduces a critical approach to the study of victims of crime, questioning many of the previously prevalent orthodoxies.

Spalek, B. (2006) *Crime Victims: theory, policy and practice*. Hampshire: Palgrave Macmillan.

An insightful book and a useful introduction to victimology.

Walklate, S. (2006) *Imagining the Victim of Crime*. Maidenhead: McGraw-Hill/Open University Press.

A very interesting and thoughtful reflection on victimology. This book makes for interesting reading with useful debates on current developments in victimology in a world post-9/11.

Walklate, S. (ed) (2007) *Handbook of Victims and Victimology*. Devon: Willan Publishing.

A useful handbook offering a selection of thought-provoking chapters from a wide range of respected authors. Very accessible and a valuable source of up-to-date information.

Williams, B. (2005) *Victims of Crime: Justice Rebalanced?* London: Jessica Kingsley.

An up-to-date account of policy and research relevant to the position of victims of crime, paying particular attention to community justice and restorative justice.

Zedner, L. (2002) 'Victims' in M. Maguire, R. Morgan, and R. Reiner (eds) *The Oxford Handbook of Criminology* (3rd edn). Oxford: Oxford University Press.

This chapter succinctly summarizes current academic knowledge about victims and witnesses of crime and their place in the criminal justice system.

WEB LINKS

http://www.victimology.nl

An extremely useful site, which provides two databases, one on research and the other on victim services. It also includes a wide range of documents such as international conventions, a news section, and links with other victimological websites worldwide.

http://www.restorativepractices.org

A US-based site giving information about conferences and news as well as access to an online library and an eforum on restorative justice.

http://www.restorativejustice.org.uk/

The Restorative Justice Consortium was formed in 1997 bringing together a wide range of organizations with an interest in Restorative Justice.

http://www.victimsupport.org/

Victim Support is an independent charity which helps people cope with the effects of crime. The site provides information on police and court procedure, on compensation and insurance matters, and on victim-related issues.

REFERENCES

Amir, M. (1971) *Patterns of Forcible Rape*. Chicago: University of Chicago Press.

Ashworth, A. (2000) 'Victims' rights, defendants' rights and criminal procedure' in A. Crawford and J. Goodey (eds) *Integrating a Victim Perspective within Criminal Justice*. Aldershot: Ashgate.

Boswell, G. (1999) 'Young offenders who commit grave crimes: the criminal justice response' in H. Kemshall and J. Pritchard (eds) *Good Practice in Working with Violence*. London: Jessica Kingsley.

Bowling, B. (1998) *Violent Racism: Victimisation, Policing and Social Context*. Oxford: Clarendon.

Brienen, M.E.I. and Hoegen, E.H. (2000) *Victims of Crime in 22 European Criminal Justice Systems*. Nijmegen: Wolf Legal Publications.

Chouhan, K. (2002) 'Race issues in probation' in D. Ward, J. Scott, and M. Lacey (eds) *Probation: Working for Justice* (2nd edn). Oxford: Oxford University Press.

Criminal Justice Online (2002) *Justice for All—CJS White Paper Published—the Executive Summary*, <http://www.cjsonline.gov.uk/downloads/application/pdf/CJS%20White%20Paper%20-%20Justice%20For%20All.pdf>.

Crown Prosecution Service, Department of Health and Home Office (2002) *Provision of Therapy for Vulnerable or Intimidated Witnesses Prior to a Criminal Trial: Practice Guidance*. London: Home Office.

Curry, D., Knight, V., Owens-Rawle, D., Patel, S., and Semenchuk, M. (2004) *Restorative Justice in the Juvenile Secure Estate*. London: Youth Justice Board.

Doerner, W.G. and Lab, S.P. (2002) *Victimology* (3rd edn). Cincinnati: Anderson.

Downes, D. and Morgan, R. (2002) 'The politics of law and order' in M. Maguire, R. Morgan, and R. Reiner (eds) *The Oxford Handbook of Criminology* (3rd edn). Oxford: Oxford University Press.

Elias, R. (1993) *Victims Still: the Political Manipulation of Crime Victims*. London: Sage.

Erez, E. (1997) 'Victim Harm, Impact Statements and Victim Satisfaction with Justice: an Australian Experience', *International Review of Victimology*, 5 (37): 37–60.

Erez, E. and Rogers, L. (1999) 'The Effects of Victim Impact Statements on Criminal Justice Outcomes and Processes: the Perspectives of Legal Professionals', *British Journal of Criminology*, 39 (2): 216–39.

Erez, E. and Tontodonato, P. (1992) 'Victim Participation in Sentencing and Satisfaction with Justice', *Justice Quarterly*, 9: 393–417.

Garland, D. (2001) *The Culture of Control: Crime and Social Order in Contemporary Society*. Oxford: Oxford University Press.

Gottfredson, M.R. (1984) *Victims of Crime: the Dimensions of Risk*. London: Home Office (Research Study XX).

Her Majesty's Inspectorate of Probation (HMIP) (2003) *Valuing the Victim: an Inspection into National Victim Contact Arrangements*. London: Home Office.

Home Office (1990) *Victim's Charter: a Statement of the Rights of Victims*. London: Home Office Public Relations Branch.

Home Office (1996) *The Victim's Charter: a Statement of Service Standards for Victims of Crime*. London: Home Office Communications Directorate.

Home Office (2002) *A Better Deal for Victims and Witnesses*. London: Home Office.

Home Office (2003) *Restorative Justice: the Government's Strategy*. London: Home Office Communications Directorate.

Hoyle, C. (2007) 'Feminism, victimology and domestic violence' in S. Walklate (ed) *Handbook of Victims and Victimology*. Cullompton: Willan Publishing, pp. 146–174.

Hoyle, C., Cape, E., Morgan, R., and Sanders, A. (1998) *Evaluation of the One Stop Shop and Victim Statement Pilot Projects*. London: Home Office Research and Development Directorate.

Johnstone, G. (2002) *Restorative Justice: Ideas, Values, Debates*. Cullompton: Willan.

Kennedy, H. (1993) *Eve was Framed: Women and British Justice*. London: Chatto & Windus.

Kershaw, C., Chivite-Matthews, A., Thomas, C., and Aust, R. (2001) *The 2001 British Crime Survey: Home Office Statistical Bulletin 18/01*. London: Home Office.

Koffman, L. (1996) *Crime Surveys and Victims of Crime*. Cardiff: University of Wales Press.

Maguire, M. and Kynch, J. (2000) *Public Perceptions and Victims' Experiences of Victim Support: Findings from the 1998 British Crime Survey*. London: Home Office RDSD.

Mawby, R. (2003) 'The provision of victim support and assistance programmes: a cross-national perspective' in P. Davies, P. Francis, and V. Jupp (eds) *Victimisation: Theory, Research and Practice*. Basingstoke: Palgrave Macmillan.

Mawby, R.I. and Walklate, S. (1994) *Critical Victimology: International Perspectives*. London: Sage.

McManus, J. (2002) 'Systems not Words? Some Organisational Response to Hate Crimes', *Criminal Justice Matters* 48, Summer, 44–5.

Mendelsohn, B. (1956) 'Une nouvelle branche de la science bio-pyscho-sociale: victimologie', *Revue Internationale de Criminologie et de Police Technique*: 10–31.

Moran, L.J. (2001) 'Affairs of the Heart: Critical Reflections on Hate Crime', *Law and Critique*, 12(3), 1–15.

MORI (2004) Views of the probation victim contact scheme: Research Conducted for National Probation Service.

Mullender, A. (1996) *Rethinking Domestic Violence: the Social Work and Probation Response*. London: Routledge.

MVA Consultancy (2000) *The 2000 Scottish Crime Survey*. Edinburgh: Scottish Executive.

Newton, E. (2003) 'A study of the policies and procedures implemented by the probation service with respect to victims of serious crime', *British Journal of Community Justice* 2(1) 25–36.

O'Mahony, D., Geary, R., McEvoy, K., and Morison, J. (2000) *Crime, Community and Locale: the Northern Ireland Communities Crime Survey*. Aldershot: Ashgate.

Radford, J. (2001) 'Feminist research' in E. McLaughlin and J. Muncie (eds) *The Sage Dictionary of Criminology*. London: Sage, 121–3.

Reeves, H. and Mulley, K. (2000) 'The new status of victims in the UK: opportunities and threats' in A. Crawford and J. Goodey (eds) *Integrating a Victim Perspective within Criminal Justice*. Aldershot: Ashgate.

Sanders, A., Creaton, J., Bird, S., and Weber, L. (1997) *Victims with Learning Disabilities: Negotiating the Criminal Justice System*. Oxford: University of Oxford Centre for Criminological Research.

Sanders, A., Hoyle, C., Morgan, R., and Cape, E. (2001) 'Victim Impact Statements: don't work, can't work', *Criminal Law Review* 447–58.

Shakespeare, T. (1996) 'Power and prejudice: issues of gender, sexuality and disability' in L. Barton (ed) *Disability and Society: Emerging Issues and Insights*. Harlow: Longman.

Spackman, P. (2000) (ed) *Victim Support Handbook: Helping People Cope with Crime*. London: Hodder and Stoughton.

Temkin, J. (1987) *Rape and the Legal Process*. London: Sweet and Maxwell.

Temkin, J. (2002) *Rape and the Legal Process* (2nd edn). Oxford: Oxford University Press.

Tudor, B. (2002) 'Probation work with victims of crime' in B. Williams (ed) *Reparation and Victim-focused Social Work*. London: Jessica Kingsley.

Van Dijk, J. (2000) 'Implications of the International Crime Victims Survey for a victim perspective' in A. Crawford and J. Goodey (eds) *Integrating a Victim Perspective within Criminal Justice*. Aldershot: Ashgate.

Von Hentig, H. (1948) *The Criminal and his Victim*. New Haven: Yale University Press.

Victim Support (1995) 'The Rights of Victims of Crime', policy paper. London: Victim Support.

Walklate, S. (2002) 'Victim Impact Statements' in B. Williams (ed) *Reparation and Victim-Focused Social Work*. London: Jessica Kingsley.

Wemmers, J.-A. (1996) *Victims in the Criminal Justice System*. Amsterdam: Kugler.

Williams, B. (1999) *Working with Victims of Crime: Policies, Politics and Practice*. London: Jessica Kingsley.

Williams, B. (2002) 'Justice for victims of crime' in D. Ward, J. Scott, and M. Lacey (eds) *Probation: Working for Justice* (2nd edn). Oxford: Oxford University Press.

Williams, B. (2005) *Victims of Crime: Justice Rebalanced?* London: Jessica Kingsley.

Wolfgang, M. (1958) *Patterns in Criminal Homicide*. Philadelphia: University of Pennsylvania Press.

Zedner, L. (2002) 'Victims' in M. Maguire, R. Morgan, and R. Reiner (eds) *The Oxford Handbook of Criminology* (3rd edn). Oxford: Oxford University Press.

NOTES

1. We would like to thank Hannah Chong and Azrini Wahidin for revising the original chapter. Professor Brian Williams died suddenly and tragically on 17 March 2007. He was Professor of Community Justice and Victimology at De Montfort University, Leicester.

2. One might speculate that male victims in particular tend to wish to avoid a fuss and put the incident behind them. Some victims will not want contact with the probation service because they view it as an offender orientated service. Others will view the incident as relatively minor, and still others may lack confidence in the criminal justice system as a whole.

3. A notable exception is South Africa, where there are insufficient resources available to set up a general compensation scheme, but the near-defunct arrangements to compensate victims of terrorism cover property as well as personal injuries.

25 Policing

Trevor Jones

INTRODUCTION

The study of policing now forms a major sub-field within criminology. Policing research is undertaken by a diverse range of bodies, including universities, national and local government, market research agencies, think tanks, pressure groups, and, of course, the police themselves (Newburn and Reiner, 2007). This chapter provides a broad introduction to some of the main themes within this large body of work. The first section discusses the definition of 'policing', and briefly outlines some of the factors contributing to its growth as an area of interest within criminology. The second section examines what the police actually do in practice and discusses two contrasting models of policing. The third section explores several key debates within the policing literature. The primary focus is upon policing in England and Wales,[1] although the similar themes are visible across most western industrial democracies.

BACKGROUND

Criminological studies of policing have focused traditionally upon the activities of the specialist state agency—'the police'—tasked with law enforcement, crime investigation, public reassurance, and peace-keeping. This 'state-centric' approach (Shearing, 2006) has strong conceptual, empirical, and normative implications. It implies a conceptual conflation of 'policing' with 'what the police do', a way of thinking about policing that has proved remarkably resilient. It suggests that in empirical terms public constabularies are the dominant providers of policing services in contemporary societies. Finally, it implies that policing *should* be provided primarily by state institutions. All these implications have come under question in recent years.

Beginning with the conceptual issues, writers have attempted to provide clear definitions of policing that capture the complex range of activities and agencies involved in the authorization and provision of policing services. As discussed further below, the law enforcement, investigation, peacekeeping, and other activities undertaken by state *police* institutions can be viewed as a subset of a broader range of *policing* functions authorized and undertaken by a variety of state, commercial, voluntary, and community bodies. Both of these are themselves subsets of the wider system of social controls (Jones, 2008). Working definitions of policing must therefore be sufficiently specific to capture the distinctive features of policing within the broader mesh of formal and informal social controls, but at the same time be general enough to include the range of activities undertaken by, or on behalf of, non-state bodies. One such definition denotes policing as 'organized forms of order maintenance, peacekeeping, rule or law enforcement, crime investigation and prevention...undertaken by individuals or organizations where such activities are viewed by them and/or others as a...key defining part of their purpose' (Jones and Newburn, 1998: 18–19).

The traditional exclusive focus on state policing has been challenged by empirical research that has demonstrated how 'policing' activities are now undertaken by a range of public, commercial, and voluntary agencies as well as the public police (Bayley and Shearing, 1994; Johnston, 1992, 2000; Jones and Newburn, 1998). Regulation, order maintenance, and law enforcement activities are increasingly 'pluralized' in contemporary societies and the public police are one among many policing bodies (Jones and Newburn, 2006). This changed policing landscape includes a burgeoning commercial security sector (Johnston, 1992; Jones and Newburn, 1998), new forms of public sector policing provision such as local authority patrol forces and municipal police forces (Loader, 2000), the creation of new patrolling ranks—such as 'Police Community Support Officers' (PCSOs)—within public police organizations (Johnston, 2007), the development of informal policing forms such as vigilantism (Johnston, 1996), and the emergence of transnational policing forms above the nation state (Sheptycki, 2000).

The literature on plural policing, as well as challenging dominant empirical understandings of *what policing is*, has stimulated normative debates about *how policing should be* (Jones, 2007). On the one hand, there are concerns about the standard of service provided by non-state policing forms, and about the perceived lack of public accountability of private policing agents. It can be argued that private policing exacerbates social polarization and aggravates feelings of insecurity. Against this, some authors have argued that non-state forms of security provision and governance provide an important opportunity to develop more equitable and effective forms of security provision in local communities (Johnston and Shearing, 2003; Shearing 2006). On this view, the authorities should seek to facilitate the participation of disadvantaged groups in security markets, and help communities to develop their own locally designed forms of private governance (Wood, 2006).

Although non-state policing forms play an increasingly important role within policing generally, it is important not to underplay the continuing importance of state-organized arrangements. Some commentators have argued that state policing should be viewed as something more than 'one node among many' (Crawford, 2008), and a number of authors have provided compelling arguments in favour of retaining a conception of policing as a social good, and one which should be promoted and organized—if not always directly delivered—by democratically accountable collective political institutions (Loader and Walker, 2001). Thus, whilst acknowledging the important conceptual, empirical, and normative contributions of recent research on pluralization, the remainder of this chapter will, for the most part, focus upon state-organized policing arrangements.

Prior to the 1960s, the police and policing were rather invisible within criminology (Reiner, 1997). The central focus of the 'criminological enterprise' for the first part of the twentieth century was 'criminals', and the challenge was to identify them, discover what was different about them, and, later, to develop interventions to address offending behaviour. To the extent that policing was considered at all by academics, it was in rather straightforward terms as the agency providing institutional responses to the more sociologically interesting concept of crime. From the late 1960s onwards, however, this was challenged by the emergence of 'labelling' perspectives that demonstrated the socially constructed nature of crime (Becker, 1963; Lemert, 1964). These new approaches analysed crime and deviance as the product of complex interactions between individuals and the social audience. From this 'interactionist' viewpoint, the operation of criminal justice agencies—and particularly the police—was absolutely vital. In order to fully comprehend the problem of crime and its construction, criminologists needed a detailed knowledge and understanding of police interactions with members of the public, the factors that shape police attitudes and behaviour, and the ways in which organizational policies are formed and translated (or not) into practice (Reiner, 1997). Subsequent developments in critical criminology also placed policing centre stage to analyses of crime and deviance, this time as a key weapon deployed by the capitalist state to control the working classes, demonize marginal groups, and maintain the existing system of class relations (Hall *et al.*, 1978).

In addition to these developments in academic thinking, social and political developments contributed more generally to a growing awareness of—and critical discussion about—policing and the police (Newburn, 2008). From the 1950s to the mid-1990s there were large and sustained increases in recorded crime which frequently became a source of criticism of the police. Sporadic outbreaks of urban disorder in the larger English cities fuelled concerns about law and order. During the 1970s and 1980s, large-scale industrial disputes brought the police service into controversial and sometimes violent conflict with pickets, culminating in the 1984/85 Miners' Strike which had a lasting impact on British policing. More generally, throughout the past 30 years public concerns about law and order have been stimulated and exploited by politicians of all parties 'talking tough' on crime in order to enhance their electoral popularity (Downes and Morgan, 2007). Various other developments have kept policing at the top of the political agenda. A series of high profile miscarriages of justice during the 1980s and 1990s damaged public confidence in the police, and focused attention on police corruption and malpractice (Rozenberg, 1992). Growing inequality and social divisions have continued to highlight the uneven impact of adversarial policing on different social groups, most visible in the arena of race relations (Phillips and Bowling, 2007). And in common with other public services, there has been an ongoing obsession with issues of performance which has been a central driver in attempts to reform the public police under both Conservative and Labour governments. Such developments have contributed to much more critical scrutiny of policing, and a decline in levels of public confidence in the police from the high water mark of police legitimacy in the 1950s (Reiner, 2000). Nevertheless, it is clear that the police institution retains a significant, perhaps unique, cultural and symbolic significance in England and Wales (Loader and Mulcahy, 2003). Though public support for the police has declined, it remains high relative to public confidence in other institutions such as the press and government. Public demands for increased levels of policing remain as strident as ever, typified by the frequent call for 'more bobbies on the beat' (Loader, 1997; Morgan and Newburn, 1997). Finally, representations of the police remain a central part of our popular culture, with crime and policing stories providing a core part of both news reporting and popular fiction on film and television (Reiner, 2007, 2008; Leishman and Mason, 2003; Clarke, 2001). Despite the increasing tide of criticism and scrutiny of the police over recent decades, we retain a peculiar attachment to, and fascination with, the police institution.

What do the police do?

Policing functions

The American sociologist Egon Bittner, highlighted two core defining characteristics of the (public) police (Bittner, 1980). The first concerned the very broad functional mandate of the police that makes them an omnibus or 'catch all' public service, for which it is 'all but impossible to imagine a human problem which could not be their proper business' (quoted in Jones and Newburn, 1998: 248). The second key feature highlighted by Bittner was the distinctive legal capacity that the police bring to this broad mandate— their access to the legitimate use of force.

Within this broad and flexible functional mandate, there is little doubt that 'crime-fighting' is central to the occupational self-image of many police officers, as well as the wider representations of policing in media and public debate. However, the strong conclusion of research on what the police actually do is that crime-related activities only take up a minority of the everyday work of most police officers (Punch, 1979; Morgan and Newburn, 1997; PA Consulting Group, 2001). For example, Skogan's (1990) analysis of the British Crime Survey showed that broader 'service' functions are the staple diet of police work, and that 'most public-initiated encounters reflected the integration of the police into the routines of everyday life'. The police are called upon to preserve tranquillity, ease the flow of traffic, serve as a clearing house for reports of a variety of community problems, assist in civil emergencies, and help people find their way. However, this view has been challenged in a number of ways. For example, Shapland and Vagg's (1988) analysis suggested that 'potential crime' accounted for over half of all calls to the police. Reiner (2000) argued that changes in the organization of police forces have expanded the number of law-enforcement specialists, and increased the involvement of uniformed officers in the investigation of routine crime. The primary focus of government reforms since the early 1990s has been upon improving police performance in crime-oriented areas of work, a development reinforced by official discourse about the main job of the police being to 'catch criminals' (see for example, Home Office, 1993). The emphasis on demonstrable improvements in statistical performance indicators (such as 'sanction detections', 'offences brought to justice', 'detection rates' etc) has clearly refocused policing—and the wider public image of policing—towards crime-oriented activities. Thus, while the view of the police as primarily 'crime-fighters' remains a gross simplification of the realities of everyday police work, dealing with crime remains not only important symbolically to policing, but a key part of how police effectiveness is perceived by politicians, the general public, and the police themselves.

Nevertheless, most research on what police officers actually do in practice supports the view that the primary police task is peace-keeping or 'order maintenance'. The majority of day-to-day police activity involves settling of disputes without recourse to formal legal powers (Reiner, 2000). This arises from the wide level of discretion devolved to front-line police officers. It is a distinctive feature of policing that scope for discretion increases for officers the further they are down the police hierarchy (Manning, 1977). Policing activities are 'low visibility' and much policing involves interactions with individuals of low social power that take place away from the gaze of supervisors or the general public. In addition, it is not possible to legislate in advance for the wide range of possible situations that police officers may face, and thus professional discretion is a necessary and inevitable part of doing policing. Officers will not invoke the law in every situation where a crime has been committed, but in circumstances where they believe that a crime has been committed *and* they deem it appropriate to apply their legal powers. Decisions to enforce the law are often made in pursuit of the broader objective of 'peacekeeping'. This was recognized by Lord Scarman in his 1981 report on the Brixton riots, when he argued that in situations where law enforcement may conflict with maintaining the public peace, it is the latter that must take priority (Scarman, 1981).

These order maintenance activities come in many different forms. Most frequently, they involve mediation by officers in relatively minor disputes or providing a visible police patrol presence at public events such as football matches or demonstrations. However, they can also include major 'paramilitary-style' interventions of organized force to deal with serious outbreaks of public disorder (Waddington, 2008). It is in these situations that public order policing is at its most morally ambiguous and contentious, because they inevitably require the upholding and maintenance of a particular order. Ultimately, at least to some degree, this involves the protection of vested interests that benefit from a continuation of the status quo. Waddington has argued that modern professional police responses to large-scale disorder require a degree of paramilitary organization, equipment, and tactics. In particular, strong central 'quasi-military' forms of command and control in these situations enable a targeted and disciplined application of force in contrast with tactics that allow individual officers to take *ad hoc* defensive action. On this view, officers acting as part of a disciplined group under the direct command of a senior officer are less likely to commit acts of individual over-aggression or other kinds of indiscipline. Lines of accountability in such situations are much clearer in that it is the commanding officer who has clear responsibility for the officers' behaviour (Waddington, 1993). Against this, critics have argued that the development of paramilitary public order policing tactics has transformed the nature of policing in England and Wales (Jefferson, 1993). In particular, it has encouraged police forces to prepare for the worst case scenario in their public order planning strategies, building in expectations of trouble. Such expectations become self-fulfilling when aggressive police tactics provoke similar responses from crowds and spirals of disorder develop. Jefferson thus argues that the equipment, tactics, and mindset of paramilitary public order policing actually generate crowd violence and disorder, rather than control it (Jefferson, 1990, 1993).

Models of policing

As Newburn and Reiner (2007) note, the policing field is characterized by the frequent appearance, and re-appearance, of 'new' models of police work 'each claming to reorient and refashion policing in ways that represent a more or less radical departure from traditional methods' (2007: 928). Here, we consider briefly two contrasting models of delivering policing services, 'community policing' and 'zero tolerance policing' (ZTP).

Community policing

Most police forces in contemporary democracies claim to support 'community policing'. However, what precisely this means in terms of practical policing strategies and tactics is difficult to pin down. Indeed, as Bayley (1994) has noted, it has been defined so broadly that almost any kind of policing activity can potentially be included under its remit. In general terms, community policing suggests that policing should be undertaken in partnership with the public, that citizens are co-producers of policing, and that control of crime and disorder is not the responsibility of the police alone but shared with other branches of government, commercial bodies, voluntary groups, and individual members of the public (Tilley, 2008). This implies a broad social role for the police and that they should not be seen simply as enforcers of the law, but as delivering a range of order maintenance and social service functions as well. Another key theme within discussions of community policing is that policing strategies should be proactive. The police should not simply respond to calls from the public or reports of crime, but should attempt to identify and address the complex problems that underpin problems of crime and disorder (Newburn and Reiner, 2007). Community policing also implies organizational reforms of the traditional militaristic police hierarchy, with core responsibilities devolved to front line officers, multi-functional units attached to particular localities, and organizational emphasis on team work and problem-solving (Bayley, 1994). In practice, a range of policies and practices have been introduced under the mantle of community policing. These have included the attachment of permanent beat officers to small local areas, a range of policies designed to facilitate non-adversarial contact and exchange between the police and particular community groups, building new forms of community support such as neighbourhood watch and crime prevention panels, and improving consultation between the police and particular community groups (Newburn and Reiner, 2007).

Whilst community policing philosophies have been enormously influential in contemporary policing systems, research has produced mixed findings about the effectiveness of such approaches. Part of the problem lies in the lack of clarity about what exactly is involved. Even where clear policy prescriptions can be identified, research has uncovered significant problems of planning and implementation (Newburn and Reiner, 2007). Nevertheless, many of the policing initiatives listed above have—either on their own or in combination—formed a central part of community policing policies introduced periodically in England and Wales since the 1970s. The most recent manifestation of this kind of approach can be seen in the Government's current 'Neighbourhood Policing' programme (Home Office, 2005).

Zero-tolerance policing

'Zero tolerance policing' (ZTP) is associated with a vigorous enforcement-oriented policing approach that focuses upon minor offences and 'disorder' as much as upon more serious crimes. During the 1990s, there was considerable attention paid by the British media to developments in the policing of New York City where there had been very significant drops in crime. This became associated, at least in popular consciousness, with a 'zero tolerance' approach to policing (Jones and Newburn, 2007). Concern about growing levels of street crime led UK politicians from both main parties to gaze across the Atlantic for inspiration and call for the introduction of police strategies similar to those adopted in New York City under the then mayor Rudolph Giuliani and his police chief, William Bratton (Harcourt, 2001). The policing strategies associated with 'Zero Tolerance' have been variously described as 'Quality of Life', 'Order Maintenance', or 'Broken Windows' policing. This last term derives from the famous *Atlantic Monthly* article by US academics James Q. Wilson and George Kelling (Wilson and Kelling, 1982).

The article focused upon the relationship between 'disorders' (graffiti, public drunkenness, prostitution, vandalism, begging, etc) and the growth of more serious crime. It suggested that serious crimes and lower level disorder are linked in a 'kind of developmental sequence'. Neighbourhood disorder signals that nobody cares. Disorders and incivilities, left unchallenged, result in reduced use of public spaces by residents, and also signal to potential law-breakers that community controls and surveillance are weak. The authors argued that it was important for the police to deal firmly with disorderly behaviour in local areas in order to have an impact on serious crime. 'ZTP' (and associated approaches) are associated with a number of concrete policing practices introduced in New York City by Commissioner Bratton. These included a vastly increased uniformed presence on the streets, a vigorous law-enforcement response to minor crime and disorder, the use of civil remedies against those perceived to be involved in criminal activities, enhanced accountability of local police managers for crime and disorder in their areas, and aggressive action against street crimes (Jones and Newburn, 2007). These policing practices became associated with massive drops in recorded crime in New York, although there has been vigorous (and at times, bitter) debate about the relative contribution of policing practices and other factors (Bratton, 1997; Bowling, 1999; Harcourt, 2001). Concerns have also been raised about the potential impact of aggressive enforcement-oriented policing approaches upon police-community relations in general, and upon the incidence of police brutality and aggression in particular (Greene, 1999).

Both the terminology and the concrete policing practices associated with ZTP as developed in New York have been resisted by most senior police officers in the UK, and experiments with 'New York' style policing have been rather limited (Jones and Newburn, 2007). However, the broader ideas associated with 'Broken Windows' have been extremely influential over wider government policy on crime and anti-social behaviour. New Labour's adoption of such approaches is evidenced by the title and the contents of the 1998 Crime and Disorder Act, the more recent Anti-Social Behaviour Act 2003, and the architecture of government anti-social behaviour policy more generally (Burney, 2005).

REVIEW QUESTIONS

1 What are the core policing functions?

2 What kinds of things do police officers actually spend most of their time doing?

3 What are the key elements of community policing and how might they be implemented?

4 What does 'Zero Tolerance Policing' mean in practice and what are its associated benefits and disadvantages?

Key debates in contemporary policing

This section focuses upon a selected number of issues that have formed the subject of important contemporary debates about policing. Space restrictions mean that a number of important issues cannot be covered, and the reader is referred to other key works for further information about these. In particular, there is no discussion of the historical development of policing institutions (Rawlings, 2002), the emergence of transnational policing arrangements (Sheptycki, 2000), the legal powers of the police (Sanders and Young, 2008), or debates about policing and counter-terrorism (Innes and Thiel, 2008).

Police occupational cultures

As noted above, police constables operate with a considerable degree of discretion, a situation that arises from the practical realities of police work (such as its relatively 'invisible' nature) and from established common law traditions ('constabulary independence'). It is clear that the law and organizational rules can only set broad parameters for police behaviour, and certainly does not determine the pattern of policing on the ground (Smith, 1986). A key question for police researchers has concerned the degree to which informal working cultures shape the ways in which officers use their discretion.

Occupational police cultures can be defined as beliefs, norms, working practices, and informal rules that help police officers to make sense of their world (Reiner, 2000). The early observational studies of policing—mainly focused on uniformed patrol officers— suggested there was a relatively stable set of dimensions that appeared to characterize 'cop culture' in a range of different societies. Skolnick (1966) highlighted how tensions associated with policing in liberal societies appeared to foster a common set of cultural responses. Police officers face the problem of constant pressure for results, combined with the difficult position of being symbols of social authority in a way which sets them apart from their fellow citizens. Skolnick argued that these structural problems tend to generate a series of traits within a shared police sub-culture, and highlighted in particular suspicion, social isolation/group solidarity, and conservatism. Other studies added further elements to the standard 'list' of features that are said to characterize 'cop culture'. These include the sense of mission, cynicism/pragmatism, machismo, and racial prejudice (Reiner, 2000).[2] Although as Waddington (1999) points out, cop culture has tended to be discussed in pejorative terms, it is important to understand the relationship between these cultural tendencies and the structural realities of policing. Furthermore, they should not be assumed automatically to be universal and always negative. For example, police officers are trained and socialized to suspect that things are not always as they seem. Whilst this is arguably an important skill for effective police work, it can also lead to the unfair stereotyping of particular groups or individuals. Group solidarity can be linked to the mutual interdependence between police officers, who may face potentially dangerous situations in which they are outnumbered by hostile members of the public. The need to rely upon colleagues to back each other up in difficult situations helps to foster a strong sense of in-group loyalty. However, this strong group identification brings with it the danger of negatively stereotyping 'outsiders', and also a marked tendency to close ranks in the face of investigations of police malpractice. Though racial prejudice and machismo can never be regarded as positive, it is also important to understand the complex dynamics via which these traits also arise and are perpetuated in the police organization. Crucially, they are linked to the experience of 'doing policing' in societies characterized by structural inequalities of race and gender. They are also connected to the practical realities of new recruits 'learning on the job' in the company of more experienced officers (Jones, 1998).

An important question is how far can these cultural tendencies be explained with reference to the individual dispositions that police recruits bring to the job? Some research has suggested that police recruits tend to be more authoritarian than other comparable groups in the population (Coleman and Gorman, 1982). However, most research on this matter suggests that occupational police subcultures are better understood as a collective cultural adaptation to the everyday realities of police work, rather than being the product of individual personality traits (Newburn and Reiner, 2007). Thus, whilst reforming the police organization in order to eliminate the negative aspects of police culture has been seen as a prerequisite for better policing, this is a far more difficult task than simply weeding out individual officers with inappropriate attitudes. For example, once we accept occupational culture as a complex collective phenomenon, we can begin to understand the limitations on traditional approaches to changing the culture. Interventions such as better recruitment practices or improved 'cultural awareness' training tend to individualize problems such as prejudice, and take insufficient account of the fact that much policing is learned on the streets.

Recent work has presented a more sophisticated notion of occupational police culture. In particular, it has highlighted the fact that too often 'cop culture' is discussed as if it is a universal and homogenous phenomenon (Chan, 1996). Indeed, it is more accurate to talk about 'police cultures', given the noted differences within and between police forces. For example, there appear to be significant contrasts in occupational cultures between different functional specialisms, officers of different ranks, and urban and rural force areas (Westmarland, 2008). In addition, authors have challenged the idea that cop culture provides a straightforward explanation of deviant police behaviour. Waddington (1999) argues that 'canteen culture' is primarily an oral phenomenon that involves the telling of 'war stories' away from the front-line of policing. Many of these verbal accounts of policing as told by one officer to another bear little relation to the more mundane reality of police work. For Waddington, this demonstrates that the oral culture fulfils a number of functions for the officers who participate within it. It helps bolster occupational self-esteem, and provides mutual reassurance that they are doing a dangerous and valuable job. It provides a gloss that enables officers to cope—practically and emotionally—with the often depressing, difficult, and messy situations with which they are faced (Reiner, 2000). Finally, although elements of this oral culture are undoubtedly unpalatable, it cannot be related to practical police behaviour in a straightforward causal way. Individual officers are not helpless in the face of an all-pervasive culture, but actively interpret and react to it (Waddington, 1999). We therefore need to understand the ways in which individual officers resist and rework the occupational cultures in which they find themselves.

Policing a diverse society

During recent decades, Britain, along with most western industrial societies, has experienced increasing social and cultural diversity. For example, social differences along lines of religion, age, gender, region, nationality, ethnicity, sexuality, and lifestyles are becoming more important as a source of individual and group identity. At the same time, social and economic inequality has increased substantially over the past 20 years (Morgan and Newburn, 1997). An important challenge for contemporary policing is to balance and respond to conflicting demands from an increasingly diverse society. However, a central finding of much policing research is that the adversarial aspects of policing have always been experienced disproportionately by those at the lower end of the social hierarchy (Reiner, 2000). The unemployed, the poor, people living in inner-city areas, immigrants, and ethnic minorities consistently find themselves more likely to be on the end of police powers (see also Chapter 18 on race and ethnicity and Chapter 11 on violence). We will focus here on the arena of race relations, although it should be noted that similar arguments have applied to the policing experiences of other social groups. In particular, concerns have been raised about the experiences of women and LGB (lesbian, gay, and bisexual) people both as police officers, and also as receivers of policing services (Heidensohn, 2008; Williams and Robinson, 2004). In addition, as society has become more diverse during the latter half of the twentieth century, police relations with a range of other minority groups have come under scrutiny (Jones and Newburn, 2001).

The subject of crime, ethnicity, and policing remains highly controversial and explanations have too-often been reduced to those entirely related to police racism, or alternatively, to alleged higher offending rates among minority ethnic groups. Recent work has provided a more sophisticated understanding of the different forms of racial discrimination that operate within the police organization and in wider society (Phillips and Bowling, 2007). It has also highlighted the important impact of wider structural patterns of disadvantage that disproportionately place some ethnic minority communities in the geographical places and social groups that are more likely to be on the end of adversarial policing. The research also continues to demonstrate that, despite over 20 years of official attention to the issue, it is clear that relationships between the police and minority ethnic communities remain problematic in a number of respects (Bowling, Parmar and Phillips, 2008). First, considering the dimension of suspects/offenders, it is clear that ethnic minority people (and especially black people) are substantially over-represented in police stop and arrest statistics. Recent data at the national level shows very stark differences, with black people about seven times as likely as whites (on average) to be stopped by the police, and about three and a half times as likely overall to be arrested (Ministry of Justice, 2007). Second, there is evidence that ethnic minorities remain 'under-protected' as well as 'over-policed'. Particular concerns have been raised about levels of racist-harassment and violence (Bowling, 1998). The police service has come under strong criticism for failure to deal effectively with such crimes, although it is accepted that significant improvements have been made in recent years. Despite over two decades of official attention, ethnic minorities remain markedly under-represented among police officers. The most recent figures show that ethnic minority officers account for less than 4 per cent of total police strength, compared to 7 per cent of the working population (Ministry of Justice, 2007). Difficulties in attracting sufficient numbers of ethnic minority recruits and the relatively high resignation rates among ethnic minority officers have been related to anticipated and actual experiences of racism from colleagues and the general public (HMIC, 2000).

There are a number of possible explanations for these different experiences of policing. Direct discrimination by individual police officers is most probably a contributory factor, given what we know about the history of racial prejudice within occupational police cultures (see above). Direct discrimination is also suggested by the fact that racial disproportions are widest for the offence categories in which police officers have the greatest discretion to target, such as drugs possession or minor public order offences (Smith, 1997). However, questions have been raised about the degree to which levels of stated prejudice within the oral police culture are put into practice in police behaviour (Smith and Gray, 1985; Waddington, 1999). More recent official attention has been applied to the concept of 'institutional discrimination' highlighted in the MacPherson Report into the racist murder of the black teenager Stephen Lawrence. MacPherson defined institutional racism as unwitting and unintentional discrimination that is built into organizational policies and practices, with the (sometimes unintended) effect of disadvantaging members of particular ethnic groups. This clearly moves us towards a more sophisticated notion of discrimination, one in which discriminatory practices arise out of the everyday functioning of an organization rather than being equated simply with examples of individual racial discrimination. However, the concept as outlined by MacPherson has itself come under criticism for its lack of specificity, and its failure to identify the particular policies, and the organizational dynamics that underpin them, that lead to discriminatory outcomes (McLaughlin and Murji, 1999; Lea, 2000).

On the other hand, there is evidence that factors other than police discrimination (direct and institutional) contribute at a more fundamental level to problematic relationships. For example, although definitive conclusions cannot be drawn, there is some evidence that there are disproportionately high numbers of some ethnic minority groups involved in crime and disorder (Smith, 1997). This should not be a contentious finding given what we know about wider patterns of racial disadvantage, and associations with offending of socio-economic problems such as unemployment and poverty (Dickinson, 1993). In addition, as mentioned above, these wider structural features often work to place ethnic minorities at greater risk of police attention, in a very practical sense. For example, a number of factors, including higher levels of unemployment and more school exclusions among young black people, mean that they are disproportionately 'available' in public places for police stops (MVA and Miller, 2000; Waddington *et al.*, 2004). It is increasingly recognized that socio-economic disadvantage contributes both to higher offending and greater targeting by the police. This, in turn, helps further generate mutual hostility between the police and some ethnic minority groups, which fosters resentment on the part of the community and prejudice within the police organization. In turn, these processes help to reinforce and exacerbate the wider patterns of ethnic disadvantage (Lea and Young, 1984). As Reiner (2000) has stated, 'the police are reproducers rather than creators of social injustice, although their prejudices may amplify it'. Police reformers must focus their attention upon these amplification effects in order to bring about improvements within the framework of policing policy (Jones, 1998). But it is difficult to avoid the conclusion that, without a more general reduction in socio-economic inequality and racial disadvantage, changes in policing policy alone can only bring about rather limited improvements.

Police effectiveness and performance

In recent years, the issue of police performance has been the central concern of political interest in policing in England and Wales. By the early 1990s there was heightened official concern that, despite ever-increasing amounts of public expenditure devoted to the police, crime rates had continued to rise, whilst detection rates had fallen substantially (Jones and Newburn, 1997). Since this time, however, there have been substantial falls in crime as recorded by the British Crime Survey, although it is unclear what contribution policing has made to these falls (Maguire, 2007). Despite the recent evidence of decreasing victimization, an obsession with promoting police effectiveness remains central to government attempts to reform the police service.

The roots of the current police reform programme can be detected during the early 1980s, when the then Conservative Government began to apply market disciplines to a range of public services. The process began when the Government's 'Financial Management Initiative' (designed to promote economy, efficiency, and effectiveness in public services) was extended to the police service in 1983. This was the first significant attempt to bring about more central budgetary control of policing by linking increases in police staffing levels to evidence that police forces had 'civilianized' posts. Since the mid-1980s the Audit Commission has been increasingly influential, promoting 'value for money' within police forces. During the 1990s, government reforms during the 1990s were underpinned by a 'rigorous instrumentalism' with the key focus being to promote efficient and effective service delivery (Walker, 2000: 98). The Police and Magistrates Courts Act 1994 introduced a range of reforms, including the introduction of a 'purchaser-provider' split between police authority and force, the development of national policing objectives and key performance indicators, the introduction of costed local 'business plans' for policing, the appointment of independent members to police authorities to make them more 'businesslike', the encouragement of charging for some police services and the promotion of sponsorship, and the devolution of budgetary controls to the local level (Jones, 2008).

There have been particular concerns about police performance in the arena of crime investigation and control. These areas of policing have been shaped increasingly by economic forms of thinking over recent years (Maguire, 2008). The Audit Commission has promoted a more 'proactive' strategy in contrast to more traditional case-based methods of detective work (Audit Commission, 1993). This includes a more calculative and risk-oriented approach towards crime investigation, including crime management, case screening, the increasing use of surveillance technologies, and more systematic quantitative methods of crime analysis (Johnston, 2000). These developments are currently being systematically introduced across all police forces in England and Wales with the development of the National Intelligence Model (NIM), which provides a 'business model' for the organization of police crime control activities (Maguire, 2008).

These policy trends have been further encouraged by Labour administrations since 1997. Two of the most significant developments within this were the stringent national planning framework introduced by the Police Reform Act 2002, and the establishment of the Police Standards Unit—a Home Office Unit with a brief to promote improvements in 'under-performing' police force areas—in the same year. These developments have been accompanied by an ever more strident rhetoric on the part of government ministers expressing frustration at levels of police performance and the need for more radical reform (Travis, 2002). Another example of this heightened political concern with police performance was the Street Crime Action Group that was established in March 2003. This involved direct central intervention in day-to-day policing by senior government ministers, with senior officers in ten target force areas required to report on a regular basis to government ministers on progress towards targets (Home Office, 2002). Strong concerns have arisen about the efficacy of crude statistical indicators as measures of police effectiveness, and about some of the negative organizational side-effects arising from intensive performance management regimes (Senior *et al.*, 2007).

Police governance and accountability

Whilst debates about police governance and accountability have been less salient in recent discussions of British policing, the issue remains of central importance in a democratic society. A central part of the debate on police accountability has concerned the governance of policing policies concerned with overall priorities, resource-allocation, and policing styles. A key finding of research on police governance has been the progressive centralization of control over policing policy in England and Wales (Jones, 2008). The 1964 Police Act divided responsibility for the framing and monitoring of police policy between a 'tripartite structure' comprising chief constables, the Home Office, and local government (in the form of police authorities). It is clear that the local element of this structure became increasingly weakened over the latter part of the twentieth century. This was related to a variety of factors. For example the Home Office has taken a much more proactive role in promoting central government priorities and has exerted greater control over the training and promotion of senior police officers (Reiner, 2000). Local police authorities have traditionally been weak in terms of legal powers, and rather reluctant to use the few powers that they do have (Jones and Newburn, 1997). In addition, the senior officers' professional association—the Association of Chief Police Officers (ACPO)—has emerged as a significant policy-making and lobbying body at the national level (Savage *et al.*, 2000).

A further illustration of growing central control over policing policy is the emergence of national policing organizations during the late 1990s, including the National Criminal Intelligence Service (NCIS) and the National Crime Squad (NCS) (Johnston, 2000). These bodies were later subsumed within a single national policing organization with the establishment of the Serious and Organised Crime Agency (SOCA) in 2006. SOCA also incorporated a number of other existing national policing functions including Her Majesty's Revenue and Customs' role in investigating drug trafficking and criminal finance, and the UK Immigration Service's work in tackling organized immigration crime. Part of the justification for the establishment of SOCA was that many provincial forces were considered too small to be able to effectively provide these functions. In 2005 it seemed that further radical centralization of control over policing was imminent, when the then Home Secretary Charles Clarke proposed a radical restructuring of police organization in England and Wales into a much smaller number of large regional forces. This raised strong criticisms about the lack of local accountability in the structures proposed, though supporters of the restructuring argued that effective local accountability mechanisms could be developed at 'Basic Command Unit' level. However, a combination of the lack of statutory powers of local bodies, and the likelihood that local police chiefs would be constrained by regional and national influences, cast doubts on how accountable to the local democratic process such large forces would be. In the event, the proposed restructuring became mired in controversy, and was postponed indefinitely following a change of Home Secretary in 2006.

Most recently, there have been indications from both main political parties that they wish to enhance the local electoral input into the governance of policing. A Conservative policy document called for a return to localized police forces, but responsible to elected sheriffs (based on the system in certain parts of the USA) (Loveday and Reid, 2003). The Labour Party also remains enamoured with US-style solutions, and floated the idea of placing local police services under the control of directly elected mayors, or introducing direct election to police authorities (to replace the current system of appointment from constituent local authorities). The Government flirted with a more direct form of local police accountability by considering the introduction of local elected community panels as part of its move towards Neighbourhood Policing. However, they were later to retreat from this move towards greater local electoral accountability of policing (McLaughlin, 2007).

The pluralization of policing poses significant challenges for the development of effective systems of governance and accountability. Loader (2000) has proposed the establishment of local, regional, and national 'Policing Commissions' with a statutory responsibility to monitor and control *policing* policy as exercised by a wide range of policing agencies and institutions. This kind of institutional approach was adopted by the Patten Commission on reforming policing in Northern Ireland (Patten, 1999). The Commission recommended that local policing units be answerable to 'District Policing Partnership Boards'—a committee of the local authority that would have the power to 'buy-in' extra local policing resources from providers other than the public police. It also recommended that at force level, a 'Policing Board' (and not a 'Police Board') should be established that would have substantially more powers than the existing police authority (Walker, 2000). This would have responsibility for regulating all policing providers including the commercial security industry, and co-ordinating provision across policing networks.

Police accountability can also be considered in terms of the accountability and control of police officers as they go about their day-to-day activities. There have been significant developments regarding the regulation of police behaviour in particular cases. Two of the most significant involve the regulation and control of police powers in dealing with suspects in criminal investigations, and the development of an effective complaints mechanisms for the police. Although space prevents a detailed discussion, the Police and Criminal Evidence Act 1984 introduced a number of regulations over the powers held by the police over suspects in custody. These included things such as the introduction of a custody officer to monitor visits to suspects detained in police cells, time limits for how long a person can be held without charge, the right to legal representation, and tape recording of interviews. Whilst a number of criticisms have been raised regarding the impact of PACE (Sanders and Young, 2008), the balance of research does suggest that there has been a significant effect on police behaviour within the police station, and possibly on wider detective culture (Maguire, 2002). Whatever the ongoing problems about controlling police discretion via the imposition of rules, it seems fair to say that the police are certainly more accountable than they were for their use of powers in particular investigations. Turning to the areas of police complaints mechanisms, until recently a major criticism of the arrangements has focused around the independence (or rather the perceived lack of it) of the complaints process from the police organization. Ultimately, police officers have investigated serious complaints against other officers, although there was an independent element in the supervision of such investigations in the form of the Police Complaints Authority (PCA) (Maguire and Corbett, 1991). The Police Reform

Act 2002 established the Independent Police Complaints Commission (IPCC), staffed entirely by non-police officers and with a greater remit and more powers than the old PCA. It remains to be seen exactly what impact these new arrangements will have on the individual dimension of police accountability, but it is likely to be significant.

CONCLUSION

This chapter has presented a broad overview of some of the key themes surrounding policing and the provision of security in Britain today. It has demonstrated how the study of policing emerged from a position of relative invisibility during the 1960s, to the forefront of debate in the latter years of the twentieth century. For much of the past 40 years, this renewed academic and political interest in policing has focused on the state institution known as 'the police'. Recent years, however, have seen a growing focus upon the idea of fragmentation and pluralization of policing which has led some commentators to question the relevance of a continued focus on public constabularies. This chapter has had a slightly different emphasis. Although there have been some highly significant developments within the policing systems of the UK (such as the growth of commercial security), it still seems that for the forseeable future at least, state-organized policing arrangements will remain central to security provision. Thus, the primary focus of the discussion has been on traditional police forces, what they do, how they do it, and what key debates have arisen in relation to them. These include the issue of the nature, sources, and dimensions of police occupational cultures, and how they might relate to problematic behaviour by police officers. Also important is the challenge of providing equitable policing services to an increasingly diverse society in which a range of groups make contrasting demands upon the police. A central theme in recent government policy has concerned police performance and effectiveness, and, finally, there is the challenge of how best to make the police accountable to the publics they serve. Although the policing landscape has undoubtedly become considerably more complex in recent decades, these areas of debate—and others connected with the police and policing—are likely to remain hot topics of discussion amongst students, academics, and the police themselves.

QUESTIONS FOR DISCUSSION

1 What is 'cop culture' and where does it come from?

2 How and why do some ethnic minority groups experience difficult relationships with the police?

3 What ways have the Government tried to improve police effectiveness in recent years?

4 In what ways is control over policing policy becoming more centralized in England and Wales?

5 Are the police becoming more or less accountable for what they do?

GUIDE TO FURTHER READING

Jones, T. (2007) 'The Governance of Security: Pluralisation, Privatisation and Polarisation in Crime Control' in M. Maguire, R. Morgan, and R. Reiner (eds) *The Oxford Handbook of Criminology*. Oxford: Oxford University Press (4th edn).

This chapter provides a detailed review of the theoretical and empirical literature exploring contemporary developments in policing and security governance.

McLaughlin, E. (2007) *The New Policing*. London: Sage.

A detailed introduction to the key issues facing contemporary policing, providing a comprehensive overview of traditional approaches to studying the police along with a lucid treatment of more recent developments in the governance of security.

Newburn, T. (ed) (2008) *The Handbook of Policing*. Cullompton: Willan. (2nd edn)

An authoritative and comprehensive overview of British policing that draws on the expertise of both academics and senior police practitioners.

Newburn, T. and Reiner, R. (2007) 'Policing and the Police' in M. Maguire, R. Morgan, and R. Reiner (eds) *The Oxford Handbook of Criminology*. Oxford: Oxford University Press (4th edn).

This chapter provides an up-to-date and extremely detailed review of the key themes of recent British (and other) policing research and a helpful guide for further reading in the field.

Reiner, R. (2000) *The Politics of the Police*. Oxford: Oxford University Press.

This is the third edition of a widely praised book that provides a detailed review of the history, politics, and sociology of the police in England and Wales. This edition remains a key text for students, and is now comprehensively updated with a wealth of research data published during the 1990s.

DEFINITIONS OF KEY CONCEPTS

- **Governance:** this is often used as a general term to denote governing strategies originating from inside and outside the State, though with regard to policing is often used simply to refer to the constitutional and institutional arrangements for framing and monitoring the policies of the police.

- **Accountability:** the ways in which policing organizations and individuals are rendered answerable for their policies and day-to-day activities, exerted by internal and external mechanisms.

- **Policing:** organized and purposive forms of social control and regulation, involving surveillance and the threat of sanctions for discovered rule-breaking.

- **Police:** the specialist state agency tasked with law enforcement and order maintenance.

WEB LINKS

Crime reduction

http://www.crimereduction.gov.uk

A government-run website with a wealth of information on crime reduction, community safety, and policing, including up-to-date statistics on the criminal justice system, on-line reports on policing and community safety, and details of the latest policy initiatives.

Her Majesty's Inspectorate of Constabulary (HMIC)

http://inspectorates.homeoffice.gov.uk/hmic/

HMIC has a statutory responsibility to promote the efficiency and effectiveness of police forces in England and Wales via a programme of regular force inspections and reports. It has become increasingly influential in recent years in promoting the Home Office agenda on performance improvement, as well as producing influential thematic reports on such matters as race relations and equal opportunities. This website includes a range of useful information and statistics on policing in England and Wales, and also provides online access to HMIC reports.

Home Office
http://www.homeoffice.gov.uk

The Home Office is the central government department with responsibility for policing in England and Wales, and this website allows access to a wide range of relevant material for students interested in research and current policy developments on policing. In particular, students can access online a large body of Home Office research studies on policing, dating back to 1995.

Police reform in England and Wales
http://police.homeoffice.gov.uk/police-reform/

A key website for students interested in the major programme of police reform introduced by the current Labour Government. It includes key official publications such as consultation documents and summaries of recent legislation, and also the influential National Intelligence Model (NIM) for policing, and the most recent National Policing Plan.

Police services of the UK
http://www.police.uk

A police service website with important details and contact addresses for all the police forces (and related organizations) in the United Kingdom. This includes a range of relevant service-related information about current issues of concern, as well as details of police recruitment processes.

REFERENCES

Audit Commission (1993) *Helping with Enquiries: Tackling Crime Effectively.* London: Audit Commission.

Bayley, D. (1994) *Police for the Future.* New York: Oxford University Press.

Bayley, D. and Shearing, C. (1996) 'The Future of Policing' *Law and Society Review* 30(3) pp. 585–606.

Bayley, D. and Shearing, C. (2001) *The New Structure of Policing.* Washington, DC: The National Institute of Justice.

Becker, H. (1963) *Outsiders: Studies in the Sociology of Deviance.* New York: Free Press.

Bittner, E. (1980) *The Functions of the Police in Modern Society.* Cambridge, Ma: Olgeschlager, Gunn and Hain.

Bowling, B. (1998) *Violent Racism.* Oxford: Clarendon Press

Bowling, B. (1999) 'The Rise and Fall of New York Murder' *British Journal of Criminology* 39(4) pp. 531–54.

Bowling, B., Parmar, A., and Phillips, C. (2008) 'Policing Minority Ethnic Communities' in T. Newburn (ed) *The Handbook of Policing* (2nd edn). Cullompton: Devon .

Bratton, W. (1997) 'Crime is down in New York City: Blame the Police' in N. Dennis (ed) *Zero Tolerance: Policing a Free Society.* London: Institute for Economic Affairs.

Burney, E. (2005) *Making People Behave: Anti-social Behaviour, Politics and Policy.* Cullompton: Willan

Chan, J. (1996) 'Changing Police Culture' *British Journal of Criminology* 36(1) pp. 109–34.

Clarke, J. (2001) 'The Pleasures of Crime: Interrogating the Detective Story' in J. Muncie and E. McLaughlin (eds) *The Problem of Crime* (2nd edn). London: Sage.

Coleman, A. and Gorman, L. (1982) 'Conservatism, Dogmatism and Authoritarianism in British Police Officers' *Sociology* 16(1) pp. 1–11.

Crawford, A. (2008) 'Plural Policing in the UK: Policing Beyond the Police' in T. Newburn (ed) *The Handbook of Policing* (2nd edn). Cullompton: Willan.

Dickinson, D. (1993) *Crime and Unemployment.* Cambridge: Institute of Criminology.

Downes, D. and Morgan, R. (2007) 'No Turning Back: The Politics of Law and Order into the Millennium' in M. Maguire, R. Morgan, and R. Reiner (eds) *The Oxford Handbook of Criminology.* Oxford: Oxford University Press (4th edn).

Ellison, G. and Smyth, J. (2000) *The Crowned Harp: Policing Northern Ireland.* London: Pluto Press.

Greene, J. (1999) 'Zero Tolerance: A Case Study of Police Policies and Practices in New York City' *Crime and Delinquency* 45(2) pp. 171–187.

Hall, S., Critchley, C., Jefferson, T., Clarke, J., and Roberts, B. (1978) *Policing the Crisis*. London: Macmillan.

Harcourt, B. (2001) *Illusion of Order: The False Promise of Broken Windows Policing*. Cambridge, MA: Harvard University Press.

Heidensohn, F. (2008) 'Gender and Policing' in T. Newburn (ed) *The Handbook of Policing* (2nd edn). Cullompton: Willan.

Her Majesty's Inspectorate of Constabulary (HMIC) (2000) *Winning the Race: Embracing Diversity. Consolidation Inspection of Police Community and Race Relations 2000*. London: Home Office.

Home Office (1993) *Police Reform*. London: Home Office.

Home Office (2002) *Delivering the Street Crime Initiative: Partnership in Operation*. London: HMSO.

Home Office (2005) *Neighbourhood Policing: Your Police; Your Community; Our Commitment*. London: Home Office.

Innes, M. and Thiel, D. (2008) 'Policing Terror' in T. Newburn (ed) *The Handbook of Policing* (2nd edn). Cullompton: Willan.

Jefferson, T. (1990) *The Case Against Paramilitary Policing*. Milton Keynes: Open University Press.

Jefferson, T. (1993) 'Pondering Paramilitarism' *British Journal of Criminology* 33(3) pp. 374–81.

Johnston, L. (1992) *The Rebirth of Private Policing*. London: Routledge.

Johnston, L. (1996) 'What is vigilantism?' *British Journal of Criminology*, 36:2, pp. 220–36.

Johnston, L. (2000) *Policing Britain: Risk, Security and Governance*. London: Longman.

Johnston, L. (2007) '"Keeping the Family Together": Police Community Support Officers and the "Policing Extended Family" in London' *Policing and Society* 17(2) pp. 119–40.

Johnston, L. and Shearing, C. (2003) *Governing Security: Explorations in Policing and Justice*. London: Routledge.

Jones, T. (1998) 'Police and Race Relations' in R. Chadwick (ed) *The Encyclopedia of Applied Ethics*. San Diego, CA: Academic Press.

Jones, T. (2007) 'The Governance of Security: Pluralisation, Privatisation and Polarisation in Crime Control' in M. Maguire, R. Morgan, and R. Reiner (eds) *The Oxford Handbook of Criminology* (4th edn). Oxford: Oxford University Press.

Jones, T. (2008) 'Private Policing' in T. Newburn and P. Neyroud (eds) *The Dictionary of Policing*. Cullompton: Willan.

Jones, T. (2008) 'The Accountability of Policing' in T. Newburn (ed) *The Handbook of Policing* (2nd edn). Cullompton: Willan.

Jones, T. and Newburn, T. (1997) *Policing After the Act: Police Governance After the Police and Magistrates' Courts Act 1994*. London: Policy Studies Institute.

Jones, T. and Newburn, T. (1998) *Private Security and Public Policing*. Oxford: Clarendon Press.

Jones, T. and Newburn, T. (2001) *Widening Access: Improving Relations with 'Hard to Reach Groups'*. London: Home Office.

Jones, T. and Newburn, T. (2002) 'The Transformation of Policing? Understanding Current Trends in Policing Systems' *British Journal of Criminology*, 42:1, pp. 129–146.

Jones, T. and Newburn, T. (2006) (eds) *Plural Policing: A Comparative Perspective*. London: Routledge.

Jones, T. and Newburn, T. (2007) *Policy Transfer and Criminal Justice: Exploring US Influence over British Crime Control*. Maidenhead: Open University Press.

Lea, J. (2000) 'The Macpherson Report and the Question of Institutional Racism' *Howard Journal of Criminal Justice* 39(3).

Lea, J. and Young, J. (1984) *What is to be done about law and order?* Harmondsworth: Penguin.

Leishman, F. and Mason, P. (2003) *Policing and the Media: Facts, Fictions and Factions*. Cullompton: Willan.

Lemert, E. (1964) 'Social Structure, social control and deviation' in M. Clinard (ed) *Anomie and Deviant Behaviour*. New York: Free Press.

Loader, I. (1997) 'Private Security and the Demand for Protection in Contemporary Britain' *Policing and Society*, Vol. 7 pp. 143–162.

Loader, I. (2000) 'Plural Policing and Democratic Governance' *Social and Legal Studies*, 9:3, pp. 323–345.

Loader, I. and Mulcahy, A. (2003) *Policing and the Condition of England: Memory, Politics and Culture*. Oxford: Oxford University Press.

Loader, I. and Walker, N. (2001) 'Policing as a Public Good: Reconstituting the Connections between Policing and State', *Theoretical Criminology*, 5(1) pp. 9–35.

Loveday, B. and Reid, A. (2003) *Going Local: Who Should Run Britain's Police?* London: Policy Exchange.

McLaughlin, E. (2007) *The New Policing*. London: Sage.

McLaughlin, E. and Murji, K. (1999) 'After the Stephen Lawrence Inquiry' *Critical Social Policy* 19(3) pp. 371–385.

Maguire, M. (2002) 'Regulating the Police Station: The Case of the Police and Criminal Evidence Act 1984' in M. McConville and G. Wilson (eds) *The Handbook of the Criminal Justice Process*. Oxford: Oxford University Press.

Maguire, M. (2007) 'Crime Data and Statistics' in M. Maguire, R. Morgan, and R. Reiner (eds) *The Oxford Handbook of Criminology*. Oxford: Oxford University Press (4th edn).

Maguire, M. (2008) 'Criminal Investigation and Crime Control' in T. Newburn (ed) *The Handbook of Policing* (2nd edn). Cullompton: Willan.

Maguire, M. and Corbett, C. (1991) *A Study of the Police Complaints System*. London: HMSO.

Manning, P. (1977) *Police Work*. Cambridge, Ma: MIT Press.

Ministry of Justice (2007) *Statistics on Race and the Criminal Justice System 2006*. London: Ministry of Justice.

Morgan, R. and Newburn, T. (1997) *The Future of Policing*. Oxford: Oxford University Press.

MVA and Miller, J. (2000) *Profiling Populations Available for Stops and Searches*. Police Research Series Paper 131. London: Home Office.

Newburn, T. (2008) 'Introduction: Understanding Policing' in T. Newburn (ed) *The Handbook of Policing* (2nd edn). Cullompton: Willan.

Newburn, T. and Reiner, R. (2007) 'Policing and the Police' in M. Maguire, R. Morgan, and R. Reiner (eds) *The Oxford Handbook of Criminology* (4th edn). Oxford: Oxford University Press.

PA Consulting Group (2001) *Diary of a Police Officer*. Police Research Paper 149. London: Home Office.

Patten, C. (1999) *A New Beginning for Policing in Northern Ireland: The Report of the Independent Commission on Policing for Northern Ireland*. Belfast: HMSO.

Phillips, C. and Bowling, B. (2007) 'Ethnicities, Racism, Crime and Criminal Justice' in M. Maguire, R. Morgan, and R. Reiner (eds) *The Oxford Handbook of Criminology* (4th edn). Oxford: Oxford University Press.

Punch, M. (1979) 'The Secret Social Service' in S. Holdaway (ed) *The British Police*. London: Edward Arnold.

Rawlings, P. (2002) *Policing: A Short History*. Cullompton: Willan.

Reiner, R. (1997) 'Policing and the Police' in M. Maguire, R. Morgan, and R. Reiner (eds) *The Oxford Handbook of Criminology* (2nd edn). Oxford: Oxford University Press.

Reiner, R. (2000) *The Politics of the Police* (3rd edn). Oxford: Oxford University Press.

Reiner, R. (2007) 'Media-made Criminality: The Representation of Crime in the Mass Media' in M. Maguire, R. Morgan, and R. Reiner (eds) *The Oxford Handbook of Criminology*. Oxford: Oxford University Press (4th edn).

Reiner, R. (2008) 'Policing and the Media' in T. Newburn (ed) *The Handbook of Policing* (2nd edn). Cullompton: Willan.

Rozenberg, J. (1992) 'Miscarriages of Justice' in E. Stockdale and S. Casale (eds) *Criminal Justice Under Stress*. London: Blackstone Press, pp. 91–117.

Sanders, A. and Young, R. (2008) 'Police Powers' in T. Newburn (ed) *The Handbook of Policing* (2nd edn). Cullompton: Willan.

Savage, S., Charman, S., and Cope, S. (2000) 'The Policy-Making Context: Who Shapes Policing Policy?' in F. Leishman, *et al.* (eds) *Core Issues in Policing*. Harlow: Longman.

Scarman, Lord (1981) *The Brixton Disorders 10–12 April 1981: Report of an Inquiry by Lord Scarman*. London: HMSO.

Senior, P., Crowther-Dowey, C., and Long, M. (2007) *Understanding Modernisation in Criminal Justice*. Maidenhead: Open University Press

Shapland, J. and Vagg, J. (1988) *Policing by the Public*. London: Routledge.

Shearing, C. (2006) 'Reflections on the Refusal to Acknowledge Private Governments' in J. Wood and B. Dupont (eds) *Democracy, Society and the Governance of Security*. Cambridge: Cambridge University Press.

Sheptycki, J. (ed) (2000) *Issues in Transnational Policing*. London: Routledge.

Skogan, W. (1990) *The Police and Public in England and Wales: A British Crime Survey Report*. London: HMSO.

Skolnick, J. (1966) *Justice Without Trial: Law Enforcement in a Democratic Society*. New York: Wiley.

Smith, D.J. (1986) 'The Framework of Law and Policing Practice' in J. Beynon and C. Bourn (eds) *The Police: Powers, Procedures and Proprieties*. Oxford: Pergamon Press.

Smith, D. J. (1997) 'Ethnic Origins, Crime and Criminal Justice' in M. Maguire, R. Morgan, and R. Reiner (eds) *The Oxford Handbook of Criminology* (2nd edn). Oxford: Oxford University Press.

Smith, D.J. and Gray. J. (1985) *Police and People in London*. London: Policy Studies Institute.

Travis, A. (2002) 'Met Police Get Six Month Deadline To Tackle Crime'. *Guardian* 15 February.

Tilley, N. (2008) 'Modern Approaches to Policing: Community, Problem-oriented and Intelligence-led' in T. Newburn (ed) *The Handbook of Policing* (2nd edn). Cullompton: Willan.

Waddington, P.A.J. (1993) 'The Case Against Paramilitary Policing Considered' *British Journal of Criminology* 33(3) pp. 352–66.

Waddington, P.A.J. (1999) 'Police (Canteen) Sub-Culture: An Appreciation' *British Journal of Criminology* 39(2) pp. 286–308.

Waddington, P.A.J. (2008) 'Police Use of Force, Firearms and Riot Control' in T. Newburn (ed) *The Handbook of Policing* (2nd edn). Cullompton: Devon.

Waddington, P.A.J., Stenson, K., and Don, D. (2004) 'In Proportion: Race and Police Stop and Search' *British Journal of Criminology* 44(6) pp. 889–914.

Walker, N. (2000) *Policing in a Changing Constitutional Order.* London: Sweet and Maxwell.

Westmarland, L. (2008) 'Police Cultures' in T. Newburn (ed) *The Handbook of Policing* (2nd edn). Cullompton: Devon.

Williams, M. and Robinson, A.L. (2004) 'Problems and Prospects with Policing the Lesbian, Gay and Bisexual Community in Wales' *Policing and Society* 14(3) pp. 213–232.

Wilson, J.Q. and Kelling, G. (1982) 'Broken Windows' *The Atlantic Monthly*, March pp. 29–37.

Wood, J. (2006) 'Research and Innovation in the Field of Security: A Nodal Governance View' in J. Wood and B. Dupont (eds) *Democracy, Society and the Governance of Security.* Cambridge: Cambridge University Press.

NOTES

1. For more information about the policing arrangements in Scotland and Northern Ireland, the reader is referred to Walker (2000), and Ellison and Smyth (2000) respectively.

2. Readers should note that although the term 'canteen culture' is still used regularly in discussions about the police, the landmark ethnographic studies of British policing that did so much to raise awareness about police working cultures in this country are now over 20 years old.

26 Community sentences and offender management

Anne Worrall

INTRODUCTION

When the topic of punishment is discussed, many people think first about prison. Yet the vast majority of people who commit crimes and are detected are dealt with by measures that do not involve imprisonment. Approximately 1.8 million offenders were found guilty or were cautioned in 2006 (Ministry of Justice, 2007a) and, of these, approximately 96,000 were sent to prison. The remainder were cautioned, discharged, fined, or placed on community sentences. This chapter explores and explains the history, philosophies, current practices, and policy debates surrounding those measures which are, often mistakenly, frequently referred to as 'alternatives to prison'. In this chapter, it will be argued that community sentences should not be viewed merely as 'alternatives' to prison but should be understood as representing a different sphere of penal regulation which is based on enabling and requiring offenders to take responsibility for changing their own lives and behaviour without the physical constraints of imprisonment. The following section will provide a brief introduction to the key concept of offender management and related terminology. There will then follow a more detailed description of the range of sentences available to courts, the relevant legislation, and the extent to which these sentences are used. A brief history of the Probation Service—the agency responsible for most community sentences—will follow, concluding with the creation of the National Probation Service in 2001 and the National Offender Management Service in 2004. The chapter then proceeds to an analysis and discussion of the main issues and problems presented by offender management, culminating in an exploration of the impact of the 'What Works' agenda, which has dominated developments in this area over the past decade. The concluding section of the chapter will summarize the key facts, concepts, and debates relating to this topic.

BACKGROUND

There is no single generic term for punishment that does not involve imprisonment. The most commonly used terms are 'alternatives to custody' or 'non-custodial sentences', but 'community punishment', 'community corrections', 'community penalties', and 'community sentences' are now widely recognized terms, though the word 'community' in this context means little more than 'not in prison'. The term 'community' is difficult to define because it has different meanings in different contexts. It conjures up images of neighbourliness, mutual aid, and a positive sense of belonging, while, at the same time, blurring the boundaries of responsibility between the State and the individual. In relation to crime, it is not clear whether 'the community' is tolerant, resourceful, and healing or intolerant, fearful, and punitive (Worrall and Hoy, 2005). The extent to which the 'community' is involved in community sentences in practice is generally very limited and the implication that such sentences enhance social inclusion, rather than exacerbate social exclusion, is also debatable (see Chapter 16 on the concept of social exclusion). The phrase 'punishment in the community' entered penal vocabulary in a government discussion paper in

1988 (Home Office, 1988) and was an attempt to dislodge prison from its central position in penal thinking. It became integrated into legislation in the Criminal Justice Act 1991, which was the overarching legal framework for sentencing until the Criminal Justice Act 2003 introduced the 'community order'.

It is possible to classify non-custodial sentences in three ways: self-regulatory, financial, and supervisory (Worrall and Hoy, 2005). Self-regulatory penalties involve some form of public admonition or reprimand which is assumed to be sufficiently shaming of itself to deter the offender from further lawbreaking. Financial penalties are of two kinds: fines are both retributive and deterrent (see Chapter 22) in purpose and are paid to the central administration of a criminal justice system, whilst compensation is paid (through the courts) to the victim of a crime and is intended to provide reparation. Supervisory sentences are imposed when courts believe that the offender is unable to stop committing crimes without support or surveillance and they may contain one or more of three elements:

(a) rehabilitation (through education, therapeutic programmes, counselling, and welfare advice);

(b) reparation (through unpaid work for the community); and

(c) incapacitation (through curfews and electronic monitoring).

Some community sentences have long histories, while others have been introduced more recently. For example, the origins of probation (the main form of supervision) can be traced back to the late nineteenth century, whereas community service (unpaid work) was introduced in the 1970s, and electronic monitoring in the 1980s, initially as a mechanism for reducing the numbers of offenders being remanded in custody to await trial or sentence. Expansion in the use of supervisory sentences since the 1970s has been due to the desire of governments to be seen to be finding less expensive, but equally demanding, alternatives to imprisonment. This has been termed the 'decarceration' debate and resulted from a loss of confidence in the 1950s and 1960s in the 'rehabilitative ideal' (based on the discredited therapeutic possibilities of institutions). In reality, such expansion has been an accompaniment, rather than an alternative, to a rising prison population (Scull, 1984; Cohen, 1985).

It could be argued that community sentences might have several advantages over imprisonment. They allow offenders to retain family, work, and social ties while, at the same time, giving them the opportunity to repair the damage they have done to the community and resolve the personal and social problems which may have led to their offending in the first place. They enable offenders to avoid the stigma of imprisonment and the risk of becoming embedded in a criminal culture as a result of constant association with other prisoners. Community sentences are also less costly to administer than imprisonment (Worrall and Hoy, 2005). Despite these apparent advantages, community sentences have an 'image' problem. Although many more offenders receive some form of community punishment than are imprisoned, penal debates and policies focus overwhelmingly on prisons and neglect other forms of punishment (Windlesham, 1993). Attempts to raise the profile of community sentences encounter a number of obstacles.

First, and of most significance, is the public and media perception that community punishment is but a poor substitute for the 'real punishment' of prison. Viewed as 'soft options', community sentences are often represented in policy documents as weak and undemanding 'let offs', which do not command public confidence. There is, therefore, a constant search among advocates of community sentences to include more and more demanding conditions which distinguish 'intermediate sentences' (as they are sometimes called) from traditional welfare-oriented supervision (Byrne et al., 1992). Second is the obstacle of unfair and inconsistent sentencing. Despite increasingly sophisticated guidelines on the use of community sentences, there remain concerns that certain groups of offenders are over-represented in prison for reasons that may have little to do with the seriousness of their offences. Community sentences tend to be available only to the relatively advantaged socially; for example, those with sufficient money to pay a fine or those who are perceived to be able to benefit from supervision. Third is the obstacle of 'net-widening', a term which entered criminal justice vocabulary in the 1960s in the wake of labelling theory (see Chapter 4). With the proliferation of alternatives to custody comes the danger that instead of keeping people out of prison, community sentences will simply draw more and more people into the 'net' of the criminal justice system (Cohen, 1985) if sentencers use them for offenders who would have previously been discharged or fined. This process of 'up tariffing' increases the likelihood that they will eventually end up in prison. The fourth obstacle is that of enforcement. Ensuring compliance with community sentences is notoriously difficult (Hedderman, 2003; Hedderman and Hough, 2004) and courts have the right to send to prison any offender who fails to pay a fine or who breaches the conditions of a supervisory order. In this way, community sentencing always functions 'in the shadow' of imprisonment.

Types of community sentences and sentencing trends

We have already seen that there is no agreement on a collective name for penalties that do not involve imprisonment. It is also the case that there is no agreement on whether or not the term 'community sentences' should include sentences that do not involve some form of supervision by the Probation Service (see next section). For the purposes of this exercise and in order to provide a comprehensive introduction to the full range of non-custodial sentences, we will use the term in this broader sense.

Self-regulatory sentences are those which do not impose any immediate sanction on an offender. They assume that the very act of being detected, arrested, and, in some cases, taken to court, will cause sufficient shame to either deter or reform the offender, without need of further penalty. Formal police cautions, reprimands, and warnings are used very widely for juvenile offenders, especially those committing first or minor offences. They are also available for adults but are used less frequently. Overall, the cautioning rate fell from 40 per cent of all known offenders in 1995 to 32 per cent of all known offenders in 2000 but rose again to 41 per cent in 2006 (Ministry of Justice, 2007a). For adults, the most common self-regulatory sentence is known as a 'conditional discharge'. This involves a court appearance but the offender is put 'on trust' for a period of time. If they reoffend during that period, they are liable to be re-sentenced for the original offence, as well as for the new one. The use of conditional discharges has also declined steadily over the past decade (Mair, 2004a), and in 2006 only 5 per cent of all known offenders were given this sentence by the criminal courts (Ministry of Justice, 2007a). Other self-regulatory sentences are available for special situations but are used less frequently than those described here. For example, it is possible for a court to 'bind over' people 'to keep the peace' for a specified length of time. The Criminal Justice Act 2003 has also revived the infrequently used suspended prison sentence, adding specific conditions to it, and this has leapt in popularity, with over 32,000 such orders being made in 2006 (Ministry of Justice, 2007b). Arguably, this should now be categorized as a supervisory sentence because sentencers can require offenders to comply with the same requirements as those sentenced to community orders (described below).

Financial penalties remain the most commonly imposed sentences in the courts of England and Wales, although their use has reduced over the past decade (Moore, 2003). The two main types of financial penalty are fines and compensation orders. Advocates of the fine argue that it is a very flexible sentence which can take account of the offender's ability to pay as well as the seriousness of the offence. Thus, it combines elements of retribution (reflecting the seriousness of a crime), deterrence (convincing the offender that crime, literally, 'does not pay'), and reparation (paying society and/or the victim back for harm done). However, many people are either unable or unwilling to pay fines and they are then sent to prison 'in default'. In an attempt to resolve this problem, in the early 1990s, courts experimented with 'unit fines' which involved a specific formula for matching an offender's disposable income with the seriousness of their offence (Home Office, 1990). However, it was unpopular with sentencers, who believed that it was fettering their sentencing discretion, and the experiment was discontinued in 1993. There are large numbers of offenders who go to prison for 'fine default' but, because they spend only a few days there on average, their numbers are under-represented in prison population statistics (Ministry of Justice, 2007b: 89). Aware of this problem, courts have become more reluctant to impose fines, especially on women, who often do not have an independent source of income and who are responsible for the care of children (Hedderman and Gelsthorpe, 1997), and on unemployed offenders. Critics of this practice have argued that the use of financial penalties should be resuscitated to prevent the 'silting up' of probation caseloads with low risk offenders (Morgan, 2003). Compensation to a victim can be ordered as a separate sentence or as an adjunct to any other sentence. It is also possible for courts to confiscate the proceeds from crime.

Supervisory sentences come in many forms and it is confusing that, since the creation of the National Probation Service in 2001, the traditional names for the main sentences have been changed, not once but twice. Under the Criminal Justice Act 2003, which was implemented in 2005, all formerly separate orders were subsumed under the generic term 'community sentence' to form part of the 'menu' of basic requirements that sentencers could choose from when passing sentence (Gibson, 2004). Probation Orders became Community Rehabilitation Orders (CRO), then 'supervision'; Community Service Orders became Community Punishment Orders (CPO), then 'unpaid work'; Combination Orders (which combine probation and community service) became Community Punishment and Rehabilitation Orders (CPRO), but then disappeared, although sentencers can still require offenders to undertake 'unpaid work' and to participate in 'supervision'. In addition to these main components, the new community orders can now also include any combination of the following requirements: activities (for example, participating in activities related to seeking employment); accredited offending behaviour programmes; prohibited activities (for example, not possessing, using, or carrying a firearm); curfew (with or without electronic monitoring); exclusion (from a specific place); residence (at an approved address); mental health treatment; drug rehabilitation; alcohol treatment; and attendance centre (for offenders aged under 25). Traditionally, supervisory sentences have aimed to reform or rehabilitate offenders through advice, counselling, treatment, and constructive activity. Sentences involving unpaid work also contain strong elements of reparation to the community. Increasingly, however, the term 'supervision' is accompanied by the terms 'intensive' and/or 'monitoring', reflecting a change of ethos towards the principle of 'incapacitation'. Restricting offenders' liberty, checking on their whereabouts, and gathering ever more information about them, are routine features of contemporary supervision. The use of electronic monitoring to ensure compliance with curfew requirements is but an extreme example of current trends towards 'incapacitation in the community'.

The Ministry of Justice produces annual *Offender Management Caseload Statistics* and these are now available on the Ministry of Justice website (<http://www.justice.gov.uk/ publications/statistics.htm>). Figure 26.1 shows the trends in supervisory sentences over the past decade It should be noted that, prior to the implementation of the Criminal Justice Act 2003 (in 2005) orders involving supervision, unpaid work—or both—could be counted separately. However, with the introduction of the community order, these were subsumed under the generic heading of 'community sentences'. In order to give a simple and comprehensible picture of sentencing trends, the following table has combined the statistics for all orders on men and women since 1996. As can be seen, the total number of orders for men increased from around 99,000 in 1996 to 115,000 in 2005, falling slightly to 108,000 in 2006. For women, the numbers rose from around 16,000 in 1996 to 21,000 in 2004, falling slightly to 20,000 in 2006.

Supervision (formerly known as probation orders or community rehabilitation orders)

Supervision can be traced back to 1907 when the probation order was established in England and Wales. Its traditional purpose was to offer advice, assistance, and friendship to offenders, in the belief that they could thus be reformed or rehabilitated. These two

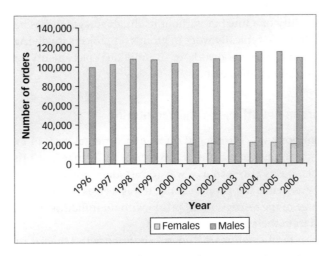

Figure 26.1 Persons starting community sentences by gender

Source: Based on data from Table 3.1, Offender Management Caseload Statistics 2006, Ministry of Justice (2007b).

terms are frequently used interchangeably and there is no consensus about their defin-itions. However, 'reform' (when used in relation to an individual rather than an insti-tution) tends to refer to a change of mind or will (as in 'reformed character'), whereas 'rehabilitation' has more deterministic overtones, requiring a change of circumstances (personal, social, or medical) (Worrall and Hoy, 2005: 11). More emphasis is now placed on restricting offenders' liberty, protecting the public, and preventing reoffending. Offenders are selected for probation through a process of assessment by a probation officer who advises, or writes a report for, the sentencing court. Supervision, which can be between six months and three years in length, requires the offender to maintain contact with their supervising officer and to tell their supervisor about changes in their circumstances. Failure to comply with these conditions constitutes a breach of the pro-bation order and the offender can be re-sentenced, usually to a period of imprisonment. The development of the generic community order allows for supervision to be combined with one or more of 11 further requirements as listed in the previous section.

Unpaid work (formerly known as community service or community punishment orders)

Requiring offenders to undertake unpaid work can be traced back to 1973 when Community Service was introduced in England and Wales (its predecessor, hard labour has a much longer history) and requires offenders to undertake unpaid work in the com-munity for a period ranging from 60 to 240 hours. It was introduced because of concern about rising prison populations and the apparent ineffectiveness of probation orders to reduce reoffending. It has a chameleon-like ability to adapt its aims and objectives to fit almost every traditional justification of punishment—retribution (visible hard work), reparation (unpaid work for the community), deterrence (working for no reward), incapacitation (restriction of liberty), and rehabilitation (learning skills and/or achiev-ing something of worth). This has made it very popular with sentencers, who see it as having the flexibility of a fine but without its disadvantages. It has been described as a fine on time. Offenders typically work in groups on projects involving land restoration, painting, decorating, and woodwork, or in individual placements with charity shops, voluntary organizations, and so on.

Curfew requirement with electronic monitoring

Electronic monitoring was introduced on an experimental basis in England and Wales in the 1980s for a number of reasons. It was seen as a way to reduce prison overcrowding and prison costs. It was also seen as a way to introduce privatization to punishment in the community as well as to prisons. Finally, it was seen as a sophisticated way to subject offenders to some of the restrictions of prison without inflicting on them the damage of being removed from their home environment.

Electronic monitoring requires offenders to be fitted with a special anklet which is con-nected electronically to a telephone which is, in turn, connected to a call centre, whence regular checks are made on the offender's whereabouts. Offenders have individualized schedules requiring them to be at home between certain hours. There are now two distinct ways in which electronic monitoring is used to enable offenders to live in the community. First, courts can include curfew requirements with electronic monitoring in a community sentence. Second, prisoners may be released several weeks before the end of their sentence, on condition that they are monitored. Both measures have been available nationally since 1999 and provide a strong element of surveillance. In 2006, 8,734 curfew requirements with electronic monitoring were made (Ministry of Justice, 2007b). By October 2005, 119,000 prisoners had been released on home detention curfew and, of these, only 3.4 per cent had been convicted, cautioned, or were awaiting prosecution (Mactaggart, 2006 cited in Cavadino and Dignan, 2007: 308).

Although most of the early technological problems relating to 'tagging' have now been overcome, there remain other matters of concern. Some people argue that it is an infringement of civil liberties and encourages 'net-widening' (resulting in more minor offenders being tagged who would not have gone to prison anyway). Others point to the visible stigma of the tag (or, alternatively, the danger that it becomes a 'badge of honour' for some young offenders). Yet others have suggested that confining certain offenders to their homes may place a strain on other members of their family.

Drug rehabilitation requirement (formerly known as drug treatment and testing orders)

Drug Treatment and Testing Orders were introduced with the Crime and Disorder Act 1998. In 2004, at their height, approximately 25,000 orders were made, of which around 70 per cent were made on men (Ministry of Justice, 2007b). Under the Criminal Justice Act 2003, drug rehabilitation is included as a requirement of community order, and is most commonly used in combination with supervision or supervision and attendance at an accredited programme (see Chapter 10). Together these measures constitute a government response to the increasing number of offenders who appear to commit crimes to finance their drug use and they are aimed at those offenders who are willing to cooperate with treatment, supervision, and urine testing. They have been criticized for making drug treatment compulsory and for over-simplifying the link between drug use and crime. As with other penal innovations, they have also been criticized for being used for 'petty' offenders (thus contributing to a process of net-widening), for not taking sufficient account of the needs of women and minority ethnic offenders, and for not providing an appropriate level of social support to ensure that treatment is sustained (Rumgay, 2004). The drug rehabilitation requirement is discussed in more detail in Chapter 10.

REVIEW QUESTIONS

1 What different types of community penalties are there?

2 What principles of sentencing underpin these different sentences?

3 What have been the main features of trends in community sentencing over the past decade?

The National Probation Service and National Offender Management Service (NOMS)

There is a broad consensus that the earliest recognizable 'probation officers' were the 'police court missionaries' who worked in London courts in the last quarter of the nineteenth century. Their job was to rescue and befriend drunken offenders, setting them on the path to redemption. Secular probation officers have been a presence in all criminal courts since the early twentieth century, and, from the 1930s, they were trained as social workers, influenced by 'welfare' and 'medical' models of delinquency (Chui and Nellis, 2003). From the 1970s, however, such models became discredited and probation officers became increasingly influenced by 'non-treatment paradigms' (Bottoms and McWilliams, 1979) and increasingly exercised about securing the correct balance between 'care' and 'control' in their work with offenders. By the end of the twentieth century, probation officers had to accept that their role was to 'confront, control and monitor' and not merely to 'advise, assist and befriend' (Worrall and Hoy, 2005). Organizationally, until 2001, each of the 54 area Probation Services was managed autonomously, although most of the Service's funding came from the Home Office. Each Probation Service had its own Chief Probation Officer and, like the police, there was no centralized organization or spokesperson for the Service. Until the 1980s, the Home Office did not really interfere at all with the running of local Probation Services, but in 1984, it produced a Statement of National Objectives and Priorities (SNOP). The content of SNOP was not particularly contentious, but the fact that it had been produced at all certainly was and it proved to be the start of a debate lasting almost two decades on the management of the Probation Service. By the 1990s, all area Services were required to meet National Standards of practice and policy and, by the middle of the decade, training for probation officers (which had previously constituted a specialism within social work training courses) had been separated completely from social work training. By the end of that decade, the Government was mooting the abolition of the name 'Probation' altogether and considering the merger of probation and prisons into one correctional service (Home Office, 1998; Raynor, 2007). This caused much protest and the eventual compromise was the creation in 2001 of a centralized National Probation Service with a Director. The number of areas was reduced to 42, and, as we have already seen, the names of the main court orders were changed. These changes both reflected and confirmed a major change of ethos for the Probation Service and, as Chui and Nellis muse, 'continuity with the past may be less than meets the eye' (2003: 1).

The National Probation Service now views itself, first and foremost, as a law enforcement agency delivering community penalties (National Probation Service, 2001). However, this was not to be the end of the restructuring story and in 2003, the Carter Review (Carter, 2003) and subsequent government response (Home Office, 2004a) proposed a new National Offender Management Service (NOMS) which would finally bring together the Prison and Probation Services (from June 2004) to provide 'end-to-end management of all offenders, whether they are serving sentences in prison, the community or both' (Home Office, 2004b: 1). This has implications for work with offenders because the focus is no longer on the welfare of the offender (with some ill-defined hope that this will lead in some way to desistance from crime) but on clearly defined goals of reducing reoffending and protecting the public. Every offender who goes to prison or is placed on a community order is subject to an assessment of their risk of reoffending and of causing serious harm. There are various methods of calculating risk but the most widely used is a system called the Offender Assessment System (OASys) (Burnett, Baker, and Roberts, 2007; Kemshall and Wood, 2007) which is usually completed electronically. Following the development of the National Offender Management Model (NOMS, 2006), work with offenders is now divided into four 'tiers', depending on levels of risk and danger-ousness. Tier one offenders are to be punished; tier two offenders are to be punished and helped; tier three offenders punished, helped, and changed; tier four offenders punished, helped, changed, and controlled (NOMS, 2006). Central to this approach are the con-cepts of compliance of enforcement—ensuring that offenders meet the requirements of their orders. Returning an offender to court for non-compliance with an order (known as 'breaching'), which was seen in the past as an admission of failure by the probation officer, is now viewed as essential to the credibility of orders and an act of strength (Hedderman, 2003; Hedderman and Hough, 2004).

REVIEW QUESTIONS

1 In what ways has the Probation Service changed since its early days in the late nineteenth century?

2 What are the priorities of the National Offender Management Service?

Ways of understanding the politics of punishment in the community

In this section we consider three different ways of explaining and understanding (or theorizing) about the development of community penalties. We draw on Stan Cohen's analysis of the history of 'social control talk' (1983) which juxtaposes three models of correctional change: 'uneven progress', 'benevolence gone wrong', and 'it's all a con' (1983: 104–106).

Uneven progress

Accepting that, in an imperfect world, progress will never be unimpeded, Cohen describes, first, an optimistic conservative rhetoric which argues that penal reform has been steady and that alternatives to custody represent the enlightened values of an ever more civilized society. Before the end of the nineteenth century, the only non-custodial sentences (apart from the death penalty) used regularly by courts were fines and release on recognizances (the equivalent of cautions, binding over, and discharges—see above). Most histories of the probation service place it within the humanitarian considerations of Victorian and Edwardian penal reformers, but Raynor and Vanstone (2002) provide a more critical summary which emphasizes the dimension of 'moral training'. An increasing confidence in both their material wealth and their scientific knowledge led reformers to believe that crime was a social disease for which a cure was possible through 'specific practices of normalization, classification, categorization and discrimination between criminal types' (Garland, 1985: 32). Social control could now be achieved 'through attention to the material, social and psychological welfare of criminals' (Worrall and Hoy, 2005: 4) without the need for physical incarceration. Throughout the twentieth century a range of non-custodial penalties developed, adding increasing numbers of conditions and restrictions on offenders' freedom, while stopping short of incarcerating them. As discussed earlier in this chapter, the criminal courts are now able to impose a range of requirements on offenders. The aim of all these measures is to prevent offenders from reoffending without resorting to sending them to prison. In this way, it is argued, the public is more likely to be protected in the longer term because imprisonment protects the public for only a short while, and, by cutting offenders' social ties and fuelling their resentment, may make them more likely to reoffend in the future (Hagan, 1994; Maruna, 2000; Farrall, 2002).

Benevolence gone wrong

But the rehabilitative ideal came increasingly under attack in the 1960s and 1970s for both ideological and pragmatic reasons. Ideologically, attempts at offender rehabilitation were regarded as, on the one hand, intrusive and an infringement of civil liberties and, on the other hand, as a 'soft option'—an indulgence of middle-class liberals out of touch with the 'real' world of crime victimization. Pragmatically, it seemed that rehabilitation just did not 'work' and, in some cases, made matters worse (Worrall and Hoy, 2005: 24).

Cohen's second account of penal change reflects this disillusion with rehabilitation which characterized much of symbolic interactionist theorizing about crime and deviance (see Chapter 4) and the 'nothing works' approach to punishment. Rather than seeking reform, this model suggests, we should be looking for ways to manage both the system and individual criminal careers so as to cause the least damage, cost, and inconvenience to the rest of society. However, after a decade of defensiveness and soul-searching in the 1980s, advocates of rehabilitation slowly regained confidence with the discovery of what is now termed the 'What Works'—or 'evidence-based'—approach, which we will consider in more detail later in this chapter. For Cohen, however, these developments (though he wrote before the term 'What Works' was coined) represented a process of official mystification.

It's all a con

Cohen's third model presents a conspiracy of the powerful to mystify and obfuscate. He argues that humanism, good intentions, professional knowledge, and reform rhetoric did not simply result in change 'for the better'. They also involved the exercise of power and the social construction (see Chapter 1) of offenders as certain 'types' of people (or objects of knowledge) about whom it is both possible and desirable to accumulate information and make judgements. The decarcerated criminal is one such new object of knowledge about whom new bodies of information must be accumulated. Community-based programmes, far from reducing the restrictions on offenders who might otherwise have been sent to prison, create a new category of offenders who are controlled or disciplined by other mechanisms. The boundaries between freedom and confinement become blurred. The 'net' of social control is thus thrown ever wider into the community, its thinner mesh designed to trap ever smaller 'fish' who would previously have been subject to financial or self-regulatory penalties. Once caught in the net, the penetration of disciplinary intervention is ever deeper, reaching every aspect of the offender's life.

REVIEW QUESTIONS

1 How might we explain the historical development of community penalties?

2 Which explanation do you find the most convincing and why?

Diversity and punishment in the community

Traditionally, the probation order was the sentence 'of choice' for women (see Chapter 17). They were considered ideally suited to being 'advised, assisted and befriended' (to adapt the former mission statement of the probation service). But the influence of feminist perspectives on criminal justice led many probation officers to be concerned that too many women were being placed on probation and, more significantly, too early in their criminal careers. The good intentions of probation officers in recommending supervisory sentences for women appeared to result in 'net-widening' and ultimately accelerating a woman's journey to custody. There was an assumption (informed by theories of labelling and deviancy amplification) that diverting women from probation would automatically reduce the numbers in prison. As Eaton (1986) and Worrall (1990) demonstrated, probation officers' court reports (known then as social inquiry reports, now pre-sentence reports) constructed women within the ideological constraints of the family and inadvertently reinforced sentencers' stereotyped views on 'good' and 'bad' women. This emerging gender awareness among probation officers resulted in a concerted effort to write non- or anti-discriminatory reports which strove to avoid collusion with such stereotyping.

The effort was partially successful in that fewer women were placed on probation for minor offences, and for a while in the early 1990s, there was some cause for optimism. The Criminal Justice Act 1991, based on the principle of 'just deserts', *should* have resulted in a fairer deal for women criminals. If sentencing was to depend predominantly on the seriousness of the current offence, the implication should have been that fewer women would go to prison for relatively minor offences, however frequently committed. But as the prison population rose, this did not seem to happen. As the female prison population rose steadily from 1,500 in 1992 (Home Office, 1993) to 4,300 in

2002 (Councell, 2003) it has remained at around 4,500 since (see the weekly prison population bulletins published by HM Prison Service at <http://www.hmprisonservice. gov.uk/resourcecentre/publicationsdocuments/>), it became clear that the traditional probation order (now supervision) was seen as insufficiently punitive for women who were no longer regarded as in need of 'help'. So the focus turned to sentences involving unpaid work.

There is nothing in theory or in law to debar women from doing unpaid work but sentencers have always had ambivalent feelings about sentencing women in this way (Worrall and Hoy, 2005: 129). Research has suggested that there is greater inconsistency in the use of unpaid work for women than for men and that in the past women have been more likely than men to receive community service orders for their first offence (Hine and Thomas, 1995). It has always been viewed by courts as not quite an appropriate sentence for women and the practicalities have always been an obstacle—the absence of childcare facilities being the main problem (Howard League, 1999). There is debate about what constitutes appropriate work for women on such orders. Should they be encouraged to broaden their horizons and do 'male' work or should they stick to what they know in order to get through the hours?

The problems surrounding unpaid work for women are well-known but by no means unresolvable. What is required is a change in the attitude that regards community service as predominantly a punishment for 'fit, young men' (Worrall and Hoy, 2005: 133). Better childcare arrangements, more female supervisors, and consideration for the kind of working environments most suitable for women would also result in greater use. Whatever the perceived disadvantages to women of doing unpaid work, they cannot possibly outweigh the disadvantages of imprisoning those same women.

The use of community sentences for black and Asian offenders has also been controversial (Durrance and Williams, 2003). It is well established that black offenders, in particular, are over-represented in prison in relation to their distribution in the general population: 26 per cent of the male and 28 per cent of the female prison population was from a minority ethnic group on 20 June 2006 (Ministry of Justice, 2007b). What is less clear is whether or not this over-representation is due to discrimination (either direct or indirect) within society and/or the criminal justice system and what contribution, if any, the Probation Service makes to that discrimination. Research literature is inconclusive (Powis and Walmsley, 2002) but there is widespread concern that community sentences are not meeting the needs of black and Asian offenders. This may be because the theoretical underpinnings of contemporary rehabilitative programmes (see below) fail to take sufficient account of the particular experiences of poverty, racism, and exclusion of many black and Asian offenders. Projects which seek to combine the cognitive behavioural approaches that characterize contemporary probation intervention with approaches that emphasize issues of identity and empowerment may be the most promising (Lewis *et al.*, 2006; Gelsthorpe and McIvor, 2007). The proportion of minority ethnic probation officers is steadily increasing and in 2006/07 approximately 16 per cent of probation staff were from black and minority ethnic backgrounds (Ministry of Justice, 2008), reflecting exactly the proportion of offenders subject to supervision (Ministry of Justice, 2007b).

Soft options? Community sentences and populist punitiveness

The policy of 'bifurcation' (separating out the 'minor' from the 'dangerous' criminals) has been a feature of the politicization of crime in the past two decades and has allowed successive governments to sustain a paradoxical rhetoric of supporting alternatives to prison while arguing that there are many 'dangerous' criminals for whom alternatives are simply not 'suitable'. Since 'dangerousness' (as politically defined) is very much 'in the eye of the beholder', this line of official rhetoric has given rise to the concept of 'populist punitiveness' (see Chapter 21 for a discussion of this concept), which has resulted in the chronic under-use and under-resourcing of alternatives to custody. Raynor and Vanstone (2002) discuss populist punitiveness and its impact on the use of community sentences. They argue that 'crime-related issues [are] defined by political elites as problems of insufficient punishment or as being "soft" on criminals' (2002: 69). By playing on understandable public concerns about crime, supporting biased media coverage and fuelling moral panics, it is argued that politicians use crime-related issues to manipulate public opinion. Within this discourse, the only acceptable kind of community sentence is a 'tough' one, the implication being that most community sentences are far from 'tough'. The dialogue between probation or community corrections officers and governments (for a detailed account of one such dialogue, see Worrall and Hoy, 2005) has been one centred on the so-called 'strengthening' of community sentences by means of increasingly unrealistic 'conditions' that have to be met by offenders. Carlen (1989) has referred to this process as being one which disregards 'sentencing feasibility'. Practitioners often refer to it as 'setting an offender up to fail'.

This 'toughness' has resulted in a range of penalties known in the USA as 'intermediate sanctions'—penalties that 'fit' between traditional probation orders and prison. Intermediate sanctions involve a greater intensity of supervision, coupled with greater monitoring or surveillance (Byrne, Lurigio, and Petersilia, 1992). Towards the end of the twentieth century partnerships between police forces and Probation Services have resulted in prolific (or persistent) offender projects in England and Wales, which represent an extension of the theoretical underpinnings, policy objectives, and multi-agency practices of previous intensive supervision schemes. Combining penal philosophies of deterrence, incapacitation, and rehabilitation, they seek to provide a mix of frequent contact, access to treatment (particularly drugs treatment) and community facilities, and constant monitoring. They also seek to demonstrate cost-effectiveness and increased public safety.

The major departure from previous projects, however, is their avoidance of the pitfall of relying on offenders to reduce their own rates of reoffending. This was always the weakest link in the chain and the one which consistently undermined claims of success. Instead, it is now accepted that prompt re-arrest (resulting from increased intelligence and monitoring) is also a measure of success. There is, however, a serious flaw in this logic. The possibility that a project could claim success entirely on the basis of arrests and order breaches does seem to be somewhat at odds with the spirit of the exercise. Nevertheless, the reality of modern corrections demands that those who do not respond promptly to the 'carrot' of rehabilitative efforts should experience the 'stick' of enforcement (Farrall, Mawby, and Worrall, 2007).

REVIEW QUESTIONS

1 What is meant by the term 'populist punitiveness' in relation to community sentences?

2 In what ways have community sentences been 'strengthened' in response to calls for greater public protection?

Community sentences and the 'What Works' agenda

The nature of probation intervention has changed radically in the past two decades. Personal counselling, based on psychotherapeutic approaches, has been replaced by cognitive behavioural programmes, based on social learning theory. Rather than attempting to change the whole personality or circumstances of an offender, cognitive behavioural programmes focus on specific unacceptable behaviours and seek to modify these by correcting distortions in the way offenders think about their crime. Offenders are required to accept full responsibility for their actions (instead of blaming the victim or their circumstances), empathize with the victim of their offences, and expand their repertoire of responses to those situations which have previously triggered a criminal response. Programmes may focus on generic cognitive skills or cover a range of specific problem behaviours such as anger management, drink-impaired driving, and sex offending.

These programmes collectively form the 'What Works?' agenda. The etymology of this phrase lies in a famously pessimistic remark made in 1974 by a criminologist called Robert Martinson (1974) to the effect that 'nothing works' in penal interventions. The disillusion which followed this conclusion (supported by research findings at the time) led to a loss of confidence in probation which lasted until the early 1990s when the 'discovery' of cognitive behavioural programmes (initially in North America) gave rise to a series of conferences entitled 'What Works?' (McGuire, 1995). The phrase caught the imagination of politicians and professionals and now dominates probation intervention in the English-speaking world. Evaluation research gives cause for cautious optimism in respect of the effectiveness of such programmes in reducing reoffending but critics have argued that enthusiasm for the cognitive behavioural approach should not result in the neglect of other provision such as basic literacy skills and social skills. Nor should the wider social problems that may lead people into crime be overlooked (Mair, 2004b; Raynor, 2007).

CONCLUSION

In this chapter we have explored the range of punishments which do not involve incarceration that are available to courts. The aim of the chapter has been to demonstrate that, despite the overwhelming focus of the media, penal policy, and academic literature on prison and imprisonment, the vast majority of people who commit crimes and are detected are punished in ways that require them to self-regulate, pay money, or cooperate with some form of supervision or monitoring of their behaviour—within their own communities. We have identified a number of advantages to dealing with offenders in this way. Apart from the high cost of imprisonment, allowing offenders to remain in conditions of freedom enables them to retain family, social, and employment ties, all of which may reduce the likelihood of reoffending. It also avoids the stigma of imprisonment, which is a major contributor to persistent offending. We have also demonstrated the ways in which community penalties can meet the conventional requirements of the principles of punishment, providing opportunities for retribution, deterrence, incapacitation, rehabilitation, and reparation.

The chapter has provided an overview of the historical and political development of community penalties, suggesting a number of different ways of theorizing (or explaining) that development. It has traced the main features of the National Probation Service over the past century and the changes which have taken it from its religious origins, through to a secular social work profession and its culmination in the twenty-first century as a law enforcement agency concerned primarily with public protection.

However, we have also discussed a number of issues and problems related to community penalties. These include the 'image' of community sentences as being 'soft options' and poor substitutes for imprisonment. The recent history of community penalties has been characterized by the need to respond to populist punitiveness by making such sentences 'tougher'. This has involved a proliferation of additional requirements, combinations of orders, increased intensity of contact, and even close collaboration with the Police and Prison Services. Ultimately, it has involved the National Probation Service in accepting physical restrictions on an offender's liberty, such as electronic monitoring, compulsory drug treatment, and even prompt rearrest and incarceration, as being measures of success, rather than measures which undermine the fundamental values of the Service.

The chapter has also explored the issue of diversity and the potential for discrimination in the implementation of community penalties. The particular needs of women offenders and those from minority ethnic groups have been highlighted. Finally, some of the ideas that are central to the 'What Works' agenda for offender rehabilitation have been introduced.

Although it remains the case that research into community sentences is overshadowed by research into prisons, there now exists an interesting and accessible body of research literature in this area (Mair, 2004b and 2007). Much of the recent research can be found on the Home Office and Ministry of Justice websites and the details of some key recent books are set out at the end of this chapter.

QUESTIONS FOR DISCUSSION

1 What are the advantages and disadvantages of dealing with offenders in the community rather than sending them to prison?

2 To what extent do community sentences meet the requirements of punishment for retribution, deterrence, incapacitation, rehabilitation, and/or reparation?

3 Which of the existing community sentences are most suitable for women and why?

4 What are the central principles of the 'What Works' agenda and what are its implications for the treatment of offenders?

5 How, if at all, should community sentences contribute to the reduction of the prison population?

GUIDE TO FURTHER READING

Canton, R. and Hancock, D. (2007) *Dictionary of Probation and Offender Management*. Cullompton: Willan Publishing.

An excellent reference book for clarifying all those policy and practice issues that other texts never explain in quite enough detail.

Gelsthorpe, L. and Morgan, R. (2007) *Handbook of Probation*. Cullompton: Willan Publishing.

The current state-of-the-art edited collection about probation and offender management.

Mair, G. (ed) (2004) *What Matters in Probation*. Cullompton: Willan Publishing.

A very lively, critical, and controversial examination of the 'What Works' agenda for offender rehabilitation.

Raynor, P. (2007) 'Community Penalties: Probation, "What Works" and offender management' in M. Maguire, R. Morgan, and R. Reiner (eds) *The Oxford Handbook of Criminology* (4th edn). Oxford: Oxford University Press.

A comprehensive and balanced resumé of the key issues and debates surrounding community penalties.

Worrall, A. and Hoy, C. (2005) *Punishment in the Community: Managing offenders, making choices*. Cullompton: Willan Publishing.

A recent and critical introductory text.

WEB LINKS

http://www.homeoffice.gov.uk

The Home Office website continues to provide a wealth of information and statistics about crime and criminal justice policy, practice, and research. It also provides links to many other relevant websites.

http://www.inspectorates.homeoffice.gov.uk

This website contains all the prison and probation inspectors' thematic reports.

http://www.justice.gov.uk

The new Ministry of Justice website now has responsibility for information, research, and statistics relating to offender management (prisons and probation).

http://www.noms.justice.gov.uk

The new National Offender Management website hosted by the Ministry of Justice.

http://www.probation.homeoffice.gov.uk

The National Probation Service website provides useful information about various aspects of policy and practice relating to the management of offenders in the community.

REFERENCES

Bottoms, A. and McWilliams, W. (1979) 'A Non-treatment Paradigm for Probation Practice', *British Journal of Social Work*, 9 (2): 159–202.

Burnett, R., Baker, K., and Roberts, C. (2007) 'Assessment, supervision and intervention: fundamental practice in probation' in L. Gelsthorpe and R. Morgan (eds) *Handbook of Probation*. Cullompton: Willan Publishing.

Byrne, J., Lurigio, A., and Petersilia, J. (1992) *Smart Sentencing: the Emergence of Intermediate Sanctions*. London: Sage.

Carlen, P. (1989) 'Crime, inequality and sentencing' in P. Carlen and D. Cook (eds) *Paying for Crime*. Milton Keynes: Open University Press.

Carter, P. (2003) *Managing Offenders, Changing Lives*. London: Home Office.

Cavadino, M. and Dignan, J. (2007) *The Penal System: An Introduction* (4th edn). London: Sage.

Chui, W.H. and Nellis, M. (eds) (2003) *Moving Probation Forward: Evidence, Arguments and Practice*. Harlow: Pearson Longman.

Cohen, S. (1983) 'Social control talk: telling stories about correctional change', in D. Garland and P. Young (eds) *The Power to Punish*. London: Heinemann.

Cohen, S. (1985) *Visions of Social Control*. Cambridge: Polity Press.

Councell, R. (2003) *The Prison Population in 2002: A Statistical Review*, Findings 228. London: Home Office.

Durrance, P. and Williams, P. (2003) 'Broadening the agenda around what works for black and Asian offenders', *Probation Journal*, 50 (3) 211–24.

Eaton, M. (1986) *Justice for Women?* Milton Keynes: Open University Press.

Farrall, S. (2002) *Rethinking what Works with Offenders: Probation, Social Context and Desistance from Crime*. Cullompton: Willan Publishing.

Farrall. S., Mawby, R., and Worrall, A. (2007) 'Prolific/persistent offenders and desistance' in L. Gelsthorpe and R. Morgan (eds) *Handbook of Probation*. Cullompton: Willan Publishing.

Gelsthorpe, L. and McIvor, G. (2007) 'Difference and diversity in probation', in L. Gelsthorpe and R. Morgan (eds) *Handbook of Probation*. Cullompton: Willan Publishing.

Garland, D. (1985) *Punishment and Welfare: A History of Penal Strategies*. Aldershot: Gower.

Gibson. B. (2004) *Criminal Justice Act 2003: A Guide to the New Procedures and Sentencing*. Winchester: Waterside Press.

Hagan, J. (1994) *Crime and Disrepute*. Thousand Oaks: Pine Forge.

Hedderman, C. (2003) 'Enforcing supervision and encouraging compliance', in W. Chui and M. Nellis (eds) (2003) *Moving Probation Forward: Evidence, Arguments and Practice*. Harlow: Pearson Longman.

Hedderman, C. and Gelsthorpe, L. (1997) *Understanding the Sentencing of Women*, Home Office Research Study 170. London: HMSO.

Hedderman, C. and Hough, M. (2004) 'Getting tough or being effective: what matters?' in G. Mair (ed) *What Matters in Probation*. Cullompton: Willan Publishing.

Hine, J. and Thomas, N. (1995) 'Evaluating work with offenders: community service orders', in G. McIvor (ed) *Working with Offenders*, Research Highlights in Social Work 26. London: Jessica Kingsley.

Home Office (1984) *Statement of National Objectives and Priorities*. London: HMSO.

Home Office (1988) *Punishment, Custody and the Community*. London: HMSO.

Home Office (1990) *Crime, Justice and Protecting the Public*. London: HMSO.

Home Office (1993) *Prison Statistics England and Wales 1992*. London: HMSO.

Home Office (1998) *Joining Forces to Protect the Public: Prisons-Probation—A Consultation Document*. London: Home Office.

Home Office (2003) *Prison Statistics England and Wales 2001*. London: Home Office.

Home Office (2004a) *Reducing Crime, Changing Lives*. London: Home Office.

Home Office (2004b) *Reducing Crime, Changing Lives* (press release 5/2004). London: Home Office.

Howard League (1999) *Do Women Paint Fences Too? Women's Experience of Community Service*. London: Howard League for Penal Reform.

Kemshall, H. and Wood, J. (2007) 'High risk offenders and public protection' in L. Gelsthorpe and R. Morgan (eds) *Handbook of Probation*. Cullompton: Willan Publishing.

Lewis, S., Raynor, P., Smith, D., and Wardak, A. (eds) (2006) *Race and Probation*. Cullompton: Willan Publishing.

McGuire, J. (ed) (1995) *What Works: Reducing Reoffending*. Chichester: John Wiley.

Mair, G. (2004a) 'Diversionary and non-supervisory approaches to dealing with offenders' in A. Bottoms, S. Rex, and G. Robinson (eds) *Alternatives to Prison: Options for an insecure society*. Cullompton: Willan.

Mair, G. (ed) (2004b) *What Matters in Probation*. Cullompton: Willan.

Mair, G. (2007) 'Research on community penalties' in R. King and E. Wincup (eds) *Doing Research on Crime and Justice* (2nd edn). Oxford: Oxford University Press.

Martinson, R. (1974) 'What works? Questions and answers about prison reform', *The Public Interest*, 35: 22–54.

Maruna, S. (2000) *Making Good: How Ex-Convicts Reform and Rebuild their Lives*. Washington DC: American Psychological Association.

Ministry of Justice (2007a) *Criminal Statistics 2006 England and Wales*. London: National Statistics.

Ministry of Justice (2007b) *Offender Management Caseload Statistics 2006*. London: National Statistics

Ministry of Justice (2008) *Statistics on Race and the Criminal Justice System 2006/7*. London: National Statistics.

Moore, R. (2003) 'The use of financial penalties and the amounts imposed: the need for a new approach', *Criminal Law Review*, January: 13–27.

Morgan, R. (2003) 'Thinking about the demand for probation services', Probation Journal, 50(1): 7–19.

NOMS (National Offender Management Service) (2006) *The NOMS Offender Management Model*. London: NOMS.

National Probation Service (2001) *A New Choreography: An Integrated Strategy for the National Probation service for England and Wales—Strategic Framework 2001–2004*. London: Home Office.

Powis, B. and Walmsley, R. (2002) *Programmes for black and Asian offenders on probation: lessons for developing practice*, Home Office Research Study 250. London, Home Office.

Raynor, P. (2007) 'Community penalties: probation, "what works" and offender management', in M. Maguire, R. Morgan, and R. Reiner (eds) *The Oxford Handbook of Criminology*. Oxford: Oxford University Press.

Raynor, P. and Vanstone, M. (2002) *Understanding Community Penalties*. Buckingham: Open University Press.

Rumgay, J. (2004) 'Dealing with substance-misusing offenders in the community' in A. Bottoms, S. Rex, and G. Robinson (eds) *Alternatives to Prison: Options for an Insecure Society*. Cullompton: Willan.

Scull, A. (1984) *Decarceration: Community Treatment and the Deviant*. Cambridge: Polity Press.

Windlesham, Lord (1993) *Responses to Crime*, Vol. 2. Oxford: Oxford University Press.

Worrall, A. (1990) *Offending Women: Female Lawbreakers and the Criminal Justice System*. London: Routledge.

Worrall, A. and Hoy, C. (2005) Punishment in the Community: Managing Offenders, Making Choices (2nd edn). Cullompton: Willan.

27 Prisons

Roger Matthews

INTRODUCTION

Imprisonment has been the dominant form of punishment in western societies for the last 200 years. In that period, however, the role, scale, and functions of imprisonment have changed considerably. Since its inception the modern prison has been the focus of debate and controversy. From the early period of construction at the modern prison at the beginning of the nineteenth century through to the perceived 'crisis' of imprisonment at the end of the twentieth century, prison has been subject to critical examination. The recent growth in the size of the prison population in England and Wales, together with the adoption of a policy of mass incarceration over the last 20 years in America with in excess of two million people incarcerated in State, Federal, and local prisons, has raised issues about the use and costs of imprisonment. In this chapter we will explore the contours of these changes and attempt to understand something about the processes involved. Taking a historical perspective, the aim will be to outline some of the more significant developments in incarceration over the last two centuries, focusing particularly on the role and impact of imprisonment, changes in its scale and purpose, as well as an examination of who goes to prison and the relation between prison and the wider community. In the course of examining these issues a number of key themes will be discussed, while providing an introduction to the terminology and some of the central concepts that have become associated with this topic.

BACKGROUND

The word 'prison' is a generic term applied to a range of institutions that hold captives. The word 'prison' also tends to have a different meaning in American and British contexts, and while Americans commonly use terms such as 'correctional facilities' and 'jails' to describe different types of custodial institutions, the British tend to mainly use the generic term 'prison' (McConville, 1995). It is also necessary to distinguish between different types of prisons. In America, the term prison is reserved for State and Federal segregative institutions for offenders sentenced to imprisonment for more than one year. The term 'jail' is normally used for those institutions that hold prisoners who are sentenced to less than one year. In UK prisons, the Prison Service allocates prisoners according to an assessment of their security risk. There are four main categories of prisoners ranging from A to D. Category A prisoners are those deemed to be highly dangerous. Category B prisoners are those for whom the very highest conditions of security are not necessary but for whom escape must be made very difficult. Category C prisoners are those that cannot be trusted in open conditions but are felt to have a low probability of trying to escape. Category D prisoners are those that can be trusted in open conditions. There are also remand prisons, or 'local prisons' as they are sometimes called, that hold those awaiting trial or sentence. These are designated as category B prisons. There are also dispersal prisons which are top security prisons holding Category A prisoners in the UK and 'Supermax' prisons in the USA, which, as the name suggests, are designed to provide maximum security and tend to involve the restricted mobility of inmates. Young offenders between the ages of 15 and 21 are held in Young Offender Institutions. Women are held in all-female prisons, or in separate all-female wings within male prisons.

The birth of the modern prison

We can identify the birth of the modern prison with some precision. In the UK the modern prison was introduced in 1842 with the construction of Pentonville Prison in London. Pentonville Prison, which still stands on its original site, became the model for the construction of many local prisons in the decades that followed and attracted world-wide attention. This modern prison was a different kind of institution from forms of confinement and 'prisons' such as Newgate that had been in operation in the eighteenth century that functioned mainly as sites of containment and as places of detention for those awaiting trial or paying off their debts. The new generation of prisons that were built in the course of the nineteenth century in both Europe and America were distin-guished, according to Michel Foucault (1977), from previous forms of confinement by three essential characteristics—the focus on labour discipline, the introduction of new forms of spatial design and control, and the use of more finely calibrated time-based punishments.

In prisons such as Newgate, in the eighteenth century, it was difficult to distinguish the prisoners from the visitors except that the former were often chained in irons. The jail appeared as a kind of lodging house with some inhabitants living in ease and others in squalor. Some prisoners gambled while others stood drinking at the prison tap. These were privately run establishments and jailers made a living from selling beer and provid-ing other services to those who could afford them. Debtors, who made up a significant percentage of the detainees, tended to live in separate quarters—sometimes with their families. Evangelical campaigners, such as John Howard and Elizabeth Fry, and philan-thropists, like Jonas Hanway, campaigned against the conditions, abuses, lack of discip-line, and poor hygiene in these institutions, and argued for the creation of a well-ordered prison that was quiet and functional (McGowan, 1995). These and other like-minded reformers were instrumental in campaigning for the introduction of the modern 'well-ordered' prison in the nineteenth century (Rothman, 1971).

The new model prisons like Pentonville that were introduced in the nineteenth cen-tury were designed as 'total institutions'. Erving Goffman (1968) identifies 'total institu-tions' as those in which the inmates are largely cut off from their families, their work, and their communities. In relation to prisons this meant the exclusion of the public and casual visitors. In these quiet and orderly institutions convicts were required to wear uniforms and masks, and conversation and pleasure was strictly outlawed. The main focus of these modern prisons was labour discipline. As Jeremy Bentham suggested, one of the main purposes of the Victorian prison was 'to grind rogues honest'. Through the application of labour, prisons, it was claimed, would instil discipline and the habits of industry. Through a mixture of hard work and reflection on their transgressions prison-ers would, it was believed, come to see the error of their ways and become law abiding and productive workers. While male prisoners were mostly sentenced to 'hard labour', which involved industrial labour, women prisoners typically spent their days cleaning and mending (Zedner, 1991).

The aim of making prisons productive and self-financing through the manufacture of goods was, however, undermined by the fact that most prisoners had poor work skills and little motivation. It was also the case that trade unions objected to what they saw as unfair competition from unpaid prisoners. Consequently, restrictions were placed on the goods that could be manufactured in prison, and increasingly through the nineteenth century the emphasis on productive labour gave way to the introduction of unproductive forms of labour involving the use of the tread wheel and the crank.

Changes in the design and the use of space within the modern prison were also significant. Prison cells were to be of a uniform size and prisons were constructed along new lines with a series of wings radiating from a central point. The aim of this design was to maximize the control and surveillance of prisoners with the least amount of staff. The epitome of the use of surveillance to control the activities of prisoners was the panoptical design (Foucault, 1977). Although this design maximized the surveillance of prisoners by employing a central vantage point from which all prisoners could be observed—without the observer being seen by the prisoners—this model was in fact only employed in a limited number of prisons such as Stateville in America and a few panopticon-inspired prisons in the Netherlands and Spain (Jacobs, 1977). Although the radial design predominated for most of the nineteenth century, ongoing debates about the best type of design reflected a continuing preoccupation with spatial control as a way of maintaining order in prisons (Evans, 1982).

Time represents the third important dimension of the modern prison. The prison became a punishment of measured time. The attractiveness of imprisonment as a form of punishment was the ability to link the period of time served to the perceived seriousness of the crime committed. Previous systems of detention appeared arbitrary and unfair. Linking the use of imprisonment to a certain number of months or years of confinement gave the prison an objectivity and solidity not found in previous forms of punishment. The ultimate attractiveness of time-based punishments is that they have social and universal quality, they operate independently of each individual, and they embody an element of formal equality before the law.

Thus the modern prison was distinguished from previous forms of punishment by its construction around the three elements of labour discipline, spatial design and control, and the use of a time-based punishment (Matthews, 1999). Although the nature of these three elements was to change over time they remained the key distinguishing features of the modern prison. Indeed it was these three elements that contributed, as Michel Foucault (1977) argued, to the 'naturalness' and acceptability of the prison.

REVIEW QUESTIONS

1 In what ways was the modern nineteenth century prison different from the 'prisons' that operated in the eighteenth century.

2 Why was the design of the prison of such importance to nineteenth-century reformers? ·

3 In what ways was the modern prison linked to the factory?

The demise and re-expansion of the prison

Imprisonment became the dominant form of punishment in the nineteenth century. The number of people incarcerated grew during the century and a number of new prisons were built. However, towards the end of the century prisons increasingly became the object of critical scrutiny. As a social experiment in reforming offenders the prison became widely viewed as failing, while the costs of incarceration were increasing. The problem of making a profit from the production of goods became more pronounced as the century went on and overcrowding, corruption, and cruelty became more evident. Confinement in small cells was increasingly seen as being detrimental to the health and wellbeing of prisoners, and reports of brutality by prison staff were widespread. There were growing concerns about security and control as a result of reports of repeated escapes and riots. The Gladstone Committee in 1895 pronounced that the prison was a failing institution and that as a consequence of the evidence that it gathered on the operation of the prison system 'a sweeping indictment had been laid against the whole prison administration' (Ignatieff, 1978).

Prison, it appeared, had little apparent effect on criminal behaviour, and the growth of recidivism and violent crime were seen to indicate the failure of prisons to reform offenders or to act as a general deterrent. The numbers of people in prison peaked on both sides of the Atlantic. As Rusche and Kirchheimer (2005) pointed out, changing economic conditions during the age of imperialism, together with changing working practices, affected the significance of labour discipline in prison. At the same time there was a reorientation of sentencing policy away from strict proportionality as it became increasingly directed towards the rehabilitation of offenders. These changes came to redefine the role of imprisonment. At this point in time there was a shift to a Fordist mode of production, with its emphasis on the reproduction of labour power rather than solely on labour discipline, and this involved a growing focus on the socialization of the young, the development of the modern 'cornflake' family, and the introduction of compulsory education (Melossi, 1979).

The growth of the welfare state at the beginning of the twentieth century signalled a significant change in the nature of social control. The aim was to develop more inclusive forms of regulation tied to providing support to individuals and their families principally through the expansion of social work, which, as Jacques Donzelot (1979) pointed out, became the agency that was able to link problematic individuals to the family, the school, and the court. The growing emphasis on trying to address problems in the community represented a shift in the form of regulation and a consequent expansion of *inclusive* forms of social control (Cohen, 1985). The prison with its emphasis on exclusion became less prominent and its use more restricted, and increasingly came to operate as a back-up sanction to what David Garland (1981) has referred to as the 'welfare sanction'. Thus for most of the twentieth century the dominant forms of social control oscillated between exclusion associated with imprisonment on one side, and the more inclusive strategies linked to the operation of the welfare sanction on the other.

In England the number of people imprisoned fell from just under 33,000 in 1880 to around 14,000 by 1931. Other European counties experienced equally dramatic levels of decrease (see Rusche and Kirchheimer, 2005: Chapter 1X). The average daily population of women imprisoned in England decreased from 1,249 in 1860 to 302 in 1890 (Zedner, 1991). Women were sent in increasing numbers to newly established reformatories designed to train and re-socialize them into domesticity (Rafter, 1983). Similarly, juveniles were also increasingly redirected towards reformatories or given probation as an alternative to custody. On the basis of these trends across Europe, Rusche and Kirchheimer concluded, in 1939 when they wrote their classic text *Punishment and Social Structure*, that the decline of the prison would continue towards the end of the century and that the fine would become more widely used. For them the prison was essentially a nineteenth-century institution that was becoming increasingly anachronistic. However, it has become apparent in the post-war period that Rusche and Kirchheimer's predictions have not materialized. On the contrary, the scale of imprisonment has increased in many European countries and the increase in the number of people incarcerated has been particularly pronounced in America.

The question that arises is why this re-expansion of the prison occurred. American penologists have suggested that the increase in the use of incarceration during the 1980s and 1990s was largely the result of the 'war on drugs' that provided the justification for the deployment of harsher policies towards certain types of drug user. Michael Tonry (1995), for example, has argued that it was the focus on crack cocaine that was the drug of choice amongst poor African-Americans living in the inner cities of America that fuelled the dramatic expansion in the use of imprisonment, and also resulted in the growing racial disproportionality amongst the prison population. However, the increase in the scale of imprisonment in England and Wales and other European countries cannot be explained as a function of the 'war against drugs'. Although the numbers of people incarcerated for drug-related offences has increased in recent years this increase only accounts for a small proportion of the total increase in the number of people imprisoned. An alternative explanation for the growth in the use of imprisonment is the perceived increase in punitiveness. It is argued that both politicians and the public have become increasingly punitive in recent years, and that this punitiveness has been translated into longer prison sentences and the more widespread use of imprisonment (Pratt, 2007). However, the evidence that has been presented to explain this apparent surge in punitiveness is less than convincing, and it would seem that the explanation for the growth of imprisonment over the last two decades lies elsewhere (Matthews, 2005; Meyer and O'Malley, 2005).

REVIEW QUESTIONS

1 What were the achievements and failures of the modern nineteenth-century prison?

2 What factors account for the increased use of prison in the second half of the twentieth century?

3 To what extent can the increase in the prison population over the last two decades be explained by an increase in punitiveness?

Who goes to prison?

One in sixteen of the general population in England and Wales, it is estimated, will spend some time in prison in the course of their lives (Harvey and Pease, 1987). In America it is one in twenty (Bonczar and Beck, 1997). These general figures, however, mask significant differences in the sections of the population who make up the prison population since this population is not drawn evenly from across the whole of society. We can examine the composition of the prison population by a number of different criteria—age, gender, race, offence type, and social class.

It is important to note the difference between prison population and prison admissions—what is sometimes referred to as *stock* and *flow*. The size and nature of the prison population at any time is a function of the number of people sentenced to imprisonment and the length of time they actually serve. Thus it is possible that there could be a decrease in the number of people sent to prison in a period, but that if the period of time served increases significantly the average daily prison population could rise. Similarly, changes in the lengths of sentences issued to different categories of offenders will affect the composition of the prison population.

The custodial population tends to be mainly made up of those between 18 and 40 years of age, although there has been a 'greying' of the prison population in recent years with an increase in the number sentenced to long terms of imprisonment (see Chapter 20). Males make up the vast majority of the prison population in England and Wales, and women comprise just under 6 per cent, although it should be noted that the number of women in prison in England and Wales has almost doubled over the past decade (Carlen and Worrall, 2004). In February 2003 one in four of those in prison were drawn from minority ethnic groups. It is estimated that the incarceration for those defined as 'black' is seven times that of whites, while approximately one in eight of the prison population are foreign nationals (Prison Reform Trust, 2005). The number of juveniles in custody is a frequent point of reference. A survey carried out by the United Nations in 2002 found that the rate of juvenile/youth custody per 100,000 of the population was 38.40 per 100,000 in America and 18.26 per 100,000 in England and Wales. According to these statistics, England and Wales currently incarcerate young people at a higher rate than any other country in Europe (Muncie, 2005).

The background of those in prison typically involves a history of marginalization, deprivation, and poor achievement. Those in prison tend to have low educational levels, few skills, and poor work histories. Nearly half of all prisoners have been excluded from school. One third did not have permanent accommodation prior to imprisonment (Social Exclusion Unit, 2002) (see Table 27.1). A survey carried out by Nick Davies (2004) found that over 70 per cent of prisoners suffer from two or more mental health disorders.

If we look at the composition of the prison population by offence type it is apparent there have been significant changes over the last decade or so. For male prisoners there has been an increase in the number imprisoned for violence, burglary, robbery, and drug offences between 1992 and 2002 (Councell, 2003). There has also been an increase in the number of women imprisoned for violence-related offences, but the

Table 27.1 Characteristics of the prison population

Characteristic	General population	Prison population
Ran away from home as a child	11%	47% of male sentenced prisoners and 50% of female sentenced prisoners
Taken into care as a child	2%	27%
Regularly truanted from school	3%	30%
Excluded from school	2%	49% of male and 33% of female sentenced prisoners
No qualifications	15%	52% of men and 71% of women
Numeracy at or below Level 1 (the level expected of an 11 year-old)	23%	65%
Reading ability at or below Level 1	21–23%	48%
Unemployed before imprisonment	5%	67%
Homeless	0.9%	32%
Suffer from two or more mental disorders	5% of men and 2% of women	72% of male sentenced prisoners and 70% of female sentenced prisoners
Psychotic disorder	0.5% of men and 0.6% of women	7% of male sentenced prisoners and 14% of female sentenced prisoners
Drug use in the previous year	13% of men and 8% of women	66% of male sentenced prisoners and 55% of female sentenced prisoners
Hazardous drinking	38% of men and 15% of women	63% of male sentenced prisoners and 39% of female sentenced prisoners

Source: Social Exclusion Unit Report: 'Reducing re-offending by ex-prisoners', July 2002.

most dramatic change has been the number imprisoned for drug-related offences (see Figures 27.1 and 27.2). A further significant change is an increase in the number of people serving life sentences. In March 2005 there were 5,800 prisoners serving life sentences in England and Wales compared to 4,000 in 1998 and 3,000 in 1992.

Figure 27.1 Male prison population under an immediate sentence 1992 and 2002

Source: Home Office, 2003.

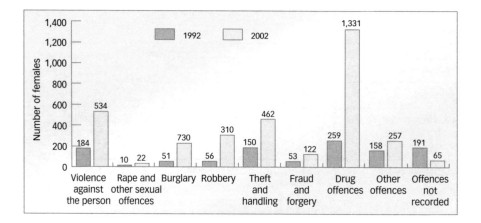

Figure 27.2 Female prison population under an immediate sentence 1992 and 2002

Source: Home Office, 2003.

REVIEW QUESTIONS

1 Prison is a form of punishment reserved mainly for the poor and the powerless. Discuss.

2 What are the implications of such a high percentage of prisoners being mentally ill?

3 In what ways is women's experience of incarceration different from that of men?

Order and control in prison

Since the number of inmates in most prisons on any one day normally exceeds the number of staff, why do prisoners not try to take control of the prison and escape? This question not only raises issues about how order and control are routinely achieved in prison, but also has implications for how order and control are achieved in the wider society. Another way of posing this question is why do people conform or adapt to situations that they find oppressive or constraining? To some extent order and control are achieved in prison through the mobilization of its three basic elements—labour, space, and time. Despite the problems of engaging in profitable forms of production in prison, most prisons engage inmates in some form of labour even if it is only working in the prison grounds, in the kitchen, or cleaning up. It is seen as important to keep prisoners occupied as much as possible, and the aim of instilling some form of work discipline in prisoners remains an objective of prison authorities. Prisoners are also controlled through spatial segregation and by the organized distribution of bodies so that forms of congregation are limited. High walls and continuous surveillance also make escape difficult. For those who try to escape, solitary confinement has been used historically as a form of punishment. Order in prison is also achieved through the use of a strict time-table that structures the prisoner's day and is used to establish routines and orchestrate activities. For those who misbehave, adding time onto the existing sentence has been a widely used sanction.

Apart from these basic organizing themes there are a number of other ways in which order and discipline is maintained in prison. Some penologists have emphasized the role of subcultures within prison that serve to establish normative codes amongst inmates, establishing a set of informal rules or an 'inmate code' which sets out how inmates should behave towards reach other and the prison authorities (Clemmer, 1940). From this perspective it is argued that it is not so much that order is imposed, but negotiated, and that rather than the custodians being omnipotent, achieving order is a continuous process of negotiation and struggle (Sykes, 1958). In some prisons it has been suggested that the inmates exercise considerable control in relation to each other (Edgar *et al.*, 2003). American research has drawn attention to the role of gangs in prison and the considerable degree of control that they exercise (Elsner, 2006).

Order and disciple is routinely achieved through the use of incentives and disincentives. Virtually all prison regimes employ some version of a 'stick and carrot' approach which includes a loss of privileges, on one hand, to being given more attractive forms of work, increased number of visits, and other 'perks' on the other. Of particular significance in relation to good behaviour is the issue of parole and early release. To the extent that early release is based on assessment of 'good behaviour', prisoners have a major incentive to demonstrate compliance. Apart from the traditional range of incentives and disincentives, the prisons department deal with problems of order in prisons by identifying 'troublemakers' in certain prisons on the basis of risk assessments and transferring them to other prisons.

Violence, however, is an endemic feature of prisons and it tends to take a number of forms—interpersonal violence between inmates or between inmates and staff, and collective violence in the form of riots and disturbances. Research on prisons in England and Wales carried out in the 1990s revealed that remand centres and Young Offenders Institutions had the largest number of assaults on inmates and reports of fighting. Serious violence is significantly higher in men's than in women's prisons (Bottoms, 1999). King and McDermott's (1995) study of five prisons in England and Wales, which employed self-completion questionnaires, reported that 12.5 per cent of their sample said that they had been assaulted at some time while in their current prisons; 6.8 per cent of respondents claimed to have been sexually attacked; and 33 per cent said that they had been threatened with violence. Although the authors note that much prison violence is not reported, they conclude from the research that inmates behave differently in different prison settings, and that different prison regimes, systems of management, variations in design and the like can all have an impact on the level and frequency of violence in prison.

In response to reports of violence and abuse there are mechanisms in place in the prison system for expressing grievances and exercising accountability. Every prison in England and Wales is served by a Board of Visitors and body of lay volunteers. Boards of Visitors were involved in disciplinary hearings until 1992 when they were relieved of this duty as it was held that it was incompatible with their role as inspecting prisons and hearing prisoners' grievances. Prisoners are now expected to refer complaints to unit managers or their duty governor, and they still have the option to refer complaints to the prisons ombudsman or their MP. These is also a prison inspectorate that makes announced and unannounced visits to prisons and has provided some of the most critical accounts of the conditions and management of prisons in recent years (Home Office, 2007).

The key indicators of breakdown of order in prisons are riots and disturbances. The distinction between riots and disturbances is that riots involve collective actions that aim to take control of the whole or part of the prison, while disturbances tend to involve more localized and short-lived disruptions. There is no consensus on the causes of riots, but the Woolf Report (1991) is seen as providing an authoritative analysis of the conditions and processes that led up to the riots at Strangeways prison in Manchester in 1990. Lord Woolf argued that if riots were to be avoided there needed to be a proper balance between 'security, control and justice' within prisons, although the report placed the primary emphasis on control and made it clear that the delivery of 'justice' was dependent on the maintenance of an adequate level of security (Sim, 1994a). What was clear, however, from the Woolf report was that there is no single cause of riots, whether it is poor conditions or a 'toxic mix' of prisoners. Riots, as Rod Morgan (1997) has argued, tend to be the outcome of what he refers to as a 'disorder amplification spiral' in which poor conditions are linked to a growing sense of injustice and the polarization of relations between staff and inmates. When this process is set in motion, any one of a number of 'triggers' can turn anger and frustration into a riot.

Another outcome of this process of the breakdown of control is the intensification of a sense of anomie and insecurity amongst prisoners, which allows stronger prisoners to exercise greater control over weaker and more vulnerable prisoners. This scenario is seen as producing the conditions for an increase in the suicides in prison, particularly when those being victimized are isolated (Leibling 1992). In 2004 the number of suicides in prison in England and Wales was 95, 13 of which were women and 5 were under 21 years of age. This is the highest number of suicides recorded in one year.

Does prison work?

The question 'does prison work?' is deceptively difficult to answer. While on one side there are conservative criminologists like Charles Murray (1997) and John Dilulio (1987) in America and conservative politicians like Michael Howard in the UK who claim unequivocally that prison works to reduce crime, there is a wide body of liberal opinion that flatly denies that this is the case. The truth is somewhere in between and a closer examination of the issue reveals that there are a number of dimensions to this question and consequently a range of possible answers. Thus while some commentators might argue that prisons work to deter potential offenders and thereby reduce crime, they might simultaneously deny that prisons work to reform or rehabilitate offenders.

If by the phrase 'prison works' we mean that it acts as an instrument for simply punishing offenders then we might concede the truth of the statement. However, this immediately raises the question of whether it works any better than other forms of punishment. In terms of general deterrence, the effectiveness of the sanction of imprisonment to deter prospective offenders from committing crime is extremely difficult to determine with any precision. The extent to which people think about the possible punishments for crimes they might commit is difficult to determine and whether they think about the possibility of imprisonment is even less certain (Wilson, 1983).

In terms of rehabilitation, we have seen the development of an impressive array of programmes in prisons in recent years to address what the authorities describe as the 'criminogenic needs' of offenders. Under the slogan of 'Making Prisons Work' the Government has introduced a number of programmes designed to address drug use and violence amongst prisoners as well as to develop education and training programmes. However well intentioned these programmes might be, critics of incarceration have argued that the nature of imprisonment militates against rehabilitation and that prisons tend to debilitate rather than rehabilitate offenders (Goffman, 1968; Mathieson, 1990).

In the same way, the claim associated with Robert Martinson's (1974) review of rehabilitation programmes that 'nothing works' has served to undermine rehabilitation as a rationale for imprisonment (Bottoms and Preston, 1980). Although Martinson and others have qualified and criticized this conclusion and pointed out that the research results indicate that some programmes work for some people under some conditions, the general belief that rehabilitation programmes are of limited value has persisted (Pawson and Tilley, 1997; Martinson, 1979; Palmer, 1975). The dismissal of the ideal of rehabilitation has, however, been challenged by some penologists. Indeed, it has been argued that rehabilitation is the only justification for imprisonment that obligates the State to care for offender's needs and welfare (Cullen and Gilbert, 1982). It is also the case that the widespread critiques of rehabilitation in the 1970s and 1980s led to a greater emphasis on incapacitation and the warehousing of prisoners.

One of the major obstacles to properly evaluating the effects of rehabilitation programmes as well as the effects of specific deterrence is that they are predominantly assessed in relation to recidivism. Recidivism, however, is a difficult and unreliable measure (Maltz, 1984). This is primarily because the concept of recidivism is conceived as involving four different processes—reoffending, rearrest, reconviction, and prison re-entry. It is, however, possible that individuals might reoffend without being rearrested or reconvicted. Thus the level of recidivism can change depending on which of the four elements is taken as the point of reference. At the same time, offenders may commit less serious crimes less often after leaving prison but they can still count as recidivists and be seen as examples of the 'failure' of incarceration.

A more complex and difficult question to answer in relation to the claim that prison works is whether a five-year sentence, for example, works better than a two-year sentence. Some critics have argued that there is a diminishing effect in extending the length of sentences beyond a certain period of time because individuals' personal time horizons do not allow them to adequately conceptualize the meaning of time beyond a certain number of years in the future (Cohen and Taylor, 1972). An equally perplexing question is whether a short period of imprisonment is likely to have any impact on rehabilitation or a greater effect on specific deterrence than a fine or a non-custodial sentence.

An equally difficult question is whether the increased use of imprisonment in both Britain and America has reduced crime levels, as some observers claim. Certainly, there is a correlation between the increased use of imprisonment and the decline in both countries in recent years. But are these changes causally linked? Other countries have reported a decrease in crime while prison numbers have remained stable or declined, while in others both crime rates and imprisonment rates have increased simultaneously (Jacobson, 2005). These variations demonstrate at the very least that any suggestion that a drop in crime rates is likely to result from the increased use of prison needs to be treated with extreme caution. We also know that the level of crime in any period is influenced by a range of social and economic factors that operate independently of imprisonment and other forms of punishment. The available evidence suggests that, while the increased use of imprisonment may convey a significant message about 'getting tough' on crime, the impact of imprisonment on what are generally considered to be the most serious crimes—murder, violence, rape, and sexual offence—appears to be limited. If a deterrent effect is in operation it is more likely to be effective in relation to the prospective offenders' assessment of their likelihood of being caught, rather than the nature and severity of the available sanctions (Currie, 1998).

One variant on the claim that prison works is the claim that 'prison pays'. That is, some criminologists argue that there are significant financial savings to be made by removing offenders from the community and locking them up (Dilulio and Piehl, 1991; Wilson and Abraham, 1992). Those that have argued that 'prison pays' have examined the number and cost of crimes committed by offenders in the period before incarceration and then tried to work out the amount saved by removing the offender from the community.

This cost is then compared to the cost of incarceration, and where the cost of crimes that have been predicted to have been committed is less than the cost of imprisoning offenders it is argued that 'prison pays'. There are problems in this analysis in relation to which costs are taken into account and how they are calculated. In particular, the costs of the 'collateral damage' associated with incarceration, which disrupts families, neighbourhoods, and communities sustaining cycles of disadvantage are not normally taken into account (Mauer and Chesney-Lind, 2002). It is also the case that the experience of imprisonment can further marginalize individuals and adversely affect their opportunities on the job market. Indeed, in the words of one government report published during the Thatcher years 'prison can be an expensive way of making bad people worse' (Home Office, 1988). Moreover, a significant proportion of offenders enter prison at or near the peak of their offending and the assumption that they would have carried on offending at the same rate year on year may not be justified. Also offending patterns change with age and as those in prison grow older it is likely that their level of offending would predictably decline.

The arguments that 'prison works' or 'prison pays' are generally weakened by the fact that most of the advocates assume that the option is between sending people to prison or doing nothing. But doing nothing is never in practice an option. There are alternative means available to prevent and respond to crime, and the critical question is whether the enormous sums of money spent on prisons could be more usefully employed in other ways.

REVIEW QUESTIONS

1 Critically evaluate Charles Murray's claim that 'prison works'.

2 Imprisonment can be an expensive way of making bad people worse. Discuss.

3 How useful is recidivism as a measure of the effectiveness of imprisonment?

The crisis of imprisonment

The term 'crisis' has become increasingly associated with imprisonment in recent years. But what exactly does it mean to say that the prison is in a state of 'crisis'. Is the term crisis a synonym for 'problems' or 'tensions' in the prison system, or does it signify something deeper and more serious? It is clear in newspaper reports and academic publications that different commentators provide different examples of what they consider constitutes the 'crisis' and it is not clear whether these different points of reference are different aspects of the same crisis or whether they represent different forms of crisis (King and McDermott, 1989).

In their book *British Prisons* Mike Fitzgerald and Joe Sim (1979) argue that there are in fact a series of 'crises' that have become associated with imprisonment and that these involve a crisis of visibility, authority, conditions, containment, and legitimacy. The crisis of visibility refers to the limited public access and information regarding the prison system. The segregated nature of imprisonment and restrictions on entry mean that the day-to-day activities that go on in prison are largely shielded from public view. This, it is argued, provides the conditions for abuse, maltreatment, and other excesses within prisons. It was not until the late 1980s that television cameras were allowed to film in prisons and different agencies were allowed regular access to certain prisons. Consequently, in previous periods prisoners resorted to roof-top protests in order to make themselves visible and to bring attention to their grievances.

The crisis of authority involves the perceived undermining of the traditional forms of authority and discipline exercised in prisons, particularly as they have become more accessible and accountable. Prison staff complain that changes in prison rules and working practices have undermined their authority in prisons and made it harder to maintain order. The declining support for the rehabilitative ideal during the 1970s and 1980s brought into question the professional ideology of prison staff and the shift towards incapacitation and the warehousing of prisoners which intensified the problems of maintaining order in prisons. In 2007 prison officers went on strike over pay and conditions, and prison overcrowding was cited as one of the factors that increased pressures on prison staff (Campbell, 2007).

The crisis of conditions refers to the poor and in some cases deteriorating conditions in a number of prisons. Many of the remand prisons in England and Wales, for example, were built in the Victorian era and are in a poor state of repair. In these prisons and elsewhere in the prison system the level of overcrowding has become a major point of concern as prison populations increase. At the end of 2004 some 16,000 prisons were sleeping two in a cell designed for one, and many of these cells have unscreened toilets. In March 2005 it was found that 82 out of 139 prisons were overcrowded (Prison Reform Trust, 2005). Overcrowding has the effect of not only making the physical conditions in prison worse, but also affects the time out of cells, recreational activities, and other forms of association amongst prisoners. It also puts increasing pressure on staff–inmate relations. Worsening conditions can also lead to crises of containment since these processes directly and indirectly affect control and security in prisons. As prison conditions worsen and overcrowding increases the possibility of disturbances in prison increases, as does the likelihood of escape. One response to the overcrowding in certain prisons has been to move prisoners around the country to prisons where there are vacant beds. This process, however, causes disruption and difficulties for prisoners and their families who have to travel further to visit them.

These various 'crises' have been well documented in the criminological literature, but Fitzgerald and Sim (1979) argue that the 'crisis' facing the prison system goes far beyond the *internal* problems facing the prison system. For Fitzgerald and Sim, resolving the specific crises of visibility, authority, containment, and conditions would—even if it were possible—not entirely solve the crisis of imprisonment because there is, they argue; 'no evidence to suggest that if we had hygienic, clean, antiseptic, single occupant cells throughout the penal system, there would be no crisis' (1979: 19). Instead, they suggest there is an underlying crisis, which 'reveals the essential bankruptcy of penal policy' and which 'transcends the prisons walls' (1979: 24). This involves what they refer to as the 'crisis of legitimacy' involving external processes and wider dimensions of politics and power. The prison, the authors argue, suffers from two fundamental flaws. First, they claim that prison simply does not work and that the high levels of recidivism are testimony to its failure; secondly, that 'imprisonment is consistently invoked against the marginal working classes' and it is part of 'a class based legal system' which singles out particular groups of offenders for punishment. The implications of this 'crisis of legitimacy' are that there is no real justification for the continued use of imprisonment and that prisons should be abolished (Sim, 1994b).

Paul Cavadino and James Dignan (2002) have taken up the issue of the prison crisis and, like Fitzgerald and Sim, make a distinction between the internal and external nature of the 'crisis', distinguishing between what they see as a material crisis which they describe as a 'crisis of penological resources' on one side, and an ideological crisis, or a 'crisis of legitimacy', on the other. However, they see the 'crisis of legitimacy' in a very different way from Fitzgerald and Sim. For Cavadino and Dignan the crisis of legitimacy centres around the sense of injustice amongst inmates. Thus rather than focus on the way in which the prison is linked to wider political processes, Cavadino and Dignan tend to locate the legitimacy crisis within the penal sphere itself, and it is seen, on one hand, as the culmination 'of all the individual crises' within the penal system, while they also claim that it operates on a distinctly different 'ideological' plane. From what they describe as a radical pluralist position, the 'crisis' can be overcome by increasing resources and by addressing instances of injustice. It is not clear, however, from their account if these two options are exclusive or for that matter how they relate to each other.

A similar approach to the penal crisis is adopted by Richard Sparks and Anthony Bottoms (1995) who focus in particular on the issue of legitimacy. For them prisons lose their legitimacy when the rules and procedures are not followed or when staff do not operate professionally. In line with the approach advocated by Lord Woolf (1991) in his review of the Strangeways riots, Bottoms and Sparks suggest that improved systems of justice within prisons will improve security and control within prisons.

Thus, there remains a tension and uncertainty in the criminological literature over the precise meaning of the 'crisis of imprisonment'. Articles in the media that frequently refer to the prisons 'crisis' tend to focus on the conditions in prison or overcrowding. Criminologists, however, like Cavadino and Dignan and Bottoms and Sparks, tend to see the 'crisis' on two levels—one as a crisis of conditions and the other as a crisis of legitimacy. For them legitimacy is mainly seen in procedural terms, while for Fitzgerald and Sim the 'crisis of legitimacy' goes far beyond the penal sphere and is bound up with wider political and economic changes that increasingly call into question the role of imprisonment and its class-based nature (Reiman, 2004). It has, however, been claimed that the growth in prison population over the last decade or so indicates that there is little sign of a crisis of imprisonment if by crisis we mean the imminent breakdown and demise of imprisonment (Morgan, 1997). However, there may be no contradiction between the expansion of the prison and its growing legitimacy deficit.

REVIEW QUESTIONS

1 How useful is the concept of 'prison crisis' in identifying the current state of imprisonment?

2 Would dealing with the injustices that occur in prison overcome the problem of legitimation?

3 What evidence is there that prisons are in a deepening crisis?

CONCLUSION

Predicting the future is always a precarious business. However, in recognizing that the prison system is facing a series of 'crises', it is important to think about the development of an appropriate response. Francis Cullen and John Wright (1996) have suggested that there is, in essence, two ways forward for penal reform. One involves the adoption of what they call the 'punishment paradigm', which is associated with conservative criminologists like Charles Murray and John Dilulio. The other option they refer to as the 'progressive paradigm', which is associated with a more liberal approach. The punishment paradigm claims that crime can be effectively reduced through the increased use of imprisonment, but that the use of imprisonment needs to be rationalized in order to reduce costs. Consequently, the preferred option for some conservative criminologists is to contract out the running of prisons to private operators, or alternatively to build high-tech prisons that rely on new forms of design and surveillance that are able to operate with a reduced number of staff (Beyens and Snacken, 1996; Harding, 1997). Staff costs account for some 80 per cent of the running costs of the prison and therefore any attempt to significantly reduce overall costs will necessarily involve reducing the number of staff or alternatively reducing the amount that they are paid. Another way of reducing costs is to limit the number of training and rehabilitation programmes offered in prison and to keep prisoners locked up in their cells for a greater percentage of their time. Consequently, within this approach there is a tendency towards penal austerity and the warehousing of prisoners.

The more liberal 'progressive paradigm' as outlined by Cullen and Wright (1996) takes a different approach. It claims that the punishment paradigm has persistently failed to reduce crime and claims that the large financial investments that have been made in prisons have brought only marginal and diminishing returns (Currie, 1998). Liberal critics point to public opinion surveys that suggest that the general public do not support an increase in the use of imprisonment. They also argue that prisons should be used *as* punishment rather than *for* punishment. The penalty of imprisonment is the deprivation of liberty for a specified period of time. In that time the aim should be to address the needs of offenders and develop rehabilitative programmes, rather than prisons serving as 'schools of crime', which only serve to release dangerous and disillusioned offenders back into neighbourhoods that already have more than their fair share of problems. Rehabilitation, it is argued, offers a humane and effective way to reduce crime and improve the lives of certain groups of offenders.

In the meantime the various 'crises' confronting the prison have motivated policy makers, activists, and practitioners alike to develop strategies to reduce reliance on imprisonment. Over the past two or three decades a number of measures have been developed to achieve this objective. The measures adopted include the development of alternatives to custody, introducing new sentencing policies and guidelines, and extending the use of early release from prison. In brief, any strategy designed to reduce the number of people in prison must divert people away from prison or reduce the period of time they spend in prison. The first element of this strategy is seen to be dependent on changing the nature of sentencing and increasing the availability of non-custodial sanctions. Changing sentencing policies is, however, a complex business. Deciding when prison is appropriate, the duration of a prison sentence, and where alternative sanctions should be used raises complex moral and legal concerns (Hudson, 2003).

Discussions about the role of rehabilitation have also been affected by the development of what Malcolm Feeley and Jonathon Simon (1992) have referred to as 'The New Penology'. These authors argue that the 'old' penal strategies that were directed at the reform or rehabilitation of the individual are being increasingly replaced by a 'New Penology' that is based on risk analysis and is more concerned with the management of the underclass rather than its reform. In this actuarial approach the authors claim that the role of imprisonment is changing and that its rationale is gravitating towards incapacitation rather than rehabilitation.

Finally, it was suggested above that the modern prison was constructed in relation to three central elements—labour discipline, time, and space. At the beginning of the nineteenth century developing a mode of punishment around these elements seemed obvious and 'natural'. However, it has been argued that the preoccupation with labour discipline is less evident in the contemporary prison system and that there are changes in the significance of time and space in the 'information society' in which the notion of confinement as mode of punishment appears less appropriate. Consequently, there is a general shift towards what Giles Deleuze (1995) has called the 'control society' in which social control becomes continuous and comprehensive, relying increasingly on monitoring and surveillance. As the 'control society' develops, he suggests, future generations will look back with nostalgia at the notion of punishing people by confining them to limited spaces for a designated period of time.

QUESTIONS FOR DISCUSSION

1 What could be done to reduce the size of the prison population?
2 To what extent is it reasonable to suggest that the 'old penology' is being superseded by the 'new penology'?
3 Is there a case for defending the continued use of rehabilitation programmes in prison?

GUIDE TO FURTHER READING

Matthews, R. (2002) *Imprisonment*. London: Ashgate.
This book contains approximately 20 classic articles on imprisonment.

Jewkes Y. and Johnstone H. (2006) *Prison Readings: A Critical Introduction to Prisons and Imprisonment*. Cullompton: Willan.
This is another useful collection of articles on different aspects of imprisonment.

Carlen, P. (2002) *Women and Punishment*: The Struggle for Justice. Cullompton: Willan.
This is a collection of articles focusing particularly on the relationship between women and punishment.

Mauer, M. (1999) *Race to Incarcerate*. New York: The New Press.
This book examines the relationship between crime control and the use of imprisonment and in particular the significance of class and race in relation to the increased use of imprisonment.

Ramsbotham, D. (2003) Prisongate: *The Shocking State of Britain's Prisons and the need for Visionary Change*. London: The Free Press.
This book is written by a former prison inspector and provides a unique insight into the state of the prison system and the politics of penal reform.

Crow, I. (2001) *The Treatment and Rehabilitation of Offenders*. London: Sage.
This book examines the concepts of treatment and rehabilitation in prisons and discusses the role of different agencies in developing types of intervention.

WEB LINKS

http://www.homeoffice.gov.uk

The home office site provides details of news and developments in prisons as well as publications on the penal system. It also has a useful link to HM Chief Inspectorate of Prisons and Probation which contains inspection reports and thematic reviews.

http://www.justice.gov.uk/

This site covers the work and activities of the recently established Ministry of Justice. It contains a useful link to the National Offender Management Service (NOMS) which provides details of NOMS' role in reducing reoffending and of its publications.

http://www.hmprisonservice.gov.uk

This site provides information about the operation of prisons throughout England and Wales. It includes a visitors' guide, an insight into the prison system, as well as providing prison population figures.

http://www.howardleague.org

This site contains details of the work of the Howard League in relation to penal reform, news of developments in the penal system, as well as listing a number of publications.

http://www.prisonreformtrust.org.uk

In a similar way to the Howard League, the prison reform trust website contains information on their current activities as well as listing a number of publications on different aspects of the penal system and prison reform.

http://www.niprisonservice.gov.uk

This site provides information on the operation of the prison system in Northern Ireland as well as providing some useful links to other organizations involved with the issues relating to imprisonment.

http://www.ppo.gov.uk

This site provides details of the work of the Prisons and Probation Ombudsman, which deals mainly with complaints from prisoners and those subject to probation supervision. It also contains a reasonably comprehensive listing of organizations that deal with different aspects of imprisonment and lists their respective websites.

REFERENCES

Beyens, K. and Snacken S. (1996) 'Prison Privatization: An International Perspective' in R. Matthews and P. Francis (eds) *Prisons 2000*. London: Macmillan.

Bonczar, T. and Beck, A. (1997) *Lifetime Likelihood of Going to State or Federal Prison*.

Bottoms, A. (1999) 'Interpersonal violence and social order in prison' in *Crime and Justice*, Vol. 26.

Bureau of Justice Statistics. US Department of Justice.

Bottoms, A. and Preston, R. (1980) *The Coming Penal Crisis*, Edinburgh: Scottish Academic Press.

Campbell, D. (2007) 'Simmering Anger That Finally Boiled Over' *The Guardian*. 30 August.

Carlen, P. and Worrall, A. (2004) *Analysing women's imprisonment*. Cullompton: Willan.

Cavadino, P. and Dignan, J. (2002) *The Penal System: An Introduction*. London: Sage.

Clemmer, D. (1940) *The Prison Community*. New York: Holt, Rinehart and Winston.

Cohen, S. (1985) *Visions of Social Control*. Cambridge: Polity Press.

Cohen, S. and Taylor, L. (1972) *Psychological Survival*. Harmondsworth: Penguin.

Councell, R. (2003) *The Prison Population in 2002: A Statistical Review*. Findings 228. London: HMSO.

Cullen, F. and Gilbert, K. (1982) *Reaffirming Rehabilitation*. Cincinnati: Anderson Publishing.

Cullen, F. and Wright J. (1996) 'The Future of Corrections' in B. Maguire and P. Radosh (eds) *The Past, Present and Future of American Criminal Justice.* New York: General Hall.

Currie, E. (1998) *Crime and Punishment in America.* New York: Metropolitan Books.

Deleuze, G. (1995) *Negotiations.* New York: Columbia University Press.

Davies, N. (2004) 'Scandal of Society's Misfits Dumped in Jail'. *Guardian,* 6 December.

Dilulio, J. (1987) *Governing Prisons.* New York: Free Press.

Dilulio, J. and Piehl, A. (1991) 'Does Prison Pay?' *Brookings Review,* Fall. Part 4: 29–35.

Donzelot, J. (1979) *The Policing of Families.* London: Hutchinson.

Edgar, K., O'Donnell, I., and Martin, C. (2003) *Prison Violence: The Dynamics of Conflict, Fear and Power.* Cullompton: Willan.

Elsner, A. (2006) *Gates of Injustice.* New York: Pearson Education.

Evans, R. (1982) *The Fabrication of Virtue: English Prison Architecture 1750–1840.* Cambridge: Cambridge University Press.

Feeley, M. and Simon, J. (1992) 'The new penology: notes on the emerging strategy of corrections and its implications', *Criminology,* 30, 4, 449–474.

Fitzgerald, M. and Sim, J. (1979) *British Prisons.* Oxford: Blackwell.

Foucault, M. (1977) *Discipline and Punish: The Birth of the Prison.* London: Allen Lane.

Garland, D. (1981) 'The Birth of the Welfare Sanction' *British Journal of Law and Society,* Vol. 8: 29–45.

Goffman, A. (1968) *Asylums.* Harmondsworth: Pelican.

Harding, R. (1997) *Private Prisons and Public Accountability.* Buckingham: Open University Press.

Harvey, L. and Pease, K. (1987) 'Prevalence of Imprisonment in England and Wales' *British Journal of Criminology,* Vol. 27: 65–69.

Home Office (1988) *Punishment, Custody and the Community.* Cmnd 424. London: HMSO.

Home Office (2000) *The Prison Population in 2002: A statistical review.* Findings, No. 288, London: Home Office.

Home Office (2007) *HM Inspectorate Annual Report 2005–06.* London. HMSO.

Hudson, B. (2003) *Justice in the Risk Society.* London: Sage.

Ignatieff, M. 1978) *A Just Measure of Pain: The Penitentiary in the Industrial Revolution 1750–1850.* London: Macmillan.

Jacobs, J. (1977) *Stateville: The Penitentiary in Mass Society.* University of Chicago Press.

Jacobson, M. (2005) *Downsizing Prisons.* New York: New York University Press.

King, R. and McDermott, K. (1989) 'British Prisons 1970–1987: The Ever-Deepening Crisis' *British Journal of Criminology,* Vol. 29 No, 2: 107–128.

King, R. and McDermott, K. (1995) *The State of Our Prisons.* Oxford: Clarendon Press.

Leibling, A. (1992) *Suicides in Prison.* London: Routledge.

Maltz, M. (1984) *Recidivism.* Orlando: Academic Press.

Martinson, R. (1974) 'What Works? Questions and Answers About Prison Reform' *Public Interest,* 35: 22–54.

Martinson, R. (1979) 'Symposium on Sentencing' *Hofra Law Review,* Vol. 7 No. 2: 243–258.

Matthews, R. (1999) *Doing Time: An Introduction to the Sociology of Imprisonment.* London: Palgrave.

Matthews, R. (2005) 'The Myth of Punitiveness' *Theoretical Criminology,* Vol. 9 No. 2: 175–201.

Mathieson, T. (1990) *Prison on Trial.* London: Sage.

Mauer, M. and Chesney-Lind, M. (2002) *Invisible Punishment: The Collateral Consequences of Mass Imprisonment.* New York: The New Press.

McConville, S. (1995) 'The Victorian Prison: England 1865–1965' in N. Morris and D. Rothman (eds) *The Oxford History of the Prison.* New York: Oxford University Press.

McGowan, R. (1995) 'The Well-Ordered Prison: England, 1780–1865' in N. Morris and D.J. Rothman (eds) *The Oxford History of the Prison: The Practice of Punishment in Western Society.* Oxford: Oxford University Press.

Melossi, D. (1979) 'Institutions of Social Control and Capitalist Organisation of Work' in National Deviancy Conference (ed) *Capitalism and The Rule of Law.* London: Hutchinson.

Meyer, J. and O'Malley, P. (2005) 'Missing the punitive turn? Canadian criminal justice, "balance", and penal modernism,' in J. Pratt, D. Brown, M. Brown, S. Hallsworth, and W. Morrison (eds) *The New Punitiveness: Trends, Theories, Perspectives.* Devon: Willan.

Morgan, R. (1997) 'The Aims of Imprisonment Revisited' in A. Liebling and T. Ward (eds) *Deaths in Custody: International Perspectives*. London: Whiting and Birch.

Murray, C. (1997) *Does Prison Work?* London: Institute of Economic Affairs.

Muncie, J. (2005) 'The Globalisation of Crime Control—The Case of Youth and Juvenile Justice: Neo-Liberalism, Policy Convergence and International Conventions' *Theoretical Criminology*, Vol. 9 No. 1: 35–64.

Palmer, T. (1975) 'Martinson Revisited' *Journal of Research in Crime and Delinquency*, Vol. 12: 133–192.

Pawson, R. and Tilley, N. (1997) *Realistic Evaluation*. London: Sage.

Pratt, J. (2007) *Penal Populism*. London: Routledge.

Prison Reform Trust (2005) *Prison Fact File. Bromley Briefings*. London: PRT.

Rafter, N. (183) 'Prisons For Women 1870–1980' in M. Tonry and N. Morris (eds.) *Crime and Justice: An Annual Review of Research*, Vol. 5: University of Chicago Press.

Reiman, J. (2004) *The Rich Get Richer and the Poor Get Prison* (7th edn). Boston: Pearson.

Rothman, D. (1971) *The Discovery of the Asylum: Social Order and Disorder in the New Republic*. Boston: Little Brown and Co.

Rusche, G. and Kirchheimer, O. (2005) *Punishment and Social Structure*. New Brunswick: Transaction.

Sim, J. (1994a) 'Reforming the Penal Wasteland? A Critical Review of the Woolf Report' in E. Player and M. Jenkins (eds.) *Prisons After Woolf: Reform Through Riot*. London: Routledge.

Sim, J. (1994b) 'The Abolitionist Approach: A British Perspective' in A. Duff et al. (eds) *Penal Theory and Practice*. Manchester: Manchester University Press.

Social Exclusion Unit (2002) *Reducing Re-Offending by Ex-Offenders*. London: ODPM.

Sparks, R. and Bottoms, A. (1995) 'Legitimacy and Order in Prisons' *British Journal of Sociology*, Vol. 46 No. 1: 45–62.

Sparks, R. Bottoms, A., and Hay, W. (1996) *Prisons and the Problem of Order*. Oxford: Clarendon Press.

Sykes, G. (1958) *Society of Captives*. Princeton, NJ: Princeton University Press.

Tonry, M. (1995) *Malign Neglect; Race Crime and Punishment in America*. New York: Oxford University Press.

Wilson, J. (1983) *Thinking About Crime*. New York: Basic Books.

Wilson J. and Abraham, A. (1992) 'Does Crime Pay?' *Justice Quarterly*. Vol. 9 No. 3: 359–377.

Woolf, Lord (1991) *Prison Disturbances April 1990*. London: HMSO.

Worsley, R. (2007) *Young People in Custody 2004–2006*. HM Inspectorate of Prisons. London: HMSO.

Zedner, L. (1991) Women, Crime and Custody in Victorian England. Oxford: Clarendon.

GLOSSARY OF TERMS

Abolitionism A political and criminological perspective that advocates the radical transformation/replacement of modern punishment forms with a more reflexive and multifaceted approach capable of better understanding dominant ideological constructions of crime.

Accountability The ways in which organizations and individuals are rendered answerable for their policies and day-to-day activities, exerted by internal and external mechanisms.

Acquisitive crime A term used to categorize economically motivated crimes.

Actuarial justice A term coined by Malcolm Feeley and Jonathan Simon to try to characterize a possible emerging aspect of criminal law and criminal justice. The term derives from 'actuary', meaning a statistician who works for an insurance company to calculate risks, premiums and pay-outs. Actuarial justice thus suggests a form of justice based on calculation of risks, and the statistical use of past data to predict the likelihood of future events.

Administrative criminology A form of practical policy-relevant criminology that focuses almost exclusively on the nature of the criminal event and the particular setting in which it occurs. Under this perspective, the offender is considered only as a 'rational actor' who makes calculated decisions about the costs and benefits of criminal action. Administrative criminologists seek to reduce the opportunities for crime, thus making the costs/risks of crime outweigh the potential benefits.

Aetiological crisis The majority of post-war criminology was predicated on the basis that poor social conditions caused crime. Consequently, if a meaningful reduction in crime was to occur, then governments needed to implement a series of social democratic policies specifically aimed at reducing unemployment and raising general living standards. Despite substantial improvements in the Western world in these and other areas during the years 1950–70, recorded crime soared to unprecedented levels. This refutation of the then major thinking in the social sciences has been described by Jock Young as the 'aetiological crisis'.

Aetiology The philosophy of causation; the study of causes.

Ageism Discrimination or prejudice against people because of their age or presumed age.

Appeal The initial decisions made by magistrates' or Crown Courts can be challenged by a convicted defendant (or in some cases by the prosecution). This is known as an 'appeal' and can be either on the question of the correctness of the conviction itself or the appropriateness of the sentence. The appeal will be to a higher court—this will normally be to the Crown Court from the magistrates' or to the Court of Appeal from the Crown Court.

Atavism The recurrence of certain primitive characteristics that were present in an ancestor but have not occurred in intermediate generations.

Behaviourism A psychological approach (first promoted by J.B. Watson in 1913) that stresses that the only proper subject matter for scientific study in psychology is directly observable behaviour.

Bifurcation A dual-edged approach to the problem of offending which allows governments to reserve custody for the most serious offenders and to use community penalties for not-so-serious offenders. In practice, it often involves a more punitive approach across the whole range of punishments.

Binge drinking Refers to the consumption of large amounts of alcohol in a single drinking session.

Business cycle (or economic) cycle The ups and downs often seen simultaneously in most parts of a country's economy. They tend to repeat at fairly regular time intervals. This involves shifts over time between periods of relatively rapid growth of output (recovery and prosperity), alternating with periods of recession or relatively slow economic growth.

Civilizing process Concept developed by Norbert Elias (1897–1990) to refer to the pacification of medieval society through the development of self-restraint, social regulation and increasing repugnance towards violence.

Cognition A somewhat inexact, indeterminate term that encompasses concepts such as memory, imagery, intelligence and reasoning. Often described as 'a synonym for thinking'.

Community notification Allowing communities to know when a sexual offender who may pose a risk has moved into their midst. This policy is not pursued in the UK, but is in the USA where it is sometimes known as 'Megan's Law'.

The policy is premised on the idea that information on the offender known to the professionals and practitioners working with the offender should not be held only by those professionals and practitioners and that with such 'notification' the community will be better able to protect itself.

Community penalties In its broadest sense, this term refers to any sentence that does not involve imprisonment and therefore includes cautions, discharges and fines as well as sentences involving supervision or monitoring. In its narrower sense, the term refers to community orders.

Conscious mind Being aware (cognisant) of one's actions and emotions. Actions undertaken by the conscious mind are intentional.

Consumer expenditure (or in shorthand consumption): The money from income, savings, or from borrowing spent on the purchase of currently produced goods and services. Consumption tends to increase as income increases, but not by as much.

Corporate crime Illegal acts or omissions which are the result of deliberate decision-making or culpable negligence within a corporation.

Corporation Used here to denote all companies registered under the UK Companies Acts, from the smallest limited liability company to the largest multinational.

Corporatism A word used to describe an approach to criminal justice based on centralization, government intervention and cooperation of agencies and professionals working towards common goals. Typically, it has also been associated with the use of targets, and prescribed ways of working.

Crime count The number of offences occurring within a given referent of time and space, for example, the number of burglary offences in England and Wales per year.

Crime flux A concept that defines the crime rate as a product of the prevalence of victims in the population, and the frequency with which they are victimized.

Crime frequency How the counts of criminal offences are distributed amongst a population, for example, how many people are victims, and how frequently are they victimized.

Crime markets A market that deals specifically with the acquisition, distribution and consumption of illegal goods and services.

Crime rate The measure that gives an index of crime occurring in a particular jurisdiction for a specific time period.

Crime statistics The accounts that the State compiles of the actions of its agencies concerning those acts which the law proscribes.

Crime victimization surveys Large-scale sample surveys of general populations whose purpose is to estimate, describe and explain the distribution of crime victimization and victims.

Criminal law This is the regulation of conduct by the creation of criminal offences—laws, made by Parliament, that forbid particular conduct and lay down punishments. Nowadays the courts no longer create new offences, although their decisions shape the boundaries of offences.

Criminological psychology A sub-discipline existing broadly at the interface between psychology and criminology that seeks to apply psychology to help explain criminal behaviour.

Criminological verstehen Sympathetic or affective understanding regarding the situated experiences and emotions of criminals, crime control agents and crime victims.

Cultural criminology A distinct theoretical, methodological and interventionist approach to the study of crime that places criminality and its control in the context of culture; that is, it views crime and the agencies and institutions of crime control as cultural products—as creative constructs. As such they must be read in terms of the meanings they carry. With its focus on situated meaning, identity, space, style, and media culture, along with its commitment to understand and account for the ongoing transformations and fluctuations associated with hypercapitalism, cultural criminology is an attempt to create a 'post' or 'late' modern theory of crime.

Culture The symbolic environment created by social groups; the meaningful way of life shared by group members.

Cybercrime Criminal activities which take place in 'virtual' space using networked technologies. They cut across national boundaries, which has implications for law enforcement and punishment.

Dangerousness An individual's actions or behaviour pattern considered dangerous to the safety of that individual or other people—a person may be so disposed by individual characteristics or by pre-disposing circumstances in their immediate environment—the behaviour is usually associated with elements of unpredictability.

Decarceration Refers to policies and practices that aim to reduce the numbers of offenders in prison by providing alternative measures for dealing with them in the community. Theoretically, the debate about decarceration was at its height in the 1960s and 1970s and included reduction in the use of other institutions, most notably psychiatric hospitals. With the dramatic increase in the prison population in the 1990s, the term and the debate has largely fallen into disuse.

Defence representation A key element of a fair trial is that of 'equality of arms'—that the prosecution and defence are allowed the same facilities to put their case. An individual defendant will never have the same resources as the State but the State must provide for adequate representation of offenders, whether in the police station or in court. The criminal justice system also provides for defendants to be assisted by lawyers, paid out of public funds.

Deterrence The idea that crime can be reduced if people fear the punishment they may receive if they offend.

Discipline A term used by Michel Foucault to describe a method by which some people can efficiently control others, and which he claims is at the heart of modern public institutions such as the prison, school and hospital. Discipline is the analysis and 'correction' of others' behaviour, especially in relation to time and space, and is a key part of his understanding of how surveillance operates and what it is trying to achieve.

Discrimination The unfavourable treatment based on a person's colour, age, sexuality, gender or ethnicity.

Diversion strategy Describes efforts to minimize young offenders' involvement with the formal youth justice system, steering them away from the more punitive sentences such as custody, and where possible keeping them out of the system entirely.

Edgework The momentary integration of subcultural practices with experiences of extreme risk and excitement.

Elder The blanket label of the 'elderly' can perpetuate a stereotype that the elderly population constitutes a homogeneous social group. The term elder will be used as a generic term to define those persons over the age of fifty in recognition of the positive aspects that older age can confer.

Empathy The ability to identify mentally with another person and thus understand how others feel.

Empirical research Research based upon the analysis of data rather than conceptual analysis.

Environmental criminology A form of criminology that focuses on the complex relationships that exist between crime, space and environment.

Ethnicity The problem that arises from using the biological concept of 'race' to describe social phenomena has led some theorists to reject the term 'race' in favour of 'ethnicity'. Like the terms 'race' and 'racism', 'ethnicity' has no universally agreed definition. The term ethnicity characterizes social groups based upon a shared identity rooted in geographical, cultural, historical factors and migratory patterns.

Ethnography The study of groups of people in their natural setting, typically involving the researcher being present for extended periods of time in order to collect data systematically about their daily activities and the meanings they attach to them.

Evaluation A form of research, which prioritises solving practical problems over the generation of new theoretical knowledge.

Experiments An approach to social research which involves emulating the approach of the natural scientists by collecting data from an 'experimental' and a 'comparison' group to test a hypothesis.

'Fair trial' and criminal procedure Procedural laws govern the actions of law enforcement agencies. In the pre-trial process, such laws provide legal powers for the police enabling them to arrest and detain suspects. The rules also ensure that suspects are treated with due respect. Equally important are trial procedures—the idea of a 'fair trial' is enshrined in many human rights conventions and this idea governs such matters as the way in which defendants can defend themselves from accusations, the roles of the judge, as well as of the prosecuting or defending lawyers, the presentation of evidence, the questioning of witnesses and the taking of verdicts.

Fear of crime General term that suffers from lack of clarity in its definition. Generally taken to refer to concern, worry or anxiety about crime but there is research evidence that it may be a conduit for broader concerns about change and uncertainty. At the start of the twenty-first century the focus for the police has broadened to encompass a reassurance agenda as politicians struggle with falling recorded crime levels and rising levels of public anxiety.

Focus groups A data collection method which takes advantages of the dynamic interaction of groups to collect largely qualitative data.

Folk devil As constructed by the mass media and public officials, a public identity that comes to embody a larger sense of threat and social insecurity.

Functionalism A structuralist perspective, which argues that, although crime and deviance are problematic, they also serve a social function by contributing to the smooth running of the social system as a whole (see Chapter 4).

Gender A socially constructed phenomenon that refers to differences ascribed by society relating to expectations about appropriate social and cultural roles.

Generalizabilty The extent to which research findings can be applied beyond the sample being studied; for example, to other groups or to different locations.

Gerontology Interest in the study of human ageing has grown steadily throughout the twenty-first century. Gerontology is a broad discipline, which encompasses psychological, biological and social analyses of ageing. It is also the study of social welfare and social policy focused on ageing. The various stands within gerontology seek to problematize the construction of ageing and to identify the conditions experienced by elders in society. Gerontology raises questions about the role of the State in management of old age to issues about the purpose of growing old within the context of a postmodern life-course.

Governance This is often used as a general term to denote governing strategies originating from inside and outside the State, though in this volume is used more straightforwardly to refer to the constitutional and institutional arrangements for framing and monitoring the policies of the police.

Governmentality A term invented by Michel Foucault to describe certain specific techniques developed over the centuries by governments and the State, so as to exercise power over populations as a whole. It complements 'discipline', which refers to the operation of power at the level of public institutions.

Gross Domestic Product (GDP) The total value of all goods and services produced within a country during a specified period (most commonly per year).

Hegemonic masculinity The prevailing idealized cultural conception of dominant (hegemonic) masculinity involving the dominance of women, heterosexuality, the pursuit of sexual gratification and independence. This is a cultural resource enacted to maintain domination over 'subordinate masculinities'.

Hegemony The dominance of one particular ideology, resulting in the empowerment of particular values, beliefs and practices over others and frequently resulting in the naturalization of those values, beliefs and practices throughout the social body.

History from below A form of historical narrative developed and popularized in the 1960s. This form of history focuses on the study and analysis of the lives of 'ordinary' individuals within society as well as individuals and regions that were not previously considered historically important. This has given rise to the important developments in such fields as women's history, black history, and gay and lesbian history.

Home Office Counting Rules Official instructions that set out how, and in what ways, incidents are to be recorded and counted as offences.

Hypothesis A theoretical assertion about the relationship between two or more variables which can be tested.

Ideal type An abstract model of a phenomenon which illustrates a generalization for descriptive purposes. For example, in the context of victimization, the 'ideal victim' is an innocent, elderly, vulnerable person. This does not imply that such people are typical of victims of crime—rather, it shows how many people think about victims and suggests a commonsense understanding which should be challenged and tested by research.

Incapacitation Punishment which calculates the risk of future crimes and uses a custodial setting to remove the offender from society to protect the public from further harm.

Institutionalized racism The term 'institutionalized racism' was first introduced in 1968 by Carmichael and Hamilton in their seminal text, *Black Power: The Politics of Liberation in America*. Common to most definitions of institutionalized racism is the collective failure of an organization to provide an appropriate service to people because of their colour, culture, or ethnic origin.

Interviews A data collection method based upon the posing of a series of questions, usually face-to-face but sometimes using more indirect approaches (for example, telephone).

Intimate (domestic) violence Predominantly (but not exclusively) violence against women and children within the family, which can take many forms including physical assault, rape and sexual violence, psychological or emotional violence, torture, financial abuse including dowry-related violence, and control of movement and of social contacts.

Jurisprudence The science or philosophy of law.

Justice model One that places the offence at the centre, regarding it as an act of will. It is to be dealt with by punishment set to reflect the seriousness of the crime. The justice model also emphasizes the legal rights of offenders, for example, to representation in court.

Labelling theory A criminological theory that locates the meaning of human activity not in the activity itself, but in others' reactions to it.

Late modernity A period in the historical development of capitalism characterized by individualization, globalization, personal insecurity, hyperconsumption and the decline of large-scale collective initiatives such as the welfare state.

Legal psychology A sub-discipline of psychology specifically concerned with the application of psychological knowledge and research to the process of law.

Life-Course A term that has replaced the term life stages to reflect holistic understanding of the ageing process. The blurring of the life-course problematizes negative 'ageist' stereotypes and practices and in turn produces more accurate and positive images that imply that later life is a time for vitality, creativity, empowerment and resourcefulness—all attainable in old age.

Mafia A term often used to describe an organized crime group consisting of particular ethnic members, for example, Sicilian Mafia, Russian Mafia. It has also been used in reference to individuals and groups who deal specifically in illegal protection.

Managerialism The use of a more corporatist strategy to deal with crime. The 'managerial' approach aims not necessarily to deliver 'welfare' or 'justice', but to find the most efficient and effective way of managing a visible crime problem.

Media Any technological form of communication or expression designed to impart meaning (television, newspapers, Internet, radio, brochures, road signs, advertising billboards).

Meta-analyses When a number of studies on a particular research area are reviewed and assessed in a bid to find some overall conclusions.

Method triangulation The practice of using more than one research method when conducting empirical research.

Moral entrepreneur A powerful person or group seeking to impose a moral agenda by creating a new category of crime and crime control.

Moral panic As generated by the mass media and public authorities, the public's belief that a particular crime or criminal is symptomatic of larger moral failures and social harms.

National Crime Recording Standard A protocol to standardize crime recording practices amongst police forces, with effect from April 2002.

Neighbourhood Watch Voluntary organizations that are devoted to preventing crime and disorder in local neighbourhoods. Members are not expected to intervene in possible criminal incidents but to be the eyes and ears of the police by being alert to unusual activity. Grew rapidly in numbers during the 1980s as part of the Conservative government's emphasis on active citizenship.

Netwidening A term used to identify the counter-intuitive problem posed by the proliferation of 'alternatives' to prison. There is a risk that innovative non-custodial sentences might be used by sentencers for offenders who would previously have received *less* severe sentences rather than *more* severe sentences. If this happens, it means that *more*, rather than *fewer* offenders are likely to end up in prison. In this way, the *net* of criminal justice intervention is thrown *wider*.

Night-time economy Used to describe bars, pubs, nightclubs and fast-food outlets, often clustered in town and city centres.

Normalization thesis Particularly associated with the work of Howard Parker and his colleagues who argue that recreational drug use has become a central component of contemporary youth culture.

Nothing works The notion that became popular in the 1970s and 1980s that nothing could be done to reduce re-offending. It fitted well with the anti-welfarist views of the time, which have now been replaced by the more nuanced view that some interventions work for some offenders in some situations.

Observation A research method which involves watching, and sometimes participating in, social activities.

Offender Management A term increasingly used to describe the process of working with offenders at different stages of the criminal justice process with the aspiration of preventing reoffending. The nature and extent of 'management' is determined by the level of risk and harm the offender is judged to pose to the public.

Organizational culture Culture has been defined as 'the way we do things around here', and while organizations themselves tend to have their distinct cultures, these often take distinct forms within different parts of an organization.

Organizational structure Refers to the lines of authority, decision-making, accountability, management systems and the relationships between constituent parts of an organization.

Organized crime A generic description of any criminal activities carried out by a group of two or more people. Official usage of this term specifies that the groups engaged in these activities are motivated by profit, operate over a period of time and are willing to use violence as well as actively seeking to influence those across the legal divide such as the police, politicians, bankers and so on who can further their cause. Organized crime is not a legal term.

Patriarchy Refers to a system of social structure and practices in which men dominate.

Phenomenology A method of philosophical investigation that seeks to describe and understand experienced phenomena. Although phenomenological methodologies are deliberately complex and opaque, one could say that the 'goal' of phenomenology is to challenge and question the foundational knowledge claims.

Phrenology Phrenology is the study of the structure of the skull to determine a person's character and mental capacity. It is associated with the work of the Austrian physician Franz Joseph Gall (1758–1828). Gall was one of the first to consider the brain as the home of all mental activities.

Physiognomy Physiognomy is the interpretation of outward appearance, especially the features of the face, to discover a person's predominant temper and character.

Police The specialist state agency tasked with law enforcement and order maintenance.

Policing Organized and purposive forms of social control and regulation, involving surveillance and the threat of sanctions for discovered rule-breaking.

Positivism Positivism is a form of empiricism that was established by the sociologist Auguste Comte in the nineteenth century. Rejecting metaphysical or theological explanations, it attempted to emulate the methods of natural science. Thus only scientific or empirical investigation and observation will enable a true understanding of social structures and institutions.

Post-disciplinary Refers to theories of surveillance and/or punishment that derive from, and accept in part, Foucault's theory of technologies of power and of discipline, but which argue that the disciplinary historical phase is in the process of being superseded by a new technology of power.

Problem drug use Problem drug use involves dependency, regular excessive use or use which creates serious health risks (for example, injecting) and it is usually associated with the use of Class A drugs.

Proportionality A philosophical ideal stating that punishment should be proportionate to the criminal act.

Prosecution and trial In its technical sense, 'prosecution' means bringing an offender in front of a properly constituted tribunal (the magistrates' or Crown Court) in order to test the validity of a formal accusation made against the defendant. The obligation is on the State as prosecutor to satisfy the tribunal that the accusation is true beyond reasonable doubt. The preparation of a case for trial and the presentation of that case is predominantly undertaken by the Crown Prosecution Service, although other agencies such as Customs and Excise and Inland Revenue may take responsibility for mounting their own prosecutions.

Psychometrics The measurement (typically via questionnaires or inventories) of psychological characteristics such as intelligence, personality and creativity.

Punitive populism (or variants on it such as populist punitiveness, penal populism) The pursuit of a set of penal policies to win votes rather than to reduce crime rates or to promote justice. Central to this strategy is the support of imprisonment and, generally, the advocacy of tough measures to deal with offenders.

Qualitative data Textual, visual or audio data which are not amenable to measurement, provide an insight into social phenomena (for example, crime, sentencing, victimization) and convey, for example, subjective interpretations of meaning.

Quantitative data Numerical data which measure social phenomena (for example, crime, sentencing, victimization), typically through some form of counting and subsequent statistical manipulation.

Quantitative history Quantitative history involves the use of empirical, statistical historical data (such as census returns, crop yields, tax records) in the study of historical topics. It is often associated with the emergence of social history, which borrowed methodologies from the social sciences.

Questionnaires A standardised research instrument used to collect data from respondents about a particular topic.

Race The terms race and ethnicity have been used interchangeably but are not synonymous. Current notions of race are centred exclusively on visible (usually skin colour) distinctions among populations, although its historical origins and usage were broader and included religious and linguistic groups (such as Jews or the Irish) who were considered to be 'races'.

Racism Many authors define racism as a 'doctrine, dogma, ideology, or set of beliefs'. All definitions of racism have a set of common themes—typically the belief that certain groups are innately, biologically, socially, morally superior to other groups, based upon an assumption held about them.

Racist violence Any incident, including threats, harassment, emotional and physical harm, which is perceived to be racist by the victim, or any other person.

Rational choice theory of crime A classical model of human choice that assumes that offenders rationally calculate the costs and benefits of committing a crime. The rational choice theory is the leading perspective behind the majority of contemporary situational crime prevention initiatives.

Rational economic (wo)man An ideal type economists use to derive theories about human behaviour. The assumption is that, faced with choices and given their preferences, individuals will always act in such a way as to optimize their economic well-being. They weigh up the costs and benefits of different actions and choose the one that will leave them the best off.

Recession (economic recession) Defined formally by economists as occurring when the amount of goods and services produced by a country's economy falls in two successive quarters. A sustained recession, such as that in the 1930s, is often referred to as a depression. A recession will lead to fewer jobs and higher levels of unemployment.

Recreational drug use Characteristically centred on the use of cannabis and 'dance drugs' (for example, ecstasy), recreational drug use may be frequent but does not involve excessive use, dependency or serious risks to health.

Reflexive A heightened degree of self understanding and reflection about one's theorizing or particular standpoint/position; from the Latin term *Reflectere*, meaning 'to turn back on oneself'.

Regulation Within criminology, this term implies the control of business activity within the framework of a set of rules, by an agency or by dedicated personnel assigned to ensure compliance with those rules.

Rehabilitation The belief that it is possible to tackle the factors that cause offenders to commit crimes and so reduce or prevent re-offending. The focus is usually on individual factors such as employability, problem substance use, and anger management.

Relativism The perspective that knowledge is relative and contingent rather than absolute and determined.

Resettlement Refers to a long tradition of work which aims to reintegrate imprisoned offenders back into the community.

Restoration In the History of England the term 'Restoration' has a specific meaning in as much as it is used to describe the process whereby Charles II regained the English throne after the Parliamentarian rule in the wake of the English Civil War. More commonly, though, the Restoration period refers to the subsequent years of Charles II's reign (1660–85).

Restorative justice An approach to criminal justice which aims to restore victims, offenders and the wider community as far as possible to the position they were in before the offence was committed, by involving them in the decision-making process and attempting to reconcile their conflicts through informal (but structured) discussion. Mechanisms for implementing RJ include victim–offender mediation; direct or indirect reparation; family group conferences; changes to sentencing arrangements which involve wider community representation; and community involvement in supervising offenders using circles of support and accountability.

Retribution/Just desert Punishment that seeks to express social disapproval and concern but which is proportionate to the harm caused by the crime.

Revisionist history Historical revisionism is the re-examination and reviewing of the stories told as history with an eye to updating them with more recently discovered, more unbiased or more accurate information. Broadly, it is the approach that history as it has been traditionally told may not be entirely accurate and may be subject to review. Revisionist history challenges orthodox and traditional approaches to an historical problem. A revisionist history of crime offers new perspectives to the orthodox (often called *Whig*) version that many historians accept.

Risk assessment The activity of collating information on an individual, their immediate circumstances and social environment with a view to assessing the likelihood of particular behaviour patterns occurring in the future. This may divide into clinical collection and assessment, and actuarial assessment; the latter implying a statistical analysis based on particular categories of people. In the case of sexual offenders this is an increasingly formalized and coordinated activity sometimes using risk assessment 'instruments'.

Risk factors Increasingly used to refer to individual or social factors which increase the probability of involvement in crime.

Risk management The activity of using a risk assessment to manage the future risk an individual may pose. In the case of sexual offending this is an increasingly formalized and coordinated activity involving various forms of containment and incapacitation to achieve public protection (for example, supervision, registration, routine surveillance, longer custodial or hospital detention).

'Rule of law' The idea of the 'rule of law' is that individuals and the State should regulate their conduct according to the law. Laws must be created in a constitutionally proper fashion to be effective, normally through legislation passed by Parliament but such statutory offences can be contrasted with 'common law' offences which are based on the decisions of courts. Law enforcement agencies such as the police, the prosecution, the courts or prisons can only exercise their powers (such as those of investigation, trial or detention) where they have legal authority to do so.

Self-regulation Self-regulation refers to the expectation that most people are capable of complying with the law most of the time, not because of the fear of punishment but because they have internalized the values and norms of society and consider that it is in their own interests, and the interests of those that matter to them, to comply. If they occasionally break the law then it is assumed that this will produce a sufficient feeling of guilt and shame for them to *regulate* their behaviour without either restrictions or assistance from other people. The ultimate aim of criminal justice policy, therefore, is to produce *self-regulating* citizens who require minimal outside intervention to be law-abiding.

Sex Refers to biological criteria for classifying persons as male or female.

Sexism Refers to oppressive attitudes and behaviours directed towards either sex.

Sexual offending The commission of acts of a sexual nature against a person without that person's consent (for example, rape, indecent assault) or where that person lacks the capacity to consent (for example, because they are a child, have learning difficulties, or are otherwise incapacitated); these acts may be accompanied by violence or the threat of violence. The commission of acts of a sexual nature that are 'prohibited' by law (for example, between members of the same family, or abuse of a position of trust).

Situational crime prevention An approach to crime prevention involving the management, design or implementation of the immediate environment in which crimes occur in order to reduce opportunities for crime.

Social control A term used in various different ways in criminology. In the context of surveillance, its most frequent use is to claim (following Marxist theories of class conflict and domination) that the essential 'function' of surveillance is to help the State gather information on individuals or groups it perceives as representing a threat to its (class-based) interests, and/or to prevent such threats from arising in the first place.

Social exclusion A term used to describe people or areas suffering from a combination of problems such as unemployment, poor skills, low incomes, poor housing, high crime environments, bad health and family breakdown. It is distinguished from financial poverty and focused rather on constricted access to civil, political and social rights and opportunities.

Social interactionism A theoretical approach that stresses the interactions between individuals as 'symbolic and linguistic exchanges'. Within this rubric, crime is understood as a product of social interaction.

Style A symbolic medium for the display of collective identity and affiliation; style often serves also as the medium for others' attempts at surveillance and control.

Subculture The distinctive symbolic environment of a criminal group, often embodying language, rituals and symbols that, when considered in relation to the study of crime and deviance, run counter to the legal constraints and conventional understandings proffered by mainstream society.

Tautology/Tautological (In theoretical terms) something that relies upon circular reasoning.

Thatcherism A label given to a set of political values associated with Margaret Thatcher, the Conservative Prime Minister of the UK from 1979 until 1990. Economically committed to allowing markets to operate freely and opposed to supporting firms or industries that performed badly, its policies involved privatizing nationalized industries, reducing state expenditure particularly on welfare. Its advocates believed the Welfare State was to blame for the growth in a 'dependency culture' where people relied on State handouts rather than working and providing for themselves and their families.

Time series data Refers to data collected from a particular geographical unit—town, region or country—at fixed intervals—daily, weekly, monthly, quarterly, annually—for example, annual recorded crime in England for each year from 1950 to 2003. Time series analysis refers to statistical techniques that examine how the measurement varies over time. In contrast, cross-section data is collected for a particular time period across different geographic units, for example, recorded crime in each local authority in the UK in 2004.

Total institution An organization which controls all aspects of people's daily lives. Primarily associated with the work of sociologist Erving Goffman, who saw the total institution as a social microcosm which was controlled by an hegemony with clear hierarchies and sets of rules. Examples include prisons, schools, mental institutions and workhouses.

Traditional crime Those acts upon which criminal justice agencies—and criminologists—have typically focused their energies, such as interpersonal violence, theft, burglary, the use and distribution of illegal substances, public order offences, and so on; also frequently referred to as 'street' crime or 'conventional' crime.

Transnational organized crime A relatively recent term that is applied to activities carried out by crime groups across jurisdictions, either by the same group or in collaboration with others. It is intended to reflect the globalizing tendency of organized crime.

Unconscious mind The part of the mind that is inaccessible to the conscious mind but which still affects behaviour and emotions.

Unemployment The State of being available and able to work but unable to find a paid job. In practice, difficult to identify and measure. For example, government rules as to the meaning of 'available for work' or eligibility for benefit can change, altering the numbers counted as unemployed without the material position of any particular individual altering.

Validity The extent to which the conclusions reached are credible and plausible.

Verdicts and sentencing At the end of a trial, the magistrates (or the jury in a Crown Court) will bring in a verdict—this derives from the Latin for a 'true statement'. This verdict will be guilty or not guilty. After a verdict of guilty, the court will proceed to sentence. A sentence is a court order which specifies the penalty (from fines to community-based sanctions to imprisonment) to be imposed and which gives legal authority to agencies such as probation or the prison service to enforce that penalty.

Victim blaming Ways of thinking about the causes of criminal victimization which seek explanations from the individual victim's conduct and the victim's relationship with the offender, rather than looking for wider social factors which help to explain victimization. In the context of police investigations, victim blaming can take the form of disbelieving the victim's report of a crime being committed, or giving some types of incident lower priority on the grounds that the victim is less deserving than others.

Victim impact statements A mechanism for allowing victims of crime to give a written statement of the impact of the offence upon them, materially and emotionally, so that courts and other criminal justice agencies can take this information into account. An apparently straightforward and sensible innovation which has been controversial and largely ineffective in practice.

Victimology A sub-discipline of criminology. It is concerned with the study of victims of crime; the causes, nature and impact of victimization; and the dynamics of relationships between victims, offenders and the environments in which victimization occur.

Violence Behaviour that intentionally threatens or does physical harm, and involves the infliction of emotional, psychological, sexual, physical and material damage.

Welfare model One in which offending is taken to be a symptom of psychological or social deprivation. The response rests with providing expert-led treatment in order to meet the individuals' needs and so reduce offending.

Welfare State A State which takes the responsibility for providing basic services to its population. Through systems of social security it guarantees to meet people's basic needs for housing, health, education and income.

'What works' In its narrowest sense, 'What works' refers to a movement that emerged in the 1980s and 1990s in North America and spread worldwide. Its aim has been to revive interest in offender rehabilitation through the promotion of programmes for offenders, based on cognitive behavioural psychology and supported by scientific evidence of success in reducing rates of re-offending. The term is intended to counteract the claim that 'nothing works' in offender rehabilitation. In its broader sense, the term has come to refer to a very wide-ranging and controversial political and ideological agenda that emphasizes individual responsibility for offending and minimizes the role of social determinants.

Whig History A term used to describe the views of some eighteenth and nineteenth century British historians that British history was a march of progress whose inevitable outcome was the constitutional monarchy. It takes its name from the British Whigs, advocates of the power of Parliament, who opposed the Tories, supporters of the power of the King and the aristocracy. Whig history is criticized for its overemphasis of the roles played by key political figures and for downplaying the historical importance of the struggles between different classes and groups.

White-collar crime Offences committed by people of relatively high status or enjoying relatively high levels of trust, and made possible by their legitimate employment.

INDEX

Q